W9-CMU-932

SOCIOLOGY
AN INTRODUCTION

SOCIOLOGY
AN INTRODUCTION

K. ISHWARAN
Editor

Addison-Wesley Publishers
Limited
Don Mills, Ontario • Reading, Massachusetts • Menlo Park, California
Wokingham, England • Amsterdam • Sydney
Tokyo • Madrid • Bogota • Santiago • San Juan

Copyright © 1986 Addison-Wesley Publishers Limited. All rights reserved. No part of this publication may be reproduced, stored in a retrieval system, or transmitted, in any form or by any means electronic, mechanical, photocopying, recording, or otherwise, without the prior written permission of the publisher.

The publishers wish to thank the following sources for photographs used in this book. We will gladly receive information enabling us to rectify any errors in references or credits.

MILLER SERVICES

4, 8, 16, 18, 26, 30, 32, 35, 37, 43, 54, 62, 70, 73, 80, 97, 99, 102, 108, 112, 114, 119, 121, 126, 132, 139, 140, 141, 142, 143, 144, 146, 147, 152, 160, 164, 169, 170, 173, 186, 193, 200, 203, 214, 216, 228, 234, 236, 245, 254, 257, 259, 264, 266, 272, 274, 284, 295, 300, 310, 314, 316, 322, 324, 327, 329, 331, 334, 338, 340, 342, 363, 365, 371, 373, 377, 384, 389, 391, 393, 396, 399, 400, 408, 427, 433, 443, 454, 460, 480, 484, 487, 490, 502, 506, 510, 532, 535, 538, 540, 549, 551, 554, 564, 576, 577, 591, 602.

CANAPRESS

12, 20, 28, 39, 42, 44, 53, 103, 127, 162, 212, 232, 239, 242, 287, 289, 297, 337, 343, 347, 350, 369, 419, 421, 424, 450, 453, 456, 467, 470, 476, 478, 494, 509, 516, 529, 544, 560, 561, 563, 590, 597, 598, 600.

NATIONAL FILM BOARD

6, 68, 90, 110, 361, 446, 463, 464, 586.

TOM SHIELDS CREATIVE AND EDITORIAL SERVICES

opposite 3, 23, 50, 56, 66, 81, 115, 179, 213, 422, 497, 546, 547, 584.

MANITOBA ARCHIVE

47, 558, 579.

PUBLIC ARCHIVE OF CANADA

358, 418.

VANCOUVER PUBLIC LIBRARY

438.

CO-ORDINATING EDITOR: *Craig Doyle*
DEVELOPMENTAL EDITOR: *Sonia Paine*
COPY EDITOR: *Janet Thomas*
DESIGN: *Brant Cowie/Artplus*
PHOTO RESEARCH: *Francine Geraci*
TYPESETTING: *Compeer Typographic Services Limited*

CANADIAN CATALOGUING IN PUBLICATION DATA
  Main entry under title:
  Sociology, an introduction

  Bibliography: p.
  Includes index.
  ISBN 0-201-11650-2

  1. Sociology.   I. Ishwaran, K., 1922–

  HM66.S32 1986   301   C85-090839-6

Printed and bound in Canada by John Deyell Company

A B C D E   90 89 88 87 86

To
Arundhati, our daughter
and
L. Doreen Hopkins, the late Director and Founder of Bayview Glen

Contents

Detailed Contents

Contributors

Alan B. Anderson is Associate Professor of Sociology at the University of Saskatchewan. He was educated at Harvard University, Queen's University (B.A. 1961), the University of Edinburgh, the University of Toronto, the Graduate Faculty of Political and Social Science within the New School for Social Research in New York City (M.A. 1967), and the University of Saskatchewan (Ph.D. 1972).

Gordon Darroch received his B.A. from the University of Western Ontario and his M.A. and Ph.D. from Duke University. He has taught in Sociology at Duke and at York University since 1967. He has been Director of the York Institute for Social Research since 1983.

Leo Driedger is Professor of Sociology at the University of Manitoba, Winnipeg. He did his graduate studies at the Universities of Chicago and Michigan State. He is the author and editor of five books on ethnicity, and his seventy publications appear in a score of chapters in books and twenty-five scholarly journals.

Desmond Ellis obtained his Ph.D. at Washington University of St. Louis and is currently teaching sociology at York University. He is also Co-ordinator of the Lamarsh Research Program on Violence and Conflict Resolution at York University.

Dennis Forcese is Professor and Dean of the Faculty of Social Sciences at Carleton University. He earned his B.A. and M.A. from the University of Manitoba and his Ph.D. from Washington University of St. Louis. Other publications include *Stages of Social Research* (with S. Richer, Prentice-Hall, N.J., 1970), and *The Canadian Class Structure* (McGraw-Hill Ryerson, 1975; 1980).

Sheldon Goldenberg was born in Toronto and educated at the University of Toronto, University of Michigan, and Northwestern University. He received his Ph.D. from Northwestern in 1974. Recent papers have dealt with the acquisition of identity and public participation programs in major natural resource development projects on the sociology of knowledge.

R. Alan Hedley is Professor and Chairman of the Department of Sociology at the University of Victoria. He earned his Ph.D. in 1971 at the University of Oregon, and has conducted extensive industrial and organizational research in Britain, the United States, Australia, and Canada.

Kathleen Herman has studied at the University of Alberta, the University of Toronto, and the University of California at Berkeley. She is now an Associate Professor in the Department of Sociology at Queen's University in Kingston.

K. Ishwaran is Professor of Sociology at York University, Toronto. He holds a Ph.D. from Karnatak, a B.Litt. from Oxford, and a D.Litt. from Leiden. He has published ten original books on Canada, Holland and India and edited fifty books. Professor Ishwaran is also the editor of three well-known international journals.

Noel Iverson earned his Ph.D. at University of Minnesota. He is now Professor of Sociology at the University of New Brunswick, Canada. He has written articles on theory, comparative socioeconomics, urbanization, and social change.

Charles Langford Jones is a Professor of Sociology at the University of Toronto, and holds an adjunct appointment at McMaster University. He studied at Cambridge University and the London School of Economics and obtained his Ph.D. from Edinburgh University, Scotland. His substantive interests are in subjective aspects of stratification and in women in the workforce.

Warren Kalbach earned his Ph.D. from the University of Washington in 1960. He is presently Professor and Associate Chairman for Sociology at University of Toronto, Erindale Campus. His other publications include: *The Adjustment of Immigrants and Their Descendents*, Ottawa: Information Canada, 1980; and co-author with W.W. McVey, *The Demographic Bases of Canadian Society*, Toronto: McGraw-Hill Ryerson, 1971.

John H. Kunkel obtained his Ph.D. from the University of Michigan in 1960 and is now a professor at the University of Western Ontario. At present his major research interest is social psychology, and his academic hobby is the analysis of personality theories.

Jayant Lele is presently Professor in the Departments of Political Studies and Sociology, Queen's University at Kingston. After graduating from the University of Poona he completed his Ph.D. at Cornell University. His publications include *Elite Pluralism and Class Rule* (Toronto, 1981) and *Tradition and Modernity in Bhakti Movements* (Leiden, 1981), as well as numerous articles in major journals.

Eugen Lupri is Professor of Sociology at the University of Calgary. He was educated in the Federal Republic of Germany and in the United States. In 1969, he joined the Department of Sociology, University of Calgary, to teach courses in theory, family, and comparative sociology.

Marlene Mackie is currently Professor of Sociology at the University of Calgary, where she teaches collective behavior, gender relations, and social psychology. She received her Ph.D. from the University of Alberta in 1971.

Peter McGahan is currently Dean of Faculty, University of New Brunswick at Saint John. He received his Ph.D. from Fordham University. He is the author of *Urban Sociology in Canada* (1982) and *Police Images of a City* (1984). He has engaged in research on the structure of urban neighborhoods, the ecology of crime, and the evolution of urban communities.

David A. Nock is currently Chairman and Associate Professor of Sociology at Lakehead University, Thunder Bay. He received his B.A. and M.A. from Carleton University and a Ph.D. from the University of Alberta.

Karl Peter, Professor of Sociology, received his degree at the University of Alberta in Edmonton, where he also held a teaching position. He subsequently taught at the University of Waterloo, Ontario before coming to Simon Fraser University in 1968. His best-known publications deal with the Hutterite communities of Western Canada.

Robert Presthus did his graduate work at the Universities of Chicago and London. Formerly University Professor of Politics at York University and Editor of *Administrative Science Quarterly*, he has written widely on political and organizational behavior.

Robert A. Stebbins received his Ph.D. in 1964 from the University of Minnesota. He assumed his present position at the University of Calgary in 1976 where he was Head of the Department of Sociology until 1982.

Nico Stehr is Professor of Sociology at the University of Alberta, Edmonton. His work has been published in the *Canadian Journal of Sociology*, the *British Journal of Sociology*, and the *American Sociological Review*. He is also one of the founding editors of the *Canadian Journal of Sociology*.

A.H. Turrittin obtained his Ph.D. in sociology at the University of Minnesota in 1969, and is a specialist in the area of social stratification and social mobility. He is presently chairperson of the Department of Sociology, Faculty of Arts, York University.

Axel Van Den Berg is Assistant Professor of Sociology at McGill University. His work has been published in the *American Journal of Sociology*, the *Canadian Review of Sociology and Anthropology*, and the *Canadian Journal of Sociology*.

Donald Von Eschen is currently Associate Professor at the Department of Sociology, McGill University. He earned his M.A. at University of Chicago and his Ph.D. at Johns Hopkins University. His interests include political and economic sociology, stratification, and social change.

Preface

Some two hundred years ago, when sociology began to emerge as a systematic scientific discipline, its founding fathers — Comte, Durkheim, Marx, and Weber — were primarily concerned with the implications for social life arising from the industrial revolution and rapid changes in rural life. Today, sociologists are involved in making sense of the changes in what has been frequently described as post-industrial society. Nevertheless, the problems of pre-industrial, industrial, and post-industrial societies, despite their differences in scale and complexity, are not totally unrelated: they are still in all cases problems arising from the effort to create, sustain, and change human life. It is for this reason that this book brings to beginners in sociology not just differences of awareness, but the continuum of insights into human and social life provided by the sociologists of yesterday and today.

I have attempted to stress the following aspects of the sociological study in order to make this book an effective, interesting tool of learning and teaching:

1. *A Cross-cultural Emphasis.* Historically, sociology as a discipline came into being with its focus on Western European societies and, for many decades, continued to grow within that limited perspective. However, with changing global circumstances, sociology has slowly widened its outlook. It has gone beyond the traditional perspective in that it now frequently tends to investigate a society in the context of other societies and vice versa.

2. *The Inter-play of Theory and Research.* This book has been organized under the influence of the intellectual excitement in the broad field of sociology as a whole. The basic general principle of this volume, containing a wide range of contributions from experienced sociologists who have spent many years in developing their knowledge and ideas as researchers and teachers, is to communicate the intellectual adventures and excitement of modern sociology to those about to discover the field of sociology for themselves. Instead of leaving abstract ideas, concepts, and theories to stand by themselves, it has been attempted throughout this volume to illustrate concepts, theories, and methods by providing concrete examples, thus making students aware of the inter-play of theory and research. With regard to theory, attention has been drawn not only to classical theorists such as Durkheim, Marx, and Weber, but also to many modern theorists such as Parsons and other contemporary thinkers who have enriched or modified the classical traditions.

3. *Perspective.* It is a common observation that sociologists often "brand" each other in terms of this or that theoretical and research orientation;

however, this book does not claim to belong to any particular "brand." In the preparation of this book, it has been my concern to provide beginners in sociology with the essentials of sociology as a science; therefore, our contributors have not stressed the importance of certain concepts and theories over others in exposing the reader to the wealth of investigative awareness in sociology today.

Organization of the Book

Presentation of Topics. The chapters in this volume reflect a logical progression. Divided into six parts, each part in the book focuses on and elucidates a major sociological theme or field. The three chapters in Part I outline the major features of the historical, methodological, and theoretical aspects of sociology, indicating in the process the meaning and scope of sociology as a developing discipline. Part II is concerned with problems, patterns, and processes related to the ways in which the individual becomes a social individual: how one learns the meaning and purpose of one's culture, appropriately functions in it, or fails to do so. Part III deals with the ways human individuals cope with their larger sociocultural contexts through micro and macro social processes and formations. Part IV focuses on a number of basic human institutions: family, religion, education, politics, and economy. Part V deals with stratification, or social inequality — a major feature of most societies, western or non-western. Special attention has been given here to the issues of stratification or inequality based on race, ethnicity, gender, and age. Part VI draws attention to social issues that have proved convulsive in a wide range of modern societies: population, urbanization, social movements, and social change — especially the change arising from industrialization.

Flexible Approach. The organization of this book leaves a great deal of freedom to instructors to combine and re-combine the chapters in full or in parts, to accomplish the objectives of their own teaching programs.

Pedagogical Aids. This book contains an introduction to each part, providing an overview of the areas to be discussed. Every chapter contains an outline of the topics to be discussed within that chapter, and ends with a summary that condenses the most important ideas into several paragraphs, emphasizing the basic concepts in the chapter. A glossary at the end of each chapter, containing specific definitions of the major concepts covered, acts as a condensed dictionary for the student. Following the glossary, each chapter contains an annotated reading list, designed to encourage the student to explore specific topics.

Instructor's Manual

A testbank, containing over 700 multiple-choice questions, is available as manual or on disk for microcomputers.

With Thanks

The publication of this book is made possible by our contributors, who willingly gave of their time and expertise in going through several revisions of their chapters. They gave us all the needed attention and co-operation in making this an interesting, readable, and teachable text. I wish to express my indebtedness to each one of them for the high quality of their contributions.

I am also deeply indebted to the many dozens of reviewers who read the manuscript and offered valuable comments and suggestions, which certainly helped to improve the quality of the book.

Richard Kitowski, former acquisitions editor, was chiefly responsible in getting this book into production. To Sonia Paine, developmental editor, and the staff of Addison-Wesley who gave their countless hours of assistance, I remain sincerely thankful.

K. Ishwaran

Introduction to Sociology

Part I is designed to provide you with the basic understanding of what sociology is, what theoretical approaches sociologists use in exploring how human society is organized, and how they go about doing their research.

Chapter 1 explores the nature of sociology, its place among the social sciences, and its major approaches. Durkheim, Marx, and Weber — the three dominant thinkers of sociology — are discussed here in terms of their methods, theories, and several areas of their studies. In reading about the origin and development of sociology in Europe and America, you will find insights into your own society and the issues concerning it.

Chapter 2 shows how social life can be looked at from a number of angles and analyzed at levels. For purposes of organizing sociological research and knowledge systematically, sociologists have developed several approaches, variously called theoretical models, perspectives, or paradigms.

Chapter 3, on "doing social research," deals with some of the basic methods used by sociologists in collecting their data and interpreting it. They choose the role of a detective in searching for answers to the complex issues of society. In doing so, they are guided by their chosen theoretical perspective, as theory and methods are interdependent.

CHAPTER ONE

Sociology: An Overview

SHELDON GOLDENBERG

All of us are insatiably curious about our own behavior and that of others. We would like to be able to understand why people act as they do. Every time we predict which team will win the Stanley Cup or Super Bowl, we engage in countless subtle calculations of the factors affecting performance. Each time we try to decide what to wear on a date or to a party, the decision reflects our social sensitivity, as well as our budget. Each conversation we have, each relationship that we are part of, involves our continual assessment of what is going on and what meanings are conveyed. In a very real sense then, all of us are social investigators and experimenters simply by virtue of being human.

Social science originates in just such mundane concerns. Still, the step from the everyday sort of common-sense knowledge we all possess to social science is a considerable one. Its premise is that questions about human behavior are answerable if one proceeds in a scientific manner. Human behavior is not random; it is ordered, and the pattern can be understood and used to interpret and even to predict the form of future behavior. It is this quest to discover the *patterns* of human behavior that characterizes the social sciences. It is the *manner* in which the quest is conducted that makes it a science. It is the selection of a *perspective* or set of key explanatory variables that distinguishes sociology from its sister social sciences.

Culture may be defined as everything about us that is not physically inherited. These Japanese women share not only their language, but a common sense of aesthetics with regard to this tea ceremony and its tradition.

SOCIOLOGY AMONG THE SOCIAL SCIENCES

All social sciences, and many of the natural sciences and humanities too, are attempts to understand and ultimately explain human behavior. Many of the same questions can be asked in different fields. For example, why do revolutions occur in some countries and not in others? Why do some marriages end in divorce while others do not? Why is the GNP higher in some countries than others? Why do some people become killers? Why do men and women behave differently? All these questions could be asked in

the fields of psychology, sociology, anthropology, political science, perhaps even in history and biology. All seek common features in terms of which patterns or regularities of behavior can be described and explained.

Perhaps the most basic feature of all the social sciences is their common belief that *culture* is thought to have more explanatory power than inherited physiological, genetic, or other hereditary attributes. Culture is defined broadly as everything that is not physically inherited. It therefore includes language, concepts of right and wrong, of beauty, ugliness, truth, justice, and pain, and all of our attitudes, values, and beliefs. All social scientists, whatever their particular choice of key explanatory variables, tend to focus attention on cultural features to begin their search. It is this approach that distinguishes the social sciences from the natural sciences, where emphasis tends to fall on the "natural" rather than on the "man-made" or social factors.

It is not as easy to make distinctions among the social sciences as it is to distinguish social from natural sciences: while there are questions and substantive areas of concern that do not overlap equally among social sciences, there are many that do. Discipline boundaries are therefore to a great extent arbitrary and political. It is not easy to say at what point a question or issue concerning government, for example, ceases to be of interest to a sociologist and becomes the "territory" of the political scientist. All the social sciences overlap to some extent, and distinctions therefore cannot be securely based on field limits. Social psychology, for example, lies precisely in the area where sociology and psychology overlap. It is often taught in both departments, though not in the same way. One could not accurately define either discipline without mentioning social psychology, but it is the exclusive domain of neither.

SOCIOLOGY AS PERSPECTIVE

In practice, one can get a sense of what sociology is by recognizing that there are very general differences in the *perspectives* employed by different social sciences. That is, they tend to deal with variation in human behavior from somewhat different positions, and by reference to different sets of explanatory factors.

It is this difference in perspective that allows us to say that most pyschologists focus on individuals and most sociologists on groups. It is this difference that allows us to suggest sociologists tend to ask questions about variations in behavior that most often seem to call for answers in terms of group characteristics or location in social structure, while psychologists tend to seek answers in terms

of individual motives and characteristics. Political scientists might answer the same questions with a different set of explanatory variables in mind, as would anthropologists, for instance. *The choice of explanatory variables in most cases is what we mean by the "perspective" of the discipline.* The sociological perspective is one that seeks to relate aspects of social structure to variations in people's behavior.

It is the development of a sociological imagination or perspective that enables one to relate "personal troubles of milieu" to "public issues of social structure," as C.W. Mills argued some years ago (Mills, 1959). For the sociologist, human behavior is understood only in light of the broader context, and this broadening of the issue, this ability "to stand farther back" and see the influence of context, is central to the perspective. For the sociologist, individuals are usually less important than the general characteristics they embody and the patterns of behavior they exemplify.

MAJOR PERSPECTIVES IN SOCIOLOGY

Within the field of sociology itself, there are two broad perspectives or categories of explanatory variables — one group is derived from a *structural* position, the other from a *social-psychological* position. The two types of explanatory schema are in some ways complementary and in some ways contradictory. The questions they ask differ; the premises differ; the methodologies differ. And most students will tend to find one perspective more convincing or apt than the other.

The Macro-Structural Perspective: Major Premises

It was Emile Durkheim, the great French sociologist, who suggested the basic position of the structuralist. The world is full of "*social facts*" that are not reducible to psychological states or to characteristics of individuals. They exist in their own right, outside of and transcending individuals. This may sound complex but it is a simple

A job description spells out a person's role within an organization, and implies certain rights and responsibilities.

idea. For example, the law is a social fact; it is an institution in our society rather than an individual attribute. It stands outside each of us but affects our behavior in many ways. The law preceded our existence, and though we may affect it, it will survive us. It is an element of social *structure*, and such social structures (i.e., social facts) transcend and encompass individuals. Because it focuses attention on factors larger than individuals, this structural approach is referred to as macrosociology. From this perspective, it is apparent that social structure is *external*, in a sense, and *coercive*. In addition, changes in social structure produce changes in behavior, to the extent that they are *systematically* and causally related. This system premise is another basic element of structuralist thought. To structural analysts, the idea that society is an *interdependent system* implies that a change in any one part will have effects elsewhere. These "ripple effects" may be obvious or not, desirable or not, revolutionary or minor. They will result in some change in the system and some people will view such change as disruptive, while others will view it as positive or adaptive.

Three Variants of the Structural Perspective

Within the general perspective of structuralism just introduced, there are at least three different major explanantory foci. These three are: a focus on society as *system of interdependent positions*; an *ecological* focus on the shape of the system itself and the effects of spatial arrangements on people; and lastly a focus on the *normative* structure of society.

Society as a System of Interdependent Positions

Perhaps the most fundamental tenet of structuralist analysis is not only that human behavior is patterned and repetitive, but that these patterns can be related systematically to the social features of the society. One feature that is frequently used to anchor description of patterns is the idea of society as a system of *interdependent* positions or *statuses*. Thus, there are parents and children, teachers and students, friends and enemies — all statuses occupied by individuals in the system. For example, a woman may be a doctor, mother, daughter, wife, or sister. Each position carries its powers, obligations, expectations, and prerogatives, which are fairly well codified, though most often only informally. Jobs have job descriptions that spell out the *role* of the person holding a particular status. Marriage contracts do likewise. As yet, there are no codified rules for parenting or for sistering, but there are expectations that are strongly patterned. The key here is the notion of regularity or pattern. Any and all incumbents will have about the same general *script*, as it were, and therefore all who occupy a similar position

will perform the same role, at least to a degree. This suggests that if one can discover the various statuses occupied by any individual, knowledge of the relevant scripts or role requirements will allow one to expect and predict behavior in most situations, with a degree of error since particular individuals either may not know the script or may not care to perform in accordance with it. The description and analysis of such scripts and their relationship to statuses is then one variety of structural analysis.

People having the same status in society tend to look at things and to conduct themselves in the same way. This makes *stratification* another key feature of social life, and much of our behavior is said to be explicable in terms of this variable. Stratification to the sociologist means just about what it means to the geologist — the layering of society into differentiated strata in which there is more similarity within a stratum than there is between other strata. But insofar as society is viewed as stratified, there are layers piled on top of one another, *in relationships of super- and subordination*. It is by reference to these relationships that sociologists move from analysis of stratum to analysis of social class. The upper "class" is said to be "higher" than the lower "class," and more powerful as well. Most of us think we can interpret, explain, and even predict a good deal of people's behavior, given no more information about their circumstances than their social class or position in the stratification system of the society. The premise of such a belief is that people usually display patterns of behavior common to their class position. In other words, "class" provides us with a very important and accurate set of scripts or prescriptions for behavior. If you were to tell sociologists these class circumstances then, they might well claim to be able to explain and predict specific behavior. They might even claim to be able to manipulate behavior, to the extent that position in the stratification system could be systematically altered. This is a powerful and somewhat scary claim with grave ethical considerations.

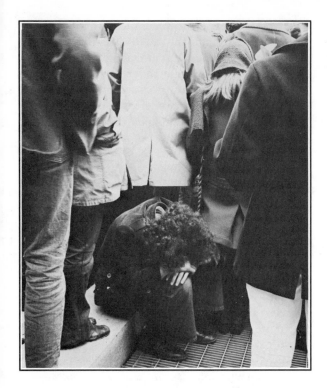

Human ecology takes into account the environment of people in relationship to one another, in settings ranging from the classroom to city streets, where crime and aberrant behavior are often linked to density.

The Ecological Approach

A second variant of the structural perspective involves analysis of the manner in which the physical arrangements of people in space affects their behavior. This focus is termed the "ecological" approach, and human ecology refers to this relationship of people to one another within their geographic and physical environment. Again, the structuralist believes that regularities exist and that such patterns can be used to predict and understand behavior. Thus, it is widely believed that density is related to pathological or aberrant behavior, and this explains in part the higher rates of homicide, drug addition, suicide, and mental illness in more densely populated locations. A full explanation would require that one spell out the mechanism(s) by which density affects behavior, which is hard to do. It is worth noting here again that density is not an individual attribute. It is a characteristic of social structure outside of individuals but affecting their behavior. Other examples of this perspective might include analysis of the implications of apartment-dwelling on child-rearing; analysis of the ways in which the seating arrangements in a classroom affect the level of participation; or analysis of the implications of assembly-line work arrangements for the morale and productivity of laborers.

The Normative Approach

There is a third important variety of structural analysis that is again slightly different from those we have illustrated thus far. In this variant, the focus is on the *normative structure* of the society, or on the set of rules and standards that guide our conduct. Norms regulate our behavior in a myriad of ways, many of which we are normally unaware of. Norms can be thought of as a constraining, shaping force outside of us, controlling everything from the length of our hair and our preferred family size to the socially prescribed distance favored on the bus, in the classroom, or at a dance. Some structuralists focus their attention on the descriptions of various aspects of the normative structure of society.

Norms come in several sizes, as well as in all shapes, and are appropriate to all circumstances. They are "graded" in terms of importance, reflecting to some extent the level of consensus about how important the areas they regulate may be. Thus, there are laws, which are simply norms embodied in legislated form and set down, as for example, in the criminal code. Next there are norms that are not as important. These norms are not set down in legislation, but are widely shared within the society. They are called the *mores* of the culture. Somewhat less important, less agreed-upon, and more quickly changing norms are called *fads* and fashions. Thus, one form of structural analysis might well set out to fully describe the normative structure of a society at any one time, or as it changes over time. Behavior will be explained insofar as it can be attributed to a set of regulating norms. For example, we might suggest that your classmates have in many instances not so much chosen or decided to attend university as they have simply gone along with their friends and with the expectation that university is what follows high school. Or we might suggest that young people will get married at about the age of twenty, simply because that is the "appropriate" age for marriage in our society, and conformity to the norms is expected.

Obviously we do not always know of or conform to all norms. Legislation can be enforced by institutional agents of *social control*, such as the police and the judiciary. Less formal norms, too, are coercive and are enforced by the rewards and punishments that sociologists call *positive* and *negative sanctions*. People tend to repeat positively reinforced behavior and they usually learn to avoid behavior that is negatively reinforced. Furthermore, it is generally true that the more important the norm, the stronger the punishment for its violation, while relatively unimportant norms are correspondingly associated with less severe sanctions. A full catalogue of the normative order will therefore also involve a corresponding catalogue of associated sanctions, from the death penalty to a sarcastic remark; from a medal to a smile.

Summary of Perspectives

To summarize briefly then, the macro-structural approach involves explanation of human behavior by reference to *independent variables* (explanatory variables) that are located in the larger social structure of society. These are outside of and transcend the individual. They are coercive to an extent and they shape all our behavior by obvious and subtle ways, of which we may or may not be aware. Three varieties of the overall perspective have been discussed here. These include focus upon society as a system of interdependent positions; the physical and social arrangement of people in relation to their environment; and emphasis on the normative structure of the society and corresponding sanctions. The premise of the structuralist is that there are regularities of behavior displayed by large numbers of people who share similar circumstances. These circumstances, whether social positions, roles, physical locations, or normative constraints, explain the patterns of behavior that are observable. Changing the circumstances will result in changes in behavior. While these points do not by any means exhaust the implications of a macro-structural perspective, they can give you a good starting place and a reference point for further discussion.

The Micro-Interpretive Perspective

Let us begin this section with a closer examination of norms or rules for conduct. Norms are key elements of culture, and they are learned. This learning process is called *socialization*. There are two essential points to be recognized in this connection. The first is that all rules are ambiguous and elastic, spelling out in most instances a range sometimes narrow and sometimes broad, of acceptable behavior. For example, how long should a man's hair be? What does it mean to be "on time" or "late" for an engagement? How much talking is acceptable during a lecture? Clearly all norms are *conditional*, and the conditions are not completely specifiable. It is not always obvious when such rules are violated. They may be bent without being broken. Again, whether a rule is broken or not may depend on who the actor is, or on the circumstances, including various features of the audience involved. Secondly, everything depends on our ability to understand the situation as an instance to which a particular rule is applicable. In other words, *we decide* when a situation is "new." We decide which rule applies, and often there are conflicting rules. These points make it clear that while one might describe the norms, the description may have limited utility. To the micro-interpretive sociologist, it is the *meaning and relative importance* of the norms for the individuals whose behavior we would like to understand that is critical. Only if we can discover these things can we understand how the norms affect behavior.

The micro-interpretive perspective, then, is significantly different from the structural. It is far more individualistic; hence the description *micro-interpretive*. This perspective tends to deal with social reality as it is understood by the actors themselves. It is therefore closely related to social psychology. The basic premise of the micro-interpretive perspective is that one must understand social behavior from the "inside," or as the actors understand it. This is in sharp contrast to the external focus of structuralists. It was Max Weber who defined the subject matter of sociology as the study of "intentional behavior," thereby introducing our concern with the actor's intentions. The internal focus is closely related to a view of the social world as a symbolic one, in which people interact largely through the manipulation of symbols. Such symbols primarily include language, but we also communicate through the unspoken language of gestures and through the manipulation of other symbols, such as cars, clothing, houses, and grades. From this perspective, sociology is properly construed as the study of "*symbolic interaction*" among human beings. The American, George Herbert Mead, is generally considered to be one of the originators of this view of society.

One basic aspect of this approach is its concern with what W.I. Thomas, another American contributor to the symbolic interaction school of sociology, called "the definition of the situation." Thomas's dictum says that "if a situation is defined as real, it is real in its consequences." This suggests that people act in accordance with what they believe to be true, whether it is in fact true or not. Knowledge of the objective situation is insufficient, since where the subjective and the objective differ, people will act in terms of what they believe to be true, and knowledge of their definition of the situation will be required if we are to make sense of

their behavior. Suppose, for example, that the airplane you are on hits a pocket of turbulence. Some experienced fliers will scarcely take notice of what is for them only a momentary and normal inconvenience. Other passengers will react differently. Some may even begin praying for their souls, convinced that the end is close at hand. The variation in behavior may be considerable, and explicable only if we can find out what they believe the situation to be.

Interpretive sociology, then, focuses on the motivations, intentions, and subjective states of the actors. For such theorists, reality is not simply out there, external and coercive. It is *negotiated* and created through interaction. If someone were to yell "Fire!" in a crowded theatre, there could be a panic, and people could be injured in the rush toward the exits. If an airplane were full of novice passengers, they too could panic. It is for this reason that the captain will normally use the cabin radio to explain the situation to the passengers, thereby structuring their symbolic definitions of the situation and trying to allay their alarm by helping to negotiate a picture of their reality as basically safe and only temporarily disrupted.

Interpretive sociology has as many variants as structural sociology, but its basic premises are few and simple. The proper study of society requires a concentration on *meanings*, as these are created, negotiated, and transmitted among people. Reality is flexible and ambiguous, and there is considerable range and variation of behavior displayed by human beings in any particular circumstance. Only by learning the definitions of the situation held by the actor can we comprehend behavior. Again, while there is far more that could be said, these ideas are a start and provide a reference point for comparison and further elaboration.

THE SCIENTIFIC STATUS OF SOCIOLOGY

While some sociologists consider it appropriate to use the methods of the natural sciences in dealing with human social behavior, others are convinced that this is both inappropriate and impossible. The issue involves both different views of the basic nature of science and different views of the methods appropriate to the conduct of social science in particular.

The Classical View:
Science as a Context-Free Institution

Most of the early sociologists, and some current ones as well, were adherents of a "classical" view of science. According to this view, all scientists seek to discover *universal* and *permanent laws* according to which the universe is ordered. Science is viewed as a set of time-tested *procedures* emphasizing the *systematic* collection and *objective* scrutiny of *empirical* evidence gathered as necessary to *test theoretically* generated hypotheses. The objective body of knowledge gathered in this way is considered to be the substantive findings of the science involved. These findings can be considered to be guidelines to accurate prediction and to manipulation of outcomes. Thus, water is expected to boil at 212°F and I can make it do so. Science as an institution is free of any contaminating effects of its social context because of the strict guidelines for its proper conduct and scrutiny.

In conducting social science, the adherents of the classical view advocate the goals and adopt methods as close to those of the natural sciences as possible. Thus, quantitative analysis is emphasized, and experiments and descriptive surveys are considered appropriate tools. Scientists themselves are expected to be impartial in testing their ideas. This objectivity and methodological rigor make it possible for scientists of differing cultural backgrounds or political beliefs to come to agreement as to the validity of any scientific claims to knowledge. While the adherents of the classical view of science acknowledge that there are problems in matching the procedures and findings of sociology to their model, it is their view that such problems are temporary and surmountable. The social sciences are latecomers, after all, and one can

hardly expect them to rival the natural sciences, which have been developing far longer. According to this classical view then, the goals and the methods of the natural and social sciences are identical or very closely matched, and these goals and methods are available and wholly appropriate. If pressed, the sociologists who take this position might describe themselves as "social engineers" who feel that they can alter people's behavior by manipulating the relevant parts of the social structure. Thus, penal reform can make prisons more successful rehabilitative institutions if we have correctly understood the manner in which environment affects behavior, and if we can shape that environment.

The Critical View
The Unique Character of Social Science

Critics of the classical view have taken a variety of positions. Some have argued that social science is qualitatively different from natural science, and that both the goals and the methods to achieve them are not now and can never be the same. These critics argue that the self-consciousness that characterizes human behavior makes it unique. Whereas chemicals cannot change minds and neutrons have no intentions, human behavior is creative, and it is also affected by the process of being studied. This latter feature makes it impossible to produce knowledge that is generalizable to behavior in other classrooms from the one in which the principal is sitting in on the lesson! This issue of the responsiveness of the subjects to the act of studying them is called *reactivity*, and as you might imagine, it is a serious problem with which social scientists have to contend, and one which some of these critics suggest requires a substantially different approach to the subject matter. Of even greater importance is the human ability to hold "internal conversations" in which one may change one's mind, rehearse behavior before the act and modify it in accordance with one's perception of how various potential acts would be understood and received. To some sociologists,

Dr. Margaret Mead, one of the best-known anthropologists of this century, visits with friends on a field trip to Bali in 1957. Ideally, the social scientist sets aside personal cultural "baggage" in order to understand the group under investigation. Mead's early work on adolescent sexuality among Samoans, whom she incorrectly perceived to be without inhibitions, was subsequently shown to have been flawed by her own expectations.

these characteristics of social action necessitate methods that seek to gain access to the actor's thoughts and intentions. For these critics, the goal of social science is often neither successful prediction of behavior nor successful manipulation of the social structure; it is understanding behavior from the perspective of the actor. This kind of understanding was called *verstehen* by Max Weber, and it is both goal and method of sociology as some practise it. As a method, verstehen is based on intuitive and introspective reasoning, and on the ability to identify with the subjects so that one can claim to share their intentions and moti-

vations and so understand their behavior "as if it were your own." The common-sense idea of "putting yourself in someone else's shoes" is another way of defining verstehen as method.

Many related methods have been developed in the social sciences as people attempt to enter the minds of actors. One of the most commonly employed among sociologists and anthropologists is a field work strategy called *participant observation*. The premise of "p.o.," as it is popularly called, is that trained investigators can come to share the "universe of discourse" of those they are interested in studying, through participating in their society as if they were "authentic" members. In this process, investigators strive to acquire a working understanding of the culture of the subject group in the same way any group member acquires such understanding, i.e., by experiencing socialization within the group. The investigator "sets aside" personal cultural baggage or standards, understandings, rules for interpreting and getting along in the world, and learns a new set, from the inside, as a child does growing up in a new culture. Now the social scientist, in order to stay one, must set aside personal culture, but keep it within reach, as it were, since the object is not simply to become a member of the group under investigation, but to study it. This ability to keep a foot in each camp, to be "marginal" to two cultures, is a tricky piece of balancing and a skill both difficult to acquire and hard to maintain.

For some critics of the classical position then, social science is a unique field requiring new but exacting tools for the achievement of goals different from those of the natural sciences.

Science as a Contextual Institution

Other critics have been even more radical in their critique of science. They question the objectivity and impartiality of any scientific work. They view science as a social study and hence as a contextual product of its time and place. For them, it is not that human behavior is a unique subject matter requiring a different method of study. For them, all science is again the same, and *it is our view of science itself that must change*. Social resources enter into both the discovery and dissemination of knowledge. It makes a difference who you know, how much research money is made available in your area, and how many publishing outlets there are. On occasion, revolutions occur in scientific thought, overturning past findings and calling into question the status of both the body of presumed knowledge and the criteria and means for its assessment. First-year university students are often made forcefully aware of this when the chemistry professor, for example, begins the

course with the advice that you forget everything you've been taught in high school, since it is all now obsolete! According to this critique, science is not cumulative; it is competitive, and the real rules simply are not those described by the classical view.

Given these competing views, the status of sociology as a science is no doubt unclear to you at this point, but it ought really to be no more unclear than the scientific status of chemistry and astronomy. Even the scientific relativists just described do not argue that sociology is not a science. They suggest that our notion of science itself must be revised. In their analysis, science simply does not operate in the way the classical view suggests, nor is it capable of producing knowledge of the kind suggested. There are no laws; there are only tentative and temporary generalizations. There are no impartial and objective scientists, immune to differences in prestige, funding, and publication. Such knowledge as we have at any time may well not be cumulative; it may be overthrown in some future scientific revolution.

What we know is always the product of our time and space. In general, the critics emphasize the relativity of science as a social institution, like all others. For the most radical, as a consequence, no particular methodology is indicated, nor are any prescribed. The only stipulation is that knowledge claims must be critically assessed in a competitive marketplace of ideas and evaluated by wise and skeptical "shoppers."

Science: Sociological Perspective and Method

One's view of the status of sociology as a science of human behavior has fairly clear implications for the methods one adopts. The choice of a structural or interpretive perspective is related both to choice of method and to one's view of sociology as a science.

Taken jointly, a belief in the classical perspective on science coupled with a structural orientation in sociology tends to imply what most practitioners would call a "hard" or quantitative orientation in methods. A critical perspective on science coupled with an interpretive view of sociology tends to imply a "soft" or qualitative methods preference. Both orientations and the range between are represented in the sociological literature.

MAJOR FIGURES AND THE DEVELOPMENT OF SOCIOLOGICAL THOUGHT

Introduction

Men have always asked questions that we now consider to be sociological. Long ago, Socrates speculated on the consequences of different forms of government and on the effectiveness of various strategies of teaching, as well as on the optimum size, shape, and administration of cities. Nonetheless, it was Auguste Comte (1798–1857) who coined the term "sociology" and explicitly launched an infant science for the study of human societies. Herbert Spencer (1820–1903) was another early influence who conceptualized society as an organism and sought to apply many of Charles Darwin's theses concerning evolution to the analysis of societies.

Durkheim, Marx, and Weber

By common agreement among sociologists, the three central figures in the development of the sociology discipline are Emile Durkheim, Karl Marx, and Max Weber. Although there have been many other influential theorists, none have had so broad and deep an impact as these three. Emile Durkheim (1858–1917) has already been introduced as the key figure in the development of the structural perspective. His specific contributions deal with the division of labor and its implications, with suicide, with sociological methods, and with religion. Durkheim was an adherent of the classical view of science, and he sought in his career to establish sociology as a legitimate, independent social science. His emphasis on "social facts" as external to the individual is the basis of structuralism. Durkheim emphatically denied that human social behavior could be explained adequately from a psychological and individualistic perspective.

Karl Marx was a brilliant observer of the human condition. He is revered by economists, philosophers, and political scientists, as well as sociologists. Marx (1818–1883) is of course best known for his work on social conflict and class interests. It is in this connection that he is considered by sociologists to be the originator of the conflict perspective. His famous writings include *The Communist Manifesto*, written with Friedrich Engels in 1848, and *Das Kapital*, his major treatise. Marx was a revolutionary thinker and an activist whose view of science was very different from Durkheim's. He sought to change society and his supporters and exponents have certainly done so. Marx's statements and analyses of the role of workers and owners, of the interests of bourgeoisie and proletariat, are a touchstone to which many modern sociologists regularly return. His analyses of science, of labor, religion, and of the family, are radical and challenging. They remain powerful challenges to us today. Certainly, regardless of their orientation, virtually all current sociologists recognize the importance of social class and the potential of class conflict. Many would agree with Marx as to the primacy of economic factors in explaining behavior of all kinds.

Max Weber (1864–1920) is the last to be dealt with of this trio of the most influential of the founding fathers. He has already been mentioned in association with the micro-interpretive perspective and its focus on social action as intentional behavior. In this respect, Weber's views stand in contrast to those of Durkheim. While both were interested in creating an independent science of sociology, their views of its proper subject matter and the related methodology for describing and analyzing it were different. It is largely because the differences were so clearly stated and the implications so fully explored that modern sociologists are forced to return to the works of Durkheim, Marx, and Weber. Weber is usually thought of first as a critic of Marx. In fact, it is often said that his work consists largely of a dialogue or debate with Marx. Certainly his best known work (*The Protestant Ethic and the Spirit of Capitalism*) argues in favor of the independent influence of ideology on aspects of social structure — a thesis directly opposed to Marx, whose view was that "ideology" was "superstructure" and without influence, while economic arrangements were causal and basic. Among Weber's other influential writings, some concern the proper subject matter and method of sociology, as in *Science as a Vocation* and *The Methodology of the Social Sciences*, where the ideas of verstehen and of "value-free" sociology are explored. In his advocacy of a value-free sociology, Weber took issue very definitely with Marx's belief in the scientist as a man of action, committed to changing society. Weber's "classical" scientist was an analyst, set aside in this capacity from society, and seeking to avoid allowing personal, political, religious, or cultural values to affect scientific studies. Weber's prominent contributions include as well his central writings on the nature of bureaucracy and the impact of the process of bureaucratization.

All three of these authors were brilliant scholars of great breadth and depth. While their work stands out from the rest, outlining and foreshadowing most of the main thrusts of subsequent research in the sociology discipline, there have been many other theorists of great, if not so broad, insight and influence.

European and American Origins of Sociology

Sociology originated in the wake of the French Revolution. In those waning days of the eighteenth century and throughout the first half of the nineteenth century, European society experienced profound change, politically and otherwise. Revolutions caused radical changes in many govern-

ments, and the nature of economic production was fundamentally changed with the advent of industrialization. The Industrial Revolution in turn produced basic changes in all social arrangements. In Europe, extensive urbanization took place at this same time. Many of the forerunners of modern sociology concerned themselves with trying to grasp the essence or emerging nature of an industrial, urban society with its changed class and political structures. These social scientists spent their careers striving to foresee the implications of the new society for familiar institutions such as the family, the educational system, the political and legal structures, and religion. They sought to comprehend the mechanisms of change in order to be able to predict and possibly to control it.

For the early sociologists, theirs was a transitional generation, and most of them did not view the transition as favorable. Their pessimism is evident in some of their work; their profound unease is clear in most of it. Many of these men sought to capture the nature of the changes by describing them in terms of dichotomies. Thus, Tönnies (1855–1936), for example, spoke of a movement from *gemeinschaft* to *gesellschaft*, and Durkheim (1858–1917) described a shift from *mechanical* to *organic solidarity*. Sir Henry Maine spoke of change from *status* to *contract* relationships, and Thomas Horton Cooley wrote of *primary* and *secondary* relationships. Robert Redfield later, but in the same vein, described a transition from *folk* to *urban* societies, and, most recently, Talcott Parsons wrote of *ascription* versus *achievement*, *particularism* versus *universalism*, and other dichotomies. Whereas all of these concepts differ in some ways, they are also closely related, and one can get a better understanding of these thinkers if one views their dichotomies as different aspects of the *same* shift in societal emphasis that all tried so hard to grasp and comprehend. (See Figure 1-1.)

Before we discuss each of these dichotomies, it would be wise to point out that in Max Weber's

The Industrial Revolution radically changed all social arrangements. Workers, among them many women, migrated to cities in order to find employment, as with this match factory, circa 1871.

terms, each of these is an *ideal type* rather than an empirical reality. Furthermore, it has been said that these social scientists intentionally oversimplified in creating paired contrasts that are really the black and white ends of a mostly grey continuum. In reality, the polar extremes of a continuum are never reached, but they serve as reference points in describing trends that approach them. Thus, "ideal" in this context means only a "purified" form unmixed with others, clearly embodying the concept. There is no value judgement attached, or implied.

Durkheim felt that the very glue that holds societies together was changing in a fundamental

Figure 1–1.

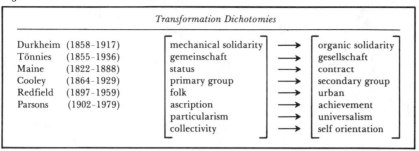

Transformation Dichotomies		
Durkheim (1858–1917)	mechanical solidarity	⟶ organic solidarity
Tönnies (1855–1936)	gemeinschaft	⟶ gesellschaft
Maine (1822–1888)	status	⟶ contract
Cooley (1864–1929)	primary group	⟶ secondary group
Redfield (1897–1959)	folk	⟶ urban
Parsons (1902–1979)	ascription	⟶ achievement
	particularism	⟶ universalism
	collectivity	⟶ self orientation

way. At an earlier time, societies were aggregates of basically like individuals, and the cohesion or solidarity of a society was based on the likeness or similarity of the individuals who made it up. In the newly emerging societal forms foreseen by Durkheim, people were becoming more unlike yet more dependent on one another. The division of labor was proceeding, based on specialization rather than generalization, and this meant that no individual could survive without depending on other specialists to supplement his or her talents and abilities. The new order was a solidarity based on interdependence, which Durkheim called organic solidarity.

Ferdinand Tönnies's dichotomy was an attempt to capture the spirit of the transformation from an earlier community-oriented life toward one that was increasingly market-oriented with impersonality and commercial-contractual relationships predominant. Sir Henry Maine's dichotomy focused primarily on this emergence of contract as a new basis for expectations and guarantees of performance. Cooley's related conception of movement from primary to secondary groups and relationships referred to the transition from a way of life in which most groups were small and intimate, and relationships all-encompassing and general, to the emerging forms that appeared to him to focus on larger groups and involve relationships that were increasingly narrowly specialized. Most people in these new forms of association knew one another only in terms of the specific context in which they met, i.e., as teacher or customer only. Cooley's view was that people were becoming segmented personalities playing impersonal roles to others they knew fleetingly and only superficially.

Part and parcel of this qualitative change was the rapid urbanization of society. Robert Redfield directed our attention particularly to this aspect of change from a rural or folk society to its modern, urban form. Other twentieth-century authors, too, have written about the distinctive characteristics of urban life.

Talcott Parsons sought to capture a number of aspects of the dichotomies in his conception of the transformation of society. Perhaps the key element in his thought concerned the transition from an emphasis on *ascription* and ascriptive characteristics to *achievement*. Ascribed characteristics are those an individual is born with, such as gender, ethnicity, or race—characteristics that are unchangeable (or very difficult to change, though easier to camouflage). Achieved characteristics are earned. According to Parsons, one way of describing the changes in the nature of society was to focus on the shift in opportunity and reward from ascription, i.e., who you are—to achievement, i.e., what you can do.

In sum then, and oversimplifying still more to make the case most clearly, all of these thinkers described the advent of a new social order that they alleged to be impersonal, competitive, contractual, and restricted to relatively superficial contracts. People were said to be increasingly

Some sociologists have described cities as collections of alienated individuals, struggling to create meaning in a complex world in which possessions are valued above relationships.

The examination of the validity of the intuitions and analyses of these sociological forefathers has been our basic inheritance as sociologists of the latter part of the twentieth century. Modern sociologists have been profoundly influenced by all of these authors. Their original concerns with the possibility and the potential of a science of human behavior remain current, and are perhaps more hotly debated today than they were earlier. Many of the basic concepts and premises of these authors have become integral parts of the sociological perspective, as we have seen in earlier discussions of macro- and micro-sociological perspectives. Durkheim's views of society are widely characterized as the foundations of modern structural-functionalism. Marx's views of the fundamental dialectic and conflict basis of order in society have given rise to an entire school of sociology loosely called the conflict approach. Weber is a major precursor of modern symbolic interactionism, which is the foundation of most micro-sociological schools of thought. And yet it is an oversimplification to say that Weber, for example, can be accurately categorized as a micro-sociologist. As we argued earlier, the categories are oversimplifications that are introduced only to make it easier to grasp some of the points of contrast among different perspectives. None of the great sociologists were exclusively exemplars of one or another approach. They were first of all social scientists, following their reasoning wherever it led, not confined by strict and arbitrary adherence to either macro- or micro-levels, to either structural functionalism or conflict.

specialized and dependent on one another, but forced simultaneously to rely on contract to enforce and regulate their responsibilities, the moreso since few could be expected to stay in one place long enough to create primary relationships outside of their families. Possessions were said to be the only things valued and there appeared to be no other standard of value. Cities were described as collections of anonymous and alienated individuals struggling to create meaning in lives that were increasingly complex but essentially meaningless.

Sociology arrived in the United States in the late nineteenth century. It did not reach Canada until considerably later. The discipline flourished in the United States and new directions were soon established in response to the specific American context. From the 1920s to the 1940s what came to be known as the "Chicago School" dominated American sociology. At the University of Chicago, Robert Park and Ernest Burgess took this city as their focal concern and shifted sociological attention to the "social problems" of the city. Their concern with "social pathology" developed just as the central ideas of social work were being introduced and this too happened in Chicago — a city characterized at the time by heavy immigration from rural areas and abroad, and displaying very evident signs of disorganization and "uprootedness." In this context, the emerging focus of American sociology on the empirical study of poverty and gangs, of prostitutes and criminals, was hardly surprising. And when one considers that a great many of these sociologists had rural backgrounds themselves and were either ministers or the sons of ministers, the orientation of their work is again made more understandable. It was during this same period that George Herbert Mead was creating much of the body of symbolic interaction theory, focusing his attention on issues of socialization and the acquisition of a self.

Modern American sociology is no longer dominated so clearly by any single department in the United States. Major contributors have come from Harvard and Columbia, from Michigan, Wisconsin, and Berkeley, while many other influential sociologists are now widely distributed throughout the universities of the United States. American sociologists have trained individuals from elsewhere and have themselves been exported (to Canada, for example), carrying with them an agenda of both methods and substantive areas of interest that has been of great influence all over the world. Indeed, it is to the implications of this export of American sociology that we now turn.

THE ISSUE OF NATIONAL SOCIOLOGIES

National Sociologies and Context-Free Science

The foregoing description of the origins and development of sociology has made it clear that context and current events have always shaped the focus of the sociology discipline. The turmoil of the political and industrial revolutions in Europe gave rise to sociology and led to its concern with

the issues of solidarity, of the impact of bureaucratization, industrialization, and of urbanization. Once sociology as a science was transplanted to the United States, additional issues arose from the American environment, and sociologists turned their attention to social problems and their amelioration and to more quantitative and empirical studies on a smaller scale than those favored in Europe. Such considerations emphasize the point that sociology responds to and reflects its context. It is a science, but it is not a context-free science that is the same no matter where it is practised or by whom. It is this responsiveness, this *ethnocentrism*, that leads to a number of thorny scientific and political issues.

Ethnocentrism is the belief, implicit or explicit, that your own group, culture, or society is central, and provides the yardstick against which other cultures or societies can be measured. It is illustrated most graphically in the case of European missionaries arriving in Africa or the Pacific islands and seeking to convert the natives, not only to the "true religion," but also to European clothing! Classical science is not supposed to be ethnocentric. It is supposed to strive for universals, rather than statements that are context or culture specific. Yet sociology clearly has been strongly influenced by its environment, and one therefore can legitimately wonder whether any "universals" it may claim to have discovered might be true only in their country of origin.

If the findings of sociology were society-specific, it would be imperative that each society developed its own national variety of sociology. Otherwise, solutions that worked in one context could be disruptive failures in another society to which they had been illegitimately generalized. Furthermore, issues of importance to one society are not necessarily the issues of importance to another. This suggests again that national priorities and interests ought to set the agenda for sociologists, and that they ought not to assume that their studies must be limited by what has been decided elsewhere.

In Canada, until recently, most social science has been conducted by Americans or Europeans, or those trained in the United States or Europe. What difference has this made?

Let me offer one particular example. Race Relations is a course commonly offered in Sociology departments. It is an area to which considerable research attention has been devoted. Most students in Sociology at one time or another take at least one course in this area. Yet the subject matter is not the same in all societies. In the early 1960s, Canadian universities expanded enormously and most of the faculty was hired from abroad. This situation produced the peculiar circumstance in which many Canadian students in Race Relations courses in Canada studied the history and sociology of relationships among blacks and whites in the United States. The teachers hired from abroad were unfamiliar with Canadian materials and with the Canadian situation. They therefore quite naturally fell back on prior training and interests acquired at that time. The result was absurd. The 1960s was a period of considerable tension in Canada among French- and English-speaking people, and many other minorities (Indians and eastern European ethnics, for example) were awakening and mobilizing. Yet this material was not taught in Canada, even in courses called Race Relations. Furthermore, and possibly even more distressing, the area attracted little of the attention, interest, or research that would have been required to develop it in the context of Canadian society.

French-English relations in Canada are not equivalent to those among blacks and whites in the United States, though the comparison is useful and suggestive. The study of the differences that variations in context make is one of the ways of defining sociology, and it requires real comparisons actually done, not assumed. It follows that a Canadian sociology will in some ways be different from its American or British counterpart, even as the societies differ. Yet this is still not the end of the implications of this debate, for

Since the 1960s, many ethnic groups and other minorities within Canada have mobilized in order to preserve their rights, as well as their heritage. Here, a native dancer participates in a rally to guarantee aboriginal rights in the Canadian Constitution (1983).

another issue concerns the methods and theories themselves and their cultural content.

It is the view of classical scientists that theory is theory and method is method. There is no cultural content that contaminates these, for science is culture-free as a process and institution. The quest for objectivity means precisely this: that cultural or social context will be irrelevant. An Israeli and an Iraqi might agree with a Russian or an American that a conclusion is warranted, if all are scientists and the study in question has been objectively conducted.

The scientific relativist is much more aware of the social context of science, and of its status as a social product. This means that both theories and methods will change over time, as fashions change. This suggests in turn that sociology as practised in the United States may not be the appropriate kind of model for practitioners in Asia, Africa, or Canada, who may develop indigenous theories and methods that differ from those advocated in Berkeley or Harvard, London or Paris, and be no less accurate or appropriate for being different. If European sociology is more theoretical, more qualitatively inclined, more philosophical and historical, and American sociology is more empirical and quantitative, cannot Canadian sociology be different, too, growing from its unique context and heritage? Once again, the issue concerns the source of standards, and their evaluation. For the classical scientist, there is only one truth and only one science. For the relativist, there are many truths, and all are only temporary and tentatively held. There are many methods that claim to be valid, all of which must be carefully and continually tested in many different ways if we are to be able to distinguish the useful from the useless. In our concern that sociology be a science, we do continually seek wider and wider generalizations. We would like to achieve a sociology of race and ethnic relations, for example, that is equally applicable to *all* societies, but at the same time we must be cautious, fully aware that it is both easy to overgeneralize and crucial that we not do so.

The Quest for a Canadian Sociology

Sociology has a brief history in Canada. The first department of Sociology (McGill's) was not begun until 1923, and Sociology was taught in a joint department of Political Economy at the University of Toronto from 1939 until 1963. As of the late 1960s, there were probably fewer than one hundred sociologists in all of Canada. The Canadian Sociological and Anthropological Association did not come into existence until 1965 and the flagship journal of Canadian sociology, the *Canadian Review of Sociology and Anthropology*, began publication in 1964. Only a handful of Ph.D.'s had been awarded in Canada throughout the decade of the 1960s, but it was in the 1960s that the picture changed dramatically.

In the 1960s, the baby-boom generation came of age to attend university. At the same time, higher education was given a strong boost by a government that had decided that increased education was the key to national development. Parenthetically, it is important to note that even this commitment to increasing the availability of higher education was imported from the United States, and is one example of a strategy that had some success in the United States while backfiring in important ways in Canada. In the 1960s, the universities of the west were opened and others expanded. Since there were virtually no Canadian Ph.D.'s, Canada was forced to import professors to staff her new universities. These faculty members came from the United States and Europe. In Sociology they were overwhelmingly American, or American-trained, although French-Canadian schools tended to recruit more heavily from France. In fact, it was during this period that anglophone and francophone sociology in Canada diverged considerably, as anglophone sociology was pulled toward the American model of quantitative survey research on fairly specific topics, while francophone research emphasized issues of national survival and ethnic identity, and utilized a wider variety of historical methods and a more philosophical approach.

In line with the argument presented to this point, it has been the differing concerns and contexts of anglophone and francophone sociology that have influenced their directions. From the 1930s through to the late 1950s, sociology in Canada was a fairly typical Canadian hybrid of European and American orientations and methods. It was strongly historical and shared the European macro-level emphasis. In addition, the many case studies of industrialization and its impacts, particularly in Québec, were written after the fashion of the Chicago School. Subsequently, under the leadership of Harold Innis at the University of Toronto, economic considerations were emphasized and the initial outlines of our grave concern with Canada's economic relationships with other societies was formulated in Innis's "staples theory." S.D. Clark is another more recent exemplar of this infant indigenous Canadian sociology mixed with history and political economy, as is John Porter (arguably Canada's most famous sociologist), author of *The Vertical Mosaic*, the seminal and influential study of Canada's stratification system.

The massive influence of the American newcomers in the 1960s effectively delayed the coming of age of any Canadian sociology that might have borne the imprint of its own national society. Throughout the 1960s and into the 1970s, anglophone sociology in particular was dominated by these imports, and relatively little research attention was paid to the more particularly Canadian issues, such as regional disparities, economic and cultural dependency, the impact of multinationals, and the impact of changing immigration patterns. In addition, as has been argued, even when sociologists did look at issues of great importance to Canada, they often displayed a tendency to ignore the Canadian features, while concentrating on those in common with the United States. Thus the study of social problems gave short shrift to Indian Rights, and the study of minorities paid little attention to French Canadians.

In the late 1960s and early 1970s, this issue was brought to public attention by articles and books calling for the Canadianization of our universities and preferential hiring practices that would see Canadian Ph.D.'s hired before others, and a demand for courses in Canadian studies and the use of Canadian texts in social science courses. These recent trends have continued into the 1980s and a more vigorous, potentially different, and particularly Canadian sociology is now taking shape. This sociology is sensitive to Canadian issues and to Canadian perspectives. It no longer so slavishly follows the American lead.

The issue of national sociologies turns out to be much the same as the issue of the nature of science. In both instances, there has been long and hot debate between cultural relativists and classical absolutists. In both instances, the battle is between those who seek universals and those who believe that such a search, while commendable, will be fruitless, since different societal contexts inevitably set different parameters within which scientists work. Fortunately, sociology is a broad enterprise and there is certainly room in it for sociologists engaged in the creation of uniquely national sociology, and for those whose goal remains a universal sociology as free of uniquely national features as they can make it.

WHAT'S IT GOOD FOR? APPLICATIONS OF SOCIOLOGY

Students with a degree in Sociology may have any of a wide variety of substantive course backgrounds. Some may have extensive methodological and statistical training; some may have none. Some may have macro-structural orientations while others may lean to the micro-interpretive perspective. Possession of a degree therefore tells us little about the student's "real" background, beyond the fact that the individual has a degree in social science.

Students with such degrees have a wide range of occupational choices, and they compete favorably with students who have other undergraduate degrees. Sociology backgrounds may be an advantage to students wishing to pursue a career in social welfare agencies, or in any capacity in government or industry in which research design, data collection, analysis, and presentation are important. Since our society is increasingly concerned with information as a prerequisite to marketing or policy in government and out, these skills are increasingly highly valued. Students whose

Sociology background includes statistics and methods therefore possess a considerable and growing advantage in the marketplace. Sociology students who know that they wish to go on into Law, Management, Environmental Design, Social Welfare, or Criminology, can select from a wide variety of courses those most appropriate for them. Certainly a background in Sociology can prove helpful in all of these areas.

More generally speaking, sociologists study all the institutional arrangements in which we live, and sociologists have come to learn a reasonable amount about how these institutions work. Thus, the study of the family may help you decide what might happen in the future, in the event that you and your spouse should both be working. You may have have other questions. What are the effects, if any, of parent absence on child-rearing? How does retirement most often affect marital satisfaction? What is the "normal" pattern of behavior that culminates in divorce? Are there ways in other societies in which mobility may occur in a less disruptive manner than it does in North America? How can ties be maintained over time, and across generations and cultural barriers? Whether you go on into social work or whether you simply live in a family, such information can help you by making you more aware of the factors that affect your behavior.

The same types of illustrations could be multiplied for every relationship you are involved in, whether at school, at work, or among friends. We learn in sociology that there is great variety in social arrangements and behavior; that there are other options that are deemed appropriate, acceptable, and succesful in some circumstances. We may learn that organizations, for example, can be structured other than according to a formal bureaucratic model, and that they can still achieve their goals, or achieve them even more successfully. We may learn that there are a wide variety of family forms that work for different people under some circumstances, and that no one form is permanent or more "correct" than another.

As a science, sociology can lead to a deeper understanding of every relationship you are involved in, whether at school, at work, or among friends.

We may learn that cities are not everywhere alienating and dangerous environments, and we may learn what factors can make cities more humane and hospitable. The primary value of sociology is that it sensitizes us to ways in which behavior is shaped by factors of which we may well have been unaware. This sensitization, this awareness, gives us the power and the responsibility to take a greater hand in shaping our own behavior.

We learn to recognize and evaluate aspects of our own lives and society as compared to others, and as compared to what they might be. Along the way, we learn to be tolerant of differences rather than ethnocentric. We learn that while there are norms, we can choose to conform to them or not. This choice becomes yours as a result of your sociological exposure. It is a choice worth having.

SUMMARY

1. Sociology is more accurately understood as a perspective than as a substantive field.

2. As a social science, sociology emphasizes the preeminence of cultural contributions in making sense of human behavior.

3. Though there is much overlap, the differences among social sciences are primarily differences in the choice of explanatory and key independent variables.

4. Among sociologists, there are two primary sets of such explanantory variables. One such set could be termed macro-structural, the other micro-interpretive. The choice of focus affects and reflects the questions asked, and the methods used.

5. The macro-structural perspective has three main aspects:
   i. network of interdependent positions
   ii. ecological structure
   iii. normative structure

In all cases, social factors are thought of as outside of and transcending the individual, and shaping human behavior.

6. The micro-interpretive perspective is based on symbolic interaction. The key premise is that "if a situation is defined as real, it is real in its consequences." The study of sociology involves examination of how people create and negotiate the meanings of their "reality."

7. Adherents of a classical view of science believe they can discover patterns of recurrent elements in behavior that are causally and systematically related to one another. They seek generalizable knowledge based on empirical methods that are replicable.

8. Adherents of a more humanistic view of the sociology discipline are primarily interested in comprehending the meaning of behavior. They may or may not be concerned with generalizing, and may or may not rely on different methods.

9. The three most influential founders of sociology are Durkheim, Marx, and Weber. Each contributed widely to our methods, to our theories, and to several substantive areas of study.

10. As a discipline, sociology traces its roots to the great revolutions, both political and economic, of recent history. The early sociologists wrote in an attempt to understand and foresee the social implications of such dramatic and drastic changes.

11. Sociology today still grapples with the intuitions and analyses of these fathers of the discipline. Their views are still our inspiration and our challenge.

12. The issue of national sociologies, including the quest for a Canadian sociology, is a reflection of the growing awareness of the effects of social context even on the institution of science. The quest for a Canadian sociology reflects a belief that these contextual features are of great importance and that they can be dealt with positively.

13. While a background in Sociology is helpful preparation for many subsequent careers, it is its broader impact on the students' ability to understand their world that makes sociology valuable.

GLOSSARY

Culture. Everything expressed by humans that is not physically inherited, including values, attitudes, and behavior.

Definition of the situation. Thomas's dictum that "if a situation is defined as real, it is real in its consequences."

Determinism. The idea that there is not free choice; that all behavior is fixed and could not be otherwise.

Ethnocentrism. The belief that your own group, culture, or society is correct, and is the yardstick against which others are to be measured.

Explanatory variables. Variables that are expected to explain why other variables change as they do.

Human ecology. The relationship of humans to territory.

Internalization. The process whereby that which is learned is taken into oneself and made a part of one's personality.

Macro-structural. A focus on variables that transcend individuals, are external and coercive, and are related to other similar features of the society in systematic fashion.

Mode (modal). The most frequently occurring category or score.

Norm. Regulation, rule, guideline, or standard of what is expected or what is acceptable behavior.

Paradigm. A model.

Perspectives. The point of view by which emphasis is placed on one or another variable as most basic.

Positivism. A hard version of classical science in which concern is with a search for laws quantification and manipulation.

Reactivity. The idea that the data can be affected by the investigator's presence.

Recidivism. Repetition of criminal activity.

Relativism. The idea that nothing is universal. Everything is contingent or conditional, dependent on its relationship to other things.

Replication. Repetition of a study to corroborate or retest it.

Role. The expected behavior associated with a status.

Sanction. Positive or negative reinforcements, rewards or punishments.

Socialization. The process of learning.

Status. A position in the system of interdependent positions held by individuals in society's structure.

Stratification. The system of layering in a society by which some strata are super- and others subordinate.

Symbolic interactionism. The school of sociology that is heavily social psychological and emphasizes the aspects of meaning negotiation.

Transformation dichotomies. The various dichotomies expressed by many classical authors to try to capture the dramatic changes from pre-industrial, small scale societies to the emerging industrial and urban ones.

Value judgement. A judgement of the moral qualities of some act, i.e., that it is "good" or "bad."

Verstehen. Intuitive understanding "from inside the actor's head."

FURTHER READING

Berger, Peter L. *Invitation to Sociology: A Humanistic Perspective.* New York: Anchor Books; Doubleday and Company Inc., 1963. A book some people feel is singlehandedly responsible for attracting a great many people into the field. Well written, but students sometimes find the language a little difficult and the examples a little lengthy. Chapters 2, 4, 5, and 6 are excellent.

Hagedorn, Robert and Sanford Labovitz. *An Introduction into Sociological Orientations.* New York: John Wiley and Sons, 1973. The first two major sections in particular are clearly written discussions of the major orientations to the discipline, including points of convergence and disagreement.

Mills, C. Wright. *The Sociological Imagination.* New York: Oxford University Press, 1959. A classic in the discipline, and a book with which every student of sociology should be familiar.

Broom, Leonard and Philip Selznick. *Essentials of Sociology* (2nd. ed.). New York: Harper and Row Publishers Inc., 1979. A concise American introduction for the student who may find Berger a little too abstract. American substantive orientation and treatment, with very little comparative Canadian data.

Himmelfarb, Alexander and C.J. Richardson. *Sociology for Canadians: Images of Society.* Toronto: McGraw Hill Ryerson Limited, 1983. A thorough introduction to Canadian society and to sociology in Canada in general. A selected treatment of several major themes and institutions in Canadian society.

CHAPTER TWO

Theoretical Models in Sociology

NICO STEHR and AXEL VAN DEN BERG

*Owing to the contemporary mania for what are
called facts, we are apt to forget that an age can
only learn to know itself if the different methods
of approach, the power of formulation, and the
analysis of complex phenomena, do not lag behind
the collection of data. It is not enough that our
age should be rich in a knowledge of fundamental facts, which gives it ample scope for new experiences; it must also frame its questions adequately.
This it can only do if the tradition of theoretical
formulation is held in the same esteem as the technique of sheer fact finding.* Karl Mannheim

All scientific disciplines require theoretical models or, as they are variously called, theoretical perspectives, approaches, or paradigms, because they
make examination of certain specific questions
possible and in some sense orderly and directed
rather than haphazard, accidental, and of course,
rather uncertain. In science, theoretical models
perform the indispensable function of guiding
research by suggesting broad ways of looking at
the world, the kinds of questions that are worth
asking, and the sorts of answers that are deemed
satisfactory. Models by themselves do not provide
definite answers but they certainly provide the
questions and they thereby clearly pre-structure
the answers.

Theoretical models are of particular importance to sociology as a scientific discipline because it is after all a discipline that deals primarily with ideas and symbols, rather than objects, techniques, formulas, and the like. But models, even in sociology, remain *models*. That is, they are representations of aspects of social reality that cannot and do not claim to faithfully depict each and every feature of social reality. And importantly, there is not a single widely accepted model of social reality in sociology today but a number of diverging ones. Of course, each of the competing sociological models of social reality aspires to become the predominant model in sociology. But none has thus far succeeded, nor is it likely that a single model will become dominant in the near future.

The reasons for the greater diversity of and controversy over theoretical models in sociology as compared with the natural sciences, are themselves the subject of much debate and controversy. But there is little doubt that these differences between sociology and natural science are at least partly the result of their different subject matters. Unlike the objects studied by natural science, the subject matter of sociology, the social world, is entirely man-made; it is the product of, or rather *consists* of, human agency and is therefore presumably subject to human will. This simple statement raises a whole series of issues that appear to be extremely difficult to resolve. It not only suggests alternative ways of representing social reality, but at a deeper level, it raises questions about the very nature and purpose of social scientific knowledge. As a result, it would seem impossible to come to any agreement on which of the existing models, or combination of models, is better than the others, since even the criteria for what makes a model "better" are controversial!

All this can be clearly seen in the broad issues on which major theoretical models in sociology differ. They fall, roughly, into four broad categories. *First*, there is the problem of how to view the relation between the individual (agency) and

Karl Marx considered ethics, politics, and religion to be the products of socioeconomic relations.

the society (social structure) of which one is a member. Since society is obviously nothing more than people interacting (and yet each person's actions are the outcome of, and occur in and through, a society that the individual did not create), one can *either* ask how the actions of certain people create and change society, *or* how society (norms, institutions, and so on) shapes and conditions people's actions. *Second*, there is the question of the nature of social change: do societies evolve according to certain scientifically observable, fixed evolutionary principles or is historical development an infinite variety of choices, accidents, and struggles? *Third*, and perhaps basic to all others, is there a fixed, unalterable human nature, and if so, what are its features? *Fourth*, what is the role of (social) science in all this? Is it only to observe and explain or does it have an additional task, such as helping to create a social world that corresponds more closely to human nature, or conversely, to bring about human attitudes that correspond to the requirements of the social world, or even to help change *both* society *and* human attitudes to correspond more closely to some higher ideal or evolutionary requirement?

Obviously these are tough questions to answer. Moreover, as the third and fourth questions suggest, the issues are so closely related that they are often impossible to disentangle, let alone resolve. At any rate, they are of such a general, philosophical character that they may well be unresolvable in principle. Yet it is precisely their generality that makes them indispensable in inspiring and guiding sociological research. The major sociological models serve to suggest to the researchers in the various specialized fields — industrial sociology, for instance, or the sociology of deviance or the family — what questions to ask, what variables to take into account, and how to place their findings in the larger framework of society as a whole. Thus, the researchers in all subdisciplines of sociology necessarily rely upon one or more of the various broad theoretical models discussed in this chapter for direction and for a more comprehensive frame of reference.

These considerations also help to explain why the major theoretical models of sociology — again, in contrast to natural science — are even today closely connected with the various founders of the discipline who first formulated them, especially Auguste Comte, Karl Marx, Herbert Spencer, Emile Durkheim, Max Weber, George Herbert Mead, and Vilfredo Pareto.

Sociology today, in many ways, relies on interpretations, revisions, and elaborations of models first advanced as major sociological perspectives by one or the other of these intellectual founders

of sociology. And the main difference between sociology today and the contribution of the founders is one of content, not of theoretical intent and concepts. Therefore, despite the rapidity of sociohistorical change, our awareness of these changes and the advances made by social scientists in developing the methods of social research, the major sociological models continue to retain their relevance because the issues they deal with are of such a general and perhaps timeless character that they cannot be resolved any more easily today than a century ago.

It is not unusual for treatments of sociological theory to identify different models with individual authors, particularly the "founding fathers" just mentioned. Other ways of categorizing and presenting the major theoretical models, such as by historical period or on the basis of their different treatments of some central problem (e.g., power, inequality, community) are no less plausible. Each such classification represents, of course, a kind of model of sociological models in its own right, implying what material is relevant, why it is relevant, and how it is to be organized and presented. We have already presented the model of sociological models we will use to organize our materials by identifying four broad issue-areas on which the major perspectives tend to differ: the relation between society and the individual, social change, human nature, and the nature and purpose of sociology itself. Seen from this perspective, the major theoretical models in sociology can be said to fall into three, more or less distinct broad groups:

1. structural models
2. conflict models
3. interactionist models.

The degree to which each of these models represents a relatively *homogeneous* group of models with a *distinct* outlook and whether or not they are mutually exclusive outlooks, are matters of continuing debate within sociology that we cannot hope to resolve here. No doubt, in the course of the polemical exchanges between advocates of

Sociological models stress that social relations and institutions exist above and beyond particular individuals, and that social reality is external to the individual.

rival models, the differences between them have been emphasized, and even exaggerated, to the neglect of some of the similarities in ideas. It is worth remembering that these are virtually without exception *sociological* models, as opposed to the common-sense view of social reality, which is for the most part naively egocentric. Thus, at a minimum, they agree that the common-sense view of society is in some respects misleading. Sociological models stress time and again that social relations and institutions exist above and beyond

particular individuals, that social reality is external to the individual. Sociological models are, in other words, not as subject-centered as their common-sense counterparts.

THE STRUCTURAL (FUNCTIONAL) MODELS

The structural (functional) model in sociology traces its origins to the work of Comte, Spencer, and Durkheim in particular. Among its contemporary influential representatives are Talcott Parsons and Robert K. Merton.

Most sociological models contribute to our understanding of why social life is ordered, predictable, and patterned. Our own expectations, and the expectations of others of and during a wide range of social activities, normally are fulfilled rather than disappointed. Sociological models differ, however, when it comes to explaining either the source or the importance of social order to society.

Comte, Spencer, and Durkheim introduced a specific set of answers to the question of the prevalence of social order, or of why social cohesion is part of our normal experience and what importance it generally has for society. More recently, the structural model has been labelled the *structural-functional* perspective in sociology because, as we shall see, sociologists who have contributed to the development of the structural model frequently have asked themselves what purpose or function is served by various existing social arrangements.

The Structural Models of Comte, Spencer, and Durkheim

The specifics of the theories of Auguste Comte (1798–1857) may today be considered obsolete by sociologists, but Comte remains a central figure in the history of sociological thought for he was the founder and prophet of a new science of society that *he* called "sociology." Sociology was to be the "queen of the sciences," enabling mankind to go beyond scientifically controlling the processes of nature, by scientifically designing and administering even society itself. Sociology would, Comte firmly believed, provide the scientific understanding of the intricate relations and interactions between the various parts of the society necessary to find the right social institutions and arrangements to assure the perfect balance between order and progress. Sociology, then, was to become a practical guide to the scientifically correct organization and governance of society.

Comte sought to justify these rather large claims in his system of "positive philosophy." The evolution of the human mind, which determines the character of civilizations, social institutions, and material conditions of human life, Comte thought, is a long-term progression through three necessary successive stages: the theological or fictitious stage, in which the natural and social world are thought to be ruled by supernatural forces or beings, and in which society is dominated and ruled by priests and military men, is the first and longest stage; then come the metaphysical or abstract stage, a transitional stage in which supernatural beings are replaced by abstract, "universal" principles and society is dominated by clergymen and legal specialists; finally, there is the positive or scientific stage, in which abstract principles give way to scientific study of the immediate causes and consequences of things, and in which society will eventually be governed by an elite of industrial administrators and scientists. Roughly, in European history, the theological stage seems to have prevailed until the late Middle Ages; the metaphysical stage coincides with the period from the Renaissance until the early nineteenth century; and the positive stage, Comte believed, was just arriving in his time and would become more fully realized with the inevitable advance of science and industry.

The development of the sciences, Comte claimed, to some extent parallelled the evolution of human civilization but according to evolutionary principles of its own. Each science progresses through the three stages, too, which culminate in the positive stage when it comes to rely exclusively on the scientific methods of observation and reasoning. But the sciences develop in a fixed succession, rather than simultaneously, starting with those dealing with the least complex phenomena but of most general applicability and ending with the least general, most complex sciences, which depend for their development on the results obtained by the less complex but more general ones. Thus, the sciences became positive accord-

"Primitive" societies with only a rudimentary division of labor and minimal social inequality are highly cohesive. This Tongan woman, incidentally, is in mourning, as the mat wrapped around her indicates.

ing to a sequence that begins with mathematics, physics, and chemistry, and ends with biology and sociology. The reaching of the positive stage by sociology coincides with the positive stage in the development of mind and civilization: it provides the knowledge necessary for the scientific organization and control of that most complex of all realms, society.

In order to uncover the laws of society with a certainty and precision matching those of physics or astronomy, sociology must be divided into two main parts: *statics* deals with the requirements for maintaining social order and stability in any society, while *dynamics* will uncover the inescap-

able laws of development, which man can only ignore at his peril. The first law of statics, Comte maintained, was that social order and harmony depended most crucially on widespread acceptance of the proper values and norms and on a feeling of social solidarity. This consensus, to be maintained by the family and educational system as the prime socializing agents, he believed, was absolutely indispensable to curb the elementary selfish drives of individuals, which, if left unchecked, would wreak havoc with the social order. This idea was to become a recurrent theme in structural (functional) theorizing.

Comte did not pay a great deal of attention to dynamics, but he did point to the increasing division of labor as one inevitable trend that would necessitate an increasingly important role for governmental coordination. In general, Comte's major concern was that government and social organization was not a matter of choice that could be safely left to laymen, such as politicians or the electorate, but was a matter of scientific understanding of the "laws" of society. Thus, he felt that government should be controlled or at least guided by social scientists. Toward the end of his life he moderated his extreme reliance on science somewhat, but not his belief in rule by an enlightened elite, as he proclaimed himself the high priest of a "Religion of Humanity."

Herbert Spencer (1820–1903) was less concerned with the need for moral consensus than other theorists of the structural (functional) tradition in sociology. His major contributions lay in drawing out the implications of a close analogy he made between societies and living organisms. The entire universe, Spencer believed, developed according to a single principle of evolution, which leads from simple, homogeneous forms and structures to ever more complex and heterogeneous ones, better adapted to the constantly changing requirements of survival. Just as Charles Darwin had shown how biological species evolved by a mechanism of natural selection of those features best suited to the environment, Spencer claimed societies could also be shown to evolve according to the principle of "survival of the fittest."

This line of argument led Spencer to ideas that were to become basic to the structural (functional) approach. Living organisms, he reasoned, have a *structure*; that is, they are made up of different but interrelated parts that have a necessary role to play, or *function* to perform in assuring that the organism remains healthy and capable of successfully responding to the demands of a changing environment. If one part fails to perform its function, the survival of the organism as a whole may be at stake. In the case of society, the structure consists of vital, social processes that assure social cohesion and ultimately survival, such as arrangements for central regulation, the provision of sustenance, and distribution. These vital functions are met in societies by institutions such as the political system, the economy, the division of labor, and the family. These institutions, Spencer believed, were the result of a long evolution from simple, undifferentiated social arrangements of primitive bands, to the infinitely more complex and differentiated social structures of modern industrial society.

The division of labor and social differentiation is also a central theme in the work of the French sociologist, Emile Durkheim (1858–1917). However, not unlike his fellow countryman Comte, Durkheim was primarily concerned with its significance for the minimal social solidarity necessary to maintain a viable social order. In combining the themes that had preoccupied Comte and Spencer, Durkheim developed a structural model of society and a conception of sociology that are still relevant to contemporary sociology.

Sociology, according to Durkheim, should be concerned with the study of "social facts," that is, primarily with the social norms and expectations that people share and that influence and constrain their behavior. These norms and expectations have an almost thing-like existence external to any given individual and are felt even by those who refuse to obey them in the form of guilt feelings, peer pressure, and the like. By stressing these external, thing-like "social facts" as the proper subject-matter for sociology, Durkheim did much to develop an object-centered sociological conception of society and our place in it. Durkheim's conception emphasizes how the behavior and the motives of individuals are shaped and conditioned by the norms crystalized into social institutions.

Durkheim saw society as primarily a *moral* community, in the sense of a collectivity held together by shared sentiments and beliefs, or as he sometimes put it, by a "collective conscience." He persistently tried to show how the various features of social life, which are often seen to represent purely economic relations, are viewed as the outcome of pure self-interest (such as the division of labor, for example, or the system of market exchange) and how these are in fact moral (collective) phenomena with distinctly moral consequences. Different societies and broad social changes for Durkheim represent and result in differences in the dominant moral values of a society.

Durkheim claims that due to the advancing division of labor in society, the character of the social solidarity necessary to hold society together has undergone a major, qualitative change. Primitive societies with only a rudimentary division of labor and minimal degree of social inequality are held together by "*mechanical solidarity*," a form of solidarity based on a similarity of individuals that makes them practically interchangeable. The activities and experiences people engage in are so much alike that individuals cannot even conceive of themselves as distinct from their community: collective and individual conscience coincide almost completely. However, as the division of labor increases, so does, by definition, the number of activities and experiences people can engage in. Thus, people become aware of differences among themselves and they become aware of themselves as individuals, distinct from the community, with aspirations and needs of their own. For a society to remain viable as social differentiation increases, it must, according to Durkheim, develop a new kind of solidarity, an *"organic solidarity"* based on the individuals' awareness and acceptance of the increasing mutual dependence on each other.

The division of labor, then, poses a basic problem of integration for modern society, because it creates potentially unlimited individual aspirations and desires that no society, no matter how advanced, can ever hope to satisfy. A ruinous struggle over scarce resources can only be avoided if society can curb the aspirations of its members. What is needed is an evolving organic solidarity, a set of shared norms and values, capable of reconciling people to the rewards and satisfactions that they can realistically expect to receive.

But this requirement of a dynamic equilibrium between a progressing division of labor and an evolving value consensus opens up the danger of a gap between the two. Thus, people may be caught in a situation where they lack the appropriate moral constraints and normative guidelines to reconcile their aspirations, a situation Durkheim called *"anomie"* or rulelessness. Such a situation causes a disintegration of the social order by provoking both fierce social conflict and widespread apathetic withdrawal. In his famous study of suicide, Durkheim sought to document the existence and dangers of anomie by linking variations in suicide rates to variations in the degree of social integration of individuals, and their aspirations, into different communities.

Durkheim, like Comte, thought that sociology would provide the knowledge necessary to control the persistent threat of anomie. By close examination of the way social institutions perform cohesive functions at different stages of social development, it should be possible for sociology to suggest the appropriate values and institutions to maintain the requisite level of organic solidarity. With this in mind, Durkheim embarked upon his famous studies of the functions of religion in maintaining the moral unity of pre-modern society, and of socialism as one non-scientific attempt

to re-establish moral unity in modern society. He believed sociology could provide a scientific answer to the problem of moral unity in modern industrial society and he made a number of specific proposals himself. These chiefly had to do with the establishment of professional organizations uniting employers and employees within each industrial sector, which would, he thought, moderate class conflict, regulate the terms of exchange between sectors, serve as a communication channel between the government and the citizens, and as agencies for the development and inculcation of the values and attitudes necessary to maintain social integration.

Whatever the merits of Durkheim's specific policy recommendations, he firmly established the structural model of society as preoccupied with the functions performed by social institutions in curbing and harmonizing individual aspirations and actions by means of shared norms and beliefs.

The Modern Structural (Functional) Models

Talcott Parsons (1902–1979) emphasized the functionalist aspect of the structural model and tried to develop it into a general social theory.

To expect sociology to provide solutions to major practical problems, as Comte and Durkheim had done, was premature, in the view of Parsons. Before sociology could yield any solid causal propositions, let alone make practical policy recommendations, Parsons felt it was first necessary to map out the social world by means of an ordered and well-defined system of concepts and categories. However, in elaborating his system of concepts, Parsons did from the start accept Comte's and Durkheim's major sociological problem: how are the potentially limitless expectations and aspirations of individual men and women reconciled and harmonized to yield a relatively stable and predictable social order?

Parsons began by defining the most basic elements of a "voluntaristic theory of action": the "unit act" in actors must make subjective decisions about goals to pursue and the *means* they will utilize to achieve them, decisions that are shaped by the *situational conditions* they face and the *norms, values, and ideas* they adhere to. But, as this first conceptualization already suggests, action does not take place in social isolation. Rather, it occurs in the context of the actions of numerous others, which together form a highly interdependent *system of action*. Moreover, these systems of (inter-)action appear to be relatively regular and stable patterns; they can be conceived as structures of interrelated statuses occupied by individuals who play roles corresponding to these statuses as prescribed by apparently widely known norms, which, in turn, must derive from widely held cultural patterns. Such structures Parsons calls *social systems*, whether they be small groups or whole societies.

This conception of the social system immediately suggests the importance of *integration* as a functional problem on whose solution the survival of the system as a stable pattern depends. The question is: how are the broad cultural values produced and maintained, and how are the actors motivated so that the end result is a relatively stable and integrated pattern of roles in which each actor knows and complies with what is expected and knows what to expect of the others?

Parsons conceives of the mechanisms by which this integration is obtained along two lines. On the one hand, values and norms capable of integrating the system emerge in a *process of institutionalization*, in which actors, through complex processes of interaction, adjust their orientations and expectations to one another until a stable pattern acceptable to all is found. On the other hand, such stable patterns of expectations and behavior are maintained by two types of mechanisms that individuals will be sufficiently motivated to comply with. First, and most important, are mechanisms of *socialization*, through which the appropriate values and beliefs are internalized and come to form the individual's identity. The principle institutions that perform this all-important func-

The educational system serves to inculcate a society's values and beliefs in its youth, and helps to form the individual's identity.

tion of socialization are the family and the educational system. Second, and essentially to reinforce the socialization mechanisms, are mechanisms of *social control*, which function to resolve the strains and tensions and reduce the deviance that socialization fails to prevent. Such mechanisms range all the way from peer pressures and the law to outright physical coercion.

However, provision and integration of appropriate norms and values, and their inculcation and enforcement upon individual actors, are not the only functional requirements that must be met for a social system to survive, though they *are* the most crucial. In a further elaboration of his conceptual framework, Parsons distinguishes between four basic "functional imperatives" that any social system must meet: *adaptation*, or securing and distributing sufficient facilities from the environment to meet the physical needs (food and shelter, for instance) of the members; *goal-attainment*, or establishing agreement on collective goals and mobilizing resources to realize them; *integration*, or the coordination and harmonization of system elements, such as actors and roles and the norms and values guiding them; *latency* and *pattern maintenance*, or the motivation of actors to adopt and comply with norms and values and the elimination of tensions and strains. This is the now famous AGIL-scheme, which can be used to subdivide any social system into its componenet structures or subsystems, whose function it then is to meet the basic requirements for the survival of the system over time.

The structures or subsystems that perform these vital functions are developed slowly as the social system seeks to maintain its social cohesion while adapting to a changing environment. In other words, the social system evolves through a gradual differentiation of its structures that help maintain its stability and integrity, while at the same time enhancing its capacity for survival vis-à-vis the environment. But in keeping with the central place of cultural values in Parsons's overall conceptualization, what is most important for him is the evolution of the "paramount value pattern," which characterizes and shapes the culture, norms, and orientations of actors in the system as a whole. Parsons mentions a number of important "pattern variables;" that is, distinct patterns of values that distinguish social systems. The two most important of these are *universalism versus particularism*. This dichotomy refers to the choice between orientation toward universalistic, impersonally defined criteria of evaluation and evaluation on the basis of criteria that apply in different ways to members of, for example, different social or ethnic groups, communities, and females or males. A closely related variable is that of *achievement versus ascription*; that is, evaluation in terms

of a people's performance or assessment in terms of their origin or group membership. In the course of the process of social evolution, Parsons believed, societies have evolved more and more toward the universalism–achievement pole of the continuum; for him, advanced industrial societies, especially the United States, represent the epitome of that tendency.

Thus, in a more abstract fashion, Parsons reiterates many of the traditional themes of the structural (functional) model: the importance of a cultural value consensus in maintaining a viable balance between potentially conflicting individual expectations and aspirations, the analogy with the self-balancing organism and with organic evolution as a combination of adaptive change and maintenance of necessary stability, and finally, the explanation of social structures in terms of their functional role in all of these processes.

The contribution of Robert K. Merton (1910–   ) to the development of the structural model is in many ways designed to correct and react to some of the perceived shortcomings of the general functionalist model proposed by Parsons. In particular, Merton stresses that Parsons's general theory of society is too abstract and complex. The complexity of the model prevents it, for example, from being immediately useful in sociological research. Merton proposes instead that sociology should develop less general and abstract models that apply to smaller units or processes of society (*middle-range theories*); for example, models dealing with the problems of deviance, youth, or urban issues. Merton's reasoning is that sociological research (which should be based on models of this kind) simply is not advanced far enough to benefit effectively from highly general models, but he also believes that sociology should not completely abstain from working on general models.

Merton wants also to add to and alter the way in which the term function is employed by sociologists. He argues that the term has been used too generally; Merton emphasizes, for example, that social arrangements such as the university, facto-

Such social arrangements as universities, factories, and the army have clear-cut functions, but they also may have latent functions, which often pass unrecognized and may not be desirable.

ries, or the army, may have *manifest* functions — those which are intended by the individuals involved — as well as *latent* functions, which are unrecognized and have unintended consequences. Moreover, Merton points out that not all features of social life must necessarily have beneficial or positive functions simply by virtue of their existence; they may also have *dysfunctions*, a term Merton introduces to refer to the potential disruptive force of a social arrangement for the larger social system.

Merton finally adds the notion of functional alternatives to the meanings associated with the term functional analysis. The idea of functional alternatives is designed to alert sociologists to look for other consequences, which may well follow from certain social arrangements, or for similar results from different social processes.

To sum up, the structural (functional) model of society is primarily preoccupied with the problem of social integration. Structural (functional) theorists tend to emphasize how social institutions, and even more so, the values and norms embodied in them, shape the behavior of individuals. They also tend to view social change as a matter of an evolution of value patterns and institutional arrangements according to such abstract principles as differentiation and adaptation. Implicit in their emphasis on social order and value consensus, moreover, is a view of human nature as potentially selfish and disruptive. Finally, for some, such as Comte and Durkheim, this implies that sociology should seek to discover and help realize conditions that assure social cohesion and stability.

Because of this emphasis on the normality and even desirability of social order and integration, critics often charge that the structural (functional) model is an inherently conservative one. However, the contributors to the model have maintained that their model is a largely neutral, objective sociological model of society that is capable of dealing with problems of social change and conflict in society. Robert Merton, for example, has made an especially strong argument along these lines for his own, modified structural approach. But, as can be seen from even our brief discussion of his contributions, the gains made in terms of meeting some of the critics' objections may have to be paid for by a certain loss of the model's distinctness from the other models discussed in this chapter.

THE CONFLICT MODELS

Sociologists either view social life as generally characterized by shared values and beliefs or they see it primarily in terms of a continuous clash of conflicting interests of different groups in society. However, what is frequently presented as the conflict model constitutes anything but a single, unified theoretical approach. On the contrary, the various theories and theorists that are lumped together under this heading often differ as much from one another as they differ from theories belonging in the other major models. For example, there are those conflict theorists who believe social conflict to be part of human nature and those who believe it is only inevitable in certain types of societies. There are those who focus almost exclusively on whole societies or large institutions

and collectivities — much like functionalists tend to do — and those who are more concerned with smaller groups and even individuals, almost shading over into the *microsociological* approach discussed as the interactionist model below. Furthermore, some conflict theorists emphasize broad social change according to fixed evolutionary principles; others view social change as a chance outcome of social conflicts, and still others believe social change is largely an illusion. Finally, there are those conflict theorists who believe the mission of sociology is to criticize the established social arrangements that cause the prevalence of social conflict and coercion they see all around them, ultimately with a view of replacing those social arrangements with better, more equitable ones. And then there are conflict theorists who believe such a mission to be wholly outside the sphere of competence of science proper, because a scientific sociology should only concern itself with the determination and analysis of matters of fact, not with political and moral goals.

Not surprisingly, these differences in basic views tend to be related. Those who believe social conflict is not an aspect of human nature and that it can be alleviated by replacing present, "exploitative" social institutions with better ones, also tend to argue that sociology has a broad moral and political mission to fulfil. They furthermore tend to be somewhat more *macrosociologically* oriented than the other conflict theorists. But here, as elsewhere, there are some theorists who combine elements from a variety of general viewpoints. Finally, many, perhaps most, theorists who have been called "conflict theorists" object to that label precisely because it lumps together so many divergent theories.

However, we have retained the general label here because it has found wide acceptance and because it is not entirely unjustified. After all, conflict theorists *do* agree on some basic things. They agree that conflict is such a general feature of social life that its analysis should be of primary concern to sociologists. Furthermore, many conflict theorists also agree that the most persistent structural cause of social conflict, as well as its consequence, is inequality, although there are sharp differences of opinion about which form of inequality should be considered as the most fundamental. Nevertheless, conflict theorists distinguish themselves most clearly from structural-functionalists in that they do not treat power, prestige, or weath as collective resources serving the community as a whole, but rather as *scarce* values whose distribution and allocation is a source of continual competition and struggle between a variety of groups and individuals.

Radical-Critical Conflict Theory: Marxism

"The history of all hitherto existing society is the history of class struggles." This famous line from the *Communist Manifesto*, written more than 130 years ago by Karl Marx (1818–1883) and Friedrich Engels (1820–1895), aptly sums up why Marxism is generally viewed as the original inspiration of the conflict perspective in sociology. But the struggle of classes is not the *ultimate* cause of social change: it is only a reflection of even more profound factors that constitute the economic "base" of society.

The fundamental proposition of *historical materialism* — the name Engels later gave the doctrine — is that the economic "base" (that is, the economy) decisively shapes the sociocultural "superstructure," that is, the state and the legal system, religious and political beliefs, art, philosophy, and culture in general. In this process of determination of the superstructure by the base, the class struggle is the medium through which changes in the economy are expressed and transmitted to the sociocultural superstructure.

The economic base consists of two interrelated sets of factors whose interaction constitutes the ultimate cause of social change: the *forces of production* comprise the means of production and the level of scientific-technical development — in short, society's *technical* productive capacity; the

The most persistent cause of social conflict is inequality, although opinions differ about which form of inequality is the most fundamental and how it should be tackled.

relations of production consist of all the social relations people must, throughout history, enter into in order to produce: those between master and slave, lord and serf, capitalist and worker, as well as all the institutions of property and exchange on which such relations are based. All societies, except the most primitive and the future communist society, are class-divided societies, which means that their relations of production divide the population into two groups with sharply opposed interests: those who own and control the means of production and those who do not and who for that reason have to work for those who do to make a living. The former is the exploiting class and the latter the exploited class.

Marx and Engels distinguished a few broad types of economic system or "modes of production." These modes of production — in accordance with the fundamental materialist doctrine that the economic base determines the social superstructure — are used to distinguish broad types of society. Human history, Marx and Engels believed, is a more or less necessary succession of modes of production from primitive tribal communism, to ancient slavery, to feudalism, to capitalism, and finally, in the near future, to socialism and communism. In addition, they sometimes mention a sixth mode of production, orientalism, but its place in their historical scheme remains uncertain.

The development and succession of these modes of production is the result of the dynamic interaction between the forces and the relations of production. Initially, the newly established relations of production of each mode of production are always progressive in the sense that they stimulate an unprecedented growth of the forces of production or in society's productive capacity. This fact allows the new exploiting class to convince the exploited that the the new mode of production is in their interest, too. Thus, "the ideas of the ruling class" become for a time "the ruling ideas." But paradoxically, the very success of the exploiting class in developing the forces of production can only hasten its own eventual downfall. As the mode of production matures, its relations of production become increasingly conservative; from the initial motor of economic growth they turn into obstacles against further growth. The development of the forces of production stagnates. The exploiting and the exploited classes come to confront one another more and more directly and visibly, and it becomes more and more obvious to the latter that the exploiters do not in the least intend to share the fruits of progress with them. Thus, the exploited class comes to formulate its own distinct class consciousness in growing opposition to the exploiting class. The class struggle intensifies, until things finally come to a head in a great social revolution in which the formerly exploited class takes over the means of production, establishing its relations of production and thus becomes the new exploiting class, and the cycle then starts all over again.

Capitalism, Marx and Engels argued, is the last of the class-divided modes of production. It will be succeeded by socialism, in which classes and class exploitation will be abolished at last and forever. This is so, because under capitalism the *alienation* and dehumanization of the exploited class is carried to its extreme while at the same time capitalism is condemned, by its own dynamic forces, to develop the technical and social foundations that make an advanced, civilized society without classes possible for the first time in history. Under capitalism, the downtrodden workers will become such a huge majority that after *their* revolution there will be no one left to form a new exploited class.

The main institutions supporting capitalist relations of production are private ownership of the means of production and exchange of both commodities *and* labour on formally free markets. This divides society into two basic classes: the capitalist owners of the means of production (the "bourgeoisie") who seek to produce and sell their products on the market at a profit; and the non-owners, the workers (the "proletariat") who have nothing to sell but their labor-power which they must offer to the highest bidding capitalist — or starve.

Obviously the interests of capitalists and workers are directly opposed: the former want to hire labor at the lowest price possible so as to maximize their profit, while the latter naturally want to increase their wages as much as they can. The relationship is inherently exploitative for it could be shown, Marx claimed, that the capitalist could not possibly earn a profit except by paying his workers less in total wages than the value they were producing for him in products to be sold. But initially this was not so obvious to either the workers or even to the political economists who advocated and analyzed the new mode of production. The new system appeared vastly superior to its immediate predecessor, feudalism, in terms of developing the forces of production, as demonstrated by the Industrial Revolution, and in moral-political terms, as manifested by its slogan of "liberty, equality, and fraternity." However, as with all previous class-divided modes of production, capitalism's own economic dynamics would inevitably awaken the consciousness of the workers and lead to its eventual overthrow.

Thus, Marxism definitely shares the macrosociological outlook and broad evolutionary sweep of functionalism. Like functionalism, it focuses on institutions and collectivities to explain social change and individual behavior. But the forces that shape society, history, and the individual are quite different from those posited by functionalists. Change does not occur through steady evolution but through incessant conflict and class struggle culminating in social revolutions. However, Marxism views social conflict as undesirable and remediable, much like functionalism does, but the functionalist remedy — to put moral constraints on people's "natural" impulses to enable them to accept the "inevitable" frustrations of communal life — is not an acceptable solution to Marxists. This is because they believe both society *and* human nature are capable of *far* more dramatic change than functionalists are inclined to think. But whereas their remedies may differ, both Marxism and many functionalists (e.g., Comte, Durkheim) consider the legitimate mission of social science to be the analysis and criticsm of those social inequalities that provoke "unnecessary" social conflict and to formulate ways to abolish them. The role of social science is to actively help in the shaping of the historical process, which is to lead to a better, more equitable world. In Marxism, this stance is often referred to as "the unity of theory and praxis."

However, as the original Marxist predictions of a socialist revolution in advanced capitalism failed to materialize, that unity became increasingly precarious. The success of the Bolshevik revolution in Russia and the subsequent Soviet party dictatorship turned Marxism into a rigid orthodoxy there, mechanically applied whenever needed to justify the policy of the day. In the advanced capitalist countries, on the other hand, Marxists necessarily became increasingly preoccupied with theoretical questions as they sought to explain why

the predicted proletarian revolution had failed to come about. Typically, this has led "Western Marxism" to significantly qualify many of the basic tenets of historical materialism while seeking to integrate major themes from other sociological models.

There are basically two broad traditions in *Western Marxism*: (1.) Critical Theory stresses the role that theory must play in the quest for human emancipation, particularly by uncovering and criticizing forms of "false consciousness"; (2.) Structuralist Marxism takes itself to be a pure science of society, analyzing the reciprocal effects of social structures. Thus, many Marxists do not simply view Marxism as a doctrine, but as a systematic and comprehensive framework for the analysis of primarily capitalist society.

Critical Theory

Critical Theory was originally developed in the 1920s and early 1930s by a group of German scholars collectively known as the "Frankfurt School," the most well-known of whom were Max Horkheimer (1895-1973), Theodor Adorno (1903-1969), Herbert Marcuse (1898-1979), and Erich Fromm (1900-1980). After the rise of Hitler to power, they were forced to emigrate to the United States, where Marcuse and Fromm settled for good and achieved great fame. The failure of the expected socialist revolution and the rise, instead, of Fascism in Western Europe were the major phenomena the critical theorists attempted to come to grips with. This led them to pay considerably more attention to superstructural phenomena and to attribute much more independent causal force to them than more orthodox Marxists had done, while adopting aspects of Freudian psychology and phenomenological philosophy.

As the critical theorists see it, capitalist economic development has not led to working-class consciousness, but to acquiescence. Somehow, the system has managed to win the hearts and minds of its very victims, the workers. Thus, Marxist theory appears to have lost its practical counterpart

Herbert Marcuse combined Freudianism and Marxism in his social criticism. According to Marcuse, modern society is automatically repressive and requires violent revolution as the first step toward a Utopian society.

— a militant, socialist working-class. Therefore, theory is forced to base its criticisms of the irrationalities of the capitalist system on more abstract principles of human liberation and emancipation. On the basis of such principles, Critical Theory proposes to analyze and criticize the ideologies that contribute to the maintenance of a capitalist system, which prevents those principles from being realized, as well as the mechanisms by which such ideologies are propogated and become widely accepted. Critical Theory, then, conceives of itself as a critique of ("false") culture and consciousness from the vantage point of a truly human rationality.

Capitalist domination, the critical theorists argue, has turned out to be far more subtle and pervasive than Marx would have thought possible. It is not only, or even mainly, a matter of naked physical repression and economic exploitation, but rather one of the subtle but persistent manipulation of people's very consciousness. The acquiescence of the workers has been "bought" by offering them material affluence in a mass consumption society. But this is only possible because people are constantly exposed to the media of mass persuasion, which never cease to celebrate the virtues of new products and gadgets, of middle class affluence and material security, thus creating the very demand for even more consumption which the capitalist system is so well-equipped to meet. Moreover, the institutions of the state, the education system, and the mass media consistently exploit people's sense of belonging, cultural symbols, and various half-conscious fears to convince eveyone that this is really the best of all possible worlds. At an even deeper level, the very instrumental rationality that forms the core of all economic and scientific-technical endeavors — with its exclusive emphasis on efficiency and productivity — comes to dominate the whole culture and all consciousness. Genuine human values of substance, such as the need for personal autonomy, free creativity, and aesthetic satisfaction, are simply brushed aside by the irresistible tide of better, bigger, and more consumption. Thus, government, the media, academics, and educators all contributed to the manufacture of "One-Dimensional Man," as Marcuse has called modern, exclusively consumption-oriented man.

Recently, German philosopher-sociologist Juergen Habermas (1929–) has further developed some of these themes, borrowing from Parsonion systems theory, linguistic philosophy, phenomonology, and psychoanalysis. Habermas has tried to explain capitalism's apparent stability by depicting it as a social system, seeking to maintain equilibrium and integration by resolving tensions and imbalances between sub-systems.

In this way, Habermas believes, it is possible to discover the system's current "weak spots" because it can never entirely resolve the contradictions inherent in capitalism. Second, and perhaps more importantly, Habermas has sought to amplify the critique of instrumental rationality — that is, the belief that human reason can only apply to the choice among means but not to the determination of ends — begun by the earlier generation of critical theorists, by basing it on a linguistically inspired theory of "communicative competence." On the basis of truly and completely "undistorted" communication, Habermas believes, it must be possible to show that such ends as liberation and emancipation are indeed truly rational and therefore that their suppression in present-day society for the sake of material affluence alone is really irrational.

The ideas of the critical theorists are controversial and many are pitched at such a high level of philosophical abstraction that it is at times hard to see of what relevance they are to sociology and social research. But the shift away from the economic base to the socio-cultural superstructure is clear enough in critical theory. This shift has helped stimulate a considerable amount of sociological research and debate concerning the role of the media, education, and the family in the formation of consciousness and personality; the social orgins of fascism; the role of art and entertainment in modern society; the theory of "mass" society, although the issues raised by critical theory appear to have remained unresolved by them.

Structualist Marxism

Structuralist Marxism was originally formulated by the French philosopher Louis Althusser (1918–   ) in the 1960s as a conscious alternative to the somewhat subjective variety of Marxism represented by Critical Theory. Yet it draws on some of the same sources as the latter, notably Freudian psychoanalysis, and reaches very similar conclusions. In addition, it draws on structural linguistics, especially as adopted for social

Rapid industrialization has flooded the markets of many nations with an unprecedented number of new products and gadgets, while mass media agitate an ever-increasing consumer demand. Some sociologists sharply question whether such human values as autonomy and creativity have suffered as a consequence.

analysis by the French anthropologist, Claude Levi-Strauss.

Structuralist Marxism is by no means the first version of Marxism to proclaim itself a "rigorous science of history," but Althusserian structuralism is certainly the most radical of them all. On the basis of an intensive re-reading of all of Marx's works, Althusser claims to have discovered the radically new philosophy on which Marx's mature approach is based, even though Marx himself was unaware of it: *dialectical materialism*. According to Althusser, Marx's "mature" writings — which include only parts of *Capital* and some minor pamphlets written late in his life — are based on a radical "epistemological break" with all of his

The social origin of fascism is one of the questions that sociology seeks to address. Here, on the wall of a high school in Montréal, the word "JAPS" stands for "Jewish-American princesses (or princes)." Five Jewish students in this school had recently been beaten by classmates.

previous work. In those writings, Althusser claims, Marx established a brand-new science, the science of history and the "social formation," with a degree of rigor no less demanding than mathematics or physics.

The major discovery of this rigorous science, Althusser claims, is that the "social formation" (roughly society) is not a collection of individuals with a will and consciousness of its own, but a "structure of structures" whose interaction determines the character of the whole. Structures determine the roles people are to play. Individuals are nothing but "bearers" of the structures in which they take part. Much like Parsons, Althusser distinguishes three major "regional structures," "instances" or "levels" in each social formation: the political, the economic, and the ideological. They each perform certain necessary functions, they interact constantly, and they presuppose one another as well as the whole structure of structures they form together. What matters is which

of these is the "dominant" instance, as determined ultimately by the economic instance. Yet while one instance is always dominant and the economic always determinant, all instances are nevertheless "relatively autonomous" from one another; that is, their development is never *entirely* determined by any of the others. This explains why there is always some degree of "uneven development" between the levels of the social formation. While the contradiction between the forces and relations of production at the economic level remains fundamental, it creates a variety of secondary contradictions at the other levels, which react back upon it and which at least partially develop according to a rhythm of their own. This constant interaction between levels Althusser calls "over determination." Thus, Althusser argues, the science of the social formation does not at all predict a socialist revolution as a simple outcome of the development of the primary contradiction at the economic level. Revolution only occurs when the various contradictions "fuse" at a particular "conjuncture" (roughly, time and place), such as in Russia in October, 1917. Obviously such moments are very rare in history.

Like Critical Theory, Althusser's structuralist Marxism has provoked a great deal of controversy. Nevertheless, it has found some dedicated followers among sociologists and is credited with having opened up, for orthodox Marxists, politics and culture as legitimate subjects of study, in some degree independent of the economy. It is worth noting in general that these two versions of neo-Marxism, while starting at almost opposite ends, display some convergence: both depict modern society as a self-balancing system or structure, consisting of discrete subsystems interacting and performing functions for the equilibrium of the whole. In both versions, the system or structure has a logic and purpose of its own, which is impressed upon individuals so that they may play their assigned parts. All this is remarkably similar to Parsons's systems theory and rather far removed from any conflict model. This is not so surprising since Western Marxism attempts to resolve a problem not unlike the central problem of the structural (functional) model: how is a stable *capitalist* order possible?

Although (neo-) Marxist *theory* as such has had limited influence on sociological theory in North America, the influence of specific Marxist concepts, emphases, and explanations has been pervasive in all branches of sociology. The concept of "class" has become a major topic of debate, and an explanatory variable and focus of research in all branches dealing with macrosociological phenomena (e.g., industrial sociology, social stratification, and political sociology). The notion of "alienation" is much-debated and researched in industrial and political sociology. Worthy of separate mention is the recent emergence of a whole new Marxist-inspired perspective in the area of social change and development: World-Systems Theory, according to which internal developments in different societies are inextricably linked to their

positions in the international system of (neo-) imperialist exploitation and subjugation. Even from this incomplete listing, it is clear that the influence of Marxism on sociology has been profound indeed.

Conservative Conflict Theory: the Struggle for Power

The power struggle model was first formulated as a sociological approach by Vilfredo Pareto (1848-1923) and Gaetano Mosca (1858-1941) in deliberate opposition to Marxism. Pareto and Mosca agreed with Marxism that social life is primarily a matter of conflict and struggle and they were certainly as skeptical as Marxists are about any claims that social order is the result of free consensus. They, too, believed that ideologies and high-sounding principles are usually merely concealed attempts to promote group interests and that whatever "consensus" could be established was no doubt imposed upon the rest of society by those in power, whether by force or by deceit. However, these elite theorists, as they are sometimes called, differ from Marxism on two crucial points: they reject the proposition that all significant social conflict is *class* conflict over *economic* domination and they consider as utterly utopian the Marxist belief that widespread social conflict can be eliminated by abolishing socio-economic inequality. Not surprisingly, they also restrict the mission of social science to that of scientifically refuting such illusions.

Not unlike structural theorists, Pareto and Mosca take it for granted that human nature is basically selfish and human aspirations insatiable. However, they dismiss any claims that social norms and values can operate effectively to curb those aspirations and selfishness, considering the idea just as unrealistic as the Marxist belief that human nature can be transformed. Norms and values are nothing but rationalizations of the interests of the powerful or of those who seek power. For the most basic fact of social life is that any collectivity or organization, beyond the smallest and most primitive form, necessarily entails an unequal division of power between a dominant elite and a large, virtually powerless mass. With its power, in turn, the elite can claim a disproportionate share of wealth and prestige within the collectivity or organization. It follows from this inevitable state of affairs and the incorrigible selfishness of man that social life is an incessant struggle for power. Intermittent periods of order and stability only persist as long as no group is strong enough to challenge the elite in power. Although the ruling elite may for a time maintain its power by the appropriate mixture of force and guile, there are strong forces that in the long run tend to weaken the ruling elite and to allow counterelites to gather enough strength to eventually take power by force. Thus, history is characterized by repetitive cycles and revolutions in which elites succeed each other, or as Pareto once put it, "history is a graveyard of aristocracies."

The reasons Pareto and Mosca give for this incessant "circulation of elites" differ slightly, as do their overall theories. For Pareto, for example, the inevitability of elite formation in every branch of social activity ultimately derives from man's naturally differing endowments, talents, and inclinations, or what he called "residues." Thus, for a governing elite to successfully maintain its power, and thereby social stability, its members must possess a specific mixture of "residues" suited for government, consisting of an ability to use persuasion and fraud whenever possible, in combination with a ruthless determination to use force whenever necessary. However, as a result of a lack of overt challenges to their rule and the natural tendency to pass on the reins of power to their children (whether or not they possess the appropriate combination of residues), the governing elite will in time tend to lose its resolve to use force. Moreover, this would only result in a build-up of a frustrated counter-elite among the masses of men whose residues make them fit to rule, but whose road to power has been blocked by the incumbence of less talented members of the governing elite. Eventually, if access to the elite remains barred, the counter-elite will revolt and replace the elite that has lost the competence to rule. Usually the counter-elite obtains the support of the masses by promising equality and democracy. But as soon as it has won firm control of government, it becomes the new governing elite, not a bit less oppressive and exploitative than its predecessor. Thus, the cycle starts all over again, while things never really change.

Mosca and Pareto were skeptical about the degree to which real democratic government was possible at all. They believed that the democratic promises and slogans characteristic of modern politics were little more than "derivations" (Pareto), or "political formulas" (Mosca), designed to conceal effective elite rule or to arouse mass support for a change of elites. This thesis received strong support from the investigations of Robert Michels (1876–1936). Michels focused on the mass organizations that, at the turn of the century, professed far and away the strongest ideological commitment to democratic government: the socialist parties and labor unions. As such organizations grew in time, Michels found that authority was necessarily more and more delegated to the elected party officials. However, by virtue of their day-to-day control of the organization's business, vital information, and expertise, these elected officials came to form a self-conscious elite within their own organizations, effectively escaping control by the rank-and-file members to whom they were officially accountable. From this, Michels concluded that all large organizations, even those most strongly committed to democracy, are subject to an "Iron Law of Oligarchy."

In recent years, the power struggle model has been reiterated by German sociologist Ralf Dahrendorf (1929–   ). Inequality of wealth is not the mainspring of social conflict and social change, Dahrendorf argues, but rather inequality of power and authority, which is a universal aspect of all organized social life. Authority relations divide all collectivities into two "classes" whose interests are

By the turn of the century, labor unions were among the most vocal proponents of democracy. Here, crowds gather at Victoria Park during the Winnipeg General Strike (1919).

inherently opposed: those who share in the exercise of authority and hence wish to see the existing structures maintained, and those who are subject to that authority and hence wish to change those structures so that they can share in the exercise of authority, too. Thus, according to Dahrendorf, in principle there can be as many different class conflicts as there are associations. The degree of intensity and scope of society-wide class conflict largely depends on the degree to which the various conflicts overlap, i.e. the degree to which those who exercise authority in one type of organization (e.g., business) also form the "dominant class" in other organizations (e.g., politics). But while it may vary in intensity and scope, class conflict is an inevitable fact of social life so long as there are complex organizations requiring authority relations for their effective operation. However, class and class conflict is only one side of the "Janus-headed" character of society. The other, equally real aspect of social life, Dahrendorf concedes, is that of value consensus as expounded in the structural model of society.

Similarly, the American sociologist Gerhard Lenski (1924–   ) accepts that the value consensus approach may be fruitfully applied to some types of society, particularly simple, small-scale, tribal societies, but he claims that the power struggle model is far superior in accounting for the nature and dynamics of more complex societies. Lenski's own model is a straightforward version of the latter; it assumes that people are naturally selfish and that their appetite for foods and services is insatiable. From this, it follows that all social life necessarily involves an incessant struggle over scarce resources. Moreover, since survival is the first and most basic need of each, the threat and use of force (i.e., the threat to survival), is the most effective, ultimate weapon and sanction in that struggle. Therefore, control over the means of physical coercion and willingness to use them means power over other aspects of social life. Hence, the struggle for power and the resulting distribution of power determines the distribution of material wealth and prestige in any complex society.

Lenski's approach is in some ways a restatement of the original model formulated by Mosca and Pareto. However, unlike the latter, both Lenski and Dahrendorf are rather more impressed with the rise of formally democratic government in the advanced Western countries as a social transformation of considerable significance. Nevertheless, they clearly share the basic postulates of the power struggle model: that human nature is basically selfish; that social life is an incessant struggle for power in which those who are by nature best-equipped for the fight tend to win out; and that, hence, social conflict and social inequality are inevitable facts of social life. This approach seems to imply a more individualistic point of view than either functionalism or Marxism: social institutions do not shape the individual so much as the individual (if necessary in cooperation with others) shapes the institutions in the never-ending pursuit of power and its rewards. Finally, again unlike Marxists and some structural-functionalists, the power struggle perspective clearly seems to imply that the proper role of social science is not to engage in utopian wishful thinking, but to confront and analyze the facts as they are, however much we may personally dislike them.

Liberal Conflict Theory: the Weberian Model

Perhaps the single most influential conflict model in sociology is the one originally conceived by the German sociologist Max Weber (1864–1920). Like other conflict theorists, Weber depicts society as a precarious and constantly shifting balance of power between various groups and organizations competing for scarce resources. However, he sought to integrate the useful insights of both models into a more flexible, less dogmatic framework that could be applied more widely in the empirical analysis of different societies in different historical periods, although he believed as a matter of philosophical principle that the infinite diversity of social reality could never be fully captured by *any* single framework.

Explanation of the causes and consequences of social behavior, Weber maintained, involves more than the observation and influence of causal links "from the outside" as is done in the natural sciences. In addition to that, social acts must be understood in terms of the *meaning* they have for the actors. This idea of empathetic understanding, or *"verstehen"* in German, was to have a considerable influence on some of the interactionist perspectives (phenomenology, ethnomethodology) discussed in the next section. But for Weber, it was only one aspect of his general position of *"methodological individualism."* According to this position, organizations, institutions, or social systems (a term Weber himself would never use) do *not* have any "values," "purposes," "principles," or "requirements" — only the individuals that are members of those collectivities do. Therefore, it is not legitimate to speak of such features unless it is no more than shorthand for the "purposes," "values," and so on, of some section, or perhaps even the entirety of the membership; for that reason, it is at all times reducible to the "purposes," "principles," and so on, of identifiable individuals engaged in observable (inter-) actions. Weber therefore rejects the view that the behavior of social actors can even be explained as the simple, straightforward manifestation of pre-existing "social norms" or "class interests," as some functionalists and Marxists claim.

"Social structure," then, is never more than the conceptual shorthand used by observers and/or the actors themselves to describe perceived patterns of actions by individuals. But as much as the patterns are simply made up of individual (inter-) actions, each individual act also takes place within already pre-existing patterns to which the actors orient themselves and which help to make their actions understandable. Collectivities such as social classes or ethnic groups, and institutions such as marriage or religion, consist on the one hand of nothing but series of (inter-) actions by and between people, but on the other hand, they are also groups and institutions that influence people's orientations and purposes and hence their actions, to the extent that people identify with them. It was one of Weber's main aims to find out under what circumstances people are most likely to form and identify with collectivities, and of what sort. Somewhat ironically, Weber's "methodological individualism" led him to become almost exclusively preoccupied with macrosociological phenomena as he sought to understand how large-scale social structures influence human behavior to produce new large-scale structures.

To arrive at such understanding, Weber felt it was neither necessary nor useful to make any *a priori* assumptions about "true" human nature. The incredible variety of values, aims, and purposes that people pursue in different cultures, or even just in different groups within the same culture, simply cannot be so easily reduced to a single common denominator. Weber certainly acknowledges that much human behavior arises from purely selfish motives, and that as a result, a great deal of social conflict can be understood as struggle over scarce resources and power. But at the same time, every differentiated society provides a variety of life experiences for its members from which arise, understandably enough, differing values, norms, and ideals, which may be important to those members for their own sake. Much social conflict consists of contests between groups with conflicting *ideal interests*, which may be as irreconcilable as material interests, often even more so.

It makes good sense, Weber concedes, to look for the material interests behind the always lofty ideal proclamations of any group or individual, as Marxists and elite theorists always do. But it is not useful to assume without question that ideals can *always* be traced back to some "real" material interests that they are designed to conceal as well as promote. It seems more fruitful to start with the hypothesis that there is always a certain degree of "elective affinity" between ideal and material interests: that people's values are likely to affect what they conceive to be their material interests, just as their felt material interests make them more receptive to ideas that correspond to them. It is precisely the task of the sociologist, Weber argued, to find out under what conditions the material interests are likely to take precedence over ideal interests and under what conditions the reverse is more likely to be the case. In his extensive sociological studies of the major world religions, as well as in his famous *The Protestant Ethic and the Spirit of Capitalism*, Weber tried to trace the complex chains of effects of religious beliefs and economic and political interests *on each other*, to account for the unique historical development of the West in comparison with other civilizations.

Weber was particularly interested in the types of collectivities people form in order to pursue their felt material and ideal interests, because much of

Such institutions as marriage may be seen to consist of nothing but a series of interactions, yet they greatly influence people's life orientations and purposes.

the significant social conflict appears to be between those organized collectivities. He distinguished three major groups: classes, status groups, and political parties, corresponding to the three major sets of resources necessary to realize material and ideal interests, namely material wealth, social status (prestige), and political power. Each of these three types of resources may be valued for its own sake, but they can also — precisely *because* they are so widely valued — be used by their possessors as a basis of power; that is, wealth, status or political power enables their possessors "to realize their own will ... even against the resistance of others." In contrast to the other conflict models discussed

so far, the Weberian approach does not assign any necessary primacy to any one form of power. Power based on economic resources may become the basis of political power and prestige, as the Marxists claim, but political power can just as well be used to acquire wealth and prestige, as the power elite theorists claim, and even prestige frequently constitutes the ultimate basis of economic and political power. Therefore, Weber argues, classes, status groups, and parties must be seen as comparable "phenomena of the distribution of power within a community," the relations between which may vary and are a matter for empirical investigation.

Although Weber defines "class" on the basis of objective economic criteria like Marx, his criteria are more broadly conceived to include *all* goods, opportunities, and qualities a person may exchange for income on the commodity and/or labor markets, and which thus help determine a person's "life chances." Marx's single criterion of (non-) ownership of the means of production, then, is only *one* of Weber's criteria determining objective "class situation." Others are level of skill, formal qualifications, and labor power. To the extent that a number of people share such attributes, and as a result, the ability to obtain a certain level of income, they form a class. In principle, therefore, there could be as many "classes" as there are different skills and types of property and different income levels, but in practice, Weber claims one can distinguish four broad classes in modern capitalist societies: the manual worker; the petty bourgeoisie or small entrepreneur; the relatively property-less intelligentsia; and finally experts and those who are highly privileged by virtue of property ownership and level of education.

People may, and frequently do, act collectively on the basis of shared class situation, that is, in their perceived class interest. But Weber rejects any Marxist claims that common class-interest is in some sense the only obvious, natural or "true" basis for collective action. Whether or not people are *more* likely to be preoccupied with, and act upon class interests and engage in "class struggles" than in other types of collectivities and conflicts, depends on many conditions, such as the transparency of the connections between causes and consequences of class situation, cultural traditions, the speed and disruptiveness of technological and economic change, and so on. Classes, then, are not "natural" communities, but only possible bases for collective action, awareness of which must first be provoked by certain specific social conditions and events.

"Status groups," on the other hand *are* normally self-conscious communities. They are groups that share a sense of positive or negative social estimation of "honor" that is based on some common attribute or other such as race, ethnic origin, or religion. Status groups tend to develop distinct life styles, shared values and customs, and restrictions on the members' interactions with outsiders (especially sanctions on intimate contacts such as intermarriage), which naturally leads to a strong group consciousness and solidarity. As a result, people are often more easily mobilized to defend their status group interests than their purely economic class interests. Thus, in contrast to Marxism, Weber maintains that status groups and the struggles between them are, and are likely to remain, independently important social phenomena that cannot be easily reduced to more "basic" class interests. Weber agrees that status and wealth tend to converge in the long run, but this may be the result of successful status group claims to material privileges for its members as it equally may be due to the tendency for the wealthy to command high prestige once their lowly origins have been forgotten.

Another basis of social inequality is political power. Political power is the ability to ensure obedience to one's commands on the basis of the ability to use physical force if necessary. In most communities beyond some minimal level of social complexity, there is a central political institution or a "state," which Weber defines as the institution that claims a "monopoly of the legitimate use of physical force within a given territory." This institution issues decisions and commits actions for the community as a whole and consists of those who take those decisions and a more-or-less extensive administrative "staff," which executes them and backs them up by (the threat of) physical force, if and when necessary. Now, political parties are organizations that seek to influence the state's decision-makers and administrative staff on behalf of their members' interests, and if possible have these individuals recruited from their own ranks. Political parties in this broad sense are not a new phenomenon. They have existed as long as states have. They have represented a variety of interests, including classes, status groups, or just their members' interests, in joining the state's payrolls ("patronage" parties) and even purely ideal interests (parties "of principle").

Those who control and staff the state apparatus usually seek to legitimize their rule; that is, they seek to justify their right to demand obedience and to use physical force if necessary to obtain it. This does not mean, however, that such legitimization need be widely accepted by the subject population for the rulers' legitimate domination, or "authority," to be effective.

Weber distinguished three types of legitimate domination on the basis of their principles of legitimation: traditional, charismatic, and rational-legal domination. Each of these is characterized by its own type of organizational structure (administrative apparatus), problems, and the typical conflicts over the distribution of political power between rulers and their staffs.

Traditional domination is justified by the sacredness of ancient traditions, which presumably demand personal loyalty and obedience to those entitled to rule according to those traditions. Though rulers, too, are bound by customs and traditions, these are usually so vaguely defined as to leave rulers a great deal of discretion. Originating in the authority relations characteristic of the extended patriarchal household, the ruler considers his or her power as personal property, and staff as personal servants to be used and dismissed at will. Thus, administrative staffs under traditional domination tend to consist of the ruler's current favorites. As the traditional ruler seeks to expand his or her domain, however, typical problems of maintaining central control tend to emerge. The loyalty and actions of officials become more and more difficult to secure, and officials, especially in the more remote regions, acquire more and more independent power. The typical power struggle in any large traditional system is waged between a stratum of high officials who seek to reduce the amount of discretionary power of the central ruler, thereby increasing their own independent power, and rulers who try to maintain as much arbitrary power as possible and especially to prevent the formation of a strong status group solidarity among immediate subordinates. Both parties will try to justify their interests by appealing to the most ancient and sacred of traditions.

Charismatic domination is based on the belief in the extraordinary powers or virtues of a specific leader, and by extension, the leader's immediate disciples. Charismatic leadership is most likely to arise from severe crises and mass excitement, which appear to require exceptional leadership. It is by definition non-conventional and non-routine. The power of the charismatic leader is not bound by anything, except the ability to maintain the faith of followers in his or her exceptional gifts. But charismatic domination is inherently unstable. Charismatic movements tend to collapse, either because their leaders prove unable to cope with the crisis at hand and thus lose their charisma, or because their very success at solving the crisis reduces the demand for exceptional rule. If they do not collapse, they almost inevitably succumb to the pressure toward "routinization" exerted by the need to resolve conflict, raise taxes, or regulate leadership succession. Thus, charismatic rule tends to rapidly turn into one of the other two types of rule.

Rational-legal domination, finally, is exercised by virtue of formally enacted rules and regula-

tions that circumscribe the powers, competence, and duties of each office in detail, irrespective of the person who occupies it. Recruitment to all offices is also regulated by strictly impersonal procedures. Obedience is presumably based on commitment to impersonal rules enacted according to specified procedures and *not* on personal loyalty to the person issuing the command. This form of legitimate rule is a typically modern phenomenon. Its characteristic form of organization is modern bureaucracy, which, by virtue of its efficiency, precision, and a reliability unmatched by any other form of organization, was, according to Weber, rapidly becoming the dominant form of organization in all sectors of modern societies, whether private or public.

Weber paid a great deal of attention to the construction and analysis of the ideal-typical features of bureaucracy, although he was well aware that real-life bureaucracies only rarely approximate this *ideal type*. The main features of the ideal type are: continuous operation, duties, and required resources and authority to execute them, which are allocated and strictly limited according to impersonal criteria and rules; offices are organized in a strict hierarchy of authority; officials neither own the resources they use in the performance of their functions nor the office they occupy, and are held strictly accountable for their use of both; all transactions are recorded; officials are hired on the basis of a legal contract; they are employed full-time and rewarded by regular salaries and career opportunities; recruitment and promotion are based on unambiguous and impersonal criteria of competence and technical qualifications.

But whereas the rise of bureaucracy is a result of its undoubted superiority in terms of *formal rationality*, i.e., efficiency or dependability, Weber did not consider its growing dominance a sign of inevitable "progress" by any means. For this formal rationality may well seriously threaten certain forms of *substantive rationality*, i.e., moral values and human needs that are cherished for their own sake. The gains in equity and efficiency produced by the rise of bureaucracy, Weber feared, may be obtained only at the cost of a profound depersonalization of social relations and an irretrievable loss of personal autonomy, creativity, and freedom.

Moreover, Weber warned that the rise of bureaucratic organization in government (the civil service) and politics (political parties) could become a serious threat to legitimate political control. Because of their presumed professional expertise, their loyalty to their organization, and their *de facto* control over enormous resources and vital information, Weber believed, government bureaucrats would easily form self-conscious status groups capable of effectively deciding what policies would be pursued and what would not. Thus, there is a persistent tendency of large-scale bureaucracy to escape from the control of their legal masters and unsurp the latter's official decision-making powers. In democratic countries, this means that bureacracy is both an indispensable instrument of policy execution *and* a persistent threat to democratic government.

Weber was deeply pessimistic about mankind's chances to ever escape from the "iron cage" of bureaucracy that he saw closing in around it. Socialism — that is, a state-controlled economy — could only hasten the process of bureaucratization, he predicted, because it could only lead to an enormous expansion of state bureaucracy necessary to plan and run the economy. The only choice seemed to be one between the complete domination of society by a single "socialist" state bureaucracy *or* competition between several bureaucracies, as in advanced capitalist societies, which at least allows for some precarious control over them, and perhaps some protection of the few not yet bureaucratically organized spheres of life.

But even though he described the growing bureaucratization of modern society as a virtually inescapable trend, Weber did not believe that the enormous diversity of cultures and epochs that together make up world history could be fruitfully

The power of charismatic leaders, such as Muammar al-Qaddafi of Libya, lies in their ability to inspire and maintain faith in their leadership, however unconventional.

reduced to a single, "necessary" trend or factor. The similarities and differences between the histories of different civilizations, he felt, were matters to be established by empirical research, not philosophical speculations about the "nature" of universal history. Accordingly, Weber's own comparative research into the major world religions was intended to help explain the major factors that account for the historical emergence of modern capitalism in the West and not elsewhere. It was this research that led Weber to identify the process of growing bureaucratization as an aspect of a much older and broader but uniquely Western process of disenchantment and rationalization of the social world, which could ultimately be traced in part to the strong influence of prophetic revelation in ancient Judaism, an aspect absent in the other world religions. That was the starting point, Weber believed, of a long-term process that gradually eliminated all elements of magic, ritual, and mythology from social life, and replaced them with secular, formally rational, and methodical forms of organization based on the

The Canadian civil service represents one of the world's largest bureaucracies. Such bureaucracies, according to Max Weber, may pose a political threat.

principles of efficiency and logical consistency only. But Weber never did claim there was something "inevitable" about this long-term process. Nor did he simply consider it a matter of "progress."

Weber was personally rather ambivalent about the desirability of the disenchantment of the world. But as a matter of principle, he believed it was not for social scientists *as* scientists to pass judgements on the (un-) desirability of the socio-historical phenomenon they seek to understand. That requires the sort of moral or political judgement for which social scientists are no more competent than anyone else. Social science must limit

itself to trying to understand matters of *fact* that may provide useful information for arriving at moral judgements, but which can never replace them.

Weber's theoretical model has not inspired a separate sociological tradition to the extent that others have. Only one major theorist, the American sociologist Randall Collins (1947–), has attempted to further develop the Weberian model as a distinct, comprehensive theoretical approach, by explicitly incorporating many contributions of Marx, Durkheim, Michels, and some ideas from the interactionist model that seem to be compatible with it. Yet Weber's influence has been so pervasive that it has become hard to distinguish Weberian from plain mainstream sociology. In fact, in the core areas of *macrosociology* — political sociology, the sociology of complex organizations and social stratification — Weber's main propositions, concepts, and typologies have become the accepted orthodoxy. In addition, such areas as the sociology of culture and religion and social movements, economic sociology, the sociology of social change and law and urban sociology, have been greatly influenced by Weber's wide-ranging historical research and conceptualizations. But even this understates Weber's influence. The fact that he squarely belongs in the conflict tradition has not prevented either structural-functionalists or interactionists from claiming Weber as a major theoretical inspiration, because of his emphasis on the importance of values and beliefs as causal factors and on the importance of empathetic understanding in sociology, respectively. More than any other major theorist, then, Weber belongs to all theoretical traditions in sociology.

THE SIGNIFICANCE OF CONFLICT

Models in Sociology

There clearly is a great deal of difference *between* the various conflict models of society. Yet while they may appear to contrast as sharply with one another as they do with the other two major models, they are not necessarily wholly incompatible. Besides the synthesis attempted by Collins, the work of American sociologist and social critic C. Wright Mills (1916-1962) makes that clear. In his most famous book, *The Power Elite* (1956), Mills adopts major aspects of all three conflict models. Mills argues that American society is becoming more and more dominated by giant bureaucratic organizations in the political, military, and corporate sectors. These organizations, in turn, are run by small elites of top politicians, generals, and corporate executives that are becoming an increas-

ingly cohesive, single power elite, making all the important decisions for society as a whole without being accountable to anyone. This concentration of irresponsible power is buttressed by the emergence of a "mass society," in which the majority of the population forms a fragmented, passive, and inarticulate mass unable to formulate coherent demands, let alone influence public policy. The mass media, the educational system, the haggling at the "middle levels" of power, and mass prosperity all serve to further distract and debilitate the mass of the population into an apparently contented but certainly docile force. Thus, Mills combines elements from the Weberian and power elite models to develop a radical critique of modern U.S. society that is remarkably similar to the Marxist-inspired perspective of Critical Theory.

The conflict model is, moreover, not necessarily incompatible with certain aspects of its most evident rival, structural-functionalism. This was shown by American sociologist Lewis Coser (1913-) who, drawing on ideas of Georg Simmel (1858-1918), a German contemporary of Max Weber's, tried to combine the two in his well-known *The Functions of Social Conflict* (1956). Coser seeks to show that social conflict is not necessarily disruptive. On the contrary, conflict frequently enhances the solidarity *within* groups and eventually even *between* them, as it allows for the open expression of differences of interest and hostility, which permits negotiation and compromise, often by means of the creation of new norms and institutions capable of resolving the conflict. Thus, ironically, open social conflict may well be among those very mechanisms of social integration that functionalists commonly seek to identify, and consequently, the contrast between the conflict and structural models may not be as sharp as is often suggested by the polemics.

Nevertheless, the differences between the two models amount to more than just polemical rhetoric. Functionalists *do* tend to emphasize social order and stability as a result of social integra-

Some sociologists feel that the desire for approval is the cornerstone of social order.

Nonetheless, the structural model and the critical model share a common emphasis on social collectivities and society, rather than (as is the case in the interactionist model to be described in the next section) on the importance of the relations between much smaller social units of social life. The stress on larger social units represents the *macrosociological* emphasis, while the concern with the interaction of individuals is typical of *microsociology*.

THE INTERACTIONIST (SOCIAL-PSYCHOLOGICAL) MODELS

As we have had occasion to stress, both the structural and critical model emphasize the need to view social relations as object-centered and therefore as different from the prevailing subject-centred way of looking at social life typical of common sense. However, the common-sense view, with its emphasis on the individual, has not entirely disappeared from sociology because the interactionist model to be discussed now, follows, to some extent at least, the lead of common sense by focusing attention on the individual social actor. The interactionist model may therefore also be said to represent a more socio-psychological model than is the case for either the structural or the critical model.

Sociologists have developed a considerable range of such interactionist models, which focus on the individual and smaller social units of interaction. The most important of these models judged by the number of adherents among sociologists is known as *symbolic interactionism*; this model grew out of the work of George Herbert Mead and later, Herbert Blumer. Other interactionist models we shall examine briefly are associated with the writings of George C. Homans and are known as the *exchange model*; the *"dramaturgical" model* developed by Erving Goffman; the *phenomenological model* first devised by Alfred Schutz; and finally, the most recent model developed by Harold Garfinkel and his students, which is known as *Ethnomethodology*.

tion, and they *do* value consensus, whereas conflict theorists tend to emphasize social change and conflict as a result of the conflicts of interests and ideas that appear to be the inevitable concomitant of the competitive struggle over scarce resources. Even if and when conflict theorists such as Mills or the Critical Theorists acknowledge a high degree of stability and apparent consensus, they are apt to consider it highly precarious and attribute it primarily to the temporary ability of some dominant group to impose the views expressing *its* interests upon the rest of society. Where functionalists are likely to see genuine agreement and consensus as the basis for social order, conflict theorists of all persuasions will tend to be more skeptical and try to uncover the *conflicting* interests concealed beneath the apparent consensus.

Phenomenology and Ethnomethodology

The writings of Alfred Schutz (1899–1959) represent the first attempt to constitute a *phenomenological* model in sociology. Phenomenology is a method of inquiry into the nature of meaning, pioneered by the German philosopher Edmund Husserl (1859–1938) and adopted by Schutz for the purposes of sociology. Key concerns are the social organization of the world of everyday life and the social foundation of common sense and other forms of knowledge (for example, scientific knowledge). Generally, the interest centres on what social phenomenologists choose to call the "mundane world." More specifically, Schutz is interested in the sociological analysis of the social construction of the life-world, which is the sphere of everyday experience and expectations we all inhabit. Schutz analyzes, for instance, the kind of attitudes that prevail in everyday life; he calls it the "natural attitude" because what is most typical of our attitudes under ordinary circumstances is that we simply take for granted most of those beliefs that govern our conduct in everyday life. These attitudes are, in other words, natural to all of us until we have reason to re-examine this assumption. Individuals in the natural attitude do not, phenomenologists observe, suspend their belief in the existing material and social reality; on the contrary, they typically suspend doubt that it is anything other than it appears. Motives individuals may entertain are essentially two-fold according to Schutz, or at least the observers should distinguish between "in-order-to" motives and "because" motives. Both motives refer to meaningful reasons for the action of an individual, however, only because motives are directly accessible to the observers. "In-order-to" motives are the reasons an individual contemplates in an effort to bring about some future event. "Because" motives in contrast are retrospective views by individuals of the factors that have prompted them to act in a certain way. Schutz stresses also the unique character of each individual actor and his or her life experiences. In addition, he deals with

the life-world in terms of its stock of knowledge, that is, in terms of the means by which individuals orient themselves in everyday life. Schutz shows how this knowledge is structured in different ways depending on the relevance knowledge may have for the individual; some knowledge is rather important, other knowledge is vague and distant, or still other knowledge is knowledge about where and how to acquire it. Knowledge, therefore, is defined in a rather broad sense and covers all interpretative schemes individuals learn in order to grasp the meaning of their conduct and that of others. But the core social relation is that of face-to-face interaction, the "we-relationship." In any face-to-face encounter, actors use a stock of knowledge, or "common-sense conceptions" in terms of which they typify the other individual and are able to sustain the association with that person. Stocks of knowledge that are relevant in typical, everyday social situations are pragmatic in character, in that this kind of knowledge is primarily geared to cope with the recurring practical tasks of day-to-day social life. But Schutz is also concerned with the interaction in everyday life, although he continually emphasizes, as do all contributors to the interactionist model, the importance of individual motivation and plans; of course, such motives and plans are affected by the orientations of other social actors.

Harold Garfinkel (1917–) shares Schutz's emphasis on the analysis of features of everyday life and its mode of social organization. His contribution is known as *ethnomethodology* and derives its name from the general interest of this perspective in the *methodic* attributes of coping with the contingencies of ordinary life employed by all of us in those situations. Ethnomethodology focuses those rules and shared understandings that prevail in all spheres of everyday life. Garfinkel and his students are interested in the methods one could say individuals employ in ordinary life (the lay actor as a practical social theorist) to make sense of life and carry out their conduct in relations to other persons. Their image of the individual is one of an active person who follows but also adjusts to changing demands of everyday life. Ethnomethodology, therefore, asks the important question of how and in what way we go about our lives assuming that it is a part of *social* life; that is, how exactly is our sense of social reality constructed, maintained, and/or changed. Garfinkel stresses that we must share in certain techniques that give us the feeling for the certainty of a common world; for instance, we must share certain interpretative skills. In contrast to the lay actor, the attitude of the sociologist is to suspend belief that things are as they appear. Moreover, ethnomethodology is concerned with the kind of motive analysis Schutz has advanced. Garfinkel and his students, though, are concerned with how the "natural attitude," for example, is realized by actors in their daily life. Ethnomethodologists, one should note, have stressed the extent to which the meaning of human conduct is "indexical." Indexicality refers to the extent to which the sense of various features of conduct, including language, are dependent on the context in which they happen to occur.

The writings of Erving Goffman (1922–1982) have a comparable focus but are generally more concerned with the ways in which individual actors present themselves in social situations. Individuals who manipulate, for example, gestures to create certain impressions of themselves, are one of the primary foci of his work. Goffman is therefore less interested in the structure of social relations.

Symbolic Interactionism

Symbolic interactionism as a sociological model goes back to ideas first presented by George Herbert Mead (1863–1931) and later elaborated for sociology in particular by Herber Blumer (1900–), a student of Mead. The term symbolic interactionism (coined by Blumer) derives from the emphasis Mead and others put on what they see as the unique character of human interaction, namely that in stark contrast to the interaction among non-humans, conduct among humans involves the possession of an active mind. Humans have a creative and active self, which is both aware of itself and of others. Unlike the behavior of simpler organisms, human conduct should therefore not be seen to be governed by a mere response to external stimuli. Social interaction is shaped by self-consciousness, including of course the view others have of self and consciousness of others. It is through social interaction that self-consciousness develops in the first place, and self-consciousness is in turn essential for successful social interaction. In order to avoid disappointments in social interaction, the views of different individual "selfs," including their motives, are co-ordinated. In contrast to other sociological models, especially the structural model, the symbolic interactionist model emphasizes the active, creative individual and his or her contribution to social relationships, and thus downplays the individual's possible dependence or coercion by others.

Mead is also concerned with what might be called self-interaction. That is, the extent to which self-conversations, for example, play an important role in the development of our identity and in our response to others.

Like Mead, Herber Blumer emphasizes the need to take the subjective experience and covert behavior, as well as directly observable conduct, into consideration when explaining human conduct. But Blumer's primary focus clearly is on the point of view of the individual actor as the most important reference for such an explanation. For individuals act and imitate action, as Blumer suggests, on the basis of the meaning that specific objects have for them and the meaning the individual acquires in the course of social interaction. The received meaning of objects is, however, modified through encounters the person may have subsequently with these objects.

Exchange Theory

George C. Homans (1910–) and Peter Blau (1918–), in contrast, emphasize that the best (scientific) analysis of social behavior is to regard it as a form of exchange of both tangible and intangible services and goods, including the exchange of social approval and liking. Individuals choose the kind of exchange relations they care to enter into in the first place. Their choice, according to Homans, is based on a more or less rational calculation of the alternative costs (a "value" foregone for Homans) and benefits they expect to derive from different social relations. Individuals are therefore assumed to be capable of calculating and of predicting the advantages and outcomes of different courses of action. As a result, human behavior is seen by exchange theorists to be based on fairly straightforward and universal principles of motivation and action. Both the incidence of revolutions and the choice of a marriage partner are assumed to involve such rational calculation of advantage and disadvantages.

It can easily be seen that exchange theory favors principles of human conduct and human nature that indicate that humans are largely motivated by self-interest and that economic exchanges exemplify the nature of social relations in most other spheres of social life. Homans's analysis of social approval, for example, indicates that it is close to the role money plays in purely economic exchanges. Moreover, the persistence of social order is the outcome of a basic preference among individuals for approval from others. As a result, conformity that is said to bring about such approval is likely to be a dominant form of behavior in social groups.

Homans's work, furthermore, is based on the conviction that the basic principles of human behavior can best be studied and derived from an examination of small groups of individuals and the interpersonal relations among group members. Homans is strongly convinced that social interaction rests, in the final analysis, on certain pyschological rather than social principles, for example, the desire for social approval. Factors that refer to the makeup of individual human beings are therefore the building blocks of the explanation of social relations that exchange model offers.

These few remarks already indicate, we believe, that exchange theory may well be rather limited in its application, although this is denied by Homans. In particular, it is questionable whether an essentially subject-centred explanation of social relations — that is, an explanation that limits itself to the motives, experiences, and actions of individual persons — is helpful at all in analyzing the evolution of significant societal trends and the emergence or decline of major social institutions such as religion and politics. In such cases, the emphasis must shift, in our view, as is the case for example, for the various critical models, to the effect of social institutions and trends on individuals. Moreover, the preference for individual factors as explanations of social behavior in the exchange model make it of course doubtful that *sociology* is more than an appendix to psychology.

SUMMARY

1. Contemporary sociology is, in contrast to the sociological models developed by the eminent founders of the discipline, richer in content: that is, it contains a greater wealth of information about social relations in all spheres of life.
2. Despite this fact, the models developed earlier in the history of the discipline are still pertinent to present-day social research because the theoretical intentions and concepts they developed remain relevant, continue to be discussed, and still form the basis for most of the questions and answers formulated by sociologists.
3. At the same time, the diversity of models developed by Auguste Comte, Karl Marx, Max Weber, and Emile Durkheim, to mention the most prominent architects of sociological models, continues to persist.
4. This is evident in the fact that still central to the concerns of contemporary sociology is the range of diverse ideas about the nature of human

nature and its effect on social relations, the possible divergent impact of individual or society on social life, of the meaning and long-term direction of social change, and of the vocation of sociology itself.

5. Despite the diversity of answers to these fundamental questions and how they can be best studied, all of sociology ultimately depends on one of the models studied here: be it the structural, the conflict, or the interactionist model in any of its variants.

6. In many cases, the specific questions chosen for study may of course be quite specific and even narrow. However, even in such cases, the study of social relations will in some way refer to one of the sociological models presented in this chapter.

7. It is also the case that sociologists may choose to be informed in their work by more than one of the models presented. This fact serves as a reminder that the structural, the conflict, and the interactionist models are not necessarily mutually exclusive.

8. Thus, there ought to be an awareness of the alternative models in sociology and the implications each model may have for more concrete social research. As well, this awareness provides one with a resistance against a premature closure of discussion, and makes one more open to search for answers to the complex, changing nature of social reality.

GLOSSARY

Anomie. A state of social restlessness in which generally accepted norms guiding people's behavior have broken down, provoking both serious social conflict endangering the stability of the community, and apathetic withdrawal from communal life.

Elective affinity. The argument that people's material interests and their ideals tend to converge by a process of mutual influence, not by a unilateral determination of one by the other.

Forces and relations of production. The technical productive capacity of a society (forces of production) and the social relations between those who control the means of production and those whose labors they exploit (relations of production) form the economic "base" of a society. The dynamic interaction between the forces and relations of production is responsible for the historical succession of increasingly productive modes of production.

Historical materialism. The Marxist view of society, according to which, developments in the socio-political "superstructure" are primarily determined by developments in the economic "base."

Ideal type. A hypothetical model of some sets of phenomena in which their most characteristic or theoretically interesting features are deliberately exaggerated so as to use it not as a replica of reality, but as a standard to compare reality with.

Institutionalization. The process whereby actors create mutually acceptable roles and norms that come to form the basis of stable, predictable patterns of social interaction.

Methodological individualism. The idea that not organizations, institutions, or social structures have needs, goals, and requirements but only real people do. Therefore, all such things must be reducible to identifiable individuals engaged in observable (inter-)actions.

Mode of production. A type of society characterized by a specific set of relations of production. Marxism distinguishes six such modes of production in history: primitive communism, ancient slavery, orientalism, feudalism, capitalism, and socialism.

Paradigms. An overall theoretical perspective on the (social) reality that provides practising scientists with both the philosophical basis and the orientation they need for asking questions and looking for the answers in their research.

Pattern variables. Basic sets of values that can vary along a continuum between two opposite poles and orient the actors in different social systems, e.g. universalism versus particularism.

Universalism versus particularism. Evaluation on the basis of criteria equally applicable to all as versus to criteria that depend on the nature of the particular case.

Verstehen. Empathetic understanding. Weber believed that to fully understand social behavior, one must not only examine its external causes, but also the meaning it has for the actors themselves.

FURTHER READING

Berger, Peter and Thomas Luckmann. *The Social Construction of Reality*. New York: Doubleday, 1966. A challenging attempt to combine different sociological models into a single comprehensive perspective.

Bottomore, Tom B. *Marxist Sociology*. London: Macmillan, 1975. A very short and very readable discussion of various schools of Marxism and their relation to sociology.

Campbell, Tom. *Seven Theories of Human Society*. Oxford: Claredon Press, 1981. A succinct introduction to a wide range of contrasting theories of society.

Coser, Lewis A. *Masters of Sociological Thought: Ideas in Historical and Social Context*. New York: Harcourt Brace Jovanovich, 1977. A concise overview of the key figures in the development of sociological thought.

Coser, Lewis A. and Bernard Rosenberg (eds.). *Sociological Theory: A Book of Readings*. New York: Macmillan, 5th edition, 1982. A comprehensive selection of readings on major sociological topics by leading sociological theorists, past and present.

Gerth, Hans H. and C. Wright Mills (eds.). *From Max Weber: Essays in Sociology*. London: Routledge and Kegan Paul, 1948. A wide-ranging selection from Weber's works with an authoritative introduction on his sociology.

Gouldner, Alvin. *The Coming Crisis of Western Sociology*. New York: Basic Books, 1970. An important presentation and critique of major sociological models, in particular structural-functionalism.

Kuhn, Thomas. *The Structure of Scientific Revolutions*. Chicago: University of Chicago Press, 1962. A very important socio-historical model of the development of scientific knowledge.

McLellan, David. *The Thought of Karl Marx: An Introduction*. London: Macmillan, 2nd edition, 1980. A comprehensive introduction to the life, ideas, and works of Karl Marx.

CHAPTER THREE

Doing Social Research

CHARLES LANGFORD JONES

Theories help us to understand our social world. We do research so as to develop, check, and improve our theories. The phrase "social research" conjures up many different images: Karl Marx in the Reading Room of the British Museum, a white-coated psychologist recording what rats do as they run through a maze; a market researcher carrying out an interview over the telephone; Sheila Arnopoulos interviewing community members and leaders in francophone northern Ontario; Liza Dalby studying the Japanese Geisha through interviewing them and training to be one herself; Laud Humphreys taking the role of lookout in order to observe male homosexuals in rest rooms; Diana Russell designing a random sample survey to study women raped by their husbands; the statistician poring over computer printouts to test a hypothesis.

Role Models of Research

Research can be described romantically: to see what everyone has seen, but to think what no one has thought. Alternatively, it can be described as exploration: to use a technique that allows the researcher to gaze on some virgin aspect of social or physical reality. We sometimes liken the social scientist to the white-coated laboratory researcher of the physical or biological sciences. The sociologist can also be seen as a kind of historian, finding interpretations of events that are supported by contemporary documents, or at a broader level, fitting individual historical events into the wide sweep of a general interpretive scheme. A further role model is that of the participant observer, who immerses herself in another culture or subculture by learning the language and living as they do, emerging after several months or years to describe the structure and functioning of that culture. Sociologists also use methods of "investigative journalism," checking facts like a contemporary historian, penetrating official versions of stories, using anonymous informants, and writing up a clear "story."

Each of these aspects of sociological research will have varying appeal to different people. Some prefer to identify with the objective and antiseptic scientist image; others with the idea of being an "undercover agent" of some kind. Several sociologists have begun their careers by following one role model and have changed to another.

The Sociologist as Detective

A popular general model that could include many of the above specific ones as special cases is to view the sociologist as a "detective," though whether the detective in question is to be one of the classics, such as Poe's Auguste Dupin, Doyle's Sherlock Holmes, Chandler's Phillip Marlowe, or even television's Columbo, is left vague. The "sociologist as detective" metaphor has some usefulness in that both sociologists and detectives (real and fictional) try to solve puzzles concerned with human behavior, and both use a variety of methods to collect data bearing on the puzzle. Both assemble files of documents concerning any problem, and eventually consolidate the contents of those files when building up a "case" to be heard in a judicial or quasi-judicial setting, which has explicit rules of evidence and comes to some formal conclusion. Both work with large, modern bureaucracies, though detectives usually do much more direct reporting to their superiors than do sociologists. Both work on planned projects,

though the detective has little control of what cases will come to him, while the sociologist (if an academic) has great discretion in selecting a problem, but must then write a convincing thesis proposal or research grant application, and then see it through over a period of years, according to the stated (and self-imposed) schedule. In both cases, the file on a problem is eventually closed, though in sociology some other researcher is likely to come along and re-open it, while in detective work this is less likely.

A major difference between sociologists and detectives is that North American law operates on an adversary system, so that when a detective builds up a case, he can be sure that the defendant will have someone on his side to argue against that case. The situation in academic research is more diffuse since the sociologist has the choice of forum in which to present his results. The toughest forum is the scholarly refereed journal, in which each submitted paper is reviewed by at least two experts in the area. Such experts will not generally know the identity of the author, and will consider the article solely in terms of its academic merit. Some less tough forums are papers in conference proceedings, collected by an editor who may be a personal friend of the author, or books that have not been published by a reputable university or commercial press. In these "easier" forums, an author is much less constrained to the prevailing orthodoxy of theory and methodology, a situation that has both bad and good points. Orthodoxy may prevent the publication of poor research, but it may also stifle new approaches to problems.

Pure and Applied Research

The various steps involved in "doing research" include theoretical analysis, formulating hypotheses, designing surveys, conducting face-to-face interviews, participating in the lives of others, writing computer programs, doing statistical tests, consulting contemporary documents, working out which companies own or control other companies, but most of all, writing coherent arguments in plain language. These step-by-step activities can be satisfying in themselves, and it is important that they be done well, but they are of no value unless they are co-ordinated in the interests of attaining some overall goal, which may be theoretical or applied. A theoretical goal (or goal of pure research) would be the refinement or validation of some existing body of knowledge — perhaps, if definitive studies ever take place, the demonstration that one theory is superior to some opposing one. Applied goals have ranged from the classic nineteenth-century studies describing the nature and extent of poverty among the working class, to contemporary research on the effects of replacing social security schemes by a "negative income tax" system.

Whether the purpose of research is theoretical or applied, it will adopt a design in the selection of empirical data to support some arguments and cast doubt on others. Published research almost always comes to some conclusion and this should be reached through careful weighing of evidence. As a reader of published research, or as a writer of research proposals, one should check for the possibility of "circular reasoning" (an argument that assumes the truth of what is to be proved). As modern-day anthropologist Michael Agar says (in a discussion of participant observation methodology), "A crucially important part of any research design is that it have the capability of demonstrating the investigator's pet theory wrong."

SOCIOLOGICAL EXPLANATIONS

Levels of Analysis and Units of Analysis

Arguments in theoretical or applied sociology can always be distinguished in terms of their level of analysis. Sometimes we discuss social influences on the behavior or attitudes of individuals; for example, why do some people have criminal records while others do not? We might look for explanations in terms of the individual's level of

education, ethnic group membership, family background, type of child-rearing, and so forth. This problem is phrased at an individual level of analysis, and would likely (not necessarily) be attacked by research using data on individual persons. Alternatively, we might ask why some neighborhoods have higher crime rates than others, and give an explanation, not solely in terms of individuals, but also in terms of the emergent group characteristics of such neighborhoods. Yet another level of analysis might involve the jurisdiction of criminal law, for which we might wish to take the nation state as an example. In that case, we might explain the comparatively higher incidence of crimes of violence in the U.S.A. compared to Canada, partly in terms of individual characteristics of people in those countries, partly by reference to structural features of neighborhoods, and finally by noting the different legal and attitudinal factors regarding gun-control in the two countries. To take another example, an individual-level analysis of suicide or parasuicide (parasuicide is an unsuccessful attempt at taking one's life) would concentrate on predisposing factors in the individual's personal life, while explanation at a social level would ask (as Durkheim did 100 years ago) why some communities have higher suicide rates than others, and would use the properties of groups in addition to the properties of individuals to explain social behavior. Note that an aggregated individual property can be a group property: for example, being Catholic or Protestant is an individual-level property, but the proportion of people in a community who are Catholic is a group property. Whether one is Catholic or Protestant or Buddhist, living in a community that is mostly composed of Catholics is not the same thing as living in a community mostly composed of followers of some other faith.

Sociological explanations will usually be phrased in terms of regularities that could only be observed over a fair number of individuals, countries, or whatever is the level of analysis. Where a sociologist seems to be attempting an explanation of some

Research may include face-to-face interviewing as well as the theoretical work of hypothesis and analysis.

unique historical event, for example, the causes of the 1789 French Revolution, or of the War of 1812 between the U.S. and Canada, the explanation should be read as an attempt to consider that historical event as a particular instance of some general pattern, which might be expected to repeat itself in other times or other places where conditions are appropriate.

Variables, Networks, and Meanings

Explanations in sociology can be considered to be based on *variables*, on *structure in social networks*, or on *meaning*. The most common type of explanation is variable-centred at the individual level of analysis. Variable-centred explanations take note of the fact that every individual differs from every other individual in countless ways, and that by judicious selection of a few dimensions or cat-

egory systems for classifying the individuals, it may be possible to relate variation on some dimensions (considered as dependent or "caused") to variation on others (considered as independent or "causing"). The terms dependent and independent imply the operation of forms of causation in social processes that act in the same way for all individuals, so that an explanation can be in terms of relations between variables and at a specified level of analysis over a population of individuals, all obeying the same basic sociological laws. For explaining many individual-level characteristics, other individual-level variables such as age, sex, race, nationality, and educational qualifications comprise a useful battery of basic influences (what survey researchers call "the demographics"), to which other, more subtle dimensions of individual variation may be added, if necessary.

Neighborhood characteristics vary widely, and thus demand a tailored analysis in order to explain social behavior.

Correlations and other statistical measures are used to develop arguments about the strength of theoretically plausible causal effects. A correlation is an association between two variables, such that cases that score in one direction on one variable tend to score in the same direction on the other. Thus, people with high levels of formal education tend on the average, with some exceptions, to have high incomes. Most measures of correlation have a maximum possible value of +1.0 and this indicates perfect association. Unless otherwise stated, the association referred to is a "straight-line" one, so that as one variable changes, the other

changes in constant proportion, which is given by another coefficient called the regression slope. Correlation values near 0.0 indicate that the two variables are statistically unrelated. A correlation can also be negative, which means that cases that score in one direction on one variable tend to score in the opposite direction on the other. Thus, economists used to find that years with high unemployment tended to be years with low inflation. A major problem here is that correlation by itself does not necessarily indicate causation. Can we reduce inflation by regarding unemployment as an independent variable and deliberately increasing it? This is a question of political economy, and its practicality (aside from morality) depends on whether the observed correlation is judged to be the result of direct causation from lower unemployment rates to higher inflation. In fact, many observed correlations are called "spurious" because, while real enough, they do not arise due to direct causal links. As an example, consider the inflation of prices that took place from 1970 to 1980, and the associated increase in labor force participation by married women. The correlation is there, but is spurious, being due to complex economic and social factors that caused both inflation and the increase in women working.

Taken to an extreme, the variable-centred type of explanation can leave out some crucial social and human dimensions. In many areas of life, people do not act as individuals: their material and information resources are determined by their positions in a web of social relationships. Furthermore, people are not blind automata. They often make conscious plans and can describe their reasons for taking any course of action, and to the extent that this is important for complete explanation, such symbolic and meaning-centred aspects must be taken into account. Sociologists typically use participant observation and carefully transcribed interview materials in order to do "meaning-centred" research, and may supplement this by a survey (as Liza Dalby did when studying Geisha).

As an example of these three facets of sociological explanation, consider the fact that some high school graduates go on to study in a university or community college, while others look for a job. A variable-centred explanation leads us to expect that certain characteristics (race, ethnic group, social class background, ability) will be very differently distributed in the two groups. A network-oriented explanation leads us to look for the flow of information and interpersonal influence between the high school students and other students, their teachers, relations, and "significant others." A meaning-centred explanation suggests

Women's participation in the labor force increased dramatically during the 1970s, partly because of changing social attitudes and partly because of economic factors.

that we talk to the high school graduates concerned and establish how their actions are understandable in the context of their perceived situations.

The Measurement of Concepts

Sociological research begins with ideas, and since research is a social rather than an individual activity, these ideas are often the product of thinking and writing produced by others. Sir Isaac Newton once wrote, "If I have seen further than others, it is because I have stood on the shoulders of giants," and so in sociology, we usually find that what seem to be topical questions have been addressed before.

Deriving predictions from theory is not as easy as it sounds. What seems to be a clear concept in abstract theory may dissolve into muddy ambiguity once we wish to measure it in any specific situation. For example, the "Labor theory of value," which Marx adapted from Adam Smith implies that capitalists extract *surplus value* from the labor of workers. Theoretical definitions of this concept exist, and it should be possible to set up practical (or "operational") definitions and measure the amount of surplus value extracted in a given year, and to note trends in and correlates of this quantity. Cuneo (1978) attempted this measurement activity, using Canadian official figures as data, and came up with no less than eleven different operational definitions of surplus value. A few of them had totally different time-trends and correlates from the others, which should not be so if they were really measures of the same the oretical concept. Focusing on those that seemed the better measures, Cuneo showed a general increase in the annual amount of surplus value and (also in general accordance with Marxist theory), positive correlation with the annual incidence of strikes and lockouts. Several critical papers were later published in the same journal, and the result of the exchange was a sharpening of the concept and a greater knowledge of how to measure it.

In the measurement of individual characteristics, it is now common practice to ask several questions, rather than one. For example, in a study of robbery victimization, it might be unwise to ask the obvious question, "Were you robbed during the last six months?" The legal definition of robbery requires personal confrontation between the victim and the criminal, and survey respondents may be unaware of this and include burglaries (without confrontation) in their answer, thus upwardly biasing the estimate of robbery victimizations. A better tactic is to ask several, more simple questions that do not use terms whose legal definition differs from that of ordinary language, but which, when taken together, are an accurate operational definition of the legal concept of robbery.

Some appealing theories include concepts that are inherently difficult to measure. Thus, Granovetter put forward the idea that the "weak ties" an individual has (crudely operationalized as the people one knows, but sees less frequently than once a year) can be of crucial importance both for the individual and for the social groups he or she belongs to. This is difficult to test empirically, because it seems impossible to enumerate all the weak ties (discarded friends, casual acquaintances, old workmates) any individual has. We only know about weak ties after they have been used for something, and this is not very satisfactory, since we never know when they could have worked, but failed to.

A theory can be made untestable for all practical purposes by being studiously vague about what would constitute satisfactory measurement of its concepts. The situation is similar to that of making a bet with a friend, and on trying to collect the winnings, finding that the friend denies that the conditions of the bet were satisfied. That is not a very rewarding activity. Shearing (1973) wrote a tongue-in-cheek article, "How to make a theory untestable," in which he chided sociologists for their willingness to operate with such theories. The "weak ties" example may be a case in point.

THE BASIC RESEARCH METHODS

Using the Library: the Census and Social Indicators Research

Even in these days of computers and telephone surveys, all social research begins and ends in the library. Much of the best research and certainly the least costly never leaves it. Government documents, corporate reports, and archives are rich ground that the sociologist can mine for data. An obvious source is the Census, a giant survey of every household in the land, that has been carried out every ten years since 1851. Early reports from the

1981 Census tell us that the non-institutionalised population of Canada is now just over twenty-four million, compared with twenty-one-and-a-half million in 1971. Other "social facts" are that women have increased their participation in the paid labor force, the greatest rise being among married women (from 37 percent in 1971 to 52 percent in 1981). There has also been much growth in the proportion of women in hitherto male-dominated jobs; for example, between 1971 and 1981, the proportion of female bus drivers grew from 10 percent to 25 percent, and the proportion of female lawyers grew from 5 percent to 15 percent — but that said, 49 percent of the experienced female labor force is still concentrated in traditional "women's work" such as health, teaching, and stenographic or clerical jobs. On the language issue, 3.7 million people considered themselves able to hold a conversation in both official languages, 30 percent of these having English as their mother tongue, 61 percent French, and the remaining 9 percent some other language. That compares with 2.9 million Canadians claiming this level of bilingual proficiency in 1971; 24½ percent of these had English as their mother tongue, while 68 percent had French, and 7½ percent something else.

Census and survey data often come in tables of frequency counts and percentages, and we can use the "Population by Official Language" example to illustrate tabular presentation and interpretation.

Excellent sources for social research can be found in the library.

TABLE 3-1. **Self-reported ability to converse in the official languages**

	(Population counts)			
	English only	French only	Both	Neither
1981 Census	16 122 900	3 987 240	3 681 960	291 395
1971 Census	14 469 540	3 879 255	2 900 155	319 360

SOURCE: Canada Update 20 percent Sample from the 1981 Census.

This table contains the basic information for a variety of summary statements. Many such summaries involve the use of approximations and percentages. Thus, we rounded the 3 681 960 bilingual people at 1981 to "3.7 million," and we can express them as being 15.3 percent of the total Canadian population. (In 1981, this was 24 083 500.) We can also say that the percentage of people who are unilingual, anglophone, or francophone is still very large, at 83.6 percent in 1981, but has declined slightly from the 85.1 percent in 1971. It is also possible to express the increase in the number of bilinguals (781 805) as a percentage of the "base number" in the earlier time period (2 900 155). Thus, we could truthfully say that there has been an increase of just under 27 percent. However, while true, this could be misleading, because it mixes up the general rise in the population with the rise in the bilingual sub-population. Since the overall population increased by just under 12 percent, over the intercensal decade, we should anyway have expected the bilingual subgroup to increase in the same proportion. As well as combining a general increase with the gain of the bilingual share of the population, this example shows how growth from a comparatively small base-figure can appear spectacular. Official spokespeople often make statements that are strictly true, but disingenuous in that they appear designed to boost the image of a corporation or government program. As the saying goes, "Figures may not lie, but liars will figure."

Some research projects are "data driven." As an example, consider the study (1982) by Alex Michalos, in which he asked an atheoretical, but topical question: "Is there a difference in the quality of life in Canada and the United States of America, and if so, in which country is it better?" More precisely, he confined his study to the years 1964–1974 and used statistical measures called "social indicators." What is a social indicator? It is a measure (sometimes a rough one) of how well a country is doing in meeting the physical and social needs of its people. Michalos divided his indicators into thirteen broad areas:

1. population
2. death, disease, and health care
3. housing
4. crime and justice
5. leisure activities
6. transportation and communications
7. education
8. science and technology
9. government and organization
10. natural environment and resources
11. economics
12. religion
13. morality and social customs.

An atheoretical study can perhaps be justified by Sherlock Holmes's comment, "It is a cardinal error, Watson, to theorize without data," but there is so much data produced by modern governments in the form of "official statistics" (sometimes of dubious validity) that it is essential for the researcher to impose his own framework. Michalos focused on "quality of life" and looked for indicators of this in each of his thirteen areas. Shelter is a basic need, and one quality of life indicator is the incidence of "crowded housing" — the percentage of dwellings in which the number of persons exceeds the number of rooms. This was 11.5 percent in the U.S. at the 1960 Census, compared to 16.5 percent in Canada in the 1961 Census. Ten years later the figures showed improvement, being 8.0 percent in the U.S. and 9.4 percent in Canada. Since this information comes from the decennial census, it should be fairly reliable. Another indicator derived from the census is the percentage of one-parent families (the vast majority of single parents being female). This was 9.3 percent in the U.S. in 1960 (though 22.7 percent among non-white families), compared to 6.4 percent in Canada at 1961. This example illustrates a common problem in comparing results from different censuses or different studies. The U.S. figures are the percentage of one-parent families with at least one offspring under twenty-five years at home, while the Canadian data count one-parent families with at least one offspring under eighteen. There is no need to throw up our hands and abandon the empirical method when confronted with such problems. In research, as in other activities, we must do the best we can in an imperfect world, and make reasonable judgements about the comparability of measures with slightly different definitions. In this case, a sensible decision would surely be that little harm is done, though a research project might check on this, using survey data (where one has more control over the definitions used) to make an estimate for Canada, with the U.S. definition (or vice versa).

Quality of life can be indicated by attitudes as well as by hard facts from the census. The percentage of people disapproving of interracial marriage can be used as such an indicator, (of tolerance, or rather of intolerance). In 1968, 53 percent of a large sample of Canadians disapproved of intermarriage involving "whites" and "non-whites", while 72 percent of a sample of Americans disapproved. Americans may have become more tolerant of racial intermarriage during the 1970s, and it is possible to test this hypothesis using published results from the General Social Survey that has been carried out in the U.S. every year since 1972. The question asked was, "Do you think there should be laws against marriages between (negroes/blacks) and whites?" (Such laws exist in some countries, notably in the Republic of South Africa.) The racial-intermarriage question was only asked of whites in the years 1964 and 1972–1977, but of both whites and non-whites in 1980 and 1982. The percentages agreeing were as follows:

1964	1972	1973	1974	1975
53%	40%	38%	35%	39%

1976	1977	1980	1982
33%	28%	30%	30%

Data from Michalos's study *North American Social Report: a Comparative Study of the Quality of Life in Canada and the U.S.A. from 1964 to 1974.* Boston: D. Reidel, 1982. Page 205 of Volume 1.

As often happens with trends over time, the pattern is a bit bumpy, but seems to reflect a gradual shift. Americans slowly became more tolerant of racial intermarriage over this period.

Having found some empirical patterns (the U.S.-Canada difference in tolerance and the U.S. time-trend), we seek a parsimonious theory to explain those patterns. A good theory should explain many apparently different patterns. So why are Canadians apparently more racially tolerant than Americans, and why should Americans have become more tolerant over the years? Many studies have shown that educated people display less racial prejudice than uneducated ones, and there has been a general rise in educational opportunities over the last thirty years. As older people, who on the average had fewer educational opportunities, die off, the average educational attainment of the population increases. This has been adduced as an explanation for the American time-trend, but since there is no evidence that Canadians have higher educational levels than Americans (in fact, the reverse is the case), it is of no help in accounting for the U.S.-Canada difference.

The Search for Relevant Historical Data

As another example of library research, consider a study of the deterrent effects of capital punishment. Empirical data often bear directly on public policy issues (though it would be naive to think that such issues are resolved by empirical evidence alone). Since capital punishment is often justified in terms of its supposed deterrent effect, the majority of recent studies have concerned themselves with the situation where potential murderers might be deterred from killing because of the real possibility of being apprehended and executed. (We do not consider places where there is capital punishment for non-homicide offences, though the arguments should hold, in the same way.)

Because of uncertainties that may linger after any verdict of "guilty" (for example, Donald Mar-

Quality of life is indicated by the physical environment, especially ''crowded housing''.

We expect social theories to be consistent with one another. Phillips asks how we can believe the large number of experiments showing that people can be deterred from exhibiting aggression when they see someone else being punished for it, and at the same time, believe that capital punishment fails to deter potential murderers. Theoretical inconsistency is very disturbing and should lead to empirical studies or clarification of concepts (or both) in an attempt to resolve the inconsistency.

Having done a lot of research on human tendencies to imitate, Phillips proposed that executions could have a short-term rather than a long-term effect, perhaps similar to the impact of any propaganda or advertising campaign. If so, he argued, the yearly data on homicides, used as a criterion variable in nearly all studies, might be inappropriate, since they would be insensitive to short-term effects lasting only a few days, weeks, or months. It followed that he had to find reliable data on daily or weekly homicides in a country practising capital punishment. Much time spent studying in the library established that such data are only available for London, England, for the period 1858–1921. Why focus on weekly rather than on monthly data? Because Phillips had carried out similar studies on the effects of imitation and publicity on other social behavior and had found that weekly data seemed most appropriate.

Phillips viewed each report of a judicial execution as a "message." The week in which the execution was reported is thought of as a time period in which the "deterrent message" was sent out to the general population, and if executions have a short-term deterrent effect on homicides, the murder rate in that "experimental" week can be compared with the rate in a matched "control" period. So far as possible, the experimental and control periods should be alike, differing only in the presence or absence of the "deterrent message" and balanced on everything else. Phillips chose a control period as the combination of the weeks before and after the execution week; for example, if an execution was publicized in the week beginning

shall, Jr., an Indian convicted of murder in Sydney, Nova Scotia, spent eleven years in prison, but was released in 1983 after it became apparent that he was innocent) and because of the irrevocable nature of execution, those concerned with individual rights have argued that capital punishment should not be instituted unless there are clear grounds for believing it to have a deterrent effect.

A research paper by David Phillips (1980) begins by citing many studies that have failed to find solid grounds for believing that capital punishment has any deterrent effect, since whenever a researcher claims to show this, a critic is able to find some methodological flaw in the study.

Monday, May 1st, then the homicide rate for that week would be compared with the average of the rates for the weeks beginning Monday, April 24th and Monday, May 8th.

To test the deterrence hypothesis, we need to select a number of executions and compare the homicide rates in experimental and control periods for each one. If executions deter homicides, then murder rates in execution weeks should be lower than those in the control periods. Since the balancing of experimental and control weeks cannot be perfect, this may not be so every time, but some definite pattern should emerge in the data. On the other hand, if executions have no deterrent effect (or if the measure of homicides is a poor one since not all murders are correctly identified as such), homicides should be as frequent in execution weeks as in control weeks; in fact, the comparison of murder rates as being higher or lower in experimental weeks should be just like tossing a coin, so that about half the time the result turns out one way and half the time the other.

When Phillips used a standard casebook of notorious murderers to select twenty-two heavily publicized executions, he found three cases where there was no difference at all, four where there

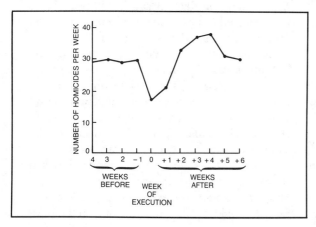

FIGURE 3-1. **The Frequency of Weekly Homicides, before, during, and after twenty-two Publicized Executions, London, 1858–1921.**

were more homicides in the execution week, and fifteen where there were fewer homicides in the execution week. Thus, heavily publicized executions did seem to have a deterrent effect. Anyone who wants to argue that these results came about because of chance fluctuations, and that there was no deterrent effect, must convince us that it is reasonably likely to find a dime come up "heads" fifteen times or more in twenty-two tosses. Try it as a private project. You will find it much easier to believe that Phillips found a deterrent effect than to believe his results came about by chance. The Phillips data can be summarized as a graph, in which the vertical axis is the number of homicides per week, and the horizontal one is elapsed time, measured from the week of the execution.

Well-publicized executions seemed to be followed by a decline in homicides, though after a two-week period the homicide rate returned to normal, and then showed a temporary rise. The count of homicides fell twenty-one short of the expected number in the week of and the week after the execution, but was nineteen higher than expected three weeks after the execution. One explanation is that potential murderers are deterred by fear. Alternatively, public executions may have served as a ritual that reinforced the moral order through dramatizing the unacceptability of murder as a way of resolving personal problems. Without further research, we cannot know the mechanism, but Phillips does seem to have shown a deterrent effect, albeit a short-lived one, that is cancelled out by the subsequent rise in homicides.

Can these results be generalized to contemporary North American society? Phillips himself points out that in strong contrast to the mid-twentieth-century U.S. experience, with its endless appeals, the English justice system of those days was swift, the murderer often being executed only a few months after the crime. In addition, the English press of those days reported executions in gruesome detail, while the modern tendency is to gloss over such unpleasantness.

The Sample Survey

Unless one has access to data on a complete population, as may happen on the rare occasions when research interests coincide with census or other official definitions, the researcher will have to face the problem of sampling (that is, of not studying the whole population) and having done so, will have to argue that people should believe the research results have "external validity" — that is, they hold beyond the particular set of data collected. Problems of this kind are usually thought of in the context of survey research, but they arise in participant observation studies, as well as in other areas.

In general, sociologists are influenced by the strength of the survey-research paradigm, and feel that research should be concerned with large and randomly drawn samples. However, it should be borne in mind that some very influential studies were based on tiny samples. Piaget's studies of language and thought were carried out on only two children, and one of the well-known Hawthorne studies of worker productivity, carried out at a Western Electric Plant in the late 1920s, was based on detailed records of only five women (Whitehead, 1938). Investigations of small samples like this are sometimes justified on the grounds that they are exploratory and designed to generate hypotheses, rather than confirm predictions. A more convincing argument is that certain social or psychological processes are the same, no matter which individuals are selected for study. The difficulty is to decide which processes are of this kind.

Surveys in which data are collected by face-to-face or telephone interview, or by a self-completion questionnaire, are the most common methods of social science data collection. The modern tendency is to draw a random sample of between 500 and 5000 individuals (depending on resources and research interests), and to devote great time and trouble in obtaining full co-operation from each person selected into the sample. The main difficulties (aside from those of phrasing sensible questions) are to first establish a reliable basis for setting up what is essentially a lottery (the "prize" being inclusion in the survey!), and second, to obtain a high response rate. Goyder (1984) has shown that personal interview studies in the U.S. average a 70 percent response rate, compared to 64 percent in Canada. Mail questionnaires typically have an even lower response, averaging around 56 percent in the U.S. and Canada. Since the characteristics of "refusers" are usually not known, it is cautious to assume the worst, and call into question the external validity of many survey-based studies. There is some evidence (Bebbington, 1970) that the hard core of non-responders are indeed different from those who co-operate, though there is also comfort in reports (Koenig et al., 1977) that in some areas, they are not.

It took many years for sociologists to be persuaded of the merits of obtaining a small but randomly selected sample and trying to get a high response rate. Even now, many sociologists are more impressed by the total sample size than by the response rate, or are satisfied with an inadequate response of the order of 40 percent or even lower. The most common error in planning a survey is to allow people to select themselves into the sample, on the basis of their own interests and available free time, rather than having a lottery-like mechanism do the selection.

Shere Hite published a best-selling book (*The Hite Report: A Nationwide Study of Female Sexuality*), which can be criticized on the basis just discussed. Hite presents her book as a scientific collation of information from over 3000 women aged seventeen to seventy-eight from across the U.S., one that represents the views of the American female population. Her conclusions may be true, but since her respondents all volunteered themselves, they may apply only to those who have the time and interest to complete questionnaires about their sex lives. Looking at how it was done, we find the study was conducted in four stages, over four years, each using a different questionnaire. The first was distributed through national mailings to various women's groups. Soon after, notices in the *Village Voice, Mademoiselle, Brides,* and *Ms* magazines told readers that they could write in for the questionnaire. In addition, *Oui* magazine ran the questionnaire in its entirety, and the paperback *Sexual Honesty by Women for Women* asked its readers to send in their replies. Apparently questionnaires II, III, and IV were distributed throughout various channels of the Women's movement and selected church newsletters. Overall, out of 100 000 questionnaires distributed, only 3000 were returned, a response rate of 3 percent. Hite ignores the issue of voluntary response, and she assumes that the large number of non-respondents held the same views as those who were prepared to reply to her questions. This may be so, but most of the history of opinion polling is against her.

A classic and widely misunderstood case is the failure of the *Literary Digest* magazine to predict the outcome of the 1936 U.S. presidential election, even when they sent out ten million mock ballots to registered voters (Bryson, 1976). Many introductory texts wrongly ascribe the failure of this poll (which predicted that Landon would beat Roosevelt by a three to two majority) to the selection of names from telephone directories and automobile registration lists (which would at that time overrepresent Republicans). In fact, the main culprit was voluntary response; only 2.3 million ballots were sent back, leaving the 7.7 million non-respondents as an unknown factor. For whatever reason, the non-respondents tended to vote for Roosevelt. The lesson is clear, though apparently very difficult to learn. Surveys must use smaller sample sizes, make them randomly selected, and devote time, money, and effort to maximizing co-operation from those selected.

Studying Social Networks

It is easy to make common-sense arguments about the importance of conceptualizing individuals as linked to others through social bonds, and to criticize standard survey research, but doing systematic research on the links that bind individuals and social roles together is difficult. Early studies were carried out in small, closed populations of co-operative individuals, such as children in schools or summer camps. In many cases, "social network" questions were added to conventional large-scale surveys (for example, Barry Wellman in Toronto and Edward Laumann in Detroit asked survey respondents about the characteristics of their closest friends). More recently, Claude Fischer reported a Californian study, in which the survey respondents reported having between eighteen and nineteen friends in their "personal social network." Current theory in the network field holds that individuals are typically involved in many more social relationships than they can remember, and that weaker relationships can be surprisingly important.

James Beniger studied the channels (1983) by which information about commonly abused drugs passed among members of ten professions in the San Francisco area. He asked sample members from the ten professions two questions:
1. During the last six months, have you given information or advice related to drugs or drug-users to anyone in this profession? (A list of the ten professions followed.)
2. During the last six months, did you receive information or advice related to drugs or drug users from anyone in this profession? (The same list of professions followed.)

The replies to these questions, together with information about the total numbers of people practising in those professions in the San Francisco area, allowed Beniger to estimate the percentages of possible links that were being used, both within any professional group and between the various groups. These are called network densities. His results showed several points:
1. The percentages were on the whole small, mostly less than 10 percent, which means that information and advice was sent and received between only a small proportion of the logically possible pairs of professionals. This may indicate

that people may prefer to use an old information channel than initiate a new one.

2. Information flows are more likely to occur within occupational groups than between them; for example, drug-relevant information passed between an estimated 32 percent of the possible pairs of Probation Officers, but only 3 percent to 5 percent of the possible links between Clinical Psychologists and Probation Officers were used. One group (Clergy) had no significant links with any of the others.

3. Most flows of information or advice between occupational groups are in one overall direction, with Physicians, Pharmacists, Probation Officers, and Psychologists at the information-giving end, and School Administrators and Teachers at the information-receiving end. Furthermore, the system is more like a chain than a cobweb. As the figure shows, there is a tendency for teachers to receive information and advice at second- or third-hand.

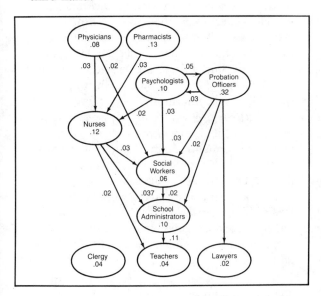

FIGURE 3-2. **Predominant Channels of Drug Information Exchange among Ten Professions in San Francisco. (Values are Estimated Upper Bounds of Densities.)**

Participant Observation (Field Research)

In this approach, the sociologist takes part in many activities of the people being studied, and through making detailed field notes, supplemented by interviews or the collection of other kinds of data, builds up a comprehensive picture of local social structure, interaction patterns, and social identities. A classic example is the description of life in an Italian-immigrant area in Boston, by William Foote Whyte (1955). As in Whyte's case, the researcher may live in the area for several months or a year, and depending on circumstances, she may or may not reveal her true identity and interests. If not, then ethical problems can arise, and this happens particularly in studies of deviant behavior, such as crime or illicit sexual activity. Choice of the people or the organization for study is often based on convenience, or some personal ties formed by the researcher. In some cases, "snowball" or "chain-referral" sampling is used, by which is meant the researcher's asking each member of the group being studied to introduce her to someone else involved in similar activities. Snowball sampling works best when there are lasting ties between members of the population being studied, and this will not always be so.

In a controversial study, Laud Humphreys (1975) collected data on the operation of "tearooms" (public lavatories used for casual sex by male homosexuals). Humphreys participated in "tearoom" activity by taking the role of "watch queen" (one who acts as lookout, and incidentally gets to watch the sex acts of others) and thus had a reason to be there regularly. His field notes (dictated into a tape recorder in his car, as soon as possible after the observations) yielded precise data on initiation patterns in tearoom pick-ups, the frequencies of different sexual behaviors, and strategies used to avoid trouble with police. Another tactic he used was to trace the addresses of "tearoom" participants through their automobile license plates, and to have them interviewed in what purported to be a general health survey.

Much debate arose on the ethics of his research practices.

In a 1977 study, Jason Ditton showed how driver-salesmen working for a large British bakery responded to management's financial control system by systematically "fiddling" their accounts. Participant observation studies often give much attention to processes of "adult socialization." Among the bread salesmen studied by Ditton, new recruits were introduced gradually to the system without having its illicit aspects spelled out in so many words. The newcomers learned that as they were responsible for balancing their accounts weekly, it was in their interest to overcharge here and there, to cover themselves against inevitable errors. They also learned that as they took over a round from some other salesman, they had to keep up the practices that salesman had been engaging in, since to start behaving honestly where the predecessor had been fiddling would reveal to the customers that they had been systematically overcharged in the last few years. They were, in fact, taking over a "situated social identity" from the previous salesman.

In sequence that is common in field research, (Whyte discusses this in an appendix), Ditton began with only vague ideas about the theories he wanted to test, and went up several blind alleys. He had started with the company by taking a summer job, and began working on the "line" in the operations of making and packaging bread products, then moved to a job in the dispatch department. During these episodes of participant observation, field notes were hurriedly made on scraps of paper in washrooms and, in addition, some personal interviews and questionnaires were used. (The questionnaires were not a success.) Finally he got a job as a driver-salesman, and this turned out to be the most interesting part of the research. As well as carrying out participant observation, he interviewed salesmen in their homes. Since he had been working at the company for several years by then, they were willing to talk freely about their fiddling and pilferage activities, and even to have him use a tape recorder.

When Ditton eventually left the field and came to construct a report, he had over 4560 hours of participant observation and thirty-four taped and typed up interviews. It took eighteen months of thinking through this material before he produced a thesis that focused largely on analyses of fiddling in the sales department. Much of the material collected in other departments was used only as background material, or was not used at all.

Ethical Aspects

Ditton's study was a "partially open" one; that is, he told many but not all of his workmates something of his research interests. He is conscious of ethical difficulties in this and, in justification, asks how ethically proper research could ever get at the truth about such institutionalized, on-the-job theft. A previous researcher had used more conventional interview methods to study similar bakery plants and had been puzzled by the fact that roundsmen had a higher standard of living than inside men. Since this researcher had not gained the confidence of the roundsmen in the way Ditton was able to, they naturally kept their criminal activities secret. When research is written up for publication, it is conventional to hide the true names of informants and the research site by using pseudonyms. However, such disguises are easily penetrated, and there would be nothing to prevent a sociologist being issued with a *subpoena*, forcing him to testify in a case brought before the notice of the authorities by his research. Clearly there are difficult problems in the path of discovering truth.

Experimentation

Experiments are distinguished by their varying emphasis on two aspects of research: first, the amount of control the sociologist has over the situation being investigated and, secondly, by the random assignment of individuals to comparison groups (sometimes called experimental group and the control group). I prefer to reserve the word experiment for studies that include random assignment aspects (not to be confused with random sampling procedures, though the two may be combined), but not everyone makes this distinction. For example, some would call the Phillips study of homicide rates "an experiment," but since randomization is absent, I would not.

Control is exerted in an experimental situation so that the researcher can measure more accurately, but primarily so that situational factors can be varied independently. As in tuning up a car, or establishing the foods to which a baby has allergic reactions, so in research, the golden rule is that each factor should be varied with all others left constant. In order to exert control (and also to save time and money), experiments are carried out on a smaller scale "model" of the naturally occurring situation. This leads to a distinction between two kinds of validity: *internal validity* is the degree to which the conclusions of the experiment stand up, within the context of the small-scale model that has been constructed; *external validity* is the degree to which one can generalize the internally valid conclusions drawn from the model to a real-world situation. If a study lacks internal validity, there is little point in discussing its generalizability.

In one of the Hawthorne studies at the Western Electric Company, five women whose job was to assemble electrical relays were taken out of the main factory floor and set up in a special "experimental" unit, so that changes could be introduced in their work conditions and payment schedules without disrupting production in the main plant. As it turned out, the control exerted in this study was not sufficient to make it easy to draw clear inferences from the data. Over the five years of the study, the Wall Street Crash of 1929 and the ensuing rapid rise in unemployment rates were

factors beyond the researchers' control, and can plausibly be argued to have influenced the operators' behavior and productivity. Here then was a study with potentially high external validity, but low internal validity. However, the data are very rich, and have stimulated much debate. Thus, even a study with low validity may have its uses.

Another example of an experiment is a study of simulated juries, reported by Valerie Hans and Anthony Doob. The researchers were concerned to demonstrate two effects: first, that jurors are more likely to consider a defendant guilty if they are told that the defendant already has a criminal record and, secondly, that jurors make up their minds differently when by themselves and when in groups. The Canada Evidence Act of 1970 allowed the criminal record of a defendant to be introduced as evidence, and the official purpose of this was specifically so that the jurors could use this information in evaluating the defendant's credibility as a witness. (The jurors were supposed to be able to separate the issue of credibility of the evidence given by the defendant from the issue of his guilt — a subtle legal distinction perhaps.)

People chosen to act as jurors in the experiment were obtained as volunteers at a museum of science and technology, and were given the task of reaching a verdict in the case before them. Each actor then read a description of a hypothetical case about a man accused of burglary. The details need not concern us here. Suffice it to say that the accused claimed an alibi that he was at the movies at the time in question, and was supported in this by the testimony of his girl friend. A randomly determined half of the "jurors" were then told that the accused had been previously convicted of burglary (these people were also given the "judge's instructions," which essentially remind the juror that prior record should be used only to determine the credibility of the defendant and should not be used to determine whether or not the defendant is guilty). Independently of this "Record versus No Record" dimension, jurors were

In the physical sciences, results are quantifiable, and controls relatively easy to establish. The challenge to the social scientist lies in determining criteria for internal validity.

also randomly assigned to comparison groups on a "Group Verdict versus Individual Verdict" dimension. In the "Group Verdict" condition, four-person mini-juries were required to come to a unanimous decision, while in the "Individual" condition, each subject served as a jury of one.

The results were striking. In the "Individual" condition, 45 percent of the verdicts were "guilty" when the defendant's record was introduced in evidence, compared to 40 percent "guilty" verdicts when there was no mention of any previous criminal record. With only twenty individuals in each of the "Record" and "No Record" conditions, the five percent difference is trivial. However, when

we look at the "Group Verdict" condition, 40 percent of the four-person mini-juries came to unanimous "guilty" verdicts in the "Record" condition, while none at all did so in the "No Record" condition. It is important to remember that the "Group Verdict" situation is more externally valid, since it more closely approximates the jury decision situation in a real courtroom. Hans and Doob were able to conclude: "Presence of a record... appears reliably to increase the probability that a defendant will be found guilty by a jury, regardless of the evidence." Strictly speaking, the conclusions can only be generalized to a population from which the people acting as jurors came. However, there is no obvious reason why the conclusion would be any different with another population of North Americans, and therefore it stands.

WRITING REPORTS (AND READING THEM)

Ideally, a report on any piece of research should summarize previous thinking in the area, identify a soluble problem, indicate the method or methods chosen to make the investigation, and outline the steps taken to do the study. Sufficient detail should be given so that someone else could repeat the research. Difficulties encountered should be reported, as should any limitations on the internal or external validity of the results. Conclusions should be stated without fanfare, and should be suitably qualified where necessary.

In practice, most writers of research reports have a point of view, and to a greater or lesser extent, are arguing for it. Professional scholarly standards require them to show how they came to their conclusions, and to discuss the limitations of their research. In addition, the enormous volume of research reports produced nowadays means that each individual report should be brief. If not, few will read it, and it may not even get published.

Thus writers of a research report have several competing aims: a *rhetorical* aim (to lead the reader to certain conclusions); a *judicial* aim (to present all the evidence, so that the reader can critique the study); and a *stylistic* aim (to get people to read the report and grasp the main points quickly). When the data have been collected and hypotheses have been tested, the writing of the report remains to be done, and it is vital that sufficient time be allowed for this crucial part of the research process. Several drafts may be required before a satisfactory final product emerges, and between those drafts, trips to the library and some further analysis of the data will very likely be necessary. Even then, if the report is submitted to a supervisor or to colleagues or to an academic journal, those external judges may point to more or less serious flaws. A number of "self-help" texts on how to write are available, and a dictionary and thesaurus are essential.

Reading a Research Report

For each book or article written, dozens, perhaps hundreds of other reports must be read, and thousands may be cursorily scanned in case they include relevant material. A quick reading of the summary and the concluding section of a report will indicate whether it is relevant, and if so, the whole paper might be read. In psychology and other sciences, it is common for authors to select certain keywords by which their articles may be characterized. This makes it easier for computer searches to be carried out by people who want to see the abstracts of all papers on a certain topic, no matter what journal they were published in. Computer searches are used in Sociology journals too, though since authors are rarely required to provide keywords, the text entered into the library's data bank may be coded by the article's title, and its abstract or keywords provided by a librarian.

The decisions to be made when reading research reports are: (1) to establish the pool of material that might be read; (2) to select the material that should be given priority; and (3) to make a judgement about the credibility of each report that is read. Having used the advice of experts in the area, and of specialist librarians, perhaps citations or

Computerized data banks have greatly facilitated research in sociology, just as in the physical sciences.

computer-aided searches, priorities can be made by using expert opinions or by the rule of thumb that papers that appear in the high-prestige journals are most worth reading. Like most rules of thumb, this is not always valid, but it serves to establish priorities. Finally, one must decide upon the credibility of each study; that is, what degree of belief should be placed in it. As mentioned, writers of research reports have competing rhetorical, judicial, and stylistic aims, and as a reader it may help you come to a conclusion about a study's credibility if you first decide whether the author was tending toward the rhetorical or the judicial. A study that tends toward the rhetorical may still be true, but there may be fewer grounds for believing it to be so, and in research, we are concerned about the grounds for belief as much with the belief itself.

SUMMARY

1. Researching a social problem gives scope for individual creativity and exercising a high order of skill in problem solving; however, it involves more mundane activities, such as writing up field notes in standard form, checking data against original sources, or verifying that a computer program produces the correct answer with test data. A researcher wants everything to be checked several times so as to be sure the results are true.

2. This chapter has emphasized the variety of approaches that can be included as "research," and has classified them as pure or applied, as being at varying levels of analysis; whether they seek explanations in terms of relationships between variables, structure in social networks, or the perceived situations of social actors. What all these approaches have in common is that they begin and end in the library, since all good research must build on previous work, and will itself be referred to by others, in later years.

3. In this sense, research is a *social* activity, involving standardized routines, that go together to expand the state of knowledge in a given field. On one account, research is carried out to test existing theory, yet, as has been shown, in some cases, there may be little agreement about how theoretical concepts should be measured, and a substantial proportion of researchers act on an opposite assumption, as if knowledge could be generated inductively, by accumulating large amounts of qualitative or quantitative data.

4. The basic research methods include: using the census and other standard reference publications in the library; searching for relevant historical data; designing and analyzing social surveys; combining data from different sources so as to estimate theoretically relevant concepts (our example was "network density"); engaging in participant observation or other kinds of field research; controlled experimentation.

5. People become specialists in one or more methodologies, and each specialty develops its own loyalty and jargon. It is all the more important then that research reports should be written in as simple and jargon-free a manner as possible. After all, the purpose of such reports is to allow others (particularly non-specialists), to see what was done and what conclusions were drawn.

GLOSSARY

Applied research. Research carried out to produce information that will have immediate practical use.

Attribute. A quality characterizing something; often used to refer to a categorical variable.

Bias. Errors that are always in the same direction and therefore do not cancel out. Also used to refer to a style of research that focuses only on data that support prior theories.

Case. The unit of analysis in the investigation. Where people are the units of analysis, the terms respondent or subject may be used.

Categorical variable. A variable that sorts the units of analysis into distinct "boxes." (For example, work situations may be divided into "working for the government," "working for a concentrated or monopoly company," and "working for a highly competitive company.") Categorical variables may have ordered categories, but it is not usually possible to do arithmetic on the values that label the "boxes."

Census. The collection of systematic data from all members of a complete population.

Coding scheme. A set of rules that a researcher makes up to guide how assistants will convert qualitative information (for example, verbal description of someone's occupation, or newspaper reports of sexual assaults) into membership in one of a set of categories.

Comparison group. A set of cases that received different treatment from some other set of cases, but are the same in other respects. Where the cases received no treatment at all, they may be called a control group.

Confirmatory research. A study planned specifically to test a clearly laid-out theoretical prediction.

Confounding. The situation where one effect is mixed up with another, often due to poor design or analysis.

Content analysis. The systematic analysis of communications in order to produce an objectively testable description of the content. For example, a sample of children's stories may be examined to detect their preoccupation with achievement motivation.

Control. In experiments, control is the isolation of the experimental situation from all irrelevant outside influences. Thus, laboratory research is inherently more controlled than field research. In analyzing data, control is achieved by restricting the analysis to a subgroup (for example, by focusing only on employed women between twenty-five and thirty-four years of age), or by using a statistical model to remove the straight-line correlation of some variable from the association between two other variables.

Correlation. The association between two variables. This term usually implies a straight-line association such that as one variable increases, the other increases in proportion. If a correlation is negative, then as one variable increases, the other decreases in proportion. It is important to remember that "correlation is not proof of causation, though a causal relationship between two variables will usually produce a correlation."

Cross-sectional survey. A study in which people are questioned on only one occasion, and are not followed up, as in a panel study or a longitudinal survey.

Cross-tabulation. A table showing the frequencies or relative frequencies of cases existing in the sample at every combination of the levels of two or more variables. Such a table has rows for the categories of one variable and columns for the categories of the other. Where a third variable is to be held controlled, its categories will form the layers of a three-dimensional table.

Demographic variable. Categorical variables that demographers and market researchers find useful for discriminating between social groups. For example, gender, age, marital status, religion, ethnic group, occupational or housing class.

Dependent variable. A variable considered to be caused by other (independent) variables being treated in data analysis.

Ecological correlation. The correlation between two variables aggregated to a higher level of analysis. For example, individual-level characteristics such as years of education completed and yearly income are said to be aggregated when averages for these variables are taken for geographical units, such as metropolitan areas, and the correlation over the aggregate units of analysis is said to be an ecological correlation. It is tempting, but fallacious to assume that an ecological correlation is a good guide to the value of the corresponding individual-level correlation.

Experiment. In the loosest sense, this may simply mean a study using empirical data, rather than speculation. A tighter definition is that experiments occur when the researcher has sufficient control to assign some cases to one ("experimental") condition, and others to a comparison (or "control") condition. A study may be strengthened if assignment to experimental or control treatments is determined by a table of random numbers, and further strengthened if those directly administering the study are kept in ignorance of the purposes of the study, or of whether any individual case is in one condition or another (the "double-blind" experiment). The terms "treatment" and "condition" are equivalent and refer to the levels of the independent variable in an experiment.

Experimenter effect. A tendency for the expectations held by people being studied (or by the research assistants supervising the study) to change their behavior, thus producing biased results.

Exploratory research. This term is classically applied to field studies involving unstructured interviewing or participant observation with convenience samples. More recently, it has been applied to a kind of rough-and-ready data analysis. In each case, the major advantage is openness to new ideas suggested by patterns in the data, but there is a danger that conclusions will be drawn too easily and generalized too widely without proper confirmatory research.

External validity. The degree to which a study's conclusions hold beyond the time, place, and sample that were associated with it.

Field research. Participant or non-participant observation, together with use of informants and contemporary records.

Field experiment. An experiment carried out in the natural environment of the social processes being studied.

Frequency distribution. A table showing the frequency count and/or the percentage value for each value of a variable, over a sample.

Generalizability. The extent to which a study's results will apply in other times and places.

Hawthorne effect. The tendency for people being studied to increase their productivity or otherwise try to please the researcher, thus biasing the research.

Hypothesis. In one usage, this means any conjecture. In another, it means a prediction derived from a larger theory.

Informant. A person who gives a researcher information about the society or organzation being studied. Using informants is widespread and indispensable, but bias can arise if informants are members of atypical subgroups or are disgruntled employees.

Interviewing. A data collection method used in survey research and case studies, and as an additional tool in participant observation. The interview may be structured or unstructured, face-to-face or over the telephone, with an individual or with a group.

Interview schedule. The questions and instructions an interviewer must use in a structured interview.

Level of measurement. The numerical operations that make sense to carry out with the scores given to variables. Sociologists most often use categorical variables, called "nominal" if there is no ordering to the categories (for example, ethnic group origin), and "ordinal" if there is. Other levels of measurement are "equal interval" (for example, income) and "ratio" (for example, distance).

Longitudinal survey. A study in which the research team goes back to members of a sample regularly, and accumulates information on changes in the life course. It is difficult and expensive to maintain contact with a large number of people in this way.

Mail survey. Self-administered questionnaires are sent to potential respondents through the mails. Response rates are typically low, unless the issues are salient to respondents.

Marginal frequencies. Also called "the marginals." These are the frequency distributions for row and column totals that appear at the side and bottom of across-tabulation. They often exclude the "no information" category, so should be used with care.

Model. A theoretical model is a simplified description of a social structure or social process. A mathematical model is the same, but the description is in the form of equations that can be manipulated according to algebraic rules. An experimental model is a smaller scale version of the social structure or process that can be set up cheaply in laboratory conditions.

Network density. The proportion of logically possible ties between people that in fact exist.

Nominal level of measurement. This occurs where the values attached to categories of a variable only represent membership or nonmembership in those categories. Thus gender may be coded "1" for male or "2" for female, without any implication that the relationship between the numbers reflects anything about the relationship between the sexes.

Nonsampling errors. Errors due to inadequacies in question-wording, interviewer training or supervision, and coding or analysis of data. Such errors will be present no matter how large the sample size (certain of them can be expected to be more prevalent with very large sample size), and cannot usually be expected to cancel out with one another.

Null hypothesis. A prediction that there is no difference between comparison groups. Typically the researcher believes there is a difference, but is unsure how large it will be. Therefore, it is easier to state his belief as one of "not no difference," that is, as a desire to refute the null hypothesis.

Open-ended questions. In interviews or self-completion questionnaires, respondents may be asked to say how they feel on some issue. Their verbatim answers can be used in exploratory research and also coded through content analysis.

Operational definition. The way a theoretical variable is practically measured. Ideally this should be close to its theoretical definition, but this may not be feasible.

Panel study. A survey in which the same respondents are asked their opinions on some issue at intervals varying from several weeks to several years. The focus is usually on stability and change of attitudes.

Participant observation. The researcher joins a social group and to some extent engages in the same activities as its members, while observing and recording what happens, either with or without the group's knowledge. Problems of ethics and of external validity may arise, but it is argued that actions cannot be understood without experiencing them from the point of view of members of the community under study.

Path analysis. A type of statistical modelling in which social processes are modelled by a causal system. Diagrams of causal arrows make this a popular device for displaying results from certain types of survey research.

Policy research. Applied research designed to help formulate and evaluate government policies.

Polling. Surveying political attitudes and voting intentions.

Probability sampling. Selection of cases from a population so that each one has a known and non-zero chance of entering the sample, the chance being determined by the throw of dice or some other mechanical random device.

Purposive sampling. Selection of cases by a method involving the judgement of the researcher or informants.

Qualitative research. Research that stresses the importance of experiencing social structures from the point of view of members of the community studied. Qualitative data are often accounts that use natural language or the slang of those being studied. Many research problems can and should be approached with both qualitative and quantitative tools.

Quantitative research. Research that stresses the importance of objective measurement, unbiased sampling methods, and statistical treatment of findings. Can often be unsatisfying unless supplemented by qualitative data.

Quasi-experiment. An experiment that is missing the component of random allocation of cases to treatments.

Questionnaire. A list of questions to be asked of respondents. Some of the questions will be the same as those successfully used in other studies.

Quota sampling. A purposive sampling method in which interviewers are told to obtain a specified number of each identified subgroup, in proportion to their representation in the population. Quotas are often set by age, economic status, and gender, so the quota might, for example, require a certain number of young full-time employed women and another number of young full-time employed men.

Random allocation. In experiments, the process of assigning cases to comparison groups by a random mechanism, such as a coin toss.

Random sampling. See probability sampling.

Rating scale. A set of ordered categories, numbers, or lines, placed beneath a statement expressing an attitude or intention. The respondent selects a category, then picks a number or checks a mark on the line, to show where he or she stands with respect to the statement.

Replication. The repetition of a research study, ideally by another researcher.

Respondent. The person who answers questions in an interview or a self-completion questionnaire.

Response rate. The percentage of people selected for a study who co-operate and take part in the study. Response rates can be increased by taking care with the design of the study.

Retrospective questioning. Asking people about events that occurred in the past. People often have poor memories, so such questions should be asked with great care.

Sample. The small number of cases taken for study and used to represent a larger population.

Sampling error. The degree to which sample estimates (for example, of a percentage) are spread around the true population value.

Sampling frame. The list that corresponds to a population, and from which a sample is selected. Electoral registers or municipal assessment lists are often used in survey research.

Secondary analysis. Research that saves the cost of data collection by analyzing data, originally collected for another purpose, by government, business, or by other academics.

Selection effect. Bias of research results due to certain types of case being overrepresented in the achieved sample, or in treatment groups.

Significance test. A method used in confirmatory research in order to decide if a difference between two groups might have occurred because of sampling error.

Snowball sample. A non-probability sample obtained by asking each respondent to name some other potential respondents. Often used in studies of deviant populations.

Social indicators. Measures (often crude) of the quality of life in a country. Examples are the infant mortality rate, the percentage of young people in higher education, and the unemployment rate.

Spurious correlation. An association between two variables that is generated, not by either causing the other, but by one or more other variables being causes of the two variables.

Structured interviewing. A highly standardized form of interviewing, in which the interviewer has little if any flexibility in the questions asked and the manner of asking them.

Survey research. An approach to studying social life by collecting data from open- and closed-ended questions to measure the variables characterizing each of a sample of respondents. The results are reported as frequency distributions, tabulations, correlations, and quotations from typical respondents. Regarded with suspicion by some, because mass media have had low standards of reporting survey research and because such research may be funded merely to legitimize policy that has already been formed.

Unit of analysis. The things being studied and which have scores on variables or network links between each other; for example people, business enterprises, metropolitan areas, countries.

Variable. A measurable property of the unit of analysis.

FURTHER READING

Berkowitz, S.E. *An Introduction to Structural Analysis: the Network Approach to Social Research.* Toronto: Butterworth, 1982. A fascinating text on the social network approach to sociology.

Erickson, B. and T.A. Nosanchuk. *Understanding Data.* Toronto: McGraw-Hill Ryerson, 1977. An excellent and fear-reducing text introducing statistical analysis.

Ferber, R., P. Sheatsley, A. Turner and J. Waksberg. *What Is a Survey?* Washington DC: American Statistical Association. Single copies of this clear and short booklet are available free from ASA, 806, 15th Street NW, Suite 640, Washington, DC 20005, U.S.A. Can also be obtained in Chinese, Greek, and Spanish translation.

Granovetter, M. *Getting a Job*. Cambridge: Harvard University Press, 1974. An honest account of what it means to single-handedly carry out and write up a small survey.

Hammond, P.E. (ed.). *Sociologists at Work*. New York: Basic Books, 1974. Recollections by eminent sociologists of how they carried out research projects in the 1940s, 1950s, and 1960s.

Katzer, Jeffrey, Kenneth H. Cook and Wayne W. Crouch. *Evaluating Information: a Guide for Users of Social Science Research*. Don Mills, Ontario: Addison-Wesley, 2nd edition, 1982. A valuable and non-technical overview of positivist research methods.

Mills, C. Wright. *The Sociological Imagination*. New York: Oxford University Press, 1959. A wonderful book, to be re-read annually, particularly the appendix, "On intellectual craftsmanship."

Mullins, C.J. *The Complete Writing Guide*. Englewood Cliffs, NJ: Prentice-Hall, 1980. An essential aid to clear presentation.

Sanders, W.B. (ed.). *The Sociologist as Detective*. New York: Praeger, 2nd edition, 1976. A discussion of similarities and differences between sociological work and detective work.

Woodward, C.A. and L.W. Chambers. *Guide to Questionnaire Construction and Question Writing*. CPHA, 1335 Carling Avenue, Suite 210, Ottawa, Ontario K1Z 8N8.

Culture, Society, and the Individual

Part II deals with the dynamic relationship between culture, society, and the individual, showing that our personality and behavior are influenced by the culture and society in which we live and grow.

Chapter 4 examines the workings of culture from a psychodynamic perspective. Your language and religion, for instance, cause you to feel, think, and behave differently from those who have a different language and religion. In this sense, we are all products of our culture, but we create and recreate it, too.

Chapter 5 discusses society at different theoretical levels and explains that the culture of our society influences our social relations, and provides its members with a distinct identity and a sense of historical continuity. As members of our society, we all enact the script given to us by our culture.

The next two chapters deal with the questions of how and why most of us tend to obey society's rules while others deviate from them. Chapter 6 is concerned with socialization — the process by which we learn to acquire our personality and identity and become members of our society. Although we continue to learn throughout life, sociologists tell us that childhood socialization is by far the most important because of its contribution to personality development and its critical role in the development of society. Chapter 7 discusses deviance from societal norms and the way society goes about controlling behavior harmful to social life.

CHAPTER FOUR

Culture

KARL PETER

Culture can be studied from various perspectives. The psychodynamic approach used in this essay is but one. Actually, the study of culture is not a prime concern of sociologists but of anthropologists. Sociologists concern themselves with *society*, and a society might contain several or many cultures as in the case of Canada, which is recognized as a multicultural society. Similarly, the same culture might be characteristic of several societies. East and West Germany, Austria, and a large part of Switzerland are very different in their societal structure, but they share the same culture. Sometimes the meanings of society and culture overlap or become synonymous. Such is the case when a homogeneous culture organizes its institutions in a self-determinate way. Norway and Denmark come close to having both unique cultures and societies.

Anthropology, in the classical sense of the discipline, studies culture in terms of the interrelationship of *culture traits* and social relations. Culture traits are ways of acting and thinking that are peculiar to a culture. They are the rules and guidelines by which the mental and behavioral activities of people are channelled. Although some of these rules may be formalized as written or unwritten laws — or codes of conduct, in which case they might overlap with the organizational requirements of a society — most of them exist in the form of an understanding that certain things ought to be done in certain ways. Norms, folkways, and mores all refer to unwritten rules. Whether you shake hands or rub noses when introduced to another person depends on the rules (in this case norms) by which the act of greeting has been regulated in your culture.

Norms, folkways, and mores are culture traits that emphasize the situational context, the customary history, or the moral connotation of behavior, respectively. An example of a norm is the following: men do not enter women's washrooms, in public places and vice versa; yet on trains and planes, where space is at a premium, both sexes do not object to using the same facilities. The situational context — the lack of space — helps to define normative behavior in different ways.

It is customary to drink tea in the wee hours of the morning in Australia, whereas a late-afternoon tea (with a sweet) is customary in Britain. In Newfoundland villages, a "lunch" is served before bedtime. All of these folkways have grown and spread through their respective cultures as a result of customs. Customs consist of imitative behavior justified by tradition.

Mores are norms that are justified by reference to accepted values. The invasion of someone's privacy is disapproved of because it violates the value of individualism as it exists in Canadian culture, for example. In the culture of Hutterites, which has a collective orientation, what is an invasion of privacy according to our understanding could be a duty of individuals to help and protect each other.

Although norms are understood by all members of society, the behavior that they prescribe often applies to certain segments only. In reflecting the values of a culture, norms are shared conceptions of what is right, wrong, good, desirable, evil, or objectionable. Societies that are highly stratified often have conflicting values. Under these circumstances, it is rather difficult to identify the relationship between values and norms. A society may value peaceful existence, but many of its norms may be highly aggressive. If educa-

tion is valued, as it is in North America, provision is made for mass education (see Chapter 13), but this does not assure the emergence of norms among students to study as hard as possible to get ahead, for example. Only homogeneous cultures have unified a value system with corresponding norms. Many social scientists in the past have emphasized individuals' capacity to internalize their culture's norms through the socialization process. According to this view, people are seen as passive recipients who think and act in accordance with these norms. This approach to the relationship between culture and personality is called "cultural determinism."

A more satisfying interpretation of this relationship sees individuals as agents who act on the cultural material presented to them, selecting, recombining, and inventing traits that are in accord with their creative mind. Although conformity to societal norms and mores is necessary to a certain degree to make an ordered life possible, human inventiveness constantly shapes and reshapes the existing cultural configuration into new untried directions. For example, many norms that in the past prescribed behavior between the sexes are no longer acceptable to the feminist segment of the population.

The study of culture, particularly from the point of view of the sociologist, includes the observation of *what is* in terms of the categories that anthropologists devised for the study of culture; but it must also include *what's going on* — the dynamic aspects of culture that are indicative of cultural change. Both the static and dynamic aspects of culture have been the topic of anthropological theories.

The anthropological school of thought that influenced sociology more than any other was *structural-functionalism*, which originated with the British anthropologists Radcliffe-Brown and Malinowski. Structural-functionalism, as you learned in previous chapters, assumes that in any given culture there is a functional relation, if not unity, between the components of social structure.

This structure is perceived as "an arrangement by which an orderly social life is maintained." Social structure "tends to adapt itself to the physical environment" and assures its "persistence by socializing the individual to acquire the traits and mental characteristics that fit him for participation in social life." (Radcliffe-Brown, 1952:193.) However, structural-functionalism attempts to study sociocultural phenomena without reference to human nature. As such, it stands in contrast to another anthropological orientation, which claims that *culture* is an expression of human nature (Kroeber and Kluckhohn, 1952), a concept that forms the basis of this essay.

THE PROBLEM OF DEFINING CULTURE

The term culture, when used in conversation, seldom elicits a response of ambiguity or miscomprehension. The apparent understanding of "culture," however, does not stem from agreement on what the term stands for, but is traceable to the difficulty of providing a precise and comprehensive definition.

During the last 100 years, scores of definitions were proposed; yet today there is no universally accepted definition. In 1952, the well-known anthropologists Kroeber and Kluckhohn wrote a critical review of the definitions of culture put forward until that time. A few examples taken from their inquiries illustrate the diversity of meaning that the term culture acquired. The anthropologist Malinowski referred to it in this way: "Culture comprises inherited artifacts, goods, technical processes, ideas, habits and values." A purely psychological twist was assigned to culture by Roheim: "By culture we shall understand the sum of all sublimations, all substitutes, or reaction formations, in short, everything in society that inhibits impulses or permits their distorted satisfaction." The shortest definition came from Herskovits: "Culture is the man-made part of the environment." And Robert Redfield defined it as "an organization of conventional understandings manifest in act and artifact, which, persisting through tradition, characterizes a human group."

If, as Kroeber and Kluckhohn (1952) observed, definitions of culture follow the fashions and trends in anthropology and sociology, one must expect that during the thirty years since these authors published their findings, other definitions have been preferred by the new sub-disciplines in anthropology and sociology. Yet even the most sophisticated ones throw light on only certain aspects of culture and therefore reveal only a fragment. As Kroeber and Kluckhohn maintain, "the totality of human culture includes the cultural phenomena of all peoples, times and places insofar as these phenomena are known or knowable." This substantive and descriptive totality, they claim, cannot be captured in single definitions, but requires a level of generalization that is attainable only in a theory of culture. Culture, then, is a general category encompassing all facets of nature and human nature in particular (Kroeber et al., 1952:365).

A discussion of the nature of culture necessarily includes a discussion of human nature, since both stand in a complimentary relation to each other.

THE NATURE OF HUMAN NATURE

Human nature is as difficult to define as culture. Some sociologists are not certain there is such a thing as human nature, but most social scientists agree that human beings have certain biological capacities, which, culturally developed, enable us to speak, think, and feel emotions. It is also generally assumed that these characteristics can be rationally controlled, although the extent of this control is not very clear. Social psychologists see human nature in terms of its unfolding in the process of socialization. From early childhood on, according to an individual's genetic constitution, cognitions, motives, attitudes, and interpersonal response traits gradually develop to form a unique personality. Symbolic interactionism takes this idea further and stresses the importance of language in the process of developing a self. The self-concept is seen as genetically based, developed under the influence of language to absorb the attitudes of others and to use these attitudes in thinking about oneself. (The chapter on socialization discusses this process in detail.) Thus, the social self is a pre-condition for all human interaction and culture. Underlying all these theoretical observations is the basic tenet that human nature stems from a set of genetically based traits that develop in a cultural environment, or that remain undeveloped if that environment is not present.

But the questions may be asked: can human nature be defined in terms of humankind's unique creative abilities? And, if human beings create culture, what is it that generated this process and keeps it going? The answers to these questions are of utmost importance for a theory of culture because they allow us to see the driving force through which human beings create and change culture. If we went back in time to the beginnings of culture, we could safely assume that the loss of instincts and the acquisition of culture must have occurred simultaneously for some time. For, instinctual behavior does not require previous knowledge, whereas culture does. In order to create culture, it meant that the early human beings had to leave the safety of instincts and rely on rational thought. This slow transformation from instinctual behavior to rational behavior seems to have occurred in association with the emergence of tool-making.

Tool-*making* intelligence is fundamentally different from tool-*using* intelligence. The act of making tools detaches the mind from the bondage of the immediate situation characteristic of animals and elevates it to the level of free thought. Tool-making is future-oriented. Past experience and future expectations had to combine in the minds of early human beings; the former depended on learning-ability characteristic of all animals, and the latter on planning ability, which in animals is taken care of by instincts and for

which human beings developed the mental activities of insight (or objectivity) and foresight. The first tools required both insight and foresight, the bases of rationality. Thus, it is rational thought that stands at the cradle of culture. Language, by which mental processes can be translated into concepts and which made the free manipulation of these concepts possible, must have developed simultaneously.

Is there a framework that enables us to understand insight and foresight — the basic elements of our rationality — in combination with our emotions and impulses? Generations of social scientists have worked on this problem.

Freud's Contribution to the Theory of Culture

Sigmund Freud, founder of the psychoanalytic movement, and his followers provided a wealth of data and theoretical formulations in this regard. In *Civilization and its Discontent* (1962), Freud was concerned with the relationship between human nature and culture. He postulated an irremediable antagonism between the demands of instinct and the restrictions that culture impose on them. The free development of sexuality, he claimed, stood in an inverse relationship to the emergence of culture. The repression of sexual instincts had an "organic" origin: repression came about when the sexual stimuli shifted from olfactory to visual excitations; the latter released male/female associations from the bondage of the sexual cycle based on smell to one based on vision.

Freud's observations on the shift from the olfactory to visual stimuli is of utmost significance for a theory of culture because this shift indicates the relative dominance of one part of the brain over the other in the structuring of cultural action. The older olfactory sense is part of a brain structure called the limbic system, whereas visual stimuli are generated and processed in the neocortex — the human brain.

It seems that if there is anything that is exclusively human about Homo sapiens, it is the structure and organization of the brain, and most likely its development paralleled the development of culture. The relationship between human rationality and human emotions is determined by the brain's internal structure and organization, and consequently, finds expression in cultural behavior. What is called human nature in this context refers to the peculiar human ability to receive and to process rational and emotional information, and to structure actions as a result of this process.

The Three Brains

The American neurophysiologist MacLean has demonstrated that the neocortex, the youngest part of our brain, acts as the mediator in discriminating and abstracting intellectual activities, but human emotional behavior continues to be under the dominance of the Limbic system that lacks discriminatory ability, verbal or symbolic capacities, and self-awareness.

Perhaps the most revealing thing about the study of man's brain is that he has inherited the structure and organization of three basic types which, for simplification, I refer to as reptilian, old mammalian and neomammalian. It cannot be overemphasized that these three brains show great differences in structure and chemistry. Yet all three must intermesh and function together as a Triune *brain. The wonder is that nature was able to hook them up and establish any kind of communication among them.*

(MacLean, 1973:7.)

According to MacLean, these three brains act like biological computers, each with its peculiar form of subjectivity and its own intelligence, its own sense of time and space, and its own memory, motor, and other functions. The reptilian brain, the oldest of the three, is programmed for stereotyped behavior, according to instructions based on ancestral learning and ancestral memory programs. This brain seems to be governed by precedent, which is illustrated by the reptile's

tendency to follow roundabout, but proven, pathways, or by operating according to some rigid schedule. The reptilian counterpart in the human brain seems to determine the persistence of cultural traditions, and obeisance to precedent in ceremonial rituals, religious convictions, legal actions, and political persuasions. It may sound presumptuous to suggest that Beethoven's symphonies could have been composed in part by the composer's reptilian brain addressing itself to the reptilian brain of the listener. Yet rhythm, harmony, and repetition could well be cultural responses partially processed by the reptilian brain.

The limbic brain, typical of the brain in lower animals, appears to represent nature's attempt to provide the reptilian brain with a thinking cap and to emancipate it from ancestral limitations. It can be compared to a primitive television screen that provides a better picture for adapting to internal and external environments. This brain plays an important role in elaborating those feelings that guide behavior with respect to the two basic life principles of self-preservation and the preservation of the species. This behavior includes hunger, thirst, nausea, suffocation, choking, racing heart, and the urge to defecate and urinate, which may combine with a variety of intense emotions such as terror, fear, anger, sadness, foreboding, strangeness, and paranoia. Some neural pathways of the limbic system, according to MacLean, elicit aggressive and violent expressions of sexual behavior. Others cause movements of the face, chewing, salivation, and swallowing. The limbic system is the seat of the olfactory sense and the connection between smell and genital functions.

The third brain, the neocortex, is the brain of insight and foresight, of reason, language, reading, writing, arithmetic, and the visual sense. It is this new brain that enables human beings to communicate and to develop culture.

If we look at the human brain as a whole, we find that nature has followed a rather strange course in its development. It has superimposed one brain over the other, instead of changing the primitive brain into more sophisticated instruments. In the normal course of evolution, fins gradually changed into feet, and gills into lungs. But in brain development, a new, superior structure became superimposed over an old one with partially overlapping functions and with no one brain in complete control.

All three brains are capable of learning. But the older structures are too crude to learn symbolic behavior such as language. The limbic brain, for example, could never aspire to conceive of the color red in terms of a three-letter word and the meaning this word stands for, but it can associate the color with such diverse things as blood, fainting, fighting, and flowers. Lacking the help and control of the neocortex, its impressions would be discharaged into emotional behavior. Considered in the light of Freudian psychology, the limbic brain would have many attributes of the unconscious Id. One could argue, however, that this brain is not at all unconscious; rather, it eludes the grasp of the intellect because its animalistic, primitive structure makes it impossible to communicate in verbal terms (MacLean, 1973:8–16).

Where does this discussion lead us in regard to the nature of human nature? Human nature, it seems, is definable in terms of the structure and organization of the three brains, each with its own input and output, and each pressing for mental and behavioral expressions in one unified personality. The often conflicting and contradictory signals that these brains release are the sources of a person's internal conflicts and anxieties. They signify the struggle between what one knows and what one feels.

Several sociological theories are founded on this dichotomy. Theories of crowd or collective behavior (the topic of Chapter 23), have summarized the frequent observation that primitive emotions are aroused when large numbers of individuals focus on the same event. The emotional reaction of a few is quickly picked up by others who are ready for the same response. Anger, fear, and insecurity, but also hope, devotion, and joy, are common components of collective behavior, expressed in all human institutions from politics to religion, sports, and economics.

The social psychology of George Herbert Mead presupposes a human nature that conceptually is divided into the "I" and the "me." The "me" is that part of the self developed in the socialization process, whereas the "I" is a biologically based readiness to respond spontaneously, unpredictably or creatively (Mead, 1963). Human actions, according to Mead, are always the result of the interaction of the "I" and the "me." Normative behavior is that kind of action where the initial impulse of the "I" is channelled into socially acceptable forms through the influence of the "me." The relative influence that the "I and the "me" can have on behavior differs widely. As mentioned previously, spontaneous forms of collective behavior might take place under conditions where the influence of the "me" is minimal. Conversely, social conformity presupposes the suppression of the "I."

Freud, whose work preceded Mead's, proposed similar categories. The "Id," the "Ego," and "Superego" are based on the same concepts regarding the nature of human nature. Human nature, as presented here, presupposes that the mental capacities of human beings can be categorized in two entities: the spontaneous readiness to experience impulses and emotions and the learning capacity to internalize norms, rules, logic, and causality as offered by the cultural environment. The impulses and emotions are the mental leftovers that remained after the instinctual equipment of Homo sapiens was dismantled. The evolutionary process that brought about this change shows an enormous amount of inventiveness in putting older structures to new uses. The interaction of Mead's "I" and "me" can be viewed as pre-programmed impulses of the older brains, standing in a feedback relationship to the learned data bank of the neocortex. This interaction perfected an information-processing system that, developing over millions of years, allowed for an entirely new approach to structuring behavior and managing the problem of survival. This new mode is what I call culture.

The natural condition of human beings is to experience conflict, for every form of behavior requires a decision. The effort required to act is attributed to motivation, and motivation is a learned mental condition that has regulated the interaction of the "I" and the "me" and made this interaction a somewhat permanent feature. To this extent, many mental conflicts are regulated through cultural conventions or traditions, and as such, are no longer recognized as conflicts. Yet the individual who is required to act in unfamiliar situations with little or no social guidance, without learned rules and conventions, will quickly become aware of the inner turmoil that precedes a decision to act in one way or another. Although this turmoil is a source of anxiety and mental illness, it is also the motor by which the human mind sharpens its consciousness, develops a sense of self, and structures its thinking processes. The explosion of cultural information that began about 30 000 years ago has sharpened the conflicts and complicated the processes by which human beings must decide how to act.

CULTURE IN THE MAKING

In the early stages of culture, material necessities naturally took precedence, thereby channelling culture-creating activities in the direction of survival. But the tools through which human beings survived were no copies of nature, but artifacts freely constructed with the use of the imagination. There is no model in nature for the bow and arrow or the wheel, and both inventions are highly abstract conceptions. Although humanity's very existence depended on nature, the cultural means by which a livelihood was extracted was accomplished through creative genius.

We can distinguish three stages in which humankind attempted to define and establish consistent relationships with the natural world. In the first, human beings oriented themselves

Native societies in British Columbia have traditionally used totem carvings to help define the human situation and its complex relationships.

toward nature and interpreted themselves in the images of nature while attributing to nature some of their own emotions. The result was spiritualism, mythology, and totemism. In the second phase, human beings sought power over nature by means of magic. The third phase sees human beings as rational beings who, having unravelled the laws of nature, use science to change nature in their own image.

Thus, culture-creating activities seem to have gone full circle: from interpreting humankind in the image of nature, humankind now remakes nature in the image of itself. How did this happen?

Meaning and Causality

The development of insight and foresight, which, as we have pointed out, allowed tool-making, led to a cultural life that secured survival. Organized work, planning, and sharing of resources were the principle means by which hunting, gathering, and scavenging in small groups were conducted. Yet it took 500 000 to 1 million years for our ancestors to graduate from the making of stone flakes to the manufacturing of purposefully shaped stone axes. Another one-and-a-half million years went by before the cave paintings in Southern France, Spain, and North Africa were created, which testify that cultural development had proceeded far beyond physical survival.

Thus, cultural achievements accelerated when insight and foresight were directed inward and to aspects of the natural environment that proved to be problematic or intriguing. Birth and death, mother and child, day and night, sleeping and waking, dreaming and reality, being and non-being, growth and decay, failure and success no longer remained isolated observations, but demanded explanation. Natural events presented themselves not only as regular occurrences but were also full of surprising irregularities. Changes in weather patterns and the seasons and the change in animal populations constituted perplexing problems that could not be resolved unless means of interpreting these events were found. The ability of using insight and foresight predisposed human beings to the notion of causality. Insight provided the cause, foresight the anticipated effect, and observation the actual outcome.

Culture, then, is in some sense a struggle to formulate causal interpretations of observable natural phenomena, including the relationship between humankind and nature. And this is precisely what the culture of archaic civilization attempted to do.

Spiritualism, Mythology, and Totemism

Meaning and causality could not have developed without language. Language, the ability to assign symbols to things and processes and to manipulate them in the mind was a skill that must have developed step by step with the emergence of culture. The first cultural task undoubtedly was humankind's ability to recognize human nature as distinct from other natural phenomena. Such an achievement was only possible when it proceeded from a reference point that was not human. This reference point was readily available in form of the natural environment in which human beings lived. To see ourselves as distinct from this environment yet part of it and to recognize our dependence on it was the first mental task. It was accomplished by throwing a mantle of meaning and causality over this relationship with nature. To this end, spiritualism, mythology, and totemism served as the earliest frameworks.

Spiritualism injected meaning and causality into objects and events by reading human emotions and intentions into them. In totemism, the characteristics of animals were used to identify and define human groups. Bonds between relatives were mediated through the totem and thereby achieved objectivity and justification through symbolic unity and shared ritual. Myths were mental frameworks of morality and value that were logically composed and internally consistent (Levi-Strauss, 1967:227).

Culture and Technique

The emergence of magic characterizes the second phase of human cultural evolution. Magic "developed along with other techniques as an expression of man's will to obtain certain results of a spiritual order. To attain them, man made use of an aggregate of rites, formulas, and procedure which, once established, did not vary." (Ellul, 1964:24.) Magic was the mediator between human beings and the "higher powers," which were assumed to exist and which directed events in a causal way. Magic made these powers subject to human manipulation and thereby secured a predetermined or desirable result. To think in magical terms showed a "scholasticism of efficiency," which humankind employed as an instrument against the environment. It was, therefore, funda-

This step pyramid at Saqqara, Egypt, predates those at Giza by at least 200 years. It has been suggested that these pyramids were not built as burial places for the pharaohs, but were intended to provide a common enterprise having deep religious significance.

mentally different from a spiritual identification with nature, which characterized the first phase (Ellul, 1964:24).

Magic laid the grounds for a leadership that was no longer based on blood or sympathetic expressions. It was the performance of ritual that counted, and the performer was believed to possess extraordinary powers and have access to secrets not attainable by ordinary individuals. Such a new selection process for leadership made the establishment of larger groupings possible. The material and spiritual well-being of these groups became dependent on magic, not so much because it produced desirable results, which it did not, but because it supplied explanations of successes

and failures, thereby creating a meaningful world. On a psychological level, magic alleviated stresses and strains, made endurance possible, and created hope.

Monotheism and culture

The third stage in humankind's culture-creating activities coincides with the creation of a monotheistic deity based on the word, the will, and the moral commands that emanated from a God. The notion of a single God who embodied the presumed causes in nature might have originated during the premagical period. But the speaking God, the God of commands who required obeisance, emerged with the founding of states such as Egypt, where a God of this sort has been documented for the third dynasty.

The connection between political leadership, social organization, and religious conceptions is striking here because the king was already perceived as the embodiment of God in the first dynasty. His powers of command as the supreme embodiment of the state were conferred on him by his religious status. Possessing powers sanctioned by God was a most effective device to elicit desired responses from large masses of people. Religious symbols proved to be a successful manipulative device to establish the power of the few over the many. In "The Riddle of the Pyramids" (1974), Mendelssohn shows convincingly that the pyramids, whose construction absorbed the wealth of ancient Egypt for over a century, were never intended to be the burial places of the pharaohs; nor did they have any other utilitarian function. It was the construction of these monuments as a common enterprise having religious significance that was meaningful. This construction required that a large and efficient bureaucracy establish effective control over the Egyptian populations, still divided along tribal lines, and subject them to its will. In other words, it disciplined the masses.

The monotheistic deity of the word and the will, of course, was basic to the Hebrews and later to Christianity. It marked the beginning of centralization, control, and authoritarianism, but it also laid the foundation for the way of thinking that characterizes science and justifies its powers over nature. It is interesting to note that Classical Greece, which was the first to liberate scientific thought from its magical predecessors, nevertheless refused to translate science into technology and thereby dominate nature. The Greeks are said to have known the principle of the steam engine, but refused to use it for technical purposes. "The rejection of technique was a deliberate, positive activity involving self-mastery, recognition of destiny and the application of a given conception of life.... It represented an apex of civilization and intelligence." (Ellul, 1964:29.)

Thus, technological achievements do not necessarily represent the highest forms of cultural development, nor do they represent the inevitable forces by which cultural development must proceed.

THE TECHNOLOGICAL TRANSFORMATION OF WESTERN CULTURE

The turning point in Western culture, according to Max Weber, came with the emergence of ascetic Protestantism during the Reformation. Ascetic Protestantism facilitated a rational systematization of thought that transformed all aspects of Western culture — science, economics, and art (Weber, 1958). It led to a disenchantment of the world and required the severance of all magical and spiritual elements that had crept into Christianity in previous centuries. God was conceptualized in a rational fashion and humankind's relation to Him had to be structured rationally. But Western civilization, which started to investigate the word of its God on a rational basis, unintentionally discovered the laws of nature instead and even made an attempt to put humankind in place of God. During the French Revolution, for example, monuments were erected to the glory of humankind and were subject to worship. Although these excesses did not last, the ideology of liberalism eventually carried the supremacy of humankind over nature into modern life.

Subsequently, Western civilization attempted to explore human nature through science. The scientific method reduces natural phenomena to the smallest indivisible elements, studies the properties of such particles, and reconstructs theories from the knowledge gained. This method was successful regarding aspects of the physical world, but it lacked the explanatory holistic qualities of totemism, mythology, magic, and religion. With the advent of scientific rationalism, humanity had difficulty understanding itself.

This malady of Western civilization was recognized as much as fifty years ago. In 1930, the English philosopher Joad wrote:

In England the men of this generation have lost their religion. It has evaporated, and withdrawing has left a vacuum. Without some cause in which to lose themselves, some creed in which to find themselves, or some loved objects of value for which to sacrifice themselves, men live lives without point and purpose. Recognizing nothing which can raise them out of the selfish, little pit of vanity and desire which is the self, they are led to turn their thoughts inwards to find in themselves at once the sole object of interest and the sole criterion, of value.... The symptoms of the malaise in terms of disillusion, cynicism, undue introspection, hysteria and neurosis, are familiar.
(In *Montague, 1964:78.)*

Fifty years before these lines were written, Nietzsche predicted that man would cry out in agony when he realized that he had left God out of his world. However, God is not quite dead yet. Robbed of His cultural and societal significance, He still lingers in an individualized and personalized form serving purely psychological functions. Called upon, or disposed of, according to the whim of the individual, He competes with social services, government programs, psychiatrists, and psychologists in trying to solve personal problems.

Lacking a religious self-interpretation, Western civilization throughout the nineteenth century busied itself with creating substitute values in the form of ideologies such as nationalism, socialism, liberalism, racism, and others. To these could be added the social sciences. In some of these ideologies, humankind was defined primarily in technological or economic terms: in capitalism, we are largely an economic entity subject to the forces of the market. In socialism, we are subject to the productive forces that are assumed to unfold according to the laws of dialectical materialism. Nationalism and racism impose on us the exclu-

sive emotional bonds of nation or race, and are, therefore, regressive to the rationally oriented mind. Classical liberalism, if definable at all, emphasizes the individual largely in opposition to unnecessary societal restrictions. Many social scientists see humanity as a functional entity in a structural system whose laws of behavior and change they are most eager to detect without being unduly bothered by the nature of humankind that is supposed to create and change that system.

Our analysis of the dynamics of Western culture from spiritualism to scientism shows a progression from the initial involvement of emotions in culture-creating activities to the dominance of the intellect, mainly framed in technological terms. There seems to be a shift from the involvement of the primitive brains to the neocortex. The primitive associations in the human mind, which formerly were involved in cultural, organizational, and mental structures, are now the source of man's irrational behavior, his anxieties, irritations, and pathologies. According to Murray Banks, a well-known psychiatrist, of any twenty-five children born in the United States today, two will be committed to a hospital for the insane during their lifetime; four will show profoundly neurotic symptoms, another four will be deeply neurotic; four will be mildly neurotic and the rest, eleven in all, can be expected to end their lives as normal human beings.

Can it be that the headlong race of Western civilization to create better tools and thereby organize culture predominately around rational tool-making activities has turned culture against us? In the next section, we explore this question further and show that, in fact, a powerfuly lobby, in the form of countercultures, aims to resist the technocratization of Western culture.

CULTURES: VARIATIONS ON AN ORIGINAL THEME

Much of the anthropological literature of the last 100 years focused on the evolution of the organi-

Buddhist monks stroll barefoot in the streets of modern Bangkok. As Buddhism addresses a wider range of human needs and capabilities than does Western technology, it is not surprising that Eastern culture has largely resisted or modified the technological rationalism of the West.

zational structure of cultures and technological development — specifically on whether cultural evolution was multilinear or unilinear. In other words, do all cultures go through the same stages of sociocultural development or are there different routes and sequences that cultures could take?

In our discussion, we emphasized mental processes rather than technological or organizational structures, although it was indicated that certain mental processes, such as monotheism in Egypt, were responsible for the development of a bureaucracy. Although three stages in the development of these processes were discussed, they were not

seen as inevitable hierarchies. Rather, these three stages were perceived as a buildup of possible mental processes that, once established, provided the bases around which cultures organized themselves.

There does not seem to be an evolutionary need for cultures to organize according to their technological development. China, Japan, and India did very well without this type of organizational principle and would have followed their own cultural course if they were not drawn by means of military force into the technological orbit of Western culture. Perhaps the infusion of Western technology into these cultures is a passing phe-

Hutterite children at Star City colony in Saskatchewan. Although much modified from its early form, Hutterite culture is still communally-based.

nomenon. Confucionism and Buddhism address a much wider range of human mental capacities than does Western technology. It is to be expected, therefore, that these cultures not only resist Western influences, but that the technological rationalism imposed on them may be modified and adapted to indigenous cultural patterns. The appeal of Islamic fundamentalism is a surprising development in this regard. In China, the economic rationality of Marxism meets head-on one of the oldest, most sophisticated and humanly balanced religious systems. The social upheavals that shook China over the last thirty years testify to the uneasiness with which the Chinese people react to technological rationalism.

We might conclude that the range from excessive rationalism to excessive emotionalism provides the playground for individual cultures to develop and allows for a limited number of variations on an original theme.

Psychocultural Dynamics and Patterns of Culture

Ruth Benedict's *Patterns of Culture*, written in 1934, considerably influenced the conceptualization of culture. The theoretical orientation of this book was taken from "The Birth of Tragedy," an essay written by Nietzsche around 1871. According to Benedict's interpretation of his theory, there are two basic opposing cultural tendencies — the Appolonian and the Dionysian. These are:

... opposing ways of arriving at the values of existence. The Dionysian pursues them through the annihilation of the ordinary bounds and limits of existence; he seeks to attain in his most valued moments escape from the boundaries imposed upon him by his five senses, to break through into another order of experience. The desire of the Dionysian, in personal experience or in ritual, is to press through it toward a certain psychological state, to achieve excess.

The Appolonian distrusts all this, and has often little idea of the nature of such experiences. He finds means to outlaw them from his conscious life. He knows but one law, measure in the Hellenic sense. He keeps the middle of the road, stays within the known map, does not meddle with disruptive psychological states....

(Benedict, 1961:78.)

Unfortunately, Benedict had no use for a third cultural orientation contained in Nietzsche's essay — the Socratic-rational orientation. It is probable that she did not include it because such a type could not be found among the tribal cultures with which she was concerned. The Socratic-rational orientation followed

... causality into the deepest layers of being; the type who not only attempted to recognize his being through his causal thinking, but believed that he was able to correct it.

(Nietzsche, 1966, Volume 1:84.)

This type of man believed that the nature of all things are fathomable and error was the only sin. To penetrate things by reasoning and to separate true knowledge from appearance and error was the only and true vocation of man and therefore valued above all others.

(Nietzsche, 1966, Volume I:86.)

This interpretation depicts Socrates wandering through the streets of Athens, finding that the high and the mighty pursued their vocations not on the basis of understanding but on instinct. Socrates condemned the existing forms of Greek art and ethics because they contained too much passion and too little intellect. Nietzsche saw in Socrates the anti-mystical counterpole to the mythical roots of Greek art, ethics, and morals. He viewed the Socratic and the Dionysian as opposites and the Appolonian as a balanced type.

An example of an excessively rational culture — the Socratic — is that of the early Hutterites. Based on a rational interpretation of God's will, this culture divided human existence into the opposing forces of the spirit and the flesh. The spirit strove toward unity with God through the strictest suppression of the flesh (which corresponds to the theme of ascetic rationalism as outlined by Max Weber). A short excursion into Hutterite history might throw some light on the problems in following such an orientation of excessive rationalism.

During the sixteenth and seventeenth centuries, when Hutterites still resided in central Europe, their preachers claimed the right to marry individuals according to the choices of the church, thereby denying marriage partners the right to act on emotions such as love and affection. They further enforced the suppression of emotions by prohibiting parent-offspring relations. Soon after birth, children were taken away from their parents and raised in communal nursing homes, where attempts were made to minimize the identification between parents and children.

These practices were derived from an interpretation of what Hutterites thought God had commanded them to do. It would serve no purpose to go into the details of this reasoning, but it is important to note that these customs originated through a rational, if selective, investigation of God's will. The same, of course, was true with respect to the communal ownership of goods, which suppressed such emotions as greed or acquisitiveness. One would have expected that over generations this group would have succeeded in socializing its members to acquire the traits and mental characteristics that fitted them for participation in this type of socio-cultural life. They had, after all, complete control over their socialization process; they were culturally distinct from their host society; they lived in isolation and self-sufficient communities and did relatively well economically; and they had a religious ideology that justified and legitimized such practices and even made them mandatory. Salvation, after all, could only be attained if such practices were strictly adhered to.

In spite of all these factors, Hutterite culture, throughout much of its history, was characterized by a struggle between the above-mentioned repressive practices and the pressure of individuals toward the re-establishment of emotional relations between spouses, parents, and children. In spite of the rules and the sanctions against disobedience, people insisted on marrying on the basis of affection and on identifying with their children. Eventually, the earlier practices had to be abandoned and extended family relations became the norm. Even the prohibition of private property became problematic. Hutterites abandoned the community of goods twice. These practices never became acceptable to the individual, despite their endorsement by Hutterite leadership. Hence, Hutterite culture today is much modified.

Recent movements in Western countries may be seen as expressions of protest against a rational-technological orientation. The counterculture movements of the 1960s were Dionysian in nature. Some aimed to achieve inner ecstacy with the use of drugs and music. As with the classical Greeks, music was the principle means of communication because it addressed the emotions directly. The current movement, concerned with the environment and pollution, may be said to be essentially Appolonian in nature in its attempt to moderate an exploitative rationality by drawing on aesthetic and moral arguments.

There can be little doubt that these modern social movements are responses to an excessive technological rationalization of the Western world. They are by no means isolated occurrences in history. Nietzsche perceived the flowering of German music during the nineteenth century as a reaction to the rationality of capitalism and the nation-state. The emergence of rock n' roll in the 1950s, with its emphasis on rhythm, voices, sexually suggestive movements, and high-decible sound tracks may be viewed as a reaction to increased rationalization (or bureaucratization) of everyday life.

SUMMARY

1. The study of culture is predominately the domain of anthropologists, whose concern is to investigate culture traits and social relations.
2. This essay uses a psychodynamic approach to the study of culture and follows Kroeber and Kluckhohn's conceptualization, which regards culture as a general category of nature — and human nature, in particular.
3. In going back to the beginning of culture, it is clear that the struggle to formulate causal interpretations of observable natural phenomena, including the relationship between humankind and nature, formed the basis of culture.
4. The range of possible cultural patterns seems to coincide with the range of what we have called human nature.
5. Throughout this chapter we have presented human nature as an ongoing process, drawing its energy and its impetus from the conflicting components of the human personality, as reflected in the structure and functioning of the human brain.
6. Human nature is a dynamic force in cultural development that follows a rational or emotional direction and generates countervailing forces when either of these principle themes becomes excessive or is creatively exhausted. Human nature not only limits sociocultural practices, but dynamically creates and changes them.

7. This creative force present in all mankind is a natural phenomenon. It is as natural as the forces of biological evolution and it has created a variety of human cultures as rich and colorful in design as anything found in the amazing variety of the plant and animal kingdom.

GLOSSARY

Appolonian. A cultural pattern wherein individuals stay within the boundaries drawn by their senses and where these individuals value moderation.

Counterculture. A movement that reacts against selected cultural trends by denying them, downgrading them, or opposing them with new or opposite trends.

Cultural configuration. Culture traits and social relationships peculiar to a given culture. It constitutes one of the major objectives in the study of culture.

Culture. A general category encompassing everything created by humankind.

Culture traits. Customary ways of acting and thinking that are peculiar to a given culture. As such, they comprise norms, mores, and folkways.

Dionysian. A cultural pattern wherein individuals attempt to break through the confinement of their senses and achieve a mental state characterized by excess.

Folkways. Customs of a local nature. They usually apply to a subgroup within a given culture, such as an ethnic group.

Mores. Norms with strong moral connotations.

Myths. Freely invented mental frameworks of morality and value, logically composed and internally consistent.

Norm. Behavior that is appropriate for a given situation. This behavior is enforced by a common understanding leading to interpersonal expectations.

Psychocultural dynamics. Process whereby shared mental states within a given population are translated into cultural patterns.

Scientism. A cultural pattern predominantly organized around rational-technological mental states.

Spiritualism. Injects meaning and causality into objects and events by reading human emotions and intentions into them.

Totemism. Utilizes the characteristics of animals to identify and define human groups whose bonds are objictified through the symbolic unity and shared ritual associated with the totem.

Values. Shared conceptions of what is right, wrong, good, desirable, evil, or objectionable.

FURTHER READING

Cohen, Yehudi A. *A Man in Adaptation: The Biosocial Background.* Chicago: Aldine Publishing, 1968.

Gehlen, Arnold. *Man in the Age of Technology.* New York: Columbia University Press, 1980.

Greenwood, Davydd J. and William A. Stini. *Nature, Culture and Human History.* New York: Harper & Row, 1977.

Gregory, Michael S., Anita Silvers and Diane Sutch. *Sociobiology and Human Nature.* San Francisco: Jossey-Bass Publishers, 1978.

Landmann, Michael. *Philosophical Anthropology.* Philadelphia: The Wesminster Press, 1974.

Leakey, Richard E. *The Making of Mankind.* New York: E. P. Dutton, 1981.

Montagu, Ashley. *Sociobiology Examined.* New York: Oxford University Press, 1980.

Morris, Richard. *Evolution and Human Nature.* New York: Seaview/Putnam, 1983.

Restak, Richard. *The Brain.* Toronto: Bantam Books, 1984.

Wilson, Edward. *On Human Nature.* London: Harvard University Press, 1978.

CHAPTER FIVE

Society

KATHLEEN HERMAN

In his powerful story *Lord of the Flies*, William Golding has provided us with an eloquent affirmation that human life outside society is not only impossible, it is unthinkable. That *human* beings are *social* beings is undeniable. Cast into an isolated and totally unfamiliar environment, the young people in Golding's story quickly realized that if they were to survive at all they had to organize themselves in such a way as to ensure a modicum of co-operation and order. It is true that these young people had had previous experience of living in society. They had already learned about roles and rules, about authority and compliance, about the division of labor and mutual dependence. Yet what is interesting is that the society they created for themselves was in many ways clearly distinct from the one they had left behind. The fundamental problem they had to resolve was the problem of order. Without order, the most pressing needs for their survival would have been quickly jeopardized. This is why many social theorists believe that to explain social order is to explain society.

But what is society? Is it any aggregate of individuals? Is it restricted to the human species, or do societies exist among other species as well? Is society a fulfillment of human nature, or is society more accurately perceived as a fetter, a constraint upon our human nature, as many theorists claim? And finally, is there a fundamental contradiction between the individual and society?

These are some of the questions addressed in this chapter. It will become apparent that the answers depend upon which theory of society is being espoused. This chapter will review several theories of society in order to show the extent to which each of them rests upon different assumptions about the nature of human nature and of society. These assumptions are the analytical foundations upon which each theory is built. They are more a matter of belief than of proof, for they are not testable, although the theories derived from them may be.

SOCIETY: THE TOTALITY OF SOCIAL RELATIONSHIPS

At one level of analysis, a society may be thought of simply as a large number of people inhabiting a common territory, engaging in some degree of regularized interaction based upon shared understandings for the furtherance of their common purposes, with some provision for their perpetuation through time. This descriptive definition accords with our common-sense notion of what we mean when we talk of "a society." Let us look at it more closely to determine how useful it is as a building block for theory.

Common territory implies at least some degree of sovereignty; in the modern world, the vehicle for the maintenance of sovereignty is the nation-state. This statement poses two problems for theory building. First, it presupposes something that needs to be explained — that is, what is the relation between state and society? Second, it assumes that all the people living within the boundaries of one nation-state necessarily constitute one society. Yet, Canada contradicts this assumption. The Royal Commission on Bilingualism and Biculturalism (1967) took the position that there were two societies within one nation, one English-speaking and the other French-speaking, each with its own distinctive culture, institutions, and aspirations. The Berger Commission's Mackenzie Valley Pipeline Inquiry (1977) speaks of the Dene (an Indian

The Inuit and Dene Indians are separate and distinct societies within Canada.

tribe in the NWT) and Inuit as "distinct peoples in history" with distinct cultures, languages, and societies that are not confined within one set of arbitrary national borders. The Task Force on Canadian Unity (1979:7) suggests that a Canadian society has yet to be created. "It seems to us that the main problem does not lie in observing or re-establishing unity," the commissioners said, "but rather in constituting it in the first place." It would seem, then, that the notion of common territory is ambiguous and problematical; its inclusion in the definition could impose premature closure on analysis.

Shared understandings, the second element in the definition, refers to the group's culture. At a very abstract general level, these shared understandings consist of a set of rights and obligations, which are embodied in the society's political constitution and legal codes. At a more concrete level, they require, at the very least, a common language. Without a common language, regularized interaction would be impossible. It is through culture, which includes the knowledge, values, and belief systems of the society's members, that social relations are reproduced through time. These regularized interactions are the society's institutions. They are the patterned ways of doing things that make possible the realization of the society's common purposes and its continuation beyond the life of its individual members. The family, the polity, the economy, religion, and education are the main institutions of society (and each will be discussed in the chapters that follow). These institutions constitute the societal structure. What is important to note here is that there is a dynamic relation between culture, social structure, and human beings, and that language is central to this relationship.

The definition cited above requires that we think of a society as a relatively autonomous, independent entity. This implies a degree of self-sufficiency that is impossible in the modern world. It no longer makes sense to talk about individual societies as though they exist in absolute isolation. They do not and cannot. All we can say is that society is the largest, most inclusive group within which social interaction for the majority of its members is controlled and contained; it is this overarching inclusiveness that enables us to distinguish a society conceptually from the less inclusive groupings that are located within it.

Furthermore, it is essential that a society be able to provide for its own continuity through succeeding generations, either by controlled reproduction or by replacement of its members from outside, or both.

The descriptive definition given at the beginning of this section, or some variant of it, is widely used in sociology even though it presents analytical difficulties. This is why some sociologists prefer a definition that is more abstract, as well as more sociological. For them, the fundamental unit of sociological analysis is not the person but the *relationship* between two or more actors, or more precisely, their *interaction*. Society, then, becomes the sum total of these relationships. Moreover, it is essential that our definition draw attention to the dynamic unity that exists, a unity of the abstract and the concrete; the general and the particular. This leads to the following definition: *Society is the total nexus of social relations and the reproduction of these relations among those human beings who comprise a clearly identifiable population with historical continuity beyond the life of its individual members.*

SOCIETY AND CULTURE

Having arrived at this definition, we can now answer two of the questions that were posed at the beginning of this chapter. Society is not just any aggregate of individuals. It is also clear that human society is qualitatively and conceptually distinct from the societies of ants, bees, or other species that display patterned regularities in their activities and that appear to have remarkable forms of social organization. Their organization, however, is founded upon instinct, which is an inherent drive that is implanted upon the organism at birth. Instinct is transmitted by heredity; it is not learned behavior, though it may be modified by learning. Instincts are automatic responses to internal or external stimuli. Moreover, they are "common to all the individual members of the species" and they emerge with a definite order and regularity in the life of the individual in close relation to the process of growth and maturation." (Fletcher in Gould and Kolb, 1964:336-37.) Thus, insects, birds, or animals engage in the same behavior wherever their particular species is found. The same cannot be said of human beings. Although we too have instinctual drives that account for much of our behavior, the way human behavior is socially organized varies considerably within the species. Let us take the sex drive as an example.

Nothing seems more natural or more "instinctive" than that people should mate in a particular way with a member of the opposite sex. Yet it is only our insistence on this myth of naturalness that hides the fact that human sexual behavior is a learned process (Gagnon and Simon, 1973). Kingsley Davis, an American sociologist who has written perceptively on the subject, tells us, "Without socialization, human beings would not even know how to copulate." He continues, "If sex is purely natural and its regulation harmful, how does it happen that human societies always and everywhere have rules governing sexual conduct?" (Davis, 1971:314-15.) What is interesting is not simply that the sex drive is socially regulated, but also that there are great variations in institutionalized sex practices. Anthropologists have documented these for many preliterate societies.

The Dani of New Guinea, for example, have "extraordinarily little interest in sex." After the birth of a child, the parents do not have intercourse with each other for five years. Furthermore, "they have few other outlets for sexuality during that time," even though nearly half the men have other wives with whom they could "have sex" if they chose to. Yet they do not (Heider, 1979: 78-79). Among the Trobrian Islanders studied by Malinowski (1929), young children were instructed in sexual matters so that girls could begin having intercourse by the age of six and the boys by the age of ten. The Lepcha of the Himalayas believe that unless girls have intercourse when they are very young they will not mature (Ford and Beach, 1951). Among the Keraki of New Guinea, the Aranda of Australia, and the Siwans of northern Africa, every male is required to engage exclusively in homosexuality before marriage, but after marriage is expected to be bisexual (Ford and Beach, 1951). In Tibet, a man can marry a mother and her daughter, and several brothers can share one wife (Fox, 1967:58).

These are only a few examples selected from

Sociality is not unique to humans. Wasps, bees, and ants all display striking patterns in their behavior and social organization.

the literature to illustrate the enormous variability in the prescriptions and proscriptions that surround sexual activity. We can safely conjecture that just as we may consider the sexual practices of these and other preliterate societies as quaint, amusing, and even distinctly odd, members of those societies no doubt would find ours just as strange if they had had anthropologists who had come to study us and interpret our sexual practices through their cultural screen.

We can conclude, therefore, that it is culture that distinguishes human societies. Culture performs for human societies the same functions that instinct performs for the societies of other species. Culture ensures the reproduction of the social relations through successive historical moments. Culture enables the society to survive and ensure its unity and continuity throughout various historical transformations. It is through culture that human beings perceive reality, and it is culture that enables us to be human. Some argue that we are not "human" at birth; we become human through the process of socialization. Since society provides the social organization through which that socialization occurs, and by means of which culture is learned and transmitted to succeeding generations, it follows that human life is unthinkable outside society.

THE INDIVIDUAL AND SOCIETY

This brings us to the last of the questions asked at the beginning of this chapter. Even though we may need society to become fully human, is there not a fundamental contradiction between the individual and society? Or, as one popular sociologist (Berger, 1963:90, 92) has phrased it, is society "more like a gigantic Alcatraz than anything else ... the walls of our imprisonment in history"? There is no easy answer to this question. There have been interminable debates about whether the individual was made for society or society made for the individual. Yet the individual *versus* society is a false antithesis. Both individual and society are notions that are complementary and indispensable to each other — they are two sides of the same coin.

At issue are opposing assumptions about human nature and society that have divided social thinkers through the ages and that continue to plague contemporary sociologists. At one extreme is the *determinist* view reflected in Berger's question, which regards human activity as being completely determined by external factors, be they biological, physical, social, or cultural. In this view, human beings are like programmed robots, devoid of free will and the capability of acting voluntarily; society is seen as an objective, external reality that exerts pressure and coercion upon the individual. Structural-functional theories of society,

discussed later in this chapter, tend to be determinist in their ontological assumptions.

At the other extreme is the *voluntaristic* or *humanist* view, which accepts human beings as rational, autonomous individuals, continuously engaged in the process of constructing and sustaining their social reality. Society is internalized within the social self, over which the individual is capable of exercising at least some degree of conscious control. In modern sociology, the theoretical schools of symbolic interactionism and phenomenology rest upon this ontological premise.

It is important to note that these are extreme positions. All theories of society fall somewhere in between or, indeed, endeavor to transcend the polarity by introducing the notion of the *dialectic*. The dialectic is a complex notion that cannot be explained in a few sentences. Suffice it to say that a dialectical view is fundamentally committed to the concept of *process*: the social world is in a continual state of becoming. To depict social arrangements as static or changeless, even when this is done as a methodological device to facilitate analysis, is to violate the essence of their being. The focus of dialectical analysis is on change, the process of transformation through which one set of social arrangements gives way to another. Furthermore, the emphasis is on totality: no part can be conceived of as separate or distinct from the whole. Everything must be studied with reference to the multiple interconnections that make up the whole of social life.

Contradiction is the principle that informs the transformation. All structural relations are contradictory in the sense that the existence of the parts is both necessary for, and yet ultimately destructive of, the relation. The contradiction can be resolved only by dissolution of the old set of relations and by replacement with a new set. This new set will also contain elements of both combination and opposition, leading to new contradictions and new transformations. It is important to know that the notion of contradiction is not synonymous with the idea of conflict; not all contra-

Many sociologists believe that the distinction between a community and a society lies in the relationships among individuals.

dictory relations stem from conflict, nor is all conflict necessarily the result of contradiction. They are two separate and distinct concepts.

Another essential principle that informs all dialectical analysis is that of *praxis*. What this means is that people themselves are the active agents in making their own history, in constructing their own social relations. This notion is contrary to evolutionary theories that seem to suggest that social arrangements change through their own inner motors, independent of the human actors who comprise them. Thus, dialectical theory is a humanist approach to understanding societies and their transformations.

Karl Marx, as you learned in previous chapters, was the first social scientist to develop a dia-

lectical theory of society. Currently, there are numerous and competing neo-Marxist theories that differ greatly in the extent to which they lean toward determinism or voluntarism; however, they all agree that the relationship between the individual and society is a dialectical one.

THE COMMUNITY AND SOCIETY

Before we turn to a discussion of particular theories of society, it is necessary to point out that a strong strand of evolutionist thought has been present in sociology from the beginning. This has led to the classification of societies based on evolutionary development from the simple to the complex, from "primitive" to "modern." Value judgements abound in such a classification, which must be approached with a good measure of caution and a healthy skepticism of its claims. As already stated in previous chapters, sociology as a distinct discipline emerged in the late nineteenth century in those countries where the industrial revolution had proceeded apace. The early sociologists did not hide their concern for what they saw as the ravages to the social fabric effected by such vast economic change. There is an element of romantic nostalgia in some of these formulations, and yet paradoxically, it is mixed with the assumption that modern society is more advanced, higher on the evolutionary scale than earlier forms.

The distinction between community and society proposed by German sociologist Ferdinand Tönnies (1855–1936) influenced evolutionary theorists. Tönnies distinguished two basic forms of human will: natural and rational will. Natural will, as its name suggests, is inherent in us by virtue of our being human. It is not consciously contrived. Community (*gemeinschaft*) is the social group in which relationships guided by natural will are dominant, whereas society (*gesellschaft*) is the social group in which relationships are based on rational (or calculative) will. According to Tönnies, both co-exist: gemeinschaft is found in the family and rural life, and gesellschaft in the city, where "money and capital are unlimited and almighty." (1957:226.) Gesellschaft is based on contract, and the state (through its legal system) replaces tradition and custom to secure the common interest. Eventually the power of the state becomes so oppressive that the masses rise up to engage in class struggle. When this happens, the "natural" feeling of community is likely to be destroyed.

Tönnies's theory is not strictly an evolutionary theory, since in his typology collectivities oscillate between a predominance of community relationships and society relationships.

Later evolutionary theorists have been much influenced by Tönnies. Among more recent writers, Robert Redfield distinguished folk from urban society; Charles Cooley, primary from secondary groups; and Howard Becker, sacred from secular society.

STRUCTURAL-FUNCTIONALISM AND THE SYSTEMS APPROACH TO SOCIETY

Emile Durkheim

Most classical and medieval philosophers believed that since human beings are by nature social beings, society is necessary for the complete development of the human personality. This largely idealist and determinist view has been incorporated into modern social science through the work of Durkheim. As has already been noted in Chapter 2, Durkheim argued that social facts are things: they are "ways of acting, thinking, and feeling, external to the individual, and endowed with a power of coercion, by reason of which they control him." (1938:3.) Thus, society for Durkheim was an independent organic and moral reality with its own laws, its own development, its own life. Individuals are constrained by external social forces (facts) that impose a normative conformity upon them. These external social forces are embodied in Durkheim's concept of the *collective conscience* (or consciousness), which consists of all those ideas that individual members of a society hold in common to accomplish shared

In our society, we have accepted responsibility for the care and support of our children, but not always of our elderly parents.

goals. For example, the common belief in our society that parents are responsible for the care and support of their children would be part of the collective conscience. The belief that adult children are responsible for the care and support of their elderly parents is, however, not yet a part of our collective conscience.

The collective conscience is made manifest through the social institutions that comprise the social structure. These institutions can be explained in terms of their contribution to the maintenance of the society as a whole. Put another way, society is a functionally interrelated system.

Durkheim analysed social phenomena, such as religion, the division of labor, crime, and suicide, in terms of the extent and the way they contribute to social solidarity. Durkheim's analysis of crime is particularly ingenious. He argued that crime is not so much an offence against any particular individual as it is an offence against the collective consciousness. Punishment, then, is the group's way of reaffirming its collectively held beliefs about the 'right' way of doing things. The chapter on social control and deviance expands this argument.

Two Types of Solidarity: Mechanical and Organic

Durkheim classified societies in terms of the way they are held together. Simple societies have a form of social solidarity, which he described as *mechanical*, whereas complex societies are held together by *organic solidarity*.

In simple societies, Durkheim postulated, the population is small and the density not very great. More important, the people who make up this small society are all more or less alike (and thus comprise a homogeneous society): there is little division of labor, except along sex lines, and each member of the society (young as well as old) engages in the same productive activity. In such simple societies, there is no sharp institutional separation: family, political, legal, moral, and religious beliefs and practices are all interrelated. The behavior of people in these societies is regulated by the collective conscience and by repressive law that discourages them from deviating from the norm. Because there is little division of labor, no institutional separation, and little individuality, there is also little conflict between the individual and the group. If conflict does occur, and it is deemed sufficiently serious to threaten the group's solidarity, harsh sanctions will be imposed (usually excommunication). Durkheim's thesis is that the cohesiveness of such simple societies is based upon the similarity and thus interchange-ability of the parts. Hence, his characterization of this solidarity as "mechanical."

In contrast, organic solidarity is the cement that holds modern societies together. The functions of society are carried out by separate institutions and so the collective conscience is likely to be weaker. Different people work at different things, have different beliefs, and different life experiences. The collective conscience, although it may exist, is less specific, less pervasive, and there is less congruence between it and the individual consciousness. Since individuals cannot be trusted to put the welfare of the collectivity above their own selfish interests, social control must be formally regulated: contractual law imposed by the state is the decisive factor in maintaining a harmony of interests. The function of the state in the "social organism" is analogous to the function of the brain in the biological organism. In such a society, the parts (that is, social institutions such as the family, the polity, or religion) are structurally separate and distinct, but at the same time they are functionally interrelated and essential for the maintenance of the whole. Organic solidarity still requires some measure of mechanical solidarity; at some level, individual differences must give way to co-operation toward the attainment of societal goals.

Anomie

Durkheim's twofold classification of society contains within it a theory of change that is premised upon population increase, both in terms of sheer numbers as well as density; that is, as the population of a society increases, the collective consciousness becomes weaker and the need for organic solidarity becomes greater. By the same token, the condition of *anomie* appears: when the old rules and ways of doing things are not longer appropriate, people do not know where to turn for moral guidance. The certainty that came from the collective conscience in a society held together by mechanical solidarity is absent. People are confused and "normless"; the society is characterized by a condition Durkheim labelled anomie (literally, "without norms"); in the extreme case, individuals without clear moral guidance and who are detached from any group may commit suicide.

Anomic suicide, Durkheim went on to argue, is but the ultimate expression of the individual autonomy that characterizes modern societies. In the absence of constraints provided by a strong collective conscience, the need arises for some other form of control to give individuals the social anchor that Durkheim believed they needed. An occupational group, such as the professions in our society, would fulfil this function, and the state would provide protection for the individual against excessive control by the occupational group. In turn, the group would buffer the control of the state.

Critique of Durkheim's Theory of Society

Durkheim provided us with many valuable insights into the role of social consensus in shaping social action. However, his commitment to the claim that social facts can be approached in the same objective way as the 'facts' of natural science, leads him to deny the place of human agency in creating and recreating society; rather, he believed that everything that happens is the outcome of a chain of causation. Hence, the charge of *social determinism*.

His theory can be criticized on ideological grounds as well, because it gives social norms a measure of autonomy and moral legitimacy. It serves to mystify rather than to explain. His theory also can be used to justify the ever-expanding role of the state in the lives of individuals in modern society.

Furthermore, the argument that the occupations are the best group in modern society to replace religion as the source of moral authority ignores the place of power and conflict in maintaining social order. It also neglects any consideration of the extent to which those who are in positions of power are able to influence the content of consensus that binds society. Struggles by individuals or groups to overthrow what they perceive to be conditions of oppression were seen by Durkheim as "pathological"; the "healthy" society is one in which order, harmony, and consensus are paramount. It is easy to see that Durkheim's functionalist theory provides ideological justification for the moral rightness of structures of inequality (stratification) and social control.

Talcott Parsons

In the first part of the twentieth century, North American sociologists, particularly those associated with the Chicago School, were preoccupied with empirical studies of social problems and social disorganization within the national and local context but without a comparative and historical framework. This trend changed in the 1950s with the work of Talcott Parsons. The task he set for himself at the outset was to develop a "general theory of action" that would bring together the insights of all previous social theory into one grand system, comparable to Newtonian theory in physics. That this was an impossible task, given the fundamentally opposing foundations of the earlier social theories, did not phase him. What is remarkable is the extent to which he succeeded. Today, even though his work has been roundly criticized and has fallen into disrepute, its influence on contemporary sociology cannot be ignored.

Following Durkheim, Parsons accepted, but went beyond, the organic analogy that society was a system of interdependent parts that functioned to maintain equilibrium. As you learned in Chapter 2, he identified four "functional imperatives" necessary for the survival of any social system: adaptation (the economic function), goal attainment (the political function), integration (social-control function), and latency (the ideological function). Parson identified four general and analytically separate subsystems of human action: the organism, personality, cultural system, and the social system. It is his insistence on this analytical separation that has led to so much criticism.

Parsons used an explicitly evolutionary model to classify three types of societies: primitive, intermediate, and modern (1966:26). As with biological evolution, the key to successful sociocultural evolution is "a generalized adaptive capacity" for "upgrading." This happens either through the internal process of differentiation or through cultural diffusion. The new social form that results is more efficient than its predecessor. Such structural changes, if they are to be sustained, require corresponding changes in the value system — the culture.

Primitive Societies

Parsons characterized "primitive" societies as those that are least differentiated. The societies of aboriginal Australia, he tells us, probably are the best examples. Kinship is the dominant organizational system, reinforced by "the overwhelming importance in all spheres of action of religious (and magical) orientations." (1966:33.) Language reinforces the collective identity and gives meaning to the society's existence. Such societies have a rigid status sysem and a normative code that prescribes stereotyped and undifferentiated behavior to ensure social solidarity. Yet even in such seemingly rigid societies, there is the potential for change.

The most likely means for change is through marriage. An element of bargaining in marriage alliances enables some lineages to gain superior control over resources. When this happens, the society reaches the "advanced primitive" level of social evolution, characterized by a system of stratification based on ownership of property. Kinship is replaced by property as the crucial organizing principle of the society. In more advanced primitive societies, such as those in the African kingdoms, a royal lineage emerges, based on wealth. In the following evolutionary stage, this upper class develops a superior culture, including a written language, which becomes the bridge between primitive and intermediate societies.

Intermediate Societies

With writing, history becomes possible, and the way is made open for imaginative innovation. This means that custom gives way to a more generalized symbolic system, principally through religion. When this happens a priesthood emerges as a specialized occupational group with some autonomy. Distinct from this development but concurrent with it is the emergence of a complex administrative system, which would not be possible without writing.

Parsons distinguishes two principal substages in this evolutionary development: the archaic and the advanced intermediate.

In the archaic society, the stratification system begun in the earlier evolutionary phase intensifies and expands into a three-tier pattern with the monarch and his court at the top; the middle group (the bureaucrats), who are responsible for the routine functioning of the society; and at the bottom, the mass of common people, including craftsmen and merchants as well as the peasants. The urban community replaces the kinship group as the most important organizational unit. Religion remains important, but reinforces the political administration in its function of social control. Parsons cites ancient Egypt and Mesopotamia as examples of archaic society.

In the advanced intermediate society (such as China, India, the Islamic empires, and Rome), writing serves more than an administrative and practical function; it is used for the accumulation of an elaborate literary and philosophical tradition. With it emerges a dichotomy between the supernatural and the natural, and this conceptual breakthrough makes possible a division of society into a superior cultural class and the common people. In India, such a process became rigidly institutionalized into a caste system.

The advanced intermediate society also undergoes considerable technological innovation and a fair degree of institutional separation. The key to continuing social evolution is the extent to which the sacred and secular orders become differentiated. This segregation in turn depends on the development of a legal code that enables specialized and relatively autonomous economic structures to emerge.

For Parsons, societal evolution is not inevitable. Failure to evolve is essentially the failure of the cultural system to adapt to change. However, he identifies two "seed-bed" societies, Israel and Greece, that produced cultural innovations of great evolutionary significance. Israel's contribution was its conception of a moral order governing human affairs controlled by a transcendental God (1966:102). Greece's contribution was its elaborate system of political thought and its ideas of justice. These contributions provided the fundamental seeds for the emergence of modern societies.

Modern Societies

According to Parsons, "The modern type of society has emerged in a single evolutionary arena, the West ... the society of Western Christendom, then, provided the base for which ... the system of modern society 'took off'." (1971:1.) Three key revolutions — the industrial, democratic, and educational — provided the "threshold points" of evolution to modern societies (1971:71–121). The industrial revolution brought about a basic change in economic organization with the development of the factory system. The democratic revolutions in France and America resulted in the separation of state and society. By the educational revolution, Parsons means the change from reliance on simple traditional techniques toward the use of scientific knowledge and technology, and an emphasis on rationality as a mode of problem-solving. This produced profound changes in the occupational system. In particular, there was a great increase in the number and kinds of occupations defined as professions. These three revolutions involved major processes of structural and

Along with the United States and Japan, the Soviet Union is acknowledged to be the most developed of modern societies. Here, the Exhibition of National Economic Achievement/Space Exhibit, Moscow.

functional differentiation. It is this high degree of differentiation, Parsons claims, that is the distinguishing feature of modern society.

The United States, the Soviet Union, and Japan are cited by Parsons as being the most developed of modern societies. The first two are the inheritors of the "take-off" in the West, whereas modernization in Japan was clearly a "reaction to the impact of the European-American system." (1966: 3.) Modern societies are more advanced and far "superior" to earlier evolutionary forms because they display a greater generalized adaptive capacity. (In Chapter 24, as you will see, Lele argues against this superiority of modern society.) In acknowledging that this is a value judgement for which he makes no apology, Parsons seems to be implying that with these three advanced modern societies, social evolution has reached its pinnacle; somehow it has come to an end.

Critique of Parsons's Theory of Society

Evolutionary theories in general have been subjected to the charge that they provide ideological justification for a certain kind of social arrangement, and Parsons's theory is no exception. His theory could be used to legitimize world domination by the few "advanced modern" societies by virtue of their hypothesized superiority. There is a large measure of ethnocentrism in the theory. Despite his supposed comparative method and his insistence on culture as the driving force in evolution, Parsons's use of history has been filtered through a Western consciousness. Moreover, Parsons's theory does not account for power and the exploitation of some societies by others in the form of imperialism and colonialism. In addition, because Parsons attributed social evolution to changes in the society's value system, his theory is considered to be culturally deterministic.

Other criticisms of Parsons's brand of functionalism include the charge that there is no room in his theory for human agency, individualism, and conflict, and that his theory is too general: it does not deal with the variability among, and the particular uniqueness of, individual societies.

Gerhard Lenski

Gerhard Lenski's classification of societies has come to be widely accepted in North American sociology. Lenski builds on Parsons's claim that societal stratification is the most likely evolutionary development. In focusing on what he calls "the structure of distributive systems" (1966:73), he classifies societies according to their means of subsistence: hunting and gathering, horticultural, agrarian, and industrial.

Hunting and gathering societies are the "most primitive of all human societies." Using the simplest of tools, they rely on foraging plants and hunting wild animals and so remain close to the subsistence level. Canada's Naskapi Indians in Labrador fall into this category. There is no or little economic surplus. Necessarily small in size, such societies are usually nomadic, their movement dictated by their search for food. Community and society are normally one. There is little occupational or institutional differentiation and little, if any, economic inequality. There is considerable cultural and individual inertia, and historical accident is the most plausible explanation for such a society's evolution to a new form.

Horticultural societies are simple or advanced. The precontact societies of North and South America, such as the Iroquois, are examples of the former. Cultivation of plants through the discovery of tools — the digging stick and the hoe (but not the plough) enables these societies to become sedentary and to form villages. The accumulation of surplus food gives them time to expend on various kinds of non-essential goods, such as houses, and to engage in leisure activities in the form of ceremonies or warfare. Economic specialization and organizations that are distinct from family and kin group develop. Some of these acquire great political significance. Although there is relative equality in material terms, a prestige system develops and leaders (chiefs) come to have considerable authority and status.

In advanced horticultural societies (such as the Aztec of Mexico), more efficient technology (including irrigation), increases the group's wealth, establishes a class stratification system and leads to a strong political organization in the form of the state, which may engage in empire-building. Slavery may be introduced, further enhancing the power of the ruling class. The ruling class, which comprises the king and his ministers, together with the priestly class, lay claim to a disproportionate share of the surplus wealth. Through inheritance, the tripartite system of economic inequality, social privilege, and political power becomes perpetuated.

Today's industrial societies differ from their predecessors in their enormous consumption of energy and greater productivity.

Agrarian societies are differentiated from horticultural societies by virtue of their technological superiority, particularly in the area of production and warfare. Urban centres develop, and occupational specialization and the division of labor are extensive. Trade and commerce, stimulated by the invention of money and writing, become a major economic activity, which serves to widen the gulf between the ruling class and the common people. The power of the nobility increases with its wealth, and eventually, it engages in an almost continuous struggle for power with the king. Despite such struggles and the exploitation of the common people, agrarian societies endured over a long time, because, Lenski tells us, "there was really no alternative." (1966:296.) Feudal societies are an example.

What makes industrial societies different from their predecessors is not only the technology, but also their greatly increased consumption of a vast array of energy sources, matched by their consumption of other resources. The age-old evolutionary trend toward ever-increasing inequality is reversed in industrial society, irrespective of the political system. The reason for this is the vast and complex knowledge base upon which industrial society rests. One of the consequences of this is that those in positions of command cannot possibly know everything that is going on beneath them and must rely on their subordinates to increase efficiency and productivity. In so doing, they give up a measure of their authority and privilege to their subordinates. At the same time, because of the vastly expanded knowledge base, production in industrial societies is much greater than in the earlier types of societies. The elite can afford to give the workers a greater share in economic surplus. This inspires greater productivity, which results in greater economic rewards for both workers and the elite. By sharing the wealth (in the form of higher wages for the workers), the elite is rewarded by greater absolute gains.

This egalitarian trend is evident in the political system as well. Although a political class system still remains, its elite status gives way in relative importance to elite status of the propertied class, identified in terms of its accumulation of private property. The occupational class system can be subdivided into several distinct "classes," each with its own world view, special interests, and position in the distribution structure. Thus, "class struggles are not nearly as pervasive a phenomenon in advanced industrial societies as Marxist theory would lead one to expect." (Lenski, 1966:418.) Rather, what struggle there is involves status groups (religious, ethnic, generational, and gender) vying for power, privilege, and prestige (1966:425).

Critique of Lenski's Theory of Society

Although Lenski does not intend his to be a theory of social evolution, it is implicit in his typology and so his theory is open to the same criticisms levelled at evolutionary theories generally, including the heavy charge of providing ideological justification for the assumed superiority of modern Western societies. Also, to argue, as Lenski does, that elite control is disappearing in industrial society is to ignore the abundant empirical evidence that shows just how wrong this assumption is. Control is becoming ever more concentrated in fewer and fewer hands, as indicated by the growth of corporations in our economy. And finally, although Lenski endeavors to avoid Parsons's extreme cultural determinism, his explanatory variable — the level of technology — is part of a society's knowledge base, and this notion clearly puts him in the idealist camp along with the other functionalists.

THE SYMBOLIC-INTERACTION APPROACH

Symbolic interactionists do not really have a theory of society as such, since they lean more toward a methodology that focuses on the individual rather than on the whole society. Also, their work is based on a nominalist ontology. What this means is that for interactionists, social phenomena can be explained only by the intentions, motives, and actions of *individuals* and not by the characteristics of whole *societies*, such as division of labor, population size, or level of technology. Furthermore, society does not exist as an objective reality external to, and imposing itself upon, human individuals; rather, society is the product of individual cognition; that is, social reality exists only in the consciousness of its creators. To grasp this reality, one has to use the method of subjective interpretation (rather than the positivist methods of the natural sciences) in order to get at the meanings that people attribute to their actions and that constitute the essence of social life. Interactionists shun determinism in any form. Although they do not deny that social factors must be taken into account, they stress that individuals create their social environment — they are not determined by it. It follows then that interactionists do not formulate law-like statements that could be universally applicable to all societies and all social behavior; their focus remains at the micro level of everyday social life. As such, it provides a healthy corrective to the functionalist idea that society is an objective and fixed order to which the individual must conform.

As you have already learned in Chapter 2, symbolic interactionism owes much to the social psychology of George Herbert Mead. Suffice it to say here that Mead offers an explanation of the process by which the attitudes of society come to be internalized by the individual while not suppressing the capacity for individual creativity and spontaneity, without which there would be nothing novel in human experience. It is this dynamic potential that makes Mead's theory so attractive to sociologists of the humanist persuasion. The fundamental problem that Mead addressed is how we become integrated selves in a rapidly changing and seemingly chaotic world; how to preserve order while accommodating change.

Critique of the Symbolic-Interactionist Approach

However insightful interactionist notions may be in helping to explain how we become social beings, it is doubtful that this approach can contribute much to our understanding of society itself. It does not, nor can it, account for the emergence and re-emergence in dissimilar societies of similar social patterns. Moreover, it neglects to deal with the phenomena of stratification, power, economic exploitation, and social oppression. By diverting attention away from such issues, interactionists, like the functionalists (though in a different way), mask fundamental social contradictions, and thus, their notions may be said to serve an ideological function. They serve a further ideological function in that, by emphasizing individualism, they affirm and reinforce the underlying liberal ideology that dominates North American society. Finally, their interpretive method makes cross-cultural and historical comparative study virtually impossible.

What is needed is a theory of society that can, in the words of C. Wright Mills, link "the personal troubles of milieu" with "the public issues of social structure," a theory informed by "the sociological imagination [which] enables us to grasp history and biography and the relations between the two within society." (1959). This is what the materialist approach provides.

THE MATERIALIST APPROACH

Sociological materialism is the theoretical school that holds that only material (economic) factors are real; in other words, the phenomenon of human consciousness or will is entirely due to material agency.

Cultural values *do* structure, give meaning to, and enable the reproduction of social arrangements that give each society its uniqueness, as Parsons says. Ideas internalized by the socialization process *do* shape individual consciousness, as Mead tells us. However, these idealist theories

are not able to explain the source of these ideas and values, nor how they are reproduced or changed, except through recourse to individualistic explanations. More specifically, idealists base their analysis of society on the overpowering normative order, the structure of rules that shape social behavior. Using the concept of social norm, idealists construct a picture of society as a set of rules, roles, and institutions. The concept of roles is the pivotal concept in these theories of society.

In contrast, the materialist theorists accept the existence of social norms, but deny their explanatory significance. They argue that social norms are merely the reflection of underlying material (economic) factors, in particular, the social relations of production. Thus, the existing ideas, values, and norms are the expression of the material interests of the dominant class, which is dominant by virtue of its ownership of the means of production. According to materialists, it is the social relations of production that must be given primacy in any attempt to explain how societies are structured and how they change.

Karl Marx

It has been said that all sociology is a debate with Marx's ghost, and up to a point this is true. Certainly the two sociologists most often cited as the fathers of modern sociology, Weber and Durkheim, were writing in response to Marx. The debate does not deny the importance of material (economic) factors in explaining society and change; rather it is over Marx's economic determinism and his insistence that cultural values and norms had no autonomy of their own vis-à-vis the economy.

The rudiments of Marx's theory of society are well known, though its complexity is little understood or appreciated. For Marx, history is a dialectical process: all social relations contain contradictions that can be traced to the material (economic) circumstances of each stage of societal development. These contradictions can be discovered and overcome through social conflict. By contradiction is meant an incompatibility between the components of social organization. In capitalist societies, the principal contradiction is that the materials produced by workers are seen as things (commodities) external to them, rather than as the embodiment of the workers through the labor expended on production. These "alien" objects come to take on a life of their own and to dominate the worker's life. For Marx, alienation is the condition of being the slave of one's own products (1966). Eventually, when the workers become conscious of their alienation and understand that its source is in the process of production, they will organize to secure their emancipation from the chains of their enslavement.

Marx does not make the claim that this is an inevitable process. "Men make their own history but not always of their own choosing," he tells us. What distinguishes human beings from all other species is their capacity for mental activity, which enables them to think about their social condition in advance of, and while acting upon, their situation. There is a unity between thinking and doing, between theory and practice. Revolution is not something that will just happen — it has to be made to happen, to be collectively achieved. And failure is always possible.

Not surprisingly, Marx distinguishes between societies on the basis of their mode of production. History is a progression from tribal to slave-owning societies, to feudalism, capitalism, and ultimately to communism. In tribal society, or primitive communism, as Marx sometimes calls it, there is communal ownership of land. Economic activities are hunting, fishing, cattle breeding, and later, agricultural production. Tools are primitive and there is little division of labor. The family is the basic social unit; and a number of families constitute a tribe under the leadership of a chief. There are no classes because there is no private ownership of the means of production. Thus, there is no need for a state.

With agricultural production, increased population, and the beginnings of trade, these tribal societies develop a system of slavery as a more efficient way of increasing their productive capacity. Such a development represents the beginning of classes and class conflicts. (Note that the introduction of slavery has a materialist base and is not simply the result of warfare.)

In feudal society the production process is small-scale farming carried out by serfs. The workers possess their own tools, though not usually the land; the family is still the production unit, and whatever division of labor exists is based on age and sex lines. Little, if any, surplus is accumulated after the serfs hand over to the nobility the share it demands for their military protection. The relations between the serfs and the aristocracy are patriarchal and fairly personal in nature. This hierarchical, though relatively benign, structure is repeated in the towns through the organization of artisans into guilds.

Over time, with new and more co-operative methods of production, this system generates an excess of production over consumption. Trade and exchange are initiated, giving rise to a merchant class. As tools become more complicated and are later replaced by machinery, the new class — the bourgeoisie — uses its economic surplus to provide the machinery, the raw materials, and the premises needed for production. The artisans, later joined by serfs, who have been dispossessed of their land, become wage workers, accepting wages in exchange for their products. The emergence of this new labor class also has a material base. As the bourgeois owners of production grow in economic power, they struggle to gain supremacy from the feudal aristocracy; the outcome is a function of superior wealth. When they succeed, the bourgeois class takes over the state. Thus is born capitalist society.

The bulk of Marx's work focuses on the analysis of capitalist society and on wage labor as the social relation of production. The nature of capitalism is based on the owners (of the means of production) accumulating profits through the appropriation of the surplus generated by the workers' labor power (after payment of production costs, including the wages needed for the reproduction of that labor power).

Marx distinguishes between a "class *in* itself" and a "class *for* itself." Only if workers become conscious of the social processes underlying their exploitation and of their common interests — only if they organize themselves to achieve these — will they become a "class *for* itself." When this happens, the workers will engage in the struggle to overthrow capitalism. Capitalism can never be corrected, Marx argued. It must be destroyed if its central contradictions are to be overcome. Only then can a fully just and humane society be created.

Critique of Marx's Theory

Much has been made of the inadequacies of Marx's economic analysis and of the fact that actual historical events appear to have falsified his theory of revolutionary change. In the West, his predicted overthrow of capitalism has not materialized, and where communist revolutions succeeded, the societies that have resulted are characterized more by tyranny and oppression than by freedom and justice. In making the claim that the most evolved society is the most desirable and that history comes to an end with its appearance, Marx seems to fall into the same trap of subjective bias as did the evolution theorists. Critics have noted that capitalism, far from collapsing, has shown a great capacity for modification and adaptation and has become ever more entrenched. Indeed, it is argued that ownership has become so widely dispersed through the share system that the owners are no longer in control — the managers are.

Neo-Marxist scholars continue to wrestle with the many difficulties and ambiguities in Marxian theory. It is not clear from Marx's writings, for example, just what is to be included in the economic base and what belongs in the superstructure. Particularly ambiguous is what constitutes productive activity. Is the economic base simply

Although no wage is paid for it, homemaking is labor. Some feminists believe that homemaking should at least be covered by the Canada/Québec Pension Plan.

the production of material things, or are mental products to be included as well? Does it include only those labor activities that yield surplus value through their exchange as commodities on the market, or are other activities for which no wage is paid also productive activities? Housewifery is the example most often cited in the last category. Is the superstructure independent of the economic base, though possibly determined by it in the end? Property law is one example sometimes cited: private ownership of the means of production could not have come into existence without some form of property law.

Although all these criticisms have some validity, Marxian theory continues to have great vital-

In Canada, capital is increasingly centralized in a few large firms, giving rise to the claim that our country is dominated economically and politically by a corporate elite.

ity. Countless scholars throughout the world, in both capitalist and socialist countries, in industrial, pre-industrial, and post-industrial societies, call themselves Marxists, albeit with little agreement between different schools. However, they all agree that it was Marx's key explanatory variables—economic factors and the social relations of production—that give his theory such power. For example, Miliband (1973) shows that in all advanced capitalist societies, the concentration of economic power leads to political power, the holders of which increasingly determine state policy and actions. Canadian sociologist Wallace

Clement (1983) applies this theory to Canada, claiming that our country is dominated by a corporate elite. There is an increasing centralization of capital in a few large firms. Clement maintains that the historical dimension is basic to Canadian political economy and to understanding social change in this country.

Scholars also agree that the dialectical method is a powerful analytical tool because it directs attention to the immanent contradictions within all social arrangements and to the complex interrelation between economic base and social superstructure, particularly with reference to the ideological content of knowledge and the normative system. The dialectical method precludes any form of determinism. The strength of Marxian sociology is that it is not writ in stone. Its very logic requires that it too be subject to dialectical analysis and change. Even Marx, in his own lifetime, in protesting against the rigid orthodoxy of some of his followers, was led to proclaim that he was not a Marxist! It is this openness, along with its methodology and its materialist ontology, that makes Marxism in all its many forms appealing to many sociologists.

THE CRITICAL APPROACH TO SOCIETY

Critical theory is a form of Marxist theory that was developed in the early 1930s by a small group of thinkers identified as "The Frankfurt School." In its earliest formulation it was not a theory of society per se, but rather a critique of traditional positivist theorizing about society. The positivist method of the natural sciences is inappropriate for the social sciences, they argued, because it treats human beings as mere facts and objects determined by external laws and forces over which they have no control. Furthermore, its insistence on the separation of fact and value obscures, and even denies, the connection between knowledge and human interests. The positivist, moreover, is taken in by the mere appearances of a phenomenon. Thus, it is the task of the critical theorist to uncover its essence.

Later writers came forth with an extensive critique of "scientism" in general, which they claim is leading modern society into a new kind of barbarism. Scientific-technological rationality has become "ideology" and the new form of domination in advanced industrial societies. Positivist sociology, they assert, is but one manifestation of this new ideology, in that it provides legitimation for the status quo and obstructs the potential for radical change.

Contemporary conflict is most likely to center around environmental concerns and issues of human survival. Here, thousands of people, including members of unions, women's groups, and political parties, march for peace along a 5 km route in Vancouver (1984).

This emphasis on ideology has led critical sociologists to focus their analysis on the cultural system (or as they prefer to call it, "the culture industry") as the principal force in late capitalist society, rather than the economic system, as Marx had posited. For them, "mass culture" has blurred, and even obliterated class distinctions, and the true nature of class society has been mystified, so that the development of a revolutionary class consciousness becomes ever more remote. The only glimmer of hope is in critical theory itself, which has as its central concern human emancipation.

To a large extent, then, critical theory becomes a critique of modern society, dominated by an impersonal power (scientific-technological rationality) and characterized by a politically quiescent "mass," which has been pacified by high consumption rates and mollified by a debased culture industry. In Chapter 24 of this volume, Lele discusses how this has come about.

Jürgen Habermas

A critical theory of society emerged in the recent work of Jürgen Habermas. In *Legitimation Crisis* (1976) and *Communication and the Evolution of Society* (1979), he outlines the elements of a reconstructed Marxist theory of society. In the first work, Habermas identifies four "crisis tendencies" in advanced capitalist society: economic, rationality, legitimation, and motivation crises. (Marx had dealt only with economic crisis.)

Habermas argues that the economic crisis that Marx predicted has been averted in advanced capitalism because of the extensive intervention of the state in the working of the economy through monetary and fiscal controls. In this way, the crisis has been shifted onto the political system to become a crisis of legitimation, wherein (1) people no longer believe in the rationality of the system and must be motivated in other ways if they are to continue to produce and keep the system going; (2) consumerism has replaced liberal values as the prime legitimator; (3) the scientific-technological rationality of the modern era has been turned into a means of ideological domination, which is so powerful that the exploited masses are no longer able to think critically; (4) communication has become so distorted that the masses come to believe that the system is really serving their best interests and not just those of the ruling elite; and finally, the cultural apparatus works to structure not simply communication but consciousness as well.

In his later work, Habermas is interested in unravelling "the specific way in which humans, in contradistinction to animals, reproduce their lives." (1979:134.) Marx had posited that it was the social relations of production that provided the key to *social reproduction*; that is, how human beings reproduce not merely their physical existence but also their way of life. Habermas adds to this theme by exploring the centrality of language in this reproduction process. Both the social relations of production *and* language constitute the irreducible elements in the explanation of the evolution of human society. Furthermore, some form of familial social organization is essential for such a development.

As for the transformation from capitalism to socialism, this rests more on the processes of democratization, which are the response to the legitimation crisis, than on class conflicts, which are the expression of economic crisis. Alongside class, new opposing social groupings based on gender, race, and age criteria have emerged in contemporary society. Conflict is more about the quality of life — about matters concerning human rights; environmental concerns; public participation in decision-making, especially about issues of human survival. Habermas believes that questions of public policy must be seen as issues for public political debate and not as technical problems to be resolved by experts. Only in this way can the "emancipatory interest" be served.

SUMMARY

1. This chapter presented four different approaches to the analysis of society. Each provides answers to questions about the relation between (1) the individual and society; (2) society and culture; and (3) society and community.

2. Despite fundamental differences, there is some common ground in each of the theories: with different emphases, they all make some use of the evolutionary model as a way of conceptualizing

the development of human society. They do not agree, however, on the inevitability of such development.

3. In positing a theory of society, the three functionalists discussed — Durkheim, Parsons and Lenski — all lean toward cultural-determinism, whereas interactionists, Marxists, and critical theorists stress human agency and the resulting indeterminancy regarding the evolutionary outcome.

4. Although all approaches recognize that culture is a necessary component in the definition of human society, there is no agreement about the extent to which it is an autonomous, external determining force or a reflexive product of social relations and the social means of production.

5. Similarly, although all approaches recognize the importance of economic forces, they disagree on whether these forces (a) determine social relations; or (b) are determined by these relations and cultural forces; or (c) whether a continuous dialectical, reciprocal process is involved.

6. All approaches agree on the centrality of language as essential to the formation and reformation of human society. Once again, there are differences regarding the place language assumes in the explanatory scheme and the extent to which it is an irreducible element that cannot be derived from other elements.

7. Finally, the theoretical approaches discussed in this chapter employ different methodological assumptions about how one might go about studying society. On the one hand, the functionalists are committed to the positivist method of the natural sciences; that is, society can be studied in the same objective way that is employed for the study of nature. On the other hand, the interactionists, Marxists, and critical theorists are committed to an interpretive methodology that attempts to understand the fundamental nature of the social world at the individual level of subjective experience.

8. Critical theorists extend this commitment even further in their claim that social science must aim at understanding the *essence* of social phenomena and not simply their *external appearance*.

GLOSSARY

Anomie. The condition of society that results when the old rules and ways of doing things are no longer appropriate and people do not know where to turn for moral guidance.

Determinism. The belief that everything that happens is the outcome of a necessary chain of causation; human action is not free.

Dialectic. The process of transformation, iniatiated by a contradiction, through which one set of social arrangements gives way to another.

Functionalism. That theoretical system that holds that society may be viewed as an entity in itself, distinguished from and not reducible to its parts, and that the system parts may be seen as fulfilling basic functions (needs) for the maintenance of the whole.

Idealism. The theoretical system that holds that the ideas that people have about themselves and their place in the world determines their position. The central concept in explaining social behavior and society is culture.

Materialism. The theoretical system that holds that only material (economic) factors are real; the phenomena of consciousness or will are determined by economic factors.

Positivism. The epistemology that seeks to apply the scientific objective methods of the natural sciences to explain and predict what happens in the social world.

Ontology. Refers to basic philosophical and metaphysical questions about the basic nature, the very essence of the phenomenon being investigated.

Social evolution. The process of development of complex societies from simpler, earlier social forms.

Social reproduction. The way in which human beings reproduce both their physical existence and their way of life.

Society. The total nexus of social relations and the reproduction of these relations among human beings who comprise a clearly identifiable population with historical continuity beyond the life of the individual members.

FURTHER READING

Functionalist theories of society:

Parsons, Talcott. *Evolutionary and Comparative Perspectives.* Englewood Cliffs, N.J.: Prentice-Hall, 1966. A brief summary of the basic tenets of Parsons's structural-functional theory of society and the evolution of society from primitive to (but not including) modern society.

Naegele, Kaspar D. "Canadian society: some reflections." In *Canadian Society: Sociological Perspectives.* B. Blishen, et al. (eds.). Toronto: Macmillan, 1961. An excellent essay that illustrates the application of the functionalist and comparative approach to the analysis of Canadian society. The non-functionalist will find considerable difficulty with the author's suggestion that Canada is on the same path (though somewhat further behind) of evolutionary development, as the United States. The criticism often levelled at functionalism — that it is ahistoric — can certainly be made of this essay. Yet it contains many useful insights.

Marxist theories of society:

Worsley, Peter. *Marx and Marxism.* Toronto: Methuen, 1982.

Bottomore, Tom. *The Frankfurt School,* 1983. Two excellent books available in the Key Sociologists series, edited by Peter Hamilton of The Open University of Britain and published by Ellis Horwood Ltd. and Tavistock. Each book provides the beginner with a short but highly substantive summary and critique of these theoretical approaches in their study of society.

Marchak, Patricia M. *Ideological Perspectives on Canada,* 2nd edition. Toronto: McGraw-Hill Ryerson, 1981. Professor Marchak identifies three ideologies from which Canadian society may be viewed. First there is the liberal-democratic version, which describes Canada as a liberal democracy, maintained by a stable, free-enterprise economy, and populated by reasonably happy and affluent workers. Juxtaposed to this is the socialist version, which sees Canada as ruled by elites and the multinational corporations, maintained by an increasingly impoverished working class. The third, more recent ideology — corporatism — differs from the first two in its values as well as its definition of the society. This is a highly readable book. Its brevity and lucidity must not be mistaken for a simplistic or cursory overview.

Clement, Wallace. *Class, Power and Property: Essays on Canadian Society.* Toronto: Methuen, 1983. Professor Clement is one of Canada's best-known sociologists who analyze Canadian society from a materialist perspective. This book is a collection of papers written over the last ten years, offering both theoretical and empirical support for his overarching thesis that Canada is dominated by a corporate elite, that there is an increasing centralization and concentration of capital in fewer and larger firms, and an increasing penetration of the economy by foreign, particularly U.S. investment. Clement insists that the historical dimension is central to Canadian political economy and basic to understanding social change.

Miliband, Ralph. *The State in Capitalist Society: The Analysis of the Western System of Power.* New York: Quartet Books, 1973. An excellent, readable example of the power of Marxist analysis, this book is essentially a critique of the functionalist view of society, of politics, and of the state. The author shows that in all advanced capitalist societies evermore concentrated economic power results in evermore power in society, in the political system, and in the determination of the state's policies and actions.

Socialization

K. ISHWARAN

You have now seen that human social life is varied, but on the whole, orderly and patterned. Yet, neither the variety nor the pattern is born with the human infant. There is nothing in the genetic endowments of human infants to predetermine their commitment to Islam and not to Christianity, to democracy and not to communism, to marrying a mother's brother's daughter rather than a stranger, to speaking English rather than Japanese. The variety and patterns are generated, as you have seen, by the difference in culture and in the structure of social relations.

It is socialization that determines individual behavior. The newborn baby becomes a member of society when it learns social roles — father, mother, son, daughter, professor, student, prime minister, or janitor — including skills to perform them. The dynamics of role-learning and role-performance begin in all societies in a family setting. Later the family is partly replaced by a variety of social contexts and situations. Unlike the family, many of these nonfamilial contexts are impersonal. In all contexts, however, there are opportunities for individual variation. Culture and society cannot, and do not, force members into a single mould. Differences arise from the interaction of biological endowments of each human being with selective aspects of socio-cultural and physical environments.

DEFINING SOCIALIZATION

In sociology, the meaning of socialization has become more precise with the widening and clarification of the field of sociology itself. Before the 1930s, most sociologists used the term to refer to the social processes that brought about conformity and harmony in social life. Later, especially under the influence of the philosopher-educationist John Dewey (1922), and also because of the insights of social interdisciplinary studies, the concept of socialization gradually acquired its modern meaning: the complex of processes by which the individual acquires a concept of self, including the skills and the motivation to function effectively in a given society. Socialization in this sense is universal. Since no human infant can survive and grow without a self-identity and the skills of role-playing, all societies have to provide a socialization process.

Moreover, socialization as a learning process continues throughout life; infants become adolescents, adolescents become adults, and problems of transition arise. These have to be met and resolved in all societies, at all times. Finally, adults grow old. New roles replace former roles. Whether an individual succeeds, is compromised, or fails in terms of certain pre-existing standards, is a different matter. What is important to recognize is the inevitability of socialization.

FUNCTIONS OF SOCIALIZATION

The first major function of socialization is to generate what is known as "personality." Personality means the totality of the characteristics that distinguish one person from another. Every human being, while growing, acquires characteristics that make him or her a distinct personality. Thus, the diversity of personality is infinite.

The second major function of socialization, related to the first, is the transmission of group requirements for personality growth. Group requirements are always present, since infants, adolescents, adults, and the elderly are always a member of some kind of a group. It is through socialization that human beings grow, survive, and acquire the cultural codes of their primary groups and of the wider society.

Canada, like the United States, is a multicultural society. People from all over the world have come to live here. Consequently, the Canadian child of a certain ethnic origin has to learn, on the one hand, about the culture of its primary groups (such as the family and peer group), and on the other hand, about the cultural codes of the wider society. This wider society encompasses a belief in democracy, for example, as well as the importance of ice hockey. In political terms, the wider society may mean simply Anglo-dominance. It is socialization that accomplishes the transformation of every citizen, regardless of ethnic origin, into Canadian persons. What has been said about Canada applies to all multi-ethnic societies and cultures.

The third function of socialization is a subfunction of the first two: the inculcation of goals and motivations related to dominant, societal goals. At different times, every society and culture may emphasize different goals as worthy of achievement. To become rich and powerful may become the dominant goal of one society; to stay poor but kind and wise may become the dominant goals in another. Human beings are capable of having a great range in goals, but they may not always be realized. The point is that as human beings form societies and interact with their changing environments, they generate goals, destroy them, reverse, and modify them.

The complex process of goal-formation is influenced by societal values learned through socialization. Some of the ways in which this happens are illustrated in studies undertaken by Max Weber (1958), Atkinson and McClelland (1948), and others. Weber showed how the values of European Protestantism encouraged the values of hard work and self-denial, which, according to him, were the basis of modern Western capitalism. Atkinson and McClelland extended this Weberian insight in their concept of "need achievement," which they related to economic development. They established need achievement scores on the basis of content analyses of cross-cultural literary sources. They argued that images that repeatedly occur in the literature of a society are likely to inspire the need to achieve what is exemplified by such images. Atkinson and McClelland thus developed the idea of measuring need achievements in various societies and proposed that if children were exposed early to goals favorable to economic development, they would more readily accept these goals in later life.

Briefly then, whatever the dominant goals of a society at any given time, its members come to acquire the motivation to pursue those goals through socialization. For a proper understanding of the mechanics of socialization, the so-called "nature versus nurture" issue must be dealt with.

BIOLOGICAL AND ENVIRONMENTAL COMPONENTS OF SOCIALIZATION

This issue arose from the impact on sociological thinking of Dawin's theory of evolution in *On the Origin of Species*: namely, which factors determined human behavior more — biological or environmental? According to Darwin, Homo sapiens was one species in the animal kingdom. Just as with other animals, what human infants became in later life was largely determined by their biologically inherited characteristics, commonly known as "instincts," "inherited traits," or "biological propensities."

From this basic idea evolved the ideology of Social Darwinism: that the superiority or inferiority of human groups — races, classes, nations — was determined by inherited traits, and there was nothing that one could do to alter the situation. Blacks, for instance, were considered inferior to whites (as demonstrated by the success of the white people's civilization) because the blacks' biologically inherited traits were supposedly inferior to those of whites. Some social scientists produced long lists of inherited traits that they thought controlled personality development and eventually the relative power of human groups.

Ideas associated with this so-called biological determinism were predominant in the late nineteenth and early twentieth centuries. Later in this century, however, a directly opposed ideology gained prominence and emphasized the importance of environment and learning processes in animals (including humans). The original, major inspiration for this new ideology was found in the implications of experiments conducted on dogs by the Russian physiologist Ivan Pavlov. An American psychologist formulated the implications as follows:

Give me a dozen healthy infants, well-informed and my own specified world to bring them up in and I will guarantee to take anyone at random and train him to become any type of specialist I might select — a doctor, lawyer, artist, merchant-chief, yes, even into beggarman and thief, regardless of his talents, penchants, tendencies, abilities, vocations and race of his ancestors.

(Watson, 1924:10.)

For Watson, therefore, formation of human personality depended entirely on environmental factors. In due course, Watson's approach developed into the behavioral perspective on various aspects of human and nonhuman behavior, including those related to personality formation. This perspective, especially as worked out by American psychologist Skinner (1971), has been used in a variety of contexts of learning, both human and non-human, including the kind of learning involved in human socialization. Skinner, in fact, pleaded that a Utopian society could be built on the basis of behaviorist principles. The behaviorist perspective of Watson and Skinner stands in contrast to biological determinism.

Studies have been attempted to establish the preeminence of biological factors in determining personality, but they have rarely managed to come up with adequate evidence to justify their conclusions. A few examples will illustrate what this means.

Studies on twins, for instance, suggest correlations between intelligence and genetic patterns. The correlation in such cases, however, is based on the assumption that no intervening variables, such as vitamin deficiency or brain damage, might be operative. Such variables explain why twins, in spite of having the same genetic pattern, become unlike, not only in intelligence but in other aspects of their personalities.

Another study (Heise, 1973) has argued that introversion, extroversion, neurosis, and other emotional states are related to heriditary factors. The evidence of this study is far from conclusive. Another study (Nettler, 1976) claimed that the potential for schizophrenia is due to inherited factors, although most studies of schizophrenia stress that the potential for this disorder becomes actual only if intervening variables (generally environmental factors) become operative. In at least one context — physical build — the relevance of hereditary factors seems obvious: tall parents often have tall offspring; fat ones have fat children. Here too, however, the operative factors are not easy to isolate; eating habits, for instance, are relevant, among other things.

This does not, of course, mean that inherited traits are of no consequence. Human beings are indeed biological organisms. Even those who emphasize environmental factors cannot, and must not, dismiss the fact that the apparently endless malleability of the human personality, as

implied in Watson's statement, is one of the main characteristics arising from human biology. What is needed is a perspective firmly based on the idea of continuous interaction between biological and environmental factors and the investigative issues.

THE SOCIAL SHAPING OF HUMAN BEINGS

It is a common-sense observation that children learn as they interact with human beings, but we rarely grasp the significance of this point. A brief review of several cases should illuminate some of the crucial aspects of the processes, patterns, and results of normal social shaping for human beings.

Frederick II was a thirteenth-century emperor in the Holy Roman Empire. He was curious to know if social isolation would have an effect on a child's learning to speak.

Frederick's folly was that he wanted to find out what kind of speech and what manners of speech children would have when they grew up, if they spoke to no one beforehand. So he bade foster mothers and nurses to suckle the children, to bathe and wash them, but in no way to prattle with them or to speak to them, for he wanted to learn whether they would speak the Hebrew language, which was the oldest, or Greek, or Latin, or Arabic, or perhaps the language of their parents, of whom they had all been born. But he laboured in vain, because the children all died. For they could not live without the patting and joyful faces and loving words of their foster mothers.
(*Machiavelli quoted in* Ross and McLaughlin, *1949:366–67.*)

The object lessons of this medieval experiment corroborated by many modern experiments are: (1) children do not learn a language except through interactions with other human beings, and (2) they die emotionally, as modernists would say, if they are deprived of normal interactions with others. It is the second lesson that is reaffirmed in the cases of feral children and children brought up in a social vacuum.

Feral Children

Feral children are those brought up by animals. Such instances occur abundantly in the myths and legends of many countries and occasionally in contemporary writings. For example, Zeus and Tarzan grew up without human social interaction. The legendary founders of Rome — Romulus and Remus — were nurtured by a wolf. There are similar instances of a Dutch fish-girl, a Bavarian swine-girl, a Lithuanian bear-boy, an Irish chicken-boy, and Indian wolf-children. Most feral children, when discovered, supposedly did not speak, were hostile to human beings, ate like savages, and rejected attempts to change them into human beings. In other words, they were savages.

It is difficult to determine whether the available accounts of feral children are fact or fiction. Bruno Bettelheim (1959:467), who studied the phenomenon of feral children, states: "The conclusion tentatively forced on us is that while there are no feral children there are some very rare examples of feral mothers, of human beings who became feral to one of their children." The phenomenon of children brought up in a social vacuum is more authentically documented.

Children Reared in a Social Vacuum

"Reared in a social vacuum" is a metaphor, for children can never be reared in a social vacuum, not in a literal sense. First, children simply do not survive in a social vacuum, and secondly, "reared" implies the presence of someone to do the rearing. Social vacuum, therefore, more accurately means social conditions that drastically limit physical, mental, and emotional development.

Kinglsey Davis (1940, 1947) reported the cases of Anna and Isabelle, both discovered in the late 1930s. Anna had been confined to her grandfather's attic since her birth in 1932. When found she could neither talk nor walk. She could not feed herself and she was bitter, indifferent, or hostile to other human beings. (It was also discovered that she was illegitimately mothered by a Mormon, and that no one wanted the child.) Anna was shunted from place to place during her first six months and was eventually returned to her mother. Once found, attempts to rehabilitate her failed, and she died a child of ten-and-a-half years old, but physically, mentally, and emotionally, only a two-year-old.

Isabelle was similar to Anna in many ways. Born in 1932, an illegitimate child, she was isolated along with her deaf-mute mother from the rest of the family in a dark room. Upon discovery, Isabelle was treated and rehabilitated. Unlike Anna, by the time Isabelle was fourteen she had become a grade 7 pupil and a well-adjusted child.

Detailed comparative studies have never been done on Anna and Isabelle. But, from what little we know about them, we can postulate three reasons why their lives proved so different. First, Isabelle may have inherited superior hereditary characteristics. Second, her rehabilitative treatment was carried out more completely and comprehensively. Third, Isabelle's social isolation was less severe than Anna's. Thus, both biological and social factors were involved in making Anna and Isabelle similar in certain ways, yet different in other ways.

Although cases such as Anna and Isabelle are rare, they do throw some light on what happens when children are reared in isolation, and therefore, hostile environments. But it is the children brought up in institutions who present a more systematic context of investigation. After all, masses of children all over the world are being brought up, not in families, but in various institutions or so-called "homes."

Children Reared in Institutions

The results of two studies of infants (Spitz, 1945 and 1946) indicate the importance of nurturing in the first years of a child's life. The first study compared four groups of infants: (1) infants from urban, professional families; (2) infants from the families in a somewhat isolated, small, fishing community; (3) infants who, born to mothers in prison, spent the first year of their life in a nursery connected with the prison; and (4) infants sent to orphanages within a few days of their birth.

At the end of a year, the children in the first three groups showed the same level of development as they had shown in the first four months of their life; in the fourth group, the average rate of development had been reduced by as much as 50 percent. In a follow-up study two years later, Spitz found that only twenty-one of the original ninety-one orphaned children were still alive. Among the twenty-one survivors in the age two-to-four group, only five could walk without help, only one could dress, and only one could speak full sentences. It was impossible for the one nurse, who had to look after from seven to twelve children, to act as surrogate mother. The plight of the orphaned children indicates the importance of "maternal caring, maternal stimulation, and maternal love" in the early years of a child's life.

Sex-Role Socialization

The majority of human beings, both male and female, are born with a wide range of capabilities. However, boys and girls are taught different ways of behaving and their sex roles are usually culturally determined. Yet biologically speaking, in all cultures, boys are capable of doing almost everything that girls do, and girls are capable of doing almost everything that boys do. In the actual socialization of boys and girls, this normal fact is ignored; in other words, sex differences cease to be a mere matter of biology and instead are invested with culturally contrived meanings. Let us see briefly what this means.

Boys are considered boys, and girls, girls, not just because of their sex differences. The totality of sex-based identity involves five factors (Clark, 1978): (1) chromosomal differences; (2) differences in hormonal balance; (3) differences in internal genitalia; (4) differences in external genitalia; and (5) differences arising from culturally assigned

meanings to sex-differences and the socialization that follows. In practice, however, those who discuss the phenomenon of sex-based identity tend to emphasize either the first four factors or the last one. It is the last factor that is of overwhelming importance to socialization.

As noted earlier, all societies recognize sex-based differences among human beings, attach meaning to these differences, and take practical steps to train human beings as functioning boys and girls, men and women. Societies, however, vary greatly in their emphases on sex-based differences and on functional differentiation based on these differences. The process begins with parental expectations, even before the baby is born. Lois Hoffman (1972:141) summarizes the literature on early sex-typing of children as follows:

.... there are sex differences in both maternal and infant behavior in the first year of life. That sex-role learning is begun so early should not be surprising. Sex is a primary status—the first one announced at birth. The mother is very much aware of it. Her early behavior towards the infant are not the deliberate efforts to teach the child his proper sex roles, but (rather) she has internalized society's views and acts accordingly.

Whether the mother's behavior toward her infant stems from deliberate efforts or from a subconscious internalization of the norms is not important, since all behavior eventually emerges from the internalization of norms, and, when needed, deliberate effort. The main point is that girls are trained to play with dolls, help in household work, wear certain clothes, and so on. Boys are trained to play with cars or guns, and to do things considered appropriate for males. When boys become men and girls women, the differences persist and are elaborated, though what is accepted in one culture may be rejected in another. For example, in many contemporary societies women are associated with the nurturing role and men with wage work. But in some parts of the world, such as in the Marquesan Island society in the western Pacific, men are involved in cooking, cleaning and baby care; in the Philippines, some men work as domestic servants while some women are pharmacists.

It must be noted that because of a variety of forces, among which technological change is foremost, sex-based role differences have come under attack, especially in certain segments of Western and modernizing societies. Women today occupy a great variety of occupations — a change that has been partly instigated by the women's liberation movement. Despite the increased participation of women in the work force, the universal practice of sex-based socialization has not yet vanished. Its persistence emphasizes the significance of culture in shaping the individual.

In Canada, as in most complex societies, socialization of role differences extends to the wider society of which the family is a part. The school, the peer group, and increasingly the media, have become major agents of socialization. Sociologists use the concepts of instrumental and expressive roles to study role behavior (Parsons and Bales, 1955). Instrumental roles signify the roles related to specific task performance; expressive roles are personal and are emotionally oriented. Among French Canadians, children turn to the mother for aid, advice, and comfort. Provision of such emotional support constitutes an expressive role. The differentiation of instrumental and expressive roles in relation to parents prevails also among Jewish Canadians, Dutch Canadians, and Hutterites, as well as the ranchers and small farmers in the Canadian Prairies (Ishwaran, 1976).

Thus, in Canada as in all societies, the family establishes the foundations for the sex-based role-differentiation in socialization, and in Canada, as in other societies where education is provided for all children, the school continues the process. The school thus reaffirms and elaborates the framework of sex-based roles, which in time influences all other roles. The school plays its part in this process in many ways, especially in the images

Reading is a potent instrument of socialization. Images that repeatedly occur in a society's literature will inspire the need to achieve what those images exemplify.

portrayed in reading material. According to one observer,

The typical family scene shows daddy reading the newspaper while mommy sews. It is even more unusual to find a woman behind the wheel of a car; males are involved in a greater variety of enterprises than are females.... Girls play primarily with dolls and associated paraphernalia, flowers, and skipping ropes, while boys prefer balls, bikes, boats, games, guns, toy vehicles, and wagons. Unisex toys were to be hoops, paints and clay, stuffed toys and blocks.

(Pyke, 1975:68–69.)

A study of some 7500 Canadian children between the ages of ten and sixteen shows that

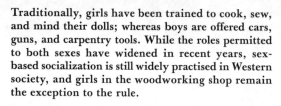

Traditionally, girls have been trained to cook, sew, and mind their dolls; whereas boys are offered cars, guns, and carpentry tools. While the roles permitted to both sexes have widened in recent years, sex-based socialization is still widely practised in Western society, and girls in the woodworking shop remain the exception to the rule.

children have a well-developed consciousness of expectations of sex-specific roles. Children's learning about these roles is influenced by their class background. Working-class children tend to have more traditional and stereotypical views about gender relations (Lambert, 1969). These findings are supported by a more recent study showing that even by the kindergarten stage, children have internalized societal norms for the sexes. Asked about their occupational goals, 83 percent of the girls and 97 percent of the boys named occupations that were sex-linked (Schlossberg and Goodman, 1972). Another study of ten-to-thirteen-year-old children in Vancouver (cited by Kimball, 1977) reports that 70 percent of the girls chose to be nurses, and 80 percent of the boys opted to be doctors.

Preconditions of Socialization

Before socialization can take place three conditions must be present: (1) an ongoing society that provides a meaningful context; (2) requisite biological inheritance; and (3) human nature (Elkin and Handel, 1984). The first precondition implies that in the absence of a society, there can be no standards or expectations in terms of which a child can be socialized. In other words, socialization can take place only in a pre-existing system of social relations — that is, in a societal context. As the child is socialized, it may grow up to accept, modify, or reject societal standards and expectations, but in their absence there can be no socialization.

The second precondition, biological inheritance, is equally important. What this means is that the biological equipment to learn and to use learning must be present for socialization to begin and continue.

The third precondition is the presence of what has been described as human nature. "Human nature is justly regarded as a comparatively permanent element in society. Always and everywhere men seek honor and dread ridicule, defer to public opinion, cherish their goods and their children, and admire courage, generosity and success. It is always safe to assume that people are and have been human." (Cooley, 1909:27.) Human nature, continues Cooley, stems from the ability to form groups based on face-to-face relations. Such primary groups — the family, the playground, the neighborhood — says Cooley, are found everywhere, at all times and in all cultures. Since the existence of such primary groups is universal, and since a great deal of socialization takes place in them, the ability to form face-to-face relations is considered human nature. If this ability is lacking, socialization cannot take place.

TYPES OF SOCIALIZATION

Different patterns of socialization yield a staggering variety of persons. Without a systematic classificatory scheme, it would be difficult to discern the processes and patterns of socialization; therefore, sociologists have subdivided this area of study into primary, secondary, and anticipatory socialization; resocialization; reverse socialization; oversocialization; and blocked socialization.

Primary Socialization

This earliest phase of socialization is associated with the earliest years of childhood. Through interaction with members of the family, especially the mother, children develop the foundations of self-identity and the rudiments of language, which vastly increases the child's learning capacity. It is at this age that major guidelines for future socialization are internalized. Children learn basic skills from the activities of other members of the family.

In Canada, as in most societies, school continues the process of socialization begun at home.

Secondary Socialization

Secondary socialization develops largely in formal settings such as the school, the church, occupational settings, and so on. In other words, it refers to all the socialization that goes on outside the direct familial context, throughout the individual's lifetime.

The pre-established components of primary socialization, whether or not the growing child is aware of them, continue to play their roles throughout the phases of secondary socialization, as children become better able to incorporate segments of the wider world into their own personality structure, and to perform, actually or vicariously, the new roles that increasingly become relevant. The school is likely to be the most impor-

For immigrants, resocialization is necessary to function in their host society.

tant context of the early period of secondary socialization. It may happen, for instance, that working-class children, when they find themselves at schools incorporating middle-class values and skills, develop their first major awareness of tension and conflict between what they had internalized during primary socialization in familial settings and what they are required to internalize in the wider world outside the family. The quality of the subsequent phases of secondary socialization is likely to depend on the way such tensions and conflicts, inevitable in a class-based society, are resolved.

Anticipatory Socialization

Socialization associated with anticipated roles — those of adult life — is known as anticipatory socialization. Children playing at being "mummy" and "daddy" are instances of anticipatory socialization. This kind of role-playing, and indeed much of human social life, is possible because of the human ability to symbolize, imagine, and create situations that are not in the immediate present. This ability enables human beings, even young chil-

dren, to imagine themselves in the position of others, which facilitates communication.

Resocialization

This process becomes relevant when, for whatever reasons, socialization considered normal in a society does not work for individuals or certain categories of individuals.

In a significant way, resocialization means a second chance, such as the rehabilitation of criminals and delinquents, alcoholics and drug addicts, and ex-mental patients. Immigrants also have to undergo resocialization in order to function as members of their host society. The nature and the extent of resocialization vary from context to context. But all contexts imply the failure of earlier socialization — failure, that is, as preordained in any given society at any given time. Such failures, and efforts at resocialization, characterize rapidly changing socieities, such as American and Canadian societies.

Efforts at resocialization, however, do not always succeed. This is clear from the cases of relapse in the history of the mentally ill and others. Resocialization efforts, especially those carried out in large, impersonal institutions, seem to help people as long as they remain within the confines of the institution; that is, rehabilitated persons tend not to function outside the institution, in the wider world. Goffman's detailed study of asylums (1961) supports this observation and suggests thoroughgoing reconsideration of the resocialization process.

Reverse Socialization

The concept of reverse socialization indicates the reversal of the socializer/socializee — teacher/learner roles. Usually, in all societies, socializers are older than socializees. However, the roles may become reversed under certain circumstances, such as when the older generation, or the parental generation, is socialized by the younger generation. This may occur when the younger generation comes to have access to information that the older generation needs, but cannot easily obtain. A classic example of reverse socialization is that of a Polish immigrant father in Canada engaging his son or daughter as his interpreter when he has to deal with the English-speaking world. The boy or the girl in such a situation has command of a valuable social resource — the ability to communicate in English, the dominant language of the host society. If parents want to acquire this resource themselves, they may do so under the tutelage of their children.

Oversocialization

Every society usually attempts to socialize its members into as perfect exemplars of its culture as possible. Christians are expected to socialize their children, adolescents, adults, and the aged as perfect Christians. Communists, democrats, Americans, Russians, and followers of Hare Krishna are expected to do the same. Therefore, how can there be an oversocialized American, Russian, Canadian, Christian, or what have you?

The phenomenon of oversocialization arises only in multi-ethnic societies and in societies in which socialization — in the sense of internalization of norms and roles — operates in a way that discourages or punishes individuality. In multi-ethnic societies, members of certain ethnic groups may become so socialized into their own group that they may lose the capacity to appreciate and understand others in their society. Oversocialization in this context is often a strategy of self-preservation in a threatening situation. A case in point is the Québecois separatist movement, whose indoctrination program aimed at reducing commitment to the wider Canada. When ethnic groups feel threatened, they become proponents of oversocialization.

Compelling oversocialization poses problems for individuals unwilling to conform to the dictates of the dominant group. Nonconformity is likely to be interpreted by the group as a threat to its solidarity and survival. It may then apply more pressure on deviants by deliberately constructing

Every society attempts to socialize its members toward the prevailing customs or creed. Those dedicated to the Hare Krishna sect do this just as Christians do.

as much of a closed world for those members as possible. The choice is either withdrawing from the group or suffering from a sense of isolation and mental anxiety. Maykovich's study (1976) of the traditional Mennonite community in Waterloo, Ontario, shows that those children who are unable to cope with the highly integrated, closed community and to bear the pressures of oversocialization become prone to mental disorders. In the rural Holland Marsh area of Ontario, those of Dutch origin who question the norms and values of the Dutch Reformed Church either move out of the community in resentment or join another church (Ishwaran, 1977).

If the lessons of history are any guide, this kind of closure on the world through oversocialization of its members may keep things under control for some people for some of the time, but not for all people all of the time. No matter how long they may take, sooner or later they defy all closures on their world. The significance of oversocialization for present purposes is to indicate this fact and draw attention to some of its implication.

During adolescence, peer groups are often favored over parents as desirable models.

Although human beings can never become persons without socialization, oversocialization, under the circumstances noted, can transform human beings into robots.

Blocked Socialization

The concept of blocked socialization refers to situations that do not allow growing children to develop sufficient or adequate skills considered necessary to lead a normal life in the society to which they belong. Spitz's study (1945) of children brought up in formal, impersonal institutions illustrates this. Blocked socialization may occur at both primary and secondary stages of socialization. If it occurs in the primary phase, its effects are likely to appear in later life, even if the person forgets about it.

The seven-fold classification used here, though not the only such classification, was meant to draw attention to the universality of socialization and to highlight some of the major features of the process. Next we turn to some aspects of socialization in the Western world that have given rise to a variety of problems. We shall focus on three specific contexts: adolescent socialization, adult socialization, and socialization of the aged. There is no need to argue that adolescent socialization in industrialized Western societies is, and has been, a problem for most socializers — parents, teachers, employers, peacekeeping officers, and so on. The aged have become a problem, too, because more and more old people, no longer working, are staying alive longer and are becoming dependent on the support (through taxation) of increasingly fewer younger people. Adult socialization is a problem because adults who change their status from single to married are inevitably caught up between the adolescent world and the world of the aged.

PROBLEMS OF SOCIALIZATION

Adolescent Socialization

The problematic aspects of adolescent socialization in industrialized societies such as Canada and the United States may be best highlighted by comparing them with non-Western, traditional societies. We shall consider one basic theme: the continuity or discontinuity in the passage of a child into adolescence, into adulthood, and into old age.

In traditional societies, life stages are not as sharply distinguished as they are in the Western world, where a child becomes a pre-teen then a teenager before becoming an adult. In the former, as soon as a child is capable, it starts taking part in useful family chores, and is thus launched into task-oriented adulthood in a way that the Canadian child never experiences. Consequently, adolescence itself is rarely a significant phase in traditional societies.

Adolescence in modern societies is a vague category—neither child nor adult. Although physiologically mature, adolescents legally remain minors until the age of eighteen. This conflict between physiological growth and legal disability may result in what is often described as an identity crisis. In traditional societies this is unlikely to happen because no special attention is paid to a category of "half child, half man." According to anthropologist Ruth Benedict (1938), adolescents in traditional societies are inducted into adulthood by a ceremony called a *rite of passage*, which announces that a certain individual, or group of individuals, has reached adulthood, with requisite rights and obligations.

Pre-industrial Western socieities did not recognize adolescence as a separate category either. "The adolescent was invented at the same time as the steam engine. The principal architect of the latter was Watt in 1765, of the former Rousseau in 1762. Having invented the adolescent, society has been faced with two major problems: how and where to accommodate him in the social structure, and how to make his behavior accord with the specifications." (Musgrove, 1964:33.) This predicament has received attention from time to time, but we are only now beginning to understand the implications of the phenomenon of adolescence in Western societies.

In 1942, Parsons described adolescents as "having a good time," seeking pleasure through heterosexual encounters and athletic displays, behavior that resulted from cultural discontinuity. This view was later challenged by a study of adolescence in a Montréal suburb, where "a continuity in socialization between adolescents and parents" prevailed. Moreover, "the peer groups are committed to the values of the parent and further a continuity in socialization". (Westley and Elkin, 1957:243-49.) In contrast, a study of adolescents in ten high schools in Illinois reported a significant shift from home to outside contexts. Peer groups loomed larger than parents as models worth imitating (Coleman, 1961).

In a study of adolescents in a rural Dutch-Canadian community, it was the church, school, and community that were the significant agents of socializing adolescents (Ishwaran and Kwok, 1979).

All these studies, although they appear to be contradictory, draw attention to specific aspects of the phenomenon of adolescence under certain social, cultural, and environmental conditions.

Adult Socialization

As is the case with adolescents, adult socialization too has become a problem in the modern Western world. In rapidly changing social and economic conditions, adults often find themselves in a world for which their earlier socialization has not adequately equipped them. Many adults consequently find themselves in a meaningless world — even many who, by the superficial criterion of material possessions, are judged successful. Such adults need resocialization, but little has been done about this problem, even in affluent societies.

Even in old age, we are faced with learning new roles and skills in order to face the same old problems: where to live, what to do with one's time, how to pay the bills.

Socialization of the Aged

There was a time when people used to think that old age was a blessing: one had all the wisdom, all the necessary experience; one could just retire, relax, and enjoy. This, however, is not the way it is today, certainly not in modern Western societies where a great segment of the population comprises old, retired, at times physically incapacitated, and often virtually abandoned people. They are looked after, in some fashion, through the resources obtained from taxing decreasing numbers of young, working people. As Rosow (1967:291) put it, "Old age represents a devalued, unstructured role with sharp discon-

tinuities from middle age. Hence the individual enters the situation with little incentive, role specifications, or preparation. Effective socialization under these conditions is problematic and it is necessary to clarify both the conducive and inimical forces at work in the situation."

The problems of the aged are discussed in detail in Chapter 20. Suffice it to say here that the aged face the problems of learning new roles and of developing the skills to play them: where to live, whom to meet, how to move, what to do with one's time, how to pay the bills.

NONFAMILIAL AGENTS OF SOCIALIZATION

Although the primary agent of socialization is the family, the growing child soon finds itself in an environment outside the family that is much more complex. Nonfamilial agents, especially in modern Western societies, are many: the school, the mass media and religious, political, and other organizations.

The School

The school plays a crucial and varied role as a socializing agent. First of all, it provides a social context in which the child's personal dependence on parents and siblings is reconsidered by the child. Teachers and schoolmates widen the child's horizon beyond the family. Also, school standards, supposedly objective, orient the child to tasks and performance. For the first time, the child realizes that the affection bonds of the family are not the only relationships.

Apart from this delinking of the child from the family, the school ranks the child according to its class and ethnic affiliation. It is hardly surprising that children from poor families receive less education than those from rich families. In general, teachers have their own class-based prejudices, which they use, consciously or unconsciously, to train the children under their care. In addition, parents of lower-class children rarely get actively involved in the schooling of their children and in influencing the running of the schools where their children go. Under such circumstances, children are liable to grow up in two conflicting worlds — the world of the family and the world of the school. This conflict is particularly acute in the case of immigrant and native children. A Canadian study shows that in relation to other ethnic groups, the children of Asian immigrants appear more often in the lower academic stream (Lanphier, 1979).

The school plays an important role in political socialization as it draws attention to the working political system and inculcates children with political attitudes, conceptions, and beliefs. Although the family may be the first to teach loyalty to one's country, it is the school that elaborates and strengthens the content and the concepts related to that loyalty. The school is likely to attach greater importance to law and authority than to one's personal rights and to the ways of influencing the governments in getting things done (Hess and Torney, 1967).

Socialization in the school, according to the literature, is primarily conservative and traditionalist: it is preoccupied with the task of transmitting traditional skills and values, and it lags behind the rapid changes in the wider world. Critics have argued for alternative and radical orientations to promote creative ability. The demand that the school should generate attitudes and beliefs favorable to social change, and the counter-demand that it should reinforce the existing social order, force educational institutions to respond more slowly than other social institutions to the challenge of change. Whether or not schools succeed in responding to change depends on community pressure, for the community may often support the maintenance of the status quo. The functioning of the school as an agent of socialization therefore usually relates to the norms and values prevalent within the community, to family socialization experiences by the child, and to the community pressure on social institutions.

Television is a powerful—and questionable— source of socialization, whether for children or adults.

The school, it seems, reinforces the family-ascribed status of the child. In the United States, for instance, neighborhoods dominated by poor families get fewer educational resources, by far, than those dominated by higher income families (Sexton, 1961). In Britain, children are classified according to their family status: poor children are admitted into lower academic streams, irrespective of ability, whereas middle-class children of comparable ability are admitted into the upper streams (Eggleston, 1967). There is overwhelming evidence to indicate that this kind of discrimination results in stigma and a less positive image, which have far-reaching consequences for later development (Boocock, 1980).

The Mass Media

Television, radio, newspapers, magazines, and entertainment such as movies, constitute another powerful, nonfamilial source of socialization of children. Television is undoubtedly the most powerful among North American mass media, and its influence on children has been a controversial topic of debate.

TV sets are found in 99 percent of American and 98 percent of Canadian homes. Even as long ago as the 1950s, a San Francisco study found that 82 percent of the children in the sample had watched TV by their fifth year. Only 9 percent of those children had had newspapers read to them occasionally. In another U.S. study of 138 children, it was found that first-graders watched TV from twenty-two to twenty-four hours a week, sixth-graders about thirty hours, and tenth-graders about twenty-seven hours (Lyle and Hoffman, 1972). In Canada, pre-school children watch TV up to twenty hours a week, whereas children in both Canada and the United States between six and sixteen watch up to twenty-two hours. Studies also indicate that children from low-income families and poor black children watch TV more than well-to-do white children (Greenberg and Dervin, 1970). On this basis alone, it is reasonable to assume that television plays an important role in the socialization of North American children.

That the exact nature of the impact of television programs on children is inconclusive and controversial is partly so because neither the issues involved nor the evidence needed for their resolution are simple. For instance, the issue of parental concern is complex. Some parents intervene when the TV viewing interferes with the children's performance of domestic chores and schoolwork, and some believe that viewing has more advantages than disadvantages. Elkin and Handel (1984) find that parents think of television as something that reduces the burden of parental responsibilities, and on occasion enables children to acquire useful knowledge. Steiner (1963:95) summarizes the contradictions involved as follows:

... television helps to educate the child, but watching it interferes with his education. It keeps him busy and out of mischief, but it also keeps him too busy to do his chores. It keeps the kids in when you want them, which is good, except for some of the bad things they see. And it keeps them in when you don't want them, which is bad even if they see good things.

The kind of programs watched is another major issue discussed by Steiner. Educational programs, for instance, may contribute a great deal to socialization in the sense of encouraging children to develop socially useful skills and knowledge. Evidence (Stein, 1971) suggests that children exposed to prosocial programs develop a significantly higher level of acceptance, tolerance, and persistence than those habitually watching antisocial programs. An assessment of the impact of *Sesame Street*, a program created especially for preschool children, stresses its beneficial effect on children in cases where mothers and children discussed the program after viewing it.

Does the media violence make children violent? Is there a causal connection between violence and children learning to become violent? Two opposing views are currently disputed regarding the issue of violent content in many TV programs. The first view, based upon studies done in the United States until 1970, concluded that "there is every reason to believe that this mass medium is playing a significant role in generating and maintaining a high level of violence in American society including the nation's children and youth." (Bronfenbrenner, 1970.) A review of more than fifty studies, which tested more than 10 000 normal children and adolescents from different backgrounds, reached a similar conclusion: "The demonstrated teaching and instigating effects of aggressive television fare upon youth are of sufficient importance to warrant remedial action." (Leibert et al., 1973:157.)

The view that the media contribute to violence has been questioned on the basis that there is no reliable evidence supporting causal relationship between media violence and children's socialization. "Those in favor of this hypothesis tend to work on the basis of the belief that the sum of a series of inadequate experiments and surveys is 'truth' rather than in terms of the relevance and meaningfulness of this hotch-potch of research." (Howitt and Cumberbatch, 1975:334.)

Instead of focusing on the role of the media on children's socialization, Nobel (1975) suggests that it would be more fruitful to focus on what people do with media, rather than what media do to people. The shift is away from passive reception and toward active participation. Nobel suggests that children may gain relief from the pressures of daily life by watching TV, as well as acquiring role models. Violence constitutes only one aspect of the relation of TV programming and socialization.

Another nonfamilial agent of socialization is the community.

The Community

A notable example of community socialization is the Israeli kibbutz. The community's role in bringing up children right from birth has largely succeeded in transferring the loyalty of children from family to the community. Children are brought up in the community institutions as they move from infancy to adolescence: nurseries, communal dining rooms, and community schools constitute "home." Parents are allowed to see their children during feeding time in infancy, and in many kibbutzim, they may be allowed to have them on weekends. Thus, it is to the community that the child's emotions are directed, rather than to the family.

The Canadian Hutterite colony is comparable to the Israeli kibbutz. The Hutterite nuclear family enjoys far more independence than the family in the kibbutz, but it is still subordinate to the community. Until the age of three, children are cared for by family. With a child's entrance to the community school, socialization gradually shifts from the family to the community. All meals are eaten at school, including breakfast, and children are taught to respect their teachers and are introduced to their peer group — all of which result in their

identification with the community. This early socialization to Hutterite norms is essential to maintain the colony's system of communal ownership of property and of production and distribution of goods (Peter, 1979).

Religious Organizations

Churches, temples, and mosques also constitute a major source of socialization. There may have been a general decline in the role of religious institutions in North America, but some denominations still retain the function of socializing agent. Hutterite, Mennonite, and Jewish children in Canada, for example, learn to share and cherish the values of their distinctive religions. In the course of growing up, they participate in activities such as camping, sports, bazaars, and picnics, which serve to widen their social network. Religious teaching conveys to children the meaning of life and provides acceptable explanations about life crises such as illness, death, and aging (Crysdale, 1977).

Politics

By the time children reach the end of elementary school, they have usually developed some awareness of the authority structure beyond the neighborhood and family. It is possible that the child may even become attached to political figures and identify with them as role models.

A recent study of approximately 600 children in grades 4 through to 8 compared the strength of political socialization in Belleville, Ontario, with that in Watertown, New York (Landes, 1979). It was found that 17 percent of grade 4 children in Belleville and 18 percent in Watertown did not know what the word "government" meant. By the time the children reached grade 8, these percentages dropped to 7 and 3 respectively, and declined to 2 percent by grade 8 in the two cities. A high percentage of children (90 percent) in grade 5 knew about the workings of government, a concept that a greater number (98 percent) of junior-high school students understood. A larger proportion of Canadian pupils (37 percent), compared to American students (20 percent), rated their government "high" in terms of dependability. Canadian children's greater trust in their government and its role is particularly significant, despite the American government's increasing role in world politics.

The impact of political organizations on socialization has hardly been studied. But the fact remains that children, as they grow, tend to develop commitments to political leaders, organizations, and ideologies. Somehow, political socialization becomes part of the general process of socialization, probably both in a familial and nonfamilial context.

THEORETICAL PERSPECTIVES ON SOCIALIZATION

As the process that transforms human beings into social persons, socialization is a special field within the wider field of learning. This is so because, as remarked earlier, human beings (despite inherited biological limitations) must learn the specifics of role-playing; we are not born with this skill. Theoretical perspectives on socialization thus derive from learning theories. In what follows, we shall consider only those theoretical perspectives that have influences, significant investigations of all phases and types of human socialization. These perspectives are behavioral, psychoanalytical, and sociological (symbolic-interactionist).

The Behaviorist Perspective

Associated with the works of Pavlov (1849-1936) and Watson (1878-1958), the behavioral perspective studies human learning by experimenting with nonhuman animals, such as mokeys, cats, rats, and dogs. Two assumptions predominate: first, a great deal can be determined about human social learning by studying how nonhuman animals learn — specifically, when they have to learn to

modify their behavior; second, the data comes from observing actual behavior, no matter how complex. The implication of this second assumption is that there is no need to consider the impact of the mind on learning — which can never be directly studied — in order to understand how human beings learn anything, be it an elementary motor skill or a complex of social roles.

Three major concepts and many theories have resulted from this perspective: classical conditioning, operant conditioning, and conditioning through imitation. The mother concept for all three is conditioning.

Conditioning means the establishment of a connection between a stimulus and a response not naturally connected with the stimulus. Take the example of Pavlov's dog, an illustration of classical conditioning. When a bell was consistently rung before food was presented, Pavlov's dog became conditioned to salivate every time the bell was rung. There is no "natural" connection between a bell ringing and salivation, but the stimulus of a bell ringing, because of repeated association with food, became connected with the "unnatural" response of salivation. This kind of unnatural connection between stimulus and response constitutes conditioning.

Watson was among those who refused to think of human behavior as merely a variation of nonhuman behavior. Yet the fact of conditioning itself is undeniable in human behavior. The passionate response with which some human beings sacrifice their lives to defend their nation is very much a matter of conditioning, however complex the actual processes of conditioning may be in this case.

Operant conditioning, primarily associated with Skinner, is in many respects no different from classical conditioning. The fundamental difference is that in operant conditioning, the experimental subject — often a pigeon — is free to explore its environment and respond to its various aspects in whatever way it pleases. But — and this is the crux of operant conditioning—only some of the responses are rewarded. The experimenter decides which responses are to be rewarded and which to be punished or ignored. In classical conditioning, the experimenter controls only the stimulus, whereas in operant conditioning, the experimenter also controls the responses.

Both classical and operant conditioning imply controlled learning situations that are paralleled in everyday human social life. Many of our social attitudes, habits, and values are the products of classical conditioning. A child threatened by a red-haired person may learn to associate red-haired people with criminal behavior. A mother feeding an infant whenever it cried may condition it to associate eating and feeling good. Such an infant might become habituated to overeating.

Operant conditioning is clearly evident in what children learn in the family through reward and punishment. They are quick to learn that good behavior brings reward, and bad behavior, punishment. It is this reinforcing mechanism that elicits appropriate learning and is the basis for most human learning and behavior.

Conditioning through imitation is widespread in human social contexts. Both children and adults imitate models, be they film stars, boxers, saints, or baseball players. Here too, the reward/punishment mechanism is operative. If the wrong model is imitated, the imitator is punished; if the right model is imitated, the imitator is rewarded. Imitation is thus a form of conditioning through which, in a behavioral perspective, social learning—including socialization—takes place.

The most important fact to keep in mind about the behavioral perspective is that it focuses on the objective data of gross, observable behavior, without consideration of the impact on learning of anything as subjective as the mind. In contrast, the psychoanalytic perspective stresses that in order to unravel learning processes and patterns, including those related to socialization, it is necessary to go beyond the surface of the stimulus response.

The Psychoanalytical Perspective

The classical ideas of psychoanalysis come from the insights produced by the work of Freud (1856–1939), the great explorer of the human subconscious. Psychiatrist Freud developed his ideas over several decades as he tried to deal with a great variety of mental patients. His emphasis on the implications of sexuality in human relations has, until recently, been misunderstood, misinterpreted, and wildly rejected, especially by conservative thinkers. Despite Freud's central significance in the development of psychoanalysis, the controversy that his theories inspired led others to contribute to the field. Consequently, the psychoanalytical perspective on socialization is no longer just a matter of Freud's ideas alone.

Freud's ideas, together with others', are relevant to socialization because they cast light on the way human personality is formed and becomes deformed. Any attempt to understand how personality can become deformed requires first an investigation into how it is formed.

The psychoanalytical perspective, as distinguished from the behaviorist perspective, stresses especially the point that human behavior is never just a matter of conditioning people to certain stimuli so as to produce certain responses. Between the stimulus and the response, there is the complex inner world of emotions, thoughts, and instincts. Moreover, much of that world, whose foundations are established in childhood experiences, is "forgotten"—it becomes unconscious. That some experiences become unconscious does not mean that they lose their significance as regulators of future experience. What this means is that the discovery of this significance for personality formation, through the processes of socialization, becomes difficult. It also means that nothing about the inner processes can ever be known by those who follow exclusively the stimulus-response way of looking at human activities, as behaviorists do.

Social interaction gives meaning to who we are and what we do.

Sexuality is prominent in the psychoanalytical approach to personality formation, as well as socialization. But sexuality did not mean to Freud, nor does it mean to psychoanalyists today, simply copulation. Sex, in the psychoanalytic perspective, refers to the urge to form relations determined and elaborated by the awareness of male/female differences. Freud argued that at every stage of life, both male and female children are preoccupied with different parts of the body; in the oral stage (birth to one year), they are preoccupied with the mother; in the anal stage (one to three years), with the anus; and in the phallic stage (three to six years), with the genital organs. It is in the phallic stage that the child desires sexual association with the parent of the opposite sex. Freud introduced the concept of the Oedipus complex to describe the boy's sexual desire for his mother, and the Electra complex to describe the girl's desire for her father. The child's desire for the parent of the opposite sex is not, however, met because of its fear of that adult and because of the need for survival. The psychoanalytical perspective stresses the importance of sexuality in this particular sense. No doubt, different cultures perceive these differences differently. Nevertheless, a great deal of social role-learning — the central focus of the field of socialization — is concerned with how boys and girls, men and women, do relate, and according to the beliefs of the particular culture, how they should relate.

The Symbolic-Interactionist Perspective

The symbolic-interactionist perspective stresses the social, or the interactionary aspect of learning. This perspective is usually associated with George Herbert Mead, to whom you were introduced in Chapter 2. However, significant contributions have been made since Mead.

The symbolic-interactionist perspective does not reject either the behaviorist or the psychoanalytical perspective. Instead, it emphasizes that everything in the human context — role-learning, role-playing, and the rest of social learning — emerges, is consolidated, changed, protected, and given meaning through interaction. An individual, apart from being a reactor and a subjective actor, is an interactionist — that is, both an actor and a reactor. In general, social learning takes place as people interact; in particular, social roles are learned as people interact and give meaning to what we do.

These perspectives are not necessarily in conflict. Each draws attention to the extreme complexity of the issues involved in social learning and therefore in socialization. Moreover, as various paths of detailed investigation have, from time to time, been followed by different investigators, different emphases have been laid on the different ideas in each of these basic perspectives. Consequently, the perspectives should be considered as a multi-directional investigation of the complex problems, processes, patterns, and products of socialization.

One major problem of the investigation of the continuity of socialization throughout life has been the establishment of more or less stable phases in this continuity. The problem is important because systematic investigation of continuous processes is impossible until the continuity is somehow conceptualized as a succession of more or less stable phases. Many investigators have dealt with this problem and produced a variety of stage-development schemes.

THE STAGE-DEVELOPMENT THEORIES

To indicate some of the main features of development theories relevant to socialization processes, we shall focus on Freud, Erikson, Mead and Cooley, and Piaget.

Freud's Developmental Stages

In Freud's view, human development progresses through several stages from childhood onward. Both biological and social conditioning converge at all of these stages, and if things go wrong at a certain stage, the consequences will continue into the next stage, too. As mentioned, many aspects of human development are regulated by the awareness of sexual differences, and this awareness begins early in life. In retrospect, it seems that Freud overemphasized the significance of childhood experiences as the basis of later phases of personality development. Historically, however, the overemphasis was important because no significant attention had been paid to the relevance of childhood until Freud brought it into focus.

Freud identified five stages of human development: the oral stage (birth to one year); the anal stage (one to three years); the phallic stage (three to six years); the latency stage (six to adolescence); and the genital stage.

The first years of the child, which involve a great deal of sucking, relate specifically to oral gratification. What happens at this stage, as the child is trained, is crucial for later personality development. For example, if the child is either frustrated or overindulged at this stage, it may grow up to become an alcoholic, a work-compulsive, or a compulsive eater. At the anal stage, the child may have trouble with toilet training, a problem that could be damaging to later personality development. The child's preoccupation with sexuality, reflected in the joys and difficulties of elimination, may result in an "anal" personality: it may grow up to be stingy. At the phallic stage, the child discovers the pleasures of the sex organs. But this discovery takes place in a family context, with the result that the little boy in the family becomes attached to his mother and looks at his father as his sexual rival. The little girl becomes attached to her father and comes to consider her mother as her sexual rival.

While all this is going on, the child — male or female — comes to realize the pointlessness of sexual tensions: it cannot compete sexually with its parents on whom it is totally dependent. Gradually, what develops within the child is the superego — the socialized self. Comprised mainly of prohibitions, the superego controls the ego and is the centre of moral awareness. In the latency stage, the child loses interest in the opposite sex and identifies with members of the same sex. For the boy, the father becomes the role model, and for the daughter, it is the mother. The sexual bases of identification, prominent in the earlier phallic stage, do not disappear at this stage; they simply become latent. In the genital stage, they reappear again in the form of bonding, or of setting up relations. But they do so with all the experiences of the earlier stages accompanying them. By now the growing child has discovered a wider world of people — boys and girls, men and women — and the bonding ramifies.

In this scheme of development, Freud's point is that children can become "fixated" to the circumstances of any one particular stage; that is, they can, even if they look like adults, behave as if they were three-year-olds. Such people may never grow up.

Freud has been criticized for overemphasizing the relevance of childhood experience and sexuality in personality development. Yet despite the many criticisms, research has shown that childhood experiences and sexuality are crucial determinants throughout life.

Erikson's Development Framework

Erikson, initially influenced by Freud, expanded his ideas through his own comparative research.

Erikson (1963) developed an eight-stage scheme involving crises brought on by both physiological changes and relevant environmental circumstances. Each stage is characterized by a dilemma, and depending on certain circumstances, the outcome of each stage could go in one of two possible ways.

The dilemma of the first stage — the newborn — is trust versus distrust. The whole of social life, at all stages, is based on trust and is constantly challenged by distrust. The newborn child has to grapple with this fundamental fact of social life above all else. The nature of the relationship with the mother at this stage determines whether the child develops trust or distrust. As Elkin and Handel put it, "The first social achievement of the infant is his ability to let the mother out of sight without becoming anxious or enraged. This is possible when the mother has become an inner certainty as well as an outer predictability." (1984:63.) Distrust becomes the general orientation, if this does not take place.

The next stage, which occurs between the ages of eighteen months and three years, is characterized by the dilemma of autonomy versus doubt and shame. This stage of personality development depends on how the child handles and reacts to socialization practices such as toilet training. If, for example, this becomes routine, the child will experience confidence in accomplishing the task. This confidence leads to an urge for autonomy. If, however, the child has difficulties with toilet training, the experience may result in doubt and shame.

The third, fourth, and fifth years are characterized by the dilemma of initiative versus guilt. At this stage, with the rudimentary development of language skills, the child's world begins to become diversified and open to investigation. If the investigative urges are discouraged frequently, the child is liable to lose its sense of initiative and develop a sense of guilt.

The next stage — roughly between the ages of six and eleven — is the school age, in which the dilemma is between industry and inferiority. This stage is crucial in many ways, especially in giving the child the first opportunity to form bonds with people outside the family and to acquire some knowledge of society's occupational structure and technology. This stage is the first opportunity for boys and girls to try their competence at school, and through play, to achieve self-esteem among peers. If they are successful, they learn industry as opposed to inferiority.

The stage of adolescence, characterized by rapid physical growth (including puberty), is crucial in Erikson's scheme and is characterized by the dilemma of identity versus confusion. At this stage, the child confronts the problem of fitting his earlier experiences into the existence and activities of others in society. If this "fitting" effort is successful, adolescents develop a clear sense of identity or self; if it is not, they become confused in their self-conception and is their relations with others.

At the stage of young adulthood, the person (who has emerged from the adolescent struggles of identity formation in the sense noted above) has to face the dilemma of *intimacy* versus *isolation*. Such a young adult, depending on the cumulative experiences of the earlier stages, may be able to form intimate and enduring relations — erotic, friendly, and others — or experience isolation, that is, inability to form such relations.

The seventh stage in Erikson's scheme is characterized by the dilemma of *generativity* versus *stagnation*. This stage of mature adulthood may be devoted to generating children and looking after them. But generativity applies equally to any activity experienced as productive and continuously useful. This activity becomes dominant in the everyday life of the mature adult. If, however, generativity does not take place, a state of stagnation results.

The last stage, old age, also has its dilemma: *integrity* versus *despair*. If a person experiences a sense of meaningfulness and satisfaction in re-evaluating the life left behind, integrity colors the remaining years. If a sense of failure predominates, despair and meaninglessness result with dismal prospects for the remaining years.

It is important to point out that no individual passes through the life cycle in these neatly enunciated choices between dilemmas. Erikson's scheme is intended as a basic framework for investigating the variations in socialization as a continuous phenomenon.

The Cooley-Mead Developmental Stages

Cooley's ideas addressed the problems of identity or self-formation as the starting point in the transformation of human beings into social persons. Cooley's central concept was the "looking-glass self":

As we see our face, figure and dress in the glass, and are interested in them because they are ours, and pleased or otherwise with them according as they do or do not answer to what we should like them to be, so in imagination we perceive in another's mind some thought of our appearance, aims, deeds, characteristics, friends, and so on, and are variously affected by it.

(Cooley, 1962:1.)

The basic implication of this concept is that we are likely to become what we think significant others think we should become; our self — our identity — is thus a creation of the others we come to think of as significant.

George Herbert Mead developed Cooley's ideas and extended them into a personality-development scheme (1934). According to Mead, the self develops through three stages. The first stage is characterized by imitative acts. The child imitates gestures and noises in its environment that produce predictable responses from the people in the child's world, particularly from the mother. Through such "gesture conversations," the beginnings of role-play are established.

By its third year, the child engages in role-play, with the use of language skills. In this second stage, the child begins to discover a world beyond its immediate experience.

In the third stage, the child participates in organized games (for instance, hockey or baseball) and becomes aware that things are done according to patterns or rules and that they are done with reference not just to one or two persons, but to whole groups. The child learns to deal not just with its mother, but with others like its mother; not just with the father, but also with others like the father. The child's world has become more complex. It has learned, in however rudimentary a fashion, to look at the world as others might look at it and evaluate it. The child has also learned to internalize a number of the roles that affect it directly.

Central to the Cooley-Mead perpective are two important ideas shared by the behavioral school. First, primary groups provide the most significant setting for early socialization and have lasting consequences for later personality development. Second, the acquiring of a notion of self or identity comes through interaction with others. Self-hood is basically a social product and cannot be acquired in a social vacuum; society and the individual, therefore, are not separable. This view was not acceptable to Freud, who believed that the individual, driven by biological or internal impulses, is always in conflict with society.

Piaget's Developmental Perspective

The investigations of Piaget (1896–1980) into human learning have been extensive. We shall summarize only the main points. Piaget focuses on the cognitive — the intellectual aspects of human socialization. The emotional, the psychic, and all other aspects of personality development are, for research purposes, ignored.

Piaget sees four major developmental stages (1958):(1) the sensorimotor stage (birth to two years); (2) the pre-operational stage (two to seven years); (3) the concrete-operational stage (seven to eleven years); and (4) the formal-operational stage (twelve to fifteen years).

At the sensorimotor stage, the initial conceptions of space and time are learned. The pre-operational stage is dominated by play and imitation. Both processes, combined with the growing command of language, enable the child to strengthen its ego on the one hand, and on the other hand, to curb its ego by relating to others in his world. At the third stage of concrete operations, the child begins to think and adjust itself in terms of real objects and situations, even though it cannot yet distinguish between dreams and external objects. Self-evaluation at this stage, while taking into consideration the reactions of others, tends to focus on physical traits, such as weight, strength, and size. At the formal-operational stage, the growing child begins to grasp and use abstract concepts and general principles. Consequently, the growing child's world at this stage assumes the pattern of an organized whole, characterized by internal rules, roles, and functions. Also, it is at this stage that the child begins to acquire a moral sense in which the relevance of the judgements of others is recognized, thereby curbing the predominance of egocentricity in the earlier phases.

There are categories and subcategories in Piaget's scheme. The main point to remember is that Piaget is primarily concerned with the intellectual or cognitive stages of this development, and his conclusion is that this development takes place in stages, more or less fixed by age categories.

Piaget, like all other stage-development formulators, has been criticized on various grounds. Unlike Erikson, Piaget based his theory without much comparative evidence, without asking whether his age categories are applicable in all cultures, at all times. Nevertheless, Piaget's framework is a starting point for cross-cultural research.

SUMMARY

1. Socialization refers to the process by which people acquire the skills and motivations necessary

for their survival and effective functioning as members of their society. It begins at birth and continues throughout the life cycle. Learning at every stage of life influences one's self-evaluation.

2. Although investigators have been divided on the extent to which socialization is biologically determined and the extent to which it is a matter of learning, our present understanding is that both nature and nurture are necessary for the survival, stability, and continuity of society.

3. It is through socialization that children learn that life is based on sexual role differentiation. Cultures differ in these gender scripts, and their content is transmitted to children through mediation within and outside the family.

4. Socialization can occur only if three preconditions are satisfied. There must be (1) a society that provides a meaningful context; (2) the biological equipment necessary for learning; and (3) the presence of "human nature."

5. Sociologists have identified seven types of socialization that take place in the development of an individual: primary, secondary, and anticipatory socialization; resocialization; reverse socialization; oversocialization; and blocked socialization. Underlying this classification is the notion that socialization continues throughout life. As we move from one stage of life to the next, socialization patterns change according to the changing needs of each stage.

6. Socialization is carried out by a wide range of agents, beginning with some form of family. Nonfamilial agents include the school, the church, the peer group, the mass media, and various political and other organizations. At times, messages from some of these agents of socialization may conflict with those of parents. At other times, teachers, priests, and parents may all collaborate in reinforcing societal norms.

7. Several theoretical perspectives have been used from time to time to draw attention to the salient dynamics of socialization. Prominent among those currently used are: the behaviorist, the psychoanalytical, and the interactionist perspective. The crucial concept of the behaviorist perspective is conditioning; that of the interactionist perspective is internalization; and those of the psychoanalytical perspective are childhood experience, the unconscious, and sexuality. Though these perspectives often seem in conflict, they are equally important for an understanding of the dynamics of socialization from various angles and in various depths.

8. Since socialization is a continuous process from infancy to death, one major concern of some of the investigators of socialization has been to work out the phases in this continuous process. This chapter has outlined the theories of Freud, Erikson, Cooley and Mead, and Piaget.

GLOSSARY

Agents of socialization. Organizations and institutions through which culture (norms, values) is transmitted.

Anticipatory socialization. Socialization directed toward the preparation of future roles.

Conditioning. Learning through habit or training.

Ego. Refers to the conscious and rational part of the personality (Freud).

Expressive roles. Those roles that have to do with emotional fulfilment.

Id. The part of the personality that stems from biologically inherited drives, instinctual desires, and urges (Freud).

Instrumental roles. Those roles that have to do with goal attainment and task performance.

Life cycle. The various stages of growth from birth to death.

Primary groups. Small groups in which relationships are informal and intimate, and which are bound together by a sense of "we-ness."

Primary socialization. Socialization that takes place during the formative period of life.

Resocialization. The learning of new roles, norms, and values that are different from those of the past.

Reverse socialization. Socialization of the aged by the young.

Social Darwinism. The theory explaining the survival of societies in terms of an evolutionary scheme based on natural selection.

Socialization. A learning process that transforms biologically human organisms into human beings throughout the life cycle.

Subculture. A group whose members are guided by distinct norms, values, and beliefs; at the same time, members share the overall culture of the larger society.

Superego. The socialized self that internalizes the moral authority of society.

FURTHER READING

Bronfenbrenner, Urie. *Two Worlds of Childhood: U.S. and U.S.S.R.* New York: The Sage Foundation, 1970. This work deals with socialization practices in the U.S.A. and U.S.S.R., showing how the state and television have a major role in the socialization of children.

Clausen, John A. *Socialization and Society.* Boston: Little Brown and Company, 1968. This is a fine collection of eight papers written by specialists in the field. It covers a wide range of aspects of socialization. The chapters on social structure, socialization, and agents of socialization are of particular importance.

Elkin, Frederick and Gerald Handel. *The Child and Society.* New York: Random House, 4th edition, 1984. This study provides a sociological account of how children are socialized into modern society. It is written in a clear and lucid style.

Goslin, David A. *Handbook of Socialization.* Chicago: Rand McNally, 1969. A very useful reference book for students interested in socialization theory and research.

Gecas, Viktor. "The influence of social class on socialization." In *Contemporary Theories About the Family*, Volume 1, edited by Westley R. Buer et al. New York: Free Press, 1979: 365–404. This paper examines the relevance of class influence on child rearing and socialization, and provides an inventory of theoretical and empirical studies on the subject.

Ishwaran, K. (ed.). *Childhood and Adolescence in Canada.* Toronto: McGraw-Hill Ryerson, 1973. A collection of eighteen papers presenting a fairly comprehensive account of current research interests in child and adolescent socialization in Canada. It covers three major areas: socialization in the social context; means and models for child and adolescent socialization; and social structure and socialization.

Maier, Henry W. *Three Theories of Child Development.* New York: Harper & Row, 1969. A comprehensive account of the theories of Erikson, Piaget, and Sears. It explains their implications for current practice.

Whiting, Beatrice B. *Six Studies of Child Rearing.* New York: Wiley, 1963. A collection of six papers written by anthropologists on comparative child-rearing practices and personality development in small communities in Kenya, India, Okinawa, the Philippines, Mexico, and New England.

Crime, Deviance, and Social Control

DESMOND ELLIS

The characters played by Clint Eastwood in the movie *Dirty Harry* and Charles Bronson in *Death Wish* have real-life counterparts in Bernard Hugo Goetz and in 300 residents of a working-class district in Lima, Peru. On December 22, 1984, Goetz achieved instant notoriety as the subway vigilante, when he shot and wounded four teenagers who, he thought, were trying to rob him while he was riding the New York subway. Less well known are the 300 Peruvians who shouted "justice to thieves" as they beat and burned to death a seventeen-year-old boy who, they thought, was attempting to rob a house in their neighborhood.

The individuals referred to above have this in common: all took the law into their own hands because the criminal justice system was too slow and uncertain in its operation. In their view, criminals were taking over their respective cities and countries because the state was not doing a good job of protecting its citizens; therefore, citizens are justified in taking the law into their own hands.

Dr. Henry Morgentaler feels the same way about the inadequacy of the Canadian state in protecting the health and welfare of pregnant women who wish to have abortions. Since January, 1985, Dr. Morgentaler has carried out a number of abortions in his Toronto clinic — abortions that are defined by the government as illegal. Like Jesus Christ and Ghandi, Morgentaler justifies his illegal behavior on moral grounds. Doctors, he believes, ought to be allowed by law to provide

convict them of the offences for which they have been charged.

Taken together, these individuals help us avoid confusing the legal and moral realms. Their behavior and their supporters represent a challenge to the assumption of consensus with respect to the content of the criminal code and the procedures governing the operation of the justice system. More generally, the motives and behavior of these individuals, together with the societal reaction to them, raise the issue of social control.

DEFINING SOCIAL CONTROL, CRIME, AND DEVIANCE

Social control is a social process directed at the inhibition of behavior regarded as harmful or deviant by members of a social group. When the members go on to accuse, judge, and punish the person whom they have defined as deviant, informal social control is at work. Informal social-control agents include parents, peers, soccer coaches, neighbors, and public opinion, generally. Punishments or sanctions imposed by informal social-control agents include name-calling, gossip, ostracism, and ridicule. The kinds of behavior defined and judged as deviant, and/or punished, include telling lies, cheating at cards, extramarital sex, and marriage of a man to a much younger woman.

The state or government is not interested in controlling a great deal of behavior that members of various kinds of groups regard as unwanted or harmful. Thus, medical researchers are permitted to conduct experiments on animals, even though the Animal Liberation Front defines this as inhumane. Again, until recently, the Canadian government refused to make criminal the killing of baby seals, although the Greenpeace Foundation had defined this practice as inhumane. On the other hand, because of the pressure exerted by the Toronto-based group WAVE (Women Against Violence Everywhere) against "violent por-

Dr. Henry Morgentaler has defied the law in order to increase the availability of abortions to women desiring them. Although many consider his activities to be both deviant and criminal, juries have refused to convict him.

the requisite medical assistance to women who have made a difficult decision about their own bodies and about the health and welfare of both themselves and their unborn children.

The individuals referred to here see themselves as saviors, albeit of different kinds. All of them committed acts defined as criminal, but which significant segments of the population regarded as the necessary or proper thing to do. In the cases of Getz and Morgentaler, juries have refused to

nography," the federal government is considering doing something about it.

The first and necessary step in legally prohibiting an action is to define the behavior as criminal. When the state itself defines behavior as illegal and attempts to arrest, convict, and punish those who commit illegal acts, then formal social-control processes are at work.

Formal social-control agents include legislators, judges, policemen, prison guards, parole and probation workers, and crown attorneys. All of these professionally trained, bureaucratically organized agents work toward reducing crime by capturing and punishing criminals. The kinds of behavior punishable by law include murder, rape, robbery, burglary, and arson. The punishments imposed range from a small fine, to twenty-five years imprisonment, to death in some countries.

At this point, then, we can say that *formal* social-control processes are intentionally applied in a formal (written-rule) manner, with the objective of making society safer by reducing crime, whereas informal social-control processes are applied implicitly (unwritten-rule) with the aim of preserving the norms and values of a social group by reducing deviance. Where social groups define certain forms of deviance as particularly harmful or threatening to traditional values (e.g., abortion), they may convince the state to convert these forms of deviance into crimes. When this happens, formal processes are put to work, and state-imposed sanctions are added to informal sanctions.

Conversely, forms of behavior presently defined as criminal may not be regarded as criminal or deviant by most members of the public and/or influential segments of it. In such cases, formal and informal social-control processes are not supportive of each other. Prohibition in the United States during the late 1920s is a classic example of this kind of situation. Whenever "decriminalization" or "legalization" is talked about, the behavior referred to (e.g., soliciting for the purpose of profitable sex) falls into this category.

Having described some of the differences between informal and social-control processes, it would be useful to draw attention to their similarities. These, in the opinion of a number of sociologists of crime and deviance, are more important than the differences (e.g., Muncie and Fitzgerald, 1981). First, both formal and informal processes play a part in reducing crime. An obvious example is that most parents attempt to instil in their children a respect for rules, other people's property, and so on. Second, the elements that together make up the process of formal social-control also make up informal social-control processes. These elements include defining, accusing, judging, and sanctioning. Third, *ironies of social control* remain ever-present possibilities in both forms of social control. Ironies of social control refer to outcomes of social-control efforts that are unintended and opposite to those intended by social-control agents. An example of this may be a drug-control program that actually increases drug addiction.

Subjective Definitions

A subjective definition of deviance is one in which the meaning is central. In other words, we do not automatically react to behavior according to general rules; rather, we interpret and evaluate behavior in terms of the options available in the situation, the knowledge of options available to us, our ability to exercise these options, and so on.

According to Becker (1963:8–10), *deviance* is "not a quality of the act a person commits, but rather a consequence of the application by others, of rules and sanctions to an offender." A deviant is "a person to whom the label has been successfully applied." Individuals who are labelled deviant are different from each other in two respects: (1) in their personality and social situation; and (2) some deviants have broken a rule, others may not have. Given these differences, it does not make sense to search for common personalities or background factors among deviants, when the only

While most North American men believe that their wife or girl friend should not be offered as sex partners in exchange for goods or services, members of some motorcycle gangs have been known to offer their "mamas" in return for gasoline or alcohol.

thing they have in common is the label "deviant." In addition, it is unwise to assume that mere rule-breaking earns a person the label. Mistakes in labelling are common.

To the sociologist, a rule is another name for a norm. According to Becker, norms cannot be treated as given, fixed, shared, and obvious in their meaning, for at least two reasons. In many cases, if not most, there always exists an "exploitable ambiguity" between the norm and the behavior to which it refers; for example, what behavior does the legal norm (criminal law) "indecent assault on a female" prohibit? The average person might give this answer: a man uses force (or threatens to) in the process of touching or fondling those parts of a woman's body thought to be sexually arousing. The legal norm certainly prohibits this behavior, but it also covers the behavior of an old

man who gently touches the knee of a seven-year-old girl.

Moreover, the norms of some groups may be different from and/or in conflict with the norms of other groups and with those shared by many members of the society as a whole. For example, whereas many men in Canada and the United States believe that men should not offer their wife or girl friend as sex partners in exchange for goods or services, members of the Hell's Angels feel it is proper to offer their "mamas" in exchange for gasoline or alcohol (Thompson, 1966:27).

Objective Definitions

An objective definition is one in which rules or norms are taken as given, as written down or agreed upon by everyone. A deviant is simply an individual who breaks such a rule. According to Hagan (1977:13), deviance consists of "variations from a social norm," and not all variations are equally serious. Viewed as a "continuous variable," various kinds of deviance can be located at different points on a continuum of seriousness. By seriousness, Hagan means serious punishment such as fines and imprisonment are administered.

Location on this continuum is objectively determined. Hagan constructs an index that can be used for this purpose. The index consists of (1) perception of harm; (2) agreement about the norm; and (3) severity of punishment for infractions. The application of this index to various forms of deviance yields the following general conclusion: the more serious the act of deviance, (a) the greater the perceived harm resulting from this act; (b) the more widespread is agreement among members of society concerning the harmfulness of the act; and (c) the more severe is the punishment made contingent upon the act.

Hagan (1977:14) identifies three types of deviation: crimes, social deviations, and social diversions. Crimes are of two types: *predatory behavior*, such as rape, robbery, kidnapping, and premeditated murder are consensus crimes, because most Canadians have regarded these as crimes since

Confederation. *Conflict crimes* are characterized by normative disagreement: people are divided as to whether abortion, prostitution, gambling, marijuana use, and pornography should be called crimes and therefore liable to punishment by the state.

Non-criminal deviations fall into two sub-groupings: social deviations and social diversions. In the former group, Hagan locates delinquency and mental illness. Nudism and homosexuality are classified as social diversions. The major differentiating factor behind these forms of deviance is the scores they receive when Hagan's index is applied to them.

One important fact to keep in mind about objective versus subjective conceptions of deviance is that research produces variable amounts and types of criminal and noncriminal deviance when these conceptions are used in different societies or in the same society at different points in time. To a cross-cultural examination of crime and deviance we turn next.

CRIME AND DEVIANCE IN DIFFERENT SOCIETIES

According to anthropologist Edgerton (1973), eight categories of "troublesome behavior" or "deviance" are found in most societies: stealing, not sharing, suicide, violence, sexual deviance, conflict between generations, alcohol and narcotics use, mental retardation, and mental illness. Although these categories are universal, attitudes toward them and the ways in which they are viewed as being deviant do differ markedly in different societies. For example, among the Bena Bena of New Guinea, the Tikopia of the Solomon Islands, and the Mohave Indians of southwestern United States, attitudes toward suicide vary from "natural" to "mild regret" to high deviant, respectively.

The conditions under which, and the way in which, a suicide is carried out also influence the labelling of deviance cross-culturally. The Tiko-

pians do not regard as deviant the suicide of a man who swims out to sea to drown because his wife has left him. Should, however, a Tikopian man kill himself by sitting on a long, sharp spike because "he broke wind in a public gathering," his behavior would be deviant. What is true for suicide is also true for each of the universal categories identified by Edgerton.

In industrialized societies such as the United States, Canada, and Britain, Edgerton's general categories of "troublesome behavior" have been subjected to classification by legislators and other agents of their criminal justice systems. In all three countries, a distinction is made between serious and less serious offences; the former are called "felonies" and the latter "misdemeanors" in the United States. In Britain and Canada, the corresponding terms are "indictable" and "non-indictable" offences, respectively.

In the United States and Canada, the serious offence group is classified further into violent crime and property crime. Violent crime usually includes murder, rape, robbery, wounding, or serious assaults. Burglary, larceny, and car theft are classified as serious property crimes. Narcotics offences constitute a separate category. These offences are classified as serious or not serious, depending on their nature. Thus, selling hard drugs such as cocaine is an indictable offence, whereas smoking marijuana is a non-indictable offence.

In addition to violent and property offences, the less-serious offence group also includes a number of "victimless crimes" or morals offences, such as gambling, prostitution, and publishing/distributing obscene materials. Because of disagreement among citizens concerning the criminality of victimless crimes, morals offences and the enforcement of relevant laws often give rise to overt forms of legal and social conflict.

Americans and Canadians who engage in crime fall into two major groupings: "career" and "occasional" offenders, according to sociologists Clinard and Meier (1975). In their classification, non-career offenders tend to commit such violent offences as murder, assault or rape, and property offences such as stealing cars, vandalism, amateur shoplifting, or forgery. Career criminals tend to be professional pickpockets, shoplifters, bank robbers, or confidence men. Between these extremes are business corporations, business executives (white-collar criminals), and youth gangs.

Statistics on criminals and criminal offences are produced in different ways in different parts of the same country, as well in different countries. More specifically, criminal statistics involve citizens, legislators, policemen, lawyers, and judges. Variations in the behavior of any one or more of these participants will yield variations in the number and types of crime. For this reason, it is difficult to make valid cross-cultural comparisons based on official crime statistics. Therefore, in reading the tables presented here, we should consider the data as measures of crime resulting from law enforcement.

Female Crime

In almost all societies that produce crime statistics, the male rate of crime is higher than the female rate (Johnson, 1983). Moveover, the female rate is alleged to be increasing, worldwide. In an attempt to test this assertion, a survey of female crime was undertaken in over fifty societies (Wilson, 1983). One of the major findings is that there was no consistent worldwide increase in female participation in crime: the rate increased in Canada, United States, England, Wales, Germany, France, Australia, and New Zealand, but it decreased in Austria, Denmark, Ireland, Scotland, and the West Indies, and it remained stable in Barbados, Egypt, Netherlands, Pakistan, and Tunisia.

Violent and Property Crimes

In interpreting crime statistics, especially those from different countries, it should be kept in mind that statistics, because of differences in legal definitions, methods of calculation, and police processing, must be treated with caution. An example may better illustrate this point. The offences used in calculating the U.S. rate, shown in Table 7-1 , are only index offences, and are considered more serious than non-index offences. The exclusion of non-index offences from the U.S. rate and their inclusion in the rates of the other countries listed explains why the U.S. rate is so low.

Most violent and property crimes are committed by men. Since most agents of a society's criminal justice system are also men, most crimes are also officially processed by men. We refer to these jointly as crime producers: the police and those who commit crimes. As Table 7-1 shows, crime producers are most active in the United States,

TABLE 7-1. Selected Offences for Selected Countries per 100 000 Inhabitants, 1980

Country	OFFENCE						
	Homicide	Robbery	Burglary	Rape	Car theft	All Offences*	Percent Violent**
Australia	3.1	56.6	1268.3	7.7	399.2	8055.0	2.7
Canada	6.0	103.7	1497.1	14.1	436.7	11 534.6	4.8
England/Wales	1.6	30.5	1264.4	2.5	658.7	5459.0	4.2
France	3.9	65.8	512.0	3.5	398.8	4903.1	2.7
Japan	1.4	1.9	248.3	2.2	27.6	1293.6	2.2
United States	10.0	244.0	1669.0	36.0	495.0	5900.0†	9.8

*Includes homicide, sex offences, rape, serious assault, theft, aggravated theft, robbery, breaking and entering, car theft, other thefts, fraud, currency offences, and drug offences.

†Includes index offences only: criminal homicide, forcible rape, robbery, aggravated assault, burglary, larceny, motor vehicle theft, and arson.

**Includes homicide, rape, serious assault, and robbery.

SOURCE: *International Crime Statistics*, (Paris, 1979–80). The offences referred to are those known to the police.

because the U.S. rate for all the offences included in Table 7-1 is over three times greater than its index crime rate. The F.B.I.'s Uniform Crime Reports shows that the rate for all offences in 1980 is 18 306 per 100 000 inhabitants. Crime producers in Canada are the second most active group. Japan's crime producers, with a rate of only 1294, at least active.

Table 7-1 shows that North American crime producers produce more reported homicides, burglaries, robberies, and rapes than do either European or Japanese crime producers. More specifically, the average North American rate for these four offences is twice as great as the European rate. The average reported rate of rape offences for Canada and the United States is eight times greater than that for France and England combined. The average rate for the two North American and the two European countries combined is almost ten times greater than the reported rate for Japan. The average rate of car thefts for England/Wales and France is over one-and-a-half times greater than that for Canada and the United States. In all the countries listed, violent offences constitute a relatively small proportion of all offences. Crime producers in each of these countries produce far more economically motivated offences (burglary and robbery) than any other kind of offence.

These figures tell us nothing, however, about the individuals who committed crimes and their victims. An examination of some types of criminals follows.

Murder: Suspect-Victim Relationship

Being a stranger to a potential murderer seems to confer some degree of protection against being murdered (Table 7-2). For all countries included in this table, strangers account for less than 20 percent of all homicide victims.

Being acquainted with a potential murderer seems to be as risky as knowing one very well. This is true for Canada and England/Wales. U.S. statistics indicate that strangers and family members are less likely to be murdered than are acquaintances. Within the category of domestic murders, most of the victims are wives or female cohabitants: for England/Wales, they totalled 53 percent; for the United States, 32 percent; and for Canada, statistics for the years 1961–1981 reveal that almost 70 percent involved husbands and wives as both suspect and victim, of which 75 percent were wives.

From these statistics, we can conclude that wives in Canada are far more likely to be murdered by the men they live with than are wives in England/Wales and the United States. One possible reason for the low U.S. figure may be that the statistics refer only to wives, whereas the figures for the other countries include both wives and cohabitants.

Rape: Victim-Suspect Relationship

In the United States, it was found that 33 percent of the women who reported to the police were raped by men they did not know, compared to 49 percent who reported being raped by dates or

TABLE 7-2. Homicides by Victim-Suspect Relationship, 1982

Country	HOMICIDES			
	*Total	**Domestic	***Acquaintance	Stranger
Canada	609	31.0	30.4	28.1
England/Wales	576	38.0	34.0	19.0
United States	19 308	18.7	38.3	15.0

*The non-percentages do not total 100 because the "relationship unknown" percentage has not been included in the table.
**Domestic homicide victims include sons, daughters, parents, spouses, cohabitants, and other family members.
***Acquaintances include lovers, friends, business associates, and neighbors.
SOURCES: Statistics Canada; England and Wales, Criminal Statistics, Table 4.4; U.S. Uniform Crime Reports.

acquaintances (Medea and Thompson, 1974). The kind of city a woman lives in also seems to have an important bearing on whom she is raped by. In a friendly, sexually permissive city such as Los Angeles, 44 percent reported being raped by acquaintances. In the more conservative, less sexually permissive city of Boston, the corresponding figure was a mere 9 percent (Chappell et al., 1978). It is also relevant that in both cities, the majority of rapes reported had been executed by strangers.

In Canada, a study conducted by Clarke and Lewis (1977) revealed that young, unmarried, English-speaking, Canadian-born, lower-class women were the predominant victims, and their rapists tended to be older, physically unattractive, Canadian-born, lower-class males.

Compared to Canadian rape suspects, American males arrested for rape are younger and less likely to be white: the Uniform Crime Reports showed that 52 percent were under twenty-five years of age and 63 percent were black or Hispanic.

Car Theft: Age as a Correlate

Cars are valuable pieces of property and they are not difficult to steal. It is this combination that makes car theft a relatively frequent occurrence. In Canada and the United States, approximately one in every 140 to 150 registered vehicles is stolen — usually by young males. The F.B.I's Uniform Crime Reports for 1982 indicate that almost 60 percent of the persons arrested for car theft were under twenty-one years of age, and a disproportionate number are blacks or Hispanics living in cities. (Since the characteristics of car thieves are not included in Canada's statistics, relevant comparisons cannot be made.)

Statistics suggest that inequality is implicated in car theft: those who do not own cars (the young) usually steal cars from those who do — that is, white adults. What is true for the United States may well be true for each of the countries listed in Table 7-1. We shall return to inequality and the role it plays in the occurrence of serious offences.

Serious Crimes: Reported versus Not Reported

The Canadian Urban Victimization Survey (1982) was undertaken, in part, to correct the inaccuracy in the incidence and distribution of crime as reported in official (police) statistics. Just how inaccurate police statistics are in Canada may be gauged from the fact that of the 700 000 personal victimization experiences reported to interviewers, over 58 percent were not reported to the police.

As Table 7-3 indicates, three of the four serious offences included in Table 7-2 occur much more frequently than police statistics suggest. For all three countries, the proportion of unreported rapes is 69 percent. The corresponding figures for robbery and burglary are 60 percent and 43 percent, respectively. By contrast, almost all the car thefts that occur in the United States and

TABLE 7-3. **Percentage of Unreported Occurrences of Selected Types of Serious Crime**

	OFFENCE			
Country	Rape (Percent)	Robbery (Percent)	Burglary (Percent)	Car Theft (Percent)
Canada	62	55	36	30
England/Wales	74	89	52	0
United States	72	35	42	5

SOURCES: Canadian Urban Victimization Survey, Bulletin No. 1, 1983 (the figures presented are for the major Canadian cities and not for Canada as a whole); Criminal Statistics, England and Wales, 1982, Table 2A; National Opinion Research Center Survey, University of Michigan, 1966.

England/Wales are reported to the police. One reason for this is that insurance policies require that the theft be reported to the police. (The same requirement applies in Canada, and yet 30 percent of car thefts go unreported.)

Table 7-3 reveals that England/Wales tend to have the highest proportion of unreported offences, car theft excepted. The average percentage of unreported rapes, robberies, and burglaries is 72 percent. The corresponding figure for Canada is 51 percent and for the United States, 50 percent.

Taken together, the findings presented in Tables 7-1 and 7-3 indicate that societies vary, not only in the amount of crime produced by police statistics, but also in the number of homicides, rapes, burglaries, robberies, and car thefts reported by victims. In an attempt to explain these variations, sociologists have formulated a number of hypotheses. One of the more interesting and important alleges that the amount of crime a society experiences is related to the degree of inequality in that society.

Wife-abuse tends to occur most often among those groups that experience social, economic, and sexual inequalities.

Inequality and Crime

A study of homicide was conducted by John and Valerie Braithwaite (1980) in thirty-one different societies. For each country, they computed an average rate based on the rate of homicide for each of sixteen years. (Their measure of homicide, then, was reliable.) Then they obtained from each country a number of measures of income inequality and analyzed the relation between income inequality and homicide.

One of their major findings was that the greater the income inequality, the higher the rate of homicide. More specifically, societies with the highest homicide rates are those that have a relatively small proportion of wealthy individuals and a large number of poor people living in conditions of hunger. They concluded that inequality creates conditions that predispose people to violence, in general, and homicide, in particular.

Turning next to an examination of crime rates in general, we discover that the lower classes are disproportionately involved in all four of the serious crimes presented in Table 7-1. The findings reported for American males and females (Elliott and Huizinga, 1983) and for British males and females (Ouston, 1984) confirm that inequality and crime go hand in hand: as the former increases, so will the latter.

Finally, an examination of robbery, vandalism, and violence reveals the workings of gerontocracy and patriarchy, respectively. Gerontocracy refers to the rule of youth by adults, patriarchy to the domination of women by men. Inequality is one outcome of both types of rule.

While many adults may consider graffiti on school walls simply another form of vandalism, others have suggested that it is a young person's way of "equalizing" some basic social inequalities.

The domination of women by men occurs mainly in the home. This is where wife-abuse occurs most often; husbands deliver more frequent and more serious beatings to their wives than vice versa. As indicated elsewhere (Ellis, 1984), wife-abuse tends to occur more frequently in lower- and working-class homes than in middle- and upper-class homes. In other words, violence against wives occurs most frequently in social groupings experiencing a double form of inequality — class inequality based on income and wealth differential and inequality based on the greater physical strength of men and female dependence on men. These same conditions also

apply to the occurrence of rape (Clarke and Lewis, 1977) and pornography (Dworkin, 1980).

With respect to deviance and crime among youth, there are ways in which the domination of youth by adults becomes associated with various forms of criminal and deviant activity. Graffiti on school walls may be considered by adults as just another form of vandalism. From the perspective of adolescents, however, it is, as Norman Mailer has noted, a way of "putting our mark on theirs."

These considerations suggest that inequality should be part of any general sociological theory that aims to explain crime and deviance. To these theories we now turn.

THEORETICAL PERSPECTIVES

Theories that attempt to explain crime and deviance fall into one of three functionalist schools: functionalist theory, conflict theory, or symbolic-interactionist.

As you read in previous chapters, functional theory assumes that most people in society share certain basic values and norms, and that this value consensus helps keep society stable and orderly. Functional theorists study the consequences for society of such regularly recurring activities as prostitution and gambling, or ever-present groups such as the family. Durkheim, for example, maintained that crime is normal, and its punishment is reinforced by the "conform-with-the-law" values that most people share. Crime, in other words, contributes to social order.

Durkheim also believed that individuals in a society could accept and believe in norms that were not really appropriate to, or in accordance with, the conditions in which they found themselves. Examples are a rich businessman who suddenly goes bankrupt and a poor person who wins a large amount of money in a lottery. When this happens, individuals find themselves in a psychological state Durkheim called anomie. Anomie or strain is a major cause of one kind of deviant death, namely, suicide.

In contrast, conflict theorists assume not consensus but dissensus. They usually study the causes and consequences of conflict in societies characterized by inequality. The influence of Marx on students of deviance has been more direct. Central to the work of these scholars is the view that one has to understand the dynamics of class conflict in order to understand crime and delinquency. That is, the conflict central to their analyses is the conflict between those who own and/or manage the instruments of production — the bourgeoisie — and those who do not — the proletariat. According to Taylor et al. (1973), the ways in which ruling groups react to crime vary according to their class interests in preserving a capitalist form of enterprise.

Mead, the father of symbolic-interaction theory, believed that we become what we are labelled, and that meanings attached to various ways of behaving, dressing, moving are central to any analysis of the outcomes of social interaction.

Although they differ from one another, functional, interactionist, and conflict theorists also have something in common. All share the assumption that social interaction, including its criminal and deviant forms, is learned. In other words, nurture rather than nature is the major determinant in crime and deviance. With nature as a common starting point, Figure 7-1 depicts the way in which the theories covered in this chapter may be classified.

We shall discuss each of the subcategories of the major schools in turn.

Subcultural Theory

A *subculture* is a set of values and norms that are different from those characterizing the culture of the whole society. Associated with subcultural values and norms are different ways of speaking, behaving, and/or dressing. A good example of a subculture in our society is the Hell's Angels, a motorcycle gang with affiliate branches all over North America (Thompson, 1966).

A subcultural theory of crime and delinquency attempts to explain why certain class, ethnic, age, or other social groupings produce more criminals and delinquents than others. Explanation takes the form of showing that criminal and/or delinquent behavior is one way in which members of these groups attempt to solve problems created for them by the wider society. Criminal and delinquent solutions are created, taught, and learned within these groupings.

Subcultural theorists, such as Cloward and Ohlin (1960) and Cohen (1955), defining certain subcultural ways of behaving as criminal or delinquent are shared by most members of society. In other words, most of us agree that much of the behavior, the mode of dress, and the manner of speech of members of the Hell's Angels is deviant or criminal. Secondly, these theorists also assume that the most useful sociological explanation of

FIGURE 7-1. Classification of Crime and Deviance Theories

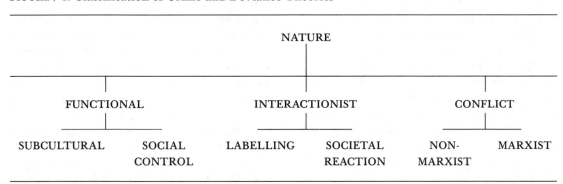

crime and delinquency is one that actually describes the process whereby members of different social groupings create criminal and delinquent subcultures, and how individuals learn to become members of such groups. Subcultures are usually created because they meet certain shared needs of members of a social group. Subcultural theorists believe that it is important to discover not only the meaning that crime and delinquency has for members, but also the motives for joining, staying in, and/or leaving delinquent and/or criminal subcultures. All of these assumptions are made by Albert Cohen, a major subcultural theorist.

Cohen's Delinquent Subcultural Theory

Cohen's theory (1955) focuses on the origin of delinquent subcultures and the interrelations between social class, status frustration, reaction formation, and delinquent subculture. We shall consider each in turn.

Social class refers to a large group that shares a similar level of education and income, values, and life style. Such groups are ranked higher/lower in terms of the status, power, and educational/occupational opportunities available to their members. Cohen's theory is based on working-class boys. The parents of these boys do their best to help motivate their children to do well in school. Compared with the parents of middle-class children, however, they may not be as highly motivated to do this, having other, perhaps more immediate and pressing economic problems to attend to, and a number of children to consider. Also, their own low level of education and income inhibit their ability to assist their children with any academic problems they may experience and to pay for educational aids that may help their children do better in school. In sum, working-class children come to school suffering from both motivational and knowledge deficits. More generally, they have learned to dress and behave in ways that may not be appropriate in a school where

middle-class teachers attempt to instil middle-class ways of dressing and behaving.

A quote from Victor Malarek's autobiographical account of "a street kid who made it" aptly illustrates this point (1984:104–05).

Sitting at my desk, I began to discover that I was different from the rest of the kids … I stuck out like a sore thumb.… I certainly dressed differently, with scuffed Oxford shoes, wrinkled grey pants … and a white starched shirt with a laundry number bleeding through the back collar. The boys in my new class, the sons of stockbrokers, lawyers, doctors, and wealthy businessmen, wore the latest fashions.…

I learned where I stood in the social pecking order from that day on. I was to be the butt of cruel jokes and cold snubs.…

The teachers got into the act as well.… My marks took a nose-dive.…

This quote also shows that if a working-class boy has been taught the value of educational achievement and if he learns that he cannot successfully compete with middle-class boys, his ambition is frustrated. He wants high grades and the status that high grades confer on him in the eyes of teachers; however, his class-related deficits prevent this from happening. He does not do as well in school as middle-class children. His own quest for status is frustrated.

According to Cohen, working-class children experiencing status frustration react by turning the values held by teachers upside down. They reject their rejectors by doing the opposite of what teaching representatives of the middle-class desire. When teachers demand promptness, they arrive late to class. When teachers emphasize respect for other people's property, they engage in vandalism. *Reaction formation* is a psychoanalytic concept that refers to the rejection of values, norms, and ways of behaving formerly believed in.

Working-class children who experience status frustration gradually come to interact more with

Perceived inequality in treatment by teachers and peers may frustrate the working-class student in his need for status.

other school failures. This group faces the same problem: frustration of their quest for status in the eyes of teachers because of poor grades. During the course of going around with each other, the members of such a group share their problems and try out various solutions, one of which is delinquent behavior. It solves the problem of status frustration by providing an opportunity for a member to gain status within the delinquent group by doing things valued in their subculture. Thus, the boy who is best at "hot-wiring" a car in order to steal it and go joyriding not only derives enjoyment in driving a car he does not own, but also earns prestige from the group for his demonstrated prowess or ability.

Applied to a society's statistics on juvenile car theft, Cohen's theory predicts that the street and the school are associated with each other in the following way: juveniles who are most likely to engage in car theft are those who are failing or who have failed in school. Since working-class boys are more likely to fail than middle-class boys, they are more likely to become car thieves. The best car thieves achieve status within their own subculture and this helps solve the strain associated with status frustration in school.

Cohen's work was influenced by Merton's theory (1938), and Cohen, in turn, influenced the work of Cloward and Ohlin (1960). Merton had assumed that those individuals who were brought up (socialized) to want to achieve the rewards society has to offer — for example, wealth — but who were denied the opportunity to achieve such rewards in legitimate ways would experience strain or anomie. Anomie, in turn, leads to deviance. Cloward and Ohlin maintained that in addition to being denied access to legitimate opportunities, the individual who becomes deviant must also have access to illigitimate opportunities or be denied access to them. Crime and deviance, then, occur as a result of differential access to *both* legitimate and illegitimate opportunities and not just the former, as Merton had maintained.

Cloward and Ohlin also extended and redirected the work of Cohen. First, they shifted the focus of attention from the school to the street and workplace. In these locations, Cohen's delinquent boys would discover few job opportunities available to them. Secondly, they differentiated between the kinds of delinquent subcultures. Depending on the opportunities that are available, individuals become members of gang-fighting, drug-oriented, or other criminal subcultures, including those specializing in car theft.

More recent formulations of subcultural theory are structural-Marxist in orientation. The delinquency of working-class juveniles is an outcome of cultural and class conflict. Delinquency is viewed as a way of adapting to or resisting constraints imposed by those who possess most of society's resources. Thus, vandalism is not a random, thoughtless act, but a way in which lower-class adolescents fight back against the middle-class adults who dominate their lives.

Another perspective of the functional school is social control.

Social-Control Theory

Social-control theories of delinquency and deviance focus on the occurrence of delinquency in terms of the strength or weakness of the individual's bond to society. People who are strongly bound to conventional society are more likely to control their deviant inclinations than those who are ambivalent toward society. *Delinquents*, then, are individuals whose deviant inclinations are least regulated because their ties to society are relatively weak.

Social-control theorists assume that (1) that human beings are preoccupied with the satisfaction of their own wants, using any means rather than legitimate means; (2) most people share norms defining certain forms of behavior as legitimate and others as illegitimate; (3) decisions as to which means to use in satisfying wants (e.g., asking, giving, exchanging, stealing, threatening, hitting), are made on the basis of rational calculation of contingent benefits and burdens; (4) theorists take as given illegitimate means (deviance) and the selection of legitimate means (conformity) to be explained; (5) a theory that explains conformity will also explain deviance; and (6) the identification of motives for deviance is irrelevant.

Hirschi's Social-Control (Bond) Theory

According to Travis Hirschi (1969), an individual's bond to society consists of four elements: attachments, investments, involvements, and beliefs. We shall consider each in turn.

Attachments refer to bonds between persons. The more we are attached to others as friends, lovers, fellow human beings, the more we tend to take their feelings, wishes, and expectations into account in deciding how to behave. The more attached we are to conventional members of society, the more likely we are to conform to rules they share and support. The loner, the person with few attachments to others, is less likely to respect norms important to others.

However, loners may remain largely conformist because of what they may lose if they are discovered behaving in illegitimate ways. Let us suppose that one of the reasons why people become loners is that they spend all their time in the quest for profit. All or much of their acquisitions and all the time and effort invested in getting ahead might be jeopardized if they engaged in deviant acts and are discovered doing so. Much of what they acquire (reputations, a wife, children, a job, a house) constitutes an investment in society. This investment, in turn, represents a stake in conformity, and the greater the stake, the more likelihood of conformist behavior.

Involvement in society is reflected in the amount of time we spend doing conventional things. Thus, those persons who become loners because they spend all their time working are doubly controlled. Being successful, they have acquired a great stake in conformity; being so busy, they do not have the time to become involved in leisure activities, let alone engaging in deviant ones.

The fourth variable is beliefs. Most people share certain values (e.g., personal security) and believe that rules supporting these values ought to be obeyed. Because they hold to these beliefs, they tend to remain conformists. At the same time, not everyone's belief in the moral "rightness" of societal values is equally strong. Those who believe less strongly feel less obliged to conform to societal rules. This remains true even though they accept, to some degree, the moral validity of the rules they break.

When Hirschi's model is applied to the problem of explaining variations in juvenile car theft, we can expect the following findings: (1) regardless of how happy their home life is, juveniles (meaning young people) who are closely supervised by their parents are less likely to be car thieves; (2) regardless of how well they are doing in school, juveniles who are strongly attached to their teachers will be less likely to engage in car theft; (3) juveniles with a low stake in conformity are more likely to be car thieves and to hang around with juvenile delinquents.

Moving now to the symbolic-interactionist school of theories of deviance, we shall consider labelling and societal-reaction together.

Labelling and Societal-Reaction Theory

A symbolic-interactionist theory of crime and deviance views labelling someone "criminal" or "deviant" as an outcome of the interaction between those who define, accuse, judge, and punish, and those who are subjected to these actions. Although such a label may have *material* consequences for those accused, such as the loss of employment, the communication that occurs is *symbolic*. *Labelling* is a verbal accusation that socially, morally and/or legally differentiates the worthy from the unworthy, the good from the bad. When sociologists study such symbolic interaction, they make the following assumptions: that one can learn more about crime and deviance by focusing on the *meanings* that "criminal" and "deviant" have for rule-makers and rule-breakers than by inquiring into the reasons or motives for rule-breaking. They also assume that it is most useful to attempt to explain, not a single or occasional act of deviance, but why individuals continue to behave in criminal and/or deviant ways. Lastly, they assume that social control is not simply a reaction to rule-breaking but a major cause of deviant and criminal careers.

Symbolic-interactionists who study deviance are either labelling or societal-reaction theorists. Labelling theorists tend to focus on how different meanings or labels are constructed and more or less successfully applied in small-scale settings such as families, bars, friendship cliques, and so on. Informal socialization and social control are the bases for their research.

Contemporary societal-reaction theorists have been influenced by Frank Tannenbaum who, in contrast to traditional theorists, conceived of societal reaction to deviant behavior as a "dramatization of evil," which actually increases the frequency of the behavior it is intended to regulate (1938). The focus on the reactions of formal social-control agents such as the police, courts, and schools, as well as the emphasis on social control and the material consequences of this process, covers such differences as exist between the two groups of interactionist theorists. These differences, it should be emphasized, are not always apparent in concrete examples of theory and research. In this connection, consider Edwin Schur's labelling approach to female crime and deviance.

Schur's Labelling Theory

In his book on women and deviance (1984), Schur deals with stigma, social power, and social control. He attempts to link the ordinary, everyday name-calling and devaluation of women that occurs in bars, the workplace, and the home with the devaluation of women in the mass media and the treatment of women under the law. For example, the reaction of the legal system to wife abuse is central to understanding why a husband who has occasionally beaten his wife becomes a "career" wife-beater.

One major implication of Schur's analysis is that as the labels or social definitions applied to women change, or become similar to those applied to men, the difference between the male and female crime rates should decrease. However, should traditional patterns of male and female socialization continue, then we should expect continued high rates of, for example, wife abuse. This outcome occurs because, traditionally, men are socialized to be aggressive, women to be passive, and the legal system's reaction to wife abuse ineffective.

Lemert's Societal-Reaction Theory

Lemert's (1951) societal-reaction theory of deviance considers the interrelation of five factors: primary deviation, societal reaction, legitimate opportunities, criminal self-concept, and secondary deviation.

Primary deviation refers to the deviant behavior engaged in just once, twice, or a few times. The primary deviant conforms to societal rules most of the time and feels quite guilty or anxious on those few occasions when he does stray. For example, a caring husband may be driven by impulse to strike his wife during an argument over his drinking. When he realizes what he has done, he feels guilty and is sorry for having behaved in a way that, for him, is out of character.

According to Ellis (forthcoming), there are many such primary deviants in Canada and the United States — most husbands who beat their wives only do so occasionally. However, some go on to become "career" wife-abusers. The major variable explaining the transition from occasional to career wife-abuser is the reaction of society's social-control agents to the husband's occasional wife-abuse.

Societal reaction refers to the punishment and/or therapy imposed on a rule-breaker by these agents, who include social workers, psychologists, counsellors, policemen, judges, and prison guards. The punishment ranges from being warned, to being arrested, and imprisoned (and made public). Along with punishment is the attachment of a stigamatizing label to the deviant. Thus, the occasional wife-abuser who is arrested, convicted, and sent to jail, and whose case is reported in his community newspaper, becomes known as a criminal and a wife-batterer.

This experience, one would expect, would deter the husband from making further assaults on his wife. Not so, says Lemert. The societal reaction itself becomes the cause of further acts of violence. This occurs because the additional, non-legal punishments inflicted upon him decrease his opportunities both for reducing the stresses that initially caused him to hit his wife, and for obtaining the support of his male friends, who do not beat their wives. He may, as a result of a criminal record, even lose his job. If the stress associated with a shortage of money had something to do with his drinking and eventual assault on his wife, then the loss of income caused by losing his job is not going to help matters. Also, his former friends may not wish to be associated with a convicted wife-abuser — and this denies him any support they may have otherwise offered.

Out of a job and without friends, the husband may begin using the children's allowance and unemployment benefits to support his drinking habit. This causes further arguments, during the course of which he hits his wife. The wife starts hitting back. The severity of the husband's violence increases, and eventually the wife is hospitalized because of one of his assaults. He is arrested, convicted, and sent to jail again. Now the husband begins to see himself as he has been labelled by the criminal justice system, by his neighbors, and former friends — as a wife-abuser. Since he has to live with this stigma, he begins to develop a rationale for his abusive behavior. Part of the rationale consists of a justification ("she had it coming") and another part consists of an attack against those who have punished him and who are really no better than he is. At this point, the wife-abusing husband becomes a secondary deviant.

Secondary deviants are, according to Lemert, individuals who, having previously been identified and punished for their criminal or deviant behavior, engage regularly in the same or similar forms of behavior because (1) they identify themselves as criminals or deviants; and/or (2) they perceive themselves as having few non-deviant options available; and/or (3) their deviance is seen as a way of attacking or defending themselves from the society that publicly labelled them as morally unworthy.

The interrelation of the above variables can be depicted diagramatically in Figure 7-2.

The third theoretical school attempting explanations of deviance is the conflict perspective.

Conflict Theory

Conflict theorists regard crime and deviance as outcomes of group conflicts. The losers of these conflicts are called "criminals" or "deviants" by the winners. The winners usually possess more wealth and authority, which is why they are winners. They use the criminal justice system to confer the stigmatized status of criminal on groups with conflicting or differing values, norms, and interests, or on members of groups who want a greater share of their (the winner's) resources. Because members of young, male, wageless, black and Indian groups are different from society's elite (the usual winners) and/or possess fewer resources (e.g., authority, property, sophistication) than do

FIGURE 7-2. Lemert's Societal Reaction Theory

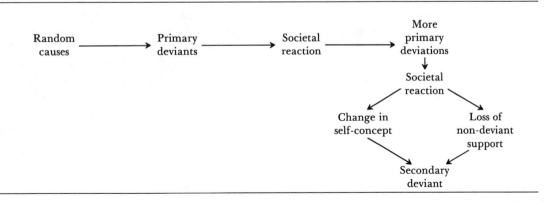

most other social groupings, they are most likely to be labelled criminal during the course of group conflict.

One of the rewards for winning intergroup conflict is the maintenance of status quo. These are usually the conditions that maintain inequality among contending groups and/or allow those who benefit most from the operation of the criminal justice system to believe that crime and deviance will be eliminated if criminals and deviants are punished more severely. For conflict theorists, then, an understanding of the sources of the unequal distribution of scarce and valued resources, such as wealth, status, property, and authority, are central to an understanding of deviance.

Subsumed under this general statement are two very different kinds of conflict theories. We shall look at these using Turk (1969) as an example of group-conflict theory and the Taylor/Walton/ Young formulation as an example of Marxist class-conflict theory.

Turk's Theory of Conflict and Criminalization

Society, for Turk, consists of a number of social groups who possess different attributes (e.g., skin color) and/or who behave in different ways. Such groups are not only different in these respects, but they are also distinguished by the amount of authority they possess. A regular and recurring feature of social life is the exercise of authority by superordinates and varying mixtures of obedience and resistance to this exercise by subordinates.

Social groups vary in the rate in which their members are labelled "criminal" by agents of the criminal justice system. The highest rates of criminality, as we have seen, occur among members of a certain age, sex, income, and racial/ethnic grouping. Why does this happen? According to Turk, the fact that some groups are more criminal than others means that they are more likely to achieve the social and legal status of "criminal" by being convicted of a criminal offence in a court of law.

Differences in criminalization refer to differences in the rate at which members of different social groups are convicted of criminal offences. A criminalization rate of twenty-five out of every 100 000 members of the former group and eight out of every 100 000 of the latter group have been convicted of a criminal offence. Criminalization occurs during the course of conflict, and conflict is most likely to occur under certain conditions.

The first condition is that the deviant attributes and/or behavior have to be defined as illegal. For example, whereas gambling by the state (lotteries) or churches (bingo) is legal, gambling on horses or football games by lower working-class individuals is illegal.

Second, for both authorities and subjects, there must be congruence between cultural norms and social norms. Cultural norms are written or spoken statements of values (e.g., free enterprise, monogamy, democracy); social norms are the rules that are actually enforced by others. The distinction here is between law in books and law actually enforced. Conflict is likely to occur whenever there is a high congruence between cultural and social norms for *both* authorities and subordinate groups.

The third condition is realized if the members of both the subordinate group and the authorities are unsophisticated. Sophistication in this case refers to the knowledge of patterns that are used to manipulate the individuals in question. Subordinate group members who are unsophisticated will not be able to preceive accurately the consequences of their behavior, and because unsophisticated authorities lack the requisite basis (knowledge) for subtle forms of manipulation and persuasion, they fall back on overt forms of coercion.

Fourth, when subordinate group members who are organized and have the support of the group, they are more likely to resist coercion by authorities than are members of unorganized groups.

Intergroup conflict occurs when all four conditions are present. The same general conditions also pertain to the criminalization of group members who, at an earlier time, were merely deviant. However, in explaining criminalization, Turk suggests that the following, more specific, criteria apply: (1) legal norms (laws); (2) congruence between legal and cultural norms on the part of the agents of the criminal justice system; (3) the relative power of the authorities, as well as norm-resisters; and (4) the relative effectiveness of socialization in the workplace, in families, schools, churches, and communities. Applied to car thieves, these criteria predict that the highest rates of criminalization will occur in communities (1) where the authorities (police, prosecutors, and judges) regard the law as safeguarding moral values and/or economic interests, and where car thieves regard the law as a means whereby business people can take advantage of the poor, who are not allowed to "rip off" people whose cars are insured anyway; (2) where the police and other agents place a high value on honesty, a cultural norm that they feel should be supported by society (that is, made into a law); (3) where the police and other law enforcers in these communities place a high value on honesty and believe that this value should be made into a law (legal norm) and that people who do not comply with this norm should be arrested and punished; (4) where the authorities are more wealthy, have greater access to control over the mass media and local politicians than members of the subordinate groups who break

Defying the law, or code of societal norms, may lead to being labelled a criminal.

FIGURE 7-3. Turk's Criminalization Theory

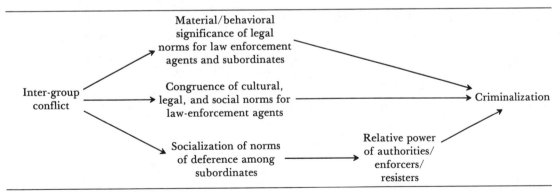

the law; and (5) where informal agents of socialization (parents, teachers, television) in these communities have not succeeded in inculcating "norms of deference" to authority. In sum, the greater the number of poorly socialized individuals in a community, the higher will be the crime rate in that group.

For Turk, then, the crime rate is simultaneously an indicator of success and of failure. By labelling group members "criminal," the authorities have (at least in the short-run) won. However, the fact that members of this group had the nerve to become norm-resisters in the first place is "a measure of failure in the mechanisms by which individuals are conditioned to accept subordination." (1969:116.)

Figure 7-3 illustrates Turk's group-conflict theory of criminalization.

Taylor, Walton, and Young's Marxist Conflict Theory

It is to Marx's definition of the capitalist mode of production as deviant that contemporary sociologists Taylor, Walton, and Young owe their inspiration. Central to their theory is the Marxist idea that all conflicts in society stem from the conflict between those who own the means of production and those who do not; all intergroup conflicts are a more or less direct manifestation of class conflict. Taylor et al. (1973) claim that class relations are the fundamental cause of the criminalization

of the poor, propertyless, and often wageless segments of society. The crimes committed by members of these groups represent an attempt by subordinates to struggle against their subjugation by the propertied classes.

In order to understand criminal behavior in relation to the social structure of power, domination, and authority, write Taylor et al., one must examine *the wider origins of the deviant act*, that is, the economic and political structure of society. *The immediate origins of the deviant act* are found in the ways in which individuals interpret and react to the contingencies generated by the economic and political structure vis-à-vis their own situation. *The nature of the actual act* must be examined in relation to the perceived alternatives available to individuals. Given the class and situational constraints on individuals, crime may, to a greater or lesser degree, be a chosen form of behavior, related in a rational way, to perceptions of the alternatives available. In reporting a deviant act, people have a choice of which social-control agent to go to — medical, welfare, or legal agents. The factors that influence their choice, Taylor et al. have called *the immediate origins of social reaction*. Social reactions to deviant behavior also have wider origins — namely, the state. The way in which the state reacts to various forms of deviation — *the wider origins of deviant reaction* — also need to be studied. The individuals who are labelled a criminal by the state react to their stigmatization in a number of ways. Just as choice

FIGURE 7-4. An Integrated Theory of Crime and Deviance

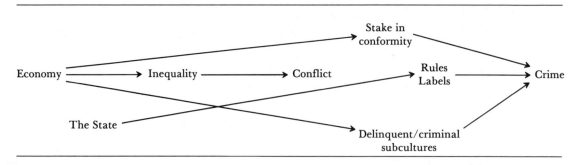

was implicated in their initial decision to commit a crime, so too is choice implicated in their reaction to the state's reaction to their deviance. Thus, *the outcome of the social reaction on the deviant's further action* must be examined, according to Taylor et al. Finally, in order to understand criminal behavior, *the nature of the deviant process as a whole* must be taken into account, meaning all six requirements identified earlier. The starting point for such an account is inequality.

Figure 7-4 illustrates that the difference in the amount of money people earn from the work they do determines the degree of inequality present in a society. In some societies, as few as 12 to 15 percent of the job-holders earn over 80 percent of the income; in others, income and wealth differentials are much lower. Inequality gives rise to conflict. Wealthy property owners, through their influence on the state, create and enforce laws that help generate economic and political conditions favorable to their interests. In the process, crimes, criminals, and deviants result. Inequality also lowers the stake in conformity of those who are least well off. The higher the proportion of individuals with relatively little to lose by being caught and punished by state agents, the higher the rate of criminality. Finally, inequality tends to be associated with residential segregation and the creation of subcultural norms and values that are conducive to violating the law.

SUMMARY

1. The relationship between social control, crime, and deviance is complex. The type of social control involved helps differentiate between deviance and crime: whereas crime invokes both informal and formal sanctions, deviance invokes only informal sanctions.

2. Social control is most usefully regarded not as a cause or a result of crime, but as a process that elicits one or another consequence under different sets of conditions and with different kinds of offences.

3. Although certain kinds of behavior or attributes may be defined as criminal or deviant in most societies, the social reactions of any one act vary a great deal from country to country. This is because the social significance of any given kind of behavior varies across societies.

4. Attempts to explain variations in the amount of crime committed by members of different social groupings are classified according to functional, interactionist, or conflict theories. These broad perspectives are further subdivided into subcultural and social-control theories (functional), theories of labelling and societal reaction (interactionist), and theories of group conflict and class conflict (conflict).

5. Inequality was found to be a common factor in several theories or explanations.

6. Each of the theories discussed was integrated into a general theory in which inequality is of central importance. Underlying this theory are the following assumptions: (1) the economy is the primary source of inequality; (2) the state formulates and enforces rules that maintain an unequal distribution of property, power, and income; and (3) inequality influences the rate of crime through its effects on interactionist, social-control, and subcultural variables.

GLOSSARY

Conflict crimes. Labels conferred upon behavior that deviates from legal norms, which some people believe ought to be conformed with and others do not.

Consensus crimes. Labels conferred upon behavior that deviates from those legal norms that most people agree ought to be conformed with.

Criminal deviance. A label conferred upon behavior that deviates from legal norms (laws) by agents of the state.

Criminalization. The process by which agents of the state produce criminals by catching suspects and convicting them.

Delinquents. Individuals whose deviant inclinations are least regulated because their ties to society are weak.

Deviance. Behavior that deviates from the norms set by members of a group.

Ironies of social control. Attempts to decrease deviance that have the reverse effect of increasing it.

Labelling. A verbal/symbolic accusation that socially, morally, and/or legally differentiates the worthy from the unworthy, the good from the bad.

Reaction formation. The psychological rejection of values, norms, and behavior previously believed in.

Social class. A large social group that shares a similar level of education and income, values, and life style.

Social control. A teaching/learning process that is specifically oriented toward the inhibition of deviant behavior.

Stratification. The hierarchical ranking of social groups on the basis of inequalities in the ownership of property and/or wealth, education, income, ethnicity, or authority.

Subculture. The complex of values and norms that is different from the content of the wider culture and that newcomers in some social groupings must learn in order to become functioning members.

FURTHER READING

Akers, R. *Problems in the Sociology of Deviance: Social Definitions and Behaviour.* Andover, Mass.: A Warner Modular Publication. Reprint #34, 1973. After reviewing labelling and behavioral definitions of deviance, the author suggests that an adequate theory of deviance is one that simultaneously explains both labelling and the deviant behavior of those labelled.

Canadian Federal-Provincial Task Force Report. *Justice for Victims of Crime.* Ottawa: Supply and Services, 1983. This report describes the situation of the victim of certain kinds of criminal offences. Victims, the report concludes, are badly treated by the criminal justice system. Proposals for improving the situation are described and evaluated.

Chambliss, W. and R. B. Seidman. *Law, Order and Power.* Reading, Mass.: Addison-Wesley, 1971. A detailed analysis of how the criminal justice system actually works. A conflict approach, the authors conclude, does a much better job of accounting for the operation of this system than does a consensus approach.

Ditton, J. *Contrology: Beyond the New Criminology.* London: Macmillan, 1979. The author goes "beyond the New Criminology" by arguing that crime (police) statistics measure only police behavior and that there are no crime waves, only crime-control waves.

Gibb, J. *Social Control.* Andover, Mass.: A Warner Modular Publication, 1972. A general review that describes the various ways in which the study of social control is significant for the study of crime and deviance.

Hagan, J. *The Disreputable Pleasures.* Toronto: McGraw Hill Ryerson, 1977. Chapters 3 and 4 contain an excellent description, comparison, and evaluation of contemporary conflict and consensus theories of crime and deviance.

Pepinsky, H. *Crime Control Strategies: An Introduction to the Study of Crime.* New York: Oxford University Press, 1980. A very good description, comparison, and evaluation of police statistics and self-report and victim surveys as measures of crime. Also useful is the attempt made by the author to relate each measure of crime to various crime-control strategies.

Solicitor General of Canada. *The Criminal in Society.* Ottawa: Supply and Services, 1973. A description of the structure and operation of the criminal justice system from the perspective of the state's social control agents.

Taylor, I., P. Walton, and J. Young. *The New Criminology: For a Social Theory of Deviance.*

London: Routledge and Kegan Paul, 1973. An excellent review of labelling, subcultural, and conflict theory from the perspective of sociologists who favor a Marxist explanation of criminal deviance.

PART III

Social Life, Social Interaction, and Processes

Part III examines social interaction, which forms the basis of social life. Interaction within social organizations and institutions results in the formation of complex patterns of social organization. Chapter 8 discusses the implications of interaction between individuals, a process that most of us take for granted. For example, imagine what would happen if we stopped interacting with people. We would lose a sense of self, and our society would cease to have any meaning for us.

Chapter 9 examines large-scale organizations, or how societies develop such structures as government, business corporations, and labor unions: complex organizations that are typical of our modern society. Organizations are often referred to as institutions, and Chapter 10 explains that organizations reveal institutional practices within power structures, whereas institutions are the sociologists' framework for conceptualizing the social order.

CHAPTER EIGHT

Social Interaction and Social Processes

JOHN H. KUNKEL

In this chapter we analyze the essence of social life: the *interaction* of two or more individuals. Most phenomena studied by sociologists consist of complex sets of interactions. In Chapter 5, for example, you saw how chains of social interaction form our institutions. Chapter 4 told of the great variety of behavior that is deemed proper in the social interactions that constitute daily life. In Chapter 6, you learned how people acquire the behavior necessary for social interaction.

Just as the interaction of individuals is the essence of social life, the essence of social interaction is the influence that individuals exert on each other's activities, beliefs, and attitudes. Indeed, much of what we do and think is the result of past and present interactions with others. It is no wonder, then, that over the years sociologists have devoted considerable effort to the analysis of interaction in dyads, small groups, and larger systems. Early in the century, Simmel (1955) proposed that society is not an ongoing entity, as some of his colleagues thought, but rather a complex system of permanent and temporary interactions. During the 1920s, Mead (1964) described how an individual's self-conception gradually develops through interactions with other people. In a famous study called *Street Corner Society* (Whyte, 1943), the author analyzes the interactions in an informal gang of young men. Later, Blau (1964) went a step farther and described the various interactions that occur in friendship cliques, offices, and communities. Later in the chapter we shall consider some of these works, but first, let us begin by considering the major determinants of people's behavior.

THE DETERMINANTS OF BEHAVIOR

In order to understand the process of mutual influence, we have to understand behavior on an individual level. Almost every human action is determined by the outcomes that a person expects on the basis of past experiences. This is especially evident in the normative behavior of people in societies, subcultures, and groups (Blake and Davis, 1964). The norm of respect for the aged, for example, implies that there are societal *sanctions* (positive and negative consequences) attached to the behavior that we choose to enact. When we meet an elderly person, most of us are likely to behave respectfully because our past experience tells us that such behavior will be sanctioned positively: people smiled at you when you helped your grandmother, while people made nasty comments when my friend did not help his grandfather with his overcoat.

The probability that an action will be repeated depends on the nature of expected consequences (Berger et al., 1974). If these are positive, then the probability of repetition increases; when the expected outcome is negative, the probability of repetition declines and eventually approaches zero. Whether the outcome is judged as positive or negative depends on the person's recent history, feelings of deprivation, and various idiosyncratic factors (Bandura, 1969). In order to predict behavior, however, we must also know the culture (and subculture) to which the individual belongs. Some tribes in West Africa, for example, consider milk unfit for human consumption, whereas in our culture, milk is considered a life-giving nutrient, especially for children.

Behavior is also affected by the relationship between expectation and actual outcome. On the one hand, if the outcome is better than what one anticipated (including effects that are not as bad as one had feared), the reward seems greater; on the other hand, if the outcome is not as great as we anticipated, we would probably think that some kind of adverse event has occurred. The phenomenon of anticipated outcome, in short, is much more complex than appears at first glance. Often, the expected consequences occur only after a long series of activities (e.g., writing a term paper), and several events follow over a period of time, such as getting a good grade, impressing friends, and avoiding a nasty letter from an uncle who pays for one's tuition.

Human behavior always occurs within a physical and social environment, and we gradually learn to associate particular aspects of that context with what happens to us; that is, certain aspects of the context become signals that indicate the likely outcomes of specific actions. Furthermore, the closer the present context is to the signals learned in the past, the greater is the likelihood that we would behave appropriately — because we expect a particular outcome on the basis of past experiences in that context (Bandura, 1969; Homans, 1974).

Many of the signals and consequences that affect our actions involve other people: the policeman in a cruiser, your professor, a letter from your parents. The major exceptions are intrinsically reinforcing actions (such as enjoying a good game of tennis), and a broad range of self-administered outcomes. Bandura (1977) suggests that most of the consequences that maintain our actions in daily life are provided by ourselves. We do "this" so often and have done "this" for so long that we might not even be aware of our self-reinforcement.

Only rarely do we experience consequences that are independent of human action. Even getting soaked to the skin in a rainstorm, for example, is the result of previous actions: you forgot your umbrella, or you did not listen to the weather report, or you should have taken a raincoat.

In summary, it is helpful to consider the major determinants of behavior — expected consequences and environmental signals — as the outer links of a three-part chain:

$$\text{signals in context} \rightarrow \text{behavior} \rightarrow \text{expected} \\ \text{consequences}$$

As we shall see later in the chapter, there are other factors that influence our actions. Most of these are internal processes, such as perception and interpretation, which mediate between the social context and the individual.

THE NATURE OF INTERACTION

Imagine that you are in a crowded elevator. No one says anything; nothing happens. Although there are many people, there is no interaction. Then you sneeze. The lady next to you frowns; you wonder if she is worried about her child catching your cold. A man behind you says in a friendly tone, "Salud." You turn and say to him, "This weather is getting to me." And then you realize that perhaps he does not understand you either. The elevator stops, and a person in the back says, "Excuse me, please." Everybody tries to make room. Within a few seconds, considerable interaction has occurred.

An interaction occurs when the behavior of two or more people is related in such a way that one individual's action is the signal for other person's actions (consequences). In the elevator, you provided a signal in sneezing, and started a chain of reaction (consequences); one person frowned and another said "salud."

But there are several complicating factors that make the study of human interaction a fascinating subject for sociologists. When the mother frowned, she made you feel uncomfortable. How do you recognize a frown and why does it make you uncomfortable? Would you apologize to her? Why might some people not feel uncomfortable? Is the person's "salud" good or bad? You search the speaker's face for clues. What language is he speaking? How should you respond? Is the other person's "excuse me, please" impatient or polite? Under what conditions would people be more likely to make an effort to be accommodating? Does it matter whether the person is a man or woman, plain or attractive?

Evidently there is more to interaction than actions (e.g., making room) or symbols (e.g., "excuse me, please"). It is true that the variety and frequency of symbols are the hallmarks of human interaction, but they cannot be considered in isolation. Equally significant are the interpretation of words and gestures, along with the ability to react appropriately. As you saw in Chapter 6, the learning of these interpretations and abilities is no small matter.

Effective social interaction requires that we know enough about the other person's culture to interpret his/her behavior and symbols correctly. This premise is aptly illustrated in Claire Mowat's first encounter with Newfoundland children, who came to visit her in the village to which she and her husband moved from mainland Canada. In her own words,

They had almost nothing to volunteer, nor were they willing to answer any questions. They just sat there in silence. I gave up trying to be a bright conversationalist and after a few words about the weather, continued doing whatever I had been doing.

And that, it took me a long time to realise, was precisely what I was supposed to do. The role of visiting children, as well as that of many adults, was simply to be there. They did not feel obliged to do or say anything, nor did they expect me to alter my daily routine for them.

(Mowat, 1984:11.)

Mrs. Mowat had previously learned to define certain behavior and symbols in a particular way: when people come to visit, one talks to them, offers them refreshments, and so on. But these definitions were inappropriate in a Newfoundland village.

Symbolic Interaction

George Herbert Mead and William I. Thomas devoted considerable effort to the analysis of verbal and nonverbal behavior, and held that they are important ingredients of human behavior. According to this symbolic-interaction perspective, as exemplified by Herbert Blumer (1969), individuals influence each other through the meanings they attach to each other's deeds, as well as words.

For example, if you see a friend walking rapidly toward you with her gaze intently fixed on a building a hundred yards away, you conclude that she is in a hurry. But then you remember her telling you last week: "We must get together some time soon." Is now the right time? You greet each other. Now you have to interpret the tone of her voice, her facial expression, and her body movements in order to determine whether she is interested in chatting with you. Perhaps she is just being polite. Thus you interpret her actions and construct the reality of the encounter — only to reinterpret and reconstruct that reality a few minutes later. And she, of course, does the same. She might ask herself: "Why is he so hesitant? Doesn't he like me?" Thus, she interprets your behavior and constructs her version of the reality of your encounter. If the realities you and she construct coincide, the interaction will continue. But if the realities do not coincide, the interaction will end quickly, and you will not be able to understand each other.

These mental processes are integral parts of our behavior, even when we are not aware of them. When two (or more) people interact, each interprets the other's words, gestures, and acts, and each behaves accordingly. Reciprocal influence is thus part of any interaction. As illustrated by the Mowat quote, the meanings that we attach to gestures and acts reflect our culture, and our interpretations reflect our experience. Mrs. Mowat was accustomed to treating visitors in a manner that was proper in her own culture. Her interpretation of the children coming to visit her was inappropriate in rural Newfoundland culture. The children, in turn, behaved the way they were taught.

The Fact of Reciprocity

There is more to reciprocity in social interaction than simply one person's affecting the behavior of another. Although it is true that actions are largely determined by contextual signals and expected consequences, this does not imply that a person is at the mercy of the environment or the victim of blind fate. Every individual plays a significant role in producing the consequences that will affect later behavior.

The degree of reciprocity depends on several cultural and social factors. One can influence the context only to the extent that one knows the culturally appropriate actions. In addition, the context must be structured in such a way that there is a definite link between one person's behavior and another individual's reactions. These requirements must be met for even the simplest reciprocal actions. On a visit to Saudi Arabia, for example, one must know the proper way of greeting a person — including words, gestures, and facial expressions — and one must know who is permitted to respond to strangers. If a Canadian visitor, for example, were to speak to a veiled lady in a bazaar, he would not receive a reply — or at least not one he would expect from his experience at home. Saudi custom prohibits a woman responding to a stranger, and indeed his boldness may have dangerous consequences for him.

The same conditions operate in the larger world, which reacts to our behavior. Interestingly enough, however, the expressions commonly used to describe actions obscure the precise link between actions and their effects on various parts of the social context. For example, it is not really true that a professor "gives" you a grade; it is more accurate to say that your performance receives an appropriate mark. Similarly, Canadian Pacific does not really "give" you a job; rather, you can do well what the company wants to have done well and therefore you are hired.

These two examples illustrate an important aspect of reciprocity: control over outcomes. You control the grade you receive by writing a good or a poor essay. And you have some control over future jobs by means of the skills and attitudes you acquire over time. Indeed, control over outcomes is such a significant component of interaction that it merits some discussion.

Control over Outcomes

During most social interactions of daily life, participants exert considerable control over one another's behavior by means of words, intonation, gestures, and body language. If I mumble a short "hi" and barely stop as we meet in a store, you will react accordingly with a quick word and be ready to move on. But if I smile broadly as I speak and stop to look at you, you too are likely to stop and exchange leisurely greetings (if you have time). Thus, I control your behavior — and the positive outcome this represents for me. In this way, I produce my own outcomes. But you also exert control over me, and thus, your outcomes represented by my behavior. If I have a lot of time and am willing to chat with you, but you are in a hurry, you can easily control my behavior: all you have to do is be short, look down the aisle, glance at your watch (and, if I'm dense, take a few steps). Now you control the outcome of your behavior — I let you go on your way.

Many studies have shown that people are greatly affected by their perceptions of who exerts control (Lefcourt, 1982). When individuals attribute the good (and bad) events of their life to their own actions, such as giving up a dead-end job or moving to another province, they have a sense of internal control. This, in turn, leads to the belief that they are effective and competent persons. The result is self-confidence, a feeling of power, and a positive self-conception. Such individuals are likely

to be more persistent in the face of difficulty (and even failure) and overcome the obstacles they face. These positive results would further increase their sense of worth.

But when individuals think that fate or chance is responsible for what happens to them, such as losing a job in a recession, they are subject to external control. As a result, they are likely to consider themselves weak, ineffective, and powerless. Such persons are likely to develop a poor self-concept, to face the future with anxiety, and to feel rather alienated from society. Apathy and a short time-frame are other consequences of a perceived lack of internal control (Rotter, 1966).

At a societal level, descriptions of peasants in Latin America, for example, and of slaves all over the world, reflect these individualistic implications of social systems that deprive people of their sense of control. Poverty, ignorance, and lack of basic skills are other factors that lead to widespread feelings of external control. A society is humane or sane to the extent that its structure and operation give people a sense of internal control (Fromm, 1955). As we saw earlier, such control depends on the individual's ability to behave in appropriate ways and on the structure of the social context. Hence, a society's socialization process should teach its citizens appropriate and effective behavior, such as basic verbal and social skills, so that they are able to cope. Also, a society should be structured in such a way that its operation produces real and inescapable evidence of strong links between behavior and its outcome — for example, a legal system that is fair and impartial.

In fact, this analysis of social interaction can be used as a means for evaluating the quality of a society. If there are problems in the society, sociologists should be able to determine what needs to be done in terms of teaching people more skills, or making the necessary adjustments in the social structure. Retraining programs and government grants aimed at stimulating economic development are examples of such efforts on the national level.

Self-Fulfilling Prophecies

Social interaction often involves predictions about other people, perhaps in the form of hopes and fears. Frequently we behave according to our predictions, and other people then react in such a way as to validate our predictions. If we had behaved differently, their reactions would probably have been different. In short, predictions tend to produce the predicted outcomes! Such self-fulfilling prophecies are also found at the societal level, as when years of inflation lead to buying habits that tend to aggravate inflation (Merton, 1968).

The power of self-fulfilling prophecies is especially evident in new situations of social interaction when few, if any, previous experiences indicate the character of the people involved. You can discover this yourself by asking an acquaintance for a date. How would you behave if you thought you might be turned down? And how would you act if you thought there might be a good chance of success? (The assumption here, of course, is that you are not smitten — love might lead you to act differently than you would if your predictions were the sole determinants of your behavior.)

The frequency and power of self-fulfilling prophecies suggest that we should make as few of them as possible. After all, they reduce the possibility of experiencing the variety and richness of social interaction inherent in our culture.

Dyads and Groups

You will notice that most examples of interaction in this chapter involve only two people. The reason for this is that in any social situation, the majority of interactions that take place at any one time are between two individuals; only rarely do we interact with three or more people simultaneously. Two-person interactions are referred to as *dyads*, and a series of dyads make up a group. The boundary of a group — who belongs and who does not — is usually determined by the frequency of interaction: those who interact often are usually considered members of a group. Friendship groups fall into this latter category.

When a person "does business" with a large institution, the interaction is of a formal, impersonal nature, involving one or more dyadic encounters with individuals working for a government agency. For example, getting a driver's licence or social insurance number, or having one's income-tax return processed, consists of a series of dyadic interactions.

One of the best studies of dyadic relationships in a clique or friendship group is Whyte's *Street Corner Society* (1943). This classic describes a group of young men who are part of Boston's Italian subculture. On the basis of observing (and participating in) this street-corner gang, Whyte was able to describe the group's social structure or "pecking order." By noting who talked to whom, when, and about what, who gave advice, followed orders, agreed and disagreed, Whyte discovered the group's status system. Doc was the acknowledged leader, and Mike and Danny were his lieutenants and closest friends. Long John was a friend of all three but otherwise not a member of the group.

Members of this gang perpetuated the status system through their interaction, for example, while bowling. The higher-status men were *expected* to bowl better than lower-status men (regardless of their actual performance). Lower-status men were verbally encouraged to bowl well — but only as long as their scores were lower than the leader's. Alec, for example, often bowled very well, as long as he played with Frank (a middle-status member) and Long John (the outsider). However, on Saturday nights, when most of the corner boys played together, Alec usually did poorly (because he was expected to).

CONTINUITY AND CHANGE IN INTERACTION

Now that we understand some of the complexities of social interaction, we can begin to analyze

Most interactions are *dyadic*, that is, they involve only two people who usually interact on a frequent basis.

the factors that maintain, change, or terminate interaction. Chief among these are balance, the nature of exchange, and fairness.

Cognitive Balance

Some social interactions continue for a long time, such as a friendship, whereas others end soon after we get to know the person. An important determinant of the length and quality of interactions is *cognitive balance*. Indeed, balance in social relations is so important that theories have been developed to describe its impact on interaction. Newcomb (1968) and others have pointed out that the partners in a relationship strive for consistency in their attitudes, beliefs, and behavior. If balance is achieved, the interaction continues. When

there is imbalance, especially in areas that are important to the participants, individuals either seek to re-establish balance in some way, or the interaction ceases.

Consider an engaged couple and their views regarding birth control in Canada. If both favor (or are against) birth control, there is cognitive balance, and we would expect the relationship to continue (other things being equal). But if one member discovers that the other has a very different view, there is imbalance. Balance can be re-established in three ways: one person's opinion can change, or the other's can be changed, or they can both agree that the topic is insignificant.

In the analysis of cognitive balance and of other aspects of interaction, the observer's assessment of relevant factors is not nearly as important as the participants' views of significant elements. To this we now turn.

Interaction as Exchange

Homans (1974) and other sociologists have analyzed social interaction from the perspective of individuals exchanging various activities. They took this one step farther and looked at social interaction in terms of the costs and benefits involved in certain behavior to the participants of an interaction. They concluded that interaction would continue as long as the benefits outweighed the costs and outcomes of alternative actions.

A well-known study by Blau (1964) analyzes important aspects of bureaucracy from such an exchange perspective. Although he derived many conclusions from a particular setting — a government agency — Blau presents considerable evidence that any hierarchically organized system contains the same elements. Co-operating, such as asking for advice, is easiest to maintain by individuals at the same status level, but difficult across levels — mainly because of the costs an individual faces when requiring assistance. When we seek help from people at our own level, the cost — admitting ignorance — is relatively low, especially if we expect to give some advice in the future (thus eliminating the cost deficit). The price of asking our superiors is higher, especially if we are supposed to know the answer. The cost of asking the advice of our subordinates is so high (e.g., loss of esteem) that it is rarely done. Part of any payment for giving advice is usually an expression of esteem, so that eventually the most knowledgeable individuals in an office have the highest status.

Almost all social interaction can be explained in terms of this exchange paradigm. The "things" that are exchanged may be objects (birthday gifts), symbols (advice), feelings (satisfaction that we could help a good friend), abstractions (knowledge that we can ask that friend for help later),

and even imaginary events (my friend really appreciated that midnight call from me).

Social exchange is always embedded in particular circumstances and in the participants' perspective. Love — as one of the more significant kinds of social exchange — is not blind, but it does involve peculiar definitions of costs and benefits. When we love someone, we do many things for the loved one even though the only "return" is the presence of the beloved, or perhaps the vague knowledge that our beloved is happy. After love ceases, we may well wonder just why we did all those things.

An important question in every exchange concerns fairness. If I do something for you, what should you give me in return and what should I expect? Norms, customs, and laws provide most answers, but sometimes we find ourselves in situations that call for improvisation. Even here, however, our feelings regarding fairness must be satisfied.

Fairness

Social interaction continues, and individuals remain members of a group depending on their assessment of the fairness with which the rewards (or aversive outcomes) are distributed. But what is fair? Sociologists have discovered that the essence of fairness lies in the relationship between an individual's behavior and the outcomes that follow it (Homans, 1974). We shall analyze two dimensions of this relationship.

Distributive Justice

Most people expect that if they contribute more to the positive outcome of a joint effort than another person, they should receive a larger portion of that outcome. For example, because Wayne Gretzky scores more goals than any other player on his team, he is paid much more. Even when we work independently, we expect that the reward will have some relationship to our performance.

We recognize that the proportions may not be exact, we accept the fact that sometimes we or others may benefit or be hurt a bit, but on the whole we stay in a group or continue with a relationship as long as we believe that the amount of positive and negative outcomes is distributed fairly.

Many studies (Homans, 1974; Walster et al., 1978) have shown that the principle of distributive justice is usually considered to be the fairest way of dividing the consequences of behavior. In general, the rule of distributive justice calls for outcomes to be proportional to one's contribution. A person's effort (rather than actual contribution) would be considered only in exceptional circumstances. Individual effort, for example, would be zero in a game of chance and large in a game of skill.

The principle of distributive justice operates in friendship and marriage, although here we usually find considerable variations, depending on the strength of the feelings involved. This strength, of course, is factored into the costs and benefits that are part of any social exchange. How long would you remain friends with a person if you did all the telephoning, paid for most of the entertainment, and did most of the visiting? What would happen if you suddenly discovered that the person does not love you after all?

When a culture prescribes such rather one-sided behavior and considers it proper—for example while dating—the idea of strict distributive justice is held in abeyance. (Consider, however, what other positive outcomes you expect from your date.) But would you go steady—or think about marriage—if you thought that you might have to continue doing most of the "work" in the relationship?

In daily life, the principle of distributive justice is complicated by such factors as differential intellectual endowment and other personal characteristics. Furthermore, in some situations it is just about impossible to assess an individual's contributions. When this happens, people tend to employ a different dimension.

Equity and Equality

When the positive and negative outcomes of behavior within an interaction are distributed on the basis of the individuals' contributions—for example, being paid for the amount of work performed—the principle of equity is said to operate. If all members of a group receive equal benefits (or negative effects) regardless of their contribution—for example, all senators receive the same salary—the principle of equality operates. Whether one or the other principle is considered fair by the participants depends on the situation, and it is not possible to say that one or the other principle is always or by nature fair. Indeed, both are fair in different circumstances.

People tend to use the equity principle—and expect others to use it—when there is a definite link between behavior and consequence, and when a person has some control over the outcome of the performance, as a baseball player does, for instance. When there is no link, or when individuals do not control the outcome of their behavior, then the equality principle is likely to be used and expected.

People who have the basic skills of life and view themselves as competent are likely to favor the equity principle in the distribution of the good things in life, whereas individuals who lack many of the basic skills and do not consider themselves very competent are likely to favor the equality principle. Whether or not our society—or life itself—is seen as fair, therefore, is closely related to the skills one has and the successful use of them. Hence we should expect that in a complex and heterogeneous society like ours, there will be a variety of judgements regarding the fairness of the "system."

MAJOR CONSEQUENCES OF INTERACTION FOR THE INDIVIDUAL

There are two major consequences of interaction that affect every individual: (1) the acquisition of new behavior through modelling, and (2) development of self-conceptions. Together, these phenomena indicate that humans are, of necessity, social beings, for without social interaction we simply would not be what we are.

Modelling and New Behavior

Animals typically learn through trial and error, whereas human beings acquire most of their new behavior patterns through observational learning and modelling (Bandura, 1969). We watch others, seek advice, or read instructions. This is true especially for complex activities, such as learning to drive a car. If people did not learn from others, life would be dangerous: you would not want to learn through trial and error which side of the road to drive on, or what kinds of mushrooms are edible. Indeed, life would be chaotic and large-scale societies would be impossible if we did not learn from others.

The modelling process involves several distinct steps. First, we pay attention to certain people and their actions. If we deem these individuals to be appropriate models, we begin to observe them and their actions, the context in which these actions occur, and the consequences of these actions. This is much more complex than simple imitation, for we also observe what happens in context. In short, we observe the signal/behavior/outcome sequence that other people experience.

Later, when we find ourselves in similar situations, we try out the actions we have observed, because we expect the kinds of positive outcomes we observed happening to the model. In a restaurant in Acapulco, you find that your neighbor's speaking Spanish to the waiter results in better service, and so you attempt to order your meal in Spanish too, with the help of your phrase book. If this proves effective, you will do the same the next time; if not, then you might give up and revert to English. Thus, we learn new behavior from models, but whether this new behavior becomes part of our repertoire depends on what happens to us (and not to the model).

People learn through modelling not only what they should and can do, but also what they should not do. Seeing a motorist get a ticket for speeding makes us slow down — at least for a while. Thus, observing a negative outcome resulting from certain behavior discourages us from engaging in that behavior. Observing the outcome of behavior has a more powerful effect than words, especially if the two do not coincide. If we see that an action has a positive outcome, we are likely to try out that action, regardless of what people say. This is why parents are notoriously unsuccessful when they tell their children to "do what I say, not what I do."

In daily life, we are surrounded by models, some of whom are official but most of whom are inadvertent. Parents try to instil the proper values in their children by modelling, as do teachers. But the peer group often serves as a more influential — though inadvertent — model. A child will often try out "bad" words, learned from other children at school or at home. The sheer novelty of these words is itself rewarding, and the fact that they are forbidden at home makes them all the more enticing.

Human learning is not restricted to the actual observation of models, for language enables us to consider role models that present themselves in newspapers, on television, and in books. Indeed, some of our models may have been dead for a while. Whether or not a person and activity is seen as a model depends on the perceived similarity of model and observer. Generally speaking, the greater the perceived similarity, the greater the probability that the person will be considered a model. Note the word "perceived." There is not much *actual* similarity between a ten-year-old boy and Wayne Gretzky, but the boy's perception may be different — especially if he looks far enough into the future. "Normal" individuals tend to place a reasonable limit on perceived similarity, whereas others aspire beyond realistically perceived models.

Whether or not a person remains our model depends largely on the results of behaving in like-fashion as the model. If the outcome is successful — in the sense of being rewarded and making our life easier or better — we are likely to continue seeing the model as appropriate. But if the behavior engaged in fails us in that the result is not rewarding, or is otherwise detrimental, then we are likely to discard the model (and perhaps look for another).

Development of Self-Conceptions

Probably the most interesting consequence of social interaction is the development of self-conceptions. Indeed, it is probable that we would not have much of a viable self-image without previous and ongoing interactions with people (Mead, 1964).

The earliest, and still the best, sociological conception of the self was proposed by Cooley. In the manner of his time (the 1920s), he spoke of the "looking-glass self": our self-conception is based on our interpretation of other people's reactions to our behavior. Such interpretations continue throughout life, and with time we might change our self-conception, depending on the people with whom we interact and the circumstances in which this interaction occurs.

It stands to reason that we cannot develop a self-image if we live in isolation; furthermore, if we interact only with a small range of people, the image will be distorted. Generally speaking, a normal and adequate self-conception is based on continuing interaction with different kinds of people in various circumstances. Even then, however, there are at least three problems that can interfere with the maintenance of an adequate self-concept and lead to changes. First, we might interpret other people's reactions incorrectly; second, people might react inappropriately to our actions; and third, it is possible that people may be unaware of our behavior and therefore behave without reference to it. Therefore, it is not at all easy to establish and maintain a realistic self-image.

According to Mead (1964), one of the most significant aspects of a normal, healthy self-concept is the ability to view ourselves as others see us —

and as we really are — within a dynamic world of other human beings. This ability should develop early in life, but it atrophies unless we practise it frequently. Social interaction keeps our self-conception in shape, just as exercise develops muscles.

As children grow and come into contact with a variety of people in all walks of life, they gradually learn to place themselves in other people's shoes. According to Mead, through interaction individuals learn to take on the role of the other person. Through years of practice, beginning with playing house as a child, individuals learn how other people act and eventually begin to understand how they feel and how they see the world. Out of such interaction empathy should develop, as well as an understanding of fellow human beings. Individuals who have not learned to take on the role of another are likely to be socially inept, for they will have difficulty predicting how people are affected by their behavior. An effective bedside manner, for example, is difficult to acquire even for a physician if he/she has never been sick.

Regarding the self, the philosopher William James (1950) distinguished between the "I" and the "Me" concepts, later elaborated by Mead (1964). The "I" is the actual self, the human being who acts, feels, and thinks. The "Me" is the person-object I observe when I put myself in the shoes of others. This distinction is useful, especially if we make it often enough. For example, the "I" may think of itself as being friendly, kind, and gentle. But when we observe ourselves as others see us, we may discover a different person — the "Me" who rarely smiles and is often gruff.

The general principle, that the self is the result of social interaction, must be combined with its corollary: the content of self-conceptions, and even some personality characteristics, are significantly affected by interactions in which the individual has been and continues to be involved. For example, when we have learned to interpret the signals others send out and to get positive responses from these people, we are likely to become optimistic, self-confident, responsible, and easygoing. Conversely, when we cannot interpret these signals and our relations with other people suffer, we are likely to become pessimistic, apathetic, irresponsible, and beset by feelings of inferiority.

The Presentation of Self in Everyday Life (Goffman, 1959) maintains that individuals act toward others in ways that are designed to present the self in the best possible light. According to Goffman, this "impression management" is a key aspect of any relationship, no matter how fleeting. A maitre d' tries to impress diners with his French accent (which may not be real) and elegant manners; secretaries convey competence through their behavior and clothes; and children jockey for playground status by using whatever criteria are in vogue in the neighborhood. The impression conveyed to others may not be an accurate reflection of one's self-concept, however. Indeed, a person might go to considerable trouble to hide feelings of inferiority or fear by presenting a tough facade. Thus, in any relationship, maintains Goffman, participants try to manage the impressions that others are bound to develop of them. To the extent that these impressions are not authentic reflections of the self, the participants are like actors on a stage. Such impression-management efforts are a significant dimension of social interaction at the group level, regardless of what the official tasks or public goals of the group might be.

PROBLEMS OF SOCIAL INTERACTION

In the rough-and-tumble ways of daily life, the ideal characteristics of social interaction are often confounded by a variety of factors. In this section we analyze two major factors that interfere with the ideal kind of social interaction described in the previous pages. First, you may not perceive other people's signals correctly, or you may see things that are not really there. In either case,

you will not react appropriately, and the interaction will suffer. Second, you may react to personal characteristics of the individuals involved rather than to their behavior. Here the reaction is inappropriate on your part, and again the interaction will be affected.

The Problem of Perception

The two most common types of misperception are: (1) the incorrect reading and interpretation of the signals that other people send out, and (2) the incorrect attribution of the causes of, and reasons for, other people's behavior.

As mentioned earlier, the signals that participants of interactions send to each other are complex: there are words, to be sure, but these are usually accompanied by facial expressions and body language. And although participants may have their tongues well under control, their faces — and especially their bodies — often tell people just what they want to hide with sweet (or nasty) words.

Generally speaking, signals conveyed by body and face are more credible than mere words, as when we feel what a person is really saying. Words, face, and body may actually transmit (deliberately or unconsciously) distinct and contradictory messages. Too, any or all of the signals may be misinterpreted or disregarded.

Both problems affect the continuation and quality of interaction. The participants may not even be aware of the roots of the difficulty. In our society, for example, men seem to have considerable difficulty in decoding the signals embedded in women's actions. A recent study, for example, indicated that men tend to misinterpret women's friendly behavior as having a deeper (sexual) interest (Abbey, 1982). This study raises the interesting question of whether it is possible to be "simply friends" with someone of the opposite sex. In such a situation, the individuals involved would have to make sure that they send accurate signals of their intentions and make accurate interpretations of their partners' signals. But how can this be done when most people are not even aware of perception problems in this area?

A similar difficulty arises in simple conversations between two people. In our culture, the normal spacial proximity between people in informal interaction, especially among friends, is greater than in some other cultures. In Latin America, good friends typically stand so close together that they almost touch. In Canada, we are likely to consider individuals who stand close to us as being aggressive (with the exception of family members). Thus, when a Brazilian stands close to a person while discussing international debts, he has no idea that his stance might be viewed as aggressive. The importance of space in social interaction is such that a separate field of study, *proxemics*, has arisen.

Misperceptions can also occur in the *attribution* of wrong causes to events in our surroundings (Kelley, 1967). It obviously makes a great difference whether you attribute failure either to the difficulty of the task or to your ineptitude, or even to the prejudice of those who evaluated your work. When people snub you at a party, does this mean that they do not like you, or is it because you have bad breath? The cause to which you attribute the snub (assuming that it was really a snub — and it may not be) determines your reaction. If you attribute the snub to dislike, you will probably leave the party and decline future invitations from the host. If you remember that you forgot to brush your teeth before going out, you may attribute the snub to your forgetfulness.

In general, individuals tend to attribute their failures to external events (including fate) or to other people, and their successes to personal factors, such as effort or skill (Weiner, 1982). Such misattribution is likely to produce difficulties later, because if failures are perceived as being caused by factors external to oneself, you may be blinded to the need for changing your ways. Social interaction can be improved only when you realize that it is necessary to change your behavior. This basic insight is the foundation of successful marriage counselling.

The Problem of Personal Characteristics

Every "someone" is a person with various characteristics. Some of these we like, some we dislike, and to some we are indifferent. A person's behavior, therefore, is colored by our perception of these characteristics as they apply to the context of the person's action. In fact, sociologists consider the positive and negative labels we attach to certain personal characteristics, called *x-factors*, as important contributors to social problems such as prejudice, discrimination, and delinquency.

Most signals in the context to which we respond during an interaction are complex amalgams of behavior and several x-factors. If an elderly woman stumbles on the sidewalk, we are likely to help her (noting the x-factors of gender and age). But if we see a young man stumble, we may well mutter something about "disgraceful drunks" (again we are aware of two x-factors: age and gender). Our reactions to the same behavior are different because the x-factors tell us that one person needs help, whereas another incurs our disrespect.

X-factors tell us what we want to hear — they do not necessarily indicate what actually exists. The young man may not have been drunk but disabled in some way. Frequently, in fact, x-factors trigger our imagination and serve as shortcuts to incorrect conclusions about individuals, situations, and behavior. In such cases, x-factors are the essence of prejudice.

When we react to a person's age, gender and/ or race rather than to his/her behavior, the link between that person's action and our own behavior is weakened and perhaps broken. Hence the individual can no longer predict and control the consequences of his/her action. As we saw earlier in the chapter, this lack of control will affect that person's future activities and perhaps even his/ her self-conception.

Many teachers favor pupils whom they consider to be bright or who come from a middle-class background; which clearly influences educational achievement.

A culture can define personal characteristics, such as race, height, or religion, as x-factors, and people may react to them positively or negatively. If we react negatively (i.e., discriminate), the person is less likely to interact with us in the future. If there are many of us, the person is likely to withdraw from contact with all those who discriminate against him/her on the basis of the x-factor. Positive reactions to an x-factor also disrupt the link between behavior and its outcomes. If we shower children with approval regardless of their actions, they will not learn the basic rules of social behavior and may well end up being selfish, spoiled brats.

Any reactions to x-factors, be they negative or positive, will have detrimental effects on an individual. In Chapter 20 you will see how gender, race, and age affect individuals and their activities. But there are other x-factors as well and sometimes they are found in places where we least expect them. Several studies have shown, for example, that teachers often react to pupils on the basis of their intelligence, occupation, income of parents, and even first names (Rosenthal and Jacobson, 1968). Many teachers tend to pay more attention to and reward with better grades pupils whom they consider to be bright or who come from a middle-class background.

The operation of such x-factors disrupts the linkage between actual performance and outcome. If this happens often in the life of students, they will probably feel discouraged and exert less effort in the future. As we saw in a preceding section, one's self-image is also likely to be affected. We can only wonder how many high school dropouts have been influenced by a teacher's incorrect perception of x-factors. A study of communities in Northern Ontario, for example, showed that teachers' differential treatment of pupils was responsible for the high correlation between the parents' social class and the children's educational achievement (Lucas, 1971).

One of the most interesting x-factors is physical attractiveness. In general, people expect physically attractive individuals to be warmer, friendlier, and socially more adept than the average or unattractive person (Berscheid and Walster, 1978). People therefore behave in ways that produce just that kind of warm and friendly reaction from the attractive individual. Here we have another example of self-fulfilling prophecy in social interaction.

Indeed, people often draw rather farfetched conclusions regarding attractive individuals, through fleeting impressions gathered on an elevator or while stopping at a traffic light. In a classic study (Dion et al., 1972) students were shown photographs of people their own age. From these, they inferred that the more attractive individuals would get better jobs, marry earlier, have happier marriages, and lead more satisfying and contented lives.

INTERACTION AND SOCIAL PROCESSES

From our knowledge of social interaction, it is possible to better understand the major social processes that characterize various cultures and occur daily in the world around us. Two significant components of social processes are *aggression* and helping (as an expression of altruism). Whereas the former leads to various problems and comes between individuals, groups, and nations, the latter results in co-operation and is at the root of humanitarian efforts.

On the societal level, these two social processes can pervade an entire nation or culture. In a famous study, anthropologist Ruth Benedict (1934) compared the peaceful, co-operative culture of the Zuni (of New Mexico) with the conflict-ridden, competitive culture of the Dobu of New Guinea. Her descriptions focused not so much on the culture as on the kind of interaction in which people typically engaged. Aggression and co-operation in daily life contribute to a culture's tone, at the same time as the culture teaches and encourages one or another kind of social interaction.

Aggression

Although many people talk about aggression and condemn it, scientific debates continue to question the actual causes of aggression and how to minimize it. Today, even the definition of aggression is problematic, since there is no consensus on what aggression really is and thus no agreement on what to do about aggressive acts.

The basic difficulty is that the label "aggression" is attached to a great variety of activities, without much agreement as to what the distinguishing features are. Even in such relatively simple situations as children's games, it is often hard to differentiate between play and genuine aggression.

The first step in analyzing aggression, therefore, is to determine which acts are truly aggressive. It is common practice to consider not only the doer's behavior itself, but also the recipient's reaction, such as pain. The circumstances, recent history, and the doer's intention are also taken into account. Finally, the relationship of the observer to the individual(s) charged with aggression matters, as when one parent says to another, "Your child is aggressive; mine is exuberant." Thus, the acts described as truly aggressive are much more limited in scope and fewer in number than appears at first glance.

Although there are several views on aggression, the emerging consensus holds that the essence of aggression is behavior that injures an individual(s) or destroys property (in cultures where property matters) *and* is considered aggressive by other people. The two important factors are a person's behavior and other people's evaluation of it. Both vary from one culture to another. According to Benedict, the peaceful Zuni consider shouting and forceful gestures toward others as aggressive and reprehensible, whereas the Dobu regard these actions and some actual violence as simply expressions of masculine prowess.

If aggression is to be eliminated, or at least reduced, we must know what causes it. Unfortunately, today there are more theories about the causes of aggression than accurate information, and all too often the programs advocated reflect one or another theory rather than valid knowledge. Any program based on faulty theories, of course, is bound to fail.

We now turn to the two major theoretical perspectives of aggression and consider their implications for solutions to the problem. Instinctual theories postulate that aggression is inborn and therefore there is little hope for its reduction. In contrast, social-learning theories postulate that aggression is learned — and thus can be changed.

The Instinctual Perspective

Sigmund Freud (1933) proposed what for many years was the most popular explanation of aggression: that it is part of human nature. Since aggressive acts are instinctual, individuals must learn to displace and sublimate their aggressive tendencies. For example, attending football games and other sports events would be a means of channelling aggression in harmless directions. Since there are few, if any, ways to displace aggression on the societal or national level, nations always face the danger of external threats.

Ethologist Konrad Lorenz (1966) proposed a theory of aggression based on his studies of animals, especially primates. He, too, postulated that aggression is instinctual in the entire animal kingdom, including human beings. These instincts are generally adaptive in that their existence helps animals cope with their environment and survive for many generations. The energy for aggressive behavior is generated internally — it does not require an outside source — and this is where the danger lies for humankind. The danger is aggravated by the fact that lower animals have developed certain inhibitions that prevent them from killing members of the same species, but human beings have not yet developed such inhibitions. Again, there is little that can be done about the problem of aggression, aside from channelling it in safe directions, such as competitive sports.

There are several problems with instinctual theories. First of all, they are extremely difficult, if not impossible, to test and their empirical bases are far from solid. Lorenz's descriptions and interpretations of animal behavior, for example, have been called into question. Secondly, human aggression takes on various forms ranging from facial expressions to combat; it occurs in some situations and not in others: identical actions are sometimes labelled aggressive and sometimes not — for instance, a good body check becomes

interference to members of the other team. It is highly unlikely that the diversity of aggressive behavior, which also varies by circumstance, is caused by instinct. Finally, it is dangerous to apply the results of animal studies to human beings; at the very least, there has to be substantial empirical support.

The Social-Learning Perspective

As mentioned, Bandura (1973) postulates that aggression is learned and therefore not an integral part of human nature. On the basis of many human studies, he concludes that aggressive acts are acquired, largely through modelling, and are maintained by positive outcomes that are self-administered or arise from the context. Thus, we learn to engage in aggressive behavior from our parents, peers, and various other people whom we observe directly or through the mass media, particularly television. Many of the consequences experienced by an aggressor are positive or neutral, and the negative outcomes (e.g., verbal reprimand or threats of retaliation) are not always significant. More often than not, the total expected outcome of aggressive acts is at least mildly positive — unless we learn to administer our own negative consequences (feelings of regret or remorse in having acted aggressively), or think that legal sanctions are likely to follow.

Reducing aggression therefore requires changing or eliminating behavior regarded as aggressive. The way to accomplish this is through behavior modification in general: changing the consequences of aggressive acts from positive or neutral to negative. This includes discouragement and punishment. In addition, instead of using aggressive means, individuals must learn more effective ways of reaching their goals. Children, for example, should be taught to achieve status through academic performance or skill in sports rather than by bullying their peers.

This social-learning view of aggression has several implications for sociologists. Since aggressive acts are learned in a social context, it is neces-

Aggression can take on numerous forms, from competitive sports to combat.

sary to change the context so that it no longer engenders aggressive behavior. The elimination of aggression is not possible unless the culture or society emphasizes the peaceful resolution of interpersonal differences and conflicts, and unless the society is structured to discourage aggressive acts. Our culture does this to some extent, but at the same time it values the "macho" image and disparages "sissies." Ideally, a society should operate in such a way that the variety of prosocial behavior of which human beings are capable will bring its citizens positive outcomes (as defined by the culture).

Prosocial Behavior

The term prosocial behavior refers to those activities that benefit other people, regardless of what happens to the actor. Chief among these is altruistic behavior, such as helping other people. We are, perhaps, more aware of antisocial behavior, but this is due largely to the mass media and our selective perception and memory. Good deeds do not catch our attention unless they are truly outstanding, and the pleasurable interaction of daily life is so routine and mundane that we quickly forget about it. In this section we consider the nature and causes of altruistic acts.

Again, we begin by considering how circumstances affect the labels we apply to behavior. The same action, that of running into a burning house to rescue a child, for instance, can be viewed as altruistic or foolhardy. The label clearly depends on the fierceness of the blaze and on who rushes in: a firefighter, the father, a stranger, or a pyromaniac. To avoid this labelling problem, we shall concentrate on one person's helping another in more or less clear-cut situations.

As with aggression, the biological perspective postulates that many selfless acts have a genetic foundation, whereas the social-learning perspective holds that they are learned. According to biologist Wilson (1975), animals and humans are genetically programmed to engage in a variety of altruistic behavior that benefits the blood relatives of the individual — where the "benefit" refers mainly to the perpetuation of the species. In the extreme form of altruism, human beings (as well as some animal species) are genetically disposed to sacrifice themselves so that the larger group — the family, community or nation — can survive.

During the last ten years, this position has been hotly debated by biologists, sociologists, and others, with no resolution in sight. The major problems with genetic explanations are that (1) the altruistic behavior among human beings varies greatly; (2) they vary among members of a population; and (3) whether or not they are effective depends on the immediate and larger situation. Indeed, it is often not clear just which actions would most benefit one's family, community, or nation. For example, one has to consider the probabilities and the frame of reference before "joining the army" turns out to be altruistic — if it ever does.

Research on human altruism leads to the conclusion that most acts labelled altruistic are learned in some way that other behavior is (Rushton, 1980). Furthermore, situational factors, such as the people involved, the nature of the problem, and the general circumstances, have been shown to be significant determinants of the help that people offer.

From studies of children, we know that altruism develops over the years, especially as children acquire the ability to put themselves in the place of other people. From parents, peers, and later from other adults in their surroundings, children learn through modelling and encouragement a variety of altruistic acts and the circumstances where such acts are appropriate. Indeed, emphasis on helping, sharing, and general concern for others is so pervasive in the family setting that by the time children become adults, they are no longer aware of how often self-reinforcement occurs. We simply feel good when we have helped others.

Just because people have learned to help others, however, does not mean that they will proffer help when it is called for. As we saw earlier, situational factors — the signals perceived in the context and the outcomes they lead one to expect — are the major determinants of human behavior. In our complex, urban-industrial society, the social environment is in constant flux and people's perceptions of it vary greatly. No wonder the expressions of altruism are so varied and perplexing. The mass media inform us of heroic deeds versus bystander apathy, or courage versus cowardice.

The act of assisting others is the last of several steps, each with its problems and uncertainties (Latane and Darley, 1970). The first step is actually noticing someone who needs help. Your perception depends on such factors as time — people in a hurry are less likely to notice individuals in trouble. Secondly, you have to interpret the situation as one requiring action. But your interpretation may be erroneous, not necessarily through your fault. When you are surrounded by calm people who do nothing even though there is smoke in the room, you will probably not worry and do nothing. When you are used to fire drills and false alarms, you may not be aware of an emergency until someone shouts, "It's real!" after the alarm goes off.

Thirdly, you must decide that it is your responsibility to do something. When you are alone with someone who is in trouble, the responsibility clearly rests on you. But when there are others, the responsibility is diffused. As long as you are alone with a person suffering a seizure, for example, you represent the only possibility of help; but when others are present, you hope that there is a person who knows more about seizures than you.

The fourth step consists of choosing a way to help. Unfortunately, most emergencies require actions about which you probably know very little. This ignorance makes it rather difficult, and sometimes impossible, to select the most effective course of action. If you see a man struck by a car, do you move him or not? (He might have a spinal injury.) You are awakened by the fire alarm in the hotel. Do you stay in your room and hope for the best, or do you lead your family out into the hall and look for the stairs? After a major hotel fire, we usually read about guests who died because they did the wrong thing, but what is right or wrong is usually not apparent until after the fire. (It depends on factors about which guests know nothing, such as the source and nature of the fire.)

Then you consider the consequences of your action. Here you think not only about the probable effectiveness of your help and the dangers of doing the wrong thing, but also of the outcomes for you personally. How dangerous is the situation? If you stop to help this person, and if you do the wrong thing, will you be sued? After all, compassion and ignorance do not make a delightful and effective combination, especially in a courtroom.

The final step is implementation. You do what you have decided is the best; or rather, you do whatever you can, which may not be the best course to follow (and we may be aware of our limitation).

In simple situations, such as giving up your lunch hour to help a classmate with her homework, it is easy to be altruistic. We quickly go through the steps outlined above and may not even be aware of them. But when we come upon an accident that just happened, our thoughts in some of these steps may be difficult to sort out.

There is more to helping others than the foregoing sequence of steps when confronting an emergency. It has been well-established that the victim's characteristics also affect our behavior (Penrod, 1983: chapter 12). Generally speaking, people are more likely to help those who are similar in socioeconomic status, race, religion, and nationality. Often we make snap judgements based on clothes and evidence of personal care (such as grooming). Furthermore, people are more likely to help those who are physically attractive. In large part, this is because attractive individuals are thought to have several other positive characteristics, as we saw earlier. There is some evidence, indeed, that this factor may be more significant than the presumed similarity of victim and helper.

Finally, people are likely to help those who are deemed not to be responsible for their plight (Lerner, 1970). A complicating factor is the frequent tendency to blame the victim, to assume that those who are in trouble got themselves into difficulty. We would expect, therefore, that we are more likely to help an old lady who has been struck by a car while crossing a street at a crosswalk than a teenager with a Walkman who has crossed a busy street in the middle of the block.

In conclusion, if it is true that aggression and altruism are affected more by learning than by instincts, and arise from our experiences and the social context rather than from our genetic makeup, then social processes such as co-operation and conflict are not natural and inescapable; they are not necessarily part of human nature. Today we know that co-operation must be learned and that conflict can be prevented — if the social context of individuals encourages the first and discourages the second.

SUMMARY

1. The interaction of two or more individuals constitutes the essence of social life. Since behavior is determined largely by expected outcomes and contextual signals (which indicate likely outcomes of our actions), interaction occurs when one person produces outcomes and/or signals for another.

2. These signals and outcomes can be actual behavior or symbols, such as words and gestures. Thus, sociologists often speak of symbolic interaction as the essence of human social life. Participants in an interaction exert reciprocal influence on each other, which in turn means that many outcomes of a person's actions are, in fact, the result of his own action. In a very real sense, therefore, an individual helps produce his own outcomes. This is most evident when society is structured in such a way as to make self-fulfilling prophecies possible.

3. Social interaction is likely to continue if the relationship is balanced and fair. That is, the partners' views of one another and their beliefs should concur, and each should receive outcomes that reflect the contribution to the relationship. When effort is related to results, rewards should be distributed equitably; but when chance is the major determinant, rewards should be distributed equally.

4. On the basis of interaction, individuals acquire new behavior and a self-image. We learn from models and their experiences what we should and should not do. And we learn who we are by relating other people's reactions to our actions. When we interact with a variety of people in different situations, we are likely to develop an adequate and valid self-conception.

5. An important dimension of any interaction is what Goffman calls "impression management," wherein the participants attempt to create impressions of themselves. Sometimes the effort to create the right impression is the raison d'être of an interaction, as for example, on a first date.

6. Another dimension of interaction is the exchange principle: we give in the expectation of getting something in return. Interaction as exchange has been useful in analyzing the social relations that occur in small groups and large bureaucracies.

7. Two major factors interfere with the smooth running of an interaction. We may misinterpret another's action and therefore respond inappropriately, or we may react to personal characteristics such as gender or age rather than to the other's behavior. In either case, the link between the other person's behavior and the expected outcome is weakened or even broken. This has repercussions for both individual behavior and future interaction.

8. Two opposing perspectives of social processes have been advanced: one based on instinct, and the other based on social learning. Aggression and altruism are two major processes that pervade societies. Lorenz maintained that aggression is inherent in human nature as it is in the animal kingdom. Bandura argued that aggression is learned through modelling.

9. Similarly, the issue of whether altruistic behaviour is genetically programmed or learned has been debated for the last ten years. It appears, from the study of human altruism, that acts labelled altruistic are learned.

GLOSSARY

Aggression. Behavior that injures individuals or destroys property and that is regarded as aggressive by others.

Attribution. The process of assigning causes to events and activities experienced by the individual.

Cognitive balance. The consistency of beliefs, attitudes, and behavior of the individuals in long-term interaction.

Distributive justice. Rules regarding the relationship between a person's contributions to an interaction and the positive (and negative) outcomes.

Dyad. A relationship composed of two individuals.

Impression management. The attempts of participants in an interaction to convey certain impressions about themselves.

Interaction. A process by which one person's behavior influences another's.

Labelling. The process of reacting not to an individual's actions but rather to the label that has become attached to the person (e.g., delinquent).

Modelling. The learning of new behavior by observing what happens to other people as they behave in a particular context and experience various outcomes.

Sanction. Positive or negative consequence of certain behavior.

Social exchange. The concept of social interaction as an exchange of goods or services.

Symbolic interaction. The conception of social interaction in terms of people's interpretations of one another's actions, including the meaning individuals attach to various behavior.

X-factors. Those personal characteristics (age, gender, race) that tend to elicit certain reactions from others.

Goffman, Erving. *The Presentation of Self in Everyday Life.* Garden City: Doubleday, 1959. The classic description of social interaction from the point of view of the participants.

Homans, George C. *Social Behaviour: Its Elementary Forms.* Revised edition. New York: Harcourt Brace Jovanovich, 1974. The best introduction to social interaction from an exchange perspective. Well-written and full of interesting examples.

Kelley, H. H. and J. W. Thibaut. *Interpersonal Relations: A Theory of Interdependence.* New York: Wiley Interscience, 1978. An advanced analysis of social interaction in terms of costs and benefits.

Rosenberg, Morris and Ralph H. Turner (eds.). *Social Psychology: Sociological Perspectives.* New York: Basic Books, 1981. A rather advanced treatment of most of the topics discussed in this chapter.

FURTHER READING

Bandura, Albert. *Social Learning Theory.* Englewood Cliffs: Prentice-Hall, 1977. A good introduction to the principles of social learning and modelling, and their application to various social phenomena.

Blau, Peter M. *Exchange and Power in Social Life.* New York: John Wiley & Sons, 1964. An excellent application of exchange theory to a variety of social phenomena, ranging from small groups to bureaucracies and institutions.

Blumer, Herbert. *Symbolic Interactionism: Perspective and Method.* Englewood Cliffs: Prentice-Hall, 1969. Although not recent, this introduction to the symbolic-interaction is good and very readable.

Formal Organizations

R. ALAN HEDLEY

In an urban-industrial society, in which most Canadians live, we occupy many roles. Some of these roles involve deep, long-lasting relationships, whereas others are of an impersonal, short-lived nature, but both are essential to our daily life. Primary relationships involve the total personality of each participant: communication is personal and intimate, and provides a source of emotional expression and gratification. Secondary relationships, in contrast, involve only specific aspects of one's personality, have a limited scope in what is communicated, are impersonal and unemotional, and are engaged in to accomplish specific goals or purposes. It is these secondary relationships that form the basis of formal, complex organizations.

The twentieth century has been called "the age of organization." In a very real sense, the emergence of large-scale organizations encompasses most aspects of everyday life in our modern age and so affects how we think and behave. The evolution of formal organization and its envelopment of contemporary industrialized society is aptly described in the following quote:

Only a lifetime ago, at the turn of the century, the social world of Western man might have been represented as a prairie on which man himself was the highest eminence. A small hill—government—rose on the horizon, but while it was larger than anything else there, it was still quite low. Today, by contrast, man's social world,

whether West or East, resembles the Himalayas. Man seems to be dwarfed by the giant mountains of large-scale organization all around him. Here is the Mount Everest of modern government. Next to it there are the armed forces, which in every country devour the lion's share of national production. Then come the towering cliffs of large business corporations and, scarcely less high and forbidding, the peaks of the large, powerful labour unions; then the huge universities, the big hospitals—all of them creatures of this century.
(*Drucker, 1964:vii.*)

Although such organizations may not be a recent creation, never before has society been structured in such an organized fashion as it is today. For example, most Canadians (76 percent) live in organized complexes called cities, and an even greater proportion earn their income in formal work organizations. In 1981, fully 93 percent of all non-agricultural workers were wage earners, that is, working in organizations as opposed to being self-employed (Statistics Canada, 1981:44). Furthermore, most Canadians work in large organizations such as public bureaucracies, industrial and commercial enterprises, educational institutions, and hospitals. Therefore, it is important to understand how these formal, complex structures work.

CHARACTERISTICS OF FORMAL ORGANIZATIONS

Organizations are extensions of ourselves. They permit achievement of goals otherwise unattainable on an individual level. For example, it is inconceivable that any one individual could engage in all the activities associated with the administration of a university, any more than it is possible for an individual to build and launch a space satellite. It is through organizations that individuals can accomplish complex objectives.

Horizontal Differentiation

One of the essential features of organizations is a *division of labor* or horizontal differentiation, whereby members participate collectively in the achievement of an organizational task. The type and degree of horizontal differentiation vary according to the nature of the task performed. For example, the complex task of automobile assembly is usually broken down according to groups of workers who vary in skill and function, who perform various operations in sequence until a car is produced. Compare this kind of extreme division of labor with the job of a family doctor who is responsible for treating a whole patient.

Vertical Differentiation

A corresponding feature of formal organizations is *vertical differentiation*, or the establishment of a hierarchy to achieve the co-ordination necessary for completing a task. Almost as soon as there is a division of labor, it is likely that someone will assume a supervisory role. Again, the degree of vertical differentiation varies according to the relative complexity of the task. Many or only a few hierarchical ranks may be established.

In the example of the automobile assembly plant, the top organizational level will be occupied by the plant manager responsible for overseeing the entire operation. On the next level may be divisional superintendents who are responsible for functions within their area of expertise. The superintendent of production ensures that sufficient raw materials have been ordered to maintain the desired level of production within the plant. This superintendent will also be in charge of the actual production operations, seeing to it that quality controls as well as volumes of output are met according to prescribed, company procedure. The superintendent of sales is responsible for providing markets for the finished products, and the superintendent of finance is in charge of cash flow, both out of and into the company. The next hierarchical level may consist of various departmental managers, and below them fore-men, and finally, the actual workers (assemblers, salespeople, and clerks). A simplified chart of a university structure illustrating both horizontal and vertical differentiation is shown in Figure 9-1.

Formalization

Another dimension of organizations is the degree of formalization or standardization — that is, the extent to which organizational operations are codified in terms of job descriptions, procedures, rules, and regulations. In those organizations with highly predictable operations and outcomes, a high degree of formalization may be introduced. For example, in some government bureaus responsible for processing many similar cases, job types and levels within jobs are defined in specific detail,

and procedures are rigidly standardized within an exhaustive system of rules and regulations. However, in bureaus where many dissimilar cases may be encountered, it is impossible to standardize operations. Instead, employees are given discretion to handle things as they see fit on a case-by-case basis.

Centralization

The final characteristic of organizations we shall consider is centralization, or the delegation of authority. Power is the ability to influence the actions of others, and it may be located at the uppermost ranks of the organization or it may be diffused throughout. Again, the nature of the task (and other factors) influences whether an organization is centralized or decentralized with regard

FIGURE 9-1.

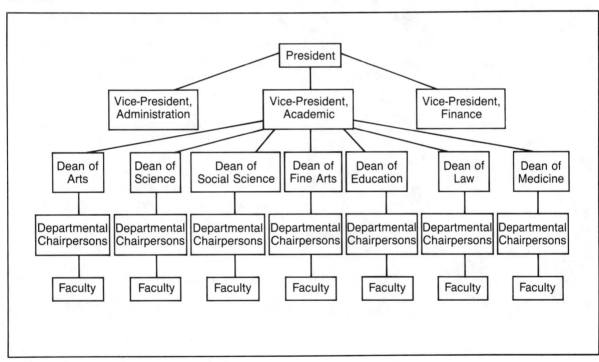

In division of labor or horizontal differentiation, as on an automobile assembly line, one complex task is broken down into a sequence of functions performed by different individuals. Here, workers at a General Motors transmission plant check gears.

to its decision-making function. An important recent development with respect to the centralization of power is the computer revolution and the significant advances in information and communications technology. For example, it is now possible for managers, geographically remote from their various operations, to have instant access and up-to-the-minute information on all facets of their business simply by punching a few keys on their head-office terminals. (See Guiliano, 1982.) Obviously, this new technology has important implications for the locus of power within organizations. Already, the major banks have computerized their operations and introduced centralized decision-making such that local branch managers have very limited authority in comparison to what they exercised only ten to fifteen years ago.

FORMAL ORGANIZATION DEFINED

A definition of formal organization is difficult because it must apply to all the many different social structures we characterize as organizations. What do business corporations, universities, hospitals, prisons, governments, churches, labor unions, and armies have in common? They are collectivities that are purposively established on a continuous basis to accomplish a defined set of goals. They are horizontally and vertically differentiated (i.e., there is a division of labor, and power is hierarchically distributed), the positions being connected by a communications system and bound by rules and regulations.

LEVELS OF ANALYSIS

How Organizations Are Studied

It is important to note at the outset that the study of organizations can involve different levels of analysis. This means that different researchers may be interested in different questions in their investigation of organizations and therefore collect different kinds of data.

Decision-making power in an organization may be centralized or decentralized, depending on the task at hand.

Basically, researchers are interested in dependent variables — in how and why they vary in terms of independent or causal variables. Depending on which dependent variables they select, they may be involved in one of four different levels of analyses.

1. Individual level. Some researchers are interested in what members of an organization think and how they behave as a consequence of their participation in organizations. Thus, the focus of research is on the individual, and the researcher may study such dependent variables as job satisfaction, productivity, perceived self-control, absenteeism, and so on. Why are some people more satisfied or more productive than others? What contributes to individual feelings of self-control? Under what conditions are people more or less absent? Typically, research on this aspect of organization is gathered by a questionnaire survey or through a personal interview of all or a sample of members. Some research on this level is conducted through participant observation.

2. Group level. Other researchers are interested in the functioning of groups within different organizational contexts. Their dependent variables involve, for example, group cohesiveness and morale, group interaction, the attributes of leaders in relation to other group members, conflict, and productivity. Research at the group level can encompass field experiments, sociometric surveys, interviews, and participant observation.

3. Organizational-elements level. At a more abstract level of analysis, some researchers are concerned with the composition, structure, and functioning of organizations. Why are some organizations "tall" (i.e., have many hierarchical levels) while others are relatively "flat"? Under which conditions can formalization be introduced? What are the determinants of centralization? Why

What do business corporations, universities, hospitals, prisons, governments, churches, labor unions, and armies have in common? They are collectivities purposely established to accomplish a defined set of goals.

are some organizations of similar size, and that manufacture exactly the same products, more productive than others? Research on these aspects of organization is conducted by secondary analysis (systematic search of existing organizational records) or by interviewing key informants (often personnel managers and chief executive officers). The unit of analysis in this type of research is some element or characteristic of organization, and therefore it is necessary to compare and contrast many organizations in order to arrive at satisfactory answers.

4. **Global organizational level.** The most general or abstract level is the anlaysis of entire organizations as composite entities. At this level, researchers may be interested in the relationship of organizations to their environment, or in the relation between organizations. Other researchers may compare and contrast large complexes of organizations, for example, the relative profitability of various manufacturing industries. Does the organizational mix within industries explain profit-

ability, or is the technology employed within and between industries a more important factor? Reasearch at the global level generally involves secondary data — company records, or government or other institutional data.

It may be seen that interest in organizations can occur on several levels, and involve an extremely wide variety of research problems. Even though researchers may be interested in the same theoretical concept, e.g., productivity, the level of analysis they select will involve them in examining very different issues. You will note that examples of productivity or profitability (a measure of productivity) were provided for each of the four levels of analyses. Yet the researchers involved in these projects would have very little in common with each other and it would make no sense for them to pool their findings. This is why it is extremely important to keep in mind the level of analysis when engaging in or assessing research on formal organizations.

MAJOR PERSPECTIVES ON ORGANIZATIONS

The emergence of modern organizations can be traced back to the Industrial Revolution in England at the end of the eighteenth century. With the harnessing of inanimate energy (James Watt discovered the steam engine in 1784), it was both possible and at the same time necessary to build large machinery capable of producing great volumes of output. It was possible because, for the first time, the capacity of the tools and equipment could exceed the limits of human physical power. Mechanical rather than human power was the driving force. However, the construction of this equipment was also relatively expensive compared with human labor. Therefore, in order to achieve *economies of scale* — increased volume of output at reduced costs per unit of output — it became necessary to build large complexes of machinery. In this way, the first factories, which comprised large-scale work organizations, came into existence.

In order to function to capacity, these factories demanded much human labor to operate the machinery. In response to this demand, the industrial towns of the English Midlands and north country sprouted, and newly formed factories dotted the countryside. With the surge of workers in these factories came problems of organization.

Table 9-1 presents a chronology and summary of the major perspectives used in the study of organizations. Generally, the movement from the rational-economic perspective in the early 1900s

TABLE 9-1. **Major Perspectives on Organizations**

Perspective	Major proponents	Approximate date of introduction	Critical Features
Rational-Economic	(a) Weber	1900	The ideal type of rational organization (bureaucracy) contains certain essential features: (1) hierarchical ranking, (2) functional specialization, (3) written records, (4) rules, (5) appointment based on merit.
	(b) Taylor	1910	An engineering model of work organization wherein managers are responsible for specifying precisely to workers: (1) the type of work to be done, (2) the method of performance, (3) the time necessary for completion.
Human Relations	Mayo	1930	A perspective that recognizes the importance of social relations and the informal social structure in the attainment of organizational goals.
Conflict Theory	Dahrendorf	1955	A model of organization that focuses on the inherent conflict among organizational participants, which arises from the unequal distribution of power and authority.
Open-Systems Theory	Thompson	1965	A perspective that recognizes the importance of the environment on the structure and operation of organizations. There is constant interaction and adjustment of an organization to its environment.
Contingency Theory	Lawrence and Lorsch	1970	An open-systems derivative that asserts that there is no one best method of organization. Contingencies such as the kind of environment, technology and organizational tasks and personnel all influence organizational structure.

With the Industrial Revolution, mechanical rather than human power became the driving force, paving the way for the modern technological era.

to present-day contingency theory may be seen as a movement from certainty to uncertainty. Early scholars and practitioners assumed that there was an ideal type of organization that would be able to handle any exigency that might arise under any conditions. Later scholars, after actually studying how organizations work and behave, came to the conclusion that there is no one best type of organization. Instead, the particular organizational structure that emerges is in response to a whole set of complex factors. We shall briefly examine these perspectives in this section.

Bureaucracy

Max Weber, pioneer of the study of organizations, proposed that the ideal type of organization for the pursuit of rational, complex objectives was a bureaucracy (Weber, 1964:329–41). According to Weber, all bureaucratic organizations should contain the following features:

1. A hierarchy. All bureaucracies should have graded levels of authority, with each level reporting and being responsible to the level immediately above, and with the person at the apex of the hierarchy having ultimate authority for all dealings within the organization.

2. Functional specialization. Tasks should be assigned on the basis of specialized competence. Thus, there should be clear areas of jurisdiction and delimited spheres of duty within all bureaucracies.

3. Written records. The life of a bureaucratic organization ideally lasts longer than that of any one individual. Written records or files constitute the mechanism by which this continuity is established.

4. Rules and regulations. These should cover every experience that an organization might encounter.

5. Appointment based on merit. The sole criterion for appointment to a position or promotion within a bureaucracy should be based on merit or achievement.

Because of these features, Weber believed that organizations based on bureaucracy are technically superior to more traditional organizations in the achievement of objectives.

Scientific Management

Frederick Taylor, an American engineer, was also concerned with devising the best system to accomplish organizational goals (Taylor, 1911). His approach, called scientific management, began from the principle that it is the duty of managers to assume responsibility for organizing *all* aspects of work — what workers do, how they do it, and how long it takes them. Furthermore, managers must organize the activities of all workers into a co-ordinated system of efficient output.

The basis of scientific management is task specialization; that is, the dividing and subdividing of work into its essential task elements, which can then be performed by individuals with a minimum of training and instruction. (Henry Ford later adopted Taylor's principles in the construction of the world's first automobile assembly line.) Thus, all responsibility for the organization of work lies with management; workers are responsible only for the performance of explicitly defined, standardized tasks. In this way, workers become simple appendages to the tools and equipment with which they are working.

Both Taylor and Weber sought to establish systems of organization that could be universally applied to accomplish any limited set of objectives. Weber was a sociologist concerned with the total operation of complex organizations; Taylor was a manager interested in somewhat more limited endeavors, but both assumed that it was possible to arrive at the one best method of organization. The major difference between the two was that Taylor was interested in applying this knowledge to actual work organizations, whereas Weber devised general abstract principles of organization.

Human Relations

Elton Mayo (1960) and his colleagues at the Harvard Business School introduced the first note of uncertainty into the study of organizations. As a result of a number of experiments in a telephone assembly plant (the Hawthorne experiments), they discovered both a formal and an informal structure within organizations.

The formal structure refers to the blueprint or design for organizational behavior: that is, what *should* take place according to the rules and regulations, prescribed channels of communication, stated operating procedures, and official chains of command. In other words, the formal structure is an empirical approximation of Weber's ideal bureaucracy.

The informal structure refers to what actually takes place within the organization, which may not be consistent with the formal structure; in other words, "the actual personal interrelations existing among members of the organization which are not represented by, or are inadequately represented by, the formal organization." (Roethlisberger and Dickson, 1964:566.) Thus, the informal structure may either complement or run counter to the formally specified goals of the organization.

Discovery of the informal structure meant that just because organizations are designed in a certain fashion (e.g., Weber's bureaucracy) does not mean that they will necessarily operate in this way. Examples of the informal structure running counter to organizational design are (1) when friends are chosen for positions over more qualified candidates; (2) when rules are often circumscribed according to common operating procedure; and (3) when written records contain what is supposed to be on file, but not necessarily what actually occurred. In short, although many of the conclusions drawn by the Hawthorne researchers are still in doubt (Franke and Kaul, 1978), their findings gave rise to the first questioning of whether we can assume an organization will operate in the way we specify it should.

Conflict

This perspective on organizations comes from Marxist theory. According to Dahrendorf (1959), all members of an organization do not share the same interests and goals. Specifically, conflict of interest occurs between ranks within an organization. Managers and owners do not have the same objectives as do workers on the shop floor; often their objectives are antithetical to each other. Because of the unequal distribution of power and authority within organizations, conflict is endemic. Recognition of this fact strengthens the notion that it cannot be assumed that the formally stated goals of an organization (management objectives) are the goals of all members. An obvious and dramatic example of this fact is a prison. Prison officials have different goals than the inmates. A researcher who studies both groups will come away with very different accounts as to how the prison (organization) actually functions.

Open-Systems Theory

A relatively recent perspective introduces even more uncertainty into the study of organizations. Thompson (1967) pointed out that organizations interact with their environment in crucial ways and therefore cannot be studied as closed systems impervious to the effects of the larger society of which they are a part. Thus, in their study of organizations, open-systems researchers are concerned with such factors as labor supply, raw material, and competition as they affect organizational structure and process. For example, factories located near large available pools of labor employ a different recruitment strategy than do more isolated factories. Similarly, organizations in a highly competitive environment operate differently than organizations that have a monopoly over resources.

Open-systems theory thus assumes a state of flux and uncertainty rather than certainty. Through complex feedback mechanisms, organizations must continually adjust and adapt to their environment. Because environmental conditions everywhere are different and are themselves in a state of flux, no one structure is assumed to be best for all organizations; rather, the structure evolves in response to a particular environment.

Contingency Theory

Originally coined by Lawrence and Lorsch (1967), contingency theory focuses on those factors that contribute to task uncertainty: the nature of the environment, the type of technology employed to produce particular goods or services, and the kind and level of information that must be processed in order to achieve adequate organizational performance. The nature of the structure and process is contingent upon these and other factors. No longer do reseachers look for the one best way to organize; instead, they attempt to specify those variables that produce variation in structure and performance. In so doing, they hope to uncover complex relationships that both explain and predict the variance in organizational design.

"If Weber can be credited with emphasizing the structural features of organizations, he can also be charged with having set back their systematic empirical analyses by his use of the ideal-type model which implied, or was interpreted as implying, that all modern [bureaucratic] organizations were similar in their structural characteristics." (Scott, 1975:2.) Rather, in the contemporary empirical study of organizations, one is struck by the diversity as opposed to the uniformity that constitutes organizational life.

ORGANIZATIONAL CONTINGENCIES

Variables Affecting Organizations

Most contemporary research on organizations is involved with identifying those factors or contingencies that cause organizations to be different from one another. The most important are the size and technology of the organization, and environment.

Size of the Organization

Systematic research on organizations has been concerned with how the size of an organization (usually measured by the number of organizational participants) affects its structure and functions. And specifically, what effect has size on the administrative component of an organization? Traditionally, the argument for an increase in organizational size has been that economies of scale can be realized: a large organization can be managed with a proportionately smaller administrative overhead than a small organization; therefore, it will be more efficient, in that relatively more human resources can be focused on achieving the organizational objectives that have been set. Generally, research findings confirm the hypothesis that with increasing size the administrative overhead is proportionately smaller (Hall, 1982:56–63).

Other structural factors that have been studied in relation to size include formalization and centralization. Again, the results are not clearcut, but they suggest that as organizations become larger they also become more formalized (standardized impersonal control mechanisms are brought into play), and authority is delegated to a greater number of managers on all levels.

Technology

The first large-scale comparative study of the effects of technology on an organization was conducted by Woodward (1965) in approximately 100 British manufacturing firms. First, she classified these companies according to three major types of production technology: (1) unit production — the manufacture of items according to individual customer requirements (e.g., made-to-measure suits); (2) mass production — the manufacture of items for stock or inventory (e.g., off-the-rack suits, automobiles); and (3) process production — continuous production such that the "product" is measured in volume, weight or length (e.g., chemicals, food, petroleum). Woodward also constructed an index of business success, by which she rated the firms. Finally, she grouped all the firms into their appropriate technological types and then sought to determine whether certain structural features were the same for firms employing a common technology but different across technological type.

Some of Woodward's results are reported in Table 9-2. She found a direct relation between technical complexity (process production is technically more complex than unit production) and vertical differentiation — that is, firms employing process production have more hierarchical levels than do either mass- or unit-production firms. Furthermore, she determined that the most successful firms were grouped in the modal or most frequently occupied category (the circled numbers in Table 9-2.) of each technological type. Thus, not only did she find a significant relation between technology and structure, but she also provided evidence to confirm that there is no one best way to structure an organization. The appropriate structure is contingent upon a host of factors, including technology.

Other findings from this pioneer research are (1) as technical complexity increases, the percentage of total operating costs allocated to labor decreases; and (2) with increasing complexity, there is a marked tendency for the administrative component of an organization to increase proportionately.

Subsequent research on the relation between technology and structure has introduced confusion. Some researchers have corroborated Woodward's original findings, whereas others have refuted them. The major contention appears to be whether it is technology or size that is the major determinant of structure (Hall, 1982:63–69). However, given that structure is contingent upon many variables, researchers are now concluding that both technology and size have an effect on structure. Depending on the type of organization studied (manufacturing or service, for example, public or private), either technology or size determines the greater part of variation in structure.

TABLE 9-2. **Number of Hierarchical Levels in British Manufacturing Firms by Type of Production Technology**

Levels of Management	Production Technology			Total Firms
	Unit	Mass	Process	
8 or more	0%	3%	20%	8%
7	0	6	20	9
6	0	10	(28)	12
5	0	23	24	16
4	12	(52)	8	26
3	(75)	6	0	25
2	12	0	0	4
Total	99%*	100%	100%	100%
(Number of Firms)	(24)	(31)	(25)	(80)

*Figure does not equal 100 due to rounding.

SOURCE: Adapted from Woodward, 1965:52.

FIGURE 9-2.

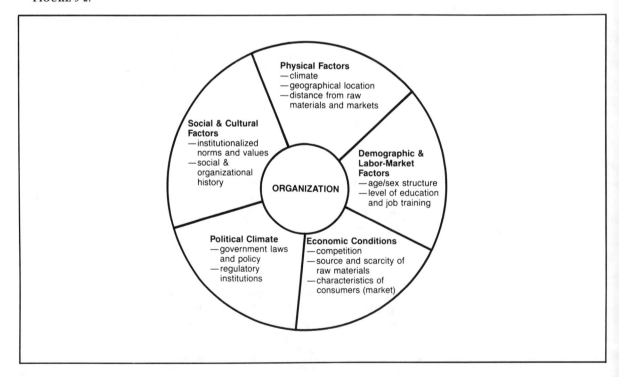

Environment

The environment of an organization constitutes everything that is *not* the organization—interrelated factors, which are only now being examined systematically and comprehensively. Figure 9-2 presents the major components of the environment with which organizations interact. Physical factors such as climate, geographical location, and distance from raw materials and markets are important to organizations, particularly if their operations involve dealing directly with the physical environment. For example, the location of oil rigs off the coast of Newfoundland is of strategic importance to oil companies in terms of cost and safety considerations. The estimated cost of drilling operations in some locations may preclude companies from preceeding further. In fact, all offshore drilling was prohibitively expensive before the price increases in oil in the early 1970s. Similarly, remotely located mines must ensure that

In figure:

Physical Factors
—climate
—geographical location
—distance from raw materials and markets

Social & Cultural Factors
—institutionalized norms and values
—social & organizational history

Demographic & Labor-Market Factors
—age/sex structure
—level of education and job training

ORGANIZATION

Political Climate
—government laws and policy
—regulatory institutions

Economic Conditions
—competition
—source and scarcity of raw materials
—characteristics of consumers (market)

their ore is of sufficiently high grade to warrant the heavy transportation costs involved in bringing the ore to the nearest available smelter. Whereas physical factors are more important to some organizations than others, they place constraints on all organizations.

Demographic and labor-market factors are also of importance to organizations. For example, the declining birth rate in Canada and the United States has severe implications for companies manufacturing baby products (diapers, for example). Either they must diversify their product lines, accept a reduced volume of sales, or go out of business. Provincial and state governments and local school boards must also deal with declining enrollments, which result from demographic changes in the population. On the other hand, the declining birth rate, together with the continuing improved standard of living in North America, has meant that the total population is aging. These same demographic facts have quite different repercussions for other organizations which provide goods and services to the elderly (e.g. pension plans, health and welfare schemes, nursing homes, and various products aimed directly at the aged). Consequently, demographic shifts in a population can either constrain or facilitate organizations as they attempt to achieve their objectives.

With regard to labor-market factors, it is imperative that organizations locate in areas in which there is (or they can attract) the staff necessary to carry on operations. Depending on the organization and its objectives, a large pool of highly skilled professionals and technicians of various types may be required. If this were the case, it would be necessary to establish operations in a relatively large urban area where one could be sure of a significant proportion of the population being highly educated. For these reasons alone, it is currently impossible to develop "high-tech" industry in Third World or underdeveloped countries.

Economic conditions in the environment are extremely important factors that organizations must deal with constantly. For example, the presence or lack of competition obviously has implications for an organization's performance, and it is an aspect of the environment that many organizations have increasingly attempted to control through the process of mergers and takeovers.

The prospect of economic competition in industrialized countries has resulted in increasing concentration of organizations in industrial sectors, with the result that relatively few organizations account for greater proportions of manufacturing assets, value-added through production and number of people employed. In Canada, "industrial sectors in which four enterprises have accounted for 80 percent or more of these indices ... have included, since 1948, cotton textiles, motor vehicles, petroleum refineries, tobacco, breweries, distilleries, rubber tires, and aircraft and parts manufacture." (Smucker, 1980:90.) Consequently, the response on the part of many organizations to competition in the environment has been to control this factor through consolidation; hence, the growth of corporations.

Social and cultural factors in the environment also impinge upon organizations. Institutionalized norms and values, for example, are reflected in organizational performance. Research in this area has questioned whether organizations in different cultures are becoming more alike because they increasingly have similar goals and employ the same type of technology (the convergence hypothesis), or whether organizations in different cultures are different from one another because of their different social and cultural environments (the cultural diversity hypothesis). As with most complex questions, one cannot answer in "either this or that" terms. Yet there is evidence to suggest that organizations throughout the world are becoming more alike, but that distinct cultural differences remain (Form, 1979).

The political climate, too, constrains organizations. In Ontario alone, there are now 292 provincial regulatory institutions (e.g., agencies, boards, commissions, and advisory, research, and other public bodies), most of which have been established to control the activities of business organizations (Bresner and Leigh-Bell, 1978). This number does not include federal, regional, and municipal regulatory bodies.

Government acts and policy reflect societal values and goals. For example, immediately after the great price increases in oil in the 1970s, Canadians indicated their desire to become self-sufficient with regard to energy. Government policy was thereby drafted to encourage exploration. The giant Alberta tar-sands consortium of public and private organizations was one significant result. Thus, the political climate as well as the other environmental factors discussed above have important implications for organizational performance. Because this environment is always in flux, its impact on organizations is variable, and their actions and interactions can in turn modify the environment. An example is the move of several large companies from Montréal to Toronto in the wake of "official" language legislation.

One of the major tasks adopted by researchers is to grasp all of the contingencies that affect the structure and function of organizations. This involves first of all a simple but laborious description of each of these contingencies, together with an assessment of their impact under a variety of conditions. When this point has been reached, it should then be possible for researchers to make reasonably accurate predictions about the likely consequences should particular organizations engage in specified courses of action. Although systematic research is relatively new, spanning only five decades, researchers are currently in a position where they have a grasp of the problems. Perhaps the next fifty years will reveal some of the solutions.

EMERGENT ORGANIZATIONAL FORMS

Two important types of organizations that have emerged in response to changes and constraints in the environment are professional organizations and multinational corporations. Professional organizations, which are different from traditional bureaucracies, came about as a result of a general increase in the educational level of society (Wood and Kumar, 1982:78); a greater need for specialized knowledge in the achievement of organizational objectives (Brown and Schneck, 1979); and the increasing importance of the tertiary or service sector in the economy (Hall, 1975: 17–24).

Canadian statistics reflect these facts. Fifty years ago only 6 percent of the labor force was comprised of professionals (Kubat and Thornton, 1974:154), whereas today the corresponding figure is 16 percent or almost two million (Statistics Canada, 1982:53). Also, the goods-producing sectors of the economy (agriculture, forestry, fishing, mining, manufacturing, and construction) accounted for 60 percent of the work force in 1931 (Kubat and Thornton, 1974:154), but only 30 percent of the current labor force (ibid). The service sector (commerce, health, education, finance, transportation, communications) employs fully 70 percent of the labor force today, and it is this sector in which most professionals work. The influx of professionals which these changes have brought has affected both how organizations are structured and how they function.

The other emergent organizational form, the *multinational corporation*, is one that is familiar

TABLE 9-3. **Foreign Control in Canadian Industry, 1977**

Type of Industry	Foreign Control	
	Asset value (in millions)	Percent of Industry
Manufacturing	$112,007	54
Mining	37,351	51
Trade	13,922	22
Services	4,665	18
Construction	2,223	12
Agriculture, forestry, fishing	353	8
Utilities	6,147	7

SOURCE: Adapted from Foreign Investment Review Agency, 1980:2.

to Canadians in that a significant proportion of Canadian industry is controlled by foreign interests. (See Table 9-3) Indeed, multinational corporations have become overwhelmingly dominant in international investment, production, trade, finance, and technology (Lall and Streeten, 1977: 11). Reasons for the emergence of multinationals include the quest for raw materials, expansion of existing markets, relatively cheap foreign production costs (including labor), favorable host-government policies and concessions, economies of scale, and the desire to maintain competitive advantage (Gherson, 1980; Lall and Streeten, 1977).

Let us now examine in more detail each of these organizational forms.

Professional Organizations

Basically there are two ways in which an organization can achieve a complex goal: by breaking down the objective into its component parts with various individuals becoming responsible for the achievement of simple tasks, or by training all persons to do all of the skills necessary to attain the objective and then by working more or less independently toward its achievement. This is the basic distinction between a bureaucratic and a professional organization. Bureaucracies are involved in the division and subdivision of goals such that with the appropriate co-ordination and control, the entire task can be achieved with no one actually having all the requisite skills to accomplish it on his or her own. In contrast, professional organizations teach each professional all the skills required for task completion.

From this basic distinction between bureaucratic and professional organizations, other implications follow. Below are juxtaposed the essential features of the bureaucratic and professional models of organization.

BUREAUCRATIC MODEL

1. **Division of labor.** Assumes that complex objectives will be broken down into specific task elements; these elements are then assigned to participants according to their functional area of competence.
2. **Hierarchical authority.** The basis of control lies in the hierarchical level of the position; organizational rank rather than knowledge becomes the grounds for assuming authority.
3. **Rules and regulations.** The participant's actions are governed by a *specific* set of rules and regulations established by the organization, which are designed to cover any exigency that may arise.
4. **Full working-capacity of the official.** Involves participants in the notion of a career with, and loyalty to, the organization.

PROFESSIONAL MODEL

1. **Systematic theory.** Presumes mastery by all professionals of that body of knowledge that constitutes the profession's major focus of interest.
2. **Professional authority.** Possession of a unique fund of knowledge, considered essential to society, places the professional in the logically necessary position either of being responsible for his or her own actions or of being controlled by other professionals who have the requisite knowledge upon which to judge performance.
3. **Code of ethics.** The professional's actions are governed by a *general* code of ethics established by the profession, which is internalized during the long training period by the professional to the point where the professional code and the individual's code are one.
4. **Professional culture.** Arises out of the formal and informal social interaction among professionals and involves commitment to the profession and what it stands for.

Because of the different bases for organization, conflict can and does occur between the bureaucratic and professional models. This is demonstrated when a significant proportion of bureaucratic organizations is comprised of professionals, which is increasingly becoming the case (Brown and Schneck, 1979). For example, a study (Hall, 1968) found that the greatest conflict between professional and bureaucratic modes of work is the source of authority. To the extent that hierarchical authority is imposed on professionals, there is an almost corresponding loss in their feeling of autonomy. Professionals strongly resist supervision from uninformed laymen, regardless of the latter's rank within the organization. As mentioned above, only professional colleagues with similar expertise are deemed competent to judge professional performance.

Although the potential for conflict between professionals and bureaucrats is strong, it does not necessarily occur. Depending on the perceived costs and benefits to both, accommodation and adaptation do take place. For, professionals increasingly need organizations both as contexts of work and custodians of scarce resources (money and equipment, for instance), and organizations, in their sophisticated development of various goods and services, increasingly need the specialized talents of professionals. But each side pays its price: for professionals, there is an erosion of (professional) autonomy; for organizations, an adjustment to their structure and process.

Out of the bargain develops the professional organization. Generally, what occurs is the carving out of an area of professional jurisdiction within an overall bureaucratic system of control. Within this defined area, professional norms of work organization are applied, provided that the outcome is consonant with bureaucratic expectations. In other words, both professional and bureaucratic models can be accommodated in a sort of uneasy alliance (Hedley, 1977).

Compared with a traditional bureaucratic structure, a professional organization is (1) more flexible with regard to rules and procedures; (2) is more task-oriented as opposed to being organized according to strict functional jurisdictions; (3) engages more in horizontal, collaborative communication and decision-making; and (4) is more responsive to change in the environment. The professional organization is thus an emergent organizational form precisely because it represents an adaptation to these changes in its environment.

Multinational Corporations

The impact that multinational corporations have on the world economy is dramatic. (See Table 9-4.) For many of them, their annual volume of sales exceeds the annual *gross national product* (i.e., the total market value of all the goods and services produced) of some not-so-small countries. In the view of the U.S. Tariff Commission, "It is beyond dispute that the spread of multinational business ranks with the development of the steam engine, electric power, and the automobile as one of the major events of modern economic history." (Cited in Lall and Streeten, 1977:15.)

A multinational corporation is an organization that "directly controls both the preparation and sale of goods and services in two or more countries." (Smucker, 1980:112.) Basically, this can occur in one of two ways: either a national corporation attains direct control of an existing foreign company, or it establishes a new subsidiary in a foreign country. Control is achieved through ownership of more than 50 percent of the voting stock of a company, although effective control can often be exercised through having a good deal less than this figure.

Multinational corporations represent a logical and rational step on the part of organizations to control their environment. Whether it be access to raw materials, cheap labor costs, or expanded markets by operating in two or more countries, organizations can achieve economic advantages and increase their profit margins substantially. Some of the "protective" strategies adopted by multinational corporations are truly phenomenal in their wizardry. For example, in order not to report high profits and therefore be subject to high rates of tax, many multinational corporations import raw materials and components from their affiliated companies at inflated prices, thereby reducing officially declared profits. Alternatively, finished goods are exported to subsidiaries at deflated prices, again accomplishing the same purpose of artificially lower profits.

This strategy, known as *transfer pricing*, is made possible by the exchange of goods, services, and technology across national boundaries, but within organizational units of the same firm. Murdoch (1980:246) reports that "the most notorious example of transfer pricing is from a study by Vaitsos of the pharmaceutical industry in Colombia. In 1968 total profits were reported as only 6.7 percent of multinational investment. However, when overpricing of goods sold by multinationals to their own Colombian subsidiaries, plus royalties paid for the imported technology, were calculated, return on investment rose to 136 percent!"

Many such mechanisms exist whereby multinationals, through trading across national boundaries and operating in several countries with different local conditions (including different rates of taxation), manipulate the environment to their advantage. Recently, their efforts have been facilitated by the advent of electronic data-processing and high-tech communications. No longer is it necessary to make *physical* financial transactions across borders; instead, transfer can be accomplished electronically, thus avoiding detection but further increasing control over the environment.

It is obvious that the multinational corporation as an emergent organizational form has substantial implications for existing patterns of relations among nations. So successful have these organizations been in manipulating and controlling their environmental contingencies that the balance of power in the world has shifted dramatically in favor of these freewheeling transnational giants.

TABLE 9-4. **Nations and Multinational Corporations: A Comparison of the Gross National Products of Selected Nations and the Annual Sales Volumes of Selected Corporations, 1980–81, in Billions of Dollars**

Nation or Corporation	GNP or Sales	Nation or Corporation	GNP or Sales
Saudi Arabia	$117.1	Israel	$17.6
Exxon	115.0	Safeway	16.6
Austria	76.7	K Mart	16.5
South Africa	66.4	Canadian Pacific	12.6
General Motors	62.8	Chrysler	10.8
Texaco	59.4	Singapore	10.8
Norway	59.1	Boeing	9.8
British Petroleum	49.2	Guatemala	8.3
Standard Oil of California	45.2	RCA Victor	8.0
Greece	43.4	Burma	6.3
Ford	38.2	Colgate-Palmolive	5.3
Algeria	37.1	Lockheed	5.2
Gulf Oil	30.5	Ghana	5.0
China	28.6	Zimbabwe	4.8
Sears Roebuck	27.4	McDonald's	2.5
General Electric	27.2	Macmillan & Bloedel	2.3
Egypt	25.2	Jamaica	2.3

SOURCES: *Moody's Handbook of Common Stocks, 1982;* and *World Population Data Sheets of the Population Reference Bureau, 1981 and 1982.* Adapted from a similar table in Lenski and Lenski, 1978:413.

SUMMARY

1. Although large, complex organizations have been in society for hundreds of years, only since the Industrial Revolution have they evolved into the characteristic form in which our society is structured. Formal organizations are the vehicles by which we achieve most of the objectives necessary for survival in a modern economy.

2. The modern study of organizations first began in the early 1900s with Max Weber, who was concerned to design an organization that would be ideal for the accomplishment of any set of objectives. This organization is a bureaucracy, in which positions are designated according to function (division of labor) and stratified according to authority (hierarchy).

3. However, discovery of the informal structure of organizations by subsequent researchers revealed that organizations do not always function in the ways that they are designed. Also, all members of an organization do not share the same goals. (The conflict between management and workers is a case in point.)

4. Finally, it was discovered that organizations do not operate independently of their environment. Depending on a host of interrelated factors, two otherwise similar organizations may have to be structured differently and operate differently in order to achieve similar goals.

5. Some of the important contingencies that account for variation in organizational structure and performance are size, technology, and environmental factors. Organizations, in turn, affect the environment of which they are a part.

6. Two emergent organizational forms — the professional organization and the multinational corporation — represent attempts on the part of some organizations to adapt to a changing environment and in so doing, to gain increased control over that environment.

7. Multinational corporations, by engaging in transnational imports and exports, manipulate their environment in ways impossible were these organizations to remain within the confines of one political boundary. Through the strategy of transfer pricing, multinational corporations increase both their control over the environment as well as their profit margins.

8. The study of organizations has changed significantly over the decades. Researchers now realize the complexities involved in organizational performance and the fact that this occurs in a dynamic, ever-changing environment.

GLOSSARY

Bureaucracy. An ideal type of rational organization that is characterized by hierarchical ranking, functional specialization, written records and files, rules and regulations, and appointment based on merit.

Division of labor. Functional specialization according to area of competence.

Economies of scale. Increased volume of output at reduced costs per unit of output.

Formalization (standardization). The extent to which organizational procedures and practices are explicitly regulated.

Formal organization. A collectivity that is purposively established on a relatively continuous basis to accomplish some defined set of goals. It is horizontally and vertically differentiated, the positions being connected by a communications system, and bound by rules and regulations.

Gross national product (GNP). The total market value of all goods and services produced.

Horizontal differentiation (division of labor). Functional specialization wherein organizational members are assigned tasks according to their special area of competence.

Multinational corporation. An organization that directly controls the production and distribution of goods or services in two or more countries.

Professional organization. An organization comprised of a significant proportion of professionals that is relatively flexible with regard to rules and procedures, task-oriented, and engages predominantly in horizontal, collaborative communication and decision-making.

Technology. The means employed to produce goods and provide services. Technology can be of three kinds: unit production, mass production, or process production.

Transfer pricing. A strategy employed by multinational firms whereby they exchange goods, services, and technology at artificially set prices across national boundaries, but within organizational units of the same firm.

Vertical differentiation (hierarchy). The extent to which an organization is stratified according to ranks of authority.

FURTHER READING

Anderson, John and M. Gunderson. *Union-Management Relations in Canada*. Don Mills, Ontario: Addison-Wesley, 1982. A comprehensive collection of articles dealing with all aspects of the Canadian industrial-relations system, including a comparison of Canada with the United States and Europe.

Britton, John N. H. and J. M. Gilmore. *The Weakest Link: A Technological Perspective on Canadian Industrial Underdevelopment*. Toronto: University of Toronto Press, 1978. An examination of the Canadian manufacturing sector, including a review of foreign control in Canadian industry.

Hall, Richard H. *Organizations: Structure and Process*. Englewood Cliffs, N.J.: Prentice-Hall, 1982. Now in its third edition, this standard text on organizations is written by one of the reputed experts in the field.

Lammers, Cornelis J. and D. J. Hickson (eds.). *Organizations Alike and Unlike: International and Interinstitutional Studies in the Sociology of Organizations*. London: Routledge and Kegan Paul, 1979. Studies of convergence and divergence in comparative organization research.

Scott, W. Richard. *Organizations: Rational, Natural, and Open Systems*. Englewood Cliffs, N.J.: Prentice-Hall, 1981. A textbook on organizations describing in detail the major perspectives that have been used in organizational research.

Smucker, Joseph. *Industrialization in Canada*. Scarborough, Ontario: Prentice-Hall, 1980. A history of industrialization in Canada and an examination of business corporations and the trade-union movement.

Wood, W. K. and P. Kumar (eds.). *The Current Industrial Relations Scene in Canada*. Kingston, Ontario: Industrial Relations Centre, Queen's University, 1978. An up-to-date compilation of statistics relating to the Canadian economy, manpower, and labor markets; labor legislation and policy; collective bargaining; and industrial relations.

CHAPTER TEN

Social Institutions and Functions

GORDON DARROCH

In the everyday use of the term, institutions are places such as schools, churches, hospitals, factories, prisons, and asylums. We also speak of long-established centres of activity, such as the Montréal Stock Exchange, Toronto's Maple Leaf Gardens, or Vancouver's University of British Columbia as major institutions of their communities. And we often hear of certain individuals having become "institutions in their own time": the long-lasting politician, the powerful corporate executive, the rock-star.

These familiar uses of the term may appear to be barely related, yet they share important shades of meaning, as this chapter will reveal. Most people read and use the term institutions regularly, although few, perhaps, could easily provide an exact definition. Consider the comment by the artistic director of the Winnipeg Folk Festival in a recent newspaper article: "The Winnipeg Folk Festival, in my opinion, has become an institution here; I am very wary, though, of it being institutionalized." (*The Globe and Mail*, 7 July 1984.) We can assume that readers of the morning paper readily understood the general meaning of the terms in this context. And although the artistic director of the festival was not attempting a sociological analysis, his use of the terms is not far from those common in sociology. Like many sociological concepts, the notion of a social institution is rooted in everyday language, yet has taken on specific theoretical meanings. It would be most convenient if, in this transition from everyday use to analytic use, the concept had acquired a single, widely shared meaning. However, the sociological meaning of institution varies widely, and the variations reflect different theoretical orientations or perspectives in sociological thought.

In this chapter, we consider how these variations reflect the major theoretical perspectives. Other chapters in this book discuss in detail specific institutions, such as the family, religion, education, politics, and the economy.

An excursion through the varieties of meaning of a single concept may seem an unnecessary complication in an introduction. But there are at least two good reasons for the analysis. First, an understanding of the concept of institutions is an essential ingredient in what C. Wright Mills (1959) called the "sociological imagination." A sociological imagination allows one to recognize that our personal life is directly connected to wider social arrangements — to the institutions that make up the larger society. Thus, the story of our life is profoundly shaped by changes in institutions, or as Mills would say, shaped by history. Sociological imagination is, Mills argued (1959:7), "The capacity to range from the most impersonal and remote transformations to the most intimate features of the human self — and to see the relations between the two."

Secondly, and directly related to the development of sociological imagination, is the fact that there are different approaches to the study of institutions, just as Chapter 2 revealed the many theoretical models of sociology itself. The liveliness and importance of sociological thought derives from theoretical debates and competing approaches, not from conventions and consensus.

DEFINITIONS OF SOCIAL INSTITUTIONS

A Working Definition

Two related elements can be seen in the everyday uses of the term institutions. (1) Social relations in places we call institutions, such as schools, factories, prisons, and asylums, follow well-established patterns. Compare playgrounds, sporting events, or a protest demonstration, which are not referred to as institutions. (2) The term seems to be applied to situations in which there is some structure of power, and often a distinctive authority structure. In the school, there is the division between teachers and students, in the hospital and prison between staff and inmates, and in the factory, there is the division between manager or supervisor and workers. We can draw from these observations a preliminary working definition: *Institutions are established social practices that entail some form of authority.*

It is important at this point to distinguish between institutions and organizations. The difference is frequently unclear in sociological writing, just as it is often not clear in everyday speech. Organizations are social arrangements designed to accomplish specific goals, as discussed in detail in Chapter 9. Institutions are large systems or structures within which organizations exist. For example, the church on the corner is an organization, whereas the religious system it represents is a social institution. Similarly, we distinguish between the school and the educational system, between the corporation and the economy, between your family and the family or kinship system of the community, between the provincial legislature, say, and the state or larger political system of which it is one part.

It is worth noting that these apparently straightforward distinctions are not always easy to maintain. Some authors will refer to *formal institutions* rather than organizations (Katz, Doucet, and Stern, 1982: Chapter 9), others simply use the term *institutions* (Goffman, 1961). The reason for this is that specific organizations reflect larger institutional practices and authority structures; we might say they embody or exemplify them. So the study of prisons, corporations, or hospitals can also be a study of the larger institutional systems they represent. In fact, some important studies of institutions begin with the study of a single organization. (See for example, Goffman, 1961, or recently, Clement, 1981.)

The working definition given above also reveals a fundamental difference between sociological approaches to the study of institutions. It is a difference discussed throughout this chapter. On the one hand, there are established social practices. On the other hand, there is authority. Most discussions of institutions emphasize one or the other of these elements, sometimes exclusively. But one question is basic to all institutional analysis — the question of how social order is routinely maintained. Simply put, how is it that the major institutions of our society are not disrupted or torn apart by the differences among us in our interests, resources, and capabilities? For the moment, what we call the functional perspective on institutions takes established social practices as the key to the question, since they reflect shared understandings and well-socialized forms of interaction among people. The alternative power-conflict perspectives emphasize the second element of the definition, that power and the way it becomes legitimized are the keys to institutional order.

Of course, the question of social *order* is only one side of the coin; it raises the question of the sources and directions of institutional *change*. But the question of order is a basic point of reference around which we can compare alternative perspectives on institutions.

One other element should be added to our working definition. It was noted that in ordinary speech, the term "institution" is often applied to specific agencies or organizations: a stock exchange, a hospital, a university. The usage also often implies that these are long-established and influential organizations. Furthermore, when we sometimes label particular individuals as "institutions," we mean that they have become highly influential in the community. Apparently, the shared meaning in these cases is that the person or organization has come to set standards for the community; they provide points of reference to

be emulated or imitated, by which we measure the actions or performances of others.

Again, everyday speech shares a key element with the more formal sociological concept. If institutions are social practices, they are practices that are guided by principles or standards that have become widely known among members of the community. This is why we say institutions are "established" practices. Specific standards of conduct are referred to as social norms, or "rules of the game," which may be written, as in the case of the law, or unwritten and enforced by informal sanctions. Norms are usually distinguished from basic values and beliefs, but both are involved in any social institution.

Taking all the elements discussed above now gives the following working definition: *Institutions are social practices, established in conformity with principles or standards that have become widely known in the community, and upheld by power or authority.* In our discussion of various sociological perspectives, definitions taken from each will be introduced; they will certainly differ from this working definition, but the particular emphasis of the perspective in question will be more readily apparent when compared to it.

Functionalist Definitions

The most widely known approach to social institutions is called functional or structural-functional. Many introductions to institutional analysis adopt this perspective to the exclusion of any other.

In the functionalist perspective, institutions are (1) the main social means through which human activities are organized, and (2) they are established to serve basic needs or solve the basic problems that seem to be universal to ordered social life. The definition and the perspective it represents emphasize three characteristics of institutions. First, that they "function" to fulfil certain basic needs or resolve universal human problems. Second, institutions are made up of a set of social roles (such as those of parents, children, or teach-

Individuals may come to be "institutions" through exerting a powerful influence on the community. The Beatles, for instance, set standards that are still felt and emulated by contemporary popular musicians.

ers) that are maintained and integrated by a shared normative order. Third, institutions are an expression of a fundamental social consensus on certain basic values. The norms or standards applying to particular social roles are versions or translations of the more fundamental values.

An even more formal definition is worth considering. One of the most influential functionalists, Talcott Parsons, stated: "An *institution* will be said to be a complex of institutionalized role integrates which is of strategic structural significance in the social system in question. The institution should be considered to be a higher order

unit of social structure than the role, and indeed it is made up of a plurality of interdependent role patterns or components of them." (1951:38-39.)

Now this definition is convoluted and confusing, partly because it is out of context, but largely because it is too abstract to be of much help. Luckily, a careful translation has been provided by C. Wright Mills (1959:29):

Men act with and against one another. Each takes into account what others expect. When such mutual expectations are sufficiently definite and durable, we call them standards. Each man also expects that others are going to react to what he does. We call these expected reactions sanctions. Some of them seem very gratifying, some do not. When men are guided by standards and sanctions, we may say that they are playing roles together ... an institution is probably best defined as a more or less stable set of roles. When within some institution—or an entire society composed of such institutions—the standards and sanctions no longer grip men, we may speak, with Durkheim, of anomie. At one extreme, then, are institutions, with standards and sanctions all neat and orderly. At the other extreme, there is anomie: as Yeats says, the center does not hold; or, as I say, the normative order has broken down.

The widespread use of functional approaches stems partly from a very persuasive answer to the question of order—specifically, functionalists suggest how culture accounts for social structure. In other words, the view assumes that values and norms emerging in everyday interaction are largely sufficient to maintain orderly patterns of behavior.

Power-Conflict Definition

Non-functionalist views emphasize not the smooth integration of roles by consensus on values, but the operation of power, though perhaps in subtle ways. Power is a central element in all conflict theories of institutions.

To his translation of Parson's functional definition, Mills added the question, "Have you ever been in an army, a factory—or for that matter a family? Well, those are institutions. Within them, the expectations of some men seem just a little more urgent that those of anyone else. That is because, as we say, they have more power." (1959: 29-30.) Mills's own argument was that the "good ideas" he found in a functional definition of institutions had to be balanced by recognizing that if institutions were clusters of roles, the roles were always arranged or graded in terms of authority. As noted above, authority is a key sociological concept, for it implies that power is taken to be legit-

imate, or at the very least, not routinely resisted. We shall explore these critical issues in more detail.

Definitions of institutions that take power or authority to be at their core have been given considerable emphasis by some prominent sociologists. The most concise is that of Stinchombe (1963:108): "By an 'institution' I mean a structure in which powerful people are committed to some value or interest."

Whereas functionalists view institutions as beginning with values shared by the whole community or society and expressing them through normative regulation of behavior, by placing power at the centre, the conflict perspective takes social values to be expressions of the interests of specific groups or classes. Stinchcombe comments further (1968:108): "The key to institutionalizing a value is to concentrate power in the hands of those who believe in that value ... whatever values or interests are defended by the various power centres of a society or groups are said to be institutionalized in that group."

This view of institutions as concentrations of interests and centres of power was developed in an earlier analysis of specific organizations (Selznick, 1957). It has the particular merit of providing an explanation of the "lasting power" or historical continuity of institutions. To put it in other words, it accounts for their stability in the face of either indifference to the values or in the face of real opposition to them.

Interpretations of institutions that focus on power also have the advantage of insisting that we look beyond the surface appearances of institutions—the appearance that all is well and there is little or no conflict—to a deeper source of their structure and stability: the greater power of some over others. In this respect, they also take conflict to be as commonplace in social life as harmony. The conflict may, however, be submerged and kept in check by both subtle and unintended means, as well as by obvious devices of social control such as the courts, police, military, and so forth.

Social order is based on shared standards, but these may be imposed as a form of social control.

INSTITUTIONAL ORDER: THE ACCEPTANCE OF AND RESISTANCE TO NORMS

As we suggested, one can view competing perspectives on institutions in terms of their answer to the question of how social order is maintained. The problem of social order may seem so elementary that it barely warrants analysis at all. After all, social life goes on and social organization appears all around us. Only rarely is there widespread disruption of the orderliness of everyday life, much less of the major institutional realms of the economy, of the political system, or of the

family. The significance of the question, however, can be seen if it is asked in a slightly different way: how do people come to know and to abide by the shared standards or understandings that guide their actions?

Other chapters in this book examine the question in detail, especially in terms of the processes of socialization. In the current context, what is important is that the way the question is posed and answered reveals a basic theoretical difference in the analysis of social institutions. Functional analyses strongly tend to emphasize the significance of socialization and the internalization of norms as part of the individual's own morality. Power-conflict analysts are much more skeptical. Socialization is not so benign, they argue. We do not just learn to fulfil our social roles; we are often compelled to learn and fulfil them. When, they ask, does socialization become social control?

The problem of how to distinguish socialization from social control is as fundamental as any question in the study of social institutions. The working definition, given earlier, was intentionally cautious with regard to this issue. It suggested only that the institutional standards or principles (norms) that regulated social practices were *widely known*. In effect, the definition hedged the question of whether widely *recognized* standards were also widely *accepted* by members of the community.

This issue will be considered in presenting each perspective. For the moment, we note that for any member of a community there is undoubtedly a difference between social actions that are based simply on a knowledge or understanding of what is expected or required in the given situation, and the internalization of the standards or norms. This distinction can be illustrated by drawing on Goffman's analysis (1961) of "total institutions."

By total institutions Goffman meant organizations that were also residential communities. The residents lead a largely confined and formally administered life. Hospital patients, inmates of asylums and prisons, children in boarding schools and summer camps, monks and nuns in monasteries, and prisoners in concentration camps all share a basically similar round of life, and perhaps, experiences. Goffman is clearly using the term institution to mean a special kind of organization, but he elaborates it into a full analysis of institutional life in contemporary society. One comparison in his provocative analysis, however, will serve to underline the difference between acceptance or internalization of norms and the mere tolerance of them.

Consider two total institutions, the concentration camp and the monastery. In the former, the inmates are expected by their countries to reject the standards of the camps and to resist actively their incarceration and their superiors, whenever it is feasible. At the same time, prisoners of war have a clear understanding of what is expected of them in the camps. In the terms used before, there is routine conformity to the role expectations and the norms. But it is clear that the conformity is superficial — the consequence of raw power.

The monastery, too, requires a recognition of the rules and expected practices. For both superiors and initiates, the intention is to achieve complete harmony of interests and motives. In this case, we are clear that the members wish to *internalize* the values of the community — to be one. This is complete socialization. Goffman (1961:91) provides this account:

People in the world are forced to obey manmade laws and workaday restrictions. Contemplative nuns freely elect to obey a monastic rule inspired by God. The girl pounding her typewriter may be pounding for nothing but dollars' sake and wishing she could stop. The Poor Clare sweeping the monastery cloisters is doing it for God's sake and prefers sweeping, at that particular hour, to any other occupation in the world.

Of course, the examples are extreme cases, but they serve to illustrate the issue. To summarize, functional theories and definitions of institutions imply that the values and norms regulating conduct are not only widely agreed on, but largely internalized as the actors' own motives. Power conflict perspectives often reserve judgement on the question of the sharing of values and the internalization of standards; they argue that standards and values come to be widely accepted for very different reasons, under different historical conditions. Goffman's typist conforming to the norms of the workplace, because she lacks options, is just one example.

In this context, both functional and power-conflict perspectives on institutions also differ with respect to the significance they attribute to resistance to and breaking of rules, and with respect to interpreting the sources of these violations. Functional approaches tend to treat violations as deviance, resulting from a breakdown in the processes that produce conformity, or as anomie, resulting from the breakdown of institutions themselves. The emphasis is often on a failure of socialization; in other words, on lapses in early and consistent learning of social values, or on rapid social change. The alternative perspective on institutions tends to view the breaking of rules and social conflict as a result of differences between groups in their interests and conditions of life, in their relative ability to organize and advocate their interests, and the extent to which rules or laws can be enforced.

In the sections that follow, we discuss perspectives on social institutions under the two broad labels of functionalist and power-conflict approaches. Obviously this simplifies the world of institutional analysis a great deal. Each perspective could be subdivided several times to reflect important internal differences and subtleties. Only one such division will be made in this discussion, because it is of such importance: between Marxist perspectives within the power-conflict school and other conflict perspectives. Stinchcombe's definition and approach cited above, for example, places power squarely at the centre of institutional analysis, but it is not Marxist.

In this Buddhist monastery, socialization is achieved through a common acceptance of not only rules but of shared goals.

The Functionalist Perspective: Analysis

Following Durkheim, functionalists came to argue that social order was only secondarily the result of external constraint — the imposition of norms by concrete sanctions, punishments, and rewards, for example, in the operation of the law. To reiterate the functional view: members of society fulfil their role expectations and conform to normative standards primarily because they internalize those norms and the values they represent; they come to adopt the standards as their own, as internal and self-imposed guides. In a word, the norms become their conscience.

Parsons has argued that Durkheim himself began with the view that norms could be understood as external constraints that control individuals from the outside. However, Parsons (1937: 378–90) noted that Durkheim, in his later work, came to recognize that norms are constituted or recreated in everyday social interaction, as well as the regulators of that interaction. To put it another way, we conform to norms as external standards, but we also affirm and reproduce the normative order at the very same time.

This emphasis in functionalist thought is a fundamental insight into the intimate relationship between social values, social interaction, and institutional order. Functionalists also provide an account of how norms are learned in the first place and how they are passed from generation to generation. This account focuses on socialization, especially in childhood. All new members of a community, but children in particular, tend to be taught a more-or-less consistent set of those expectations previously shared and reproduced by the other adult members of the community. As a result, it is argued, there is great stability in the general normative order from generation to generation.

In the next step in the analysis, functionalists argue that the variations in the socialization process, from one person and community to another, are limited and governed by adherence to very general values and beliefs. Consider the case of the family. Despite the diversity of family types in Canadian society, parents everywhere tend to teach their children, and especially male children, to be prepared to be competitive and achievement-oriented because those are the values of the larger society. To do otherwise is thought to be irresponsible: failing to prepare the children for the "jungle" out there. Similarly, we accept and we expect the school system to use standards of competitive grading because those are the accepted norms in the economy.

Functionalists also argue that there is orderliness in the way in which various institutional realms mesh together. As discussed previously, each institutional realm is viewed as a complex of roles that complements and is co-ordinated with the others. This co-ordination is a result of the general consensus on cultural values, which governs the whole society. Some institutions, such as the family, the educational system, and religion, specifically sustain the cultural values and reinforce them over time.

A final emphasis focuses on the separation of institutional realms. In less complex societies, it is argued, the institutional realms are deeply intertwined; a member of these societies might not distinguish, say, between kinship obligations, gift-giving, and economic activity as separate spheres and might be engaged in all three simultaneously. Functionalists argue that the evolution of modern industrial society has involved both increas-

ing institutional complexity and the progressive differentiation of institutional spheres. One knows precisely when one is engaged in the economy, the family, worship, or play; indeed, these activities often take place in different settings and at distinct times of the day or week.

A brief example of a functionalist analysis of the family will serve to indicate both the general logic of the approach, and coincidentally, how very familiar in sociological literature and in popular culture this form of analysis is. Studies of the family are often conducted from a functionalist perspective, particularly in comparative cross-cultural analysis.

Functionalists note that the family seems to have progressively lost certain functions with the advance of industrial society. Consider the family farm or industry, where the members of the family all contributed to production. The family, they suggest, has been largely stripped of its productive functions and become a simple unit of consumption in modern urban society. Similarly, it is argued, the educational functions of the family have increasingly slipped away and been replaced by the educational system of the larger society. These are functionalist examples of the institutional differentiation of modern society.

Moreover, functionalists argue (Parsons and Bales, cited in Worsley et al., 1977:180) that the family has not only lost some functions, but it has also become more specialized in function. They say there are two functions that the family carries out in modern society more effectively than it did in the past: primary socialization — that is, the socialization of young children — and the fostering of adult stability by the provision of privacy and refuge from the world outside. The fact that the modern family is devoted largely to these two functions has contributed both to the stability of the family unit itself and to the stability of the society. Clearly social order in contemporary society remains the central focus in this analysis.

Even in this sketch some of the appeal of a functionalist analysis can readily be seen. It is both internally consistent and is in keeping with a familiar idea that the smooth "fitting" of individuals and institutions to the needs of a society is determined by the twin criteria of efficiency and social order. The critics of functionalist accounts focus precisely on these familiar qualities.

The Functionalist Perspective: Criticisms

Functional theory has been widely and continuously criticized. Mills's comments on Parsons, cited earlier, were part of the early critique. The 1960s, in particular, generated a large amount of literature that argued that functionalism was a-historical and based on politically conservative assumptions. In this discussion, we shall briefly examine criticisms of the three main tenants of functional theory set out earlier and indicate how each is related to alternative perspectives that we have included under the rubric of power-conflict perspectives.

In one sense, the most characteristic feature of functional analyses of institutions is the claim that institutions are organized to serve basic social needs. The critics wonder what these needs are. They point out that although almost everyone can agree that societies as entities appear to accomplish certain basic tasks — there has to be an economy of some sort, and some form of government, and children have to be raised — it is never obvious what exactly the functional prerequisites or needs are, or how many there might be. (See Demerath and Peterson, 1967, for selected articles.) The reader can easily pursue this troublesome aspect of functionalism by making up a list of those needs of society that seem most urgent. One quickly finds there are many possibilities and no guide as to how to select among them. Your list is probably as good as mine, but they are not likely to be the same.

The notion of basic societal needs has been attacked on other grounds. Giddens (1977:111) argues that societies or communities cannot be assumed to have any particular needs independent of the interests of their members: needs are simply wants. For example, a society does not have a "desire" to survive independent of the desires of its members to continue in some political alliance. Thus, for Canada to continue as a national state is a political issue. A referendum can be held on whether or not a political entity called Canada should exist at all, or whether it should include Québec. However, Canada as such has no system-need to survive as if it were a biological entity. Or consider the idea that societies need to maintain order or stability. This is a common functionalist assumption. But what about the orderliness of a repressive society — a slave society, one based on apartheid, or one that arbitrarily suspends civil rights? What is the source of their order? Or, one can ask, is orderliness and the forces that sustain it often serving the interests or needs of those who are most privileged? Alternatively, would fundamental changes, not order, best serve the social needs of disadvantaged groups? Clearly any simple statement about a system-need for order is open to question, and it seems, impossible to verify.

The second main criticism of functional analysis takes aim at the idea that institutions are collections of social roles held together through the role-players' internalization of norms and values. Two main criticisms were given a classic statement by Dennis Wrong (1961).

In the first place, Wrong argued, the idea that individuals simultaneously conform to and reproduce standards of social conduct or the normative order, renders individuals as almost completely moulded by the social institutions themselves. In contrast, Wrong drew largely on the work of Freud to emphasize that people are social beings, but not essentially socialized beings. Our character, he argued, is not entirely forged by the internalization of norms and through reinforcement in everyday interaction with others. In other words, people do not conform automatically, free from tension and stress.

Extremely repressive societies can be highly organized. Some sociologists question whose interests are being served when such an "orderly" society is based on the suspension of civil rights, or on *apartheid*, as in the case of South Africa.

To this basic criticism, Wrong grafted a second: functionalists tend to ignore power. What about the capacity of some people to *impose* normative definitions on others? Wrong recognizes that there are elements of power and authority in *all* institutions. This is obviously true of the state, the courts, the police agencies, and legislation, but it is also true of the economy, the school system, and the family as well. Wrong insisted that institutional order is maintained everywhere, even in the face of discontent and through forms of repression.

Many others have also taken up the criticism that institutional order is at least as much a product of the exercise of power as of processes of internalization. We face here a version of the complicated, but essential question, noted earlier: how do we distinguish socialization from social control?

The last of the major functionalist assumptions about institutions has not been spared a critical barrage: that institutional order in general is based on a widespread social consensus on basic values. The critics argue that, in the long run, conflict over values and over the distribution of material goods has been more characteristic of the history of any society than consensus. It should be pointed out here that it is with regard to basic moral notions of what is good — for example, that Canadian society should be moving toward an ever-improving standard of living, or that we should having equality before the law — that functionalists believe there is consensus. The basic problem of this notion of social consensus is that it tends to be a "view from the top." One may confuse a dominant set of values and moral codes for the values and convictions of the members of the society as a whole. For example, minority and subordinate cultures and their particular values may be set aside as relatively unimportant or even deviant. One important critique argues that the major class-divisions of capitalist society actually foster distinct and rival subcultures, in which there are dominant and subordinate versions of central social values rather than a single overarching culture (Parkin, 1972). Others emphasize the variations in political culture between regions or between ethnic groups (Dreidger, 1978). The critics argue that these variations are more significant in the social and political fabric of a society such as Canada than broad cultural commonalities.

The diversity of approaches loosely labelled "conflict theory" are distinguished more for their shared criticism of functionalism than by a shared perspective. Nevertheless, the work of two very different nineteenth-century sociologists, Karl Marx and Max Weber, provides the foundations of conflict theory. We shall distinguish Marxist from Weberian approaches throughout the next section.

Marxist Perspectives: Analysis

In all conflict perspectives, distinguishing between institutional realms is much less evident than in functionalist perspectives. Indeed, "institution" is seldom defined and refers to such aspects of society as the "market" or "private property."

Speaking of the market and of private property as institutions seems rather different than speaking of the school system, the family, or the economy. Yet there are basic similarities, for each refers to specific clusters of rights, meanings, obligations, and practices. For example, private property entails a legally defined set of rights, practices, and forms of conduct (as given in the terms of a contract or in relations between employers and employees) and is backed by the authority of the state (in law, the courts, and ultimately, by force of state agencies). In this usage, property is not a "thing" that is owned, but a form that particular social relationships take. The working definition of institutions offered at the outset covers both the more specific and broader definitions, though Marxists, like all conflict theorists, are most attuned to the subtleties of power and social control.

The market and private property are at the core of Marxist analysis of Western capitalist society. As the reader saw in Chapter 2, they are regarded as the key institutions of the capitalist mode of production.

Two points warrant specific comment. First, in Marxist analysis there is a particular notion of the relationship between these economic institutions and all other institutional realms of society. Whereas non-Marxists, especially functionalists, treat economic institutions as one institutional realm among many, in Marxist analysis the institutions of the labor market and of property are the core of the capitalist "mode of production." The mode of production is the way that capital and labor, instruments of production and people, are organized to produce goods and services. Thus, the mode of production is not just an economic institution, but economic and social relationships at once, and the foundation of all other major institutions of the society.

Secondly, there is a difference in emphasis between Marxists and other theorists in the uses of the terms social structure and social institution. This point is increasingly important in sociological analysis of institutional forms. Often, however, the two concepts are used interchangeably simply to describe stable patterns of social relationships; for example, by "structure" of the Catholic Church is meant the church hierarchy and its organization; by "structure" of the Canadian economy is meant the flow of goods and services among firms and between producers and consumers.

In contrast, there is a notion of human relationships in which basic structures are said to underlie everyday interaction and communication. In this context, the structures are basic rules or forms that give rise to social practices and hence to institutional life. A simple analogy is the idea that genetic structures give rise to particular species and individuals, or that the rules of our language — grammar — underlie our ability to carry on meaningful conversations. The point here is that Marxist thought shares in this second tendency to seek explanations of institutional life in terms of basic structures that lie beneath the surface patterns. The fundamental structure is the class structure.

In summary, Marxists tend to use the term social structure in a different sense than functionalists, though the casual reader will often not recognize the difference. For Marxists, the core institutions of the capitalist mode of production, private property, and the market, and the interests they generate, give rise to a social order that is inherited and imposed on individuals, though it may also be changed, even revolutionized, by collective action. Functionalists, in contrast, imply that institutional order is primarily negotiated and internalized as a moral commitment of individuals to their community.

We now turn to the specifics of a Marxist analysis. Because capitalist society is seen as based on an exploitative relationship between capital and wage labor, the interests of both are inherently in conflict. Hence class conflict is endemic to capitalism. Class interests are generated, on the one hand, by the rights of private property in pursuit of profit, and on the other, by the fact that the livelihood and way of life of wage- and salary-workers depends solely upon them selling their skills and capacity to produce, that is, selling their labor power. Therefore, Marxists argue, class conflict is fundamental — it can be likened to a single geological fault-line running beneath the whole surface of everyday social relationships. The conflict takes complex forms and only sporadically

finds overt and coherent expression. In this respect, Marxist analysis is essentially revolutionary with regard to institutional change: in the long run, increasing consciousness and expression of class conflict come to revolutionize a society. In the short run, however, Marxists agree the conflict is often deflected or contained.

If all institutional realms of society — political, legal, religious, educational, and so forth — derive their essential character from capitalism's class conflict, these other institutions tend, in complex ways, to foster or at least seldom to endanger the operation of the core institutions of private property and the labor market. This is especially so, Marxists argue, with regard to the state and its political and legal institutions.

Consider the importance of law in countries such as Canada, the United States, or Great Britain, in which the liberal idea of the rule of law is deeply established. The fundamental form of law in these societies is contract law. From a Marxist perspective, the basic contract is that contract between employers and workers, which sets the terms by which the worker agrees to work so many hours and the employer agrees to pay a specific wage. In historical perspective, the contract represents a radical transformation in the relationship between workers and employers. The contract embodies the understanding that the employer has no responsibility to the worker other than to pay the wage: there is no additional responsibility for the worker's security, housing, health, the education of children, or whatever. The relationship is wholly economic. Marx took this purely economic relationship, represented by the contract, to typify capitalism.

Marx could contrast capitalist relationships, say, to those of feudalism, in which the lord or master was obliged by tradition and social pressure to provide a variety of services to serfs and ordinary workers, including minimal security and a place in the community. In return, the serf owed to his lord field products, labor for the repair and upkeep of the lands, and other services. The mutual obliga-

between employee and employer in capitalism is an even deeper deception. The workers' freedom is only formal, since the law favors the already powerful. Workers could be denied their livelihood, for example, by being fired, but do not have similar ways of affecting the employer's well-being. In addition, workers may not have the resources to go to court to fight a broken contract, whereas the employer is more likely able to marshal the force of the law.

In Marx's own analysis, it was this sort of institutionalized illusion of equality that characterized liberal or bourgeois society, and in masking exploitation through legal guarantees of equality, actually perpetuated the social order of inequality and exploitation.

Marxist Perspectives: Criticisms

Perhaps the most general criticism of Marxist theory is that it emphasizes the deterministic over the voluntaristic in human affairs; people tend to be considered as products of social structural forces, as passive recipients, or at least, as agents of those forces, rather than as creative, willing actors who shape society and give relationships meaning. The criticism is often misplaced, as in the case of suggesting that Marx's work implied simply that technological change, rather than the organization of production or class struggle, is the basis of institutional forms and change. Yet, more subtle forms of the criticism are closer to the mark. Three versions of the criticism are considered. One criticism raises the question of how a Marxist analysis can specify the relationship between capitalist society and the particular historical form that institutions take within capitalism. Consider an argument that educational institutions directly serve to maintain capitalist society, and hence, in the long run, primarily serve the interests of a capitalist class. They do this, for example, in the way the classroom is organized. The organization imitates that of the factory or office and teaches work discipline and respect for supervisory authority. Moreover, the school system inculcates values of

Marxists consider that the core institutions of the capitalist system are private property and the market. Together, they generate a social order that is inherited and imposed on indviduals. Whether one agrees with this approach or not, Place Victoria seems a fitting monument to both the system and the Montréal Stock Exchange, which it houses.

tions were hardly equal, however. Surplus value produced by serfs and peasants was extracted by the ruling class, despite the fact that the dominance of lord over serf was legitimated within the particular cultural conditions of feudal society.

More important to the Marxist analysis is the argument that the legal and contractual equality

individual competition and achievement that directly reinforce the central values of capitalist culture. A similar Marxist argument maintains that the nuclear family is central to the maintenance of capitalism in its orientation to the values of individualism, hierarchy, and obedience.

Critics (Worsley et al., 1977:201) take issue with such analyses by pointing to their failure to account for the great variety of forms that educational institutions or families take in capitalist societies, or of their changes under capitalism. They point out that there are very significant differences in the way we educate and socialize children — for example, in public and private schools, in technical colleges and universities, in day-care facilities, in families with one and with two working parents, in simple nuclear families and in extended families, in families with many and with few children, and so on. An analysis of education or the family, or of any other institution, is insufficient if it merely asserts that the institution is organized to correspond to capitalism's needs. An adequate explanation would have to specify at least how class structure or conflict sets limits on the ways the institution is organized. A fuller explanation would also have to show how specific institutional forms emerged under specific historical, political, and ideological circumstances.

A second related criticism of Marxist analysis of institutions raises the question of the relative independence of various institutional spheres. As noted, many Marxists argue that although there is some autonomy among the economy, the state, and the educational systems, in the end, the determining factor is the organization of production.

This question of the "relative autonomy" of various institutional realms is the subject of an important debate *within* Marxist circles, but it is the critics of Marxism that argue there are other independent sources of institutional growth and variation beyond productive relations. Indeed, they maintain that religion or the kinship system, for example, are structures of power that affect economic institutions at least as much as they are

influenced by them. Some argue that beliefs and values themselves may set the course upon which subsequent, institutional change follows. Others simply argue that although all institutions are not equal in influence, no one realm can dominate, and some are highly interdependent. (See Mills, 1956; Porter, 1965.)

Finally, critics state that the theory has little or nothing to say about those interests and forms of conflict that are *not* expressions of class divisions. One way to put this criticism is to ask what forms of institutional conflict would remain should the sources of class conflict disappear in the emergence of a socialist society (Giddens, 1977:101). What about the strains, stresses, and divisions of interest in the contemporary family — do they derive mainly from class conflict? What about the sources of ethnic, racial, national, and religious conflict that appear to be so much a part of the contemporary world (Parkin, 1979)? In the end, this criticism takes issue with Marxist's apparent reduction or simplification of institutional conflict to a narrow and exclusive source.

Non-Marxist Conflict Perspectives: Analysis

The term conflict theory has been used as a catch-all label to identify all forms of non-functionalist theory. The term seems to derive from the work of Ralph Dahrendorf (1959) in a study that undertook to examine the application of Marx's theory to contemporary society. The many strands of conflict theory are actually drawn from both functionalism and Marxism; a conflict perspective attempts to bridge the two.

Non-Marxist conflict theory focuses mainly on the distribution of power as the ultimate basis of institutional order and on conflicts over that distribution. These analyses often emphasize not only the significance of sheer power, coercion, or social control, but also the processes that *legitimize* the structures of power. The central place of legitimacy was raised earlier in the discussion of social order. Much of the scholarship that pursues the question of legitimacy follows in the tradition of Max Weber.

Weber emphasized the thoroughly political nature of social institutions. He approached the problem of institutional order largely by considering the methods of social control available to a ruling group (Benson, 1978:29). It is especially with respect to legitimacy and compliance — the willingness of people to accept authority or tolerate the exercise of power — that Weber's theoretical legacy is reflected in the analysis of institutions.

The question of how institutions come to be legitimate in the eyes of most people, and hence acquire stability over time, often draws on Weber's distinction between *acceptance* of an authority structure and *agreement* with its central ideology or values. We can distinguish, for example, between the motives we have for going along with the way things are, even if they benefit others more (often it seems most sensible not to "buck the system"), and truly accepting or believing the justifications offered for the status quo. The distinction has the merit of acknowledging the complexity of the sources of institutional order. As one interpreter of Weber succinctly translated his argument, "Citizens may grumble about this and that, but as isolated individuals they do not see what can be done to change the situation. Sheer unreflecting *habit* becomes a widespread motive for compliance. What begins as resentment and frustration often ends in apathy and resignation, because the personal cost of kicking against the traces is too high." (Benson, 1973:33.)

An example of this perspective can be found in the work of Parkin (1972). His analysis takes for granted that social inequality cuts across all institutional realms of contemporary societies. Thus, the central sociological question is the familiar one: what sustains the legitimacy of these institutions and prevents the inequality of condition among people from driving them to radical reform or to revolution? Parkin's answer revolves around the notion that there are three, more-or-less distinct subcultures in contemporary capitalist societies: the dominant, the subordinate, and the radical. It is the values of the dominant subculture that are largely represented in the major institutions of a society. In a sense, they are the "official" versions of social values that provide a moral framework for the entire society. As a result of the routine institutional support they receive, they are often taken as the standards for appropriate behavior throughout society. Parkin would argue that functionalists mistake these dominant standards for true social consensus, simply because they are most prominent and receive more media coverage and other forms of official support.

In contrast, Parkin suggests the subordinate subculture is a "negotiated" version of the dominant value system; people ascribe to versions of the dominant standards in order to accommodate and adapt to restrictive economic and social circumstances. The dominant values are "stretched to meet the contingencies of everyday life of restricted resources." (Parkin, 1972:96.) For working-class people, this is just a sensible accommodation of their aspirations to the facts of life and of "making do." But the key issue is that at the same time, their adaptations serve to legitimate and give support to the existing institutional order. Thus, the accommodation to economic insecurity and to limited options breeds a sort of fatalism or resignation that is reflected in such statements as, "That's just the way things are. . . . Why beat your head against the wall. . . . All we can do is make the best of it." (Hoggart; 1958, cited in Parkin, 1972:90.) Again, from a conflict perspective, the central focus is the interplay between the power in institutions and the processes that legitimate that power.

Non-Marxist Conflict Perspectives: Criticisms

It is always a risky business to occupy a middle ground in theoretical and ideological debates. The most telling critiques of the non-Marxist conflict perspective reflect their positions of compromise

Resignation to restrictive social and economic conditions legitimates the values of the dominant culture.

between Marxist and functionalist analyses. Two such criticisms will serve to illustrate the main issues.

Marxist critics focus on the failure of the conflict perspective to assess the directions and patterns of change of major institutional realms. If conflict arises from multiple, cross-cutting sources, then larger historical patterns become lost in the description of myriad forms of smaller conflicts of interest and of allegiance. More strongly, Marxists can argue that the perspective fails to have sufficient sense of the potentiality of human life; thus, institutional analysis may provide a detailed description of the features of current institutional arrangements, but is unable to measure these against the possibilities of change, especially radical change.

Functionalist critics of a conflict view of institutions have suggested that the orientation is not so much a theoretical point of view, but a largely romanticized response to the scale and apparent intractability of contemporary institutions. Conflict theory, they say, may decry the dehumanizing character of the institutions of a "mass society" but tends to exaggerate the differences between contemporary and historical institutions, thus idealizing the past. (Shils, 1963:30, cited in Wrong, 1970: 46–47.)

SOCIAL HISTORY AND INSTITUTIONAL ANALYSIS

Perhaps the two most familiar and encompassing institutions of our society are the state and the labor market. The rapid and parallel expansion of the state, as we know it (and are ambivalent about it), and of labor markets took place mainly in the late 1700s and early 1800s in the Western world. Our everyday familiarity with these institutions makes it difficult to appreciate the recency and revolutionary character of their growth, or indeed, to see how they are related. Consider that in Canada, in the 1860s and 1870s, most people still made a living by working their own land, or working in their own workshops; only some were beginning to rely completely on work for wages as their sole means of making a living. Today, just over 100 years later, it is only the exceptional family that maintains itself outside of the labor market — simply, very few of us are self-employed and can control the tools and places of our work. And again, the change has been accompanied by the rise of every kind of state agency — in education, welfare, health, the justice system, and in the economy.

Just as we have seen that there are differences in perspectives on institutional analysis, so there are differences in the interpretation of how these transitions took place. Some emphasize that the basic changes were those of the expansion of capitalism itself. First, there was the increase in the numbers of people dependent upon wages for their livelihood. The accompanying loss of many social functions performed by the family and by the community, such as the care of the elderly and the ill, the education of children, and the extension of mutual aid to those in need, left a social vacuum (Braverman, 1974:279–80). Into this gap stepped the state, spinning out formal organizations or taking over those that had begun as private philanthropic agencies (Katz, Doucet, and Stern, 1982: 357–62). This interpretation takes its cues from a largely Marxist perspective.

An alternative formulation tends to be Weberian; it emphasizes the significance of the rise of the state itself, not as a direct handmaiden of the growth of a capitalist economy, but as an independent political phenomenon. In this view, the expansion of the modern state in European countries, between the seventeenth and nineteenth centuries, created the conditions under which the increasing commercialization of the economy and the expansion of wage labor were facilitated (Tilly, 1981). The difference is one of emphasis, perhaps, and not so significant as to distract us from the general similarity. The interpretations agree that these were the two most fundamental transformations in the making of the modern world. Moreover, they also largely agree that these twin institutional formations of the contemporary Western world generated a plethora of more specialized formal organizations. If the rise of the modern state and of labor markets were relatively recent, the growth of the organizational web of modern society was a true revolution; its basic features were set in place within the first fifty to seventy-five years of the last century, within a single person's lifetime (Katz, Doucet, and Stern, 1982:354).

Whatever interpretation we put on these transformations, a historical perspective also makes clear that the main features of contemporary life are changing — they are not given to us as commandments written in stone. We are led to wonder which historical paths were missed and which alternative institutional arrangements could have emerged (Tilly, 1981:212–13). Institutional analysis should remind us that we are not at the end of history; despite powerful historical continuities, we collectively shape our institutional environment.

SUMMARY

1. There are many uses of the concept institution in social analysis. The differences tend to reflect different theoretical perspectives. A definition that reflects the main elements of the domi-

nant perspectives is: "Institutions are social practices, established in conformity with principles or standards that have become widely known in the community, and upheld by power or authority."

2. Functional or structural-functional perspectives on institutions emphasize three defining characteristics: (1) that they fulfil basic "needs" of societies; (2) that they are made up of a cluster of social "roles" held together by shared values; and (3) that the institutions are expressions of a basic social consensus on basic values.

3. Alternative perspectives on institutions emphasize that they are concentrations of interests and power of specific groups.

4. Functional and "power" perspectives on institutions differ greatly with respect to the significance they attribute to deviance from and resistance to institutional practices, and with respect to their analysis of the sources of deviance and resistance.

5. The question of how social order is maintained is the core of institutional analysis. The differing perspectives may be best distinguished in terms of how they answer the question of order.

6. The central merit of a functional analysis of institutions is that social control is not primarily seen as a result of external constraint, but as a combination of regulation and constitutive affirmation of social standards or norms. We simultaneously conform to and recreate normative order all the time.

7. Among the main criticisms of functional analysis of institutions is the argument that there are no truly identifiable "needs" of societies as a whole — "needs are the "wants" or interests of particular social groups. Another key criticism is that people are not mainly "role" players, moulded by socialization and internalization of values, but are social beings subject to much internal tension and stress, and are commonly nonconformist or otherwise resistant to norms.

8. Marxist analysis of institutions should be distinguished from other conflict perspectives, which are often derived from the work of Max Weber.

9. A distinctive merit of Marxist accounts of institutions is the systematic, theoretical explanation of the processes by which the basic character of all institutions is intimately related to the character of class exploitation and conflict.

10. Among the major criticisms of Marxist institutional analysis is the charge that the deterministic or controlling elements of social structure are emphasized at the expense of an analysis of the creative, changing, and voluntaristic aspects of human action.

11. Non-Marxist conflict theory emphasizes power at the core of institutions, rather than value consensus or exploitation. It follows that the view also focuses on the processes of legitimating or justifying the hierarchical nature of institutions. The main criticism of conflict perspectives derives from the apparent failure to bridge both functional and Marxist perspectives successfully.

12. The most characteristic feature of contemporary society is the formal, bureaucratic institution. Almost all aspects of social life are now conducted in separate institutional settings — hospitals, offices, factories, government bureaucracies, schools, prisons, asylums. Their institutional origins are surprisingly recent; most have emerged in the last 100 years or so. Their growth must be understood as a historically specific and alterable consequence of the rise of the state and the growth of labor markets.

GLOSSARY

Anomie. A social condition in which accustomed rules and standards are made irrelevant by social changes; derived from Durkheim.

Authority. The right to exercise power, conferred by its acceptance as legitimate. Following Max Weber, there are several modes of legitimating authority and differences in the degree of consent.

Exploitation. Broadly, getting something for nothing; specifically in Marxist thought, a process of extracting surplus value from another class.

Institutionalization. A process by which social practices become established as a durable feature of social relationships by a combination of legitimating the practice as particularly valid ("this is the right way") and backing it by power ("if you don't accept it as the right way, you will be sanctioned").

Internalization. The process of learning to translate social values and norms into inner, personal convictions and commitment.

Legitimation. Any social process tending to make existing institutional arrangements acceptable or, at least, tolerated.

Normative order. A system of social norms or "rules of the game"; a moral order; culture.

Political-economy. A tradition of social science analysis that focusses on the interpenetration of political and economic institutions. In Canada, especially identified with the work of Harold Innis.

Social groups. A social collectivity defined by common characteristics.

Social norms. Social standards or rules that guide social practices and reflect widely shared expectations of acceptable behaviour.

Social structures. Stable patterns of relationships between individuals and groups that are maintained by both legitimation and power.

Social reproduction. In Marxist thought especially, the means by which class relationships are maintained over time in social relationships and in cultural patterns.

Socialization. The process of learning accepted social standards and practices; learning a culture. The learning may be of dominant, subordinate or subcultural standards, or all of them.

State. A more or less related system embracing all levels of government, government agencies, the military and police systems, the judiciary and the related bureaucracies of each.

Total institutions. Formally organized institutions in which the inmates reside, for some period, and lead a round of life administered by officials (prisons, hospitals, monasteries, holiday camps, boarding schools, asylums and the like).

FURTHER READING

Eisenstadt, Samuel N. "Social Institutions." *International Encyclopedia of Social Sciences.* Volume 14:409–29, D. Sills (ed.). New York: MacMillan Co. and Free Press, 1968. A careful overview of a version of structural-functional perspective on institutions, including a particular concern with comparative analysis.

Goffman, Erving. *Asylums: Essays on the Social Situation of Mental Patients and other Inmates.* Garden City, New York: Anchor Books, 1961. A classic, detailed analysis of the encompassing and regimented worlds of "total institutions," such as prisons, naval vessels, boarding schools, monasteries, and asylums. A lively introduction to the analysis of institutionalization in formal institutions.

Katz, Michael B., Michael J. Doucet and Mark J. Stern. *The Social Organization of Early Industrial Capitalism.* Cambridge, Mass.: Harvard University Press, 1982. An unusual interpretation of central aspects of nineteenth-century social history in Canada and the U.S. that examines the institutional roots of contemporary society.

Mills, C. Wright. *The Sociological Imagination.* London: Oxford University Press, 1959. An influential, slim book on the conduct of social science in general and its moral implications. Provides a critical, but especially clear orientation to the analysis that links institutional changes to individual experiences.

Palmer, Bryan D. *Working Class Experience: The Rise and Reconstitution of Canadian Labour, 1800–1980.* Toronto: Butterworth, 1983. A sweeping, descriptive narrative that sets out the major historical patterns of class conflict and institutional change accompanying the growth of capitalist industrialization in Canada.

Panitch, Leo (ed.). *The Canadian State: Political Economy and Political Power.* Toronto: University of Toronto Press, 1977. The most comprehensive collection of essays critically examining the nature and role of the state in Canada.

The best essays exemplify the value of a Marxist-oriented institutional analysis of the interplay of economy and politics.

Parr, Joy (ed.). *Childhood and Family in Canadian History.* Toronto: McClelland and Stewart, 1982. A collection of readings revealing various historical dimensions of the character of family life and childhood experiences.

Parsons, Talcott. *The Structure of Social Action.* New York: Free Press, 1937. A difficult, but classic discussion of the "Hobbesian Problem" of social order, especially drawing from the work of Weber and Durkheim.

Porter, John. *The Vertical Mosaic: An Analysis of Social Class and Power in Canada.* Toronto: University of Toronto Press, 1965. The path-breaking analysis of the structure of Canadian institutional life. The emphasis on ethnicity is somewhat misplaced, but the chapters on elites and on the linkages between major institutions are essential reading.

Wrong, Dennis H. "The Oversocialized conception of man in modern society." *American Sociological Review,* 26, 2 (April, 1961), pages 183–93. This article challenges basic assumptions in functional theory that deal with the relations between institutions and individuals, especially regarding the question of "social order."

Wrong, Dennis H. "Postscript." *Skeptical Sociology,* pages 47–54. New York: Columbia University Press, 1976. This is an update of a twenty-year-old, but still relevant statement. (See above.)

Social Institutions

Part IV introduces you to the social institutions that regulate, pattern, and even predict social life. Whether simple or complex, whether pre-industrial or industrial, societies need basic institutions to fulfil essential individual and societal needs.

The five chapters in this section explore five basic social institutions: the family, religion, education, politics and government, and the economy. The institution of family socializes the young and provides them with physical and emotional security. Religion serves society by giving meaning to life and reassuring us in times of crisis. Education provides the formal training of the young and focuses on the transmission of specialized skills to them. Political institutions regulate the ways of acquiring power and exercising it within a given territorial unit. It is closely related to the economy, through which the production and distribution of goods and services are carried out. Indeed, these institutions are so interwoven that a change in any one of them brings changes to the others.

CHAPTER ELEVEN

The Family

EUGEN LUPRI

Throughout history, thinkers, philosophers, and writers have disputed what constitutes an ideal family and how it ought to function in society. Their ideas took the form of religious pronouncements, political doctrines, or philosophical speculations. Today, scholars and lay people alike agree that intimacy, love, and companionship, which are private and personal experiences, are necessary ingredients in family life. Because almost all of us are members of a family, we have strong feelings about the subject.

The sociological study of the family raises one of the most pressing problems of contemporary sociology: how the normative and the actual converge. Problems of objectivity abound in family research because what ought to be is so easily confused with what is. The normative perspective (what ought to be), for example, pervaded Frederic Le Play's famous *Les Ouvriers Européens* (1855), which is considered to be the first socio-

The nuclear unit of mother, father, and children is only one variation of the family relationship. Communal living is common in China and Israel, where a number of families may live and work together.

logical study of the family based on systematic research. As European society shifted from an agrarian to an industrial economy, Le Play observed a rapid decline of the patriarchal peasant family and a lack of stability in the worker's fam-

ily. His aim was to reestablish the patriarchal "stem" family, in which authority was vested in the father and property was held in common under the patriarch. In other words, Le Play's research was aimed not at discovering what the family is in a given society at a given moment in its history, but rather what the family ought to be.

It is no business of sociology, however, to advocate or to deplore social change. Its basic task is to study social processes, social structure, and social change — including family change — from a scientific point of view. Sociologists view the family, along with religion, education, politics, and the economy, as a social institution. Interaction within the family is social interaction. The focus, however, is on social and cultural factors that shape family structure and functioning, not on psychological or personality attributes.

It is particularly difficult, however, to gain any degree of scientific detachment in the field of endeavor that touches upon our central values and personal preferences. Rapid family change is a frightening experience to most of us. The aims of sociology are to understand and analyze family change and stability, and to explore future trends and their implications for both the individual and the society. Such a sociological perspective serves those whose lives are affected by family change — nearly everyone.

THE FAMILY: A BASIC AND UNIVERSAL SOCIAL INSTITUTION

Let us look at a few general characteristics that set the family apart from other social institutions. It may be safely said that the family, as a social institution, is as old as human culture. In fact, some anthropologists maintain that marriage and the family are older than culture because human beings inherited both mating and family life from higher animal species. For example, ethologists — students of animal behavior — have called our attention to forms of social organization among savannah baboons (mating practices, patterns of affiliation and dominance, troop cohesiveness) that are similar to human family organization.

The family is also considered a universal institution, since it is found in all societies. Moreover, Murdock's (1949) study of 250 societies showed that the nuclear family is also universal; it exists in all cultures at all times, either as a part of a larger structure or as an independent unit. Although Murdock's conclusion has been widely accepted, critics argue that his conception of the family as a nuclear unit with four functions (common residence, economic co-operation, socialization, and reproduction) is simply too narrow to include certain exceptions, such as the family in the early kibbutz system in Israel and the Nayer tribes of southern India.

The family is also the most basic of all social institutions. Almost every person is born into a family, called the family of orientation, and most persons establish their own family of procreation; all but about 10 percent of Canadians marry, for example. In contrast, the roles associated with religious, educational, political, and economic institutions are more marginal, in that a person may play little or no role in them. Among all peoples, the family is a basic institution because individuals are linked through it to the larger social structure.

Finally, the family is also the most multifunctional of all social institutions, even though in our society many of its traditional functions have been taken over by other institutions. Child rearing, education, religion, protection, procreation, and economic production are managed by the family in most societies. In Canada, the family performed most of these functions until comparatively recently, before our society became industrialized, urbanized, specialized, and secular. Many would argue that affection and companionship are the sole enduring family functions, but even these are sought and found increasingly outside the family.

THE FAMILY IN SOCIETY: CROSS-CULTURAL PERSPECTIVES

Defining the Family: An Impossible Task

The traditional typical family — a working husband, a full-time housewife, and one or two children — today represents only one of many family forms in Canada. Many Canadian wives work outside the home; one out of nine families is a single-parent family, and the majority of these are headed by women. Of all married couples, 10 to 15 percent do not have children, and estimates show that about 10 percent of all couples cohabit without marriage.

The great variety of family structures across societies forces continual redefinition. As Goode (1982:8–10) has argued, the family is not a single entity that can be captured by a neat formula. Many social units can be thought of as "more or less" families, since they are more or less similar to the conventional type (husband, wife, and children). Much of this graded similarity can be traced to the role relations in the traditional (conventional) unit. The following characteristics are typical of most traditional role patterns: (1) at least two adults of opposite sex reside together; (2) who engage in some kind of a division of labor; (3) who interact socially at both the emotional and task-oriented levels; (4) who share food, sex, companionship, and other activities; (5) the adults have parental relations with their children and the children have filial relations with their parents, who exercise some authority over their children and assume responsibility for their protection, co-operation, and nurturance; (6) sibling relations exist among the children themselves, which may include a range of obligations to help one another. Such a description of role patterns helps us to synthesize a wide range of social situations where some kind of family structure exists. It also helps us to gain a better insight into the ways in which our own society is changing.

Non-family households are an important sociological category, as they represent living arrangements that exhibit many family-like characteristics. In fact, the non-family households of today are a viable base for the family of tomorrow.

Thus far we have used the terms family and marriage interchangeably, but it is essential to distinguish between them. The family is a relatively durable unit of two or more members who are related by blood, marriage, or adoption, and who share a common residence. A family is formed through marriage, which is a formal and socially accepted sexual union between two or more people. The family is embedded within a larger network of relatives — the extended family. Relatives are associated either through marriage (affinal kin) or by common blood (consanguine kin). Husband-wife ties are affinal kinship ties, as distinguished from parent-child or brother-sister ties, which are consanguineal.

However the family is defined and elaborated within a cultural context, all societies have developed a set of rules that govern marriage, family, and kin groups, and that structure interaction between them.

Variation in Family and Kinship Organization
Family Types

Comparative family research has identified three main types of families: (1) nuclear, or elementary, family; (2) extended family; and (3) the polygamous, or composite, family.

The nuclear family in its complete form consists of a husband, a wife, and their offspring, natural or adopted. It can also consist of one parent and a child, a brother and a sister, or a childless couple. The nuclear family lives in its own residential unit, separate from other relatives. It is identical to the Canadian census definition of economic family in that it refers to any two persons who are related by blood, marriage, or adoption, and who share a common residence. The conjugal family is a nuclear family based on the husband-wife relationship.

Cross-cultural evidence suggests that nuclear families are combined into larger units in one of two ways. When they are combined through the parent-child relationship, that is through blood ties, they are called extended families; when combined through plural marriage they are called polygamous families. The extended family comprises two or more nuclear families related by blood and sharing a common residence. Murdock (1949) notes that nearly half of his 250 societies had some form of extended family. Recent historical research, however, has dispelled the belief that the extended-family system was the most prevalent family organization of pre-industrial Europe. Even in those times, nuclear households predominated. Emily Nett (1981) has reached similar conclusions about the Canadian family of the past.

The extended family has a number of advantages over the nuclear family: continuity, through time; maintenance of family tradition; keeping the family property intact; assured protection for children at all times; assured care of the sick and the elderly; and finally, a sense of belonging, stability, and permanence (Leslie, 1979:35–38).

The second way of combining the nuclear family into composite families is through plural marriage. Polygamy involves plural spouses, whereas monogamy involves one spouse. The most common form of polygamy is called polygyny, an arrangement consisting of one husband with two or more wives. If the arrangement consists of one wife with two or more husbands, it is called polyandry. The third form is group marriage, the marriage of several men to several women.

In his sample of 554 societies, Murdock (1957) found 415 that were polygynous, ninety-three that were monogamous, and four that were polyandrous. (The remaining number of societies could not be classified into any one category.) Since the sex ratio in most societies is roughly 1:1, polygyny is not widespread even in a society in which it is preferred; rather, it exists along with monogamy.

Group marriage is quite rare. When it does occur, it is usually found along with polyandry. The Todas of southern India, for example, practised fraternal polyandry (in which the wife's husbands are brothers), which occasionally slips into group marriage.

A Tibetan family from Nepal. Tibet is traditionally a polyandrous society, in which a woman may have two or more husbands. This practice provides an effective means of birth control, since polyandrous women bear the same number of children, on average, as monogamous women. The custom has declined among Tibetans who have left their homeland to live among other cultures.

Monogamy is the marriage form preferred by most individuals, including Canadians. High divorce rates and high remarriage rates produce serial monogamy—more than one partner over a period of time, but only one partner at one time.

Rules of Residence, Descent, and Authority

The spatial arrangement of newlywed couples is referred to as rules of residence. In over half of Murdock's sample, the bride moves in with her husband's family or to an adjacent dwelling. This residence pattern is called patrilocal. Less frequent is matrilocal residence, in which the groom moves in with his bride's family. If a couple can choose to live with either set of parents, the pattern is bilocal. If a couple establishes their own household independent of their parents, a neolocal residence pattern prevails. The neolocal system is preferred in our own society.

Closely related to rules of residence are rules of descent. The system is called patrilineal when inheritance and descent are traced through the male line: sons inherit from their fathers and pass their inheritance on to their sons. Specific forms of patrilineal descent are primogeniture, in which the inheritance passes to the eldest son, and ultimogeniture, in which the youngest son receives all the property. In Canada, names are generally passed down the male line: a bride assumes her groom's family name. Today, however, wives sometimes choose to retain their family name, though the children generally take their father's name. In matrilineal societies, by contrast, lineage is traced through the female line. In Canada, the preferred rule of descent is bilateral; no distinction is made between paternal and maternal parents, and children inherit equally from both sides.

All social organizations tend to have hierarchies, and the family is no exception. If the power and authority are vested in males, the system is referred to as patriarchal. The ancient Hebrew, Greek, and Roman, as well as the Hindu, Chinese, and Japanese societies are examples of patriarchies. If the family is extended and includes several males, the oldest male usually wields the greatest power. This type of family hierarchy has been most common throughout history and throughout the world. In a matriarchal system, power and authority are vested in females; documented examples of this system, however, are rare. Moreover, even in societies that follow matrilineal rules of descent, inheritance, and residence, power tends to be held by males and hence is regarded as patriarchal.

Preferred Partners

No culture is indifferent to the question, who marries whom? In fact, all known societies tend to place restrictions on choice of marriage and sexual partners. The rules that govern the choice of partners provide a network of obligations and prohibitions designed to integrate the internal arrangement of family life with the external demands of the larger society.

Two basic systems of mate selection exist. Some societies prescribe exogamy, or marriage outside one's own group. Exogamy is often found in tribal societies, where almost everybody is related by blood or marriage. In contrast, endogamy prescribes the choice of mates from within certain groups. The classic example of endogamy is the Hindu system in India, where the choice of one's spouse is restricted not only to one's own caste, but even to one's own subdivision within the caste.

The exogamy rule is an extension of the incest taboo: the prohibition of marriage and sexual relations between people who are closely related. Incest taboos appear to be universal. In almost all societies, this rule applies to parent-child and brother-sister relations and many societies, including Canada, extend incest taboos to first cousins and other close relatives. Marriage between brothers and sisters, however, was not forbidden in the royal family of ancient Egypt, but was actually encouraged to keep the property intact (Middleton, 1962).

To sum up, family patterns around the world exhibit a great deal of variation. But universality also exists; all societies seem to have a more or less reliable arrangement for producing, sustaining, nurturing, and socializing offspring. Let us examine family functions.

Family Functions

The family is seen to perform several functions, not only for the continued existence of society, but for the individual's survival as well. Such a claim has its roots in the structural-functional approach to the family, a perspective that will be discussed later.

Socialization. In Chapter 6, socialization was defined as the process by which a person learns

Work, once the focus of family life, has diminished in importance with the industrialization of society.

and internalizes the ways and norms of a particular cultural group. Socialization begins within the family and continues throughout life. Because the human infant is helpless for a longer period than any other animal and depends on others for its survival, the family is responsible for its care, disciplining, nurturing, and inculcation of basic values.

Sexual Regulation. All societies regulate sexual behavior in some fashion. As pointed out, an almost universal taboo exists against incest,

and marriage is the most universally accepted outlet for sexual behavior. If all rules against extramarital sex were eliminated, the stable bond necessary for the socialization of children would be severely damaged; the family, as a setting conducive for the development of intimacy and companionship among adults, would also suffer.

Although every society has norms that govern sexual conduct, they differ widely within any given society and from one generation to the next. In colonial New England, sexual permissiveness was attacked by the Puritans because it undermined the Judeo-Christian ideal of marriage and the home. In contrast, Inuit men offer their wife to a visitor travelling without his wife as a token of their hospitality. In Newfoundland villages, the first child of a married couple was often conceived before marriage, and such an event was commonly regarded as the proper time to marry.

In a recent national survey among a representative cross-section of adult Canadians, 73 percent considered extramarital sex "always wrong." Canadian women disapproved of sexual intercourse outside marriage more often than did Canadian men. The same survey showed that the Canadian public appears far more willing to tolerate premarital sex than extramarital sex. Adultery — voluntary sexual intercourse with a married person of the opposite sex other than the spouse — is an admissible ground for divorce under the current law.

In his worldwide survey, Murdock found that only 20 percent of all societies allowed sexual intercourse outside marriage. A closer examination, however, revealed that about two-thirds of the societies allowed such a relationship if the partner was a potential future mate. Where adultery is permitted, it is usually limited to a special situation, occasion, or kin relationship.

Reproduction. By regulating sexual activity, the family ensures that children will be born to replace the society's dying members. Thus the family serves as an institutional arrangement for reproduction. As we pointed out earlier, it also designates the roles of father and mother for child care. Other arrangements are theoretically possible, and many societies arrange to accept children produced outside a marriage relationship. But no society has established a set of norms and values for procreation outside the family.

Economic Co-operation. The family plays a vital economic function in all human socie-

ties. In earlier times, the family operated as a production unit. In peasant and craft societies, for example, the husband, wife, and children formed a co-operative work team with no clear-cut division between familial and work roles. In industrial societies, however, the separation of work and home has prevailed. Economic support in the form of income is derived from labor performed outside the home. In economic terms, the family has changed from a commodity-producing to a commodity-consuming unit.

The sex-based division of labor is socially constructed. However, whatever the nature of the division of labor at home and on the job, the husband, wife, and often their children co-operate in running the family household. In this sense, the family plays an important economic role in all societies, including our own.

Affection, Intimacy, and Emotional Support. In previous chapters we reviewed studies showing that emotional attachment and affection are vital for human development. Many authorities insist that affection is a specific function of the modern family.

We must be cautious, however, not to overdraw or overemphasize the functional significance of the family as a primary group for the well-being of the individual, young or old. Dysfunctional aspects such as family violence, child abuse, wife-beating, mental cruelty, and physical brutality are by no means infrequent in past and present family life. In fact, the family has a double-edged significance for the individual: it provides a group setting that may help or impede self-actualization, self-fulfillment, and personal happiness.

One may also argue that the family is not the only group that can provide emotional support, affection, intimacy, and companionship. As discussed earlier, the biological link between parent and child is less significant than the social link and interaction. Furthermore, some people prefer to live alone and relate meaningfully to a network of close friends. "Singlehood" and communes are on the increase as viable alternatives to the traditional family.

Social Placement. Being born into a family has consequences for one's future. Each Canadian child starts out in the class position of its family, and this ascribed status affects the child's life chances. Family socialization practices also affect the opportunities for individual achievement. Even achieved statuses, which are based on one's individual performance (education, occupation, marriage), are greatly influenced by one's membership in a family of orientation.

These family functions — socialization, sexual regulation, reproduction, affection, economic cooperation, and social placement — are often referred to as universals in the sense that they are constants. In reality, however, the family's ability to perform certain tasks and to fulfil certain needs varies widely from one society to another and from generation to generation. Furthermore, these family functions may serve society as a whole, but not necessarily the individual. The producing of children may be beneficial to society for various reasons, whereas an unwanted pregnancy may be seen as a burden to an individual couple. Infertility may bring sorrow and disappointment to a young couple who want children of their own, but overpopulation may bring starvation to a whole society. Thus, as Goode (1982) argues, it is more meaningful to view the family functions as variables than as constants.

THE FAMILY AND SOCIETY: THEORETICAL PERSPECTIVES

German sociologist, Ralf Dahrendorf (1965), once remarked that a theory is a net we cast to catch the fish worth catching. The meshes determine and limit the size of fish we want. This analogy is quite appropriate, for a theory is a highly selective view, rather than an all-inclusive view of social reality. Different theoretical models emphasize different features of social reality.

Family research has been, and still is, guided by several competing theoretical perspectives. We shall limit our discussion to a few of the most prominent.

The Structure-Functionalist Perspective

Functionalists view society and its subsystems as made up of interdependent parts or elements that form an integrative system. Through boundary maintenance, a self-regulating property of all systems, the family contributes to the maintenance and stability of the whole. Thus, the family is conceived as a subsystem, performing an integrative role in society through its core functions of socialization, sexual regulation, reproduction, economic co-operation, and status placement.

The family itself can also be viewed as a social system of interacting individuals. A functional analysis of family integration focuses on the roles played by the mother, father, and child, and how these family roles contribute to the stability or instability of the family unit. The parent-child or the husband-wife relationship may in turn be viewed as a subsystem of the total family.

Functionalists, such as Parsons (1955), argue that the traditional household division of labor by gender, in which the man pursues a paid career and the woman tends the home, is necessary to maintain family integration and stability. The father's roles are those of provider and protector, and as such, are *instrumental*. The mother's roles are called *expressive* roles because they centre on supportive and nurturant tasks, which are anchored primarily in the internal affairs of the family. Role differentiation on the basis of gender within the family is assumed to be a necessary mechanism for preventing disruptive competition between husband and wife, mother and father. There is conflicting evidence on whether or not these roles must be segregated by gender or whether segregation promotes role performance.

For functionalists, the nuclear family of mother, father, and children occupies a central position in our social structure. It is seen as a necessary unit for the socialization of children and for the maintenance of stable, well-adjusted adults (Parsons, 1955). The core function of emotional support, for example, contributes to the well-being of the husband, the wife, and their children. Emotionally stable individuals, in turn, will be better prepared to participate in and serve society.

Because functionalists emphasize stability, integration, and social order based on value consensus, they regard rapid change — including changes in the family — as detrimental. More recently, however, those who view the family from a conflict perspective have presented a radical challenge to these functionalist notions.

Conflict Theory

Like functionalism, conflict theory views society, including the family, as consisting of many parts. Unlike functionalism, however, conflict theory assumes that social order and integration are achieved, not by value consensus and institutions, but through coercion and domination.

The origin of the conflict theory of the family is often traced to the work of Fredrich Engels. In *The Origin of the Family, Private Property, and the State*, first published in 1884, he described the family in capitalist society as the most exploitative social institution. "The first class antagonism appearing in history coincides with the development of the antagonism of man and wife in monogamy, and the first class oppression with that of the female by the male sex." (1902:79.) Engels believed that with the end of capitalism, all human relationships, including family relations, would be different. His view of marriage and the family is dialectic, that is, governed by inherent contradictions and conflict that give rise to change. Such a view differs strikingly from the functionalists' rendition of the family, which assumes adaptation rather than opposition, harmony rather than exploitation, equilibrium rather than disequilibrium, value consensus rather than coercive domination.

Until very recently, contemporary sociologists have disregarded the conflict perspective as a viable approach to family studies. Strongly influenced by the assumptions of structure-functionalism, researchers either ignored reports that spouses (particularly husbands) frequently used physical force and domination to settle domestic disputes, or they simply treated marital violence as a deviation from the norm of familial harmony.

In the last decade, a great many studies have yielded evidence of family conflict and violence, such as abused children, battered wives, and family murder. Research shows that violence is more common and more severe than functionalist theory suggested. Sprey argues for the need to see the family as "system in conflict" because the family embraces a great deal of compulsiveness. For one thing, marriage is not entirely voluntary; on the contrary, "non-participation — remaining single — is often a voluntary decision." (Sprey 1979:702.) Another compulsive element in the family system involves children: they cannot choose their parents. Sprey, like Marx and Engels, views the family as a network of relations characterized by an "ongoing confrontation between its members, a confrontation between individuals with conflicting interests in their common situation." (1979:704.)

Feminist scholars have taken the conflict approach, arguing that women's inequality at home and on the job results from an unequal distribution of scarce resources. Men wield political power and control the economic resources in both the family and the economy and thus can treat women as a subordinate group. Marriage is a contractual arrangement that reflects and reinforces this male-dominant relationship. Hence, marital conflict has its roots in the unequal distribution of authority and of family and societal resources.

The conflict approach is a most necessary corrective to the functionalist view of marriage and the family. Both are essential to understand the social dynamics of today's family.

Symbolic-Interaction Theory

Symbolic interaction is a social-psychological approach to the study of the family. It originated with George Herbert Mead, who, as you will recall from the chapter on socialization, coined such important concepts as the self, the I and me. Mead's fundamental insight — that social interaction is symbolic — entered family sociology through Burgess's (1926) proposal that the family be studied as a "unity of interacting persons." This perspective emphasizes the importance of viewing family relationships and roles (husband, father, wife, mother, parent, child) in the social context within which they occur. Thus, the focus is on marital and familial interaction.

Marital interaction is symbolic interaction. Social life requires communication, and marriage, more than any other enduring social relationship, is mediated by symbols. Not only words but also nonverbal communication, such as gestures and even silence, can be defined as symbolic. The interactionists who study the family argue, therefore, that we must grasp the meaning that symbols convey (Stryker, 1972). As spouses interact with one another they attach shared meanings to their interactions, and these take on symbolic forms. For example, it is not the word love that is important, but rather the meaning attached to it. In marriage, to communicate meaningfully means to communicate symbolically, and vice versa.

To maintain a satisfactory, intimate relationship, symbolic-interaction theory tells us that couples must redefine themselves continually in relation to one another. If they are unable to do so, disagreements develop and conflict is likely to occur. Likewise, when a wife's desire to pursue a career is in accord with her husband's expectation, studies indicate that marital conflict over the division of labor is less likely to occur. Both predictions can be derived from a basic tenet of symbolic interaction theory: "meanings are handled in, and modified through, an interpretive process used by the persons with the things they encounter." (Blumer, 1969:2.)

The area of parent-child relations provides an illustration of the usefulness of the interactionist perspective for family studies. When their children mature, parents are faced with difficult role transitions. When children seek independence at maturity, mothers and fathers must shake off the roles they had assumed in caring for dependent children. The meaning attached to the parent-child relationship needs to be redefined by both parties as children become adults and parents themselves.

The Family Development Approach

The family development approach derives many of its concepts and assumptions from diverse sources. From the structural-functional approach it borrows the concepts of status, role, and norm, particularly as they involve age and sex roles, along with the functionalist notions of boundary maintenance and the equilibrium-seeking family as a social system. The concepts of role-playing, role-taking, reciprocity of roles, and role differentiation are taken from the symbolic-interactionist perspective. From occupational sociology are borrowed the concept of career as a sequence of roles and the view of the family as a convergence of the careers of husband and wife, and later of children and parents (Hill and Mattessich, 1979). These concepts have been organized in a relatively unified framework that emphasizes the processual and developmental sequences of family formation, expansion, contraction, and dissolution — in other words, the life cycle of the family.

Family life-cycle analysis, as proposed by developmental theorists, assumes fluidity, change, and transition in family structure and functioning. The entire family system is viewed as a process over time rather than as a static unit at certain points in time. As the family interacts and intersects with other systems such as the economy, structural con-

In recent years, the single-parent family has become more common in Canada.

straints and critical role transitions may become evident as sources of family change and modification. In addition, certain developmental "tasks" occur at crucial points in a family's history. A failure at a critical transition point may be a potential stress point.

The social historian Hareven suggests that the life-cycle approach allows us to understand better the ever-changing nature of family life. Viewing the family as intersecting with the larger society, and viewing it synchronically, results in the differentiation of two types of time: "family" time and "social" time (Hareven, 1974:325). Family time designates such changes in the family life cycle as courtship, marriage, childbirth, children leaving home, grandparenthood, widowhood, and death of a family member. These life-cycle events follow rhythms that originate within the family system. In contrast, social time designates changing conditions that are external to the family and that take place in the larger society: changes in the occupational structure, settlement pattern, and policies and legislation all affect family behavior.

The developmental approach sensitizes the sociologist to the intersecting of roles in two main areas of life: family and work. If we focus on how and when the family and work roles of both partners mesh, our attention is directed to a potential source of stress that may cause family change or modification.

MARRIAGE AND FAMILY LIFE IN CANADA

Statistics Canada (1980:25) defines the "census family" as consisting of "husband and wife (with or without children who have never married, regardless of age), or of a lone-parent with one or more children (who have never married, regardless of age) living in the same dwelling." The term lone-parent was adopted officially in the 1976 census to describe families with one parent only, of married (spouse absent), separated, divorced, widowed, or never-married marital status. Persons living in a "common-law," "consensual," or "casual" union are included as "now married." (Statistics Canada, 1980.) A family with both spouses or two parents present is referred to as a "husband-wife family."

The definition of family influences who are eligible for various benefits. For this reason, Statistics Canada also uses "economic family," which is defined as "two or more persons resident in the same household, and related by blood, marriage, or adoption." (1980:25.) This definition resembles our definition of nuclear family, which stresses the sharing of common residence by persons who are related in some way.

In 1981, there were 6.3 million families in Canada. Of these, 5.6 million (88.7 percent) were husband-wife families and close to 714 000 (11.3 percent) were single-parent families. Of the latter, 83 percent were headed by women and 17 percent by men (Statistics Canada, 1985). Although single-parent families make up a small proportion of the total (11.3 percent), they have been increasing at a faster rate than husband-wife families.

Persons who are related by blood, marriage, or adoption and who share a common residence also constitute a "family household," whereas those who live alone or who are unrelated and share a common dwelling constitute a "non-family household." The proportion of family households has decreased from 84.5 percent in 1966 to 75.2 percent in 1981, and non-family households have increased from 15.5 percent to 24.8 percent during the same period. This change represents a 62.5 percent increase in non-family households over fifteen years (Statistics Canada, 1985). The members of non-family households are survivors of former single-family households (Kalbach, 1983:35).

The Life Cycle of the Canadian Family

The life cycle comprises family formation (marrying, remarrying, or cohabiting), expansion (childbearing and child rearing), contraction (children or spouse leaves home and family dissolution (widowhood, divorce, or separation). With a current life expectancy of almost seventy-nine years for women and close to seventy-two years for men (Statistics Canada, 1985), the family life cycle may cover half a century or more for couples who stay together.

Stages of family life vary in length not only from family to family but also from generation to generation. A general decline in the age of first marriage, combined with increased longevity and the preference for fewer children have lengthened the time that most couples spend in the empty-nest stage and in retirement, with consequences that we shall explore later.

Mate Selection

In traditional societies, the individual's field of eligible partners is severely restricted by kinship obligations and economic considerations. Personal preferences based on love were almost nonexistent, because they were considered irrelevant to marriage. In fact, in many of today's developing countries and in parts of southern Europe, marriage for love is "considered a luxury and a privilege of the rich." (Safilios-Rothschild, 1977:19.) Canadian men and women, in contrast are, theoretically, free to choose anyone to whom they feel attracted and whomever they fall in love with. Romantic love is a concept difficult to define, but let us describe it here as simply a strong emotional attachment. This attachment, which may lead to a durable sexual and intimate relationship, is considered the proper basis for marriage in societies espousing freedom of choice.

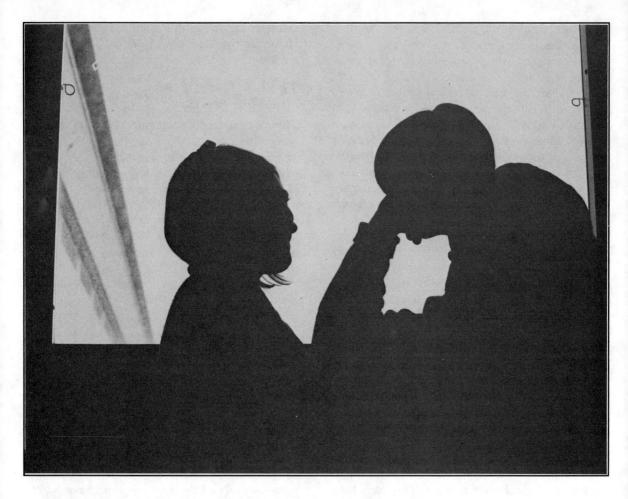

In North America, romantic love is considered the ideal and proper basis for marriage.

In an attempt to formulate a model of heterosexual love, Larson (1976: 133–46) conceptualizes the developmental process of love in five stages. First, people meet and begin to establish rapport ("I feel at ease when with my partner"). Second is the stage of limited transparency ("I feel free to tell my partner things I would not generally tell anyone else"). At this stage, commitment to one another begins to develop. This commitment is the stepping stone for the third stage of mutual dependencies ("I feel incomplete when I am not with my partner"). The fourth stage is fulfillment of personality needs, and the final stage is vital transparency ("I find it easy and natural to be totally honest and open with my partner"). At this stage, the couple have achieved total openness and total self-exposure with the mutual assurance of complete trust. From a symbolic-interactionist point of view, they have acquired the ability to share meanings and to communicate symbolically.

In most Western societies, love is considered both a necessary and sufficient basis for marriage. This romantic notion frequently leads courting couples to ignore differences in nationality, religion, age, race, or social class. It is also commonly believed that true love will render trivial, or even insignificant, any difference in personality and character.

Does research substantiate the notions of "opposites attract" or "like marry like?" Two general concepts, called homogamy and heterogamy, provide answers to these questions. Marital homogamy refers to the possession of similar attributes or characteristics in husband and wife; marital heterogamy refers to the possession of dissimilar ones. When Canadian men and women marry, for example, they generally choose partners very close to their own ages. In fact, the ages at first marriage for Canadian brides and grooms, as well as the age differences between them, have declined between 1921 and 1981. In 1921, the median age for brides was 25.5 years and for grooms 29.9 years, a difference of almost four and one-half years. By 1981, the comparable ages had decreased to 23.5 years and 25.7 years, respectively (Statistics Canada, 1985). Although the average ages at first marriage for both brides and grooms have been rising again since the mid-seventies, it is unlikely that they will increase to their 1921 level. Estimates show that about 10 percent of brides and grooms marry at the same age.

Comparison with the United States and European countries indicate the operation of similar age-homogamy-related norms. These norms themselves are a function of age, because the difference in ages between brides and grooms increases with age at marriage. Thus we may generalize that age homogamy prevails among younger couples, while age heterogamy is more common among remarried and older first-married couples.

The extent to which religious homogamy or heterogamy is practised varies considerably by faith. As shown in Table 11.1, only about one of two Anglican brides marries an Anglican. A comparison of the 1971 figures with those of 1978 shows that a trend toward religious heterogamy is present in all religious groups. It should be noted, how-

ever, that the degree of either religious homogamy or heterogamy in any society is usually related to the proportion of persons of a given belief in the general population and to their geographical distribution in the country. Canadians of the Jewish faith, for example, not only comprise a very small minority (1.4 percent of the total population), but are also more likely to live in metropolitan centres than in small communities.

Evidence shows that ethnic homogamy is particularly relevant for the native Indian segment of our population and for those of Francophone origin. Statistics Canada reported that in 1971, 92 percent of native Indian marriages, 88.5 percent of Francopone marriages, and 79.5 percent of those of British origin were ethnically homogamous. In contrast, people of Scandinavian background are much more likely to marry outside their ethnic group. More recent data on marriage suggest a trend toward greater ethnic heterogamy in Canadian society.

One exception to the rule that "like marry like" is the tendency in our society for men to marry women below their social status. The opposite, however, is true for women. This tendency, called

TABLE 11-1. **Percentage of Brides Having Same Religious Affiliation as Grooms, Canada, 1971 and 1978**

Affiliation of Groom	Percent of Brides With Same Affiliation	
	1971	1978
Jewish	89.0	72.7
Roman Catholic	88.2	58.0
Mennonite	75.9	63.2
Greek Orthodox	63.8	43.6
United Church	61.6	46.9
Anglican	49.6	34.9
Baptist	45.8	38.2
Lutheran	44.5	25.3
Presbyterian	36.7	25.9

SOURCE: Vital Statistics, Col. II, Marriages and Divorces, Statistics Canada, 1978.

TABLE 11-2. **Marital Status of the Canadian Population Aged Fifteen and Over, 1981 and 1971**

Marital Status	1981		1971	
	Women	Men	Women	Men
Married*	59.7%	62.1%	61.1%	62.8%
Separated	2.7	2.2	2.7	2.2
Widowed	10.0	2.2	9.8	2.5
Divorced	3.1	2.2	1.3	1.0
Single**	24.5	31.3	25.0	31.6
Total	100.0%	100.0%	100.0%	100.0%
Total Persons (000's)	9605	9257	7656	7532

  * Includes those living common law.
** Never married.

SOURCE: Adapted from Statistics Canada, 1985, Table 6.

marriage gradient, has at least two implications (Leslie, 1979). One is that except for the very top and the very bottom of the gradient, men have a wider choice of wives than women do of husbands. The other implication is that the marriage gradient keeps some of the highest-status women and the lowest-status men from marrying.

Family Formation: Newly Married Couples

The family life cycle begins with marriages, and most Canadians marry. In 1981, about three out of five Canadian women and men fifteen years and over were married. As shown in Table 11.2 , the proportions of married persons decreased slightly from 1971 to 1981. The percentages of divorced

women and men, however, more than doubled during the last decade.

We can safely assume that about nine out of ten adults will marry at least once. In 1981, one-quarter (26.6 percent) of all marriages were remarriages for at least one partner (1981 Census). Of those who divorce, seven out of ten remarry within five years. The families that result from these remarriages are called "reconstituted" or "blended" families. Many of those who do not remarry constitute "single-parent" families. Blended and single-parent families are rapidly increasing, and we shall discuss this trend later.

The historical trends for marriage and divorce are shown in Table 11-3. The marriage rate (the number of marriages per 100 000 population)

FIGURE 11-1. Divorce rate, Canada: 1970–1983.

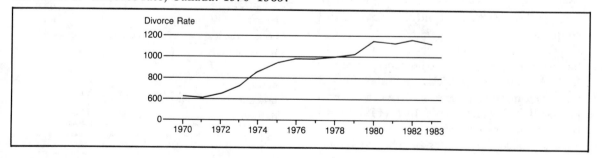

fluctuates greatly for a number of reasons. Much of the recent increase can be explained by the changing age structure of Canada's population. As a result of the baby boom, there are now more persons in the prime marriageable age group (twenty to thirty-four years) than in the past (Statistics Canada, 1979a:3). Another factor is the business cycle: the rate declines during periods of economic recession and increases during periods of prosperity. (It also tends to rise at the beginning of a war and again after the war.)

Marriage is becoming less popular than in the past. The divorce rate had been rising at an unprecedented rate up to 1982, as shown in Figure 11-1. In 1983, however, it took a nose dive: at that year the number of divorces had declined by almost 2000 (Table 11-3). Remarriage rates are also high, but it appears that both Canadian men and women in the younger age groups tend to postpone marriage. Cohabitation among young and old is gaining acceptance, and there is an increase in the number of younger Canadians, both women and men, who remain single (Peters, 1983:287; Statistics Canada, 1985, Table 7).

According to family development theory, the transition from singlehood to marriage or remarriage is a critical time for the couple. It entails a structural change from their family of orientation to their own family of procreation (an unfamiliar husband-wife relationship; however, marriage today is frequently preceded by cohabitation).

The new conjugal relationship focuses sharply on meeting the needs of two individuals who must begin to interact as a couple. From a symbolic-interactionist view, personal and societal expectations combine to exert a certain amount of pressure to interact in this way. Establishing these early marital roles always brings into play the contradiction between developing a couple identity and maintaining an individual identity. Another dilemma lies at the heart of marital interaction itself: giving up one's independence in order to satisfy the other's needs. Thus, conflict and contradition, as well as happiness and adjustment, are inherent elements of living together.

American, European, and Canadian studies of newly married couples seem to indicate that satisfaction in marriage, love, and companionship is higher at this early stage than at any other time (Campbell, 1975; Lupri and Frideres, 1981; Rhyne, 1981). Conflict and disagreement, however, are not uncommon at this time. A significant number of Canadian divorces occur at the end of the third year of marriage. Ishwaran (1983:28–29) claims that in Canada "in 1976 there were 156 divorces within the first year of marriage." Unwanted pregnancy is a source of marital strife, and the probability of eventual divorce is higher for those who marry young.

Research tells us that marital problems are not only common among newlyweds, as we would expect, but that these conflicts in early marriage do not necessarily lead to divorce at this time. Instead, they carry over into future family stages.

Family Expansion: Parenthood

Family expansion means the beginning of parenthood. Depending on the number, timing and spacing of children (if any), the expansion process may last twenty-five years or more. Viewed from the position of the parents, the expansion period constitutes the family of procreation.

The most important decision faced by young couples is whether or not to have children. Most Canadian couples do have children, but the downward trend in the birth rate that began in the early 1960s appears to be continuing into the 1980s. The percentage of families with four or more children has declined. In short, Canadian families are becoming smaller. In 1971, husband-wife families had 1.7 children on average; by 1981, the figure had dropped to 1.3. The corresponding figures for lone-parent families were 1.8 and 1.7 (Statistics Canada, 1985, Table 16).

Couples who become parents usually do so within the first two years of their marriage. The average interval between marriage and first birth dropped sharply to just under one year in 1975 and 1976. The average interval between fourth and fifth births rose from 1.4 to 1.9 years (Kalbach, 1983:41). Statistics show that an increasing number of Canadian women are postponing childbearing and reducing the number of children because of their work outside the home (Statistics Canada, 1979a). Voluntarily childless marriages are also increasing (Veevers, 1980). In 1981, 15 percent of all families were childless (Statistics Canada, 1985:4). It is estimated that by the turn of the century, one out of five married women between thirty and thirty-five will never have borne a child. This proportion would represent a four-fold increase over the present figures (Grindstaff, 1975:21). The trends among Canadian couples to have few children and to have them early reduce the period of family expansion significantly. These trends, along with the fact that children tend to leave home at an earlier age, mean that many couples will spend a longer time alone in the future.

Marital Satisfaction or Disenchantment. The birth of the first child is a potential stress point because the baby's arrival interrupts the established relationship between husband and wife; they must now assume the role of parents. As the twosome becomes a threesome, a foursome, and so on, family interaction becomes more complex. This complexity is not the result of size per se, but of a qualitative change in interaction. Enlarging any group, particularly a primary group like the family, affects the proximity, density, and intimacy of the interaction matrix.

The shifting of the mother's attention to the newborn child may make the husband jealous, which, in turn, may harm the couple's emotional bond. The presence of children may interfere with the couple's sex life, which has already been interrupted by pregnancy. In addition, child care must be provided and a new marital division of labor established, if the mother chooses to work outside the home.

It has been suggested that two marriages exist within each marriage: "his" and "hers" (Bernard, 1972.) In other words, husbands and wives do not perceive marriage in the same way. From the symbolic-interactionist perspective, each partner attaches a different set of meanings to the same reality. A Canadian survey (Rhyne, 1981) found that Canadian husbands and wives assess their marriages differently. Women reported that they were less satisfied than men with all aspects of the marital experience, with the exception of sexual needs. In the U.S., also, "more wives than husbands consider their marriage unhappy, have considered separation or divorce, have regretted their marriages, and fewer report positive companionship." (Bernard, 1972:28.)

Though most couples experience considerable rewards from parenthood, marital satisfaction at this stage declines sharply for both husband and wife, as Figure 11.2 reveals. One reason for loss of satisfaction is "generally an inescapable consequence of the passage of time in a marriage." (Pineo, 1961:11.) Another reason, which we may infer from the functionalist as well as the symbolic-interactionist perspective, is that the role of the mother takes priority over the role of the wife and companion. Role incompatibility — the extent to which the demands of one role clash with the demands of other roles — may help explain the sharp decline in marital satisfaction at this stage.

Two important dimensions of the husband-wife relationship are the division of labor and of power. In a provocative study, Young and Willmott (1975) contend that technological change and the rise of feminism have contributed to an emerging role symmetry in contemporary marriage. The characteristics of the symmetrical family are: (1) it is a consumer rather than a productive unit; (2) a nuclear unit rather than an extended one; (3) instrumental

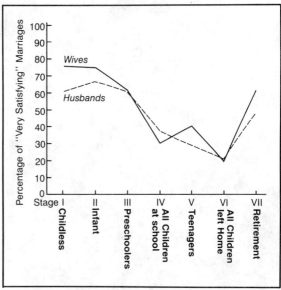

FIGURE 11-2. Marital Satisfaction by Life Cycle.

SOURCE: Eugen Lupri and James Frieders, "The Quality of Marriage and the Passage of Time," *Canadian Journal of Sociology*, Vol. 6:3, 1980.

As a family grows, the established relationship between husband and wife may come under stress.

and expressive roles are no longer gender-linked, as structural-functional theory had assumed, but are shared by both husband and wife; (4) wives are more likely to work outside the home; (5) men are more likely than in the past to be involved in the home; (6) husband and wife make all decisions jointly; and (7) equality pervades all family relationships, including those involving children.

Division of Labor. As more and more Canadian wives and mothers have taken jobs outside the home, there has been increased pressure on husbands to share household tasks and child care equally with wives. Canadian time-budget studies, however, show no dramatic changes in traditional roles. In a Vancouver study (Meissner et al., 1975), it was found that the husband's overall contribution to housework, measured in hours, remained essentially the same, whether or not the wife worked outside the home (age

and educational level of husband did not affect the husband's contribution either). Similarly, a study of working mothers in the U.S. (Cook, 1975:28) concluded: "Whether married women work or not, they get little assistance with housework from their husbands. When they work, they must still carry the major responsibility for care of home and children." Similar conclusions were reached in an international study that examined time records of men and women in twelve countries (Lupri and Symons, 1982).

To be sure, sexual equality is still pursued in Canadian marriages, but it remains largely an ideal, not an accomplished fact. Wives everywhere still continue to bear the major responsibilities for child care and housework. This inequality may explain why it is predominantly wives that are disenchanted with marriage.

Division of Power. Because marriage consists of two partners who must make decisions,

While most working women still assume prime responsibility for running the household, gender roles are now less likely to determine the division of labor in North American families.

power relations develop. Power is defined here as the ability of an individual to impose her or his will on another person and thereby influence the behavior of other members of a social group, despite their resistance (Weber, 1947:152). The emotional bond that links partners in a companionate marriage affects, and is affected by, each partner's power and the way in which it is wielded it in the family. One of three power relations can emerge: the husband-dominant pattern, the wife-dominant pattern, or wife-husband equality.

According to exchange theory, control of resources is the most important determinant of power in marriage. A classic study of marriage by Blood and Wolfe (1960) found that a husband's power within the marriage tended to increase in proportion to the amount of resources he could muster, such as education, income, occupation, and socioeconomic status. Similarly, a wife who was gainfully employed had more to say than a wife who was not.

Contrary to these findings, a 1975 Calgary study (Brinkerhoff and Lupri, 1983) found that wives who work for pay do not have more marital power than those who do not work. Indeed, working wives have slightly less power than do housewives. Furthermore, husband dominance appears to be more prevalent among couples of both the upper and the lower classes. These findings, however, do confirm the one link between employment and marital power: non-working husbands had the lowest decision-making score of any comparison group.

Another line of criticism has come from feminist scholars. As noted previously, the resources that supposedly confer marital power are those that earn money. The talents, skills, and services that the housewife brings into a marriage (cooking, cleaning, child care) do not increase her power, no matter how essential they are to the well-being of the family or of the society at large. Feminists have justifiably pointed out a strong male bias in conceptualizing and measuring marital power (Eichler, 1981).

Companionate marriage based on role symmetry is slowly growing in popularity among young, modern, urban, middle-class couples. Affection, intimacy, understanding, and equality are important ingredients of companiate marriages. Seen from a symbolic-interactionist perspective, the sharing of tasks and decision-making is not rigidly prescribed but is based on daily interaction that includes an interpretive process, through which couples define and redefine the meaning of their relationship.

Family Contraction: Marriage in Middle and Later Years

The family contraction period encompasses the middle and later years, a time span of twenty-five years or more. Several critical transition points are experienced during this period: children leaving the home (the empty-nest syndrome), preretirement, and retirement. In addition, widowhood is prevalent in later years, particularly among women.

Types of Marital Relations. Cuber and Harroff (1965) developed a typology of marital relationships in the middle years. A conflict-habituated relationship is characterized by much bickering, nagging, and quarrelling. Couples feed on conflict, which in a way holds the marriage together for a whole lifetime.

A devitalized marriage is very common. In the early years, the partners were deeply in love, and communication was extensive and deep. However, by the middle years, "the relationship has become a void. The original zest is gone. There is little overt tension and conflict, but the interplay between the pair has become apathetic, lifeless. It is intended, usually by both, that it continue indefinitely, despite its numbness." (1965:49.) Outside commitments — career, community, children — have become more important than the marital relationship.

Passive-congenial marriage is similar to the devitalized type, except that the relationship was passive from the start. The partners never experienced the excitement and joy of being in love — nor the disillusionment and disenchantment of the devitalized marriage. Both partners emphasize a successful career, high status, or political achievement rather than love. In other words, the marriage is utilitarian.

A vital relationship approximates the ideal marriage. Only about one-sixth of the couples studied by Cuber and Harroff fell into this category. The partners are "intensely bound together psychologically in important life matters. Their sharing and their togetherness is genuine. It provides the life essence for both man and woman." (1965:59.) Conflict and tension exist, as they do in every meaningful relationship, but the partners feel a strong desire and commitment to resolve them quickly, to forgive, and to forget.

A total relationship is even more vital. Work and play are shared. Affection, mutual trust, and togetherness permeate all aspects of life, inside and outside the marriage. The partners have indeed become one, as if neither has a separate existence. Total marriages are exceedingly rare.

To be sure, these five relationships are ideal-typical constructs, but they do present aspects of real-life marriage in the middle and later years.

The Empty Nest. When children leave the home, a marriage becomes as it was in the early years in at least one respect: the couple is alone again. This is a critical transition period in which couples grow closer together or move farther apart. They may rediscover themselves or face each other as total strangers. In this stage, marital satisfaction reaches an all-time low for many Canadian couples (Rhyne, 1981). Parent-child relationships also take on a new dimension; children have become independent adults and are beginning to establish their own families and in so doing, their parents become grandparents. This release from obligations of parental responsibility leaves an impressive amount of free time, especially for the housewife. Her retirement from the role of mother often results in a shift of energies to nonfamilial areas such as work outside the home, community service, or leisure-time activities.

The "empty-nest syndrome" has recently gained worldwide attention as a cause of depression in middle-aged women. As seen in Figure 11.2 , Canadian couples experience a temporary period of disenchantment with marriage at this time, but then an upswing takes place for both husband and wife. To be sure, the greater a wife's investment in her children as her source of personal fulfillment, the greater the depres-

The retirement years can offer a couple renewed opportunity for companionship and a reassessment of gender roles.

sion caused by the empty nest. (Similarly, the greater a husband's ego investment in his job, the greater his depression before or at retirement.)

In general, however, if the empty-nest syndrome is experienced at all, it is relatively short-lived. An increase in marital happiness during the postparental period stems from couples rediscovering themselves after the children have gone, from extra-familial activities, or from both causes (Lupri and Frideres, 1981).

Marriage in Retirement Years. Retirement from an occupation, especially if it is involuntary, may be a critical transition point, particularly for the husband and especially if he is the sole breadwinner. Like marriage at the honeymoon stage, the retirement years are characterized, in all classes, by joint activity, within and outside the home; retirement often brings about a meshing of sex-based roles. As the relationship becomes more egalitarian, couples experience greater happiness together in old age.

Gerontological studies on the family dispel the myth that older Canadians are abandoned by their children and the notion that the elderly are devoid of sexual and emotional feelings. The need for intimacy, companionship, and affection persists throughout life.

Family Dissolution: Divorce or Widowhood

Up to this point we have discussed three phases of the family life cycle: family formation, expansion and contraction. The fourth and last stage, family dissolution, can result from divorce, separation, desertion, or the death of a spouse. We will organize our discussion of family dissolution around two critical role transitions or role exits: divorce and widowhood. No discussion of contemporary marriage would be complete without some attention to divorce and widowhood.

Divorce

In an issue of *Maclean's* magazine (21 March 1983) divorce was featured as the cover story. *Maclean's* claim that nearly half of all marriages in Canada end in divorce was based on a comparison of the number of divorces with the number of marriages in 1980. However, it is misleading to say that nearly half of Canadian marriages in 1980 ended in divorce because very few of the couples who were divorced in 1980 were also married that year. A valid divorce rate must compare the number of divorces in one year with the total number of marriages that exist in that year.

Let us look at some trends and make a few cautious statements about the future. In Québec, under the Civil Code of 1866, married women had no legal status whatever. Nearly a century later, the Divorce Act (1968) not only provided Canada with its first uniform divorce code but also liberalized divorce by expanding the grounds. By accepting "marital breakdown" as grounds for divorce, for example, the new law gave legal recognition to a social reality that had existed for a long time.

TABLE 11-3. Number of Marriages and Divorces and Marriage and Divorce Rates per 100 000 Population for Canada, 1921–1984

Year	Marriages		Divorces	
	Number	Rate	Number	Rate
1921	71 254	790	558	6.4
1931	68 239	640	700	6.8
1941	124 644	1060	2462	21.4
1946	137 398	1090	7757	63.1
1951	128 408	920	5270	37.6
1956	132 713	830	6002	37.3
1961	128 475	700	6563	36.0
1968	167 538	790	11 343	54.7
1969	179 413	920	26 079	123.8
1971	191 324	890	29 672	137.6
1976	193 343	840	54 207	235.8
1980	191 069	800	62 019	259.1
1981	190 082	780	67 671	278.0
1982	188 360	760	70 436	285.9
1983	184 675	740	68 567	275.5
1984	185 592	740	65 172	259.4

SOURCE: Statistics Canada, Yearbooks 1941 to 1975 and Catalogue No. 84-205. Vital Statistics, Vol. II. Marriages and Divorces, 1978, Catalogue No. 84-205; 1980, 1981, Table 10, 16–17; 1982, 1983, 1984 Catalogue No. 84-205, Vital Statistics, Vol. II, Marriages and Divorces, 1984.

This reality is made strikingly clear when we observe the divorce rates over time (Table 11-3). We find a steady increase in the divorce rate from 1921 through the 1940s, a somewhat larger increase through the 1950s and 1960s, and a most dramatic increase between 1971 and 1982. The "social reality" principle is borne out when we compare the crude rate for 1968 (54.7) with that of the following year (123.8): it more than doubled within one year. This rate jumped, no doubt, because the 1968 Divorce Act facilitated the legal dissolution of marriages that had been broken for a number of years. Between 1968 to 1982, there is a fivefold increase in the divorce rate, and the number rose from 11 343 in 1968 to an all-time high of over 70 000 in 1982. In 1983, however, the rate

dipped slightly and the actual number dropped by almost 2000. The downward trend continued in 1984. Divorce rates, not unlike marriage rates, tend to rise during periods of prosperity and decline in times of economic hardship. During troubled times, people postpone making vital decisions that will change their life circumstances.

As we might expect, the incidence of divorce varies by province (Table 11-4). Alberta leads the way with 364.2 divorces per 100 000 population, followed closely by British Columbia (358.5), and to a lesser extent by Ontario (281.7). Newfoundland (95.8), Prince Edward Island (191.0), and New Brunswick (187.4) show consistently lower rates.

The provinces with high divorce rates — Alberta, British Columbia, and Ontario — also have the highest rates of female participation in the labor force. This parallel trend often leads to the premature conclusion that wives who work outside the home contribute to the high divorce rate in Canada and in other industrialized countries. We cannot tell from these data, however, whether marital strain leads women to seek

TABLE 11-4. Number of Divorces and Divorce Rate per 100 000 Population by Province, Canada, 1980.

Province	Number	Rate
CANADA	62 019	259.1
Newfoundland	555	95.8
Prince Edward Island	163	131.0
Nova Scotia	2313	271.3
New Brunswick	1326	187.4
Quebec	13 899	220.2
Ontario	22 442	281.7
Manitoba	2282	221.7
Saskatchewan	1836	189.3
Alberta	7580	364.2
British Columbia	9464	358.5

SOURCE: Statistics Canada, 1982: Vital Statistics, Vol. II, Table 10, 16–17.

employment or whether work for pay leads to marital strain.

Early age at marriage correlates with the incidence of divorce. So do low income, urban residence, and the "financial stress exacerbated by early childbearing." (Boyd, 1983:255.) The presence of children in the home is becoming less of a deterrent to divorce; of all couples divorced in 1969, for example, 45.1 percent had children. In 1978, this proportion increased to 55.1 percent (Statistics Canada, 1978). In 1980, the median duration of marriage before divorce was 9.9 years (Peters, 1983:279), a drop of five years since 1969 when the duration was 14.9 years. The ideal of "right to happiness" characteristic of contemporary marriages accounts for divorce rates but also high rates of remarriage. According to Statistics Canada (1983), about three out of four divorced persons remarry sooner or later. Men are more likely to remarry than women. In 1983, almost one out of three (29.4 percent) marriages were remarriages, of which 90 percent included at least one partner with previous divorce experience.

Widowhood

Although this discussion has been concerned with divorce and its rise in our society, many marriages do not end in divorce, but last until the death of one of the spouses. This is a transition point for the survivor. Today, it is a demographic fact of life that women outlive men by a substantial margin. In 1981, for example, life expectancy at birth was estimated to be 71.8 years for Canadian men and almost 79 years for women (Statistics Canada, 1984). Population projections show that the gap in longevity between Canadian men and women will increase for some time to come.

Since women generally marry men older than themselves, it is not surprising that among women sixty-five and older, nearly half (49 percent) are widows and only two out of five are mar-

ried. Among men of the same age group, three out of four are married and only 13.1 percent are widowed. In 1981, the ratio of widows to widowers among older Canadians was about five to one (Statistics Canada, 1984).

Widowhood entails the loss of old roles and the acquisition of new ones. Although widows and widowers have different life circumstances, they have certain problems in common as a result of their spouse's death. These problems relate to economic factors, isolation, and loneliness.

Most widows today suffer a considerable drop in income, for most did not work outside the home and if they did, it was not until their children were grown, and then only in low-paying jobs. As of 1981, nearly 60 percent of unmarried Canadian women aged sixty-five and over reported an income below the poverty line (Dulude, 1981:34). Widowers have higher incomes than widows but reportedly face economic hardship, mainly because they have to pay for services formerly supplied by their late wives. If they are left with small children, this added cost may create a heavy burden.

The second major problem faced by widows and widowers is emotional and social isolation. The loss of an intimate relationship cannot be alleviated merely by alternative relationships, particularly in the first few years of widowhood. The widowed are also likely to experience social isolation because of the lack of a network of involvements with peers, friends, neighbors, and the like. Emotional and social isolation cause loneliness, which, studies show, is the greatest problem facing widows and widowers.

Despite these problems, many widowed persons make a relatively good adjustment after a few years. Older widows appear to adjust better than younger ones (Blau, 1981) because widowhood in later years is expected, particularly by women. New sources of societal support are emerging, such as self-help "widows" groups.

Family Violence

The modern family represents a paradox: while it provides a private setting for the development of love, companionship, and intimacy, it also provides a setting for the expression of hostility, conflict, and violence. In the last decade, a great many studies have documented that family conflict and family violence (e.g., child abuse, wife-battering, murder) are not at all rare social occurrences. In fact, the growing prevalence of violence within the private confines of the home has become a social problem of considerable magnitude. It prompted a U.S. research team to label the "marriage license a hitting license." (Straus, Gelles, and Steinmetz, 1980.) The exact extent of family violence is difficult to assess, however, because so much of it is hidden from public scrutiny.

The available Canadian information on the victims of spouse abuse is obtained largely from residents of transition houses and women's shelters. Because much spousal violence is unreported, the figures based on these and other sources are substantial underestimates. According to the best available estimates, one in ten Canadian women, married or cohabiting, is battered by her male partner (MacLeod, 1980). One out of three women will be involved in a battering relationship at one time in her life. One out of five murders in Canada is committed by a husband against his wife. It has been estimated that in 1979, the International Year of the Child, close to 60 000 Canadian children were abused physically by their parents (Nett, 1983). A recent U.S. study on family violence indicated that almost 4 percent of children aged three to seventeen years are abused each year (Strauss, Gelles, and Steinmetz, 1980).

Family sociologists cannot isolate one specific factor to account for child abuse, but the various studies tend to suggest a pattern: those who were abused as children are likely to grow up to be abusers. Violence appears to be a learned response: persons who experienced violence in their family of orientation also tend to experience violence in marriage. Furthermore, the more violence that women experience as children, the more reluctant they are to leave their abusive husbands. The fewer resources women have, the less power they have, and the more they depend on their male partners without calling for outside help (Gelles, 1979).

To obtain a more realistic picture of spousal violence, a 1981 Calgary study of 562 matched couples, married or living together, collected basic information on the extent of violent acts in the home (Lupri, 1985). In a self-administered questionnaire, women and men were asked separately to indicate how often they had committed violent acts against their respective partners in the previous year (1980).

The percentages below refer to those women and men who admitted to having initiated the following eight violent acts against their respective partner:

	Women	Men
	%	%
threatened to hit or throw something at the other:		
once last year	8.9	10.5
twice or more last year	10.8	6.8
pushed, grabbed, or shoved the other:		
once last year	7.8	9.8
twice	3.8	3.4
three times or more	3.4	1.8
hit or tried to hit the other:		
once last year	7.5	5.7
twice or more	6.5	3.1
slapped the other:		
once last year	5.2	4.1
twice or more	2.6	1.8
kicked, bit, or hit the other with a fist:		
once last year	3.7	2.1
twice or more	2.7	1.1

beat up the other:

at least once last year	1.8	1.7

threatened the other with a knife or gun:

at least once last year	1.3	0.6
		(3 cases)

used a knife or gun on the other:

	1 case	none

Several inferences can be drawn from these results. First, spousal violence is more common than suggested by the family harmony model discussed earlier. Second, spousal violence in the home embraces both wife-beating *and* husband-beating. Third, spousal abuse is rarely a one-time occurrence. In fact, violence between partners becomes highly patterned: it persists. Fourth, because these "violent incidents" are self-reported it is safe to assume that not everyone told us about all the violence in his or her home. The true figures may well be double those based on what respondents were willing to admit. Fifth, there is no reason to believe that these figures are unique to Calgary. On the contrary, U.S. national surveys indicate that spousal violence is widespread and to be found in all parts of the country, among all segments of the population, young and old, rich and poor. Spousal violence is somewhat more prevalent among couples of the lower socioeconomic classes because they are more likely than couples from the middle or upper classes to be strained by financial hardships, unemployment, and unwanted pregnancy. And finally, the results make evident that marriage is a dialectic relationship: seemingly contradictory processes of love and intimacy exist simultaneously with conflict and violence. As Simmel (1950) observed cogently, the more intimate social relations are, the more likely they are to give rise to conflict.

Change and Diversity in Family Life

Let us sum up our analysis of family life in Canada. Our study was guided by the developmental perspective, an approach that organizes its analysis around the major stages of the life cycle. Theoretically, this dialectic and dynamic overview of family formation, expansion, contraction, and dissolution focuses not only on the important dimension of time, but also on inherent changes. In fact, each period produces transition strains, which may accumulate and eventually bring about further changes in family structure and functioning. The management of these conflicts acquires structure and in time results in the emergence of variant family forms such as dual-working, lone-parent, and blended families, to which we now turn.

EMERGING FAMILY VARIANTS

The Dual-working Marriage

Today, women are an integral part of the Canadian economy. However, it was not until World War II that demographic forces, economic expansion, and changes in ideology and values combined to draw masses of women into the marketplace. More recently, the proportion of married women in the work force has grown so dramatically that we have come almost full circle since the preindustrial era.

As Table 11-5. shows, over the last 50 years labor-force-participation rates for women increased from 20 percent in 1931 to 52 percent in 1981 — or by two and one-half times. In the same period, the rate for married women increased from 4 to 52 percent. In other words, one out of every two Canadian wives is working outside the home today. As we would expect, the rate for divorced women (not shown) is even higher than that for single women: in 1983, almost two out of three divorced women were gainfully employed (Statistics Canada, 1985).

A major factor in women's labor-force participation is education: the higher the level of education obtained, the higher the rate of participation. In 1983, for example, women with less than nine years of education had a participation rate of 26.4 percent, those with a high-

TABLE 11-5. Female Labor-Force Participation
Rates by Marital Status, Canada,
1931–81

| Year | Participation Rate* | | | |
| | Married | Single | Other | Total Female |
	%	%	%	%
1931	4	47	21	20
1941	4	50	20	21
1951	11	58	19	24
1961	22	54	23	30
1971	33	48	28	37
1976	43	56	31	45
1981	51	62	35	51

SOURCE: 1931–1976 data adapted from Lupri and Mills (1983:50); 1981 data from Statistics Canada, 1981.

* Defined as the percentage of all persons aged 15 years and over who are in the labor force. The participation rate for married women is that percentage of all married women in the population who are in the labor force.

school diploma had 54.2 percent, and those with a university degree had a rate of 75.8 percent (Statistics Canada, 1985).

A comparative study by Lupri and Mills (1985) shows that mothers' participation in the workforce has shown considerable growth; in particular, young mothers with small children are remaining in or re-entering the economy in unprecedented numbers.

These two patterns — the increase in employment among married women and among young mothers — indicate the following changes in the Canadian family: (1) the ever-increasing intersecting of women's roles in family and in work; (2) that wives, young and old, share increasingly the financial burden of maintaining a household; (3) that the number of families in which both parents work is likely to grow; (4) that work is becoming crucial to both women's and men's sense of identity; and (5) that the dual-working marriage is no longer a variant form, but is rapidly becoming the dominant one in our society.

In the future, home and child-care responsibilities may come to be shared more evenly, as working wives exert more pressure on their husbands.

The Lone-parent Family

More than any other family form, the single-parent family challenges the traditional family unit. Separation, divorce, desertion, the death of a spouse, or the decision not to marry are the contributing factors behind this trend.

In previous generations, most women and men experienced marriage, parenthood, and widowhood. Some single-parent families existed, particularly after both wars, but they resulted from widowhood. Today, the high incidence of divorce is responsible for the increase in lone-parent families. As a result, women and men today are likely to experience six stages in their life cycle: marriage, parenthood, divorce, single parenthood, remarriage, and widowhood.

Between 1961 and 1981, the number of single-parent families doubled. In 1981, one family out of every nine (11.3 percent) was headed by a single parent, compared to less than one out of every ten (9.8 percent) in 1976. The majority are headed by women (82.6 percent in 1981), which is due to three factors: (1) mothers are more likely than fathers to obtain custody of children when a marriage is dissolved; (2) in recent years, an increasing number of women choose not to marry and are raising their child(ren) alone; and (3) men of all ages have a greater propensity to remarry.

This trend, from a two-parent to a one-parent family, has important economic implications, particularly for those families headed by women. Separated and divorced women are more likely to work outside the home than are married women. (Lone-parent families headed by men earn almost twice as much as those headed by women.) Child care is a major expense for single mothers. Fatigue, exhaustion, and role overload are common complaints of single working mothers.

When one parent is permanently absent, does the relationship between parent and child change, and how are children affected? Schlesinger, who has researched the subject in Canada, states: "The one-parent heads of families are conscientious parents striving to bring their children to healthy maturity with as much capability for finding happiness as they would have it if they had both father and mother in an intact family." (1978:vii.) American studies report similar findings. It seems, therefore, that single parents do not pose a serious threat to their children's well-being. Single parenthood also provides opportunities for growth and change. For many, the problems are manageable, compared to the hopelessness of an unhappy marriage.

The Blended Family

Divorce does not seem to discourage people from marrying again, and they do so fairly quickly; the median time between divorce and remarriage is about four years. Remarriage for many people who have children leads to blended families — the third variant form with which we are concerned.

In 1983, 29.4 percent of all marriages that took place in Canada were remarriages (Statistics Canada, 1985). Among the women and men who remarried, eight combinations were possible, and these occurred with the following frequencies:

	% of Total Remarriages
Divorced man, single woman	30.7
Divorced man, divorced woman	29.7
Divorced man, widowed woman	3.0
Single man, divorced woman	24.8
Single man, widowed woman	2.1
Widowed man, widowed woman	4.7
Widowed man, divorced woman	3.2
Widowed man, single woman	1.7

How do second marriages differ from first marriages? First of all, people who remarry are in a later stage of their life cycle and therefore have different expectations of their new marriage. This was found to be true in a Toronto study of a sample of ninety-two second marriages (Schlesinger, 1978).

Many couples seemed to have less idealistic, but more realistic expectations of their second marriage. Couples repeatedly reported greater happiness, more mutual affection, and greater consensus on major issues, goals, and values in their second marriages. American studies have reached similar conclusions.

Remarriages that involve children are called blended or reconstituted families. Single-parent families often become part of a blended family. According to Visher and Visher (1979), five structural dimensions, each laden with potential difficulties, emerge in blended families. First, spouses and children in blended families have lost a primary relationship. Children may mourn the loss of one of their parents, and anger and hostility may be displaced onto the new step-parent. Second, the children's loyalty may be divided between the parent with whom they live and the absent parent; children are often forced to take sides. Third, the new step-parent is often forced to compete with the children for their affection. It is not unusual for the step-parent to be excluded from the parent/child relationship. Fourth, step-parent roles and nomenclature are often ambiguous: is he or she supposed to act as a parent or a friend? The use of first names to refer to step-parents is becoming quite common, but it is awkward for the biological children if they address their father as "Dad" while the stepchildren call him by his first name. And fifth, many children in blended families are members of two households. Each household may have different rules and expectations, which may lead to further confusion and ambiguity.

Appropriate terms are also lacking for the new complex of extended-family relationships, including aunts, uncles, cousins, and grandparents. The absence of proper terms is both a symptom and a cause of some of the problems faced by members of reconstituted families. Thus, despite its growing prevalence, the blended family is characterized by incomplete institutionalization.

Alternatives to Marriage

Our discussion of dual-working marriages, one-parent families, and blended families shows that long-standing assumptions about the roles and responsibilities of husbands and wives are being called into question. One alternative is to remain single, either voluntarily (those who are postponing marriage or remarriage for some finite period of time, those who were married and do not want to remarry, and those who wish to remain single) or involuntarily (those who want to marry, including the widowed, divorced, and the never-married).

Another alternative to marriage is to cohabit or live common-law. In recent years, living together has become very popular, not only among the young but also among older men and women (Hobart, 1983). American census figures for 1981 indicated that about ten percent of men and women aged eighteen or older were cohabiting. Estimates for the Canadian population are similar (Hobart, 1983; Fels, 1981). In 1980, slightly more than half of all American cohabiting couples were under twenty-five years of age, slightly more than one-fourth were between twenty-five and forty-four, and one-fifth were forty-five years and older.

Much cohabitation is short-lived. The longer a couple lives together, the greater the likelihood that a marriage will follow. In general, although the relationship of unmarried couples may be seen as an alternative to marriage, it is not unlike the relationship of many married couples.

SUMMARY

1. Sociologists view the family as a key primary group with strong intimate ties, as a network of roles and structures, and as an institution organized around the meeting of basic individual and societal needs.

2. The nuclear family is considered universal because it fulfils four functions fundamental to human life: sexual regulation, reproduction, economic co-operation, and nurturance. To these we have added emotional support and social placement.

3. Family forms vary greatly throughout the world.

(a) Based on the number of spouses, there are monogamous, polygamous, (polygynous, polyandrous) and group marriages.

(b) According to marital residence, there are patrilocal, matrilocal, and neolocal arrangements.

(c) According to rules of descent and inheritance, there are patrilineal, matrilineal, and bilateral societies.

(d) According to the source of authority, there are patriarchal, matriarchal, and egalitarian families.

(e) According to rules prescribing marriage partners there are endogamous and exogamous marriages.

4. Four prominent theoretical approaches to the family were highlighted. Functionalism focuses on the stability and variability of family structures in terms of the functions they perform for both the individual and society. Conflict theory views the family as an arena for gender inequality, sexual asymmetry, and conflict. Conflict is seen as a source of change. Symbolic interaction views marriage as a dynamic process of reciprocal interaction wherein the partners continuously define and redefine their relationship. Family development theory focuses on the major stages of the life cycle: family formation, expansion, contraction, and termination.

5. Industrialization and urbanization have been responsible for changing the traditional family unit.

6. The typical Canadian family is monogamous, neolocal, endogamous, bilateral, and aspiring to egalitarianism. As Canadians, we enjoy an almost unrestricted choice of preferred partners. This choice is governed by romantic ideals rather than

pragmatic considerations. Homogamy, however, prevails in that Canadians marry others with similar social characteristics. In marriage we seek personal fulfillment, intimacy, affection, and companionship — high expectations that place great pressure on the conjugal bond.

7. Marriage in the formation period is usually characterized by happiness. Parenthood is often a source of strain on husbands and wives. The contraction period, when children leave the home, can be a time of rediscovery for many middle-aged couples.

8. Marriage can be terminated by divorce, separation, desertion, or the death of one of the spouses. Divorce in Canada is on the increase, notwithstanding a recent downward trend. The high divorce rate is related to several factors: the liberalization of the divorce laws, economic prosperity, changing family and gender roles, the high rate of mobility, and the high expectations with which men and women enter marriage. However, divorce does not deter Canadians from marrying again: almost four out of five divorced persons do so within five years.

9. Widowhood is most prevalent among women sixty-five years and older. In fact, every second Canadian woman in that age group is widowed. The widowed face three major problems in our society: economic insecurity, social isolation, and loneliness.

10. The family shows no sign of disappearing. However, the basic structure is changing in Canada. The family unit is smaller. Childless marriages are increasingly common. Because of the high rates of divorce and remarriage involving children, there has been an increase in single-parent and reconstituted (blended) families. Furthermore, the reproductive function of the family will be shared increasingly with unmarried women. Singlehood will become a viable alternative to marriage.

11. Family violence is a reality and attracting more and more public attention as well as profes-ⁿ sional scrutiny.

12. Economic co-operation between spouses will continue, but in the form of dual-working marriages. Today, more than half of all Canadian wives work for pay. Hence, the future Canadian family will tend to be symmetrical: husbands and wives will share both paid work and domestic tasks more equally, but wives are more likely to lead the way and press for equality.

GLOSSARY

Affinal family. A system in which kin are traced through marital ties.

Bilateral descent. A system by which kinship is traced equally through relatives of both the father and the mother.

Conjugal family. A kinship system in which marital ties take precedence over blood ties.

Consanguine family. A kinship system in which blood ties are emphasized over marital ties.

Egalitarian family. A family in which the husband and wife share equal power and tasks.

Endogamy. The practice of choosing a mate from within one's own group.

Exogamy. The practice of marrying outside one's own group.

Expressive role. The role that focuses on the home and the nurturing and rearing of children.

Extended family. A family that consists of one or more nuclear family units plus many of their relatives, such as grandparents, grandchildren, uncles, aunts, and cousins.

Family of orientation. The family into which people are born and in which the major part of their socialization takes place.

Family of procreation. The family people create when they marry and have children.

Heterogamy. The selection of a spouse on the basis of characteristics that are dissimilar to one's own.

Homogamy. The selection of a spouse on the basis of characteristics that are similar to one's own, such as age and education.

Incest taboo. A rule forbidding marriage or sexual relations between persons who are closely related biologically.

Instrumental role. The role that focuses on economic functions in the family.

Matriarchal family. A system in which authority and power are vested in females.

Matrilineal descent. A system in which kinship is traced through the female line.

Matrilocal residence. The practice in which a newly married couple lives with the bride's family.

Monogamy. The marriage of one person to another.

Neolocal residence. The practice in which a newly married couple sets up a residence separate from both spouses' parents' home.

Nuclear family. Any two persons who are related by blood, marriage, or adoption and who share a common residence.

Patriarchal family. A system in which the authority and power are vested in males.

Patrilineal descent. A system in which kinship is traced through the male line.

Patrilocal residence. The practice in which a newly married couple lives with the groom's family.

Polygamy. The marriage of plural spouses.

Polygyny. The marriage of one husband to several wives.

Polyandry. The marriage of one wife to several husbands.

FURTHER READING

Canadian Journal of Sociology, 6(3), 1981. A special issue devoted to various theoretical, historical, and empirical aspects of the Canadian family.

Eichler, Margrit. *Families in Canada Today. Recent Changes and Their Policy Consequences.* Toronto: Gage, 1983. A thorough analysis of major issues and policies affecting the modern Canadian family by a leading feminist scholar.

Goode, William J. *World Revolution and Family Patterns.* New York: Free Press, 1963. A comprehensive review of the effects of industrialization on family structure throughout the world by a leading scholar in the field.

Ishwaran, K. (ed.). *The Canadian Family.* Toronto: Gage, 1983. This is one of the most recent and up-to-date collections of articles on the Canadian family by sociologists, demographers, and social psychologists.

Larsons, Lyle E. (ed.). *The Canadian Family in Comparative Perspective.* Scarborough, Ontario: Prentice-Hall, 1976. An introduction to the Canadian family in comparative terms.

Leslie, Gerald. *The Family in Social Context.* 5th edition. New York: Oxford University Press, 1981. An excellent text on the American family with a historical and comparative perspective.

Lupri, Eugen (ed.). *The Changing Position of Women in Family and Society: A Cross-national Comparison.* Leiden: E.J. Brill, 1983. Leading social scientists from eighteen countries, both capitalist and socialist, examine how the articulation of women's family and work roles is shaped by ideology, type of economy, and social change.

Scanzoni, John. *Shaping Tomorrow's Family.* Beverly Hills: Sage Publishers, 1983. An excellent account of the family, present and future, by one of the U.S.'s leading family sociologists.

Shorter, Edward. *The Making of the Modern Family.* New York: Basic Books, 1975. A social history of the Western family from 1750 to the present day.

Stephens, William N. *The Family in Cross-Cultural Perspective.* New York: Holt, Rinehart and Winston, 1963. The most comprehensive account of family practices (plural marriage, kinship, mate choice, sex restrictions, roles of husband and wife, power and deference, child rearing) in various cultures.

Religion

D.A. NOCK

As everyone is aware, there exists a stupendous variety of religious groups and organizations. The Judeo-Christian tradition, which is the dominant religious culture in Canada, encompasses both powerful religious organizations and small religious bodies that wield no power at all. The influence of Roman Catholicism with its hundreds of millions of adherents, for example, has stretched over centuries and continents, whereas the Church of Scientology has a much shorter history and wields little power.

A TAXONOMY OF RELIGIOUS GROUPS

The sociology of religion uses the typological approach or church-sect method of analysis to arrive at a taxonomy of religion. This method was pioneered by Max Weber and Ernst Troeltsch, both Germans, who contributed a great deal to the analysis of religion in the nineteenth century.

The taxonomy of religious groups began with theologian Troeltsch's definitions of church and sect based on the history of Christianity from its beginnings until about 1800. Sociologists, however, found that not all religious groups fit into these two categories and so "cult" and "denomination" were added. Still later, sociologists redefined these terms in a more sophisticated and sociological manner, and this process continues as religious bodies themselves change through time.

Before we proceed, it should be pointed out that some of these terms, particularly cult and sect, have been used by the mass media and the general public in conjunction with practices or beliefs that are interpreted as negative compared to mainstream religious practices and beliefs. Sociology does not include such emotional and subjective elements in its definitions.

Sects

According to sociologists, a *sect* is a religious group within a conventional religious tradition that finds itself in a high degree of tension with the wider society (Stark and Bainbridge, 1981:131). From the sect's viewpoint, however, the wider society is governed by worldly, unsaved, and sinful people, rather than by God's laws, as defined by that sect. The Jehovah's Witnesses, for example, believe that a person may put their salvation in jeopardy by disobeying what they perceive as God's law; namely, that the infusion of blood into human beings is forbidden. Thus, they refuse blood transfusions not only for themselves but also for their children, even when these are deemed necessary to save life. This belief has often placed Jehovah's Witnesses in a high degree of tension with the Canadian medical and legal authorities.

Some religious sects believe that to be "Christ-like" entails avoidance of bearing weapons and of participating in wars. The Hutterites and the Amish, in particular, are known for their pacifist philosophy. The Doukhobors emigrated to Canada because of the repeated insistence of the Russian state that they enrol in compulsory military conscription.

In the nineteenth century, the Mormons found themselves in conflict with the wider society because of their commitment to polygamy. This practice was a religious necessity for Mormons, especially for their leaders, who believed that they could strengthen their religiosity by producing more offspring to people new worlds. However, most of America (and later Canada) thought such a practice was sinful and carnal, rather than religiously sanctioned. As a result, Mormons abandoned the practice in the 1890s (White, 1978).

It was stated that sects remain within a conventional religious tradition, and in North America this means Judeo-Christianity. However, sects are at odds with most churches and denominations, which they feel are too lax and have compromised the Christian gospel too much. God is not usually viewed as a kindly savior who will forgive a multitude of sins, but rather as one who is intent on dividing the few sheep (the saved) from the many goats (the damned). For most of us, it is our occupation that is the main source of status. If we go to a party, we are likely to be asked "what we do," and not what religion we belong to. To members of a sect, however, religious affiliation and particularly commitment to personal salvation, and (sometimes) the salvation of others, is what counts in life.

Sects comprise a small percentage of the Christian population. In Canada, over 80 percent of the population claims to be affiliated with churches or denominations, whereas only 5 percent belongs to sects. Yet a great deal of sociological analysis has been devoted to the sect. Bryan Wilson, a British sociologist, has attempted a typology of sects.

Conversionist sects believe that the world is evil and sinful, but by conversion to a real rather than nominal Christianity, the world's sinfulness can be lessened. This sect regards the outside world as "corrupted because man is corrupted. If man can be changed then the world will be changed." (Wilson, 1969:364.) Conversion is considered as a powerfully emotional experience in a person's biography and is often referred to as the "born-again" experience or "the experience of second birth." The born-again experience is a feeling of peace and joy that stems from Christ's entering the heart of believers and relieving them of sinfulness. Membership is determined by this particular event. Thereafter, believers are expected to demonstrate their salvation by avoidance of "non-Christian" pursuits, such as playing cards,

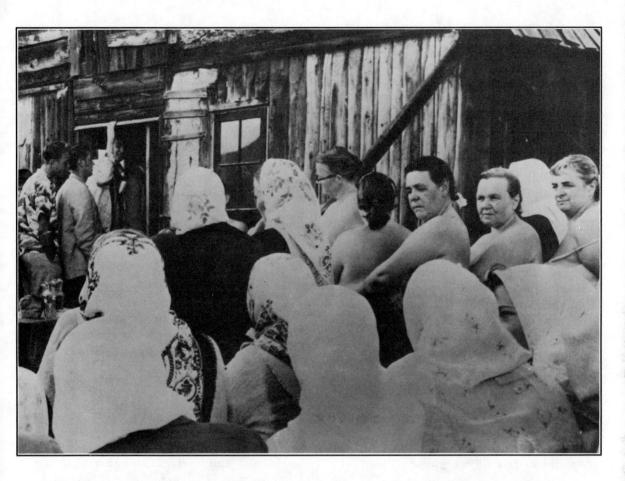

This sect of Reformed Doukhobors (formerly known as the Sons of Freedom) left Russia generations ago to settle in the Kootenay area of British Columbia. They believe that everyone must return to the life style that their ancestors knew hundreds of years ago, and have sought recognition through such anti-social acts as bombing, arson, and disrobing in public.

dancing, gambling, going to movies and plays, dressing in immodest ways, and other such frivolous activities.

Adventist sects believe the world is so evil that the only way to change it is through the intervention of God and the second coming of Jesus, who will overcome evil by setting up a Divine Kingdom.

As Wilson (1969) suggests, "The members of these sects occupy themselves actively in prophetic exegesis, in comparisons of inspired texts and between (sic) the predictions of the sect and contemporary events. They often have long-drawn-out internal debates elaborating prospects of the future." The adventist sect relies on certain sections of the Bible, such as the Books of Daniel and Revelation, which are capable of encouraging rather involved interpretations of prophecy. Today, adventist groups tend to be more cautious about predicting the exact date of the "end times." In the past, one prediction of the end was August, 1844. It was as a result of trying to reinterpret this prophetic failure that such groups as Jehovah's Witnesses and Seventh-Day Adventists arose.

A third type of sect is the introversionists, whose response to the evil of the world is "neither to convert the population nor to expect the world's overturn, but simply in retiring from it to enjoy the security gained by personal holiness." (Wilson, 366.) The introversionists feel that the world is so evil that living within it at all is a threat to salvation. The less extreme introversionist groups live alongside other people (as in cities), but raise extensive barriers to interaction outside the sect. The Chassidic (Hassidic) Jews are an example. In Montréal, they can be recognized by their distinct appearance; fathers and sons wear black, flat-topped hats, black trousers, and long, black coats (even in summer); mothers and daughters wear simple, gray apparel. They have their own schools and synagogues, and engage in occupations supported by the sect alone.

More extreme introversionists form segregated communities or neighborhoods: Hutterites are an example. The Hutterites believe the New Testament teaches the importance of living communally and avoiding possession of personal property. They also feel that those who do not share such a life style have missed the basic teachings of Christianity and thus will not achieve salvation.

Cults

Cults are like sects in that they are in conflict with the beliefs of the wider society. But whereas sects operate within the dominant religious tradition of society, cults do not. As Stark and Bainbridge (1979:125) express it, "the cult is something new and represents an independent religious tradition in the society." Perhaps one should add, however, that especially in the past, cults were often eclectic and syncretic religious movements that borrowed concepts from the Judeo-Christian heritage but in an unorthodox or ahistorical fashion. As one observer put it, "cults tend to blend alien religious or psychological notions with Christian doctrine with a view to obtaining a more 'adequate' or 'modern' faith." (Mann, 1971:6.)

Despite its name, sociologists Stark and Bainbridge define Christian Science as a cult.

Christian Science was founded in the 1870s by Mary Baker Eddy, a New Englander. According to her, matter is "mortal error" and is "unreal." It is the "infinite mind" that is real. "There is no life, truth, intelligence, no substance in matter." (Eddy, 1934:468.)

Christian Science is thus at odds with traditional Christianity, with its doctrines of material and physical reality. Specifically, "... the only reality of sin, sickness or death is the awful fact that unrealities seem real to human, erring belief, until God strips off their disguise ... all inharmony of mortal mind is illusion, possessing neither reality nor identity ... sin, sickness and death are to be classified as effects of error. Christ came to destroy the belief of sin." (Eddy, 1934:472–73.) Thus, the aim of Christian Scientists is to overcome the illusions of sin, sickness, and death by teaching the real truth, which alerts the believer to his or her spiritual reality. If this were fully so, the believer would not be subject to illness, and at an advanced stage of knowledge, even death. In traditional Christianity, sin is one of the major concepts and Jesus is seen as an intermediary who intervenes on behalf of humanity to ask God for the forgiveness of human sin (the doctrine of the atonement). The miracles performed by Jesus, and his crucifixion and resurrection are interpreted as indications that he was "the first man to understand the truth of divine science." (Eddy, 1934:124.)

Christian Science places great stress on spiritual healing, and much of Mrs. Eddy's book *Science and Health* is taken up with testimonials of people who claimed cures. It is important to understand that Christian Science belief is not that mind (or spirit) can *affect* matter and material reality (a belief that is consistent with conventional Christianity), but that matter itself is unreal and therefore an illusion.

Another cult that began in the nineteenth century is Spiritualism and its French and Latin cousin, Spiritism. The essential distinction between these is that Spiritism accepts the belief in reincarnation whereas Spiritualism does not. Although Spiritualism has more ancient precursors, its modern development stems from about 1848, when odd, ghostly happenings occurred in the Fox family of upper New York State. It appeared that odd noises and rappings were caused by a dead man who claimed to be "the spirit of a pedlar who had been murdered in the house some four or five years earlier and that he had been buried in the cellar." (Nelson, 1969:4.) Soon, mediums emerged who could call forth such spirits at seances.

In "mental medianship," it is this form of spiritualism that survived; the medium transmits messages, either by voice or in writing, without the use of material aids and manifestations. Soon a number of mediums emerged who claimed to give a full range of teaching about the spiritual dimension of reality.

As in Christian Science, spiritualism tends to diverge with conventional Christianity on the doctrine of sin. One medium was Emma H. Britten, who taught that spiritualism:

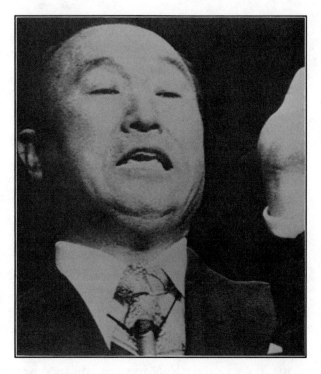

Sun Myung Moon, founder of the Unification Church, has drawn censure from established churches and government over his cult's unorthodox practices.

dispels the doctrine of eternal punishment, and substitutes the cheering assurance of eternal progress ... sweeps away the idea of a personal Devil ... denies the immoral and social corrupting doctrine of any vicarious atonements for sin, and on the testimony of millions of immortal spirits, solemnly affirms that every guilty soul must arise and become its own Savior ... (and) demolishes the absurd and materialistic conception of the theological heaven and hell.

(Nelson, 1968:209–10.)

In the past, sociologists tended to distinguish between sects and cults mainly or solely on the basis of its belief system, or more generally on the relation of sect and cult to the conventional religious tradition of a society. Cults represented a break with the conventional religious tradition, whereas sects were deemed a variation on the conventional religious tradition.

Since both sects and cults are alien to the religious outlook of the majority of the population, there is a tendency to confuse them. Sociologists, however, have recently engaged in empirical work that shows that cults and sects appeal to different types of people. In the United States, cult movements were found to be concentrated in the west, especially in the Pacific region (Stark and Bainbridge, 1981:145). In Canada, cults are also concentrated in British Columbia and the Canadian West (Stark and Bainbridge, 1982). Even for Christian Science, which began in New England, the membership rate is higher in California and the west than in the region of its birth. As early as 1926, the membership rate per million population in the Pacific region was 3491 compared to New England's 1613. In Canada, the overall cult rate per million was 4.3 in 1971, with British Columbia showing the greatest concentration at 13.1 per million population (Bainbridge and Stark, 1982).

Although one might expect that sects and cults would be found alongside one another, sects are stronger where cults are weak. "While California is home for 167 cults (a rate of 7.9 per million), it has only 29 sects for a rate of 1.37 per million." (Stark and Bainbridge, 1981:147.) As already stated, cults and sects are different in a significant way, since sects hark back to the conventional religious tradition, whereas cults deviate from it and seek to devise a new religious tradition.

What is it about the Pacific region, compared with other parts of the United States and Canada, that attracts cult membership? The answer lies in two factors: religious affiliation and mobility. In the Pacific region, religious affiliation is lowest and mobility is highest. Canadian census figures support the first factor: "no religious affiliation" was the response of 1.7 percent of the population in the Atlantic region, compared to 13.1 percent in British Columbia (the highest rate of all regions). In other words, allegiance to the conventional religious tradition is lowest exactly where the cults are strongest. Data also shows that British Columbia has the highest rate of migration. According to Stark and Bainbridge (1982:356), "Moving to a new town removes the individual from the particular local church congregation which used to provide affiliation without necessarily placing the individual in a new congregation."

Denominations

The term *denomination* may be defined as the conventional religious tradition found in a pluralistic, industrial-capitalist society. Most denominations did not start out as such, but have evolved either from sect movements or from the large churches, such as the Church of England.

A pluralistic society is one where many points of view, ideas, and subcultures exist and are tolerated. Our economic system is pluralistic in that companies compete within a framework of acknowledged rules, and this is also true of our political parties. These circumstances are different from those found in a *monopolistic* society, in which churches rather than denominations operate. In contrast to the Church of England, for example, denominations such as the United Church are not allied to the state and are thus not formally sanctioned by the state. In Canada and the United States, religious toleration is normal, and denominations respond to this situation by recognizing that there are several, or even many ways of arriving at salvation, whereas sects and churches both share the view that salvation is found only in them and nowhere else.

Another way in which the denomination reflects its surrounding climate is by its general acceptance of a democratic ethos in its leadership and a pragmatic outlook. In the church, "the authority of the episcopal and priestly orders" rests "on a divinely instituted commission to teach." (Martin, 1962:7.) In contrast, the sect is sometimes led or inspired by a charismatic leader who feels that God speaks in a special way to him or her. The denomination does not normally validate its sense of direction and leadership by claiming a special charisma for its leader. In fact, members of denominations tend to be distrustful of avowals of personal charisma; every believer can achieve his or her salvation on the basis of personal knowledge, reading of scripture, and good behavior. Neither personal charismatic experience nor a priestly hierarchy is needed for a correct spiritual relationship.

Generally speaking, denomination members do not see themselves as an elect, as do sect members. The denomination accepts as members anyone who wishes to belong and does not set complicated standards of knowledge or attendance for membership. Because of the tolerance of points of view found in denominations, there is usually a percentage of the membership who are as committed to religious views as conversionist or adventist sectarians. However, these members are left in the uncomfortable position of a minority in a religious group whose outlook tends toward laxity. As Martin points out, "the denomination is characterized by moderation ..." (1962:7), which, together with the other characteristics of tolerance and pluralism, distinguish denominations from sects and churches.

A typical denomination in Canada is the United Church, the largest Protestant body. It was formed in 1925 as a result of a union among the Congregationalists, the Presbyterians (derived from the established church in Scotland), and the Methodists (formally a conversionist sect, which, by 1925 was losing its sect characteristics). The United Church is typical of the denomination in that it is "a betwixt and between institution ... an invention of Anglo-American Christianity, designed to make possible free and equal church life in the era of voluntary religious association." (Marty, 1980:1.)

As mentioned, the denomination is characterized by a relative laxness regarding attendance, behavior, and beliefs. One becomes a member by birth and socialization rather than by merit as defined by commitment. In the United Church, a surprising number of members do not believe in the basic doctrines of Christianity. For example, data from 1975 show that only 41 percent believed that "Jesus is the Divine Son of God," and 23 percent believed he was "only a man." Only 63 percent could identify the Apostle Peter; only 33 percent felt a "certainty of having found life's meaning," and only 54 percent expressed a belief in life after death (MacLeod, 1979:8).

MacLeod summarizes his data by stating that the United Church represents an amalgam of theological pluralism. Many members are "Christian agnostics, who may be defined as those members who express doubt and uncertainty about the traditional beliefs." About 20 percent of the members had a strong religious commitment and knowledge; the rest were "unfocused" and "fragmented." (MacLeod, 1979:10.)

Churches

Churches, in the fullest sense of the word, do not exist in modern, pluralistic societies; rather, churches were typical of monopolistic, hierarchical, agrarian societies. The European feudal societies are an example, and their power was supported and legitimized by the church. This role of the church was made especially clear when acceptance of the social order by the peasant population broke down.

When rebellious voices challenged the right of the governing class to control the economic surplus produced by the peasants, the clergy usually defended the elite, asserting that their power had been given them by God and any challenge to it was a challenge to His authority. By legitimating the actions of the governing class in this way, the clergy reduced the need for costly coercive efforts.
(Lenski and Lenski, 1971:220–21.)

Sometimes, the religious-political alliance was based on a formal fusion between state and church, as occurred in England under Henry VIII, as well as in Scandinavia. In England, the church received great grants of land and buildings from the government as endowments. The bishops were considered to be equals of the aristocracy, and for that reason were given places in the House of Lords. In fact, many bishops were from the aristocracy and gentry, and were usually the non-inheriting second or third sons.

It was the original intention of the British government to set up the same sort of state church alliance in Upper Canada. One-seventh of all land was given to Ontario for the maintenance "of the Protestant clergy" in 1791 (usually interpreted to mean the Church of England), and only the Church of England clergymen were allowed to perform marriages. However, in Upper Canada, the pluralistic and relatively egalitarian farming population of the early nineteenth century resisted this attempt to transpose the English system, and by the 1850s, the denominational system had triumphed.

Not all churches were allied with one government or state. The Roman Catholic church, in particular, represented a universal church that was in alliance with many states. "Before the rise of strong national states, an agricultural feudal society with shifting political boundaries accorded well enough with forms of religious organization that symbolized a widespread overall unity." (Nottingham, 1971:234.) However, with modernity evolved pluralistic societies. "In these urbanized, heterogeneous and individualistic societies no new churches have been born. The climate of opinion (as well as the social structure) of (such) societies is, on the whole, unfavourable to established churches. In such societies already existing church establishments, whether universal or merely national in their claims to allegiance, have had to accept, either willingly or unwillingly, an approximately denominational status." (Nottingham, 1971:234.)

The church was essentially a hierarchical religious organization led by bishops and archbishops and priestly intermediaries who interpreted the scripture and dogma on behalf of the laity. Through adherence to the teachings of the church, salvation could be achieved. The hierarchical structure of the church mirrored the agrarian feudal society in its anti-democratic nature. As the industrial-capitalist societies developed, with a concomitant ideology of pluralism and democracy, an absolute and all-powerful system of authority seemed out-of-date. As a result, the church gave way to the denomination, in which lay-participation in decision-making proved more compatible with the prevailing spirit of the times. In Canada, this trend is illustrated in a 1973

National Film Board film, "Challenge for the Church," in which a Roman Catholic bishop states that the bishop is seen now as more of a brother figure than as the authoritarian, paternal figure of the past.

We now turn to a discussion of religious leadership.

CHARISMATIC LEADERSHIP AND OTHER FORMS OF RELIGIOUS AUTHORITY

Sociologists have long wondered about the origin of religious groups and conclude that charismatic leaders were a major factor. According to Weber (1968:49), charisma will be applied to a certain quality of an individual by virtue of which he is set apart from ordinary men and treated as endowed with supernatural, superhuman, or at least specifically exceptional powers or qualities. These "are regarded as of divine origin or as exemplary, and on the basis of them the individual concerned is treated as a leader." Because charismatic authority is first manifested by the evidence of a miracle attributed to the leader (Weber, 1968:49), it is impossible to prove such a claim scientifically and so, without followers, the charismatic leader would be regarded by the nonbelievers as misguided, deluded, mischievous, or mentally ill. This is, in fact, how the charismatic leader is regarded by most people who belong to the conventional religious tradition of the society in question.

Let us look at Jesus as an example of a charismatic leader. Jesus scandalized the conventional religious tradition of his society, which was Jewish. He was crucified at the insistence of the religious leaders for making improper claims about his own religious authority. By the time of his trial, however, he had a large following, for his healing miracles and his miracles over the forces of nature (for example, walking on water and calming of storms) validated his claim. His followers believed that he had conquered death, so that even his death became affirmation of his charismatic powers.

The Mormons also had a charismatic leader, namely, Joseph Smith. Smith claimed to have had a religious history of Americans presented to him on golden plates by an angel. He denounced the Christianity of his day as having fallen away from true religion and he proposed to found a reconstituted Christianity with himself as "seer, revelator and prophet." As such, he advocated economic socialism, polygamy, and the necessity for the elect to be geographically and politically separate from the nonbelieving Americans. He was arrested and lynched in 1844 by a mob as a result of opposition to his religious and social ideas.

Charismatic leaders feel certain of their calling even when they must face massive hostility, as did Jesus and Joseph Smith. As Weber (1968:49) writes, "No prophet has ever regarded his quality as dependent on the attitudes of the masses toward him." Even if it was not their intention at first, charismatic leaders tend to alienate state, social, and religious leaders because of their insistence that no compromise with God's law is possible.

Charismatic authority can be contrasted with rational-legal authority, which is based on "a belief in the 'legality' of patterns of normative rules and the right of those elevated to authority under such rules to issue command." (1968:46.) A third form of authority is traditional in nature and rests "on an established belief in the sanctity of immemorial traditions and the legitimacy of the status of those exercising authority under them." (1968:48.) As an Anglican, you would accord respect to the clergy not usually because you feel that they have a privileged relationship to God that has been demonstrated by signs and miracles. Rather, such respect is accorded because of the legality of their position within the church and because you accept that it is rational to have ministers as religious specialists and experts to act as guides. Many Roman Catholics accept the authority of the Pope partly on such legal-rational grounds and partly on the grounds of the ancient and traditional respect accorded to the Bishop of Rome.

Relating this discussion to our classification of religious groups, we see that sects and cults tend to base their claims of legitimacy more on charismatic authority, whereas denominations and churches usually claim rational-legal and traditional authority. Denominations are bureaucratic organizations usually staffed by a hierarchy of leaders whose claim to authority lies in their certification by colleges, bishops, and other church officials. When change is deemed necessary, the decision is a result of conventions, synods, and colloquia, or at least based on the traditional respect paid to senior authority figures such as popes, archbishops, and so on.

In the history of most charismatic-led religious groups, the charismatic element usually disappears fairly quickly. This is true for several reasons. First, after the charismatic leaders die, their successors may not be accorded charismatic authority, and they themselves may have been in awe of their leader and so disinclined to adopt the mantle. Secondly, the charismatic leader may wish to retain a monopoly over charisma. Thus, in the life of Joseph Smith, several other newly-converted Mormons claimed charismatic authority only to be "disfellowshipped" by Smith himself. Finally, if a sect or cult is successful in widening its appeal, it will lose its element of tension with the wider society. Charismatic leaders, who often create tension rather than reduce it, will then not be recognized.

A final but crucial point is that charisma is not simply a function of the personality of charismatic leaders. If their message has neither relation nor appeal to the society, it could not win a following for them. Jesus' claim to be a charismatic leader of the most compelling kind was rejected by the Jewish power elite. However, Judaism, under the oppression of the Romans, did hope for a divine savior, and since Jesus did claim a special relationship to God, verging on identity with God, many Jews were initially inclined to give him a sympathetic hearing. In the case of Smith, polygamy, economic socialism, and political autonomy obviously went against the grain of nineteenth-century America. However, at a time when Americans had already adopted a messianic view of their own role in world affairs (that they had become the most favoured nation in the world), Mormonism held some attraction in its belief that revelation had not ended in Asia and Europe, but that the Americans had a long religious history of their own, and that Christ had visited America centuries before.

Thus, charismatic leaders normally preach messages with an underlying appeal to some individuals, or in some cases, to specific subcultures or social groups. There is a certain range of messages that will make sense to a population, and the charismatic leader must restrict his or her message within that range, or risk being denied recognition as a charismatic leader.

Also of importance to sociologists is how one religious type changes into another.

THE TRANSITION OF RELIGIOUS TYPES FROM MINORITY TO CONVENTIONAL STATUS

As we have seen, the degree of charisma tolerated by a religious group tends to decrease as it moves from sect or cult to church or denomination, or to put it differently, from minority to conventional status. We shall discuss four factors that influence such a transition.

It is probable that most sects and cults retain minority status throughout their organizational history. However, if a religious movement succeeds in attracting large numbers of adherents, its degree of conflict with the wider society decreases, since more members of the wider society are likely to become members of the religious group. As more citizens become members, especially those with influential positions in the state institutions, the feeling of separation from the majority culture

that characterized the sect is likely to disappear. It is hard to preach against members of the power elite if they are members of the congregation.

A second factor that changes the character of a sect or cult has to do with charisma. In the beginning, the cult or sect often had a compelling leader, whose charisma bound the immediate generation of followers. The children of this first generation will have been socialized into accepting the stories about the charismatic leader, and some of the leader's disciples will likely still be alive to transmit a sense of reality connected with the original leader. After several generations, however, the stories about the original leader, as well as his or her message, will seem historical, perhaps even archaic. Thus, commitment of such subsequent generations to the teaching of the original leader will wane. For example, the last apostle after Christ's death was probably St. John, who died about 100 A.D. Four or five hundred years later, the sense of contact with a charismatic leader had been lost.

A third factor in the transition process is persecution — that is, it may alter the original oppositional stance of the sect or cult. In the nineteenth century, Mormons were subject to continuing government legislation in the United States.

The nature of this legislation belies the centrality of polygamy. All major acts contained provisions for destroying the Mormon economy and polity. They disfranchised polygamists, established electoral commissions, added a voter registration oath, abolished women's suffrage, and disincorporated the Mormon church. The church was fined and its properties placed under federal receivership — forcing it into debt. Only by abandoning their economic and political institutions (such as economic socialism), along with polygamy, could the Mormons regain their property and be permitted to continue their activities.

(White, 1978:171.)

Religious ritual can be an important factor in an individual's socialization. The Australian aborigine boy is being painted for his initiation, in which he will perform the *koraberie* dance; the Jewish boy is learning to put on *teffilin* (phylacteries) prior to his bar mitzvah. Both will be considered adults after these ceremonies.

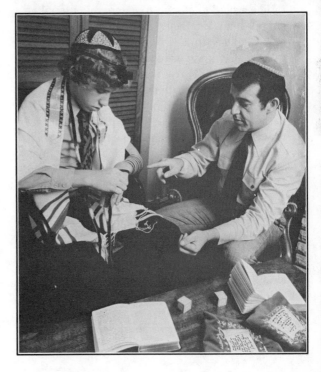

Only a minority of Mormons practised polygamy, but since Mormon leaders were expected to set an example, many of the arrested polygamists were leaders. With the attack on Mormon property and citizenship, the very existence of the group was at stake. With the abandonment of the beliefs and practices that offended majority Americans, "contemporary Mormonism can easily be conceived as a denomination or church." (White, 1978:175.)

A fourth factor is often associated with the transition from sect or cult to denomination and church. Sects usually demand ascetic behavior of its members in response to the call for personal holiness. Such behavior prohibits liquor, drugs, extra- and premarital sex, dancing, and so on, while encouraging participation and even devotion to religious activities. For example, conscientious behavior on the job is seen as a religious duty. By working hard in capitalist societies, one cannot but help accumulate surplus funds with which to buy material possessions. John Wesley is quoted as saying that "Methodists in every place grow diligent and frugal; consequently they increase in goods." (Hill, 1980:125.) Studies have confirmed that sect values merge with dominant values and thus add to the likelihood of economic success. With increasing wealth comes an increasing stake in the status quo and a decreasing likelihood that the successful person will wish to identify with forces that question the wider society and state. (The story of the rich young ruler in the New Testament provides testimony on this point.) Thus, as the degree of economic success in a sect increases, so does the likelihood of the commitment to strict guidelines to salvation as prescribed by sects decrease.

The evolution of sects to a denominational or church status is a theme in Canadian sociologist S.D. Clark's celebrated work, *Church and Sect in Canada*. Clark was intrigued with the prevalence of the sect and the relative weakness of mainline churches in rural frontiers, spanning the breadth of Canada in time and place, from Nova Scotia in the 1780s to Alberta in the 1930s. On the rural frontiers, the settlers resented the more educated, emotionally cold, and upper-class orientations characteristic of the clergy of the established churches. They sought a more emotional religion led by spirit-filled leaders from their own ranks, such as Henry Alline, who believed that the established clergy were "enemies to the power of religion." (Clark, 1971:22.) However, as the rural areas became better established and grew in wealth, the sects either became less influential or lost their original sect characteristics. By 1850, about seventy-five years after Alline's ministry, "tendencies in religious organization in the older-settled parts of the Maritime region were moving strongly away from any considerable emphasis upon evangelical methods and revivalist techniques." (Clark, 1971:261.) Specifically,

The great proportion of the inhabitants in the older communities by 1850 had become fully incorporated into the society of which they were a part. They had secured social status and were no longer dependent upon membership in the evangelical sect ... the result was an increasing reluctance to sacrifice other interests to the exclusive interest of religion. If the evangelical denominations were to survive they had to abandon the conflict position of the sect ... and accept a more accommodating position.

(Clark, 1971:261–62.)

As the older rural areas lost their commitment, new areas of frontier development opened and the disadvantaged position of the frontier settlers once again encouraged the proliferation of sects.

Sociologists have often wondered about the basis for religious affiliation, especially in modern industrial-capitalist societies where membership is voluntary and in which *secularization* has begun. A number of factors have been advanced and to these we now turn.

FACTORS AFFECTING RELIGIOUS MEMBERSHIP

Socialization

Canadians are exposed to religion at an early age through socialization; that is, learning the religious beliefs of their parents as children. In addition, studies show that these same children, as adults, tend to expose their own children to religion, even if they had stopped participating in church attendance in adolescence and early adulthood. They seem to feel that exposure to religion will be a "good thing" for their children. According to a survey (Bibby, 1980:405), persons who said that their father's religious commitment

Muslims in Ottawa pray during Eid ul-Fitr, the festival of thanksgiving that ends the month-long, daytime fast of Ramadan.

had been strong in their childhood were twice as likely to attend church services weekly in adulthood, as compared to those whose father's commitment had been weak. Canadian psychologists have also found that the reported emphasis placed on religion in one's childhood home is one of the best predictors of later religiosity (Hunsberger and Brown, 1984:239).

Membership in a religious group is also related to ethnic affiliation. Thus, most Roman Catholics in Canada come from French, British (Irish), or Italian backgrounds (85%); most Anglicans from a British and especially English background (85%); most Lutherans from a German or Scandinavian background (63%); most Presbyterians (85%) and United Church members (79%) from a British background; and most Mennonites and Hutterites from a German or Dutch background (88%) (Hiller, 1976). The ethnic variable, however, is starting to break down, partly as a result of intermarriage, and partly because assimilation is taking its toll.

Another means of increasing the membership of religious organizations is by subcultural switching.

Subcultural Switching

From the data in the previous sector, it seems that mainstream religious affiliation is relatively unchanging. But what about sects and cults that emphasize conversion and membership by tests of merit? Two studies that addressed this question examined sects in Alberta that could be defined as conversionist. The stimulus behind these studies was a spate of literature that suggested sects had been reporting dramatic increases in membership, having succeeded in converting nominal Christians or those of secular outlook. According to the studies, however, most new "conversions" were simply recruits from other conversionist sects, not from secular people or nominal Christians. New members consisted of reaffiliated Evangelicals (72.1 percent), birth-right Evangelicals (those with Evangelical parents or guardians, 18.5 percent), and true converts or proselytes (8.5 percent). As Bibby and Binkeroff (1976:355) conclude: "This suggests that conservative (religious) growth is mainly a matter of *retaining* those who are already familiar with evangelical culture. It is not, in North America at least, a matter of making significant inroads outside that culture."

In the second study, Bo and Peep were a middle-aged couple who promised their followers that flying saucers would be landing to take believers to a heaven in the skies. Most of Bo's and Peep's converts had been frequent seekers in the cultic milieu. The researchers state, "Before they joined, members of the UFO cult shared a metaphysical world-view in which reincarnation, disincarnate spirits, psychic powers, lost continents, flying saucers, and ascended masters are taken for granted. It is perpetuated by a cultic milieu that exists in virtually every large community in the country." (Balch and Taylor, 1977:850.)

Another confirmation of this subcultural thesis is provided by a study already mentioned that found cults to be disproportionately centred on the American West Coast in 1926, a fact that remains true in the 1970s and 1980s (Stark and Bainbridge, 1979).

One can conclude from such studies that (1) true conversions are rare even in sects and cults where we might expect them; and (2) previous socialization and subcultural affiliation are responsible for most religious commitment, even in small religious groups that are outside the conventional religious tradition.

Kinship and Friendship Networks

Let us persist in asking how true conversions occur when they *do* occur, as rare as that may be. What would happen if our father or mother or closest friend became a member of a religious group with a strongly proselytizing orientation? Is it not likely that we would give a closer hearing to such kin and close friends than to strangers stopping at our doors or stopping us in the streets?

In a study of conversions to Mormonism in Washington state, it was found that 50 percent of conversions took place in the home of a Mormon friend or relative. In another 34 percent of cases, conversion occurred after an appointment with missionaries set up by a Mormon friend or relative. "When Mormon missionaries merely go from door to door without the aid of social bonds, the success rate is only 0.1 percent." (Stark and Bainbridge, 1980:1383.) In a study of defections from a cult, it was found that only 14 percent of those related to cult leaders left the cult, whereas 67 percent of those who had no relationship to cult leaders defected. The authors conclude, "Humans desire interpersonal bonds, and they will try to protect them from rupture even if that may mean accepting a new faith." (1980:1393–94.)

The "Comfort" Hypothesis and Deprivation

Another important basis for religious affiliation and conversion is material deprivation. Sociologists have found that, at least in their origin, sects tend to be supported by persons of working-class or poor, rural backgrounds, as Mann (1955) demonstrated for Alberta in the 1940s. Sect members tend to be the sort of people who do not feel comfortable in churches and denominations, led as they have been in the past by middle- and upper-class people and characterized by a ritualistic rather than an emotional style.

Social deprivation stems from "the differential distribution of highly regarded attributes. In our society, for example, we regard youth more highly than old age, and greater rewards tend to go to men rather than to women." (Glock and Stark, 1965:247.) The fact that Christian Science membership is predominantly female seems related to this social-deprivation theory. Christian Science women also have access to leadership roles denied them in the conventional religious tradition and in the male-dominated society of North America. That social deprivation may account for the predominance of women in Christian Science is confirmed in an article by England (1954), who found that 88 percent of letter writers to the *Christian Science Journal* were women, and that a high percentage of these women cited personal suffering as reasons for writing. Another socially devalued status group in North America is that of black people, and the appeal of sects and cults to blacks seems related to social deprivation.

In Canada, Bibby (1980:407) found that those with an income under $5000 were over six times as likely to describe themselves as religious as those earning $25 000 and more, and the under-$5000 group scored 14 percent higher on the question of weekly church attendance than those earning $25 000 and more. We have already seen that religious commitment is stronger among older people and women. U.S. data also indicate a correlation of age and gender to religious commitment. "The important point is that among people who are attracted to membership, the church wins a greater commitment from those whose attributes are less highly esteemed by the general society.... The church offers a refuge for those who are denied access to valued achievements and rewards in everyday American life." (Glock et al., 1967:106-07.)

Adolescent Strain

Also of interest to sociologists has been what are often called "the new religions" of the 1960s and '70s. These are cult-like movements that have appealed to adolescents and young adults — exactly those persons least likely, according to commitment correlates, to be religiously involved. Such young people have opted for an intense religious commitment instead of a sabbatical from religious involvement experienced by most youth. A Canadian film, "Ticket to Heaven," is about a young man from Toronto who, despite himself, gets involved in a religious commune when he visits a friend in California. The story illustrates the power of the emotional element of cults that draw members into its fold.

A number of sociological observers have attributed the growth of such movements to the prolonging of adolescence in North American society, a situation due partly to the many years of education necessary to qualify for a job, and more recently, by the shortage of jobs. In contrast, young adults in other societies are committed to adult responsibilities by their mid-teen years. One observer concludes that the modern cults "seem to appeal most to young people who are still at an unsettled stage in their lives. As these young people mature and become more settled, they may abandon these groups." (Wuthnow, 1976:293.)

Let us now turn to the Canadian scene to find out how religious our society is.

RELIGION IN CANADA

Religious Membership by Groups

Canadians are asked to give their religious affiliation as part of the Canadian census, and although "no religious preference" is an option, this is still

A Hindu community in Bombay, India gathers to honor Lord Krishna by breaking an earthenware pot of milk and butter.

a relatively minor response. In 1981, for example, only 7.4 percent of the population responded in this way. The 1981 census reported that 91.2 percent of the Canadian population still define themselves as either Christian or Jewish. It is on the basis of this sort of imposing figure that we can speak of a conventional religious tradition. Other religions represented in Canada include Islam, Buddhism, Hinduism, Confucianism, Taoism, and Sikhism, and together they accounted for only 290 105 Canadians. The small remainder of the population belonged either to native Indian and Inuit religions, or to a small number of non-Christian cults.

Thus, most Canadians (73.1 percent) belong to denominations that originated as churches in pre-industrial, hierarchical, agrarian Europe. The breakdown is as follows: Catholic (47.3%); Anglican (10.1%); Lutheran (2.9%); Presbyterian (3.4%); Eastern Orthodox (1.5%); and United Church of Canada (about 7.9%). Counting only the percentage of the population with a religious preference, this makes for a total of 79 percent.

The remaining 21 percent of the Christian population belong either to sects or to former sects that have evolved into denominations or cults. The Methodist sect joined the Presbyterians to become the United Church of Canada. Many Baptist groups have become denominational, as well. Cults included Spiritualists, Theosophists, New-Thought-Unity-Metaphysists, and others, comprising less than 1 percent of the population. About 5 percent belong to sects such as Pentecostal and Jehovah's Witnesses.

The breakdown by religious tradition is illustrated diagramatically below:

	Percentage		Percentage
Judeo-Christian	91.2	Jewish	1.2
No religious preference	7.4	Christian	90.0
Other religions	1.4		
	100.00		

The breakdown by religious group (Judeo-Christian only) is as follows:

	Percentage
Denominations (formerly churches)	73.1
Denominations (formerly sects)	12.0
Modern sects and Jews	6.2
	91.3 (error due to rounding)

If one looks at the United States as the most comparable country to Canada from a religious viewpoint, a pattern emerges. In Canada, about 68 percent of the population belongs to the current or former established religions of Britain or France. Much of the Christian population in the United States, in contrast, belong to the Baptist (20 percent), Methodist (8 percent), and other sects and denominations that were never established state churches. As Fallding (1978:146) summarizes, "This means that American mainline Protestantism has a much greater admixture of the radical reformation. Or to say it in another way, Canadian protestantism is more directly derived from Roman Catholicism."

Could Canada's rather different religious composition have implications for the nature of Canadian society as a whole? A number of sociologists in both Canada and the United States observed that Canada is a society with different values and social structures from those of the United States. Generally speaking, the picture that emerges is of a more bureaucratic, conservative, elitist, and state-oriented country with a healthy respect for authority. In contrast, the United States is seen as more individualistic, competitive, and committed to entrepreneurial capitalism, rather than state-supported enterprise, and as being more democratic, egalitarian, and less accepting of authority. One sociologist thinks it possible that such differences are attributable to the underlying religious composition of the two countries. "In the United States, Protestantism was integral with the pursuit of distinctive nationhood; in Canada, which is a traditional society by comparison, it (Protestantism) upheld the established authority and promoted national unity. Religious freedom in the United States generated sectarianism, and in Canada, the quest for church union." (Fallding, 1978:141.)

Sociologists and other observers have speculated whether such differences will persist in the face of American influence on Canada's economic and military institutions, and particularly on the mass media. Horowitz (1973) felt that these differences would be obliterated with a continuous American presence. Canadian philosopher George Grant (1965) and historian Donald Creighton (1970) also shared this point of view. In addition, the increasing secularization of Canadian society would seem to be making religious affiliation of decreased salience in Canada.

Secularization in Canadian Society

Secularization is a process wherein religion's role in society increasingly diminishes. In the Canadian context, this process has already begun, in that religious organizations have lost control over a number of important social institutions, such as higher education. Until the twentieth century, virtually all colleges and universities (with the exception of the University of Toronto) were church-supported and sponsored. The University of Ottawa was Roman Catholic, McMaster and Acadia were Baptist, Bishop's University was Anglican, Wilfred Laurier was Lutheran, Mount St. Vincent was Roman Catholic, and so on. However, as a result of funding formulas from government, which discriminated against religiously affiliated institutions, many were forced to sever their religious ties — such as Wilfred Laurier and the University of Ottawa. The new universities — for example, on the Prairies — tended to be government-supported and therefore religiously neutral — or to put it more strongly, secular.

In the past, religious organizations were also involved in primary and secondary education and in health-care institutions. As the modern state (with its own ethos of democracy, universality of citizenship, scientism, and religious neutrality) developed in the last century or so, there has been a marked tendency to remove religious institutions from control, either with or without their consent.

Perhaps the most dramatic example of secularization in Canada occurred in Québec in the 1960s. Until that time, the church had retained its control in education (at all levels), health and welfare, the intellectual and cultural fields (for example, several daily newspapers were church-controlled or inspired), and even politics. During the "Quiet Revolution," however, the church lost most of its control to the quickly growing Québec state, staffed by a university-trained civil service that looked on the church as largely anachronistic — although a Roman Catholic, former Prime Minister Trudeau, was part of a group of young intellectuals, who in the 1950s inspired the magazine *Cité Libre*. This group supported the view that the church should restrict itself to activities that were entirely and directly religious in nature.

Secularization can be easily measured on the basis of certain empirical criteria, such as church attendance. The Canadian Gallup poll organization has regularly asked the question, "Did you,

yourself, happen to attend church or synagogue in the last seven days?" There has been a persistent increase in a negative response to this question. In 1946, 67 percent said they had attended; in 1957, 60 percent; in 1965, 55 percent; in 1975, 41 percent; and in 1985, only 32 percent.

This decline in regular attendance has been particularly marked among Roman Catholics: in 1957, 87 percent claimed to have attended, whereas only 50 percent attended in 1984. Among Protestants, who have always been less frequent attenders, the proportion fell from 43 percent to 29 percent in 1984. Another way to measure secularization is the response to the census question on religious identification. In 1971, 4.3 percent of the population registered no religious affiliation and by 1981 this figure had risen to 7.4 percent. (See Table 12-1.)

Going beyond census and poll responses, Reginald Bibby (1983:108) classified responses to a series of questions according to religious commitment and belief. "Some 43% of Canadians describe themselves as religiously committed, all but 2% to Christianity. Approximately 25% tend to see themselves as a-religious, while 21% claim

TABLE 12-1. Percentage of Population with No Religious Affiliation, by Province, 1971 and 1981

Province	1971	1981
Newfoundland	0.4	.78
Prince Edward Island	1.0	2.6
Nova Scotia	2.4	4.0
New Brunswick	1.9	2.85
Québec	1.3	2.0
Ontario	4.5	7.2
Manitoba	4.3	7.5
Saskatchewan	3.7	6.3
Alberta	6.7	11.7
British Columbia	13.1	20.9
Canada	4.3	7.4

SOURCE: Census of Canada, 1981; Bainbridge and Stark, 1982, page 359.

to be non-religious. Some 7% have interest in religion, but do not profess commitment. The other 4% offer highly individualized views of both religion and their posture toward it."

Thus, it seems clear that although a strong majority of Canadians are still willing to identify themselves as part of the Judeo-Christian tradition, their commitment and knowledge are low and decreasing. It is still sociologically valid to refer to Judeo-Christianity as the conventional religious tradition at this time, but if current trends continue, this may cease to be true in the next century.

Canadian sociologists have attempted to study the causes of secularization on the basis of a number of variables. Among them are region, urbanization, gender, and age.

Region

If we measure religious commitment simply by church or synagogue attendance, a 1984 Gallup Poll shows that the conventional religious tradition is strongest in the Atlantic provinces (46 percent said they had attended in the last week) and Québec (45 percent), middling in Ontario (35 percent), and weakest in the Prairies and British Columbia (23 percent). A possible reason for this is geographical mobility. With regard to the weak commitment to a conventional religion on the Pacific coast of both Canada and the United States, Stark and Bainbridge attribute this to the high degree of mobility into and within these areas. Conversely, geographical mobility is low in Québec and the Atlantic region. In addition, the Atlantic region does not have any large cities with an urban life style.

Urbanization

According to Mol (1976:249), "The difference in attendance between cities and towns is ... an average of about 10 percent," with cities defined as having more than 100 000 inhabitants and towns between 2500 and 100 000. Bibby's research also shows this correlation (1977:453). With regard

to belief in God's existence, 62 percent of small-town dwellers had no doubts, compared to 141 percent city people. When asked about weekly church attendance, 39 percent of small-town and rural people answered "yes," compared to 26 percent of city dwellers.

Gender

Another difference in commitment is gender-related, with women indicating greater religiosity. Forty percent of women compared to 31 percent of men responded affirmatively to the question, "Did you attend church or synagogue within the last week?" (Gallup, 25 June 1984.) In answer to the question whether organized religion is "a relevant part of your life," 48 percent of women responded "yes," as opposed to 39 percent of men. This is true not only of Canada. "The Canadian population is not different from those in other Western industrialized nations in that more women than men attend church." (Mol, 1976:244.)

Explanations for this gender difference vary from the psychological to the notion that religion is a family-related activity, and it is the female parent who is more responsible for the latter. Mol suggests (1976:245) that in Western societies, "both religion and women (are) traditionally preoccupied with conflict resolving, emotionally healing, integrative, and expressive functions, whereas men are more involved in competitive, differentiating, and instrumental activities."

Age

Since age tends to be associated with religiosity, the gender gap may be explained partly by the fact that more women survive into old age than men, and as widows are more apt to seek spiritual solace for their sense of aloneness. At any rate, the aged are the most regular attenders of religious services and feel most committed to organized religion. In response to the question, "Did you, yourself, happen to attend church or synagogue in the last seven days?", 45 percent of persons aged fifty and over stated "yes," compared to 36 percent for the thirty- to forty-nine age group, and 25 percent of the adolescent and young adult group aged eighteen to twenty-nine years (Gallup, 25 June 1984). In response to the question about whether organized religion is "a relevant part of your life at present," 54 percent of those aged fifty years and over responded "yes," compared to 43 percent for the thirty- to forty-nine years group and 33 percent for those aged eighteen to twenty-nine years old. This pattern is not surprising, since it is obvious that Judeo-Christianity held a stronger influence over the population in the past, and the greater religiosity of those born in 1934 and earlier may simply reflect the social-cultural patterns of the 1930s and 1940s. This seems consistent with Mol's view that "age makes a difference in denominations and countries where church attendance is at a low ebb." (1976:245.)

The pattern that emerges is the following: the religiously committed are likely to be older, female persons who live in towns or rural areas in the Atlantic provinces or Québec. The more secularized population is likely to be younger, male, and living in cities on the West Coast or in Alberta.

Now that we have taken a detailed, empirical look at certain important issues of interest to sociologists, we can turn to some of the theories used in the study of religion.

THEORETICAL VIEWS OF THE FUNCTIONS OF RELIGION

Comte

Sociology's concern with religion is as old as the subject itself. As you already know, Auguste Comte is considered to be one of the fathers of sociology. His concern was to understand the nature of the new industrial and capitalist society that was emerging out of the ruins of the hierarchical feudal society. In his view, religion was associated with the nature of pre-industrial societies, and he believed that science and reason would replace religion. As such, his work represents an early sociological theory of secularization and its inevitability in industrial societies.

Comte theorized that civilizations pass through three succeeding stages: the theological, the metaphysical, and the positive. In the theological stage, "the human mind ... supposes all phenomena to be produced by the immediate action of supernatural beings." In the second stage, "which is only a modification of the first, the mind supposes, instead of supernatural forces, veritable entities (that is, personified abstractions) inherent in all beings and capable of producing all phenomena." The positivist stage is based on "reasoning and observation, duly combined." Comte concludes that "there can be no real knowledge but that which is based on observed facts." (Thompson, 1975:38–41.) As the modern world continued its reliance on empirical science, institutions other than religion would take over societal functions previously controlled by the church.

Generally speaking, the empirical research of modern sociology does tend to bear out Comte's view that industrialization leads to secularization. But some sociologists provide alternate interpretations. Some, for example, feel that a religious outlook is built into humankind in its search for explanations of natural phenomena and for the meaning of life. Talcott Parsons tries to show that "modernization is not so much a process of secularization as of differentiation." (Baum, 1975:156.) That is to say, the growing complexity and specialization of institutions in the modern age tends to lead to a "detachment of the religious component from the non-religious spheres of social life." (Baum,156.) Thus, what occurs is not the disappearance of religion but a turning of religion to specialized, non-secular tasks.

Marx

For Karl Marx, "Man makes religion, religion does not make man." (Padover, 1978:286.) Furthermore, religion was created by humankind bound by a state and society, and as such, reflected the underlying oppression and exploitation that all state-level societies tolerate. Religion could offer consolation to those at the bottom of the social ladder. In Marx's words, religion is "a protest against real misery. Religion is the sign of the afflicted creature, the soul of a heartless world.... It is the *opium* of the people." (Padover, 285–86.) The "comfort" hypothesis discussed earlier concurs with Marx's view.

In the societies in which Marx lived and wrote about, the established churches supported and legitimated the state and power structure. "The social principles of Christianity justified slavery in antiquity, glorified medieval serfdom, and when necessary, also knew how to defend the oppression of the proletariat ... the social principles of Christianity preach the necessity of a ruling and oppressed class, and for the latter they have only the pious wish that the former will be benevolent." (Padover, 312.)

We have seen that there was an empirical basis for Marx's observations. More controversial, however, is whether religion continues to serve such a role in advanced capitalist societies, such as our own. It seems not, since with the process of secularization, religion became a more marginal influence than it had been in pre-industrial societies. "Religion ... cannot play any legitimizing role in late capitalist societies." (Varga, 1980:54.) Nevertheless, Marx's theory is important since it drew attention to the role religion plays as a compensator for deprivation.

Durkheim

Emile Durkheim agreed with Marx that religion serves to act as a sort of glue to ensure social continuity. However, Durkheim emphasized the more general need of society to provide integrating mechanisms that would ensure the continuity of society. As Durkheim writes, "sociability should be made the determining cause of religious sentiment" and some kinds of social sentiments are those "which bind me to the social entity as a whole." (Giddens, 1972:219.)

Durkheim based his analysis on a study of literature dealing with aborigines in Australia. In such a simple society, he felt he would be able to derive the most "elementary" social functions of religion. Whereas Marx and Comte studied religion in the context of state-level, class-based societies, Durkheim's unstratified, homogeneous society lacked an organized state and a complex division of labor. This ensured that Durkheim's analysis of religion would not concentrate on the role of religion in legitimating oppressive societies, since hunting-and-gathering societies lacked most institutionalized forms of inequity.

For Durkheim, society acts as a social force that moulds individuals in certain directions. This notion is seen empirically in Durkheim's study of suicide, in which he shows that membership in specific religious groups has an indirect effect on an individual's inclination toward suicide. Catholicism seems to impede suicide. Compared with Catholics, Protestants have a higher rate of suicide. The explanation for this difference, according to Durkheim, is that Catholicism forges a greater sense of identification of believers with their religion, as well as a sense of community. Thus, Catholicism, as a component of society, acted as a force to discourage suicide, whereas Protestantism lacked this power to influence worshippers (Durkheim, 1951).

Furthermore, Durkheim felt that religion acts as an agency of social legitimation where the laws, norms, values, and beliefs of a society are worshipped under the camouflage of the concept of the sacred. In worshipping the sacred in our society, we are in reality worshipping our society itself. Durkheim defined religion as "beliefs and practises which unite into one single moral community called a church, all those who adhere to them."

There are problems with such a theory. By Durkheim's criteria, it would be hard to describe persons who are idiosyncratic in their beliefs as religious. A more serious problem with Durkheim's view is that modern complex societies lack the homogeneity of the Australian tribal societies that he studied. Our modern industrialized (and therefore complex) society is composed of a multitude of subcultures, each with a differing outlook. Thus, "In modern democratic societies differences among religions are tolerated because of fundamental secular agreements, but conflicts among them can become so grievous as to endanger the delicate balance that Durkheim calls 'solidarity'." (Simpson, 1971:86.)

However, if we grant that nations as a whole may be too complex for religion to effect social unity and identity, religion may, nevertheless, serve a similar role in subcultures. A Canadian sociologist found this to be true in his study of a relatively tiny Anglican population in Ireland after Irish independence was won from Britain in 1922 (Bowen, 1983:107).

Weber

Whereas Durkheim viewed religion as an agency of social stability and continuity, Max Weber tended to see it as an agency for social change. Weber was convinced that religious ideologies affect the very socioeconomic basis of social organization. In *The Protestant Ethic and the Spirit of Capitalism* (1904), he observed that "business leaders and owners of capital, as well as the higher grades of skilled labour, and even more the higher technically and commercially trained personnel of modern enterprises, are overwhelmingly Protestant." (Weber, 1958:35.) He added, "The same thing is shown in the figures of religious affiliation almost wherever capitalism, at the time of its great expansion, has had a free hand to alter the social distribution of the population."

According to Weber, Protestantism held that a lay person was as close to God as any priest, and so Protestants did not need the hierarchical intervention of priests or bishops, as did Catholics. Lay persons could show their commitment to God by performing their duties in a conscientious way.

So the Protestant need to please God in one's everyday calling was absent in Catholicism.

Secondly, Calvinism taught that even before a person is born, God has decided an eternal fate — damnation or salvation. The majority of humankind would be damned, and only a few saved. Weber felt this placed an intolerable tension in the heart of believers, who wished reassurance of their salvation. The result — in practice, although not in theory — was that Calvinists came to feel that a sober, ascetic, upright life spent in Godfearing toil would result in worldly success, which in turn would be a sign of salvation. (In Catholicism, God was regarded as merciful, and God's intentions could be gleaned from a combination of revelation and reason.)

Protestantism, especially those groups affected by Calvinism, had indirectly and unwittingly supported the rise of capitalism. Of course, by Weber's time sociologists were already occupied with the issue of secularization, but once the wealth and capitalist success of Protestant nations were established, the religious ideology of believers was no longer so important.

In Canada, French Canadians and Roman Catholics have historically been underrepresented in the economic elite, and in managerial, technical, and foreman ranks. They have also tended to earn lower salaries. Porter's study (1968:110) found that in Halifax, Ottawa-Hull, Windsor, and Winnipeg, "higher incomes are related to Protestantism and lower incomes to Catholicism." He concluded that there is a relationship between income and religion. In relation to French, Catholic Québec, "because of its Catholic values it did not experience that cultural coalescing of Protestant dogma and commercial values that Max Weber wrote about." (1958:95.)

Weber also wrote about other religions and how they affected economic success. In the case of India, Hinduism prevented the rise of capitalism despite other favorable factors. In Hinduism exists the notions of karma (fate) and reincarnation (rebirth). A person will be reborn in future lives, and the quality of those lives depends on the evil or good done in this life. Whether you are considered good or evil depends on how well you perform the functions associated with the caste into which you were born. Those who strive to leave the caste of their birth may be seen as trying to evade their karma. The end to reincarnation is the cessation of rebirth, which is the aim of life. Thus, the aim of life is the extinguishment of individual consciousness. Weber felt "this attitude was responsible for the lack of interest in social and political life in the Indian cultural tradition" (Bendix, 1962:198), since the aim of the religion is the release from life itself.

This conception — that religious beliefs can affect the core of socioeconomic organization, remains controversial to this day. In Canada, with the rise of neo-Marxist sociology, such ideas have been losing favor in the last ten years. In explaining the economic backwardness of French Canada, it is more common today to cite the "colonial" status of Québec (Milner and Milner, 1973) or other factors such as language dominance, rather than the Protestant or Catholic ethic. However, many defenders of Weber's theories still exist, including Canada's John Porter. Gordon Marshall has attempted to vindicate Weber's assertions about the association of religion with economic enterprise in the context of Scotland (1980) and has since written a more general defence of Weber's heritage (1983). Certainly, Weber is to be credited for bringing to attention the relationship between religion, the socioeconomic system, and social change.

SUMMARY

1. The sociology of religion aspires to be as scientific as possible, and as such, uses polls, censuses, and statistical information to provide empirical data.

2. Sociologists have arrived at different classifications of religious groups, but the Weber-Troeltsch tradition of church-sect theorizing (along with other concepts, such as cult and denomination) has allowed sociologists to make some sense out of the enormous variety of religious groups.

3. Sociologists have paid particular importance to analyzing cults and sects — beyond what their statistical numbers would merit, since the formation of cult and sect do tell us a good deal about how new religious groups are established.

4. Cults are found where conventional religious affiliation is weak and geographical mobility high. Sects are found where conventional religious affiliation is high and mobility low. However, because cult and sect differ on how they relate to the conventional religious tradition, it is worthwhile to make the distinction, and as Stark and Bainbridge have shown, other empirical attributes follow the theological distinction.

5. With regard to church and denomination, the church is typical of pre-industrial agrarian societies, and the denomination is typical of complex industrial societies. An example of a denomination in Canada is the United Church.

6. Based on Gallup Poll and census surveys, Canadian researchers have been able to discern a pattern of correlation between certain variables and religiosity. The religious tend to be older, female persons living in rural areas or towns in the Atlantic provinces or in Québec. The more secularized population is likely to be younger, male, urban, and living on the West Coast or in Alberta.

7. Some sociologists have raised the point whether there is not some inverse association between modernization and industrialization on the one hand and religion on the other. Other sociologists suggest that new religions may emerge where the older ones decline (Stark and Bainbridge), that societies need religion as an integrative force for social cohesion (Durkheim), that religion may possess innovative ways to adapt to new conditions (Baum), and that secularization may simply be related to the increasing structural complexity of society, rather than to an outright rejection of religion (Parsons).

GLOSSARY

Charisma. That quality or power of a person that is believed to come directly from God or other supernatural powers.

Church. A religious organization typical of hierarchical, agrarian, monopolistic societies.

Conventional religious tradition. The religious point of view shared by the majority of people in a society and usually by the state and government.

Cult. A religious organization outside a cultural religious tradition of a society that professes novel, syncretic, and eclectic ideas that often seem bizarre to the majority of people.

Denomination. A religious organization having majority status within a pluralistic industrial-capitalist society.

Monopolistic society. One where only one religious, political, cultural, and social outlook is tolerated.

Pluralistic society. One where many religious, political, cultural, and social points of view are tolerated and encouraged.

Sect. A cultural, religious tradition that finds itself in a high degree of tension with the wider society.

Secularization. The diminuition of the social and individual significance of religion.

FURTHER READING

Baum, Gregory. *Religion and Alienation: A Theological Reading of Sociology.* Toronto: Paulist Press, 1975. A theologian's analysis of major theoretical areas, including chapters on Weber, Durkheim, Marx, and the secularization debate.

The Canadian Journal of Sociology. Special issue on *Religion*, 1976, Volume 3, No. 2. This contains articles on main-line Protestantism (H. Fallding), Mormonism (O. White), Fundamentalist religion (H. Hiller), Mennonites (Sawatsky), Roman Catholicism (K. Westhues), and Judaism (S. Schoenfeld). All of these authors keep an eye on the Canadian scene, as well as on American and other data.

Clark, S.D. *Church and Sect in Canada.* Toronto: University of Toronto Press, 1971 (1948). Although Clark dealt with church and sect in urban settings, its real contribution was to analyze the strength of sects and the weakness of churches on the rural frontiers in Canada from Nova Scotia in the 1760s to Alberta in the 1930s.

Crysdale, S. and Les Wheatcroft. *Religion in Canadian Society.* Toronto: Macmillan, 1976. This is a very useful collection of sociological and allied writing on religion in Canada and includes many articles cited in the chapter. It also contains a useful introduction to the sociological approach to religion.

Glock, Charles Y. and Rodney Stark. *Religion and Society in Tension.* Chicago: Rand McNally, 1965. This book contains a good deal of empirical data on differences between sects and denominations, and provides a clear statement of deprivation theory.

Hunter, James Davison. *American Evangelicism: Conservative Religion and the Quandary of Modernity.* New Brunswick, N.J.: Rutgers University Press, 1983. This book contains a very lucid and empirical treatment of modern Evangelicism and explains it as a reaction against modernization.

Mann, William E. *Sect, Cult and Church in Alberta.* Toronto: University of Toronto Press, 1972. This book takes a very good look at cults, sects, and churches (denominations) in Alberta during the period of the 1940s and early 1950s. It was inspired by the work of S.D. Clark but was contemporary in its setting.

McSweeney, Bill. *Roman Catholicism: The Search for Relevance.* Oxford: Basil Blackwell, 1980. This is an interesting sociological analysis of Christianity's largest component.

Nock, David A. "The historical process and the reformation of religious typologies: the case of the anglican communion." *The Sociological Review,* Volume 29, No. 3. N.S., August, 1981:521–41. This article shows the evolution of the Anglican Communion *away* from its categorization as an ecclesia (established national church) to a more universal status. The article points out that the typological exercise is subject to historical analysis and revision.

O'Toole, Roger. *Religion: Classic Sociological Approaches.* Toronto: McGraw-Hill Ryerson Ltd., 1984. This is a study of more theoretical approaches in the sociology of religion (Durkheim, Weber, Marx, and so on), with a brief chapter on the sociology of religion in Canada.

Pope, L. *Millhands and Preachers.* New Haven: Yale University Press, 1942. This book clearly shows the appeal of conversionist and adventist sects to Southern millworkers and discusses the role of religion in the socioeconomic order.

Shepherd, Gordon and Gary Shepherd. *A Kingdom Transformed: Themes in the Development of Mormonism.* Salt Lake City: University of Utah Press, 1984. This fascinating book traces the changing themes of Mormonism as presented in addresses at Mormon conferences from 1830 to the present. It shows the change in Mormonism from a sect-cult in high tension with the wider society to a lower tension "denomination." The use of content analysis shows the manner in which sociologists try to use scientific sampling procedures.

Stark, Rodney and W.S. Bainbridge. *The Future of Religion.* Berkeley: University of California Press, 1985. This book presents the bold new research by these authors on cults, sects, and denominations, and relates this material to the secularization debate.

Wilson, Bryan. *Religious Sects.* New York: McGraw-Hill, 1970. This is a very readable guide to sect analysis and distinguishes conversionist, adventist (revolutionist), and introversionist sects. Unfortunately, Wilson does not distinguish between "cult" and "sect" but subsumes the former under the latter term.

Social
Sciences

CHAPTER THIRTEEN

Education

ROBERT A. STEBBINS

To my knowledge, no one has ever tried to make
a case for the notion that education is the most
central institution in modern society, as Marx did
for the economy and Hobbes for the polity. In
fact, many contemporary social scientists hold that
there is no central institution, but several core institutions (which are covered in Part IV of this book).
Each is vitally important. Each makes its unique
contribution to the functioning of the society
and the individual. Education is one of these
institutions.

Education is the act or process by which some
people educate other people. To *educate* someone means to develop that person by fostering the
growth or expansion of his or her knowledge, wisdom, desirable qualities of mind or character,
physical health, or general competence. Education need not be confined to schools. It can occur
at home or on the job, but is usually accomplished
through a formal course of instruction.

The sociology of education has been chiefly concerned with school-based instruction, its origins
and consequences and with the vast social, political, and economic systems within which it operates. That is, it is concerned with schooling. These
are the interests of this chapter as well.

STRUCTURE OF THE CANADIAN EDUCATIONAL SYSTEM: HISTORICAL PERSPECTIVE

One reason why education is a core institution is neatly summed up by Plato: "The direction in which education starts a man will determine his future life." But core institutions are slow to develop; it has taken Canada and other industrialized nations a long time to develop their present system of primary and secondary education, both public and private. The Canadian system, as we know it today, has been evolving for more than 150 years. And current practices and techniques are not wanting for critics, which indicates that the future holds still more change.

In contrast to American and British practices, the control of education in Canada is divided up among the provinces and territories, according to their separate jurisdictions (which excludes education of native and military children). Since the 1850s, administration of educational matters has been carried out through provincial departments of education, headed by a minister of the Crown.

FIGURE 13-1. The Chain of Command in Canadian Education

Locations	Functionaries
The province or territory	Minister of the department of education
The school district	School board trustees
	Superintendent
	Assistant superintendents
The local school	Principal
	Assistant principal
	Department heads
	Teachers

The minister, a deputy, and a staff of civil servants issue curricular guidelines, provide teacher training, set teacher qualifications and, within limits, approve textbooks. Superintendents help implement these functions in the municipalities and rural districts.

District school boards have additional responsibilities, which include hiring and paying teachers, building and maintaining schools, and providing other personnel and services required to meet provincial standards of education. Members of these boards, called trustees, are nearly always elected. Increasingly, district school boards and principals are assuming tasks previously delegated to provincial departments, of supervising teachers, upgrading teacher qualifications, and modifying the courses of instruction used in the classroom. Though elected by the citizenry, school boards tend to be agents of government with whom they have considerable contact and with whom they identify (Cook and Coughlan, 1974).

Thus, there is a chain of command in education. (See Figure 13-1.) It starts in (1) the provincial or territorial government and runs through (2) each district school board, (3) superintendents of schools in a given district, (4) assistant superintendents, (5) school principals, (6) vice-principals, (7) department heads (where they exist), ending with (8) the teachers. A variety of other professional, clerical, and maintenance personnel fill out this basic structure.

The School Superintendent

The district school superintendent plays a crucial role in the chain of command in education. Ann and Robert Parelius (1978:125) describe the ideal and actual roles of this functionary:

[Ideally,] educational policy is supposed to be formulated by local school boards and carried out by the chief administrator—the school superintendent—hired by these boards. The superintendent is an employee who serves at the

pleasure of the board and who may, therefore, be dismissed when the board members decide his or her performance is unsatisfactory. In reality, however, ... the distinction between policy initiation and implementation breaks down in the daily operation of the schools. Superintendents can both initiate and sabotage policy through manipulating administrative procedures.

Superintendents are full-time professionals who can master the complicated procedures and regulations of local education to the point of submerging the wishes of the part-time, volunteer members of the board in details too complex for them to assess. Thus, under certain conditions, superintendents can be more powerful than the boards that hire and evaluate them. Indeed, the two American school boards studied by Kerr (1964) acted mainly to legitimate decisions made in the superintendent's office.

But superintendents have problems, too. Gross, Mason, and McEachern (1958: chapter 16), whose study of the role conflicts of a sample of American superintendents is still considered a landmark in the sociology of education, identified three sources of strain. (1) Most superintendents feel obliged to discharge their responsibility (delegated by the board) of hiring and firing principals and teachers on the basis of merit. Yet influential individuals and groups in the community may want other criteria to be used (e.g., religious, political, moral). (2) Because superintendents are highly visible in the community, they face incompatible expectations of how they should allocate their time. For example, competing for their time during and after working hours are local trade and professional associations, as well as their families. (3) Because of tight budgets, superintendents have difficulty in drawing up budget recommendations for the educational needs of their districts and satisfying the many individuals and groups in the community who expect them to cut down on educational expenses. In fact, this situation was defined as incompatible by 90 percent of the sample.

There is no evidence of these tensions subsiding in recent years for American superintendents (Travers, 1978:43–44). Nor does the superintendent's lot appear to be any better in Canada, although there are no data to confirm this impression (Jepson, 1976).

The Canadian educational system also includes groups of parents, organized in provincial chapters of the Canadian Home and School and Parent-Teacher Federation. However, such organizations have little influence on school and school-board activities (Brookover and Erickson 1975: 314). Indeed, "parent-teacher groups are often shaped and carefully controlled by school administrators." Teachers and other functionaries resent any community intrusion in their professional affairs. Two studies of Home and School Associations in Edmonton suggest that they are more effective in marshalling community support for their schools than anything else (McKendry and Wright, 1965). They were found to have a concern for the education of pupils, but they seldom tried to change the policies of school, school board, or provincial departments.

Professional Organizations

There are two major professional organizations in our educational system. One of them is the Canadian Education Association (founded in 1867 under another name). For many years it was primarily concerned with advancing the standards of teaching and teacher training, improving teacher ethics, and promoting the profession in the community. The founding of the Canadian Teachers' Federation in 1919, which is a federation of provincial teachers' unions, eventually forced changes in the goals of the older association.

As union-like considerations of salaries, hours, and working conditions began to gain importance among teachers, the federation attracted many new members, while the association experienced losses in membership. The welfare of pupils and the quality of classroom teaching are of prime concern to both organizations, but the federation sees

The open-plan classroom, composed of several areas of "free" space, is designed to provide a unique setting for both learning and teaching.

the strategies of organized labor (e.g., strikes and collective bargaining) as the way to implement these concerns. Such strategies, it argues, are no longer unprofessional since they are used by airplane pilots, nurses, police officers, university professors and, in modified form, physicians. For example, the number of pupils in a classroom affects the quality of education that can be provided. The number of pupils per classroom can be negotiated as part of the collective agreement between the provincial teachers' union and the school board.

Public, Separate, and Private Schools

Except in Newfoundland, New Brunswick, and Prince Edward Island, primary and secondary education is funded through local and, mostly, provincial taxes. This practice became universal by 1880, thus signalling the emergence of public education in Canada. Separate Catholic schools in Newfoundland, Québec, Ontario, Saskatchewan, and Alberta are supported by these same monies. Informal local support in Nova Scotia, New Brunswick, and Prince Edward Island also enables Catholic separate schools to operate as separate schools in those provinces. Government funding, however, forces those schools to abide by the same provincial guidelines as the public schools do. This arrangement has tended to eliminate all differences in education between separate and public schools, except for the religious-education programs of the former.

Outside the public schools, which include the Protestant and Roman Catholic schools and the schools run by the Department of National Defense, lie the private schools. They are managed privately by an individual, association, or corporation, although they may receive some provincial support. In 1982–83, private-school enrollments accounted for 4.5 percent of all primary and secondary school enrollments (Statistics Canada, 1982–83:16–17).

In the Yukon and the Northwest Territories, all education is in the hands of the federal government. Education is programmed with special reference to the problems encountered by native peoples in the modern world. Otherwise, the aims and organization of this extraprovincial educational system are much the same as elsewhere in the country.

Canada and World Education

In part, the history of primary and secondary education throughout the world is one of transition from *elite education*, or education of selected and usually privileged members of society, to *mass education*, or education of all members. By the end of World War II, mass education was growing rapidly in every country (Coombs 1968:18, 184). Moreover, there is no evidence anywhere of this trend reversing itself (UNESCO, 1980:320–47).

Although the practice of mass education is now firmly established in Britain, Canada, and the United States, this was not always the case. Historically, Canada fell midway between the class-biased elite system found in Britain until the 1960s and the mass system of American education when it became both free and compulsory in 1880 (Mifflen and Mifflen, 1982:22). The Mifflens conclude that in Canada,

. . . class bias was less open than in England, less covert than in the United States. It was nevertheless very real. The religious and ethnic basis of so much strife over such a long period effectively hid much of the class discrimination. The ideology of equal opportunity never attained the credibility in Canada which it enjoyed in the United States, but Canadians tended to be more aware of ethnic rather than social-class differences.

Compulsory education was established in Québec and Newfoundland only in 1943. It was introduced in Nova Scotia and New Brunswick in 1915 and 1905, respectively, and in Ontario in 1871.

Several hypotheses have been developed to explain the origins and growth of mass-education across the world (Ramirez and Meyers, 1980: 371–73). The functionalists argue that in order for mass education to develop, the society must have a large, well-trained supply of labor committed to the goals of industrial production. Marxist thinkers argue that this is a requirement set by the capitalist class, not an essential condition of industrialization. According to a third hypothesis, mass education follows on the heels of increased social differentiation of occupational roles in society. In other words, as societies modernize, the division of labor expands: that is, new occupations are born. The family is unable to train people to fill the many new, often highly specialized, positions. Consequently, if industrialization is to proceed at an optimum pace, it is predicted that the educational institution will assume the occupational training function.

Unfortunately, none of these hypotheses has received adequate empirical support (Meyer et al., 1977). For mass schooling has been known to precede industrialization, as in Scotland and France. What is more, cross-cultural research suggests that the hypothesis about the transfer of specialized occupational training from the family to the school is oversimplified (Herzog, 1962).

SOCIOLOGICAL THEORY IN EDUCATION

Four main sociological theories have received extensive application in the field of education. Two of them — symbolic interactionism and ethnomethodology — are *microsociological*. They focus on the different kinds of social interactions that take place among members of society. The other two are *macrosociological*. They provide frameworks for examining the organization of, and changes in, society as a whole. The functionalist and conflict theories are of this type. Since these theories are discussed in Chapter 2, this section will be concerned primarily with their application to education.

Symbolic Interaction

Let us consider one of the propositions of symbolic interaction: pupils and teachers label each other on the basis of their comportment, intellectual performance, personalities, and other criteria. Then they act toward one another with reference to the labels, goals (e.g., to instil knowledge, to make school less boring), values (e.g., learning is important, having fun is desirable), and the physical properties of the classroom relating to the goals and values. In short, pupils and teachers define classroom situations before enacting their intentions or carrying out their goals.

Pupil and teacher often respond to each other on the basis of intellectual performance, personality, appearance, and other criteria, which may lead to inaccurate labelling.

For example, teachers know from their experience with individual pupils who are the troublemakers and who are not. When a pupil who has been labelled a troublemaker is seen talking to another pupil during an assignment, the teacher tends to assume that the pupil is misbehaving again. On the basis of this definition of the situation, the teacher is inclined to take punitive action, such as issuing a harsh reminder to work in silence or an extra assignment. The possibility exists, of course, that the pupil in question was only trying to borrow a pen from a friend or seek clarification on how to complete the assignment. The symbolic interactionist proposition on labelling in the classroom alerts us to the fact that labels may lead their users to misinterpret what is going on before them.

Ethnomethodology

Recent work in ethnomethodology is frequently guided by Goffman's (1974) concept of *frame*: the hidden sets of rules and categories (of people, things, events) that are part of our cultural heritage. These are so deeply ingrained and so habitual in our everyday lives that they go largely unrecognized. For example, many pupils with experience in Canadian schooling automatically cease talking and moving about the classroom when the teacher enters. For these pupils, the rule that they be silent and attentive is so second-nature that it is, in effect, unrecognized. In Goffman's terms (1974:21, 27), human beings interact on the basis of previously and presently taken-for-granted or assumed cultural patterns of thought and behavior.

The analysis of frames has led still more recently to an interest in conversations, inasmuch as conversational routines are also based on hidden rules and categorizations (frames). Included here are certain educational sociologists with their interest in the structuring of classroom talk. We are indebted to them for the notion of "social competence." (Meighen, 1978.) According to this notion, successful classroom participants have learned how to interpret the speech and actions of other participants in the classroom and to respond sensibly (as defined by the others) to their speech and actions. This implies the integration of academic knowledge and interpersonal skills, some of which are unique to classrooms. They know, for instance, how and when to joke with the teacher, which of the teacher's mannerisms are signs of anger, and which kinds of disorderly behavior are particularly likely to be punished. When interacting, socially competent teachers and students share meanings at a level sufficient to accomplish normal schoolroom business.

Functionalism

The process of education performs both manifest and latent functions in Canadian society (Mifflen and Mifflen, 1982:284-96). Manifest functions comprise the following: (1) Our educational system provides for literacy and for general and specialized knowledge based on literacy. (2) As an agent of socialization, schools facilitate the transmission of Canadian culture to children and immigrants. (3) The educational institution, particularly at the secondary level, steers students toward certain occupational roles and away from other occupational roles. (4) By selecting and training individuals for particular occupations, edu-

cation also prepares at least some for movement upward or downward in the social-class structure.

The educational system, although not intentionally, also carries out the following latent functions: (1) Education provides social control by teaching pupils the proper ways to behave, as the middle and upper classes define "properly." Schools also counsel the less successful pupils into nonacademic streams of courses, even though it has been demonstrated that educational achievement and occupational performances are not correlated (Berg, 1970). (2) Schools also serve as a baby-sitting service for working parents and nonworking parents who want some time away from their children. (3) Local elementary schools tend to promote local traditions, for example, by teaching about local ethnic holidays, local historical events, and local festivals and pastimes.

Conflict Theory

Conflict is evident at all levels of Canadian education. Conflict theorists view school curricula as products of societal conflict. What is taught in schools is the outcome of many struggles among various groups and social classes for the opportunity to have their viewpoint accepted and imparted as "education." For example, a certain religious group wants to establish its view of biological evolution, or a certain segment of the population wants a return to the "three Rs," or a certain ethnic group wants the schools to teach a particular interpretation of that group's history. Some of these groups and segments will be more powerful and influential than their opponents, and so will be able to mold provincial school curricula to their advantage.

Marxist-oriented conflict theorists view education as an institution that reinforces existing inequalities rather than one that causes those inequalities. For example, Claude Escande (1973) demonstrates how several CEGEPs (*collèges d'enseignement général et professionel*) in Québec help perpetuate the present dual class structure of capitalist and proletariat. Each CEGEP offers a two-year program in general education leading to university and a three-year program in technology leading to the workforce. Escande found, however, that there was no increase in the number of working-class students who completed the general education program over the number who completed under the earlier system of classical colleges, which was run by the Catholic Church. In other words, the working-class student is underrepresented in both the CEGEPs and the classical colleges. Thus, the dominance of the capitalist class is assured, or at least not challenged, by the post-secondary system of education in Québec.

THE MICROSOCIOLOGY OF EDUCATION

The microsociology of education encompasses a wide range of topics. In this section we shall cover five of them as they relate to primary and secondary education: physical and temporal contexts of the classroom, teachers, pupils, teacher-pupil interaction, and peer groups.

Physical and Temporal Contexts

School-based education (as opposed to education undertaken at home and elsewhere) comprises a complex system of people, roles, relationships, groups, organizations, and processes, all contributing in their special ways to the establishment and maintenance of the classroom as the principal instructional situation. Acquiring knowledge, becoming socialized, and so on, may occasionally take place in other settings, such as field trips, school assemblies, or at home, but the classroom (open or self-contained) is where most educating is done. Here, in the interaction between teacher and pupils, is where the outcomes of struggles over government funding, teachers' salaries, curriculum content, class timetables, selection of books and equipment, building needs, policies about disorderliness, and so forth, have their ultimate impact. As important as principals, superintendents, librarians, counsellors, members of school boards, legislators, and other functionaries are, to the extent that they have no teaching responsibilities, they are fundamentally support personnel — behind-the-scenes workers in the theatre of the classroom.

And the events of the classroom are, in certain ways, analogous to the episodes of a dramatic production. Both have their props, scenery, and sequences of action. That is, both take place in *physical* and *temporal* space, or the space occupied by things and objects and the space of time as arbitrarily partitioned by human beings. Stebbins (1974:22–28, 47–58) describes these two conditions in Newfoundland primary and secondary schoolrooms, where these conditions are typical of self-contained classrooms elsewhere in North America. There are rows of desks, colored walls, blackboards, sets of windows, fluorescent lights (if the school can afford them), decorations, samples of student work posted here and there, characteristic smells (e.g., chalk dust, floor wax, perfume, food), teacher's desk, and a door or two.

It is the usual practice for pupils and teachers to enter and exit this setting according to the daily class schedule at their school. Within each class period, whether it lasts forty minutes or two hours, further structure is evident in most schoolrooms from grade 2 onward. First, there are the preliminaries of attendance-taking, collecting money for class projects, reciting prayers (in religious schools), and so forth. These are followed by the three-phase sequence of academic work, which normally begins with the presentation of a lesson. Seatwork, which is the act of pupils completing an assignment at one's desk, is next. Here teachers face a number of problems, some of which are discussed later under the heading of pupil strategies. In the recapitulation phase, teachers again take charge of the class as a unit, summarizing the lesson, clarifying misunderstandings, and perhaps illustrating certain points with exemplary student work. There are, of course, occasional, temporary diversions from this sequence, depending on the ability of the pupils, special events, and imminent holidays and vacations.

The Pupils

There are great variations among pupils, both socially and psychologically, and the factors that contribute to these variations form one area of study for microsociologists. The variations are related in complicated ways to pupils' views of schooling and to the ways their teachers and other school personnel treat them. For instance, many classrooms contain pupils from a range of socioeconomic backgrounds. It has generally been found that teachers who are middle-class identify best with pupils of that social level and higher. Often lower-class pupils receive less academic attention, more sanctioning for disorderly behavior, fewer privileges, and the like (Martin, 1970). However, this can depend on the teacher's orientation to the job: whether he or she is teacher-centred or student-centred. In a study of three Ottawa primary schools, it was found that lower-class pupils receive as much attention from student centred teachers as middle-class pupils do (Richer, 1974).

Given the tendency in North American cities for neighborhood segregation to occur by socioeconomic status, it is hardly surprising that many schools serve pupils with similar social-class backgrounds. Havighurst and Levine (1979:154) point out that U.S. schools containing mostly lower-class pupils present more severe teaching problems than those containing mostly middle- and upper-class pupils. Lower-class pupils more often fail to master basic academic skills. The lower-class child's world is chaotic, and financial and social uncertainties impede their learning at school. Teachers must somehow generate enough structure in the classroom for these pupils to acquire an education.

Low-income, on the one hand, and race and ethnicity, on the other, are frequently associated. Hence, adult blacks and people of Spanish origin in the United States are found in disproportionate numbers at the poverty level, which means that their children are more likely to be in disadvantaged positions at school than the children of white adults (U.S. Bureau of the Census, 1980: 466). Many Canadian Indian, Métis, Inuit, and black families face the same problem for the same reasons (Statistics Canada, 1980:174–75).

Studies in North America and Britain (reviewed in Stebbins, 1975:51–53) show that pupils are further categorized by their teachers and eventually by themselves according to their levels of academic performance and disorderly behavior. That is, pupils are known as low, moderate, or high achievers, and well-behaved, mischievous, or badly behaved individuals. There is a high correlation between social class and ethnicity, on the one hand, and levels of academic performance and orderliness, on the other. To illustrate, a lower-class Indian or black child is more likely to be a low-achieving disorderly pupil than a middle-class white child.

Finally, some pupils are intellectually or physically exceptional: that is, they are gifted or handicapped. The latter, if seriously blind, deaf, crippled, or retarded, may be given special programs of instruction at their neighborhood school or elsewhere. The general practice in North America is *mainstreaming*, which is to integrate the exceptional with the normal wherever possible, so as to give the former social experience with the latter (Sarason and Doris, 1979:17).

The Teachers

For several years Fuller and Brown (1975:27) have been studying students in teacher education in the United States. They have compiled the following profile of today's teacher:

The new teacher is younger and less experienced, but better qualified. Still typically a female, more and more of her colleagues are males. She has higher economic status, and is now more likely to come from a professional family background and to have an advanced degree. . . . She is geographically more mobile and is less likely to identify with her community or to live within the boundaries of the school system. This broad characterization, however, covers a multitude of group and individual differences.

Some American teachers still come from lower-class families, however, which may encourage them to identify with pupils whose backgrounds are similar to theirs (Goodwin, 1977).

No convenient, up-to-date profile is available for Canadian teachers. Nevertheless, examination of secondary sources produces a picture similar to Fuller's and Brown's. It is clear from Statistics Canada data (1972–73:44–45; 1982–83:40–41) that qualifications have risen; the proportion of teachers with bachelor's or graduate degrees increased more than 31 percent between 1972 and 1982; almost 83 percent of all teachers have degrees. In 1982, 9.8 percent of Canadian teachers held master's or doctoral degrees. Still, four to five times as many teachers held these degrees in the United States in 1980 as in Canada in 1982 (U.S. Bureau of the Census, 1981:151).

The sources cited in the preceding paragraph indicate that the average amount of teaching experience is increasing in both countries. This is probably due, in good part, to the restricted labor market of the early 1980s, during which time fewer teachers were being hired and fewer were able to find alternative jobs (Statistics Canada, 1980–81: 12–13).

An important facet of the occupation of teaching is teachers' unusually low level of commitment to it. There is evidence in both Canada and the United States, some of which is of uneven quality, that commitment to teaching is generally weak (Martin and Macdonell, 1982:111–13; Lortie, 1975: chapter 4). That is, few teachers believe they will retire in their profession. In fact, many men leave it for administration, and many women leave it, temporarily or permanently, for marriage or child-rearing, or both. A third option is to quit

education altogether, which some do if they can find a job with roughly equivalent prestige and remuneration.

The low level of value commitment can be traced, in part, to the "unstaged" nature of the career of the primary and secondary schoolteacher. That is, within the occupation of teaching, there is no set of positions to advance through. The opportunities for advancement lie in other educational fields: in administrative positions such as department head, vice-principal, principal, or in non-teaching positions such as counselling. Lortie (1975:99) describes the limited appeal of this situation for the typical teacher:

The main opportunity for making major status gains rests in leaving classroom work for full-time administration. The primary benefits earned by persistence in teaching (annual increases in pay) are the outcome of seniority and course-taking; the incentive system is not organized to respond to variations in effort and talent among classroom teachers.

In one study reported by Lortie, nearly every male teacher over forty years of age in his sample had a strong avocational interest outside teaching or a second source of income. These men appeared to be using their leisure time to compensate for their dissatisfaction with their career.

Teachers and Pupils

Although teachers know their job is to educate, and pupils know they go to school to be educated, conflict exists in the way each party attempts to reach this goal. As Waller (1932:196) describes the situation:

The teacher represents the established social order in the school, and his interest is in maintaining that order, whereas pupils have only a negative interest in that feudal superstructure. Teacher and pupil confront each other with attitudes from which the underlying hostility can never be altogether removed. Pupils are the material in which teachers are supposed to produce results. Pupils are human beings striving to realize their own results in their own way. Each of these hostile parties stands in the way of the other; in so far as the aims of either are realized, it is at the sacrifice of the aims of the other.

People enter situations with certain intentions or goals in mind, which help them define what is happening there. "The fundamental problem of school discipline may be stated as the struggle of students and teachers to establish their own definitions of situations in the life of the school." (Waller, 1932:297.) Teachers working in classrooms initially define the disorderly and academic performance situations they encounter with reference to two main goals: (1) giving intellectual training (and sometimes moral and social training) and (2) maintaining order. If these two goals are not met, a third emerges, namely, survival (Stebbins, 1975:45; Pollard, 1980).

Research in the United States, Canada, and Britain suggests that pupil goals include (1) maintaining order; (2) receiving equitable treatment from the teacher; (3) doing pleasant activities; and (4) avoiding boredom.

Both teachers and pupils have strategies for reaching their classroom goals. Stebbins (1981: 248-49) in a review of North American and British research on definitions of classroom situations, lists eight teacher strategies.

1. Domination is a common strategy, particularly among teachers of low-ability pupils. It hinges on physical force, vocal superiority, establishing rules, continuous surveillance, and the like.

2. Negotiation is another widely used strategy. It rests on the exchange of valued things, privileges, opportunities, and relationships. Flattery and ingratiation are often part of the exchange in teacher-pupil negotiations.

3. Some teachers attempt to win control of their pupils by fraternizing with them, by sharing their interests, styles of speech, fashions in clothing, and so on.

4. Removing oneself physically or psychologically from the classroom is a way some teachers evade its problems. In modified form, this strategy includes ignoring minor infractions of schoolroom rules.

5. Routines serve as a means of control, since they help pace the activities of the classroom and reduce the opportunity for side involvements.

6. Occupational therapy, such as having students draw maps or pictures or do an experiment, is also a means of controlling behavior.

7. Controlling talk through questioning, lecturing, limiting spontaneous pupil commentary, and related manoeuvres is still another strategy.

8. Finally, teachers maintain order by avoiding provocation of pupils known to be troublesome.

Research on pupils' views of classroom life is not as extensive as that on teachers' views. Nevertheless, six pupil strategies, called "counterstrategies" (Denscomb, 1980), have been identified through a survey of ethnographic studies carried out in Britain and North America. In contrast to these counterproductive devices, a seventh "benign" strategy has also been observed.

1. The forbidden acts of talking and eating in the classroom are justified by pupils as ways of making school more tolerable.

2. Pupils make noise to disturb the flow of lessons or annoy the teacher. It is most effective in self-contained classrooms.

3. Pupils engage in humor, thereby gaining a respite from the tedium of a lesson or an unpleasant seatwork task.

4. Negotiation can be initiated by pupils rather than their teacher.

5. Exploitation is used when pupils take advantage of the teacher's fraternization or avoidance-of-provocation strategies to shirk their assignments or gain an illegitimate respite from them.

Canadian adolescent values, typically endorsed by peer groups, exert great pressure on the behavior of individuals within those groups.

6. Rebellion commonly occurs when pupils evaluate the teacher as incompetent.

7. The benign co-operative strategy is used when pupils try to determine what their teachers want in the way of academic performance and give it to them.

Peer Groups

Peer groups are groups of individuals who are of more or less equal rank. Peer groups reach their maximum influence on their members in adolescence. There are aspects of peer group life that indirectly influence the schoolroom scene, such as certain leisure and deviant interests. Among the activities having a direct effect are non-academic and athletic pursuits, the consequences of which are different in the United States and Canada.

The benchmark study in this area in both countries has been James Coleman's (1961) research on American adolescents, wherein he concluded that norms different from the adult world guide their behavior. Academic ability was found to be neither honored nor despised. A strong interest in sports was, however, associated with peer popularity for boys, whereas a lack of interest in sports and a strong interest in bookish matters was stigmatizing. Being popular was more important for girls than academic success. Cohen's review of research on this topic suggests that these attitudes still prevailed in 1972.

Adolescent values are strikingly different in Canada. It was found that peers have considerable influence on the courses students take and on whether they abide by the school dress code, but only a minor influence on how they evaluate teachers or conform to school smoking rules (Alexander and Farrell, 1975). Other data show that Canadian students, both boys and girls, valued academic achievement first; girls ranked popularity second and athletics third, whereas boys reversed these two (Friesen, 1968).

THE MACROSOCIOLOGY OF EDUCATION

We began this chapter by noting that education is one of the core institutions of a modern society. It is from this point of view that the analysis of the institution of education may be seen as part of the macrosociological research. Concern with the effects of education on society and with educational inequality are two other major interests pursued by macrosociologists.

The Educational Institution

All institutions are characterized by the following six criteria: (1) they help solve large-scale, socially significant problems created by collective living; (2) they are composed of unique structural relationships and (3) distinct patterns of behavior; (4) as such, special roles are enacted within the framework of these relationships; (5) institutional behavior is frequently guided by abstract values; and (6) institutions change constantly, which means they have histories.

With regard to the institution of education, the major collective problem solved by education is socialization of the young (*primary socialization*) and, through higher education, socialization of adults (*secondary socialization*). Both the primary and secondary levels of education transmit the culture of society. The secondary- and post-secondary-level schools, including universities, allocate adult roles to their students by conferring success on some and failure on others.

There are many familiar educational patterns of behavior in our society: children walking to school each day from September through June, playing on the school grounds at recess, getting report cards, advancing (usually) from grade to grade, and engaging in team athletics are examples. Patterns exist at other levels, even though they are less visible to the public; these include annual salary settlements for teachers, annual budget decisions by government, and occasional evaluation programs by school boards.

Likewise, there are many recognizable abstract relationships in education. Most central and obvious is the teacher-pupil relationship. The teacher-parent relationship is also obvious. Behind the scenes are additional relationships of major importance, namely, those between teacher-principal, principal-superintendent, and teacher-counsellor and the sundry connections between school boards and government. Each relationship, as indicated earlier, forges a link between two different roles.

As they discharge their socialization function, schools transmit many of the society's major values. These include conforming to rules, being honest, being diligent, co-operating with others, and as Marxists point out, embracing capitalism. There are also values peculiar to the educational institution itself — for example, the values of education for all who are willing and able to acquire it (the value of mass education versus elite education), of preparing pupils for their occupational roles, and of developing an understanding of how the social and physical worlds work. With regard

Education may occur at school, at home, or on the job.

to mass-versus-elite education, although Canada has been heading toward the full adoption and implementation of mass education and toward using the educational system to prepare students for their life work, in the late 1970s it still lagged somewhat behind the United States in this respect.

Finally, like other institutions, education has a distinctive history. An outstanding example is the open-space or open-plan school. One of the earliest of these schools in North America opened in 1957 in Carson City, Michigan, from where it

spread to California and Canada (Stebbins, 1974: 62–63). Today it is common in both countries, replacing to some extent the self-contained classroom boxes that constitute the "egg-crate school" and that once dominated formal education the world over.

There are certain distinctive features of the open-plan school. It is composed of several areas of unbroken space, each of which may contain between three and five regular-sized classes. Within this space, which is designed to encourage student interaction with teachers, the latter sometimes form into teams (team teaching) to improve the process of education and facilitate further interaction among themselves. In some open-plan schools, students are allowed to advance at their own pace in individual subjects (called "continuous progress"), rather than wait until the end of the school year for formal promotion to the next grade. The open-plan concept is no mere passing fad, partly because it seems to be more harmonious with today's child-rearing practices than its predecessor was (Boocock, 1978:19). Still, its superiority over the traditional type of classroom remains generally unproved (Bennett, 1976).

The Effects of Education

The study of comparative secondary and post-secondary education has uncovered several effects of schooling on individuals, groups, and societies. Some of these effects are consistent across countries; some of them vary from one country to another.

Individual Effects

One consistent finding for all countries studied is that educated individuals experience significant intellectual achievement, compared with individuals of equal intelligence and family background who have received no education. International studies in education show higher levels of intellectual achievement in developed countries than in underdeveloped countries. Education also stimulates striking changes in individual values. People with more education are more likely to develop a rational attitude toward life; value new experience; see the links between political action, science, and progress; stress planning and organization; and take an interest in extra-local events.

Secondary and post-secondary education has been shown to be a universal factor in occupational attainment. This effect on the individual appears to be stronger in developed societies, but "educational credentials [are] entrance tickets, not certificates of technical or attitudinal skill." (Ramirez and Meyer, 1980:388.) As noted earlier in this chapter, there is little evidence that school-learning directly aids job performance. One set of occupations for which education has been found to be an especially important prerequisite are those of political elites. This is true for both established and revolutionary leadership roles everywhere in the world.

Group Effects

The comparative study of the effects of education on groups is much less common than the comparative study of its effects on individuals. Furthermore, most of it is inconclusive. For instance, it is so far unclear whether the dominance of traditional elites is threatened by the introduction of formal education systems, which provide an alternative route to high socioeconomic status. Questionable also is the evidence on group inequalities generated by educational systems. Jencks (1972) argues that education fails to reduce inequality, whereas Heyns (1978) comes to the opposite conclusion. The studies conducted in Western Europe on possible income inequality between groups and between social classes are also contradictory (Ramirez and Meyer, 1980:390).

Research findings on the effects of education on women are clearer. When the proportion of women increases in post-secondary-level education programs, so does their rate of participation in the labor force and their presence in higher-level administrative and managerial positions. Ris-

ing female enrollment in tertiary education is also associated with their expanding legal rights over their children (for those who are married) and over property.

Societal Effects

As with the examination of the effects of education on groups, its effects on societies has been little studied. The strongest and most recent findings show a positive correlation between the proportion of the population with secondary education and economic growth (Meyer et al., 1979). This holds for rich and poor countries. Additionally, there are some comparative data suggesting that mass education may have a moderate effect on the maintenance of representative government. Still, nearly all modern polities educate beyond the minimum knowledge required for effective democratic participation.

OPPORTUNITY AND EDUCATION

One controversial practice in North American and British schools that generates inequality is the tracking or streaming of pupils. Brookover and Erickson (1975:331) define this process as

. . . the arrangements in which students are placed in different curricula with somewhat different long-term goals for their learning. These are illustrated by what is commonly called college-bound and non-college-bound curricula in American secondary schools. . . . The decision concerning the choice of tracks is commonly based upon some prior measure of achievement or presumed differences in aptitude.

Many factors influence the decision to place a pupil in one stream or another. Intelligence-test scores, socioeconomic status of the pupil's family, advice of teachers and counsellors, encouragement from parents, and educational aspirations of the pupil are frequently part of the tracking formula (Rehberg and Hotchkiss, 1972). And, whatever the plans of school authorities for streaming their pupils, it appears that high-school girls, when compared with boys, tend to avoid technical and advanced courses, selecting instead those that are commercial (Sudermann, 1979).

Streaming (the term used in Canada and Britain) or tracking bears directly on occupational attainment. Furthermore, it serves the related institutional value mentioned earlier of allocating people to various occupational roles in adult life. It is believed that by means of this process, superior pupils are identified and tracked into post-secondary academic training, and weaker pupils are tracked into post-secondary commercial, industrial, trade, or general community college program.

Status or occupational attainment refers to the achievement of social rank in society. After surveying a large random sample of Americans, Blau and Duncan (1967: chapter 5) proposed the following status attainment model, which is also applicable to Canada (Harvey and Kalwa, 1983: 446). It has three stages: (1) the socioeconomic status of one's family of orientation has the greatest effect on one's educational attainment; (2) educational attainment has the greatest effect on the level of one's first full-time job (entry into the labor force); (3) current occupational status (several years after entry into labor force) is affected significantly by earlier educational attainment and the level of first full-time job. The importance of education in status attainment throughout an individual's lifetime is difficult to overestimate: "Overall, the model shows that the single most important factor in the determination of current [i.e., later] occupational status is educational attainment." (McRoberts, 1982:391.) Still, this generalization cannot be applied to occupations in the arts and in the fields of sport and entertainment, where training is often informal (Stebbins, 1984).

And educational attainment remains the single most important factor in upward social mobility when the ethnicity of the would-be climber is considered. We draw here on a study of status attainment among immigrants in Israel, Canada, and the United States (Boyd, Featherman, and Matras, 1980). Regarding immigrants to the last two countries, research demonstrates that, in general, educational level rather than ethnic background accounts for their social mobility. When compared with the first and the third generations, the second generation was found to benefit most from education, inasmuch as they reported the greatest occupational achievement. In other words, immigrants arrive in North America with various levels of education that qualify them for certain occupational positions. Their children, aided by significantly more education than they had, tend to climb the occupational prestige ladder (referred to as "upward intergenerational mobility"). The immigrants' grandchildren tend to climb even farther in occupational status, but the distance covered is not as great as the second generation. There is presumably somewhat less to attain, having started closer to the top rung.

Boyd and her colleagues also report exceptions to their generalizations; ethnic background does make a difference occasionally. Even after considering factors such as parental occupation and education, the following still acquired a higher level of education than children of other immigrants: native-born Americans of Russian, Chinese, and Japanese parentage, native-born Canadians of Polish and Ukrainian parentage, and foreign-born Canadians of American and German parentage. Foreign-born Mexicans in the United States and foreign-born Italians in Canada had significantly lower educational attainment levels than the rest.

Inequality

The foregoing information suggests that opportunities for occupational success through the Canadian educational system are far from equal for all contenders. According to functionalist theory, this is how it should be, for the educational system serves the function of allocating adult work roles. Allocation begins in the junior high schools with the practice of streaming, which, as we have seen, is itself the outcome of numerous factors. Functionalists argue that it is to a society's advantage to place its most capable members in its most difficult and important roles. These scholars hold that the secondary educational system selects such people and encourages them to seek further instruction beyond high school. Four-year colleges and universities, according to the functionalist model, are elitist institutions reserved for students too talented to be wasted filling work roles enacted by people of more modest ability.

Still, high intelligence is not as rare as the comparatively small number of university students and university graduates would have us believe (Bowles and Gintis, 1976). Moreover, many weaknesses inhere in the process by which students are placed in one stream or another in high school. The factors referred to in the preceding section attest to this. As a result, a significant number of objectively well-qualified students are shunted by the educational system into unchallenging jobs and discouraged from entering a four-year college or university.

Some of these students drop out of high school. Others, convinced that they are innately capable of doing university work, enrol in a community college hoping to upgrade their qualifications and eventually complete a university program. Research in both the United States and Canada (Clark, 1960; Pincus, 1978; Escande, 1973) indicates, however, that these students are often counselled by their college to terminate their educational ambitions at the end of their two years there.

Samuel Bowles (1971) contends that by allocating students to different streams, schools engage in propagating inequality of opportunity and reinforce the existing class structure division of labor. Yet schools cannot be held solely responsible for this situation, he says, since it is embedded in the larger culture and social structure of the society. For instance, the influence of such factors as

Many sociologists argue that the streaming of students in the educational system contributes to disaffection with the system and a high drop-out rate.

family-socioeconomic status on a school's decision to stream a pupil a certain way are often unrecognized parts of the cultural frame within which the educational decision-makers unwittingly operate.

Thus, a correlation has been found between social class and educational attainment at all levels of education: primary, secondary, and post-secondary. This correlation, which is sometimes referred to as the "correspondence principle," suggests that our schools and universities help perpetuate the existing socioeconomic divisions in society. This they do by failing to give to the lower-class students the linguistic skills, success values, learning attitudes, behavior patterns, and self-concepts of being successful that the middle- and upper-class students possess and that help them progress through the various levels of education. Obviously one's family background, as it relates to social class, is an important factor in whether one "makes it through the school system." (Porter, Porter, and Blishen, 1982.)

Given this correspondence between social class and educational achievement, efforts must be made early in the primary socialization process to raise children from the lower-class to the competitive level of their middle- and upper-class schoolmates. Anisef, Okihiro, and James (1982: 138–44) make several recommendations in this regard, four of which are presented here. First, government should implement compensatory educational programs at the pre-kindergarten level. Second, it should implement summer learning programs for the lower-class children of elementary-school age. Third, incentive programs should be established for teachers and administrators to increase post-secondary educational participation. Fourth, guidance counselling should, among other things, encourage a pupil's educational attainment to the limit of his or her academic potential.

Class inequalities are manifested in at least two ways in higher education. One of these is the proportion of lower-class students to other students. It was found that in Canada, upper-class students are more likely than other students to enter a graduate program (Harvey and Lennards, 1973). Medicine and law have the highest proportion of upper-class students while, at the other end of the spectrum, education has the lowest proportion. The recent expansion of educational opportunities at the post-secondary level has failed to increase the ratio of lower-class students to middle-class and upper-class students in Canadian universities (Pike, 1978).

Another way class inequalities are manifested in colleges and universities is through the presence and exploitation of elite schools. Clement's (1983) observations on the corporate elite indicate that certain private and public schools at the secondary level (particularly Upper Canada College and Trinity College school) and the post-secondary level (particularly McGill University and the University of Toronto) produced a disproportionate number of members of the corporate elite. Because these men (and few women) share many educational experiences, values, attitudes, goals, and the like, they constitute a network through which they can pursue their interests — interests that are peculiar to their own social class. However, the belief that similar educational background is characteristic of all elites is in doubt. Olsen (1980:74) found nearly two-thirds of Canada's governmental elite had not attended either McGill University or the University of Toronto.

Returning to the corporate elite, it is easy to see how its socially linked members could reinforce each other's faith in capitalism, marry into families of other members of the elite, and band together when necessary to assert their will on the political scene. They are members of the same clubs (e.g., Rideau, Mount Royal, St. James) and they vacation at the same exclusive resorts. They also live in the same areas of town (Clement, 1983).

ALTERNATIVES

If the tone of this chapter has seemed a little harsh at times — that the institution of education seems to have been criticized frequently — it is only because this tone is also present in the sociological literature. Certainly some sociologists defend all or much of the existing educational system, as do some parents, teachers, and administrators. But others reject significant aspects of it. They propose an assortment of alternatives, among them free schools, alternative schools, no schools (deschooling), lifelong learning and adult education, voucher plans, return to basics, and home-based learning. The first three are discussed here.

Free Schools

There are four kinds of free schools in the United States, which together constitute the free-school

Elementary school students enjoy a learning experience outside of the classroom, at the Henry Moore collection, Art Gallery of Ontario.

movement (Graubard, 1972). They have in common the principle of free choice and action for pupils. The *classical free school* resembles its prototype in Summerhill, England, founded in 1921. A boarding school, its aim is to create a warm, sensitive community of equals. It offers a full program of elementary and secondary schooling, in which attendance of classes is optional. Personality development and the development of skills and knowledge are regarded as more important than intellectual achievement for its own sake. The *parent-teacher co-operative elementary school* is closely related to, and mainly distinguished from, the classical school by the fact that parents work closely with committed, though poorly paid, teachers. Since parents are routinely

involved in the educational process, these schools tend to be located in or near the communities in which they live. They are not boarding schools.

The *free high schools* come in several forms. Some offer a radical political education to white, middle-class youth. Others are more vocationally oriented, usually catering to lower-class pupils. The "street academies" are designed to educate disadvantaged minority students. The fourth type, the *community elementary school*, is the work of citizens who believe they should control the schools. They are inclined to stress ethnic consciousness and the acquisition of basic educational skills. In contrast to the other types of free schools, community elementary schools are often strict.

From a description of free schools in Canada, it is evident that the above four types are represented in this country as well (Novak, 1975: 36-37). Novak mentions an Ontario communal-farm program, several free schools in inner-city Toronto, and various suburban free schools, all of which embrace the principle of minimal control over the learning of their pupils. The school studied by Novak, however, is best classified as an alternative school.

Alternative Schools

Some scholars treat alternative schools and free schools as synonymous. Others distinguish the two by noting that the former have gained acceptance with the school boards of North America, whereas free schools have not. This is especially true of the more radical programs of the free schools — e.g., those programs promoting ethnic pride, left-wing politics, priority of pupil enjoyment — they are apt to be shunned by the school boards. Among the American alternative schools, there are those that are "schools without walls," educating their pupils by means of visits to zoos, museums, factories, and through use of newspapers. Others are learning centres that draw pupils from the entire community instead of a single district. Educational parks, career-education centres, and specialized vocational and science schools are also alternative schools. Some alternative schools approach the Summerhill model.

Novak's alternative school in suburban Toronto was established in 1970 by the community's board of trustees. Some of its principles are the following:

1. [At school] the child shall have total personal freedom, with the only limitations being that the child does not infringe upon the rights of others, or endanger his health or safety.
2. The school will be concerned with the development of basic skills, though not necessarily in the traditional order.
3. At its inception, classes will be provided from junior kindergardten level to the equivalent of the sixth level. (Novak, 1975:41.)

Several alternative and free schools have been established in Canada, nurtured in part by the educational reform movement in the United States (Carlton, Colley, and MacKinnon, 1977:462-63). On both sides of the border, however, there is considerable skepticism about their true effectiveness.

Deschooling Society

The title of this section is also the title of a book written by one of its main proponents, Ivan Illich. He, together with John Holt (*Why Children Fail*), Paul Goodman (*Compulsory Miseducation*), Everett Reimer (*School is Dead*), and others have led the deschooling attack on the educational status quo. Meighan (1981: chapter 3) provides an excellent review of their ideas, to which we now turn.

The aim of schools, say the deschoolers, should be to prepare pupils to make a better society and to live in it effectively. In other words, schools should be future-oriented, not past-oriented as they are at present. To acquire this outlook, pupils must be taught learning skills, instead of subjects such as mathematics or English. Deschoolers see the child-learner as an explorer rather than a trainee or student. The model to follow is that of the self-taught person. Exploring learners are not ones who regurgitate what they have been taught by a teacher, but ones who synthesize knowledge from available resources, possibly even generating insights and new knowledge.

The teacher's roles in all this are those of consultant and facilitator. In the deschooling perspective, teachers respond to the initiatives of their collegial learners, the students. Deschoolers believe that mass education, because it confines teachers to an instructional role, makes poor use of their abilities, which are likely to be underdeveloped anyway if they have been trained in the standard "professional programs."

Consistent with what has just been said is the deschooling position that the best learning resources are first-hand experiences and a wide variety of secondary resources. Since these experiences and resources are found everywhere,

Increasing use of audio-visual technology, along with a recognition that learning may take many forms, has altered traditional teaching methods.

learning can occur everywhere, including schools. Thus, the "deschooling" slogan is somewhat inappropriate. Certainly, the walled, egg-crate structured edifice of modern mass education is hardly what the deschoolers have in mind. But some of them speak of "little schools" and "mini-schools," which amount to small learning co-operatives of parents, teachers, and pupils funded by government. But learning should also take place in libraries, museums, farms, streets, homes, resource centres, concert halls, factories, and shops, to mention a few non-school locations.

According to the deschoolers, assessments of learning should be conducted by other learners, or by someone designated by the individual learner for this purpose. They recommend the use of achievement profiles rather than tests and certificates. The traditional examination system, they argue, is primarily an instrument of the powerful groups in society, designed to maintain the status quo and their privileged position within it.

The deschooling proposals are not wanting for critics. Some of their objections to Illich's ideas in particular have been listed by Parelius and Parelius (1978:381). The critics ask: how are children to know what is important if their learning is never directed by anyone who knows which experiences to avoid (e.g., drug use, delinquency) and which to seek? It is also argued that a laissez-faire approach to education will only continue the current of inequality, since the rich are better at training themselves than the poor are. Illich has also been criticized for throwing out certification. This could open the door to quacks and to self-styled but fundamentally inadequate teachers, a problem Illich does acknowledge. Finally, the functionalists see, as basic to every society, a set of shared values, which, in industrial nations, the schools help transmit. They believe that if Illich's proposals were adopted, society would eventually collapse in anarchy, since the common foundation of values would crumble.

SUMMARY

1. Education is the process of educating others. To educate means to foster an expansion of knowledge, wisdom, desirable qualities of mind or character, physical health, or general competence, especially by means of formal study or instruction.

2. The British North America Act lodged control of education in Canada with the provinces. Here, in departments of education, a minister, his or her deputy, and a staff of civil servants issue curricular guidelines, provide teacher training, set teacher qualifications, and approve textbooks. Working through local school boards, superintendents help implement these functions. Farther down the chain of command are the school principals, who supervise teachers, upgrade teachers, and modify the courses of instruction used in the classroom. The Home and School Associations and the two professional organizations of teachers round out the Canadian educational system.

3. The history of primary and secondary education throughout the world is one of transition from elite education to mass education. Historically, Canada fell midway between the class-biased elite system found in Britain up to the 1960s and the mass system characteristic of American education since 1880.

4. The classroom is the focal point of the vast system of education. Primary-school pupils are more satisfied with their educational experiences in the classroom than secondary-school students. Variations in the socioeconomic and ethnic backgrounds of pupils lead to their differential treatment by teachers. Lower-class, minority-group pupils generally receive the least favorable treatment from white, middle-class teachers.

5. Teacher qualifications have been improving. But this has done little to alter weak commitment to teaching as a calling. One of the problems is the unstaged nature of this occupational career.

6. Teachers and pupils have incompatible definitions of classroom situations. Teachers use various strategies to reach their goals. Pupils use a different set of strategies for reaching theirs.

7. Regarding adolescent peer groups, in the United States boys generally rank athletics over popularity and popularity over academic success; girls rank popularity as most important. In Canada, both sexes rank academic success first. Boys rank athletics second and popularity third, while girls reverse these two.

8. The institution of education, like other institutions, meets six criteria: (1) certain important collective problems are solved; (2) there are distinctive patterns of behavior; (3) abstract relationships are evident; (4) there are special institutional roles; (5) institutions consist, in part, of values; (6) institutions have a distinct history.

9. There are many effects of education on individuals, groups, and societies. Concerning individuals, education produces intellectual achievement; change in values; rational attitudes toward life; desire for new experience; understanding of how political action, science, and progress are linked; stress on planning and organization, and interest in extra-local events. Education is also a universal factor in occupational achievement. Research on the effects of education on groups is largely inconclusive.

10. Many factors bear on the decision to place a pupil in a certain stream. Educational achievement is the single most important factor affecting level or status of first and subsequent jobs.

Family of orientation has the greatest effect on one's educational attainment. With certain exceptions, educational achievement even overrides ethnic background in the occupational structure.

11. Alternatives to traditional schools have evolved in response to the failings of traditional ways of educating children. They are known as free schools and alternative schools. There are also proponents of a deschooling society who say the aim of schools should be to prepare pupils to make a better society and to live in it effectively.

GLOSSARY

Alternative School. A school that usually allows free choice and action by its pupils within a program that is often acceptable to the district school board.

Correspondence principle. The tendency for the levels of social class and educational attainment to coincide.

Deschooling. An approach to education stressing the process and validity of acquiring knowledge through first-hand experience outside the traditional schoolroom.

Education. The act or process by which some people educate other people.

Educational Inequality. A process by which the educational system provides opportunities for occupational success to some students and not to others.

Elite Education. Education of the select, usually privileged members of society.

Frame. The hidden, or assumed sets of rules and categories (of people, things, events) that are part of our cultural heritage.

Free School. A school that allows free choice and action by its pupils within a program that is often rejected by the district school board.

Mainstreaming. The practice of integrating exceptional pupils with normal pupils to give the former social experience with the latter.

Mass Education. Education for all members of society.

Peer Groups. Groups of individuals who are more or less equal in rank.

Streaming. The process of placing pupils in different curricula that have different long-term goals for their learning.

FURTHER READING

Illich, I. *Deschooling Society.* New York: Harper & Row, 1971. The aim of schools, says Illich, should be to prepare students to make a better society and to live in it effectively. This can be accomplished, in good part, by getting educated outside the walls of the formal school.

Martin, W.B.W. and A.J. Macdonell. *Canadian Education.* 2nd edition. Scarborough, Ontario: Prentice-Hall of Canada, 1982. A textbook in the sociology of education, which concentrates chiefly on Canada.

Nelsen, R.W. and D.A. Nock (eds.). *Reading, Writing, and Riches: Education and the Socio-Economic Order in North America.* Kitchener, Ontario: Between the Lines, 1978. A comparative Marxian analysis of various aspects of the Canadian and American educational systems.

Novak, M.W. *Living and Learning in the Free School.* Toronto: McClelland and Stewart, 1975. A participant observer study of an alternative school in suburban Toronto.

Porter, J., M. Porter and B. Blishen. *Stations and Callings: Making it through the School System.* Toronto: Methuen, 1982. A study of Ontario students in grades 8, 10, and 12, which reveals the presence of educational inequality and how it favors the upper-middle-class.

Waller, W. *The Sociology of Teaching.* New York: John Wiley, 1932. The first observational study of schoolrooms by a sociologist, which looks at student-teacher interactions from a conflict perspective. This book is considered a major classic in the sociology of education.

CHAPTER FOURTEEN

Politics and Government

ROBERT PRESTHUS

Despite the pervasiveness of government today, human society has functioned for some nine-tenths of its existence without government. Indeed, the modern national state, which best symbolizes big government, emerged only about four centuries ago. Until that time, authority and its institutional agencies were transitory and personalized. Tribal chiefs, medicine men, religious leaders, feudal lords, and successful traders monopolized decisions involving critical social requisites such as defense, conflict resolution, and food-gathering. The bureaucracies that administer the modern state did not appear until early subsistence economies were superseded by money economies that provided the tax base required to sustain a large, permanent, administrative apparatus.

In effect, government was preceded temporally by the state, and both were preceded by society. This evolution was of course not linear; indeed, "stateless" polities exist today, typically in primitive tribally dominated societies (Levi-Strauss, 1963). In the West, however, the state is the common legal and instrumental form of government.

THE MODERN STATE

The state has several characteristics, including (1) a certain defined territory; (2) agencies of social control and conflict resolution (including the military and judiciary); and (3) sovereignty or ultimate control of its national affairs. The state usually enjoys legitimacy, i.e., popular moral approval, in its exercise of power but is often challenged by Marxists, by anarchists, or by revolutionaries of both the right and the left wings. Instead of accepting the state as a generally beneficent institution, operating in terms of a legal frame that ensures individual rights and security, they define the state as essentially an instrument of coercion.

Continuity is often cited as another characteristic of the state. However, it is clear that this condition varies as a result of war, foreign conquest, and post-war resolution of the outcome of international conflict. But even in cases of dissolution of defeated states, the ethnic and normative identifications of those concerned persist and may result in the re-emergence of the state, as seen in the history of smaller powers such as Poland and Czechoslovakia.

Other analyses of the state give it a rather more tenuous, philosophic characterization, perhaps most dramatically evident in the works of German idealist philosophers Hegel and von Treischke. They regard the state as a sort of free-floating, transcendental being. Hegel called the state the ultimate achievement of a rational "world spirit." The state is viewed as an end in itself. Later we shall see how inapposite this view is to modern democratic government. This idealist perception of the state is certainly foreign to English-speaking societies in which the concept of *limited government* permeates citizen values, particularly in the United States where a historic "fear of government" is enshrined in the Constitution, and specifically, in the first ten amendments to it, which limit the power of government in such vital areas as freedom of speech, association, and religion.

The Nature of Government

It is helpful to conceptualize government as the composite of human and institutional elements that activate the state. Government, in effect, is the legislature, bureaucracy, and agencies that manage the state. Whereas the state is permanent, government changes over time. Governmental authority and legitimacy stem from the state and its constitution, laws, and traditions. In Canada, "government" has still another meaning, when it is used to refer to the political party in power. In the latter context, government changes as departments and agencies change. Meanwhile, over time, and despite their external facade of permanence, bureaucracies change as the individuals who man them change. By definition, to govern means the establishing of laws and enforcing them. This is true regardless of the form of government. The differences in government occur in the process used by governments to exercise their power. Due process and the rule of law become critical elements differentiating democratic from authoritarian regimes. Meanwhile, the state persists, monopolizing legitimacy and sovereignty.

Modern government, in effect, is the vast apparatus of public agencies and individuals who carry on the task of redistributing the resources of a nation. Its responsibilities, powers, and size seem to increase geometrically. Fifteen years ago, the federal budget of Canada amounted to about fifteen billion dollars, the total public debt was only twenty billion, and national debt charges were 671 million, about 5 percent of the total federal budget. By 1982, the annual federal budget was some sixty-eight billion, net public debt reached some eighty billion, and net public debt charges had risen to about fifteen billion, 22 percent of the total budget. By 1986–87, according to government estimates, the debt will increase to 213 billion.

While many factors are involved, much of this growth is the result of public demands for more services and more subsidies. By far the largest category of federal spending is social welfare, amounting to thirty billion in 1982–83, 40 percent of the total. In addition, government itself is expansionist, often encouraging new popular demands that require new government programs. About half of federal agencies in Canada have created interest groups to make demands upon themselves (Presthus, 1974).

The growth of government has raised speculation as to the point at which its share of national wealth becomes self-defeating. A crude measure of this condition is provided by the proportion of gross national product (GNP) consumed by government. The proportion varies substantially among Western democracies, ranging from about 33 percent in the United States, to 50 percent in Canada, and rising to around 70 percent in Britain and the Scandinavian countries. Some economists argue that the resulting competition for capital between government and the private sector makes it difficult for the latter to secure, at reasonable cost, the infusions of capital required to sustain economic growth. Other economists believe that a dollar spent by government has the same economic impact as one spent by the private sector. However, the present financial crisis among Western democracies suggests that welfare capitalism may not be able to accommodate the vast costs of steadily expanding governmental services and attending deficits.

Power and Legitimacy

The state and its instrument, government, also possess a monopoly over the legal use of force or violence, seen most clearly in the standing armies maintained by every national state. This condition raises the question of the nature of power, leading in turn to the question of the nature of politics.

Politics is often defined as the study of power. Max Weber defined power as "the chance of a man or of a number of men to realize their own will in a communal action even against the resistance of others who are participating in the action." (Gerth and Mills, 1966.) Power has also been defined as the capacity to achieve intended effects. Or again, as the capacity to employ sanctions to bring about such effects. Attempts at specification have included differentiations of "influence," "authority," and "power." In this

An elderly welfare recipient plays the accordion as several hundred welfare recipients gather before the Québec National Assembly to protest what they call "the continuing deterioration in the condition of our lives".

context, "authority" has sometimes been characterized as the capacity to achieve one's ends without bringing sanctions to bear against those whom one hopes to control. Careful attempts to measure power, its scope, and the resources that underlie it exist, but the concept remains hazy (Presthus, 1964). In empirical situations, one can often recognize power, but adequate definitions often prove to be so abstract that they lose their analytical utility.

One useful alternative has been to recognize that individuals or institutions tend to exercise power in one fairly specific context. Power, in

Police uniforms and insignia represent and reinforce authority.

effect, is functionally specific. The state clearly enjoys a monopoly of power in the area of armed violence, but its power to achieve intended effects in the normative or moral sphere is limited by competing institutions such as the university, the church, and perhaps most important, the family.

Despite the tendency of the state to monopolize ultimate power, even the most authoritarian state tends to rely in part upon essentially permissive measures to ensure popular validation of its policies. Voluntary compliance with governmental dicta on the part of those governed is obviously preferable to coercive measures. Indeed, as the Vietnam experience indicates, policies widely assumed to be of questionable moral legitimacy are liable to end in disaster. It is equally clear that such vital governmental activities as tax collection rest essentially upon voluntary (however reluctant) acquiescense by most subjects.

This brings us to one of the critical political questions: "Why do men and women obey?" Emile Durkheim put the question somewhat differently, asking, "How is society possible?" Essentially, the answer is that they attribute *legitimacy* to the demands of the state and society. Here, we are again indebted to Max Weber for perhaps the most lucid and operational analysis of the sources of such legitimacy (Roth and Wittich, 1968). Essentially, three bases of legitimacy exist: traditional, charismatic, and legal-rational. Although all three bases may be seen in every modern society, Weber believed that the Western world was moving, largely under the spur of capitalism, steadily toward a system in which legal-rational norms were paramount.

Traditional Legitimacy

Traditional bases of legitimacy rely on authority that is accepted because of long-established tradition and convention. It is clear that much of the accumulated values and norms that govern our behavior is based on convention, on the "eternal yesterday."

The most significant type of traditional authority is *patriarchal*; the authority of the monarch over his subjects, the husband and father over the family, the feudal lord over his serfs and bondsmen, the prince over court officials and nobles (Roth and Wittich, 1968). As Weber shows, the norms governing such relationships are considered sacred; at times the authority of the patriarch is unchecked and arbitrary, based on emotion or unquestioned traditional values, which makes this type of legitimation irrational.

All institutions reinforce the legitimacy of tradition by various symbolic means. The dress and forms of address used in courts of law provide an example. The uniforms and insignia worn by police and military officers are also symbolic means of reinforcing traditional authority. Traditional authority rests most firmly perhaps in our unquestioned psychological acceptance of time-honored patterns of behavior and their institutional crystallizations. Obviously, even modern Western states differ in the degree to which their members honor traditional legitimacy, but compared with Third World societies, modern industrialized nations tend to appear iconoclastic. This is reflected in part in the extent to which technological change, especially in the communications field, tends to erode traditional values.

Charismatic Legitimacy

The charismatic basis of authority attributes the source of power to a person. Essentially irrational, the claim to obedience rests upon "the belief in magical powers, revelations, and hero worship." The religious leader, the political genius, and the military hero demand and receive obedience entirely on personal terms, reflecting their mystical, superhuman qualities. "Charisma" means "gift of grace." Those who possess it can function without an institutional or organizational apparatus, demanding personal sacrifice and loyalty on the basis of their exceptional powers. Christ, Ghandi, Castro, Napoleon, Franklin Delano Roosevelt, Churchill — some include Hitler — are often cited as charismatic leaders.

In time, Weber argues, pre-bureaucratic forms of charismatic leadership are succeeded by hierarchical organizational forms — a process Weber calls the "routinization of charisma." This occurs as the leader proves incapable of demonstrating his magical powers, or perhaps when mass movements (e.g., organized religion, political parties) develop the need for specialization of function, division of labor, media control, and the human and natural resources that ensure continuity. Routinization is also apparent in the tendency of revolutions to proceed through several predictable stages in which those who inspire them are succeeded by leaders who administer them — in Russia, the transition from Lenin and Trotsky to Stalin; in France, the displacement of Robespierre and Danton by Siéyès and Barras.

Charismatic legitimation is clearly more viable in pre-industrial societies where such values as nationalism, ethnicity, and religion provide a sympathetic milieu for its development. Capitalism, with its deification of science, rationality (of *means*, at least), technology, and materialism, tends to stamp out charismatic claims of legitimacy in favour of legal-rational claims.

Legal-Rational Legitimacy

As the term suggests, this third basis of legitimacy shifts the emphasis from tradition and personal magnetism to legally-based rules and regulations. Authority is held by a collectivity rather than by an individual, and decisions become depersonalized, rule-oriented, standardized. Science and bureaucracy, in effect, displace art and intuition. This shift, moreover, becomes steadily more imperative as larger and larger sectors of human behavior fall under the aegis of legal-rational claims (Presthus, 1978). In Weber's view, society moves toward the "iron cage" of history in which the range of individual freedom tends to become narrower in the service of materialistic ends and organizational demands for loyalty and predictability.

Critics of the welfare-capitalist state argue that government itself contributes significantly to this narrowing of individual discretion. Proponents of the system, however, claim that a welfare-capitalist government tends instead to ease the inequities of the privately-dominated marketplace. Here, Canada and the United States provide interesting contrasts, with Canadians often supporting government's expanding role, while many Americans tend to retain their historic fear of government mirrored in a constitution that limits government.

The analytical usefulness of Weber's typology is its generalizability. One can apply the typology fruitfully to various societies with different forms

Voting in democratic societies is considered a responsibility as well as a right.

of government and varying political ideologies. It is worthwhile repeating, however, that *all* societies exhibit all bases simultaneously. Even the most technologically advanced nations are subject to charismatic appeals, as the dynamics of political television in North America reveal. On the other hand, it is probably safe to conclude that there tends to be, cross-nationally, an uneven but roughly linear progression from conventional and charismatic bases of legitimacy toward legal-rational ones. It seems that nations that did not experience feudalism move along this path somewhat more quickly than those that have had to throw off this historical burden.

FORMS OF GOVERNMENT

The British essayist, Alexander Pope, insisted that "for forms of government let fools contest. Whatever is administered best, is best." But there's more to it than that. The things that matter regarding forms of government seem to be more a matter of political ideology than institutional arrangements or administrative expertise. The administrative structure of all modern states, regardless of ideology, is governed by executive, legislative, and judicial branches. In addition, all have a police, military, and counter-espionage apparatus, a plethora of so-called "independent" agencies and public or crown corporations, plus a number of "regulatory" agencies that attempt, without conspicuous success, to control various private sectors of society. Studies of Western legislators and bureaucracies indicate that their functions are similar. The class and educational backgrounds of their members are also similar in that they are generally found to be highly unrepresentative of the society they serve (Porter, 1965; Presthus, 1973, 1974).

Democracy

Democratic political theory begins with the ideal that individuals can and should participate in government. Considerable evidence (polls, interviews, and so on) can be found (van Loon, 1970; Verba and Nye, 1972) that challenges this positive assumption, but some of it misses the mark because the crux of democratic theory is not that individuals do participate, but that they have the *capacity* to do so. It is the obligation of government, largely through political parties, to nourish this capacity.

Ironically, as C.B. Macpherson points out (1965), until about a century ago, democracy was regarded as a bad system, since rule by "the people" or by government according to their will was thought to be fatal to individual freedom and civilized living. Not until the first World War was democracy regarded highly. Since then, as George Orwell has shown, its meaning has become somewhat blurred. Non-liberal regimes sometimes call themselves "democratic," and the greater part of the world is comprised of one-party states.

Our concern is with the main tenets of liberal-democracy, as practised in Western Europe and North America. These are capitalism, pluralism, constitutionalism, and majority rule.

Capitalism.

Capitalism is usually defined as an economic system (sustained by highly articulate symbols including "entrepreneurship," "free enterprise," "competition," "risk-taking," and so on) in which the means of production are privately owned. Private ownership of property and the sanctity of contracts are vital parts of capitalism. Equally essential is the existence of free markets, in which prices are determined by the "law" of supply and demand. In his *Wealth of Nations*, 1776, Adam Smith insisted that under the market system an "unseen hand" insured that the economic decisions of self-interested individuals best promoted the larger interests of society.

Over time, however, free markets and perfect competition were undercut by the emergence of giant corporations, which, through mergers and control of their markets, brought oligopolistic forms of competition, i.e., competition among a few large firms in most sectors of the economy. Such developments culminated in public demands for regulation of the private economy by government, resulting in a "mixed economy" of oligopoly and competition, of private and public control of economic affairs.

A basic characteristic of capitalism, although not a necessary one, is the co-existence of liberal-democracy and capitalism. Competition is a central value in both democracy and capitalism. Parties compete for control of the state, while unions and industry compete for larger shares of the wealth produced under capitalism. Corporations motivated by "profits" compete in product innovation and creative advertising. And, not least, individuals in a liberal-democracy compete for superior educational achievement, upward-mobility in the workplace, income, and social prestige.

Forms of government can usefully be distinguished by the source of their major support in the social structure (Linz, 1976). Liberal-democracy, especially in Western Europe, finds its electoral strength in the middle-class with its ideological attachment to capitalism and *constitutionalism*, which will be discussed later. In industrial countries such as Canada, the rise of labor unions sometimes brought working-class elements into leftist parties, such as the New Democratic Party (NDP), which rejected traditional liberal-

An individual can be put to death in a democratic society, but only after receiving the right of due process.

ism by the advocacy of greater state intervention in the economy and society. We shall see later how other forms of government find their major support in different segments of the electorate.

Pluralism

Another basic element in liberal-democratic theory is *pluralism*. The central idea is that power within government, and indeed the entire society, is widely dispersed. The power of the state is shared with a large number of private associations, interest groups, corporations, labor unions, and so forth. Within government itself, this concentration of power is institutionalized by the division of power among executive, legislative, and judicial agencies. In operational terms, this prin-

ciple also holds true for parliamentary systems, insofar as the bureaucracy and the judiciary enjoy considerable independence. Crown corporations, if we are to believe the Auditor-General, comprise another centre of independent power in the Canadian system.

Such fragmentation ensures, theoretically, that individuals can influence the decisions that affect them through participation (voting, consumer choice) in government and industry, and that the political system provides certain "veto points" where disenchanted individuals and groups can make their claims heard. Here again, one sees the extent to which competition is an ideal in liberal-democratic theory.

The view that the ideal of pluralism corresponds to what actually takes place in countries such as Canada has come under considerable attack during the last quarter-century. Critics have usually insisted that vital decisions, in both governmental and private spheres, are actually made by elites representing the various sub-groups affected by such decisions (Presthus, 1973; Porter, 1965; Clement, 1975; Taylor, 1969). In effect, the conditions assumed by pluralism are often modified by an unequal distribution of social and economic power.

Such critics tend to accept the dictum of the sociologist Pareto that "every people is governed by an elite." (Pareto, 1935.) Since brains, beauty, social status, and wealth are unequally distributed throughout society, individual power will be similarly distributed. Sociologists have carefully studied the extent and the process by which power tends to be concentrated through family ties, educational elitism, and *ascriptive recruitment* in the major socioeconomic sectors in Canadian and American society (Porter, 1965; Clement, 1975; Mills, 1951; Baltzell, 1958). They conclude that ascriptive bases of recruitment and promotion in most occupations tend to lodge power in the hands of such advantaged groups. Ironically, exceptions to such patterns tend to be temporary, since parents who have prospered through achievement tend to pass on their advantages to their children. Such a situation, however, prevails mainly at the top of social and economic hierarchies. It seems safe to conclude, in an imperfect world, that substantial avenues of upward-mobility have existed and persist in North American occupational life (Blau and Duncan, 1967).

Constitutionalism

A cardinal element in democratic theory and practice is constitutionalism. This concept holds that government is always limited by substantive — what a law or rule attempts to do — and procedural — the way in which a law or rule is administered — guaranties, often called the "rule of law." It should be noted that this delimitation does not interfere with the monopoly over legitimacy and violence ascribed to the state and its agents. Instead, constitutionalism often prescribes the *way* in which such powers can be exercised. For example, the democratic state, it is often said, can put a man to death, but only after he has received various historic rights of due process, such as habeas corpus, fair trial, cross examination of witnesses, counsel, and so on.

Constitutionalism was encouraged early on by liberalism and was in part motivated by economic needs for enforceable laws of contract and related business transactions. As seen in the U.S. Supreme Court until the 1930s, property rights were perhaps more zealously protected than the political rights of individuals. By the 1960s, however, the pendulum had swung to ensure meticulous protection for political and civil rights, especially for those accused of crime. By the 1980s in Canada, a similar trend was symbolized by the new Charter of Rights, which limited the power of government in political and criminal areas. It is significant that the vast majority of people in the world do not possess such rights, and that even in Western democracies, they must be constantly protected against overzealous governments. The Liberal Government's efforts (1983) to establish a new Security Agency, replete with extraordinary powers

House of Commons, Ottawa.

of investigation, including virtually unlimited wiretapping authority and undercover surveillance of unorthodox religious and political groups, provides an example.

Majority Rule

We noted earlier that democracy was once faulted because of its deification of majority rule. It seemed clear to most observers that the ordinary person rarely had the knowledge or political resources — interest, information, dialectical skill — required to participate effectively in government. In practice, government in the past and present is actually carried on by elites. A variety of institutional mechanisms are used to ensure this practice, one of which is the use of elected legislatures. Parliaments, furthermore, are typically divided into a "popular" elected house and an upper, appointed segment — the senate — the purpose of which is to curb any populist tendencies of the lower house. This mechanism persists in Canada and Britain, and it was a part of the original American constitution but soon modified in favor of an elected Senate.

Despite such structures, liberal-democratic governments do respond, often slowly and with important exceptions (such as capital punishment), to the will of the majority. The bewildering variety and scope of government programs provide impressive evidence. Government is probably somewhat less responsive when public opinion, as now, tends to prefer less government, but on the whole, majority rule tends to persist.

A corollary of majority rule, and one which many insist is indeed even more important, is respect for minorities. Free speech, for example, is one cherished element in a civilized society, clearly most significant for those who hold minority or unconventional views. The Charter of Rights guarantees the rights of minority groups or those who hold views not shared by the majority. It is a vital part of democratic theory that such rights be carefully preserved.

Socialism

Here again, wide cross-national variations exist in the interpretation and the practice of "socialism." We shall confine ourselves to the Western context of the term, referring essentially to the "democratic socialism" of Britain and the Scandinavian countries. It seems important to begin by emphasizing the moral and religious basis of socialism. The "brotherhood of man," a viable concept in British socialism, for example, deplores the inequities of income, prestige, and security of modern capitalism. William Morris, an early British socialist, dreamed of a society "in which there should be neither rich nor poor, neither master nor master's man, neither idle nor overworked, neither brain-sick brain workers, nor heart-sick hand workers, in a word, in which all men would be living in equality of condition." Whereas liberal-democracy is typically activated by or affiliated with capitalist *competition*, socialists reject the ethic of competitive materialism. Man as consumer and producer is replaced by a view of man as a co-operative being.

On the ecnomic side, socialist theory emphasizes public ownership of virtually all sectors of production. Production for use as well as profit is the aim. Here, unfortunately, one finds little evidence that public ownership provides a workable alternative to traditional capitalism. The Crown Corporation device, for example, has been widely used in Britain and Canada, but little hard evidence exists indicating that such institutions can increase productivity to reduce costs for the people who own them. Indeed, inefficiencies are often hidden by the autonomy that such corporations enjoy in the name of managerial effectiveness. Their losses are periodically wiped out by government and their top executives are sometimes chosen on a basis of political patronage. In some cases, special protective legislation covering routes and prices is introduced to ensure their survival, which again has the result of making them uncompetitive in economic terms.

Organizationally, socialist tenets are somewhat paradoxical in that they propose the reduction of the impersonality and standardization of state bureaucracies, yet the expansion of public ownership tends to aggravate this condition. Under socialism, huge state bureaucracies are typically substituted for private ones, often narrowing the periphery of individual choice. Canada's New Democratic Party stated in a recent party platform: "We want to create a society where the individual will not be dominated by any organization, public or private, and where the dead weight of one bureaucracy will not be substituted for another." Although socialists assume that state ownership brings greater responsiveness to citizen claims for service, this assumption seems questionable given the tenuous incentives for personal initiative existing in most government agencies. In any event, there are few objective criteria available to verify claims regarding the superiority of socialism in the areas of responsiveness, or productivity.

T.C. (Tommy) Douglas helped to form the New Democratic Party from the Cooperative Commonwealth Federation in 1961. Here, he is carried on the shoulders of supporters after winning the party's first leadership convention.

Ideologically, it is clear that liberal-democrats and socialists differ sharply in their perceptions of the state. Liberal-democrats tend to fear government and to seek constitutional guarantees against any arbitrary use of its power. Socialists, on the other hand, seem to trust government and to be prepared to give it virtually unlimited power. These divergent values tend to reflect opposing perceptions regarding the nature of man. Liberal-democracy, especially its conservative segment, has a far less optimistic view of man's potential. Essen-

tially Hobbesian — believing that people are motivated by the search for power — liberal-democrats insist that government is needed mainly to curb man's aggressive individualism. Socialists, *per contra*, perceive government as the great educator which can be used to enhance man's assumed innate goodness and his potential for self-realization in a co-operative society.

Canada's New Democratic Party, with origins in the 1930s, exhibits several traditional socialist values, although on the whole it works within the existing liberal-democratic system. Ideologically, the NDP believes that government is the appropriate instrument for achieving greater equality and security for the average man. In the trade-off between inflation and unemployment, the Party favors deficit spending to create jobs, with somewhat less concern for any resultant increase in inflation. With some reservations, state ownership of industrial enterprises is among the Party's policies. Although the Party presents itself as the champion of the working man, it receives only a small minority of working-class votes, and indeed its share of the aggregate vote in federal election has remained fairly constant, at about 18 percent. Perhaps this is because, compared with their peers in the United States, Canadian legislators of all parties rank much higher on policies commonly regarded as "pro-government": national medical plans, economic security for everyone, state supported employment programs. (See Table 14-1.)

TABLE 14-1. Economic Liberalism, United States versus Canadian Legislators, in percentages

Economic Liberalism*	United States		Canada	
	Federal	State	Federal	Provincial
High	21	25	56	83
Medium	55	53	43	37
Low	24	22	—	—
	(90)	(147)	(122)	(117)

* "Economic liberalism" is defined here by the following items: "That government which governs least governs best" (reverse scored); "Economic security for every man, woman and child is worth striving for, even if it means socialism"; "If unemployment is high, the government should spend money to create jobs"; "A national medicare plan is necessary to ensure that everyone receives adequate health care"; and "More federal aid to education is desirable if we are going to adequately meet present and future educational needs in this country."

SOURCE: Robert Presthus, "The politics of accommodation." In R. Preston (ed.), *Perspective on Revolution and Evolution.* Durham: Duke University Press, 1979, page 114.

Nationalism is also espoused by the NDP. This ideology may underlie in part its calls for public ownership in Canada's energy field, which is dominated by foreign ownership. Nationalism may also have been useful in cementing the Party's alliance with Canadian labor unions, many of which have been ambivalent about their position as subsidiaries of American international unions.

Some observers believe that the relative weakness of socialism, in Canada as in the United States, is due to the absence of a feudal heritage. Given the pervasiveness of socialism in Western Europe, which of course has a feudal past, this argument appears suspect. A more plausible explanation is the lack of any successful revolutionary tradition in Canada, which might have provided a broader social consensus upon which dramatic political change might have been based (Underhill, 1960).

Fascism

Fascist ideology had its roots in the 1880s when it appeared in Western Europe as a revolt against bourgeois capitalism and parliamentary socialism. Its intellectual origins were mainly French, including George Sorel's *Reflection on Violence*, which idealized violence and heroism. Fascism began as a crisis in liberalism and democracy. Parliaments were attacked as mere "talking shops," incapable of action. The "revolt was against reason and positivism, against the mediocrity of bourgeois society, and against the muddle of liberal democracy." (Sternhell, 1976.) The rationality and individualism of capitalism were also attacked, in favor of an emphasis upon race, heredity, sentiment, and feeling. In terms of the types of authority outlined earlier, fascism represents a rejection of legal-rational norms in favor of traditional and charismatic ones.

Here again, national variations are substantial, and we will confine our generalizations to German fascism. Fascism is distinguished ideologically by its "anti" attitudes. A definition of fascism,

Brown-shirted storm troopers rally in Nürnberg, Germany, for a rally of the Nazi Party in 1937. Party membership cut across economic and social classes, obliterating what might otherwise have been divisive cleavages.

given its complex and often contradictory nature, may be useful:

> ... a hypernationalist, often pan-nationalist, anti-liberal, anti-parliamentary, anti-communist, populist, and therefore anti-proletariat, partly anti-capitalist and anti-bourgeois, anti-clerical, or at least, non-clerical movement, with the aim of national social integration through a single party .... (Linz, 1976.)

Whereas the other major political ideologies exhibit reasonably consistent and often positive values, fascism thus assumes a generally negative, anti-intellectual posture. Among such negatives, anti-communism is especially vital, in part because this value enabled national socialism in Germany to enlist the support of influential middle- and upper-class elements, including industrial leaders. This thrust also helped the German Reich make its early successful incursions into Czechoslovakia, Austria, Poland, and the Rhineland, because important segments of both British and French elites were sympathetic toward this orientation. At the same time, it must be emphasized that the "national solidarity" demands of the Nazi Party dictated that it become a mass party, cutting across and obliterating all potentially devisive cleavages of class and group.

Fascist philosophy is thus at odds with the pluralism of both socialism and liberal-democracy. Instead, it seeks a *totalitarian* regime in which all social groups are subordinate to the state. No opposition is permitted to official versions of reality. Dissent is not tolerated. Allied with this condition is a repudiation of the rule of law and constitutionalism, which remain central in both liberal-democracy and democratic-socialism.

Again, whereas both the latter assume that policy requires rational discussion of alternatives and parliamentary legitimation, fascist regimes often govern by arbitrary decree. Government employs mass emotional appeal and irrational staging, often freighted with violence, to ensure mass obedience. State control of the mass media promotes irrationality and control of individual political opinion. Fascism is intensely nationalistic, and its propaganda often focuses upon real or imagined enemies, internal and external. In the German case, Jews and Communists provided domestic scapegoats, while Britain, France, and Russia were stigmatized as external threats. German fascism was also counter-revolutionary, a nihilistic reaction to the liberal Weimar Republic. Meanwhile, the Versailles Treaty following World War I, which settled heavy debts upon Germany and prevented — or attempted to prevent — the restoration of its hallowed military establishment, provided yet another unifying target.

Fascism's irrationality is again apparent in its obsession with racism and *volkisch*, with blood, soil, and fatherland. Biologically, of course, there is no such thing as a "pure" race, yet the Nazis made this myth a central element in their propaganda and used it to reconcile their savage treatment of Jews, gypsies, Communists, Russians, Poles, and other *untermensch*.

Ideology and history came together powerfully in the National Socialist Party. Such ideological elements as nationalism, racism, anti-communism, and anti-parliamentarism proved appealing to large segments of the German people. Meanwhile, the economic dislocations of the 1930s provided fertile ground for popular discontent and the search for drastic solutions. Violent nationalism was probably the main ingredient in the rise of the Nazi Party. In addition, new forms of political organization and propaganda account for its success. The creation of parliamentary political units was among its most effective stratagems.

Fascism, perhaps, found an especially fertile soil in Germany, given this country's historic patterns of hierarchical authority (Money-Kyrle, 1951). The *Fuhrenprinzip* was probably legitimated by the prestige of the German army, led mainly by members of the Prussian Junker class. Assigning party leaders decisive authority, as in the National Socialist case, must have seemed natural in this milieu. Democracy had never been viable in Germany, so that the need for elections and party reaffirmation of the leader's authority would seem out of context (Linz, 1976). Beyond this, German idealist philosophy has glorified both the national state and the heroic leader who could rise above conventional norms of behavior.

Such values, however, were not confined to German intellectuals. Elite theory, which generally contradicts democratic ideals of mass participation, was centred in Italy, in the writing of Pareto and Mosca. Italian fascism, moreover, proceeded its German counterpart. Meanwhile, British influences were at work, perhaps most strongly in Darwin's conception of the survival of the fittest and the harsh process of natural selection. Carlyle, too, eulogized the hero in terms somewhat similar to those of Nietszche in Germany. In sum, a climate of anti-democratic opinion existed throughout Western Europe, which by the early twentieth century had made a path for fascism.

Communism

The interpretations and the literature of communism are endlessly varied. Revisionists have appeared in many countries, deviating from the classical doctrines of Marx, Engels, and Lenin. One such interpretation raised the issue of whether communism could exist in only one country, despite its essential internationalism. Another concerned the extent to which, and how, communism might co-exist with nationalism, as seen in Vietnam. Indeed, there exists a veritable Marx factory, producing endless variations on the theme of "What Marx Meant." Our purpose here can perhaps be met by a very broad overview of conventional marxism, all the while recognizing such pervasive national and doctrinal differences of emphasis and substance.

Whereas fascism is anti-scientific and anti-rational, communism has an impressive intellectual base. Fashioned largely by Karl Marx, communism became at once both a science and a religion, an objective description of reality and a messianic prediction regarding historical evolution. As we read in Chapter 2, its *bête noire* is capitalism and its correlate, liberal-democracy. According to communist theory, the prime determinant of capitalist social organization and the allocation of resources is ownership of the system of production. Hence, institutions such as law, religion, and education in capitalistic countries — the social superstructure — are determined by private ownership of the means of production.

The energy necessary to uproot this condition is provided by the struggle between social classes, between the minority who possess land and capital and the masses who have only their labor to sell. The latter are exploited, essentially because the profit created by their labor is appropriated by the entrepreneur.

The religio-scientific character of Marxian doctrine is suggested by the fact that while Marx insisted that a revolution would occur inevitably because of the class struggle, communists must also organize and promote the revolution on a global scale. Marxist theory held that the working-class of all countries had more in common with each other than with propertied middle- and upper-class elements in their own country. Thus, communism was inherently international, a condition that accounts in part for the violent opposition it evoked among fascists, who as pointed out, were intensely nationalistic.

Communism provided both an intellectual and emotional appeal. Marx's analysis of capitalism and imperialism was an impressive landmark in social science. In addition, the inequalities and harshness of early capitalism, set down in great and evocative detail by Marx and Engels mainly on the basis of British data, and the promise of

communism to alleviate them, inspired considerable support among liberal and leftist intellectuals, perhaps reaching its apogee during the depression of the 1930s. The assumed benefits for working people were even more tangible. Having nothing to lose but their chains, they should press for a reordering of economic, and hence, social institutions that would end their relatively powerless role in the capitalist model of finance and production. Popular disenchantment with capitalism brought sizeable communist parties in France and Italy. In North America, the Communist Party appealed mainly to a small group of urban intellectuals, many of whom were motivated by the promise of easing inequalities of income, security, and education, which not only existed, but were legitimated under capitalism as part of the Darwinian ethic and its economic corollary, which dictated that only the fit survive. Communism, then, in theory shares with democratic socialism the ideal of equality, of a classless society.

The welfare programs that are part of contemporary society were not available in the 1930s to cushion the shock of unemployment, illness, and old age. The rise of labor unions, meanwhile, provided another instrument that partially restructured power relations between capitalists and the workers. Such instruments were mainly adopted by democratic socialism. Communism tended to regard them as mere palliatives, and thus demanded a radical realignment among the factors of production, with the state as the motivating agent.

In theory, at least, communism is *egalitarian*. The wide variations in personal income and status characteristic of capitalist and some socialist societies, such as the United States, Canada, and Britain, are anathema. Inherited wealth and privilege have been similarly deplored. "From each according to his talents, to each according to his needs" was the catechism. Yet as early as 1931, Stalin had begun to stigmatize "equality-mongering," while calling for a new sympathy for

Joe Clark shows a stiff upper lip after stepping down from the Progressive Conservative party leadership.

the intelligentia (Feldmesser, 1960; Djilas, 1976). By the end of World War II, the Soviet Union was well on the way to a stratified class structure. However, more recent information suggests that systematic efforts have been made, beginning with Khrushchev, to ease resultant inequities in income, educational opportunity, and other benchmarks of social and official rank. Apparently, part of the motivation for this change was to reduce the prestige of state officials, thereby increasing the power of the top political elite. Since all human societies reveal hierarchical distributions of power and status (Fraser, 1960), it seems likely that both the socialist and the communist search for equality may prove abortive.

In stark contrast to the pluralism seen in welfare capitalism and democratic socialism is the totalitarianism of the communist state in Russia. The Communist Party is the lodestar of all political and economic activity, as well as the ultimate source of ideological legitimacy. Although a constitution and laws do exist, the party and the government are omnipotent; in effect, they are the

law. Control is maintained through assigning party members to all strategic positions in the government hierarchy. As someone concluded of this totalitarian system, "Everything that is not compulsory is forbidden." And as Milovan Djilas (1976) has shown, such a system means the end of a classless society in favor of a "new class" of privileged state and party officials. Such are the differences between political ideology and political reality.

HOW GOVERNMENTS MAKE POLICY

It seems useful to conclude with a fairly pragmatic review of how governments function. We suggested earlier that politics was the art of the possible. A review of government in operation will make very clear that its policies are the result of accommodation among many interests. The end product is typically a compromise. This is because a variety of interests are involved in the shaping of any significant policy. Each has a point of view. In its efforts to give each interest at least part of its claims, government inevitably produces compromises, rather than neat, consistent policies.

Four discrete groups participate in the hammering out of public policy: political parties (i.e., their leaders), the bureaucracy, interest groups, and finally, the mass public.

Political Parties

Parties in democratic states are odd in that they usually have no constitutional basis, but instead they have simply evolved because of functional necessity. Some mechanism is required to operate the political system. Parties serve this end. They take on the responsibility for forming and running the government by assuming the controlling roles, hammering out major policies, and attempting to carry them out.

Parties also have the task of recruiting and nominating candidates for such roles, for testing them and bringing them into positions of increasing authority. The salience and difficulty of this task were dramatically indicated in Canada in the leadership convention of the Progressive Conservative Party in 1983, when the party leader, Joe Clark, was obliged to renounce his leadership post.

Another classical role of parties is to present and articulate critical issues, and to educate the public concerning them. Theoretically, a party is faced with an infinite number of potentially critical issues. To some extent, it can select those upon which it will choose to do battle. Some parties are historically associated with traditional policies from which they cannot easily deviate. Choice is further limited by the emergence or persistence of certain critical issues that reflect national socio-economic conditions. In Canada, unemployment is such a continuing problem, which all parties must include in their platforms and programs. During the recent past, inflation has been another dilemma that party leaders must address, and to which both socialist and welfare capitalist states contribute because of their huge annual financial deficits and long-term indebtedness.

Such issues must be publicly discussed. Parties can provide a valuable role in democratic societies by offering the electorate a meaningful choice among alternative policies. Insofar as parties are essentially concerned with gaining and maintaining power, there exists some tension between their functions of power and education. Inevitably, the party in power will present its policy outcomes in the best possible light and sometimes attempt to shift responsibility for failures elsewhere. The effort of the Liberal Party to ascribe their dismal economic performance during the late 1970s and early 1980s to "international conditions" provides one example.

This brings into view the function of the Opposition Party, a highly institutionalized part of parliamentary government. If the majority party attempts to shift responsibility or fails to address critical issues, the duty of the Opposition is to air such transgressions. In the process, the concerned public gains new insights into the matters at issue. The resultant heat, so to speak, also produces some light.

One possible dysfunction of this parliamentary process should be mentioned: the tendency for opposition to become a mere strategem whereby the opposition party can make political capital by attacking indiscriminately virtually any policy, program, or error of the government. The role of the Opposition then becomes dysfunctional, regardless of the substance of the issue concerned. Among the consequences is some confusion, if not disenchantment among the concerned public, and a possible weakening of the educational role of political parties and the extent to which voters feel able to participate in politics. (See Table 14-2.)

TABLE 14-2. Comparative Levels of Citizen Political Efficacy, United States and Canada

| | Percentage Agreeing | |
	United States*	Canadian**
"Voting is the only way people like me can have a say about how the government runs things."	68	75
"Sometimes politics and government seem so complicated that a person like me can't really understand what is going on."	69	69
"People like me don't have any say about what the government does."	34	49
	(1571)	(2721)

* American Data from 1966 Election Study, Survey Research Center. University of Michigan.
** Canadian data from John Meisel, national election survey of 1965 (unpublished data). The last item was phrased slightly different in this survey, i.e., "I don't think the government cares what people like me think."

Insofar as a critical function of competing political parties is to provide voters with meaningful policy choices, another problem arises: the tendency of major Canadian parties to agree on major policies affecting the nation's economy. Here, one must look beyond party platforms to their actual performance. In May, 1968, Pierre Elliot Trudeau, Liberal Prime Minister, declared in his party's platform: "The Government intends to hold down Federal Government spending and to keep our expenditures in line with our tax revenues. In other words, our aim is to achieve a balanced budget." By 1984, the annual deficit was over thirty billion dollars.

During the early 1980s, the three main parties generally agreed on such major policies as huge welfare programs (about 40 percent of the federal budget, 1982), deficits and deficit financing (debt service comprised 20 percent of the federal budget, 1982), and Canadianization of energy resources. Even the socialist NDP tends to work within the system, adopting the pragmatism of the two major parties. One systematic effort to differentiate the two major Canadian parties along policy lines found only three variations: in the areas of Québec and biculturalism, civil liberties, and welfare statism (Kornberg, 1967). Liberals tended to be more favorable than Conservatives toward each issue. Insofar as party differences tend to be more rhetorical than real, they fail to offer real alternatives to the electorate.

Bureaucracy

The role of appointed officials in policy-making varies considerably among democratic states. Certainly, such policy influence as occurs tends to be monopolized by *senior* civil servants who have both experience and expertise. The rotation of ministerial posts characteristic of parliamentary systems may also increase the policy influence of the bureaucracy. New ministers are likely to rely upon the experience of their deputy-ministers. It also seems clear that bureaucratic influence has increased as government's role has become more complex and pervasive. It may also be suggested that bureaucratic influence varies in proportion to the extent to which political elites are professional. If political office is merely a temporary interruption of a private occupational career, permanent officials will probably exercise greater influence than they might in systems where politics, to use Weber's term, is a vocation. In effect, expert permanent officials will tend to dominate amateur politicians. The sociologist, John Porter, argued that this situation existed in Canada. In Britain and the United States, where politics has become more of a career, one would expect the bureaucracy to have comparatively less influence upon major policy issues.

The extent to which permanent officials in Canada can shape major policy has been nicely documented (Lang, 1972). The case involves the Liberal Government's efforts to pass legislation limiting the duration of patent protection for drugs, which enabled manufacturers to maintain price levels widely thought to be exorbitant. In tracing the path of Bill-190, Lang found that the major impetus for drafting and supporting the legislation came from a small, interdepartmental committee of senior civil servants. Apparently, party leaders were lukewarm about the legislation, which in Lang's view might have died without the sustained efforts of the committee.

A classic example of bureaucratic influence involves the successful efforts of the German civil service to undercut the liberal Weimar Republic following World War I. In this instance, the antidemocratic ideology of permanent officials provided the main impulse. A contrasting example of bureaucratic neutrality may be seen in the extent to which the British Administrative Class, a small, elite corp of top officials whom one would assume to be politically "conservative," cooperated fully with the Attlee Labour Government's unprecedented program of nationalization following World War II. Clearly, generalizations are elusive, but given the expertise and continuity of higher officials, one may conclude that they have considerable influence upon policy-making in democratic states.

Interest Groups

As with political parties, interest groups have no constitutional basis, yet they have become an integral part of the political system. In part, this is because political representation is geographically based, leaving a need for occupational representation in the system. With many exceptions, interest groups tend to represent producer interests, such as the Canadian Bankers Association. At least such groups are the most powerful and have been longest in existence (Presthus, 1973).

One function of an interest group is to transmit technical information to legislators concerning the complex issues faced by modern governments. Legislators themselves state that such information is the most useful part of an interest group's role, and that they have often been influenced regarding a policy-issue by such information. This is understandable because M.P.'s cannot hope to be knowledgeable in all the areas in which they must make judgements. Each interest group tends to monopolize expertise in its own sphere and can often indicate potential consequences of proposed policies that would rarely occur to a back-bencher. Such information is often selected to favor the interest concerned, but since most critical issues provoke opposition, the M.P. usually hears many sides.

Interest groups also provide political support for M.P.'s, including campaign funds and opportunities to gain publicity through speeches before groups or honorific appointments in their organizations. Social ties between M.P.'s and lobbyists are common, in part because lobbyists for major producer groups usually enjoy liberal expense accounts. Interest groups also participate in appointing individuals to strategic government posts. Not only are they often asked to recommend appointees, but the major groups in a given occupational area usually enjoy a "veto power" over anyone recommended for an agency in their own area. Interest groups also play a role in suggesting new governmental policies, and in educating the public regarding the merits of such policies. Lazy journalists sometimes play a salient role here, since they will accept uncritically, and publish, "handouts" from interested groups, which state the latter's position on a proposed policy and probably have some political influence.

Canadian interest groups focus mainly upon the bureaucracy, which tends to handle the largest portion of group claims. In matters of great importance, groups will seek support at the cabinet level, often using their current president as their representative. Since interest groups always seek access where power lies, they spend relatively less time upon back-benchers. In the American system, such groups spend most of their time with legislators, who have comparatively more power (Presthus, 1974).

Public Participation

Here we are concerned with the extent to which the average voter or the public participates in politics and policy-making. Interesting differences exist between Canada and the United States. Evidence indicates that only about 2 percent of Canadian adults participate directly and continuously in politics (Van Loon, 1970). Voting seems to be the only area in which participation is significant, and as Figure 14-1 shows, it is strongly associated with income in the United States, but dramatically less so in Canada. In spheres such as talking about politics, campaigning for someone, and trying to convince someone how to vote, less than 5 percent of adults indicate participation. It is noteworthy that only 51.4 percent of American adults voted in the 1984 presidential election. Less than one-third of the eligible electorate elected Ronald Reagan. In Canada, 76 percent of the eligible electorate voted in the 1984 federal election. In Britain, voting in national elections rises to about 90 percent.

As Figure 14-1 shows, in the United States voting correlates strongly with the income of the voter, which seems to indicate a pervasive apathy among poorer voters. In Canada, income explains very little about voting participation.

Those who do participate directly (in ways other than voting) tend to be a highly select minority, possessing more education, higher class and occupational status, and higher income compared with their inactive counterparts (Verba and Nie, 1972). In the United States, the only exception to this generalization is found among blacks who are a highly politicized group at this point in history. A frequent correlate of high participation is high group membership, i.e., those who participate in community affairs and in interest or fraternal groups tend also to be active in politics.

Careful studies indicate that social class is the best single indicator of political participation. One exception occurs in what is called "particularistic contacting," which refers to direct, personal approaches by citizens in political elites. As Figure 14-2. shows, the association between class status and such participation in the United States is much weaker than in campaign activity, voting, and communal activity. In Canada, neither income nor education (i.e., social status) apparently had much influence upon participation. As William Mishler concludes, "The primary advantage of wealth is found at the upper levels of the political spectrum. It facilitates communication with political parties and public officials and increases opportunities for full-time political work, but there is little evidence that money discriminates between activists and apathetics in other areas [of participation]." (Mishler, 1979, page 96.) The explanation for the critical role of social status lies in the fact that political activity requires *resources*, of time, information, conceptual ability, and the capacity to express one's ideas. Such qualities tend to be associated with high levels of education and high occupational status. As Table 14-2, shows, however, substantial proportions of Canadian and American adults have *low* feelings of political efficacy.

FIGURE 14-1. Voting Participation by Income: Canada and the United States.

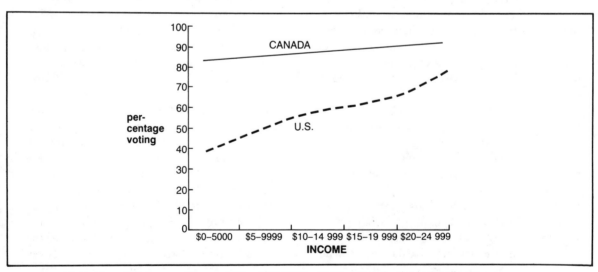

SOURCE: *Adapted from U.S. Bureau of Census, 198? and W. Mishler,* Political Participation in Canada. *Toronto: Macmillan, 1979, page 96.*

These data bring us back to the question of elite rule, in democratic societies as well as in totalitarian systems. Canadian sociologists John Porter and Wallace Clement (1965; 1975) have demonstrated that the most salient positions in Canadian society are filled by individuals from elite family backgrounds, usually of English-Protestant origin. In 1951, for example, John Porter found that only 6.7 percent of the Canadian economic elite were French Canadian, a charter group making up 40 percent of the population. Two decades later, the situation had not changed much. Among 12 741 directors of major Canadian corporations, only 9.48 were French Canadian (Presthus, 1973).

Wallace Clement found similar conditions regarding recruitment and upward-mobility among the top positions in Canadian industrial organizations. Over 80 percent of such elites are of English-Protestant origin. "Anglo" origin is reported by only 44.7 percent of the total population but by 86.6 percent of the "economic elite" (Clement, 1977). Moreover, "upper-class origin in all career avenues is consistently higher in Canada than in the United States." (Clement, 1977.) Most of the Canadian elite had attended prestige schools and universities, such as Upper Canada College in Toronto or Queen's University in Kings-

ton. Considerable social interaction occurred among and across such groups, often through membership in exclusive private clubs. In a comparative analysis of recruitment in Canadian and American industry, Clement found that 61 percent of members of the economic elite in Canada had upper-class origins, compared with 36 percent in the United States (1978). Moreover, the trend seemed to be toward increased upper-class recruitment in Canada, rising from 50 percent in 1950, to 59.4 percent in 1972 (Clement, 1977).

American sociologist C. Wright Mills argued similarly that the United States is ruled by a triumvirate of elites in three, overlapping institutional sectors: corporate, military, and political (Mills, 1951). Their members share advantaged social, economic, and ethnic statuses. Most have graduated from Ivy League universities. They interact socially and occupationally. For example, some 5000 former military officers now work in defence industries. Most of the high-level, appointive posts in Washington (Secretaries, Under-Secretaries, Deputy-Secretaries, and so on) are filled by men and women from such backgrounds. With few exceptions, studies of community power structure have reinforced the elite thesis (Hunter, 1953; Presthus, 1964; Agger, 1972).

FIGURE 14-2. **Mean Participation Rates of Six Status Groups.**

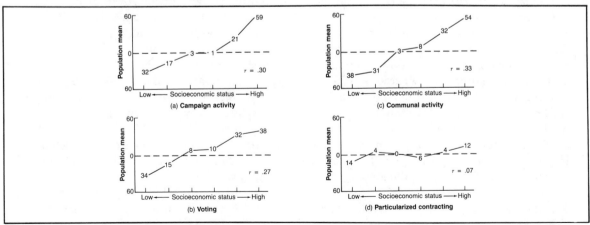

SOURCE: S. Verba and N. Nye, op. cit, p. 132.

Perhaps we may conclude that Western democracy is a unique form of government, operated under a *representative* system that to some extent insulates and isolates the average citizen from a pragmatic governing elite, which, fortunately, is usually motivated by democratic ideals and the rule of law.

SUMMARY

1. The national state, which developed about four centuries ago, has the following characteristics: a defined territory, sovereignty, and a monopoly of the legal use of force.

2. Government is essentially the human and institutional apparatus that manages the state. Its authority and legitimacy stem from the state and its constitution, laws, and traditions.

3. Power may be defined as the capacity of an individual or a group to achieve its ends, despite opposition.

4. In addition to power, the state depends upon *legitimacy* to ensure its dominance. Legitimacy may be defined as moral approval.

5. Three fundamental bases for the legitimacy of state authority exist: traditional, charismatic, and legal-rational.

6. The four forms of government most commonly seen today are: welfare-capitalism, socialism, fascism, and communism.

7. Pluralism, or the extent to which power is diffused throughout a society, is one useful criterion for differentiating the four forms of government.

8. Constitutionalism, or the extent to which a state is governed according to due process of law, is a second vital criterion differentiating the various forms of government.

9. The extent of public participation in the shaping of governmental policy provides another criterion for differentiating the four types of government.

10. Outside of voting, however, it seems that most citizens in all forms of government participate very little in political affairs. They are "spectators" rather than "participants."

GLOSSARY

Authority. The capacity to evoke compliance without (as in "power") possessing sanctions. The Weberian bases of authority are tradition, charismatic, and legal-rational.

Bureaucracy. A system of permanent, appointed officers who carry out the laws, rules and regulations of the state, in accordance with fixed and official jurisdictional areas.

Capitalism. Ideally, an economic and ideological system in which most production elements are privately owned, prices are mainly determined by free market forces of supply and demand, and the role of government in economic spheres is minimal. In the real world, traditional capitalism has been greatly modified by government intervention resulting in a "mixed economy" in Western Europe and North America.

Charisma. A highly individualistic, transitory and pre-bureaucratic type of authority, based essentially upon a personal "gift of grace" which evokes loyalty and obedience from one's followers.

Communism. More positive than fascism, communism believes in equality and the ultimate abolition of classes and of government itself. In practice, however, it has proved as repressive and totalitarian as fascist regimes. Tends to be monistic in assuming that economic structure determines the shape of entire society.

Democracy. May be defined as "government of the people, by the people, and for the people." Pure democracy, however, has rarely existed, whereas *representative* democracy is typical.

Elitism. A sociopolitical system in which power tends to be monopolized by a highly-advantaged minority.

Fascism. A political ideology characterized by negativism, being anti-democratic, anti-parliament, anti-communist, anti-clerical, anti-rational and anti-proletariat. Also totalitarian, leaving no sector of social life outside its control, while seeking national integration through a single party.

Government. The institutional apparatus that carries out the policies and programs of the state.

Legitimacy. The condition whereby the state, government and their official representatives evoke normative approval from those governed.

Participation. The process whereby individuals play a role in political affairs. The usual activities include voting, attending political meetings, contributing to a campaign fund, talking about politics, trying to convince a friend how to vote.

Patriarchy. The most important of the forms of domination existing under traditional forms of authority, usually exercised by the father, husband, elders, patron, prince and nobles.

Pluralism. A sociopolitical system in which political power is broadly shared among a large number of groups, private associations, and individuals.

Power. The capacity of an individual or a group of individuals to achieve their objectives, despite opposition.

Socialism. In its democratic form, is generally positive in its view of the nature of man, the possibility of substituting state economic planning for market determinations, and providing individual security through state welfare programs. Essentially humanitarian and collectivist, it deplores the individualistic competition often seen in liberal-democratic states.

State. The institution that claims a monopoly of the use of force in a given territory, within which it is sovereign.

FURTHER READING

Alford, Robert. *Party and Society: The Anglo-American Democracies.* Chicago: Rand McNally, 1963. An excellent comparative analysis of democratic government in Australia, Canada, Britain, and the United States.

Clement, Wallace. *The Canadian Corporate Elite.* Toronto: McClelland and Stewart, 1975. A careful analysis of elite behavior in the major economic sectors of Canada.

Doern, Bruce G. and A.W. Phidd. *The Politics and Management of Canadian Economic Policy.* Toronto: Macmillan, 1978. A review of how policy is made in the vital area of government spending.

Kornberg, Allen and W. Mishler. *Influence in Parliament.* Durham: Duke University Press, 1976. A behavioral study of interpersonal influence in the federal Parliament.

Macpherson, C.B. *The Real World of Democracy.* Toronto: Canadian Broadcasting Co., 1965. A cogent theoretical discussion of modern democracy and its problems.

Mishler, William. *Political Participation in Canada.* Toronto: Macmillan, 1979. An analysis of political values and citizen participation in Canadian politics.

Porter, John. *The Vertical Mosaic.* Toronto: University Press, 1965. The landmark study of socioeconomic power and elitism in Canadian society.

Presthus, Robert. *Elite Accommodation in Canadian Politics.* New York and London: Cambridge University Press, 1973. The definitive analysis of interest group structure and behavior in Canada.

Scott, F.R. *Essays on the Constitution.* Toronto: University of Toronto Press, 1977. A wide-ranging interpretation of constitutional issues in Canada.

Van Loon, R.J. "Political participation in Canada: the 1965 election." *Canadian Journal of Political Science*, 1970, Volume 3: 376–99. A survey-based analysis of participation levels in a federal election.

Van Loon, R.J. and M. Whittington. *The Canadian Political System.* Toronto: McGraw-Hill Ryerson, Ltd., 1981. This is the best comprehensive review of the main aspects of Canadian government.

CHAPTER FIFTEEN

Economy

NOEL IVERSON

No society can exist that has not solved the problem of providing the material means of satisfying human wants. Efforts to solve this universal problem constitute the sphere of human activity called "economy." The whole process of finding the material means of collective survival is sustained by different groups, technologies, and motives in different kinds of societies. Provisioning for man's livelihood has been the subject of a great deal of investigation and reflection, from ancient times to the present. Aristotle holds the claim to being the first to describe the process of livelihood. He called his discovery by the two names that reveal the difference between working to make money and working to meet the needs of one's group. By the word *oeconomia*, Aristotle meant production for one's own use, as in a household, village, or manor (Polanyi, 1957:53). However, what in Aristotle's time was just beginning to develop — commercial trade — was more difficult to name. This kind of practice Aristotle called *kapêlike*, or money-making by buying cheap and selling dear. He saw it as an "unnatural" activity, a form of hucksterism that benefited individuals at the expense of the community. What was then rare and to Aristotle morally suspect, the sale of goods for private profit, is now a widespread activity. In Aristotle's time, and until the formation of industrial societies in the late eighteenth century, the pursuit of a livelihood everywhere took place not in terms of the production of goods and services for sale on price-making markets (the hallmark of capitalism), but rather in terms of different modes of allocation, as we shall see.

Although there are great differences between economies, all share three basic features. (1) Every society, whether a tribe, village, nation, or empire, consists of people who must eat to stay alive and who cannot leave to chance the provision of material goods necessary for survival. The process of satisfying human material needs is called "economy." (2) All economies make use of natural resources (land), human co-operation (division of labor), and technology (tools and knowledge). This is done on an organized basis, by means of institutions and according to rules of behavior. (3) Virtually all societies make use of similar economic devices, such as market places, money, accounting methods, and trade; however, these devices differ considerably in their organization, social role, and cultural meaning from society to society. They are themselves the result of differences in social relationships and culture (Dalton, 1968: xli-xliii).

There are two ways of looking at the economy, depending on whether society is organized in terms of status or in terms of contract. Generally speaking, in primitive and ancient societies, the economy is based on social relations of status, whereas in modern societies it is based on legal contracts or exchange relations. Whatever form it takes, the economy may be understood as "an instituted process of interaction between man and his environment, which results in a continuous supply of want satisfying material means." (Polanyi, 1971b: 248.) To make sense of any economy, we must identify the institutions that give unity and stability to the economy. Without a system of law, for example, economic conduct in modern industrial societies would lack the element of security it requires, for parties to contracts would be under no legal obligation to honor their agreements. Always there must be an institutional setup — whether a system of price-making markets (safeguarded by law) or a symmetrical system of

kinship groups — to provide the basis for interactions between individuals and groups that will result in a viable economy.

MODES OF ALLOCATION OF GOODS AND SERVICES

Economic behavior is based on three distinct and overlapping principles, which can also be seen as ways of organizing a system of livelihood. They are *reciprocity*, *redistribution*, and *market exchange*. Each involves a particular set of social relationships. Let us look at each briefly.

Reciprocity

Reciprocity refers to the giving and receiving of goods and services between social groupings such as families and clans. It occurs both within a society and between societies. The archetype of reciprocal exchange is exemplified by the Kula ring of the Trobriand Islanders in the western Pacific. Travelling by outrigger canoe in a circle spanning dozens of islands stretched over hundreds of miles of ocean (the Kula ring), lifelong trading partners would periodically exchange long necklaces of red shell for bracelets of white shell. The Kula type of exchange is similar to Christmas gift-giving in Western societies.

The first striking feature of this mode of allocating goods and services is that, materially speaking, it is gainless. In primitive societies, economic activity is not performed for selfish reasons. Primitive man does not work for himself and rarely does he labor exclusively for his own family. Instead, he works for the good of his community, not out of a conscious and calculating desire to get something from others in return.

The second important point about reciprocal exchange is that it is the basis of economic *and* social conduct (primitive man makes no such distinction). Reciprocity links members of the society with one another in a complex network of social obligations. Gift exchange is primitive man's way of cementing social ties, winning allies, and avoid-

Inuit sealers typically redistribute their catch, with each family in the community receiving its prescribed portion.

ing war. Although unplanned (there is no economic policy), reciprocal behavior is guided by custom. In this way, reciprocity provides primitive societies with the staples they require, while also forming the basis of their ceremonial life. By simply meeting their obligations toward one another — without any concept of the economy — the members of primitive societies satisfy their needs.

Redistribution

In more complex societies, another mode of allocation serves to satisfy economic needs, namely, redistribution. It is usually found in conjunction with reciprocal behavior between a people and their chief. The chief, king, or emperor receives gifts in the form of tribute or taxes from his people. He accumulates a storehouse of goods, including foodstuffs, part of which he is bound by custom or law to return to his people. In primitive and archaic societies, this is usually done publicly, in the form of a ceremony accompanied by feasting. In modern societies, both capitalist and communist, the redistribution of wealth is accomplished primarily by state taxation systems, which are noticeably devoid of festive drama. What is essential is a centre (a person or an office), toward which goods and services flow and from which they are redistributed, according to need and status. This process occurs in many societies and is presided over by many kinds of authority.

Ancient societies, whose economic and political activities were based on the redistribution principle, were capable of feats of collective enterprise: the pyramids of Egypt, Hanging Gardens of Babylon, Great Wall of China, Great Temple of the

Aztec, and the unparalleled roads and stone fortresses of the Inca are examples. All societies whose economies are organized, in part or whole, by the principle of redistribution require some kind of central authority to settle the question of who gets what. In societies governed by ruling elites, this method of organizing the production and allocation of goods was usually backed up by an armed force. Kings relied on their footsoldiers and lords on their armed fellow knights to maintain the flow of goods from peasants' fields and artisans' workshops to the tables and treasure rooms of the "nonproducing part of the population, that is, to the officials, the military, and the leisure class." (Polanyi, 1957:52.) However, redistribution occurs in many kinds of societies and not all require enforcement. Small bands of hunters, for example, redistribute their goods voluntarily.

But redistribution is most fully developed in large-scale societies with highly stratified relations and centralized power. Modern industrialized communist societies such as China, Cuba, and the Soviet Union are organized by the principle of redistribution or command. Their capitalist counterparts, such as Great Britain, Japan, and the United States are, to a greater or lesser degree, organized by a different principle (although they too have redistributive modes of allocation), to which we now turn.

Market Exchange

With market exchange, we come to the modern age, whose hallmark is industrialization. In the economic sense, this means the machine production of goods and services by specialized workers, a process that renders traditional methods of production obsolete. Although today both communist and capitalist societies are involved in modernizing their economies, the first economic system associated with machine production is capitalism.

Market exchange, the essence of capitalism, refers to a two-way movement of goods between persons, each of whom seeks to gain from the transaction. What this kind of exchange does is replace all customary and personal economic relationships — whether of tribal partners, fellow guildsmen, lord and serf, or whatever — with a new, calculating, and impersonal relationship. It is a competitive relationship between buyer and seller.

Any good or service produced for sale on a market that realizes its value (price) according to what a buyer is willing to pay for it is a *commodity*. In theory, all that determines the exchange of commodities in a market is the principle of supply and demand; that is, the availability of commodities and one's ability to pay for them. In practice, however, other factors may affect the exchange of goods and services in a market — for example, a privileged group such as the Canadian Medical Association, or a powerful producer such as General Motors, or a big union such as the Teamsters, can bring pressure to bear on the fixing of salaries, prices, or wages.

Free market transactions take place in a competitive atmosphere that is indifferent to need and the use or destination of commodities. Virtually everything — land, labor and its products, and money — can be bought and sold in a market as a commodity. Indeed, some goods, such as grains, oils, and pork bellies, are sold before they are produced.

The futures market is an invention by traders in private-market economies who hope to profit by guessing correctly the forthcoming price, based on scarcity of supply of food, feed grains, and other commodities whose yield is subject to the vagaries of weather, disease, political strife, and the like. Although it can get extremely complicated, futures speculation works basically as follows: In May, a trader offers $8 a bushel for 100 000 bushels of soybeans, which he promises to deliver to Chicago in November. If the selling price of soybeans in November is $10 a bushel, he will make a handsome profit; if soybeans sell for $6 a bushel by then, he will suffer a substantial loss.

As a means of exchange of goods and services, money may take many forms. In certain islands of the South Pacific, the stone on the right will purchase a wife.

MONEY AND MARKET SOCIETY

The enormous variety, flexibility, and impersonality of market transactions is made possible by the use of money. Money is the term assigned to any quantifiable object that is used for hoarding, for payment, as a standard of value, or as a means of exchange of goods and services. In modern society, money is regarded as "general purpose" because it fulfils all the requirements of a modern economy. These are (1) means of payment, (2) standard of value, (3) store of wealth, and (4) medium of exchange. By contrast, primitive and archaic money is "special-purpose" because it serves limited requirements, such as the use of thin and thick copper wires among the Mali, a West African tribe. "Thin wires were poor man's money, exchangeable for firewood and common millet. Thick wires bought anything, including horses, slaves, or gold, indeed all the elite goods that convey standing." (Polanyi, 1977:97, 117–18.)

Generally speaking, in ancient and primitive societies the kind of money one used depended on one's status. In modern societies, the same money is available to all, and is used according to the same rules in all institutional contexts. It takes the form of general purchasing power. Modern money facilitates the calculating and quantifying spirit characteristic of market transactions, a spirit that seems alien and even inimical to nonmarket societies. The chief Finau of Tonga, a South Pacific island society, once remarked, "I understand now very well what it is that makes the Papalangis ['Europeans'] so selfish — it is this money!" (Sahlins, 1974:258.)

For market exchange to prevail, there must be an appropriate kind of society, one whose institutions and values are congenial to bargaining. In a market society, those who make their living by producing goods for sale on markets (manufacturers), or by buying cheap and selling dear (merchants), are generally well regarded. Successful businessmen — the Du Ponts, Rochschilds, Krupps, and Bronfmans — are admired and envied. What animates a society whose heroes are businessmen rather than saints, warriors, or philosopher-kings is an old desire — riches — but it is satisfied in a novel way: not by the kind of booty-taking for which the Vikings and the Mongols were renowned, nor by the direct exploitation of servile labor practised by Roman slave-owners and medieval lords. Instead, wealth is obtained by a regular and systematic deployment of capital toward the production of goods that are for sale in price-making markets. This is the hallmark of capitalist production and exchange, which emerged more than a thousand years after the decline of the Roman Empire to become the dominant mode of economic conduct in Western Europe.

The expanding production of goods by machines, rather than by hands, fed the system of market exchange that, along with the Industrial Revolution, first transformed European society and subsequently affected the entire world. This general process of machine production is known as *industrialization*. Today, it proceeds by two alternate routes: that followed by market societies of the First World (capitalist industrialized nations) and that pursued by nonmarket societies of the Second World (communist industrialized nations). Third World countries are distinguished by a mixture of economies, some inclined toward the free market, others toward state-regulated markets, but all lag behind the pace and scale of industrial development of the first two blocs of nations.

ANCIENT ECONOMY: GREECE AND ROME

No system of market-oriented production is found in the ancient world, where most work was hand work, prices were set, and wealth flowed to elites who shunned toil. While space does not permit a discussion of the range of economies found in antiquity, a review of the two best-known ones, Greece and Rome, will provide the essential characteristics of the ancient economy.

At the core of the ancient Greek and Roman systems of economy we find four dominant features that distinguish them from all other ancient economies: (1) the indispensable deployment of slave labor. (2) Land ownership: possessing land worked by slaves was the surest road to riches in antiquity). (3) The aristocracy and the wealthy generally refrained from those activities that form the basis of riches in the modern world — trade, banking, and manufacture. The elites of Greece and Rome left to individuals of low status, to non-citizens, and to resident aliens the tasks of importing food, slaves, metals, and luxury articles, the construction of houses, temples, and roads, and the manufacture of a wide range of goods — all of which provided opportunities of accumulating considerable wealth. Why? Because the citizen-elites could grow rich without participating in such activities, which they despised and regarded as inappropriate to their social standing and sense of honor. (4) Finally, there is the all but total absence of any form of capitalist enterprise (characterized by free labor, private ownership, organization for the production of goods, long-range investment of capital, planned division of labor by task, and an overall orientation to profits) and of any interest in technological innovation, outside of warfare, or improvement in production techniques.

In ancient Greece, citizenship was based on a fixed minimum property holding and "the ownership of land was an exclusive prerogative of citizens." (Finley, 1973:48.) This legal barrier between citizens and non-citizens had the effect of making it difficult, if not impossible, for many non-citizens who were engaged in trade, manufacture, and money-lending to conduct ordinary business with citizens. They could not buy and sell property, lend money, or foreclose on and accept land as security in loans with citizens. Too well-established to be torn down, this "wall between land and liquid capital" (defined in law) prevented the active pursuit of business between the two major parts of the population. Consequently, there was no significant increase of productivity and no economic rationalism among the Greeks and the Romans.

There was little interest in inventions in the ancient world. A story told by "a number of writers" illustrates this attitude:

A man—characteristically unnamed—invented unbreakable glass and demonstrated it to Tiberius in anticipation of a great reward. The emperor asked the inventor whether anyone else shared his secret, and was assured that there was no one else; whereupon his head was promptly removed, lest gold be reduced to the value of mud.
(Finley, 1982:189.)

It is striking, comments Finley, "that the inventor turned to the emperor for a reward, instead of turning to an investor for capital with which to put his invention into production." The old Romans were not troubled by the inventor's choice because they knew it was a reasonable choice, indeed the only one he could have made in an economy faced with an "extremely low level of demand." Markets for manufactured goods were local, inelastic, and even in big cities easily served by a few small craftsmen working in their own shop (Finley, 1982:190.)

THE FEUDAL INTERLUDE: ELEMENTS OF THE FEUDAL ECONOMY

Subsequent to the fall of Rome in the fifth century A.D., a rebuilding of society took place. Elements of the declining Roman plantation system (*latifundia*) were gradually combined with the agricultural economy of the Northern European village to produce what came to be known as *feudalism*. The emergence of feudalism can be seen as a series of transformations that were to lead

Under the feudal estate system, vassals and serfs served the nobility, who provided protection and goods and services in exchange for taxes, labor, and military and political support.

Western man from slave to free labor, from rural to urban life, and from agriculture to industry.

Feudalism represented a need to reconstitute society into self-contained units of livelihood. For, as Bloch (1961:39–56) has described it, the fall of Rome, precipitated by the invasions of the Northmen, meant the end of a great administrative structure of law and order and the rout of the famed Roman legions, which left the Southern Europeans exposed to the ravages of political chaos, chronic raids, disease, hunger, and death. The once-thriving towns and cities of the empire could no longer sustain a secure and stable way of life. The feudal solution to the problem of organizing a reliable mode of existence was the village, manor, and monastery, all based on agriculture.

The Estate System

Village and manor formed a complex, known as the *estate system*. It ranged in size from those estates consisting of scores of manors and villages spread over thousands of acres to others of one manor supporting a lord of meagre status. All those who lived on the territory of a manor fell under the lord's control. They were either true serfs (legally controlled by a lord) or quasi-serfs (once-free peasants who enjoyed more freedom and possessed greater rights to their land than true serfs). A small minority of tenant families on the estates were slaves, but as they mingled with serfs or were given their freedom, this category of servile labor all but vanished by the later Middle Ages. All serfs were burdened with labor services and dues (in kind or cash) for the profit of the lord, whose wealth came from the land. The soil of the manor was divided into three parts: the demesne or lord's land, the tenants' holdings, and the commons (meadows, marshes, and forests). Serfs worked the lord's land as well as their own holdings, which also supplied the lord's needs. It was on the manorial estate that the peasantry was bound to support the livelihood of the feudal aristocracy. The estate system was, like the Roman plantation system, a self-sufficient agricultural unit. But here much of the similarity between antiquity and the Middle Ages ends.

The essential features of feudalism are its hierarchical division of the agrarian population into status orders and its military-political structure of personal servitude known as vassalage. Medieval society was sharply divided between the peasantry and the aristocracy, which was also a division between those who toiled and those who did not toil. The preservation of this deep division of the population rested on the ability of the aristocracy to establish effective bonds of loyalty and support among their members, for a disunited and acrimonious nobility could not keep the peasant population servile for long. Hence, the medieval landowning aristocracy formed a social hierarchy that dominated the peasantry. At the top of this hierarchy stood the few enormously wealthy and powerful families, the great magnates, who dominated the rest of the aristocracy as well as the rest of society. All the members of the aristocracy were bound together in a vertical relationship by ties of loyalty and support; the dependence of lesser lords, called vassals, on greater lords is known by the term *vassalage*. A vassal would do homage to his lord by swearing an oath of fealty to the lord, and a vassal was expected to offer his lord military service and monetary aid when needed, in exchange for which the lord would support his vassal's interests and reward him for his loyalty by granting him land or movable wealth. This process is called *enfoeffment*, after "fief," a parcel of land.

Granting a fief served two purposes: it enabled the lord to make use of his land and it ensured his authority by organizing its use politically. Those to whom a lord granted rights to land, usually in the form of entitlement to it (and they might include rich peasants), could be counted on for their political and military support.

As for nonvassals, the serfs and quasi-serfs, it was expected and demanded that, in exchange for the lord's protection, they owed him not only labor services but also fees and dues of various kinds, including head taxes, death duties, marriage fees, as well as fees for the use of his flour mill, baking ovens, and forge. This was a system, in other words, of reciprocal rights and obligations, in which the landlords maintained undisputed authority; and it was also a system of redistributive economics, in which the lord-and-manor operated as the institutional funnel of goods and services.

The estate system produced for its own needs, which it was able to satisfy. What little external trade there was — mostly in luxury articles for the landed aristocracy — had weak economic force. Economic equality and a desire to produce only enough for their own needs and to meet the needs of their lord was the general rule among the tenant farmers of the manor.

The Urban Guilds

A similar policy prevailed in the scattered towns and cities of feudal Europe, where there evolved an organization of the guilds. Sometimes compared to modern unions, medieval guilds were associations of craftsmen (craftsmen's guilds) and tradesmen (merchants' guilds). These multipurpose associations of weavers and dyers, tinsmiths and ironmongers, stonemasons, and shipwrights sought to maintain a stable livelihood by restricting competition within the town walls and between town and countryside. These craftsmen were not in business to make money and they outlawed practices that, if left unchecked, would destroy their minutely controlled economy. Thus, besides being economic institutions, guilds also functioned as social institutions that regulated the legal, moral, political, and administrative affairs of the townspeople (Dobb, 1946:88–97).

The power of the guilds did not last, however. It was the inability of the guild producers to control the marketing of their wares on more than a local scale that "gave to merchant capital its golden opportunity." (Dobb, 1946:89.) In the growing competition to control and exploit distant markets, the artisans of the guilds were no match for the merchants of England and the continent, whose superior knowledge (which they kept secret) of distant markets and greater capital resources enabled them to become a powerful class. They often took as silent partners patricians (urban noblemen) and joined with the wealthier burghers (urban merchants) in monopolizing city administration and dominating city politics.

The class that came to dominate city life thus destroyed the spirit of near-equality that had permeated the guilds and the economic life of the medieval cities. They succeeded in gaining control of both the flow of raw materials to guild workshops and the sale of finished goods to markets beyond the legal jurisdiction of the guilds. When this happened, the stage was set for the development of early capitalist production.

As feudalism drew to a close in the fourteenth century, two major changes in the orientation of everyday life occurred: (1) in town and country, men turned from an interest in security and stability of livelihood to an interest in profits; and (2) relationships changed from paternalism and personal subservience to commercialized relations and impersonal service-for-hire. The agrarian estate system and the urban craft association were giving way to a market economy and a capitalist spirit of enterprise.

THE RISE OF MARKET SOCIETY

A general crisis spanning the whole of Europe in the fourteenth century lay waste the economy and left feudal society in disarray. Too complex to summarize this development here, suffice it to say that the result of this crisis, exacerbated by a plague that wiped out two-fifths of the entire European population, was that it left feudal society permanently transformed.

The landowners' attempts to "make the producing class pay the costs of the crisis" by exacting stiffer fees and duties caused the peasants to revolt, which had the consequence of weakening traditional relationships already shaken by the encroaching practice of substituting money payments between lords and subjects for payments in kind (Anderson, 1974:205). Many towns actively supported the rural rebellions, thus deepening the lord-peasant schism. Lords who turned against their riotous peasants, exterminating them like mad dogs, could hardly expect to keep their loyalty.

This struggle for land was linked to the same general process, the commercialization of the European economy, that drew guild artisans into conflict with merchant-capitalists. Originally promoted and protected by lords, the medieval cities gained their autonomy and became centres of trade, banking, and manufacture, thus spearheading the growth of markets and hastening the rise of capitalism (Anderson, 1974:205–08). In town and country, producers were by choice and of necessity gearing their output for cash sale in markets at greater and greater distance from the place of production. As the cost and scale (the two went together) of market-oriented production on large farms and in new factories increased, more and more small producers became unable to compete with large landowners and merchant-capitalists. They were driven into a state of propertylessness, forced to make a living by exchanging for monetary wages the only commodity they still possessed: their labor. They became, in Marx's language, members of the growing army of the proletariat: workers without property of their own on which to make a living (1967:640–48.)

Those who owned property and could hire the labor of others became a distinct class, the *bourgeoisie*. As Marx and Engels stated centuries later, the architect of a vast social and economic transformation — the bourgeoisie — was the true harbinger of the market system. Although space does not permit even a brief discussion of the origins and changing social position of the bourgeoisie (and the proletariat), or even a review of the factors that prepared the way for the bourgeoisie's historical ascendency as a class, it is important to recognize that its appearance marks the critical passage from feudal economy to market economy.

MARKET SOCIETY AND ITS THEORISTS

It is the nature of new social formations, including economic systems, to become the subject of a great deal of commentary, much of it at first confused and not a little erroneous. The market system is no exception. It has preoccupied some of the best minds of the West ever since Adam Smith (1723–1790), the father of modern economic thought, turned to the question: what is the true source of the wealth of a nation?

Smith's Optimistic Forecast

In his famous *The Wealth of Nations* (1776), Smith correctly grasped the essential feature of the early industrial economy, namely its production of goods for sale on price-making markets. His analysis of market economy focused on the social relationships which determine the share-out of the total product." (Lichtheim, 1965:169.) It was Smith who saw the labor-saving benefits derived from having ten persons divide their labor by task rather than by product (which was the way of medieval craftsmen). For example, instead of each man performing all pin-making operations himself, Smith advised that by assigning each stage of the process to a different workman, the same ten individuals could increase their daily output of pins from ten to twenty to as many as 48 000 — and with no increase in effort. In a little more than a century later, Henry Ford was to amaze the world by applying Smith's principle to the production of automobiles.

With a division of labor and with the aid of machines increasing their output, people were merely giving expression, argued Smith, to a common human tendency, self-interest. For it is through reciprocal self-interest that people are most capable of achieving a common goal, which is the satisfaction of the needs of all. By the selfish pursuit of gain Smith had in mind not the atomistic individual looking out for him/herself, but rather small groups of co-operative producers — cobblers, wheelwrights, ironsmiths, clothiers — competing with other small producers. He showed how the economic pursuit of self-interest would result in "social harmony" and "universal opulence." Furthermore, the self-regulating market would prevent any serious disruption of the livelihood of the working poor *as long as the economy remained competitive*. There had to be "perfect liberty," by which he meant the absence of any combinations of workmen or masters (unions or monopolies), or any interference by the state in the self-adjusting mechanism of the free, competi-

The principle of division of labor, on which this auto assembly line is based, is credited to eighteenth-century economist Adam Smith.

tive market. This is an important stipulation, for self-interest alone did not guarantee the self-regulatory mechanism of the market.

But the market system failed to work its wonders, as Smith felt it must if left alone. In late eighteenth-century England, vast parts of the population in the cities and in the countryside were becoming poor and miserable, and nobody understood why. Obviously, the poor were not being dealt with as Smith said they would in a free market. There had to be some underlying, pervasive force that accounted for (and therefore justified) the deepening division between the rich and the poor, argued Smith's successors, most notably David Ricardo.

Ricardo's Gloomy Vision

Ricardo (1772–1823), just twenty-seven years after Smith died, turned Smith's optimistic forecast of a society of universal opulence into a dismal image of a human jungle in which individuals and classes were locked in desperate combat. What Ricardo found when he looked at market society was "a bitter contest for supremacy": powerful and wealthy industrialists were challenging the only other class, "the great landowners," who resented the capitalists' insistence that food prices were too high. Whereas the capitalists demanded free trade, which translated into cheap food imports, the landlords were determined to protect their interests in the form of tariffs on imported grain. The capitalists insisted that only low-priced grain could keep down wages. The lines of battle over the Corn Laws were thus drawn. In studying this clash of economic interests, Ricardo concluded that the fundamental reality of economics was not co-operation and concord but vicious conflict. (As we shall see, Marx was to seize upon this aspect of Ricardo's economics.)

However, Ricardo failed to understand the workings of the market system. He mistakenly believed that the operation of the self-regulating market flowed from the inexorable laws of Nature. And since no one of his time fully grasped the laws of the self-regulating market, Ricardo's cardinal error did not lessen the widespread enthusiasm for his theory.

This failure to identify the true workings of the market system is seen in Ricardo's approach to wages. He argued that wages cannot rise above a subsistence level, and that the value (not the price) of goods is measured by the amount of labor involved in their production. This idea has been called the "iron law of wages," which was meant to account for the paradox that despite the rising productivity of British industry, the material conditions of the laboring poor were as bad as ever and growing worse. The iron law of wages kept the earnings of laborers so low that poverty was their inevitable lot.

Accepting Malthus's untested argument that the human population is regulated by the quantity of food, Ricardo concluded that the weak would succumb to "Nature's penalty," hunger. "The laws of a competitive society were put under the sanction of the jungle," where only the fittest survive (Polanyi, 1957:125). This idea was later developed by the Social Darwinists.

Yet for all Ricardo's bleak portrayal of the outcome of market competition, his labor theory of value rescued mankind from the worst consequences of Nature. "The value of a commodity, or the quantity of any other commodity for which it will exchange, depends on the relative quantity of labour which is necessary for its production, and not on the greater or less compensation which is paid for that labour." (Ricardo, 1953:11.) How then should price be arrived at in the exchange of a commodity for money? According to the amount of labor that went into producing it, replied Ricardo.

In Ricardo's answer, Marx saw his opportunity to revolutionize "bourgeois" economic thought, which he regarded as a thinly disguised defence of the status quo.

Marx's Apocalyptic Solution

Marx (1818–1883) saw that Ricardo had failed to explain where profit came from. He knew that he had to demonstrate not only where profit came from, but that it did not go to those who produced it — the workers.

This he did by analyzing the nature of capitalism. Marx argued that its essence is the pursuit of profit, which occurs by means of a particular mode of exchange. It is market exchange that "proceeds from money to money by way of commodity and which has this peculiarity: that at the end of the process of exchange you have a greater sum of money than you had initially." (Aron, 1965:125.)

Since nonmarket exchange (barter and gift-exchange) does not yield a profit, only market exchange poses a mystery: How does one end up with more than one started with? Marx thought he had solved this puzzle in his *theory of surplus value*. Going beyond Ricardo, Marx argued that the value of all products is determined by the quantity of labor incorporated in them. Labor's value is arrived at in the same way as for any other commodity and is represented by a wage paid to the worker that is equal to the amount of labor necessary to produce the goods the worker and his family need for their existence. Marx called this quantity of labor "necessary labor time." But, he argued, the hours the worker devotes to producing a value equal to what he receives in wages are less than the total number of hours he works. The difference between the worker's necessary labor time, represented by his wages, and the actual duration of his workday may be called "surplus labor time," said Marx. This belongs to the employer, not the worker, and constitutes the employer's "surplus-value" or profit (1967:184–98, 303).

Surplus-value represents, said Marx, the degree of exploitation of the worker by the capitalist. The

In the nineteenth century, the independent peddler's wagon was a welcome sight in Canada's remote rural areas, where manufactured goods were in scarce supply.

higher the surplus-value (profit), the greater the rate of exploitation. Having demonstrated to his satisfaction the essentially exploitative nature of capitalism, Marx proceeded to show why it is certain that just as slavery gave way to feudalism and feudalism to capitalism, so will capitalism eventually collapse and be replaced by socialism.

In explaining what it is that propels the course of history from simple to complex means of livelihood, Marx distinguished between the *forces of production*, which consist of the raw materials, technology, and labor power, and the *relations of production*, which appear as class relations and forms of ownership (the economic structure of society). He went on to say that (1) the forces of production are primary and determine the relations of production, and (2) at certain moments in the evolving relationship between the forces and relations of production there occurs an intense contradiction between the two that is so great that it leads to the breakdown of society's economic structure. These are revolutionary periods of history, marked by fierce class struggles.

At a certain moment in history a new class will emerge, the propertyless laborers or proletariat, which is destined to supplant the bourgeoisie and so create in socialism the modern world's first, truly classless society. No state will succeed socialism, for socialism will be perfected in communism and the final abolition of private property, class rule, and human exploitation.

Marx chose to analyze society and history from a materialist standpoint, thus relegating ideas and ideals primarily to the service of economic (class) interests. Other students of economy and society have made a strong case for a different proposition: that ideas and ideals, expressed in the context of politics, religion, art, and science, have played a decisive role in determining the shape and application of the forces of production. Wars have often been fought for ideals, often with devastating effects upon economies.

Weber's Stoical Reinterpretation

The sociologist who carried out the most brilliant reinterpretation of Marx's account of capitalism was Max Weber (1864-1920). Weber rejected Marx's materialist thesis as being too one-sided. And although he shared Marx's contention that every economic act is also a social act, he could not accept Marx's argument that the form of economy "presupposes a definite kind of society."

Weber broadened Marx's understanding of the alienation of the propertyless employee and shifted Marx's emphasis from the economically exploitative and class-ridden character of the system to a more general conception of capitalism as a way of life. For Weber saw both capitalism *and* socialism as expressions of the modern drive to rationalize life — that is, make it calculable and routine according to formal principles.

Weber added to Marx's conception of the class nature of capitalist society a dimension Marx tended to ignore, namely, *status*. This addition draws attention to "the value aspect of group relationships," for a status group is formed not simply on the basis of shared material interests (which is a class, said Weber), but also on the basis of a shared sense of honor and a certain style of life. Money and property alone do not suffice as qualifications of status, although they may lead to status. "The class position of an officer, a civil servant or a student," said Weber, "may vary greatly according to their wealth and yet not lead to a different status since upbringing and education create a common style of life." (1968:306.)

An appreciation of the vital role sometimes played by "ideal and spiritual motives" in the for-

mation of societies and their economies led Weber to conduct a series of studies of how economic and religious factors have fused to produce some of the world's great social transformations. In *The Protestant Ethic and the Spirit of Capitalism*, published in 1904-05, Weber posed the question: where did the change in moral outlook come from that made it possible for businessmen to go about their affairs in good conscience? Weber was well aware of the fact that early capitalists behaved in ways the traditional Church regarded as spiritually outrageous. His answer to this question was found in a source that others had never thought to look at: in religion itself. In religion lies the distinctive "spirit" of capitalist enterprise — and also its justification. This spirit was incubated at the dawn of the Protestant Reformation by Martin Luther and thrust into sixteenth-century European society by the revolutionary theologian of the Puritan transformation, John Calvin.

It was Calvin who, in his doctrine of predestination, provided a vision of man that helped to explain the strong sense of compulsion that seemed to underlie the everyday conduct of the individual in market society. Very few, Calvin taught, are elected for salvation; the majority are condemned to eternal damnation. This doctrine invited the followers of Calvin to lead lives of ascetic vigilance, to be hard on themselves (and others) in their unswerving pursuit of fame and fortune. Here was the key to the Protestant ethic of work. This ethic gave the early capitalists a sense of "light-hearted assurance" that they must be among God's chosen ones *because* they engaged in intense worldly activity. Although such conduct could not in itself prove anything, it was interpreted as a sign of grace and it bolstered the self-confidence of the Puritans. Those who preached Calvin's doctrines warned against all temptations of sloth, greed, and the flesh that would weaken the individual's resolve to labor faithfully and diligently in his vocation or calling.

What Weber explained was how religion legitimized gainful economic activity and made it a calling, for "now every Christian had to be a monk all his life." Now man could engage in the activity of the market, his appetite for material gain curbed only by the teachings of Protestantism. As the era of capitalism dawned, the pious Christian was encouraged to do what to Aristotle was an offence against society and to Acquinas a sin against God.

The decline of the Protestant ethic has been the subject of considerable investigation and debate since Weber raised it as a sociological question. The idea of a calling appears archaic in the modern world. Few understand it; fewer still are moved by it. Once the capitalist division of labor had been established, Calvinism's internal restraints upon economic conduct, as well as its goad to labor, were no longer necessary. Instead, the external constraints of the capitalist workplace force the individual into compliance. Weber came close to Marx's position in suggesting that mature capitalism would have no need of Puritan asceticism, for dedication to one's calling was an anachronism, concluded Weber.

The existence of many Third World economies still rests on the strength of the human back.

THE RATIONAL STATE AND MODERN ECONOMY

By 1920, the year of Weber's death, the world had undergone massive changes. Chief among these changes was the increasing role of the state in the structure and operation of the economy.

The modern state and economy, communist as well as capitalist, is a rationally ordered system of authority and production. Although the distribution of the social product (expressed as the Gross National Product, or totality of goods and services produced by a society in a year) takes place by different means (private versus public) in the two systems, in both cases the bureaucratization of life presses relentlessly onward. In both capitalist and communist industrial societies, there is a continuous erosion of traditional religious values and a general secularization of life, as science,

industry, and the state form the troika of contemporary man's journey into an uncertain future.

State Intervention: in Capitalism

The history of capitalism has been a history of state protectionism, financing, and "participation" (called "intervention" by those who regard the latter an inappropriate meddling of the state in the market). Ever since the Age of Discovery, when the New World was being opened up for conquest, followed by settlement and economic development, private entrepreneurs have found the state a ready and willing ally in their often insatiable quest for riches and profits, whether by outright seizure of native gold or by the far more lucrative exploitation of natural resources through the use of slave and cheap immigrant labor.

As early as 1672, British adventurers found government support in the launching of the Royal

African Company, which "was to deal chiefly in negroes for which there appeared to be an expanding demand in the English colonies." (Polanyi, 1966:18.) More successful were other chartered companies, notably the British East India Company (1600-1874) and the Hudson's Bay Company (1668-1869). Both were given trading monopolies and acquired quasi-government control over huge areas and their populations. These and many other nations' semi-public companies formed the advance guard of European capitalism's first wave of world expansion. As often as not, they were based upon the unlikely partnership (times were changing) of capitalist adventurer and courtly gentleman, of merchants and courtiers, whose efforts helped to open up the markets and obtain the raw materials needed by the "captains of industry" whom Carlyle felt would, with wisdom and prudence, guide the course of the Industrial Revolution.

The state has also been a chief purchaser of materials produced by private industry. Iron and steel production, for example, the "material base of the Industrial Revolution" and essential to every industrial society, was, in the nineteenth century, stimulated by the catalytic role of the state. Great Britain's iron production by 1848 was almost two million tons, more than the rest of the world put together (Landes, 1969:95). Such output, in Britain and elsewhere, was earmarked partly for state use and was often hastened in the first place by state requirements. This happened during the French Revolution when the British technique for smelting iron, known as "puddling," supplied the French with a way to produce large quantities of malleable wrought iron for manufacturing cannon. This possibility was seized upon by French entrepreneurs and officials, who collaborated closely in arms production, with the government providing interest-free loans. Hence, the state was the assured market essential for the establishment of the French iron industry.

During the two-and-a-half centuries of industrialization, there have been many instances of such crucial state support, often in the form of arms contracts, of risky and technologically innovative private ventures as the making of modern seige guns (McNeill, 1982:211-12). Prussia's early armament works, the United States' current aerospace industry, and Canada's jet aircraft program represent the time-honored practice of underwriting costly ventures in the private sector, or buying them outright, with public funds. This has always been easiest for government to do when a country's national security is deemed to be at stake.

The Military-Industrial State

Government participation in the economy has reached unparalleled dimensions with the installation of the welfare state and the advent of the horrendously expensive conventional and nuclear arms race. On the domestic front, attacks upon the problem of economic inequality and security have appeared as wars on poverty, extended federal pensions and social-security benefits, allowed for greater unemployment insurance and medical coverage, increased urban renewal and educational support schemes, public housing, mother's allowance, and welfare payments.

Military requirements have profoundly influenced the nature and direction of modern industrial societies, whose defence expenditures have reached astronomical proportions: the U.S. military budget projection for 1981-1985 is over $1 trillion (Rothschild, 1982:19). Such costs by the "military subeconomy," a fixture of most nations, have a pronounced effect upon the well-being of the vast majority of mankind and bear most heavily upon the poor (Heilbroner, 1980:183-86). Meeting rising military needs has led to what some have called the "warfare state" or the "national security state." (Its Soviet version is the "total security state.") The warfare state signifies an increasing "penetration" of market economy by political and military interests. In practical terms, this has resulted in the proliferation of close alliances between businessmen and the military, which leads to a mutual identification of interests and sharing of views, which tends to "civilianize" the military and militarize the civilian population. The network of such alliances has been called the "military-industrial complex" (McNeill, 1982: 317–61), over which the state presides. This complex is found in Western as well as in Soviet-bloc nations, although the social and political consequences of militarization are not the same for NATO Alliance and Warsaw Pact countries. However, on both sides of the Great Divide there is a common, underlying process at work: the bureaucratic management of the economy.

Ownership and Management: the Western Economy

With the rise of the modern welfare state and the development of a scientific-industrial-military order, the individual experiences the extension of formal means of control into virtually every sphere of his or her life. The long-time intimate connection between the development of the capitalist economy and the growth of the state has culminated in what Weber described as a distinguishing trait of modern capitalism, namely, the bureaucratic organization of society that tends toward "an absolutely inescapable control over our entire existence." With the retreat of the market as the organizing principle of economic life and with the growing prominence of large-scale organizations — corporations, unions, government bureaus, and military and political bodies — the need to plan, manage, and control human behavior becomes evermore pressing and is expressed more forcefully than ever before.

The ownership and management of Western economies have undergone a massive transformation since the nineteenth century. That transformation may be described in one word: *concentration*. The fierce and often ruinous competitiveness of American business enterprise during the latter half of the nineteenth century led to desperate measures as entrepreneurs sought to gain financial control of an industry. Heilbroner

(1980:109) tells of one such epic engagement between two railroad magnates, James Fisk and J.P. Morgan.

They found themselves in the uncomfortable position of each owning a terminal at the end of a single line. Like their feudal prototypes, they resolved the controversy by combat, mounting locomotives at each end and running them full tilt into each other—after which the losers still did not give up, but retired, ripping up the line and tearing down trestles as they went.

Eventually, the great men of business found a less costly way to reduce the risk of unrestrained competition. They created *monopolies* (markets served entirely by one seller) in two main ways: through mergers (buying up one's competitors) and through internal growth. They also formed *conglomerates* — by merging with corporations in a different market (International Telephone & Telegraph owns Avis, operates the Sheraton Hotel chain, and involves itself in a host of unrelated manufacturing and financial enterprises). Mergers are the most effective means of eliminating competition and thus of reducing the risk of loss to investors. So are *oligopolies* (markets shared by a few sellers), such as the division of the North American automobile market among, principally, General Motors, Ford Motors, and American Motors. In the modern system, therefore, the risk of cutthroat competition has largely been overcome by changing the structure of the market and by changing tactics. Whenever possible, administered prices (set by firms and supported by governments) replace market prices, and oligopolists have generally agreed not to disturb the market by engaging in out-and-out price warfare.

Corporations, many of them multinationals, do not merely meet the wants of consumers; they create these wants and anticipate them through continuous and costly market surveys and advertising campaigns. (In his satirical work, *The Theory of Business Enterprise*, American economist

Thorstein Veblen called this "parasitism.") In the United States, business expenditures on advertising jumped from $50 million in 1867, to $542 million in 1900, and to $33 billion in 1976. The latter figure represents one-half of the nation's "total expenditures for public elementary and secondary education," and well exceeds in purchasing power Canada's federal budget deficit of $31 billion for 1983 (Heilbroner, 1980:127).

The concentration of industry through "spontaneous internal growth" has been the fundamental tendency of capitalist enterprise in the United States, Canada, and elsewhere. About 500 U.S. corporations, in number a tiny fraction of a total of 14.7 million U.S. businesses, account for two-thirds of all industrial sales and control from 70 percent to more than 80 percent of all the assets in some sectors of the economy (Heilbroner, 1980: 119–20). Corporate concentration in Canada displays a high degree of foreign ownership, the implications of which have been the subject of a protracted and often heated debate. Of the 335 corporations in Canada for which there is information on the country that controls them, less than half (44 percent) are Canadian-owned. This means that "a significant part of Canadian industry is within the hands of big blocs of 'outside' shareholders." (Dhingra, 1983:31–32.)

As everyone knows, wealth and income are unequally distributed in all monetized societies, and the extent of such inequality varies a great deal from one country to the next. Canada's income distribution is more equal than that of most nations. Still, in 1977 the top 50 percent of the Canadian population (families and unattached individuals) owned 95 percent of the nation's wealth, leaving the bottom half with only 5 percent. Similarly, in 1977 the top 20 percent of the population earned 42 percent of the total national income, whereas the bottom 20 percent received only 3.8 percent. These disparities in wealth and income have remained fairly intact since at least 1951.

In the West, private ownership of corporations, banks, and insurance companies continues to determine in great measure the life chances of hundreds of millions of individuals. However widespread and permanent government participation in the economy is, Western capitalism remains largely a system of private ownership that controls the means of production. Modern large-scale enterprises characteristically are controlled by families who, through interrelations among the families of officers, directors, and principal shareholders of the major corporations, form the top echelon of America's family capitalists. Far from having been replaced by a managerial elite, American capitalists, since the 1920s, have grown more cohesive as competition between firms has decreased, control of markets by monopoly or oligopoly has increased, capital has become concentrated, and the alliance of bankers and industrialists has become more intimate. A similar class of family capitalists exercises domination over the Canadian economy. Moreover, the state is not a decisive owner of financial, industrial, or commercial property in the United States or Canada. It has not, by and large, usurped the property function of the capitalists, who still exert dominant control over enterprise in the capitalist economies of the West.

AUTHORITY AND FREEDOM IN INDUSTRIAL SOCIETY

One result of the structural and operational changes in the Western market system, modified and abetted by the state, is the gradual substitution of one kind of authoritarian control for another. The harsh taskmaster of early capitalism, the charismatic founder and owner of industry, brooked no interference by the state in the running of his business and regarded unions as a threat to his absolute authority. In his place today is the professional manager, operating in a bureaucratized environment, who applies routine solutions to standard problems and utilizes the "science" of human relations in securing the allegiance and compliance of workers. In the United States, Canada, and elsewhere, "there is increasing evidence of a managerial collectivism in large-scale economic enterprises (that) poses the "threat of totalitarianism." (Bendix, 1963:337-38.)

But there are countervailing appeals that weaken the authoritarian influence of the large-scale economic enterprise over the worker. Chief among these are the appeals of trade unions, which invite the worker to maintain his independence from managerial control. In the liberal-democratic societies of the West, the organized working classes, through industrial bargaining and the formation of labor parties, are capable of exercising power in opposition to the state and the corporation. Moreover, since the Great Depression, a set of entitlements, known as "citizenship rights," have been forged — rights of equal treatment before the law, the right to form political parties, the right to vote, and rights of social assistance for the needy. These underpin the freedom and preserve the economic security of citizens in Western industrial societies (Marshall, 1950).

No such safeguards exist in communist industrialized societies, where the separation of the political and the economic is not in evidence. In communist (or "state socialist") societies, the state "has a greater range of powers over the individual citizen ... than in the capitalist liberal democracies." (Giddens, 1982:176.) The powers of the state extend throughout the economy, for the state has displaced the capitalist as employer: everyone works for the state. Writing in 1916, Weber foresaw the consequences of this system of economy "in which the entrepreneur had no part. Who would then," asked Weber, "take control of and direct this new economy?" Here is his answer:

In public enterprises ... and those established by purposive associations, the powerfully and exclusively dominant figure is the official: *it is not the worker, who has a harder task to achieve anything by striking in this kind of organisation than when dealing with a private entrepreneur. It is the dictatorship of the official, not that of the worker, which, at present anyway, is on the advance.*

(Weber, 1978:260.)

In recent years, such newly industrialized countries as Taiwan, Hong Kong, and Singapore have begun to compete with the West in production of electrical components, petroleum products, and textiles.

On both sides of the line that divides capitalist and communist nations, there is at work a common, underlying process: the regulation of the economy for state purposes. It has reached total proportions in the planned economies of the communist world. However, as Weber saw, as long as "the political bureaucracy of the state and the economic bureaucracy of private enterprise ... exist alongside each other as separate bodies," economic power will not be monopolized by the state and political power can curb the exercise of economic power (Weber, 1978:255). So far, in the West, there has been no totalitarian control of the economy; only during national emergencies has the state interceded to suspend the unregulated interaction between labor and management. Such control will be achieved only when industrial leaders and union leaders are required to serve the *same* political organization, as they do in the one-party states of Eastern Europe.

SUMMARY

1. The human economy, which everywhere appears as a set of solutions to the problem of man's material livelihood, has taken many forms. A historically recent and tradition-destroying form of livelihood is the market system. It rests on the principle of producing goods and services for sale on price-making markets for private gain.

2. The entire range of human economies, past and present, may be analyzed according to three distinct and overlapping principles of allocation, namely, reciprocity, redistribution, and market exchange. While all three of these modes of allocation may be present in modern industrial societies, the latter is all but absent in primitive and archaic societies. Market exchange has been most highly developed in capitalist societies of modern times.

3. The key integrative principle of advanced capitalist and communist societies is redistribution. Thoroughly applied in communist countries, it also forms a basis, alongside the market mechanism, of much of economic life in capitalist states.

4. A capitalist economy is marked by impersonal, calculating relationships, specialization of task, generalized use of money, and a systematic deployment of capital for the production of goods destined for sale on price-making markets.

5. Ancient economies were organized along nonmarket lines and were maintained by political, military, and religious elites who commanded large forces of involuntary labor. The ownership of land and the slaves who worked the land formed the most widespread way of accumulating wealth in antiquity.

6. Feudal economy, which arose as a solution to the problem of livelihood in the aftermath of a decaying empire, was anti-market in spirit and operation. Yet it formed the basis of the Industrial Revolution and the rise of capitalism.

7. While Smith felt that by allowing the free market to operate without interference English society would be harmonious and everyone's livelihood would be improved, Ricardo said that England was locked into a bitter class struggle and that the working class, whose labor was the source of all value, would be denied its rightful share of the nation's wealth.

8. Marx saw that workers have to exchange their labor for wages because they have no significant property of their own, but that their wages are generally lower than the value of the labor they supply the capitalist. The difference between workers' wages and the value of their labor-time is the source of the capitalist's profits and the measure of his exploitation of their labor. Eventually, the struggle between the workers and the capitalists will lead to a revolutionary breakdown of capitalism, which will be succeeded by socialism and then communism, the final stage of history.

9. Weber suggested that the alienation of wage-earners and their loss of ownership of the means of production is part of a general process, affecting socialist and capitalist countries, the bureaucratic organization of economy and society. This process initially was encouraged by the Protestant Reformation, which made it possible for individuals to enrich themselves without risking the salvation of their souls. No such justification of economic conduct is necessary in the modern world.

10. Ever since its inception, the market economy has been aided in its operation by the state, which has provided corrective action to insure its optimal performance, such as by protecting and stimulating investment, underwriting research and education, and engaging in military and nonmilitary forms of spending.

11. Although its competitive race for profits was nurtured by the early state and justified by the early Puritans, capitalism has since become a bureaucratized machine that is guaranteed state support and that has found workable substitutes for free competition in market controls.

12. Modern Western economies are dominated by large-scale organizations that keep competition to a minimum by forming monopolies and oligopolies; ownership and control of significant means of production remain in the hands of small groups of interconnected family capitalists, and the state plays a major role in the regulation of enterprise.

GLOSSARY

Bourgeoisie. The class of property-owners or capitalists whose livelihood rests on their investments in commercial, banking and manufacturing ventures.

Commodity. Any good or service produced for sale on a price-making market. Includes land, labor and money, all of which may be regarded for the purposes of exchange.

Conglomerate. A super corporation, formed through mergers of corporations in different markets.

Economy. An instituted process between a people and their environment that supplies the material means for satisfying material needs.

Economic rationality. The choice among scarce means (money, labor, materials) made on the basis of the technically most efficient alternative within a situation of price-making markets.

Enfeoffment. The practice by feudal lords and monarchs of granting rewards in the form of rights to land to individuals who have pledged their loyalty or rendered some service, usually military or political, to their superior.

Estate system. An organizational complex and form of society typical of the Middle Ages, consisting of the village and the manor and dominated by a lord and his vassals.

Feudalism. A system of land tenure and labor control based on the lord-vassal-serf relationship, in which a few (lords and vassals) dominate the many (serfs and peasants) by means of their superior military power, political organization and patriarchal command of the loyalty of their tenants.

Fief. A personal contract between a lord and his vassal which entitles the vassal to certain rights, normally to the use of land but also to the exercise of authority, in exchange for his meeting certain obligations owing to the lord.

Forces of production. The raw materials, technology and labor utilized in producing goods and services.

Futures market. The practice of offering to purchase certain commodities, such as feed grains and oil, at an agreed price before they are produced, in the hope of selling them when they are available at a price higher than the one agreed to.

General-purpose money. Any article that serves as a means of payment, a standard of value, a store of wealth, or a medium of exchange.

Industrialization. The process of substituting machine-based production of goods and services for simple handicraft production.

Labor theory of value. The idea that the value of any commodity, including labor, depends on the quantity of labor-time that went into producing it.

Laissez-faire. The doctrine that an economy works best without government interference or regulation of any kind. Free trade and the self-regulating market in money, land and labor are its main tenets.

Latifundia. Large agrarian estates of antiquity owned by a class of landlords and worked by a class of involuntary, usually slave, laborers.

Market exchange. A vice-versa movement of goods and services between buyers and sellers under a market system, the purpose of which is to realize a gain.

Market system. The organization of human livelihood according to an integrated system of price-making markets, in which the value of all goods and services is determined by how much they will fetch.

Manor. The administrative hub of the medieval estate.

Monopoly. The domination of a market by one seller.

Oligopoly. A situation in which a few large sellers share a market and are able to influence the movement of prices, usually in their favor.

Protestant ethic. A religious interpretation and justification of life that regards a sober-minded and frugal dedication to work as a sign of the individual's spiritual worthiness.

Reciprocity. The exchange of goods and services between symmetrical social groupings. Common to primitive societies.

Redistribution. A form of economic integration and allocation in which goods and services are funnelled into an institutional centre and handed back to the population. Characteristic of all complex societies.

Relations of production. The class relations and forms of ownership that spring out of forces of production and constitute the economic structure of society.

Vassalage. A system of personal servitude based on an oath of loyalty sworn by a vassal, who is bound in life-long allegiance to his lord and who receives in return a landed benefit or fief.

FURTHER READING

Finley, M.I. *The Ancient Economy.* Berkeley: University of California Press, 1973. A historical and theoretical discussion of Graeco-Roman civilization and its economy by the leading English-speaking student of the subject. Erudite and a pleasure to read, it has no substitute.

Heilbroner, Robert L. *The Making of Economic Society.* 6th edition. Englewood Cliffs, N.J.: Prentice-Hall, 1980. A valuable summary of the development of modern industrial capitalism by an economist known for his lucid treatment of complex issues. Updated for the 1980s.

Landes, David S. *The Unbound Prometheus.* Cambridge: Cambridge University Press, 1969. A comprehensive history of the Industrial Revolution and its aftermath, providing a wealth of detail on the social, economic, and political effects of industrialization in Britain, France, and Germany.

McNeill, William H. *The Pursuit of Power.* Chicago: University of Chicago Press, 1982. A timely work on an important but neglected subject, its author traces the relationship since ancient times between military power, technology, and economy in the rise of empires and nations. A prodigious feat of historical synthesis, it provides a sobering glimpse of mankind's capacity for self-destruction.

Polanyi, Karl. *The Great Transformation.* Boston: Beacon Press, 1957. A masterly interpretation of the social and ethical implications of the rise of market economy in the context of political, ideological, and theoretical movements of the nineteenth century. A modern classic, it is still the only book of its kind.

Sahlins, Marshall. *Stone Age Economics.* London: Tavistock, 1974. An original and penetrating study of the nature of primitive economy and its cultural foundations. Provides a comparative and theoretical understanding of tribal economics that sheds much light on modern economic life.

Weber, Max. *The Protestant Ethic and the Spirit of Capitalism.* Translated by Talcott Parsons. New York: Charles Scribner's Sons, 1958. A famous interpretation of the historical affinity between religious ideals and (capitalist) economic action, and that continues to have vast relevance to understanding the world.

PART V

Social Inequality

The theme of this section is the many forms of social inequality that exist in all societies, including our own. In any given society, people constantly evaluate and rank one another in terms of power, prestige, and wealth. This process of grading people is known as social stratification, and sociologists inform us that there is no society that is not stratified in some way.

The notion of social inequality has a long historical development. The tendency to rank people was less evident among the historic hunting-and-gathering societies and its consequences were less marked. (Anthropological literature dealing with contemporary simple societies supports this view.) Part of the reason for this was that whatever limited resources existed, were shared. But once people began establishing stable, agrarian communities, and once individuals started producing surplus goods and accumulating these more than others, we witnessed the emergence of stratification, typical of societies today.

The chapter on stratification discusses the criteria used in ranking people and the sociological theories used to explain the existence of inequality. The remaining chapters argue that race, ethnicity, sex, and age are some of the criteria invariably used in contemporary societies to discriminate against and deny people their share of resources.

CHAPTER SIXTEEN

Social Stratification

DONALD VON ESCHEN

Anthropologists tell us that for almost all of its existence, humankind lived in small hunting-and-gathering bands, earning their living by hunting wild animals and gathering wild fruits. Studies of contemporary hunting-and-gathering societies, such as the Kung bushmen of southwest Africa or the Inuit of northern Canada, have revealed remarkably egalitarian societies, that is, members of these groups differ little in material wealth, status, and power (Service, 1979).

From the standpoint of equality, therefore, humanity seems to have been born in a state of grace. This was not to last, however, as the transition was made to agriculture, and as technology progressed. With the development of agrarian civilizations, differentiation took place, along with inequalities between the various segments of society.

In the Roman Empire, for example, as much as one-third of the population on the Italian peninsula were slaves. These slaves were acquired in the constant wars fought by Rome, and many were used to farm vast landed estates, known as latifundia. The inequality between free men and slaves was paralleled by great differences among the free population itself. The latifundia were owned by a small group of Roman aristocrats with legal privileges such as access to the principal governing body, the senate. Some of these aristocrats owned 1000 or more slaves. In contrast, most Roman citizens not only were without slaves, they also lost much of their land to the aristocracy. The dispossessed farmers, as a result, were compelled either to migrate to Rome, where they lived on welfare (state doles of grain), or to find land in the provinces, often in plots of only 1/40 000th the size of a latifundia (Hopkins, 1978).

This system eventually collapsed and was replaced in Western Europe by a system of almost as great inequalities. In feudalism (Block, 1961), the population was divided mainly into (1) a small group of titled nobles or lords, many of whom possessed one or more landed estates known as manors; and (2) a large class of peasants who lived and worked on these estates. The lord was often a kind of king, having considerable legal control over the manorial population. The peasants, known as serfs, occupied a position half-way between slavery and freedom. In contrast to slaves, they could not be sold by the lord; but in contrast to free men, they could not leave the manor without the lord's permission, and they were required to devote a substantial number of days a year to work on what was known as the "domain" land of the lord, as well as pay taxes or dues. By these means, the lord appropriated as much as half the output produced by the peasants, with the result that most peasants lived at the subsistence level. Even among the peasantry, there were substantial inequalities. Some peasants had enough land to subsist, whereas others were forced to work part of the year for the wealthier peasants as wage laborers. Another well-known example of a civilization based on inequality is India. From its early history on, Indian society has been divided into a large number of mutually exclusive groups called castes. Each has a specific caste name, generally linked to an occupation such as Brahmin (priest), Kamar (blacksmith), or Chamar (leather worker). Castes are ranked by the society in terms of status and are socially separated from one another by rules specifying what type of contact is permitted between them. Brahmins, for instance, are not permitted to accept drinking water from Chamars.

This separation is justified by the notion that some castes are purer than others, both in religious and physical senses. At the bottom of this system of ranking are the Untouchables, castes considered so polluting that most forms of social contact with them must be avoided. The villages, where perhaps 70 percent of India's population still live, are often segregated into neighborhoods according to caste. Typically, most of the land is owned by the upper castes, and members of the lower castes are often simply landless laborers, totally dependent on upper-caste families for employment. In the past, many laborers had been "bonded"; that is, they were permanently indebted to specific upper-caste families for whom they were compelled to work for minimal pay. Bondedness is now outlawed, but the dependency of lower-caste persons on the upper-castes may persist because of the former's landlessness. And most important, because a person is born into a caste and must remain in it for life, individual mobility within the caste system is impossible (Kolenda, 1978).

In industrialized societies, inequality occurs along at least five different axes: position in the economy, geographical location, ethnicity, gender, and age. Let us examine each in turn. (These variables are discussed in detail in the following chapters and so will only be mentioned here.)

INEQUALITY IN INDUSTRIALIZED SOCIETIES

Position in the Economy

Most people in industrial societies, during their working lives, derive their income from either a job and/or ownership of property, such as stocks, bonds, bank accounts or real estate, which either yield an interest or, at the time of sale, capital gains (as when land is sold at a higher price than when it was purchased).

Everyone knows, of course, that different jobs earn different incomes. Table 16-1 gives the average annual income for a range of occupations held

TABLE 16-1. Average Income of Men and Women in Selected Occupations, Canada, 1980 (full-time workers only)

	Men	Women
Physicians and surgeons	$59 834	$36 115
General managers and other senior officials (in the private sector)	46 160	24 914
Members of legislative bodies	32 120	16 167
Electrical engineers	29 379	23 761
Foremen/women in metal processing	25 639	—
Elementary and kindergarten school teachers	24 173	20 279
Construction electricians and repair persons	21 417	15 549
Tool-and-die makers	21 166	12 484
Secretaries and stenographers	18 803	12 816
Motor-vehicle mechanics and repair persons	16 550	14 091
Cashiers and tellers	14 131	10 305
Barbers and hairdressers	13 893	9 508
Laboring and other elemental work in textile processing	12 823	9 089
Waiters	11 280	8 663
Service-station attendants	11 000	8 659

SOURCE: *1981 Census of Canada*, Vol. I, Table 1.

by Canadians. For instance, doctors earn about four times as much as barbers and hairdressers. Depending on one's standards, the differences in this table may not appear too large. However, a difference of $5000 a year accumulates over a thirty-year period into $150 000, which translates into the purchase power for such luxury items as a summer cottage.

The table does not show that certain top jobs yield an astronomically high income. In 1979, for instance, the chief executive officer of Canadian Pacific earned a salary of over half a million dollars. Such top executives, moreover, often receive part of their remuneration in stocks, thus permitting them to earn an interest income as well. Generally, a high salary permits savings, which, in turn, allows the purchase of financial assets such as stocks or bonds. The ownership of such prop-

erty is unequally distributed. In 1979, the bulk of such assets (70 percent) was held by 10 percent of families, whereas the bottom half held practically none at all (Osberg, 1981:36). At the top of Canadian society, there are at least nineteen families (such as the Bronfmans and the Eatons), each of whom has a net worth of over $100 000 000 (Osberg, 1981:39). At the other extreme, about one out of eight Canadians reported themselves unemployed in 1984 (Gallup poll, reported in *Montréal Gazette*, 22 November 1984).

These extremes are somewhat modified by the fact that government taxation of incomes is progressive (in that higher incomes are taxed at a higher rate); that some government programs, such as unemployment benefits, redistribute income; and that persons in some jobs acquire private pensions. Yet studies indicate that in many industrial societies, such factors have had considerably less impact on reducing inequality than might have been expected. In Canada, for instance, the progressiveness of income taxation is negated by the regressiveness of other taxes, such as the sales tax on consumer items: people tend to pay the same proportion of their income in taxes, regardless of their income (Gillespie, 1980). Or again, a study in Britain that took account of the "ownership" of pensions still showed that the top 5 percent of the rich still owned nearly 60 percent of the wealth, and that the top *half of one percent* held 25 percent (Atkinson, 1975:129).

Differences in income and material wealth do not begin to exhaust the inequalities associated with occupation and property ownership. Studies in North America (many of which are summarized by Gilbert and Kahl, 1982, and Duberman, 1976) indicate that people in the better-paying occupations have (1) more prestige; (2) give more orders at work and take fewer; (3) have more interesting work and job security; (4) are more likely to work regular hours and do less shift work (which disrupts social life); (5) have a better social life; (6) have more political power, insofar as power results from political participation; are (7) less likely to be arrested for a crime; (9) have better physical and mental health; (9) are more likely to have a happy, stable marriage; and (10) have greater satisfaction in sexual relations.

Studies (e.g., Duberman, 1976) show further that these inequalities are paralleled by striking differences in life styles. As one moves up the ladder of success, relations between husband and wife change from separate to joint activities; social interaction goes beyond one's kin and focuses on friends; and literary and artistic tastes change. Furthermore, social interaction tends to be restricted to persons at the same socioeconomic level and manifested in segregated neighborhoods. These isolationist tendencies are particularly strong toward the top of the ladder, where a network of private secondary schools, resorts, private clubs,

débutante balls, expensive sports (horseback riding), and traditional public service for men and philanthropy for women (including patronage of the arts) combine to create an elite and an elitist life style.

Unlike the agrarian societies described earlier, there is considerable mobility across generations, the major means being through education. However, studies have shown that children from well-off families tend to do better in school, and so have an advantage over those from poorer families. Furthermore, much of the upward mobility of the latter has resulted not from exchanging positions with the offspring of well-to-do families, but from a change in the overall structure of occupations. Structural mobility occurs when the proportion of white-collar to manual-labor jobs increases, so that it is necessary to draw offspring from lower-class families to fill them. This means that while a considerable number of persons have risen across generations, substantially fewer have fallen. The result is that, to a large degree, the offspring of well-to-do families inherit favorable positions. The rigidity of such a system seems to be particularly true at the very top of the economic ladder, where elite positions are almost entirely filled by persons from well-off families (Tepperman, 1975:188).

What is perhaps most striking about the findings of these studies of Western industrial societies is how much, in spite of the absence of differential legal privileges and explicit restrictions on interaction and mobility, they parallel the inequalities in the historical agrarian societies, even if in a less extreme form.

Geographical Location

It is a notable geographical feature of the world that as one moves from temperate to tropical areas, and from the Northern to the Southern hemisphere, countries become poorer. The rich countries are almost all situated in the North, and the poor in the South, with the result that ana-

Indian section of Makkovik, Labrador. Heavily disadvantaged regions tend to display wider social and economic disparities.

lyst often speak of a north/south division of the world in terms of wealth.

The fact of the matter is, however, that the north/south problem applies not only between nations, but within them as well. As some analysts have said, every nation has a south — that is, one or more economically disadvantaged regions. The most striking current example among the industrialized nations is probably Italy. The impoverished conditions of Sicily, Sardinia, and the south are well known. One of the more recent historical examples is the American South, a region once overwhelmingly rural, characterized by widespread share-cropping, illiteracy, hookworm, repressive labor relations in mill towns and the like (Vance, 1935). Nor is Canada free from regional disparities; but the dividing axis is west/east. As Table 16-2 shows, the Maritime provinces are heavily disadvantaged.

Studies indicate that such regions tend to be doubly disadvantaged in terms of inequality. Not only are they poorer than other provinces, but economic inequality *within* them tends to be worse. Regional inequalities are often paralleled by disparities between cities and countryside. Most areas designated by the Canadian government as poverty areas, for instance, are rural, and the wheat-growing areas of Canada are especially prone to boom-bust economic cycles. Even cities form a hierarchy in terms of their economic vigor (Toronto now attracts most company head-offices), in their quality of life (Montréal has one of the world's best symphony orchestras) and physical environment (a cloud of industrial pollutants often hangs over Sudbury, where much of the terrain resembles the surface of the moon).

In short, then, the valued things of life are affected not only by one's occupation and ownership of property, but also by where one lives — in what region, town, or city.

Ethnicity

Much of the history of the agrarian societies of the past could be written in terms of ethnic or racial diversity, inequality, and conflict. For instance, the business or skilled artisans class was made up predominantly of Christian Armenians in the Islamic Ottoman Empire, of Huguenot Protestants in Catholic France, and of Jews in Spain. All of these minority groups were ultimately persecuted, and many of their members driven into exile.

As industrialization began in the West, the view emerged that the importance of ethnicity would decline, as industrialization progressed. However, ethnic inequalities have not only persisted, but their existence is due, in part, to discrimination.

An in-depth study of ethnic inequality in Canada was done by the Royal Commission on Bilingualism and Biculturalism in the 1960s. At that

TABLE 16-2. **Per capita income and unemployment rates of regions as a percentage of Canadian average.**

	Per Capita Income 1977–79	Unemployment 1981
Canada	100.0%	100.0%
Maritimes		153.4%
Newfoundland	54.7%	
Prince Edward Island	59.9%	
Nova Scotia	75.3%	
New Brunswick	67.4%	
Quebec	90.3%	136.8%
Ontario	112.0%	86.8%
Prairies		58.8%
Manitoba	93.3%	
Saskatchewan	91.9%	
Alberta	109.3%	
British Columbia	112.1%	88.2%

SOURCE: Phillips, Paul, *Regional Disparities*, Tronto: James Lorimer & Co., 1982, Tables 7.1 and 7.3, pp. 133, 135.

Historically, non-whites have ended up at the bottom of the ethnic hierarchy. American blacks and Canadian native peoples are among those who have felt the worst effects of such discrimination.

time, as Table 16-3 shows, there was a very substantial gap between the average incomes of English and French Canadians, the former earning about 25 percent more than the latter nationwide, and in Québec, more than 50 percent. These economic differences were paralleled by differences in prestige. This was strikingly demonstrated in a study by McGill psychologists (Lambert et al., 1960), in which identical texts were read to both French- and English-Canadian audiences by perfectly bilingual speakers. The audiences were asked to rank the supposedly French- and English-Canadian speakers in terms of leadership, intelligence, dependability, and character. Both audiences ranked the supposedly English-Canadian speakers more highly.

One of the most notable facts about ethnic inequality is that non-whites have historically, by and large, ended up at the bottom of the ethnic hierarchy, with American blacks and Indians being the worst off in this respect. Until the mid-1950s, blacks in Southern states occupied a position similar to the untouchable castes in India: not only were they relegated to the most menial and unpleasant work and given an inferior education, but they were also subjected to segregation on an everyday basis, such as being forced to ride at the back of buses. Although such outright segregation has ended, the position of U.S. blacks is nevertheless still low. Similarly, native Indians have fared badly in both the United States and Canada.

TABLE 16-3. Average income of anglophone and francophone men, 1970 and 1980, for various regions of Canada.

	1970 Anglo.	1970 Franco.	% Diff.	1980 Anglo.	1980 Franco.	% Diff.
Canada (not including Quebec)	$7 171	$6 353	12.8%	$17 619	$16 295	8.1%
Quebec (not including Montreal)	$6 841	$5 890	16.1%	$16 332	$15 699	4.0%
Montreal	$9 240	$6 949	33.0%	$19 892	$17 474	13.8%

SOURCE: Boulet, Jacques-André, and Laval, Lavallee, assisted by Carmer Pader and Martine Poulin, *L'évolution des disparités linguistiques de revenus de travail au Canada de 1970 à 1980*, Document No. 245, Economic Council of Canada, October 1983.

Evidence shows that there can be substantial upward mobility of some ethnic groups. Perhaps the most significant example in present-day Canada is the French Canadians. The gap in income, which nationwide was 25 percent in 1960, fell to 15 percent outside Québec by 1970, and to 8.1 percent in 1980 (Boulet and Lavallée). This change has probably been hastened by a federal government decision to promote French Canadians in the civil service, and by the passage of language-of-work legislation in Québec.

However, although some ethnic groups may rise, others, such as American blacks and Indians, suffer persistent disadvantage. North America thus appears to have an enduring underclass of ethnically disadvantaged people (even though some individuals may escape a lowly position). To a certain extent, so too do many European societies, in that much of their manual-labor force consists of "guest" workers from the Mediterranean periphery: from Algeria, Morroco, Tunesia, Yugoslavia, and Turkey (Castles and Kosack, 1973).

Inequality based on racial discrimination is the topic of Chapter 18, and gender inequality the topic of Chapter 20, and so our discussion of both is brief here.

Gender

Historically, the status of women in industrial societies has been inferior to men in terms of several dimensions: income, authority at work and in the family, rights to family income and property, political power, and sexual freedom.

One of the more interesting studies demonstrating this lower status is that of Labowitz (1974), who gave groups of students in a midwestern Canadian university a summary of a bogus scientific study to read. Each group was given a different version of the author of the study (Edward Blake, Edith Blake, Joseph Running Bear, and Marcel Fournier) and each student was then asked to evaluate the study according to a five-point scale running from highly favorable to highly unfavorable. The study was rated less favorably when it was believed to be authored by a woman and even less favorably when thought to be authored by an Indian or a French Canadian.

Over the last decade or so, the status of women has improved somewhat. One illustration of this is their increased participation in the labor force, so much so that now over 40 percent of all workers are women (Armstrong and Armstrong, 1984: 19). Furthermore, women have been entering a much wider range of occupations than before. For instance, engineering faculties in many universities, once the exclusive domain of male students, today have substantial female enrollments. Nevertheless, women have not yet attained equality. As Table 16-1. shows, women still get payed significantly less than men.

Finally, there are significant inequalities associated with age. Since this, too, will be discussed in a later chapter, we shall only touch upon it here.

Age

In Canada, children are legally under the control of their parents until the age of 16. While in school, they are also financially dependent on their parents and today, when they reach the working age, they face high unemployment rates.

At the other end of the age continuum, the elderly in most industrial societies are forced into retirement at age sixty-five (in Japan at fifty-five), whether they want to or not, with the result that their income drops precipitously. As they become more feeble, their prestige also declines.

Inequalities sometimes result not only with age itself but also with age cohorts. Whole generations may suffer disadvantages, as when a cohort comes of age in a depression, with the result that its members take longer to find jobs, are less able to find the jobs they want, and advance less rapidly in the jobs they do find. The same effects characterize the baby boom generation, which, since coming of age, has flooded the job market at a rate greater than the market can absorb. It has been argued (Easterlin, 1980) that such conditions in turn mean lower lifetime earnings, less job satisfaction, delayed marriages, more marital strain (in part because wives are forced to work, whether they want to do so or not, to supplement family income), and, for the generation as a whole, higher rates of mental illness, homicides, and suicides.

The relations between these axes of inequality are complex, and none, at least on the surface, can reduced to the others. For example, even

In most industrial societies, the elderly are forced into retirement, with the result that their income— and mobility—drops sharply.

wealthy Jews have been excluded from top social clubs, and the sons of multimillionaires are subject to the authority of their much less wealthy primary school teachers. Furthermore, one axis may intensify or decrease the impact of another. A sriking example of this is that men, as they age, tend to remain attractive to younger women, whereas older women tend to lose their attractiveness even to men of the same age. Gender, thus, mutes the impact of age for one sex and intensifies it for another.

DEFINING SOCIAL STRATIFICATION

Because inequalities are not randomly distributed but instead follow major social "fault" lines, such as occupation or age, sociologists frequently refer to *structured inequality*. More generally, sociologists refer to *social stratification*. This is because (1) people who score high in one dimension, such as power, tend also to score high in others, such as prestige; (2) whole categories of persons (e.g., doctors, waitresses) are high or low; (3) there tends to be continuity across generations as a result of restricted mobility; (4) people at a similar level of inequality share a similar life style; and (5) interact principally with each other. Thus, as one writer has put it (Kerbo, 1983:11), unequal groups may be likened to layers or strata in a geological formation.

Where stratification is absent, as in hunting-and-gathering societies, sociologists refer to classless societies. Where it does exist, an important distinction is made between an *achieved* status versus an *ascribed* status. As the term suggests, an achieved status is based on one or more characteristics that can be changed, whereas an ascribed status is based on fixed characteristics such as one's age or sex. Where mobility is possible and frequent, the stratification system is said to be open; where there is no mobility, the system is closed.

Stratified societies are sometimes categorized as slave, caste, feudal, or class societies. We have already discussed examples of these types. Slave societies, other than that of the Roman Empire, were the ancient city-states of Greece and the plantation societies of the New World, in which black slaves from Africa were imported to work in Brazil, the West Indies, and the American South. As for caste, whether this term can be applied outside India is a matter of considerable controversy. Some scholars claim it should not be, since only in India is caste justified by religion and accepted by those at the bottom of the system; others dispute the view that the Untouchables accept their position no more than did blacks in the U.S. south, so that the latter, too, can be regarded as a caste society (Berreman, 1960). Some writers apply the term caste to any group of ascribed status, so that minority groups and women are seen as having a caste-like position. The term feudal is even more disputed: one of the central issues of contention is whether the defining characteristic is serfdom or the diffusion of power to the landed aristocracy. Different definitions result in the inclusion of different societies in this type. Many writers have characterized traditional Latin American societies as feudal, particularly those in the Andean Mountains, because of large haciendas (estates), the owners of which had considerable political power, and to whom the peasants were tied in serf-like fashion.

Finally, in slave, caste, and serf societies, the lower strata are not free. Slaves and serfs were not permitted to change their employers, nor lower-caste persons their caste. In contrast, in industrialized capitalist societies, workers (the bottom stratum) are free to change employers, and their children are able to rise into a higher class, if they achieve the necessary qualifications. Where people are formally free and mobility is permitted, but where stratification nevertheless exists, the society is considered a *class society*. Canada is a class society, although, as is the case with most industrial societies, the stratification system has certain caste-like characteristics, since the position of some ethnic groups and women, for instance, is partially ascribed.

Attempts to Reduce Stratification

Those at the bottom layer of a stratified society feel hard done by. Inequality present in the industrial societies of the West has given rise to revolts. Canada has experienced (1) the union movement and the rise of the New Democratic Party (NDP), both deriving their ideology from economic position; (2) western separatism (based on regional stratification); (3) French-Canadian nationalism (based on ethnic inequalities); (4) the women's movement (based on sexual inequality); and (5) the youth rebellion of the 1960s (based partly on age inequality).

Such revolts can be either reformist, where the pattern of stratification is changed gradually through a set of reforms within the existing structure of society, or revolutionary, where a completely new society is established with one blow. Parties such as the NDP attempt to do the former. Communist revolutionary movements aim to accomplish the latter. Somewhat in-between are attempts to establish small-scale egalitarian communities within the larger society, in the hope that such communities will either survive in spite of the inequalities in the larger society or lead to the transformation of the entire society. Examples of this in-between strategy are the many utopian communities that were established in North America in the eighteenth and nineteenth centuries and the communes formed in the 1960s. In many ways, kibbutzim are representative of such communities: they are agricultural communities, increasingly with industrial pursuits, where most property is owned in common, where the members are expected to work for the common good of the community, and where goods are distributed equally.

Although most of the efforts to establish viable small-scale egalitarian communities ultimately failed, not all have done so. Kibbutzim, for instance, have shown a remarkable vitality and considerable equality. Whether such equality can be achieved at the societal level (and not just at the community level) is still questionable. Neither the reformist nor revolutionary methods has succeeded.

The greatest reformist advances have probably been made in the Scandinavian countries, of which Sweden is the best-known example. The ruling socialist party has virtually abolished poverty. The middle class is heavily taxed in order to provide health and benefits for the whole population, and progressive legislation has been passed regarding women's rights and needs. Nevertheless, inequality has not been abolished. Salaries still differ substantially according to occupations; not everyone owns property; mobility across generations is restricted, and women play a smaller role than men in both the economy and politics.

The industrialized communist societies are also far from egalitarian (Lane, 1982; 1976). Besides the fact that political power is unequally distributed, many of the same differences between occupations in pay and prestige exist as in the West; the sons of white-collar workers are more likely to attend university and be upwardly mobile than laborers' sons; the political elites have special privileges, such as the right to shop at special stores where range and quantity of goods is greater, the use of state-provided cottages, and even have servants. Although a high proportion of women work and even dominate certain professions that have been male-dominated in the West (medicine, in particular), women do not rise as high in their lines of work as men and have to do the housework when they come home from work.

In order to understand social stratification fully, it is necessary to arrive at definitive answers to four central questions:

1. What is the *pattern* of stratification in various types of societies? For industrial societies in the West, this would entail knowing (a) how much inequality there is; (b) the degree of mobility there is between strata; and (c) the extent of correlation between the various dimensions of inequality (wealth, power, prestige, authority at work, and so on).

2. What are the *causes* of inequality and of the patterns it takes? Is there a central feature of society — the economy, for instance — that lies behind the different axes of stratification? Is inequality rooted in human nature?

3. What are the *consequences* of social stratification for the functioning of society? What is its impact, for instance, on the prevalence of crime, on family stability, or on the prosperity of the economy? This question is important because many analysts believe the stratification system to be the key to the operation of the total society.

4. What are the *conditions for the reduction* of inequality? Under what conditions will movements, aimed at decreasing some form of inequality such as sexual stratification, arise? Under what conditions might they succeed in doing so?

These four questions can be summarized as those of the structure, causes, consequences, and conditions for the reduction of social stratifica-

Monkeys, chimpanzees, and gorillas exhibit social stratification through such behavior as male dominance, territoriality, and sexual division of labor. Some researchers have suggested that these proclivities are genetically determined among both animals and humans.

tion. Unfortunately, scientists have not arrived at definitive answers to each of these questions, partly because the data are inadequate. The most progress has been made on the first question, but even here there is much controversy. In fact, the first section in this chapter on stratification has probably been written with greater certainty than current knowledge warrants. As with other subfields of sociology, there exist a number of competing theories, which, in turn, are rooted in more fundamental theories of society of the sort discussed in Chapter 2.

THEORIES OF SOCIAL STRATIFICATION

We shall briefly discuss each theory in the context of industrialized societies.

Genetic Theory and Human Nature

One of the most popular and long-standing ways of explaining stratification is to attribute it to human nature. Thus, it has been argued that we are genetically programmed to be selfish, so that a struggle for income, power, and prestige is inevitable; and that we are differentially endowed with intelligence, stamina, emotional stability, and other traits needed to survive in this struggle. Furthermore, such specific social behavior, such as submission to authority, is seen as compelled by our genes.

Such genetic theories of human behavior were common in the late nineteenth and early twentieth centuries, and gave rise to a widespread eugenics movement aimed at preventing deterioration of the human population. The social consequences of these ideas led to discriminatory immigration legislation against supposedly inferior nationality groups, and to the attempted genocide of the Jews. In reaction to this inhumanity, the genetic approach nearly disappeared after World War II. In recent years, however, it has experienced a major revival, although largely shorn of explicitly racist content.

Insofar as this revival has intellectual roots, three recent developments are particularly important. The first is the use by eminent psychologists (Eysenik, 1967; Jensen, 1969) of advanced quantitative techniques, modern genetic theory, new knowledge about brain structure and the like, to argue that both intelligence and temperament are inherited.

The second is based on ethology — the study of the *social* behavior of animals (Lorenz, 1981). Ethologists have found that much social behavior of primates bears an uncanny resemblance to that of human beings (Tiger and Fox, 1971), such as dominance, territoriality, and a sexual division of labor. Because it is thought that most animal behavior is genetically determined, such similarities suggest that so, too, is human social behavior.

The third development, and the most important, is sociobiology (Barash, 1977), a new discipline that applies modern evolutionary theory to explain animal social behavior. An increasing number of analysts have extended this theory to explain human social behavior (e.g., Van den Berghe, 1978; 1979).

In their application of evolutionary theory, sociobiologists have given it an unusual twist. Traditional evolutionary theory assumes competition for survival among individual members of species. Those who have traits best-suited to their environment are selected by the environment to survive. The survivors then pass on the genes for these traits through their offspring, which eventually become the typical traits of the species. A similar survival-of-the-fittest takes place between species. Thus, in traditional evolutionary theory, the basic unit of survival is the individual or the species (the group). In contrast, for sociobiologists, it is the gene.

This sociobiological interpretation is critical, since it lies at the heart of the question of whether human beings are selfish or altruistic. Using traditional evolutionary theory, some writers (e.g., Ruston, 1980) have argued that evolution should have produced altruistic human beings, since humankind lived for most of its existence in hunting-and-gathering bands where co-operation was at a premium. Those bands whose members were unco-operative should not have survived. Thus, group selection meant that people in co-operative bands should have been better to reproduce and pass on their altruistic genes.

Sociobiologists, however, disagree with this theory. They argue that within any particular band, including co-operative bands, selfish individuals would have had a better chance to survive, since they would have let the more altruistic ones sacrifice themselves for the good of the band. Therefore, it would have been their selfish genes that would have been passed on and those of the more altruistic would have been extinguished. This process of individual selection would override that of group selection, resulting in a basically selfish human nature.

But not even individual selection is, sociobiologists argue, the fundamental mechanism. If it were, one could not account for the altruism that is present in human beings — toward kin, especially. The reason for such altruism is that kin share a proportion of genes: brothers, sisters, and children, one-half; uncles, aunts, nephews, and nieces, one-quarter; cousins, one-eighth; and so on. A gene of altruism toward kin, by causing behavior that aids the survival of kin, would aid its own survival, since a proportion of relatives carry the same gene. Since individuals will at times even sacrifice their life for kin (e.g., parents for children), the basic unit of survival is not the individual, but the gene. And the process for sociobiologists is neither group nor individual selection, but kin selection. The result is that people are neither purely selfish nor purely altruistic. Rather, they are basically selfish, but will aid kin, particularly close kin.

The evolutionary process, furthermore, according to sociobiologists, selects not just for general selfishness but for specific social behaviors, such as male attraction to younger females. The general principle is that those social behaviors are selected that aid in the survival of the individuals carrying the genes for those behaviors (otherwise the genes would not be passed on to the next generation). This means that the hidden "purpose" behind the various social behaviors in which an individual engages is the reproductive success of his or her genes. Needless to say, such motivation is largely unconscious, since most people do not recognize such bizarre motivation for their behavior.

Genetic theory, particularly sociobiology, offers an explanation for stratification along all the axes distinguished earlier. Altruism toward kin, but selfishness toward others, for instance, explains the special help parents give their children: by sending them, if they can afford it, to private secondary schools, they decrease social mobility. Particularly, good illustrations of genetic arguments are those made about sexual inequality.

It has been alleged, for instance, that women genetically have less mathematical ability than men. If so, this would put them at a disadvantage in competing in such occupations as engineering. It has also been argued that women are less aggressive and more maternal by nature. A sociobiological explanation of these difference is the following: in hunting-and-gathering societies, women not only had to bear children, but breastfeed them, as well. Their mobility was thus restricted, with the result that it was the men who specialized in hunting. Since survival in hunting was more likely if the hunter was aggressive, men were selected for this trait. Similarly, a parent specializing in child rearing would be more successful in raising a child, who would, in turn, pass on parental genes, if the parent was maternal, so women were selected for this trait. These differences in temperament mean that women are disadvantaged in the world of work, since they will fight less hard to rise and be less willing to sacrifice child rearing for a career. Or again, since women can only bear few children in a lifetime, and only before menopause, a younger woman is more advantageous to a man in perpetuating his genes and so men were selected for attraction to younger women. Since men, almost regardless of age, can impregnate women, what counts for a woman, in terms of perpetuating her genes, is a husband with the power and skills to best support her children. And because it is often older men who will have accumulated such power and skills, women were selected for attraction to them.

Arguments of this sort clearly have a conservative bias, either justifying inequality, or suggesting that it is inevitable and therefore useless to struggle against. For this reason, together with the previous horrendous consequences of genetic theories, the resurgence of genetic theories has been bitterly attacked.

Cultural and Social Environmentalism

Cultural and social environmentalism accepts one of the crucial assumptions of genetic theory — that general dispositions, such as selfishness, and individual differences in capabilities and temperament both play a major role in stratification. It disputes, however, that these are under genetic control, arguing instead that both are a result of social factors. This is argued on three grounds.

First, within evolutionary theory itself, there is reason to think that, whatever may be the case with most animals, human beings were selected for freedom from biological control of their behavior. This is because adaptation to the environment through modification of genes is an extremely slow and inefficient process compared with adaptation through the cultural innovation of patterns of social organization. Thus, once Homo sapiens started on the road toward innovation, evolution should have progressively selected for the genetic capacity to be free from genetic control and be responsive, instead, to culture.

Second, studies of societies by anthropologists, such as Margaret Mead, have revealed that the patterns of behavior existing in our own culture are far from universal. These studies, for instance, have revealed societies where people are co-operative or where men are no more aggressive than women.

Third, studies have shown that within our society, there is considerable variation among people with regard to selfishness, individual capabilities, and temperament. These variations are largely the result of two basic social processes: socialization and social frustration of human needs.

Studies (e.g., Brown, 1965; Mussen and Eisenberg, 1977) have shown that children will develop a conscience — an altruistic disposition — when parents themselves exhibit altruism; when they teach such behavior to the child consistently from an early age; when the mother is warm toward the child; when the principal disciplinary technique is not physical punishment, but withdrawal of affection; and when in both the schools and the media, altruistic and nonaggressive behavior is rewarded. Behind this process is role-modelling, to which you have been introduced in the chapter on socialization.

High achievement motivation results when children are given encouragement and the freedom to experiment.

Studies have also shown that variations between people in achievement motivation are a result of child rearing patterns (McClelland, 1961: chapter 9). High achievement motivation results when (1) parents deliberately encourage the child to achieve; (2) when the mother is warm and uses withdrawal of love as the principal disciplinary technique; and (3) when the father is non-authoritarian. (This last condition is important because children need to experiment in order to learn how to achieve.)

Finally, studies have shown that prejudice (a major factor in ethnic stratification) increases substantially when people are frustrated. A famous study by Hoveland and Sears (1940) showed that lynching of blacks by whites in the American South increased during economic recessions. Another study (Bettelheim and Janowitz, 1964) showed that prejudice was greatest among people who are

downwardly mobile. The psychological mechanism behind such behavior is that frustration creates anger and aggression.

In sum, then, general dispositions and individual differences in capabilities and temperament relevant to social stratification are under social, not biological control. Indeed, they are derivative of the stratification system itself, in such a way as to both sustain and strengthen the system. This means that once a stratification system develops, it creates the very dispositions and individual differences that perpetuate it. For example, once a sexual division of labor is established, or other forms of differential behavior are fostered between the sexes, including different temperaments, children will model their behavior on adults of the same sex and so will come to have the sexual temperaments that cause stratification along sexual lines.

More generally, because class systems mean people have different experiences and opportunities, each stratum will develop its own culture and pattern of child rearing. Lower strata, for instance, tend to develop lower aspirations, since the opportunity to advance is not great. At the same time, class systems restrict interaction between strata, since people are separated by barriers of prestige, residential segregation, and the like. Both the distinct cultures of strata and the restricted interaction across these tend to reinforce the class system. Absence of reading material around the home, for instance, makes it more difficult for the lower-strata child to pick up the cognitive skills needed for success in school; in addition, the lower aspirations of the parents means a lower probability of being socialized into having high aspirations; and confinement of interaction to people of the same class means little chance of having contact with persons who might serve as models of such aspirations. At the very bottom of a stratification system, in this view, there frequently arises a "culture of poverty" (Lewis, 1966), characterized by a high degree of fatalism, a short time-perspective, and other elements,

At the bottom of a stratification system may arise a "culture of poverty," into which children are socialized and ultimately trapped.

into which children are socialized. And so these children are unable to take advantage of opportunities even when they do arise, virtually being trapped.

But what gives rise to stratification systems in the first place? One answer is that a process of cultural selection takes place, in which aggressive cultures either conquer peaceful ones, or force the latter to imitate them in order to prevent conquest (Schmookler, 1984). Cultural and environmental theories were especially prevalent after World War II. In the late 1960s, however, they came under heavy attack on the basis that (1) empirical evidence does not reveal the existence of a culture of poverty (Goodwin, 1972); (2) the perspective placed too much emphasis on psycho-

logical dispositions and capabilities, instead of on structural factors such as plant closings, which impoverish competent and incompetent alike; (3) it overemphasizes the importance of cognitive skills of the sort picked up in school — skills that prove to be less important for many jobs relative to the skills learned on the job; and (4) the perspective itself contributes to the lower strata's being unable to get decent jobs, because its assumption that they do not have the requisite skills and motivation justifies not hiring them. The theory, in short, has the effect of blaming not the system, but the victim.

Furthermore, the theory is vague about the actual origins of *particular* systems, about why particular stratification systems have taken the form they have, and about the direction of their evolution. Marxism attempts to answer all these questions.

Marxist Theory

By now, you should have become acquainted with Marxist theory, and so here we shall focus on its relevance for explaining stratification. Marx's theory is, above all, a theory of stratification. According to Marx, it is the mode of production of a society that determines which classes exist and how life chances are distributed among them. In all types of societies, except the earliest — that is, hunting-and-gathering — Marx felt that most of the surplus (that is, production in excess of what was needed for survival) is appropriated by a small ruling class. In capitalism, as explained in Chapter 2, the way in which the surplus is appropriated leads to economic crises. These crises, along with various other changes stemming from the capitalist mode of production, will in time lead to a revolution and a new mode of production — communism — which will abolish classes. In short, this is a theory about the pattern, causes, consequences, and conditions of transformation of stratification systems.

One of the most remarkable features of Marx's theory is that most of his major predictions about capitalism failed. Successful revolution failed to materialize in the advanced capitalist countries, where Marx thought they would occur and, instead, took place in several economically underdeveloped countries such as Czarist Russia and traditional China; in these countries, the resulting communism is neither democratic nor egalitarian; and once industrialized, Communist countries have failed to show the progressiveness Marx had anticipated with regard to their economy. Instead, it has been the advanced capitalist countries that have exhibited economic dynamism.

Many critics have charged that Marx's theory failed because his predictions about the evolution of the class system, of class relations, and of the dynamics of capitalism failed to materialize (Dahrendorf, 1959). His belief that revolution would occur depended on certain changes in all of these; for example, (1) the middle class, composed of family farmers and small businessmen, would be eliminated because of the economic superiority of large firms and factory organization of production, leaving a simple two-class system (of capitalists and impoverished workers-proletarians), in which upward mobility for the proletarian class would be virtually precluded; (2) that workers would become progressively immiscerated; (3) that economic crises would become increasingly frequent and severe, causing greater unemployment; (4) that factory work would become simplified and routine, rendering it boring and alienating; (5) that this deskilling would largely eliminate economic differences between workers, homogenizing both their wages and working conditions, thus eliminating conflicts of economic interest among them; and (6) that social divisions among the working class along religious, racial, linguistic, and ethnic lines, as well as those of gender, would progressively diminish, thus permitting the unity necessary for successful revolution.

In fact, the critics charge, almost none of these changes materialized. Although the old middle class did decline, there developed a new middle class of middle-managers, salaried professionals, technicians, and clerical and sales personnel, into which many of the sons and daughters of workers rose. Far from becoming immiscerated, the wages and working conditions of workers have ameliorated substantially because of unionization and the productivity of the capitalist economy. Also important has been the democratization of the state, which has permitted workers to bring pressure on politicians to enact welfare legislation, such as old-age pensions and state-supported medical care. The state, futhermore, has learned how to moderate economic crises through tax policies, state expenditures, and manipulation of the money supply.

Not only have differences in skills persisted among workers, but if anything, a higher proportion of jobs demand more skill today than was the case in the past. In any event, major differences still remain between jobs in the organization of work (construction work, for instance, is still organized along traditional craft, instead of factory lines). Finally, social divisions among workers remain as strong as ever.

In short, the critics argue, Marx simply failed to grasp the direction of the evolution of the class system under capitalism. Marxists have responded to these failed predictions and criticisms in two ways. Some (Braverman, 1974; Domhoff, 1983) challenged the criticisms. It has been argued (1) "that much of the new middle class (the sales and clerical personnel) are really workers, since their income is low and working conditions poor"; (2) that deskilling has continued relentlessly; (3) that the state is still under the control of the capitalist class; and (4) that the welfare state does not distribute income between, but only within, classes (e.g., from young to retired workers).

Those Marxists who agree that some of Marx's predictions failed have reworked the basic theory to account for these failures. For example, it is argued that capitalism itself is responsible for the persistence of social divisions among workers, that capitalists have promoted both ethnic and sexual changes precisely to hold down wages (Reich, 1981; Szymanski, 1976). Above all, the Communist regimes that came to power in some non-industrialized countries did so largely because of their regressive agrarian modes of production (such as oppressive tenancy systems) and the very economic backwardness of these countries meant that the new revolutionary regimes could not be truly communist. Thus, the lack of democracy and equality in these countries in no way indicates that a democratic and egalitarian revolution is impossible in our own society.

In short, a sophisticated contemporary version of Marxism has emerged, one that still stresses mode of production as its major explanatory variable, and which has given rise to a large and complex body of literature. Canadian sociology has been particularly influenced by such Marxist analysis.

Functionalism

Functionalist theory is virtually the antithesis of mode-of-production Marxism. As you already know, Marxist theory concentrates on the *conflicts* of interest among members of a society, whereas functionalism focuses on their *common interests*; all members of a society benefit from a society that functions well, even if they do not benefit equally. Furthermore, the members of a society share common values and goals, and these are the collective product of all members of the society (not just the ruling class), having evolved slowly over time. Society attempts to realize these common goals in part through the political system, which concentrates power in order to achieve common aims more efficiently. Political power and the state are thus seen as resources from which society can draw for the common benefit of all, rather than as tools used by a ruling class to control subordinate classes.

Above all, functionalists argue that all societies have certain functional requirements that must be fulfilled in order to survive, and these demand a certain level of stratification. In other words, stratification is necessary for the existence and proper functioning of any society.

Stratification is necessary for several reasons. First, people must be motivated to undertake and perform conscientiously the most important functional tasks in society. Second, motivation is necessary because many of the tasks require extensive training, or because the tasks themselves are stressful, or because the skill/knowledge needed for the tasks is often scarce. Third, as a result, society needs to offer people incentives if these tasks are to be performed — and performed well. Finally, the principal incentives are differential access to such scarce rewards as prestige, income, and power, and the inevitable result is stratified society. (For the classic statement of this argument, see Davis and Moore, 1945.)

Stratification is seen as necessary not only in the economy, but in relations between men and women, between age groups, and between regions. For example, a family system is necessary for any society to function well, because children must be procreated, nurtured, and socialized. Within a family, a sexual division of labor is the most efficient arrangement. Since women bear the children and must stay home for a period during the later stages of pregnancy and the initial stages of recovery from birth, it is most efficient for the wife to specialize in housework and raising children while the husband earns the income. This sexual division of labor in turn leads to inequality; for instance, wives who work outside the home generally cannot devote as much effort to their work, and thus command lower pay. Similarly, age inequality is seen as necessary, since (1) adults must possess greater prestige and power than children if they are to socialize the latter adequately, and (2) socialization is essential for the functioning of every society.

According to the functionalists, because stratification is necessary, it benefits all members of the society, and not just those at the top of the stratification system. This is true for capitalist societies in particular. For example, it is argued that the mechanisms of distribution in capitalism reward people in proportion to their contribution to production. Since the extent to which a person contributes to production depends heavily on his or her skills, this method of distribution encourages people to invest in upgrading their skills. This, in turn, serves to increase productivity, making the entire society more prosperous. At the same time, since the contribution of workers to production increases with skill level, they receive a higher reward, thus sharing in the fruits of this increased productivity. Thus, according to this perspective, the distributional mechanisms of capitalism serve the ends of both growth and distribution (and not just the former, as claimed by Marxists).

In fact, it is held that capitalism strikes a better balance between growth and distribution than communism, for the latter tends to sacrifice the first for the second, since excessive interference of the state in the economy, the functionalists say, hinders technological advance. Similarly, capitalism is more likely to reduce ethnic stratification than communism, since it is under capitalism, for instance, that employers who discriminate and thus fail to hire the most competent workers available (regardless of race, sex, and so on), will be placed at a disadvantage in their competition with firms that do. In contrast, under communism, employers who discriminate suffer no such penalties, as competition is absent (Sowell, 1981).

In this view, the economic and other crises that arise in industrial society do not emerge, as Marxists claim, from excessive inequality, but from insufficient stratification. The current economic crises, for instance, is seen by functionalists as arising (1) partly from a shift in the balance of power from capitalists to workers, resulting in wage demands and increases that exceed the rate of productivity growth; and (2) partly from excessive democratization, whereby politicians woo voters by offering more and more government programs, leading to excessive state expenditures (Buchanon and Wagner, 1977). Japan's economy is currently functioning the most effectively, in this view, be-

cause it is in Japan where the relative power of the business class is greatest (among Western economies), where state bureaucracies have considerable autonomy from politicians, and where sexual and age stratification is still substantial. It is largely these features of Japanese society that account for the prosperity of its economy (Vogel, 1979).

Since stratification is necessary, a transition to communism cannot, say the functionalists, eliminate it. Communist societies have the same need to motivate people, the same need for a family system and the same need for adults to have sufficient power and prestige to socialize children adequately.

General Conflict Theory

General conflict theory regards both Marxism and functionalism as being in error — functionalism for being apologetic about the inequality in our society, and Marxism for being unduly optimistic and utopian in its assertion that socialism would bring equality and that the transition to socialist society is an inevitable consequence of the dynamics of capitalism. A valid theory should be neither apologetic nor utopian, but realistic.

However, general conflict theory argues that Marxism is on the right track in its emphasis on conflict — on certain groups' pursuit of particular group interests, which are generally in conflict. Marxism is also correct in asserting that stratification is an unnecessary feature of industrial society. In this respect, Marxists have contributed innovative thinking that is crucial to our understanding of stratification (Collins, 1975: 55–61).

Where Marxists go wrong is in their belief that capitalism alone is responsible for inequality in industrial society. More generally, it is the unidimensional character of Marxist theory that constitutes its fundamental flaw (Collins, 1975: chapter 2).

To begin with, Marxism gives too much weight to economic motives, failing to appreciate that concern for prestige and power are equally important goals for people. For instance, the prestige a given group obtains from denigration of another is a powerful incentive to discriminate, aside from any question of economic gain.

Marxism also fails to recognize the degree to which conflicting interests permeate virtually every area of society, not just the economy, but the family, age-group relations (Collins, 1975; chapter 5), and relations between ethnic or status groups (Blauner, 1972; chapter 1). In the family, for instance, conflicts of interest exist over who will perform the more unpleasant household tasks, whose vacation preferences will prevail, whether one partner will submit to sexual intercourse even if he or she is not interested, and so forth. Such conflicts of interest provide a powerful incentive to establish dominance — or a state of inequality. Marxism fails to see that these conflicts are very real and have a life of their own; they are not merely derivative of the economic sphere.

Furthermore, Marxism fails to perceive that it is not just ownership of the means of production that determines the distribution of income, but that other forces are also at work, such as the drive of people to restrict entry into their occupation, thus forcing up wages and salaries, as is the case with professionals and craft unions (Parkin, 1979).

Finally, Marxists fail to realize that, besides the capitalist mode of production, there are other features of the modern world that cause stratification of a society: modern technology; bureaucratization of both government and industry; the participant state (i.e., a state in which mass participation is expected); and the nation-state system (the system of competing states, each comprising a single people). All of these features of the modern world are causally linked with stratification: bureaucracy itself is a hierarchical form of organization; conflict between states inevitably generates a large military establishment with an authoritarian organization and ideology; and so forth. Since only the first of these factors, the capitalist mode of production, disappears with the transition to socialism, stratification may be expected to persist even in socialist societies.

According to general conflict theory, these features generate stratification because they affect the distribution of power and thus the ability of some people to realize their own interests at the expense of the interests of others. In addition, an unequal distribution of power is itself a form of stratification and a source of conflicting interests. Thus, general conflict theory regards power, rather than the economy, as the crucial variable (Dahrendorf, 1959; Lenski; 1966). The economy is simply one, but by no means the only factor affecting the distribution of power.

Finally, general conflict theory maintains that the fundamental conflict groups in society are not classes but status groups — groups having a distinct style of life and a high level of internal interaction, features that permit easy political mobilization. Classes are just one example of such groups and, in fact, display these characteristics to a lesser degree than ethnic and occupational groups, among others.

The most recent theory of stratification is still in the process of elaboration and involves a profound shift in focus.

World Systems Theory

All of the previous theories attempt to account for the nature, causes, and consequences of stratification, mainly by reference to factors internal to a society: to its mode of production, its functional requirements, and so on. In contrast, world systems theory refers to the external relations of societies. It argues that relations with other societies determine a society's stratification system. There is a kind of world society of which individual countries are component parts. What happens to a society, including what happens within it, is dependent largely on its position in this larger system of societies and the dynamics of this system as a whole. (See Wallerstein, 1979; Chase-Dunn and Rubinson, 1980.)

Specifically, within this world system, societies are themselves stratified, and imperialism is seen as the principal force producing this stratification. The exploitation of certain societies by others has led to the economic development of the developed exploiter societies at the expense of the underdevelopment of the exploited societies. The result has been the emergence of great economic disparities (i.e., stratification) between countries. For example, the per capita income in Canada in 1981 was $15 048 compared to $343 in India. This imperialist exploitation has taken place historically through a wide range of mechanisms: the slave trade, formal conquest (colonization), trade (in which the terms are unequal, thus benefiting some societies at the expense of others), foreign investment, and so forth.

Which countries exploit which is determined by the relative strength of their polity (countries with strong states exploiting those with weaker power), but the strength of a nation's state is, in turn, largely a consequence of its position in the world system of societies.

The mechanisms of imperialism, according to this theory, affect the structure of stratification even within individual societies. The exploiting countries concentrate within themselves the better-paying, more interesting, and less onerous jobs in the world economy (e.g., those of an engineer or executive secretary), resulting in an internal stratification system heavily biased toward the upper- and middle-strata occupations. These jobs are filled by the dominant ethnic group in these societies (essentially by whites, since the white nations have been the imperial powers). At the same time, emigration from underdeveloped countries — an emigration brought about by the disintegration of the economy of these countries because of imperialism — results in the movement of sizeable populations to the developed nations. These immigrants are relegated to the worst-paying jobs. In the end, there develops a three-tiered class system of the bourgeoisie, labor aristocracy (i.e.,

highly paid, majority-group white workers), and the *lumpen-proletariat*, such as black and Mexican Americans or Algerians in France. Exploitative relations between countries are often reproduced between regions of a country, with some developing at the expense of others, thus producing regional stratification.

The mechanisms of imperialism affect the form and character that class conflict takes. Since the lumpen-proletariat in the rich countries consists principally of colored peoples, since it is the colored societies of the world that have been subjected to imperialist exploitation, and since disadvantaged regions often are ethnically distinct, the lower classes in the world system are essentially racial/ethnic groups and so class conflict necessarily involves group conflict (Hechter, 1975).

In many ways, world systems theory is a variant of Marxism. It draws on ideas advanced in the early twentieth century by Lenin, who wrote a famous treatise on imperialism. It differs from mode-of-production Marxism in incorporating parameters outside a specific society to explain stratification, as the setting is the world.

Although it characterizes the current world system as capitalist and argues that only a transition to a socialist world system can bring about an end to inequality, many of its arguments contradict traditional Marxism. Partly for this reason, many Marxists have been highly critical of world systems theory. It is best, therefore, to regard it as a separate theory of stratification.

Each of the above theories can appeal for their plausibility to important visible characteristics of human behavior and society. Each, in effect, constitutes a comprehensive world view.

The next several chapters will examine specific aspects of stratification: class (Chapter 17), ethnic stratification (Chapter 18 focuses on race and Chapter 19 on ethnicity), and gender and age inequalities (Chapter 20).

SUMMARY

1. The first form of human social organization — hunting and gathering — was egalitarian, but once societies grew in size and technological complexity, stratification became a persistent feature of social life. In the modern world, although social-democratic countries such as Sweden have been able to reduce stratification, only small communities such as the kibbutzim have been able to eliminate it.

2. The pattern of stratification has varied greatly across societies. Among the principal forms are those of slavery, caste, feudalism, and class. The last characterizes industrial societies, along with caste-like elements that are present in the position of women and minority groups.

3. In industrial societies, stratification occurs along five social "axes": position in the economy, spatial location, ethnicity, gender, and age.

4. Sociologists disagree strongly about the causes and consequences of stratification. There are six competing theories: genetic theory, cultural and social environmentalism, Marxism, functionalism, general conflict theory, and world systems theory.

5. Genetic theory attributes stratification to such allegedly universal traits of human nature as self-ishness and to genetically determined differences among people in capability and temperament. In contrast, social and cultural environmentalism attribute such traits and differences to the social environment through socialization and socially-induced frustration, and regards the stratification system itself as one of the principal causes of these traits and individual differences.

6. Marxism argues that stratification is based on exploitation and springs from a society's mode of production. In industrial societies, this mode is capitalism. In contrast, functionalists argue that stratification is necessary for the smooth functioning of any complex society, that all members of a society benefit, even if unequally.

7. General conflict theory argues that stratification springs from (a) conflicts of interest that exist in all areas of a society, not just between employers and employees, but between men and women, ethnic groups, between the young and old; and from (b) the differential distribution of power among these groups, caused not just by the economy, but by many factors, including the state.

8. World systems theory locates the cause of stratification, not within a society, but in the relations between societies where one society is developing by exploiting and thus underdeveloping others.

GLOSSARY

Ascribed (versus achieved) status. Status that is given on the basis of characteristics over which an individual has no control, such as sex, race, or age.

Capitalism. The mode of production of most industrialized societies. The means of production are privately owned, and since most persons are without such ownership, they are compelled to work for those who do. They are thus subject to exploitation.

Caste system. A stratification system where most status is ascribed, including access to occupations.

Class society. A stratification system in which labor is formally free and in which status is achieved rather than ascribed, but where there are significant differences in social rewards.

Culture of poverty. The culture that often develops among poor people and is characterized by immediate gratification and fatalism, which together prevents them from taking advantage of economic opportunities when they do arise.

Ethology. The study of the *social* behavior of animals.

Functional requirements. Tasks that must be performed for a society to function well.

Labor aristocracy. That segment of the working class that is well paid and holds skilled jobs, generally in large firms that are unionized.

Lumpen-proletariat. That segment of the working class that is often unemployed and, when employed, holds unskilled, low-paying jobs, generally in smaller, competitive, nonunionized firms.

Mode-of-production Marxism. The economic base of a society in Marxist theory from which the structure and dynamics of society derive. The economic base includes not only the way goods and services are produced, but also the way they are appropriated from producers and redistributed to non-producers.

Sociobiology. The application of modern evolutionary and genetic theory to the study of the social behavior of animals. Its principal thesis is that the social behavior of animals is determined by their genes and is the outcome of the evolutionary process.

Status group. A social group having a common style of life and a higher degree of interaction with one another than with those in other groups. Examples are ethnic and occupational groups.

Structural (versus exchange) mobility. Mobility that results not from people exchanging positions, but from a shift in the overall structure of positions themselves.

Structured inequality/social stratification. The division of society into persistent, hierarchically-ranked social groups who differ in social rewards received, between whom social mobility is often limited, and who have distinct life styles.

FURTHER READING

Barash, David P. *Sociobiology and Behavior.* New York: Elsevier North-Holland, 1977. This is one of the best expositions of sociobiology available.

Collins, Randall. *Conflict Sociology.* New York: Academic Press, 1975. This is an excellent synthesis of general conflict theory and contains an interesting discussion of gender and age stratification.

O'Connor, James. *The Fiscal Crisis of the State.* New York: St. Martin's Press, 1973. This book gives a Marxist interpretation of the current economic crisis, relating it to changes in the class system.

Valentine, Charles. *Culture and Poverty, Critique and Counterproposals.* Chicago, Illinois: University of Chicago Press, 1968. This work both gives an exposition of the culture-of-poverty thesis and criticizes it.

Vogel, Ezra F. *Japan as Number One.* Cambridge: Harvard University Press, 1979. This book gives a functionalist explanation of Japan's economic success, relating it to the Japanese system of social stratification.

Wallerstein, Immanuel. *The Capitalist World Economy.* Cambridge, England: Cambridge University Press, 1979. A major work from the perspective of world systems theory.

CHAPTER SEVENTEEN

Inequalities of Social Class

A. H. TURRITTIN

INEQUALTIY

The facts of inequality are all around us. Some families are rich, others poor, and many are somewhere in between. Some people have a high social status or prestige, so much so that they are deferred to with great ceremony at public functions. By contrast, there are others who are looked down upon as disreputable. Individuals with sufficient political clout can pick up the telephone to speak directly with top government officials and get immediate action on a matter; others must resort to writing a letter to which they receive a polite, noncommittal form-letter in reply.

This brief description highlights the three dimensions of stratification — class, status, and power — which are the subject of this chapter, with an emphasis on class and status.

Marx, Weber, and Social Inequality

The concern with social inequality in sociology is as old as the discipline itself. Sociology's founding fathers, Karl Marx and Max Weber, were each concerned with explaining the rise of modern industrial society and the concurrent increase in corporate wealth, on the one hand, and the widespread poverty and exploitation of the new, urban working-classes on the other (Giddens, 1971).

For his time, Marx was highly perceptive about the nature of the developing capitalist-industrial system. According to him, the *bourgeoisie*, as owners of the means of production, was able to take advantage of the surplus labor to keep the wages of the *proletariat* low compared to the value of goods and services they produced. Marx discussed a number of other classes, too, such as landowners who live off rents, the intelligentsia (lawyers, journalists, writers, professors, and artists), and the petty bourgeoisie of small shopkeepers and artisans. For Marx, class is a form of property relationship, and thus structure can be understood only by careful analysis of the economy of a given society.

Writing at the turn of the twentieth century, Weber (1946) attempted a comprehensive, theoretical analysis of social stratification. Like Marx, Weber used the term *class* to refer to the economic dimension of social inequality. Like Marx, he recognized the role of property ownership in determining class position in society, but Weber stressed that what counted in determining class was one's position in the labor market. Class structure, from Weber's perspective, reflects how a society organizes and rewards jobs.

An equally important dimension of stratification is *status*. Status refers to the social standing of a group, whose appraisal stems from the deference and prestige paid to it, or from the authority attributed to it, by the larger society. For Weber, a group's status is often based on its style of life, especially on the privileges or handicaps associated with group membership. These privileges or handicaps may flow from a group's economic power, or the lack of it, but they can also be the result of factors such as special legal status. Race and ethnic-group relations often reflect status distinctions. Weber placed status struggles on a par with the conflict generated by class.

By *power*, Weber meant political power; in any society with a political system, power meant the ability of a group to influence decision-making in accord with its own interest. In democratic societies, this kind of power would normally be exercised by influencing political parties, especially the party in office. But the idea of power is general enough to apply to all organizations and associations, even to such groups as the family.

Social Inequality, Values, and Political Conflict

Human interaction may be viewed as a series of exchange relationships wherein one party gives and the other receives goods, services, advice, psychological and moral support, deference, and the like. Viewing social life in this way allows us to understand social inequality at its most basic level. From this vantage point, the concept of inequality calls attention to many kinds of unequal exchange relationships between individuals, between individuals and groups, and between groups. Observing and naming common forms of unequal exchange relationships is not only done by lay-persons in making sense of their own experience of inequality, but is the central task of sociology in the study of social stratification. Examples of unequal exchange relationships are parents' attempts to mold children as they grow up, and the patriarchial family in which women are consigned to the roles of wife, mother, and domestic laborer. On a larger scale, social inequalities also produce the redistribution of wealth to build institutions of high culture (learning, art, music), the construction of public works of all kinds, and the raising of armies. In modern times, such redistribution has made possible the advancement of science and technology, the rise of industry and mass production, the development of the welfare state with special concerns for health, education and social security, and the arms and space race.

Before we make haste to react to such outcomes of the redistribution of wealth, it is important to remember that (1) particular kinds of inequalities are not natural states but rather consequences of the ways societies structure their affairs; and therefore, (2) people collectively do have choices regarding these matters; and (3) inequalities are thus moral and political issues for the community. More generally, it should be noted that theoretical perspectives on inequalities and stratification may have strong, value biases. The functional perspective, by justifying social inequalities as being socially useful and therefore necessary, has been said to be conservative (Lenski, 1966). In contrast, mode-of-production Marxism and world-systems theory make radical and critical statements about the extent of political and economic inequality within and between societies. General conflict theories try to follow the value-neutral approach of Weber; they are largely descriptive, but with the skeptic's eye emphasize the constant struggle at all levels of society over issues of class, status, and power.

If some groups favor and promote forms of inequality, other groups resist them. In fact, inequality has often been the focus of social and religious movements aimed at change, reform, and revolution. Many different value positions regarding the acceptable extent and nature of inequality are possible. It is hoped that through the study of inequality by sociologists, the public can be offered relevant information and ideas concerning relations of equality and inequality, which can be utilized in policy-making by governments and the many private organizations that make up the larger community.

Class and Social Stratification

Class, like all concepts, can be used in two different analytical ways as either a nominal or a real concept. Class as a nominal concept is an arbitrary definition that is created as an aid to description. For example, we could speak of a two-class society of a few privileged rich and many poor. Such terms imply an arbitrary notion of level of wealth, above which a person is defined as rich and below which one is defined as poor. Class as a real concept refers to the actual existence of groups in society, whose relationship to each other reflects some form of inequality; a sense of membership in such a group and an ability to take collective action are characteristics of belonging to a class.

When sociologists speak of strata, or *socioeconomic status*, they are using nominal concepts; these imply a hierarchy of one sort or another with arbitrarily drawn divisions. For example, income quintiles for families, as reported by Statistics Canada, are based on ranking families by size of family income from high to low, then dividing the ranking into five equal parts; each division would contain a fifth of the total of all families after the ranking. The functionalist perspective, in particular, tends to examine inequality in terms of nominal concepts; functionalists are willing to acknowledge hierarchies of inequalities, such as income and prestige, but they are skeptical about acknowledging the reality of class groupings, such as the working class. By contrast, mode-of-production Marxists argue that classes are real and are ranked according to ownership of property. They also do not hesitate in pointing to the presence of a working class in Canadian society.

We have tried to be consistent in distinguishing between inequality, dimensions or kinds of inequality (class, status, and power), and social stratification, either in the nominal sense of strata or in the real sense of a social class structure. At this point, some clarification regarding the notion of *social stratification* is in order. In the previous chapter, it was noted that inequalities are structured; that is, if an individual is found at one point on a dimension of inequality, then it is likely that person will be similarly placed on other dimensions. For instance, if you have a low income, the chances are you will also have a low social status. This proposition is portrayed figuratively as a set of layers, hence the term stratification. Theorists that use a nominal scheme of social stratification often speak of social strata and describe layered pyramids or perhaps a diamond shape in order to emphasize where the majority of the population fits in a scheme of social inequality. An example of social stratification in the real group sense is the model of the class system used by mode-of-production Marxists. Weber also recognized social stratification in this latter sense. He expected that wealth, a high status, and maximum power would go together. He used the term *social class* to refer to the real grouping that results from structured inequality. Thus, a class system for him is a real system of social stratification.

Our discussion so far indicates some of the possibilities for analysis of unequal exchange relationships:

1. It is possible to isolate a particular kind of inequality and to ask how it is distributed in society (nominal descriptive).

2. It is possible to view society as a complex set of social groups that differ with regard to class, status, and power, so much so that it only makes sense to group them into a rough ranking of five or six strata (functionalists).

3. The class structure of a community may be viewed as a question for empirical investigation as to which combination of class, status, and power is embodied in self-aware class groupings (community studies).

4. Classes can be viewed as real social groups based on, say, the criterion of relationship to the means of production, with the understanding that class has important ramifications for status and power as well (Marxist).

5. A class structure may be acknowledged, but on the premise that the basis of class can vary, with wealth and power being the basis of the ruling class, but with labor-market position determining membership in other classes. (Weber and the viewpoint of general conflict theory.)

STUDYING CLASS

If classes are still strong social realities today, is it because they are the result of an uneven distribution of wealth and power? Or have classes been replaced by finely graded social distinctions that reflect how people relate to just and necessary distributions of scarce resources? Questions such as these have stimulated the search for data in support of one or another of the general perspectives on class, status, and power.

Class and the Community

The early studies of class in the United States often focused on the community, and discovering the class structure of the community was deemed essential in these projects. The most famous are those associated with social anthropologist W. Lloyd Warner and his colleagues (Warner and Lunt, 1941; Warner, 1949). Beginning in the 1930s, their studies included a New England town, a Southern town, a Midwest town, and the black community in Chicago. Classes considered as prestige or status groupings were found to be central to the total social system of these communities. In Yankee City, for example, a small, coastal city north of Boston, Warner found six status classes. But researchers in the Southern town found that the perception of status-class structure varied depending on the position of the informant interviewed. People tended to lump together the classes farthest from their own position, suggesting to the researchers that there was no consensus on the exact nature of even a local class structure.

Socioeconomic Status and Occupational Prestige

Warner and his colleagues were pioneers in developing the use of local informants to reveal the local class structure; they were also pioneers in developing quantitative scaling methods for determining socioeconomic status (SES). In large cities, and in the nation as a whole, it is too much, some critics say, to expect that people will have consistent views on either the nature of the class structure of their region or of the whole society. To continue to study social stratification in the wider community, therefore, nominal measures of SES were developed.

Today, modern SES scales are based on occupation, income, and education, and sometimes area of residence. Each of these dimensions or variables is quantified in some way and a formula is used to produce a composite score; the scores obtained can be used in turn to divide people into groups of low, medium, or high SES.

Of the three common variables used, income, and education are already scaled — income, because it comes in the form of money, and education, because it is measured by the number of years of schooling. Occupation is not as simple, since there are literally thousands of occupations in the world of work. However, sociologists have cleverly quantified even this feature of contemporary society.

Occupation is important in the study of social stratification because it is the link between family and economy. That is to say, through wages and salary earned at work, people become consumers of goods and services that contribute to a particular standard of living and life style. Jobs differ in terms of income, prestige, and power, so that, overall, occupation is indicative of all three main types of inequality.

Canadian sociologists Pineo and Porter (1967) conducted a study of occupational prestige in Canada in 1965. They asked respondents to evaluate 204 job titles regarding their perception of the general status of the job in the community. Table 17-1 gives some of their findings. The results show that not only does the public make judgements about social standing, but also that there is general agreement regarding the social status of occupations across the community. There is also some evidence that people, in assigning a status, weigh in their mind such job characteristics as the skill and education required, pay level, service to the community, and decision-making responsibilities. But, agreement regarding prestige is not equal across the class structure; there is more disagreement about the prestige given to occupations at the lower levels of Canadian society than at the top (Guppy, 1984; Guppy and Goyder, 1984).

Still another method of using occupation to study social stratification involves using an index of socioeconomic status without reference to pres-

TABLE 17-1. Occupational Prestige Scores, 1965

Occupation Title	Canada 1965
Provincial premier	90
Physician	87
County court judge	83
Catholic priest	73
Civil engineer ·	73
Owner of a manufacturing plant	69
Registered nurse	65
Economist	62
Public school teacher	60
Computer programmer	54
Policeman	52
Electrician	50
Bookkeeper	49
Farm owner and operator	44
Machinist	44
Plumber	43
Bank teller	42
Typist	42
Carpenter	40
Barber	39
Automobile repairman	38
Bus driver	36
Trailer truck driver	33
Restaurant cook	30
Assembly-line worker	28
Clerk in a store	27
Cod fisherman	23
Waitress	20
Bartender	20
Janitor	17

SOURCE: Pineo and Porter, 1967.

tige. Canadian sociologist Bernard Blishen has been creating socioeconomic indices of occupation since 1951, using sensus data. Blishen scores by themselves, or as a component of an SES scale, have been widely used in Canada to study social inequality. In the 1981 Blishen scale, a composite score is given to each of the 500 occupations used by Statistics Canada to represent the occupational structure of Canada.

Table 17-2 gives Blishen's score for thirty selected occupations, plus the information that went into the calculation of the index number: the level of education held by incumbents of a

TABLE 17-2. 1981 Blishen Occupational Scores for Selected Canadian Occupations

Occupational category*	Blishen score: total labor force	Number	Proportion in occupation with some post-secondary education or univ. degree	Average 1980 employment income for full-time workers Males	Females	Proportion of women in occupational category
Judges and magistrates	69.5	1790	93.3%	$51 795	—	—
Physicians and surgeons	68.4	40 620	100.0	59 834	$36 115	17.1%
Government administrators	66.8	23 560	73.7	31 655	21 846	20.0
Civil engineers	66.5	31 230	89.9	31 311	24 201	2.8
Police officers and detectives, government	65.9	55 110	53.3	25 336	20 459	4.1
Economists	65.6	12 165	89.6	31 034	22 225	20.2
General managers and other senior officials	63.1	86 230	62.6	46 160	24 914	9.4
Systems analysts, computer programmers, and related occupations	62.3	60 680	85.1	28 461	18 788	28.5
Elementary and kindergarten teachers	61.9	173 275	95.1	24 173	20 279	80.4
Construction electricians and repairers	56.6	56 695	25.5	21 417	15 549	1.2
Nurses: registered, graduated, and in-training	53.6	175 575	83.4	18 891	18 041	95.4
Pipefitting, plumbing, and related occs.	52.2	52 810	15.6	20 811	18 885	0.7
Machinist and machine tool setting-up occs.	51.2	46 220	20.5	19 021	11 148	2.8
Ministers of religion	48.1	22 030	89.9	12 555	9249	7.3
Motor vehicle mechanics and repairers	44.2	145 905	14.5	16 550	14 091	1.1
Bookkeepers and accounting clerks	42.6	403 340	43.1	16 830	12 616	82.1
Typists and clerk typists	40.1	100 480	38.4	16 216	11 786	97.9
Barbers, hairdressers, and related occs.	39.7	66 855	14.2	13 893	9865	75.3
Motor vehicle fabricating and assembling occupations, not elsewhere classified	39.1	29 585	13.8	18 364	12 974	15.8
Carpenters and related occupations	36.0	130 480	15.6	17 730	13 827	1.1
Bus drivers	34.2	51 240	16.0	19 313	12 298	25.0
Sales clerks and salespersons commodities, not elsewhere classified	34.1	540 585	27.0	17 053	9495	57.0
Truck drivers	33.9	266 930	11.5	18 601	13 167	2.6
Cashiers and tellers	31.9	242 270	25.4	14 131	10 305	92.7
Crop farmers	29.4	42 855	20.2	14 800	7829	8.8

Occupational category*	Blishen score: total labor force	Number	Proportion in occupation with some post-secondary education or univ. degree	Average 1980 employment income for full-time workers		Proportion of women in occupational category
				Males	Females	
Bartenders	28.1	33 945	27.5	11 295	8365	52.8
Food and beverage-serving occupations	24.8	239 430	21.1	10 884	7687	82.1
Chefs and cooks	23.2	154 955	15.2	13 025	9508	52.2
Janitors, charworkers, and cleaners	19.9	230 875	11.9	13 899	9637	41.4
Net-, trap-, and line-fishing occupations	17.6	33 310	8.1	14 326	6933	3.8

NOTE: The Statistics Canada unit group includes a diversity of occupations, but also some broad occupations have several unit groups. For example, farmers are tabulated in three unit groups, totaling 219 930 persons in 1981; crop farmers as a unit group includes wheat farmers, market gardeners, fruit farmers, and other kinds of farmers as well.

SOURCE: Blishen scores supplied by Bernard R. Blishen, Department of Sociology, York University. Educational attainment levels and employment income data were obtained from Statistics Canada (1983a, 1984c). Blishen scores are rounded off to the nearest tenth.

particular occupational group, average employment income, and the proportion of women in the occupational category.

Objective Class Position: the Marxist Perspective

For some functionalists, data such as that shown in Table 17-2. would be taken as evidence that there are no strong class lines in Canadian society, and that economic rewards match the functional importance of a job. The argument would be that jobs require different levels of skill and responsibility, and that these characteristics of a job show its social importance. Education would be taken as an indirect indicator of a job's skill and responsibility requirements.

A contrasting view is held by mode-of-production Marxists. Wright (1979) defines class according to three different kinds of control over the means of production: (1) control over how much and what is produced by a firm, as well as control over investment policy; (2) control over how items are produced in offices and plants; and (3) control over supervision. Using these three cri-

teria, Wright outlines six classes in the United States, including the three classical Marxist classes: the *bourgeoisie*, who are the owners and controllers of the main part of the nation's wealth; the *working class*, who sell their labor, whether it is physical or mental; and the *petty bourgeiosie*, who are self-employed and own their means of production.

Wright also identifies three groups occupying what he terms contradictory class locations. The growth of large-scale organizations with multiple branches and complex hierarchies of authority has lead to a considerable number of managers, technicians, foremen, and supervisors. This group occupies a contradictory class position because, although they are employees, they work on behalf of owners or directors to extract surplus value from workers. This relatively new class is further divided by Wright into two levels reflecting degrees of control within this class: top managers, middle managers, and technocrats occupy the higher level, and bottom managers, foremen, and supervisors occupy the lower. A second contradictory class includes small employers who employ up to about fifty persons. Although they are small-scale capitalists in their own right, they are often tied to large corporations and banks as dependent clients, which limits their sphere of control. To acknowledge positions characterized by considerable autonomy over the work process, occupations such as research scientist, consulting engineer, and independent artisan, Wright includes a final contradictory class location, semi-autonomous employees.

Table 17-3 illustrates Wright's scheme of six classes and shows estimates of the size of these classes based on data from several surveys done in the United States and Canada. Note that the bourgeoisie is tiny as a class, and that the majority are working class according to mode-of-production criteria.

EVOLUTION OF CLASS STRUCTURE IN CANADA

There is a widespread belief that Canada, in general, has become a middle-class society as a result of the prosperity and affluence following World War II. In a classic analysis of class structure and power in Canada, Porter (1965) refuted this idea. Tracing the evolution of class structure would require a detailed review of Canada's political, economic, and demographic history — too much of an undertaking for an introductory chapter. But one way to obtain a quick sense of class and social change is to examine the important changes that have occurred in the occupational structure. Table 17-4 covers the period from 1901 to 1981.

There is a major decline in farmers from 40 percent in 1901 to less than 6 percent in 1981. This decrease reflects the general decline in the number of independent businessmen or petty bougeoisie. If male manual workers are representative of the working class, then this class has held its own proportionally in terms of size since the turn of the century, from 42 percent in 1911, to 46 percent in 1951, to 44 percent in 1981. In terms of absolute numbers, however, male manual workers have grown from almost a million in 1911 to

TABLE 17-3. **Objective Classes in Capitalist Society**

Objective Class	Proportion of the Labor Force	
	United States	Canada
	%	%
Classical Marxist Classes		
bourgeoisie	1– 2	1.4
proletariat	41–54	62.6
petty Bourgeoisie	4.5	8.0
Wright's Contradictory Class Locations		
top managers, middle managers, and technocrats	12	2.9
bottom managers, foremen, and supervisors	18–23	13.3*
small employers	6– 7	3.5
semi-autonomous employers	5–11	8.2

* Canadian data does not include a category for bottom managers.

SOURCE: Modified from Wright, 1979, page 40, for U.S. data; and Ornstein, 1983, page 40, for Canadian data.

just over three million in 1981. By 1921, a fifth of men in the labor force were in white-collar occupations, this proportion rising to two-fifths by 1981. Every male occupational subgroup in this larger category at least doubled in proportion between 1901 and 1981, though professionals increased by a factor of four. Thus, the kinds of occupations able to support a middle- or upper-middle class life style have more than doubled since the turn of the century.

The most noteworthy feature of Table 17-4 is the remarkable growth in the size of the female labor force between 1901 and 1981. In 1901, for every woman in the labor force, there were almost seven men: in 1981, 40 percent of the labor force was female. In 1901, the majority of women were housewives; close to a third were manual workers, and over a third were in personal-service occupations (maids, servants, cleaners, cooks). In 1981,

TABLE 17-4. Occupational Change in Canada, 1901 to 1981, by Sex.

Occupational Category	Sex	Percentage Distribution for Canada by Census Year:								
		1901	1911	1921	1931	1941	1951	1961	1971	1981
White-collar	males	14.0%	14.9%	21.1%	20.2%	20.4%	25.4%	30.6%	40.0%	37.1%
	females	23.6%	30.5%	48.3%	45.5%	44.7%	55.4%	57.3%	63.0%	67.9%
proprietary and	males	4.8	5.2	8.2	6.4	6.2	8.7	9.6	13.0	8.6
managerial	females	1.2	1.6	2.0	1.6	2.0	3.0	2.9	4.0	4.2
professional	males	3.1	2.4	3.0	3.7	4.5	5.3	7.7	13.0	12.2
	females	14.7	12.7	19.1	17.8	15.6	14.4	15.5	18.0	19.0
commercial and financial (sales	males	3.2	4.4	5.2	5.7	5.2	5.4	6.6	17.0	9.5
from 1971)	females	2.4	6.7	8.4	8.4	8.8	10.5	10.2	9.0	9.6
clerical	males	2.9	3.0	4.7	4.4	4.5	5.9	6.7	7.0	6.8
	females	5.3	9.4	18.7	17.7	18.3	27.5	28.6	32.0	35.1
Service	males	2.9	3.1	3.5	4.2	4.6	6.5	8.5	7.0	9.5
(personal)*	females	42.0	37.2	26.8	33.9	34.3	21.2	22.6	22.0	15.4
Manual	males	35.2	41.6	36.2	40.4	41.5	46.3	45.2	46.0	43.9
	females	30.6	27.8	20.9	16.8	18.5	19.4	13.3	14.0	10.6
manufacturing	males	13.8	11.7	10.3	11.3	16.2	17.9	18.4	31.0	23.2
and mechanical	females	29.6	26.2	17.8	12.7	15.4	14.6	9.9	11.0	9.0
construction	males	5.4	5.5	5.5	5.7	5.8	7.1	7.1	—	10.5
	females	—	—	—	—	—	0.1	—	—	0.3
transportation &	males	5.0	6.3	5.9	7.0	7.5	9.2	9.7	7.0	6.0
communications	females	—	1.5	3.0	2.4	1.7	2.9	2.2	2.0	0.6
mining and	males	1.8	2.6	1.7	1.8	2.1	1.6	1.4	1.0	1.0
quarrying	females	—	—	—	—	—	—	—	—	—
logging	males	1.0	1.8	1.4	1.3	2.3	2.5	1.7	1.0	1.1
	females	—	—	—	—	—	—	—	—	0.1
laborers	males	8.2	13.7	11.4	13.2	7.6	8.0	6.9	6.0	2.1
	females	0.5	0.1	0.1	1.7	1.4	1.8	1.2	1.0	0.6
Primary	males	47.7	40.5	39.0	35.1	33.0	20.6	13.0	7.3	6.1
	females	3.8	4.5	3.7	3.7	2.3	2.8	4.3	2.0	2.2
agriculture	males	45.9	39.0	37.9	33.7	31.5	19.3	12.2	7.0	5.6
	females	3.8	4.4	3.7	3.6	2.3	2.8	4.3	2.0	2.2
fishing, hunting,	males	1.8	1.5	1.1	1.4	1.5	1.3	0.8	0.3	0.5
trapping	females	—	0.1	—	0.1	—	—	—	—	—
Not Stated	males	—	—	0.2	—	0.3	1.3	2.7	—	3.4
	females	—	—	0.3	—	0.2	1.2	2.5	—	3.7
Total Number	males	1 544 900	2 341 400	2 658 500	3 244 800	3 352 400	4 114 400	4 694 300	5 353 000	7 152 200
	females	237 900	357 000	485 100	663 300	831 100	1 162 200	1 763 900	2 782 000	4 853 000

NOTE: Service occupations include policemen, firemen, guards, chefs, cooks, bartenders, waiters and waitresses, porters, chambermaids, barbers, hostesses and stewards, and so on.; thus, service occupations do not correspond to what economists call the service sector of the economy. Dashes indicate fewer than 0.05 percent, or no category. Trend data between 1961 and 1971 were affected by a new system of occupational categories adopted for the 1971 census.

SOURCE: Ostry, 1967; for 1971 and 1981 data, see Statistics Canada, 1983b.

Women began entering the paid labor force in significant numbers toward the end of the nineteenth century.

19 percent were professionals — albeit mostly in female-dominated professions such as teaching and nursing, with 35 percent in the clerical category alone. Women in personal services dropped to 15 percent, and in the manual work category to 10 percent. If one considers sales, clerical, service, and manual occupations as working class, then 71 percent of working women today could be labelled working class.

In summary, an examination of trends in occupational statistics shows that there have been some important shifts in class composition in Canada. The working class remains a large class, based in blue-collar and service work, to which has been added a segment of women in low-level, white-collar jobs. Upper-level, white-collar occupations have increased significantly; this level includes a variety of new professionals that are the core of a substantial, new middle class (Mills, 1951).

Inequality of Condition in Canada

As individuals, we enter society with a number of ascribed statuses that are derived from our family

Polish shoppers purchase meat with ration cards. Communist countries exhibit a relatively low disparity between personal incomes, although Party membership can carry non-income privileges.

background. *Inequality of condition* refers to those starting points on the various dimensions of inequality. In order to focus on social inequality in Canada, it is useful to study inequalities of condition in terms of Max Weber's three dimensions of stratification, namely class, status, and power.

Income and Wealth: the Class (Material) Dimension

Inequalities of income and wealth are perhaps the most obvious forms of inequality in a money-based market economy, for they readily translate into different styles of consumption: the conspicuous consumption of the *nouveaux riches*, the suburban respectability of the middle class, the frugality of the working class, and the shabbiness of the poor.

There is an important difference between income and wealth that should be emphasized. *Income* is what is being earned by working for wages or a salary, though some professionals earn fees (doctors, lawyers, writers). By contrast, *wealth* refers to "stored up" income, such as stocks and bonds, real estate, or other forms of property,

TABLE 17-5. Before-tax Income of Families and Unattached Individuals by Quintile, 1951–83.

Income quintile	1951*	1961*	1971	1981	1983**	Upper limit of 1983 income quintile
	%	%	%	%	%	$
Highest	42.8	41.4	43.3	41.8	43.4	—
Fourth	23.3	24.5	24.9	25.2	24.9	43 383
Middle	18.3	18.3	17.6	17.6	17.0	29 840
Second	11.2	11.9	10.6	10.9	10.2	19 509
Lowest	4.4	4.2	3.6	4.6	4.4	10 465
Average in current dollars	4005	4665	8845	25 641	28 912	
Average in constant dollars (1981)	14 375	14 739	20 960	25 641	24 669	

* Excludes farm families.
** Preliminary estimates.

SOURCES: Data are found in the Statistics Canada series 13-206, now entitled Income Distributions by Size in Canada, issued annually from 1971 onward; for 1983, see Statistics Canada (1984b).

all of which can be inherited across generations. Depending on its form, wealth also can provide an income on which one can live.

From an international perspective, Canada is among the world's wealthiest nations. The average, per capita income was $8823 in 1976 (*The Economist*, 1980). This figure placed Canada at the same level as the United States, Switzerland, Sweden, and Australia; one-third more per person than in Japan or Austria; twice as much as in Britain and Israel; and three times as much as in Italy, Hong Kong, Greece, and Venezuela. Canada is also classified as having a fairly low level of income inequality. Research has shown that the best predictor of low-income inequality in a society is a high level of political democracy (Stack, 1980). The exceptions to this rule are the Eastern-Bloc Communist countries. The reasons for greater income equality in the Eastern Bloc are (1) the absence of wealth accumulation by individuals; (2) the lower pay levels of many white-collar occupations relative to those of blue-collar workers; and (3) the stronger egalitarian ideology in these countries. However, the leaders in the Eastern Bloc have non-income privileges not

available to ordinary citizens, a fact that reflects some inequality.

Income inequality in Canada can be shown by ranking income-earners, dividing the ranking into quintiles (equal fifths), and then calculating the slice of income pie obtained by each quintile group. As Table 17-5 shows, the distribution of before-tax income has remained constant over the postwar period, but it is an unequal distribution, with the top two-fifths of all families and individuals holding close to 70 percent of the before-tax income since at least 1951. These earning differences are largely owing to the different earning power of various occupations; if we look back at Table 17-2 , we see that there are significant income gaps between occupations such as truck driver and carpenter, on the one hand, and systems analyst, civil engineer, and general manager, on the other.

Income distribution has been the topic of several studies (Johnson, 1977; 1979), which argue that the gap has widened regarding individual earnings. Whereas the average worker's income was $2802 in 1946 and $4698 in 1974, for lawyers, average earnings increased from $10 142 to

Algonquin children play amid debris in a squatter settlement near a sawmill at Rapides des Cedres in northwestern Québec. Some observers have compared the health problems of Canada's native peoples to those faced by the Third World's poor.

$24 458 in the same years. These figures represent an almost doubling of real income for the average wage-earner, and almost a two-and-a-half times increase for the average lawyer, starting from a base almost four times above that of the average earner. But if the gap between incomes has been increasing through time, how is it that the family and individual income distributions have not changed significantly since 1951? One answer is that the growing inequality between occupations noticed by people like Johnson has been offset by increased family income due to ever more wives working full- or part-time (Armstrong and Armstrong, 1975).

Poverty

The lowest income quintile merits special concern, since it is proof that poverty remains a major social problem in Canada in spite of postwar affluence. The likelihood of being poor is strongest if (1) one lives in a rural area; (2) one is a single female parent with children under eighteen; (3) one's household has no income-earners; (4) one is over the age of sixty-five; (5) one is handicapped; or (6) one is a native person. Often several of these causes work together; for example, a single mother with young children is not likely to be able to work and be a parent at the same time, especially in a city or region with high unemployment. The lowest income quintile includes mainly people found in the circumstances just mentioned, and these groups are heavily dependent on government programs as their main source of livelihood.

Poverty may be defined either according to budget or income. The budget approach defines poverty in terms of a bare subsistence level for household survival (minimum basic shelter, food, clothing, and health needs), or a somewhat higher level of subsistence deemed to be adequate. Statistics Canada calculated that in 1978, the average family spent 38.5 percent of income on basic necessities. It arbitrarily defines an individual or family as low-income if 58.5 percent or more of income was spent on basic necessities. By this standard, 4.3 million Canadians lived below the poverty line in 1983, the poverty line being $19 397 for an urban family of four. The relative-income approach, developed by the Canadian Council on Social Development (1984), sets the poverty line at 50 percent of the average family income; this method leads to a poverty line somewhat higher than that of Statistics Canada: $20 125 for a family of four in 1983.

It is a myth to picture the poor as a population living off welfare or as trapped forever in a cycle of poverty. Half of all low-income families have employed heads of households. One cause of poverty for them is being caught in low-paying occupations. Others are poor because they are not employable and are heavily dependent on government "safety-net" programs for survival. These programs themselves generally provide an income of less than 60 percent of the poverty line. Unfortunately, little is known about movement in and out of poverty. A ten-year, follow-up study in the United States showed that fewer than one in twelve families in the general population stayed on welfare for more than seven years, but one in every four American families received some temporary welfare assistance in the ten-year period (Duncan et al., 1984). It has been suggested that safety-net programs and minimum-wage levels are kept deliberately low in North America so as to guarantee a sizeable pool of people willing to work at low wages (Piven and Cloward, 1971).

Sources of Income Inequality

There are both individualistic explanations and structural explanations of income inequality in Canada. Individual explanations focus on the

In spite of recent gains, fully employed women still earn 60 percent less than fully employed men.

training, ability, and experience of a person. The functionalist theory of stratification, in particular, regards training as a key variable in explaining financial success. Yet empirical research on the relationship of education to income does not support this theory. Moreover, correlating measured intelligence to income also shows virtually no direct relation (Jencks et al., 1972). By contrast, experience and age do influence income, which suggests that structural factors may be more significant in explaining income inequality.

Structural explanations focus on the institutional arrangements of society. They do not necessarily oppose individualistic variables, but constitute a shift in perspective. With respect to income, the key factor is not individual talent, but the structure of the labor market in terms of jobs and pay. The fact, for example, that fully employed women earn 60 percent less than fully employed men (even with the variable of education controlled), does not suggest that women are less talented than men, but that women have been less successful compared to men in demanding high pay from employers for the kind of work they do. The reason that age and experience affect income is understandable in structural terms, also; payment systems generally have strong career or seniority biases to them. In recent years, the structure of the labor market has received considerable attention (Montagna, 1977).

Although individualistic explanations do not help much in explaining income inequality, this does not mean that individual effort and skill are irrelevant to economic success. The greater efficacy of structural explanations, rather, reflects the complexity of the game of economic success. There are so many individuals with similar training and talent who earn different incomes that no relationship between individualistic factors and income can be deduced. By contrast, examining structural features of society — such as class, gender, and sector of the economy — shows systematic causes of inequality (Ornstein, 1983).

Inequality and Fairness

Is economic inequality good or bad for society? Are there levels of wealth and income that ought not to be acceptable? Should doctors, top professional athletes, chief executive officers, and similar high-prestige occupations be paid ten to twenty times as much as a garment worker receiving just above the minimum wage? Should corporations be required to keep jobs at home rather than expanding production in other countries? Should all wages be required to be at a level sufficient for satisfying basic subsistence needs? These are issues of distributive justice that can only be addressed and answered by taking a value position, by working out notions of fairness, by considering social as well as individual needs, and by deciding on tradeoffs between competing values.

POWER: THE POLITICAL DIMENSION

Power is the ability of one group (or individual) to work its will on other groups or individuals. Power takes different forms. When it rests on accepted values and its exercise is accepted as legitimate, it is referred to as *authority*. It can also take the form of various kinds of influence such as persuasion, domination, and manipulation. Power has a negative form in the sense that the powerful may not permit social problems to become public issues; this is termed the power of "non-decision." (Bachrach and Baratz, 1963.) For example, the discussion of the inequalities of wealth, and even of power itself, is not often presented as an issue for public debate by major political parties that have a stake in the status quo.

There are two faces to power. Functionalists point out that power is a social resource. They reason that, in order to function, groups and institutions need to make decisions, and for decision-making to be efficient, power must be delegated to leaders. Power, then, is a social resource necessary for group living. By contrast, conflict theorists stress the coercive uses of power — to manipulate and dominate — and in general, to concentrate wealth and to confer prestige and control on the key institutions of a society.

Power, as a fundamental aspect of all human relations, is found in the family, church organizations, schools, factories, as well as between organizations, levels of government, and so on. The kind of power addressed in most studies of social stratification is political power, because of the central place that state power plays in the contemporary world. Today, state and civil society are highly integrated, so much so that we count on government to achieve all sorts of ends, including setting the legal framework and policies that permit,

Peter C. Newman has written extensively on the social and economic power elite in Canada in such books as *The Acquisitors* and *The Canadian Establishment*.

moderate, or exacerbate forms of inequality. This is not to say that government is the only arena of power. One of the main issues in the study of power is the role of non-government power, particularly the power of corporations in liberal-democratic capitalist societies. Other key agencies that wield power in these societies are the military, organized labor, the church, and cultural institutions such as the mass media, to name the major ones.

The two main models of power are the elitist and the pluralist. Each tries to deal with questions such as: which individuals and groups actually make policy? Are powerful groups internally cohesive and can one speak reasonably of common interests? Is power distributed and shared among different power groups? How much access to power do subordinate groups have? The term elite is used in both of the theoretical perspectives mentioned, to refer to the uppermost decision-making positions in organizations. Thus, mention of the clerical elite would refer to the religious leaders in Canada's main religious organizations.

The elitist perspective of power has a distinguished list of exponents — Marx, Weber, Pareto, Mosca, Michels, Veblen — each with divergent views partly based on differing political persuasions. In the United States, research on power was partly stimulated by C. Wright Mills' provocative study, *The Power Elite* (1956). Mills argued that in the post-Second World War period, the elites of the corporation conglomerates, the executive branch of the federal government, and the military, formed a single power elite. According to Mills, the cold war of the 1950s legitimated the actions of the power elite; public debate on a whole range of domestic and foreign policy issues was stifled as other forums of decision-making atrophied, including democratic institutions that served as a means of power for the majority. Domhoff (1967), moved away from Mills' power-elite concept, arguing instead of the omnipotence of the upper class. He located the important power roles in the various institutional spheres of society and then showed the dominance of upper-class persons in these roles.

John Porter's *The Vertical Mosaic* (1965) was the first attempt to lay out the elite structure in Canada. He examined the social background and recruitment pattern of elite members in large corporations, the federal government bureaucracy, organized labor, the mass media, and intellectual circles; he also assessed broadly the role of corporations, the cabinet, the judiciary, the federal civil service, organized labor, the media, universities, and organized religion in Canadian society. Rejecting the notion of power elite, Porter believed that Canada's elites are integrated into a "confraternity of power," with the links between elites made through formal organizational ties (interlocking directorships), ties of kinship and friendship and elite switching. Because a pure harmony of interests does not exist between elites, one of the chief roles of government and the party system is to mediate conflicts of interests when they occur. The exception to this description is the labor elite, which is drawn primarily from a working-class background and does not have the ties that would really include it in the confraternity of power.

Porter's pluralist conception of power does not deny the elitist's contention that power is concentrated in particular groups, but rather argues that power is exercised by many different groups, and as a result, there are checks and balances in the arenas of power. Power is seen as a matter of struggle, mediation, and compromise, where there is not always one consistent winner, either the state or the corporate elite.

Porter's research, as well as more recent studies, show just how small Canadian elite groups are: in the economy, there are approximately a hundred dominant corporations. Writing about corporation directors and top executives, Peter C. Newman (1975) observes that "Canada's Establishment consists of a surprisingly compact self-perpetuating group of perhaps a thousand men who act as a kind of informal junta, linked much more closely to each other than to their country." Regarding their influence, he notes, "Although their power is waning, they still possess the ability to compel obedience, to shape events and trends — political and cultural as well as economic — in their favour." (1975: page 387.) The political elite, composed of the prime minister, provincial premiers, and federal and provincial cabinet ministers, numbered 159 persons over the period 1961 to 1973. The bureaucratic elite — top civil servants and heads of crown corporations, both federal and provincial — comprised about 350 persons in 1973 (Olsen, 1980). The "superbureaucrats," described by Campbell and Szablowski (1979), who work with the top federal political figures to set overall policy and budgets for government departments and agencies, number about a hundred individuals. Other elites, such as organized labor, the clergy, and the mass media are correspondingly small.

One feature of the Canadian elite structure is its exposure to foreign control, particularly control located in the United States. Ogmundson estimates that half of Canada's businesses and two-thirds of its unions and the media are externally controlled. Furthermore, our military policy is highly integrated with that of the United States and West-European countries. Major churches are part of international structures. "The degree to which Canada is externally dominated appears to be unusually great in a comparative perspective." (1983:248.) The dominance of U.S. multinational corporations in the Canadian economy has been a particularly controversial issue. Clement (1975) believes that this dominance is responsible for the Canadian industry's orientation toward resource-extraction rather than manufacturing, a situation that has been promoted by Canada's financial elite's serving the interests of foreign-owned firms. However, Clement's analysis has been challenged by Carroll (1982), who claims that since the early 1970s, Canadian-owned industries are on the increase, breaking to some extent the historical pattern observed by Clement.

One realization emerges from our discussion of power: that the political process — the party system, elections, the passing of laws — is only one part of a more comprehensive system of power. The economic sector, for example, is an important autonomous sector of decision-making activity. When government, industry, and other interests — such as organized labor — clash, the conflict is generally resolved outside the legislative process, although government often sets the rules of the game in advance. The historic distribution of power as reflected in the class system does mean that the scales are tipped to begin with; to use a cliché, some groups are more equal than others.

LIFE STYLES, STATUS GROUPS, AND CLASS CULTURES

Some sociologists argue that classes, in the sense of homogeneous social groups based on property relations — the working class, the middle class, or the petty bourgeoisie, for example — are no longer the social realities they once were (Moore, 1963;

Wrong, 1964). Instead, what has become more significant are status groups — groups whose identity and life style are based on such diverse factors as generation, occupation, religion, ethnicity, perhaps even on sexual orientation, or on a combination of factors not socioeconomic in origin. Because of the diversity of possible bases for status-group formation, the number of such groups could be large indeed.

For Weber, status groups lay claim to a particular honor or prestige that enables them to carry on a particular life style or set of cultural practices. Restriction of membership in some form is essential to a status group. In extreme cases, status groups even regulate choice of friends and marriage partners, and take on the characteristics of a caste. The caste system in India is probably the best example of social stratification based on a complex structuring of status groups. Large-scale societies are bound to have numerous, and an ever-changing collage of, status groups. One clue to their existence in North America is found in the world of advertising; marketing experts try to gear products to status groups such as Yuppies — the current catch phrase for young urban professionals.

We can safely say that status groups have been and will always be with us. The question is whether status groups are today more salient in the everyday life of North Americans than is class, compared to the past. Interestingly enough, the issue of whether or not classes exist today is usually phrased in terms of doubting the reality of the working class, rather than doubting the existence of the middle class or the upper class. A highly unified and class-conscious upper class is usually taken for granted, and the middle class is frequently interpreted as now being so broad as to have absorbed the working class, though perhaps leaving a residue in something called the lower class.

Drawing on the work of sociologists (e.g., Gans, 1962; Vanfossen, 1979), we shall examine five social class divisions. Even though these divisions are controversial, their labels and images are common in the public mind and often referred to by sociologists, as well.

The Upper Class

As Clement has pointed out (1975), the upper class consists mainly of families of the corporate elite. Wealth is obviously a requirement, given the role of the upper class in capitalist society and the high cost of maintaining its life style. The Canadian "establishment" has been well charted by Newman (1975). In his two latest books (1978, 1981), he describes the challenge to the old upper class by "the acquisitors," men who made their fortune by hard work, without the help of inheritance and family connections. The old upper class, prejudiced against minority ethnic and religious groups, has had to open up to this rising group whose members include Catholics, Jews, French Canadians and Chinese Canadians. These nouveaux riches are also often from Western Canada, rather than from the older industrial and financial centres of Ontario and Québec.

The Canadian upper class clearly fits Weber's notion of status group. It socializes its children in a series of private schools from the elementary level through to university. Its exclusive life style is marked by membership in private clubs, homes on large tracts of land, ingroup selection of marriage partners, reserved tables at high-class restaurants, elite hobbies such as horse-breeding and racing, and so on. Leadership training is especially important for the upper class, since their power largely rests on populating key management posts and boards of directors of corporation, universities, hospitals, foundations, and similar organizations. In terms of size, the upper class comprises only between 1 and 2 percent of the population.

The Upper-Middle and Lower-Middle Classes

The upper-middle class includes highly trained and highly paid professionals, business execu-

Many blue-collar jobs in Canada draw on the labor of a variety of ethnic subgroups.

tives, senior civil servants, and owners of small to medium-sized businesses, where the more modestly paid lower-middle class comprises white-collar semi-professionals and workers, such as school teachers, nurses, computer-systems analysts, sales personnel, supervisors, and foremen. The middle classes are paid by salaries, and in some cases, by fees.

The central value-orientation of the upper-middle class focuses on the career, with its constantly improving income and level of responsibility as one moves higher in an organization or profession. This also holds for the lower-middle class, with the exception that the opportunity for career advancement is much less. A university education is a prerequisite for upper-middle-class

occupations, whereas lower-middle-class positions are drawn from a greater variety of post-secondary training. The participation of middle-class people in the larger community, along with their high social and economic status, make their environment more predictable and gives them a high degree of control over their own fate.

Porter noted that the upper-middle-class life style rested on the "consumption" of a certain set of values: "Middle class mothers exchange opinions with each other about their obstetricians, pediatricians, and orthodontists. They discuss the relative merits of various nursery schools, private schools, ballet lessons, music classes, summer camps. They talk about their cottage communities or their touring holidays … it is the ability to consume these things … which identifies the real middle class." (1965: page 126.) Porter estimated that only the top 10 percent of families could afford to indulge in such a life style. In today's terms, to be in the top 10 percent means an annual family income of at least $60 000.

The Working Class

This is the class of the majority. It has usually been associated with blue-collar work — working with hands rather than with ideas, people, and paper. But a great deal of white-collar work is highly routine, and offices are also run like factories, giving rise to what some have suggested to be the proletarization of white-collar work (Rinehart, 1975). Because of its size, the working class encompasses many different subgroups with different life styles based on region, ethnicity, and the labor-market segment individuals occupy. Historically, the Canadian working class has drawn heavily on (1) immigrants with skilled-trade backgrounds from industrialized Britain and Germany; (2) immigrants with peasant backgrounds from Ireland, Scotland, and Southern and Eastern Europe; and (3) rural populations that have left farming in Canada itself.

Traditionally, the working class has lived in tightly knit communities close to their place of work. This pattern was generated in the early stages of industrialization when large labor forces were needed to work in mines, forests, on railways, in steel mills, packing plants, on assembly lines, and in construction. Often, small towns grew up around one or two local industries, such as mining in places such as Sudbury and Timmins in Northern Ontario. Today, with further mechanization and automation, and efforts by management to decentralize operations, the blue-collar labor forces have been considerably reduced. Also, roads and cars make it possible to live at a greater distance from one's work. Working-class communities have thus taken a buffeting from these social changes and with the recent recession, from

a wave of plant closings. At the same time, mixed-class communities have developed in urban and suburban areas.

A typical working-class person may be a semi-skilled factory employee operating an expensive and sophisticated piece of equipment. In the past, such an operative would not likely have had much education, whereas today he or she has likely completed high school and even has additional training. The value orientation of the working class at one time was described as concern for respectability and for "getting by." (Kahl, 1957). Such minimal goals may not apply to some subgroups in the working class employed in fairly secure and better paying industries. Still, the problem of maintaining an adequate standard of living is serious for the working class because competition for jobs can erode wage levels and management can treat its hourly-rated employees as expendable in times of economic crises. Often, the working-class housewife must work outside the home to improve the family's standard of living.

Some of the diversity within the working class is the result of labor market segmentation. There are three different labor markets employing working-class persons (Edwards, 1979). The first is the subordinate primary market. Jobs in this market are typically mass-production jobs in unionized industries where job security, wages, and fringe benefits are relatively high; the skills are firm-specific and mainly learned on the job. By contrast, the jobs in the independent primary market are characterized by skills learned through some formal means. For example, tradespersons such as electricians and carpenters usually learn by apprenticeship. The third segment, the secondary labor market, consists of a variety of low-skill jobs, often in small, nonunionized manufacturing firms. Much of the work in this sector is done by casual labor. When primary-market jobs disappear because of a plant shutdown, those workers who are not mobile are often forced to take this kind of employment. A substantial part of the labor force holds jobs in this sector of the economy, and because of low pay, they comprise what has been termed "the working poor."

The Lower Class: Myth or Reality?

U.S. sociologists have long written about a "lower class," members of which are at the bottom of the class structure, have the least amount of prestige, and generally live in poverty. Yet this concept can too easily fit a stereotype of disreputable poor: (1) persons who could work but choose to live off welfare; or (2) persons who live by petty crime or by prostitution, drug dealing, and other kinds of hustling activities; or (3) persons who work sporadically, earning just enough to enjoy a life style of "loose living" (leisure, sex, drugs, gambling, booze). Some people exaggerate the number of disreputable poor as part of their argument against the "safety net" government programs that help the least advantaged (Banfield, 1970).

Stereotypes aside, the notion of a lower class, or "culture of poverty," has been treated as a serious research issue by sociologists, anthropologists, and psychologists concerned about long-term implications of widespread poverty in societies with extremes of income and wealth (Lewis, 1959; Valentine, 1968; Ryan, 1971). If there is a lower class in Canada, it is perhaps best viewed as a fragment of the working class, a working poor trapped in the secondary labor market mentioned earlier.

SOCIAL MOBILITY: INEQUALITY OF RESULT

How much career mobility is there in industrial society? How rigid are class lines? How common is it to move from rags to riches? What has been the impact of technological change on getting ahead? These are some of the questions that can be answered by examining patterns of *social mobility*.

To begin with, one should expect considerable social mobility in class societies. In contrast to feudal societies, where forms of serfdom and slavery predominated, class societies formally acknowledge freedom of movement for individuals in the labor market. This factor, in combination with the expansive character of capitalist industrial societies in the West, creates dynamics favorable to social mobility.

Although there are multiple dimensions to inequality, social mobility has been studied almost exclusively in terms of occupation, in large part because this kind of information is readily available, since people are willing to give out this information about themselves. According to an international study of mobility rates (Lipset and Bendix, 1959), high and similar rates of mobility were found for all industrialized countries studied. This information was used to attack the myth that the United States was different from European countries in having a more open class structure. Not openness, but industralization was seen as the force allowing for mobility.

Table 17-6 contains data from Canadian and U.S. studies of occupational mobility done in 1973 and 1972, respectively. Since the mobility process is complex, these data are only crude indicators of it. It should be pointed out that because the information was obtained by asking a sample of men (sons) about their occupation at the time of the survey and about the occupation(s) of their fathers when they themselves were young, the data do not represent two fixed points in time. Thus, a thirty-year-old male in the Canadian study would be reporting his father's occupation as of about 1959, whereas a sixty-year-old respondent would be reporting his father's occupation as of about 1929. Also, only three occupational categories are shown. With more categories (there were seventeen in the original data), the tabular results would be different, leading to a more detailed and possibly different interpretation of the findings.

Bearing in mind these limitations, what can be said about mobility based on these two national surveys? Comparing the distribution of fathers' occupations (column 6), with that of the son's (lines 5 and 11), reveals the impact of changes in the occupational structure over time.

TABLE 17-6. Intergenerational Occupational Mobility for Canada and the United States, 1973 and 1972

Father's occupational category	Son's Occupational Category				Distribution of fathers	
	White-Collar	Blue-Collar	Farm	Total	Number	Percent
Canada, 1973						
white-collar	69.7%	29.1	1.1	99.9%	2127	24.9
blue-collar	41.5%	57.1	1.4	100.0%	4269	50.0
farm	25.6%	51.5	22.9	100.0%	2148	25.1
number of sons	3806	4162	576	8544	8544	100.0
% distribution of sons	44.5%	48.1	6.7	99.9%		
1971 labor force	40.0%	53.3	7.0	100.3%		
United States, 1972						
white-collar	66.9%	32.1	1.0	100.0%	11 563	26.9
blue-collar	38.3%	60.6	1.1	100.0%	21 534	50.1
farm	25.4%	60.0	14.6	100.0%	9886	23.0
number of sons	18 496	22 677	1781	42 944	42 983	100.0
% distribution of sons	43.0%	52.8	4.1	99.9%		
1971 labor force	48.3%	47.7	4.0	100.0%		

NOTE: The Canadian data are based on sales aged twenty-five to sixty-four. The U.S. data are based on sales aged twenty-one to sixty-four. The percentages are subject to rounding errors in the original tabular data. The white-collar category includes proprietors, sales, and clerical persons; the blue-collar category includes service workers.
SOURCE: McRoberts, 1982; Hauser and Featherman, 1973.

As pointed out earlier, this century saw a massive decline in the number of farmers, an increase in blue-collar jobs, and a recent, rapid growth of the white-collar sector. The table, then, reflects that mobility increases with changes in the social structure, namely, industrialization and technological change. This process is known as structural mobility.

The destination of the sons of blue-collar workers are shown in lines 2 and 8. The majority of these sons have stayed in the blue-collar category in both studies, with a substantial two-fifths moving upward into the white-collar sector, and a neglible proportion turning to farming. This pattern is reversed for the sons of white-collar fathers (lines 1 and 7). The majority of white-collar sons stayed in white-collar jobs, about 30 percent moved downward and very few took up farming.

The amount of mobility (as shown in Table 17-6) between generations, both upward and downward, across the white-collar/blue-collar lines is impressive. But, as has been pointed out, a greater number of occupational groups would have given a more realistic depiction of the mobility process. A summary of some of the main findings of the detailed research on American men, which are likely to be similar in Canada, makes obvious that: (1) there is a great deal of occupational mobility between generations; (2) moves upward exceed moves downward, with short moves between adjacent or nearly adjacent occupational categories being most typical; (3) long-distance mobility is rare; (for example, only 3.7 percent of self-employed professionals had fathers who were laborers, but 46.8 percent had fathers who were themselves professionals, managers, or proprietors); (4) self-employed professionals, proprietors, and farmers had the highest proportion of recruitment by inheritance; and (5) there are two class boundaries — one between blue-collar and white-collar occupations, and one between farm and blue-collar occupations. These boundaries are "semipermeable," because although there was little downward mobility across them, there was considerable upward movement across these lines. On the whole, these results suggest a rather open class-structure for the United States.

So far, we have focused on the social mobility of men only. Historically, when the study of social inequality dealt with people rather than with positions, the male head of a family was the unit of analysis. The social mobility of women was viewed as movement in a marriage market, where it was reflected in comparing the status of their family of origin with that of the males women married (Acker, 1973). The work income of a woman, if employed, and her inherited property would influence the status of her family, but her new status or class position was taken to be that of her husband's. Today, this model is deemed to be male-biased and thus inaccurate.

Education is the chief means of facilitating one's upward mobility in Canada. To this discussion we now turn.

EDUCATION, EQUALITY OF OPPORTUNITY, AND CREDENTIALISM

Until recently, Europeans viewed Canada as a land of opportunity, a place for emigrants to come for economic advancement, inexpensive or free land, religious and political freedom, or to escape military conscription. That Canada did not always live up to this image is shown by the out-migration of its population to the United States, which has occurred decade after decade. A turning point was reached with the prosperity of the 1960s when out-migration largely ended. By then the agricultural frontier had long passed, and joining the new middle class of salaried, white-collar work-

ers became the route to success. Post-secondary education became the key for travelling this route.

Economists began to talk about the importance of human capital for economic growth (Becker, 1964), and governments opened numerous new colleges and universities, encouraging higher education. Furthermore, education came to be perceived as the solution to problems of social inequality. For the lower class and other minority groups, learning basic skills would provide entry into stable, working-class occupations; for the working class, college and university education meant breaking into the world of white-collar jobs; and for the middle class, the professions beckoned through higher education and advanced degrees (Lockhart, 1979).

Much controversy surrounds the question as to whether education acts to increase the opportunities for working- or lower-class individuals, or whether it simply reinforces the class structure. Forcese (1975:81), for example, argues that because of various screening mechanisms, Canadian educational systems, rather than reducing the effects of social-class origins, favor the already privileged and are "a cause of persisting and increasingly rigid stratification." In contrast, Lorne Tepperman (1975:178) holds that schools have opened the way for advancement, and that the father's social class or ethnic origin has little effect on an individual's educational and occupational attainment.

Research on social mobility sheds light on this controversy. An analysis of the 1973 Canadian National Mobility Study (CNMS) assessed the causal relationship between social origin, educational attainment, and first job and current occupation — the latter being one's status attainment (Boyd, 1982). The results, tabulated in Table 17-7 , show how having a low status and having a high status are related to education and first job and current job, as measured by the Blishen score. A low SES predicts 8.1 years of education and a current Blishen job score of 36.2 (for males), whereas a high SES predicts 16.1 years of com-

TABLE 17-7 Predicted Attainments of Persons with Low versus High Social Origins, 1973

Social-Origin Characteristics	(A) Low Social Origins		(B) Low Social Origins but with High Education		(C) High Social Origins	
	Male	Female	Male	Female	Male	Female
father's education	3	3	3	3	16	16
mother's education	4	4	4	4	15	15
number of siblings	8	8	8	8	0	0
father's occupation	22	22	22	22	61	61
predicted education	8.1	9.6	16.1*	14.5*	16.1	14.5
predicted first job	30.3	37.6	47.9	50.6	56.2	56.5
predicted current occupation	36.2	40.1	54.5	52.2	62.4	55.8

* Assumed achieved level of education.

SOURCE: Boyd (1982), Table VI. Column B data were added.

NOTE: Educational level and number of siblings is expressed in years; the social status of occupations is expressed as a Blishen score.

pleted education and a current Blishen job score of 62.4 (for males). By referring back to Table 17-2., one can find occupations typical of scores of thirty-six and sixty-two, respectively.

Column B in Table 17-7. shows the impact of achieving the educational level of a high-status person by a low-status person. For a low-status male who completed 16.1 years of schooling, the Blishen job score would be predicted to be 54.5; it would be 52.2 for a low-status female obtaining 14.5 years of education. As can be seen from these figures, a social-class background characterized by low SES is a substantial handicap in the educational system and in obtaining a job with a high Blishen score. In contrast, a social-class background characterized by high SES brings substantial advantages. Yet higher education can overcome the disadvantages of low social origin. The opposite is also true; downward mobility can be brought on by failure to pursue higher education on the part of someone with high SES origin.

Important arguments in favor of mass education are that it enhances society's human capital, on the one hand, and provides equality of opportunity, on the other. Equality of opportu-

nity is necessary to provide an avenue for social mobility so that social stratification does not become rigid. Often, the idea of equality of opportunity is linked with the idea of *meritocracy*. Applied to mass education, this notion regards a screening system as necessary and just in public education, because such a system will ultimately find and reward the persons of talent that deserve and will fill the key leadership positions necessary for the functioning of society.

Critics who question the belief that schools have promoted greater social equality do not stand against either the importance of a society's improving human capital or the need to provide educational opportunity through mass education. They emphasize that (1) highly streamed systems of education reinforce existing social inequalities; (2) a great deal of talent is wasted by such systems; and (3) most systems of education are operated in terms of narrow, middle-class interests so that, not surprisingly, working-class youth becomes "turned off" by schooling (Bowles and Gintis, 1974). Whatever the merits of these arguments, two additional critical points need to be made.

Schools could provide a variety of education, even forms of education serving the interest of

Education is the key to upward mobility in Canada, although some critics feel that the system serves only a narrow range of middle-class interests, thus reinforcing existing social inequalities.

working-class people, for example. But these need not reflect hierarchy. That streaming in schools produces inequality of result arises mainly from the use of credentials in the economy and the inequality of rewards attached to occupations that people ultimately enter upon leaving school.

Taking a Weberian perspective, Collins (1979) argues that, in the context of the inequality of rewards, the scramble of individuals and groups to become privileged and to protect privileged positions leads to the adoption of educational requirements — credentialism — as a means to preserve and enhance social status and economic power. Schooling becomes part of the system of inequality because grades, years of education, and the completion of special programs are used in the economy as a means to sort people in ways that appear to be justified by criteria of required training, when in reality, credentials are simply part of the struggle between groups over scarce resources and rewards.

These ideas can be summed up as follows: inequality of condition is not overcome by equality of opportunity, though equality of opportunity in times of rapid social change probably does promote social mobility. But, given inequality of rewards to begin with, the outcome of equality of opportunity is inequality of result.

CORRELATES OF INEQUALITY

Virtually every aspect of social life can be looked at in terms of social inequality, whether it be showing who becomes a doctor, who participates in voluntary associations, or who gets elected to legislatures and city councils. Almost every sociological study must therefore include SES or class as a variable in its research design.

The correlates of inequality are all around us. Some are obvious and have become the basis of stereotypes, such as the beer-drinking working-man in contrast to the upper-class connoisseur of fine wines and cognacs. There are also subtle or complex correlates, complex in the sense that SES and class operate in conjunction with many other factors, so that sorting out cause and effect requires sophisticated data-gathering and data-analysis techniques.

A number of correlates have already been addressed in this chapter. Others may be gleaned by reference to the life cycle. Family size varies with socioeconomic status, as do dating patterns, sexual practices, and age of marriage. For example, the poor tend to have larger families than the affluent. Working-class youth tend to marry earlier than middle-class youth, and it is said that companionship marriage tends to be more of a middle-class value. Middle-class parents stress self-direction, and working-class parents conformity in the socialization of their children (Kohn, 1977). Close ties among members of an extended family are said to be typical of the working class, whereas middle-class persons develop friendship networks based on interests and professional requirements — the hallmark being the formal dinner and cocktail party.

Material differences between SES groups are well known. Upper-income groups may not spend more on any particular item as a percentage of income, compared with lower-income groups, but in terms of absolute dollars, the differences reflect distinct life styles. All families spend roughly 4 or 5 percent of income on recreation, but for those families with an annual income of $40 000, this means average expenditures of over $2000, compared to $800 for families with an income of less than $15 000 (Statistics Canada, 1984a). Similarly, there are proprotionate differences in spending power between income groups on such items as housing, clothing, education, and savings. Income-class differences become particularly exaggerated at retirement. Individuals who worked in low-paying jobs or at casual work frequently have little or no pension income, other than that provided by government, and are often forced to live in a cheap, single room. In contrast, people who had high-paying jobs usually have both a private pension and another through their place of employment, income which allow them to remain in their own home, own a car, and even travel.

Education, which we have already touched on, is another correlate. There are marked differences in aspirations and expectations regarding post-secondary education by socioeconomic status. Universities draw students mainly from the higher SES groups; those who graduate from high schools only, or who drop out even earlier, come mainly from the lower income groups. The most recent development in post-secondary education, community colleges, draw from a broad cross-section of Canadians.

Residence locations reflect SES because housing tracts in cities have usually been built with a particular segment of the housing market in mind. The arts draw different degrees of appreciation from different status groups; symphony concerts, dance, art galleries, and theatre are not usually attractive to those who go to wrestling matches and listen to country-and-western music. The kind of newspaper one reads (a tabloid versus *The Globe and Mail*), the type of TV program one watches ("Three's Company" versus "Fifth Estate"), and even the movies we attend all reflect the SES group we belong to.

Even health is related to socioeconomic status. The poor tend to be more afflicted by illness, to underutilize dental care, and they die younger. Workingmen are subject to industrial accidents and occupational diseases, whereas professionals and management suffer from stress-related illness.

Correlating SES with behavior not only gives descriptive information, but invites speculation regarding cause and effect, that is to say, invites the search for an appropriate, theoretical explanation. In taking up a particular correlate of inequality, it should be remembered that, because of social change, what might at one time have been considered a valid relationship may no longer be so. For example, with increasing levels of education, postwar affluence, and the rise of the mass media and mass entertainment, there may be convergences between socioeconomic groups regarding behavior, for instance, socialization of children, and how men and women relate to each other in marriage.

On balance, though, it is safe to say that inequalities will probably not lessen in the future; their forms may change, but conflict over power, status, and wealth is likely to continue. Even in a relatively affluent country such as Canada, competition from low-wage countries, competition from countries with more modern and more developed industrial systems, and declines in exports due to world recession, can lead to unemployment and consequent pressure to reduce standards of living, with some groups being more hurt than others. A general economic downturn also brings pressure on government to reduce spending on programs that help minimize the effects of inequalities of condition, especially those in the areas of health, education, and welfare. The combined effects of these processes may lead to greater social inequalities between groups. The study of social inequalities will thus remain an interesting and valuable field within sociology for the foreseeable future.

SUMMARY

1. Social inequality is conceptualized in different ways by different theoretical traditions. The dimensions of inequality, whether class is believed to be real or nominal, and the overall model of social stratification are matters that divide social thinkers.

2. Ample data exists to demonstrate social inequality. When definitions are decided, then inequality can be shown in terms of income and wealth, social status and occupational prestige, differences in forms of power, or in terms of a composite measure such as socioeconomic status.

3. The commonly held belief that Canada has become a middle-class society must be tempered by looking critically at the changing mix of occupations over the decades, for men and women separately, and the differential earnings of these occupations.

4. Poverty is still a major social problem in Canada. Research can show which groups are most vulnerable to living in poverty and thus indicate its major causes. Government "safety-net" programs are a key strategy in any society's attempt to reduce poverty, but wider issues of employment and industrial strategies are also relevant.

5. Income inequality can be explained in individualistic or structural terms, but research shows that differences in income earning power are best explained by structural factors.

6. Power relations are found throughout society — in families, schools, churches, business organizations, and so on — not just with respect to government. Still, more attention has generally been paid to power in the realm of government and the relations between government and the corporate world. Different models of power have been proposed to characterize these relationships.

7. Because the bases of status group formation are so diverse, society displays numerous status groupings. In contrast, the idea of social class is not to highlight diversity, but to help us under-

stand social inequalities in society by way of a parsimonious scheme of social stratification.

8. Class structure in industrial societies is characterized by considerable openness and, therefore, movement of individuals and groups upward and downward along the dimensions of stratification. This social mobility can be studied both within and between generations.

9. In the latter half of our century, education has become a key means of achieving social mobility. There is, however, debate concerning the extent to which education acts to increase opportunity for mobility, or whether it simply reinforces the existing class structure.

10. Class and social inequality have many ramifications for people's lives and behaviours. These correlates of class have to do with patterns of family life, dating, sexuality, socialization, consumer behaviour, attitudes toward education, use of health services, political behavior, use of media and leisure, and so on.

GLOSSARY

Authority. The legitimate exercise of power, where legitimacy refers to a general public acceptance.

Bourgeoisie. The owners or controllers of the means of production.

Class. For Max Weber, class refers to how a group derives its economic power from its position in the labor market. For Karl Marx, class also refers to the economic position of a group, but as it refers to ownership of the means of production as forms of property.

Equality of opportunity. Equal access by individuals to the means to become socially mobile — in particular, by equal access to secondary and post-secondary education.

Inequality of condition. The differences in social origins of individuals that either handicap or aid social mobility.

Inequality of result. The outcome of inequalities of condition and opportunity as a sorting of individuals into the previously existing structure of inequality or class sytem.

Petty bourgeoisie. Small property owners, small businesspeople, and independent commodity-producers (such as craftspeople, farmers, and fishermen).

Power. The ability of one group (or individual) to work its will on other groups or individuals.

Social inequality. Unequal exchange relationships between individuals, individuals and groups, and between groups.

Social mobility. Movement upward or downward between classes, or between occupations of varying prestige and economic power.

Socioeconomic status (SES). Any nominal system of sorting individuals or families into ranked categories, usually on a multidimensional scale.

Status. The social prestige accorded to an individual or group.

Working class or proletariat. The property-less class made up of individuals who work for wages.

FURTHER READING

Clement, Wallace. *The Canadian Corporate Elite: An Analysis of Economic Power.* Toronto: McClelland and Stewart, 1975. An important follow-up study of John Porter's original work on the economic elite, but with more detailed information on its internal composition as of 1972; Canada's economic history is explored and links between the economic elite and the media elite are examined.

Curtis, James E. and William G. Scott (eds.). *Social Stratification: Canada.* 2nd edition. Scarborough, Ontario: Prentice-Hall, 1979. A valuable collection of articles on inequality in Canada, which complements the authors' first anthology of articles on the same subject.

Grabb, Edward G. *Social Inequality: Classical and Contemporary Theorists.* Toronto: Holt,

Rinehart and Winston, 1984. A useful and very readable introductory essay on classical and recent theories of social inequality.

Hunter, Alfred A. *Class Tells: On Social Inequality in Canada.* Toronto: Butterworth, 1981. The most recent textbook on social inequality in Canada. Highly informative and with an innovative presentation of material.

Lenski, Gerhard E. *Power and Privilege: A Theory of Social Stratification.* New York: McGraw-Hill, 1966. An ambitious attempt to build a synthesis of theories of social inequality. The author takes an evolutionary approach and reviews social inequality in eight types of societies.

Osberg, Lars. *Economic Inequality in Canada.* Toronto: Butterworth, 1981. A thorough analysis of the economic dimension of inequality, including topics such as poverty, factor shares, human capital, intelligence, and the effects of government programs.

Porter, John. *The Vertical Mosaic.* Toronto: University of Toronto Press, 1965. Still worth reading, the classic analysis of social inequality in Canada with perceptive insights into the uniqueness of the Canadian situation.

Tepperman, Lorne. *Social Mobility in Canada.* Toronto: McGraw-Hill Ryerson, 1975. Comprehensive and insightful analysis of social mobility in Canada. The only study in this area available in book form.

CHAPTER EIGHTEEN

Inequalities of Race

LEO DRIEDGER

Before embarking on a discussion of racial inequality, distinctions between the concepts of race, racism, and inequality must be made. "Race" today is defined biologically on the basis of physical traits. As we shall see later, such a definition has complex ramifications. "Racism," as defined by Banton (1970:18), is "the doctrine that states that a man's behavior is determined by stable inherited characteristics deriving from separate racial stocks, having distinctive attributes and usually considered to stand to one another in relations of superiority and inferiority." As white Europeans increasingly came into contact with peoples around the world, and as the theory of evolution developed, there were many attempts at arranging the varieties of Homo sapiens into superior and inferior groupings. We shall return to this topic in more detail later.

Whereas racism is a negative concept, based on the belief that some races are inferior to others, the concept of inequality is an attempt to rank people more objectively on the basis of opportunities to compete in the social, economic, and political spheres of society. According to this concept, human beings have roughly the same abilities, but for many reasons they do not all have the same opportunity to fulfil their potential. In this sense, inequality is due to the social structure of a society, rather than to biological determinism. Whereas biological features are more difficult, if not impossible to change, social structures can be changed, although not easily.

CLASSIFICATION OF HUMAN BEINGS

Physical Characteristics

Today, it is generally accepted that there is no basic biological or genetic difference between the various human populations. However, the physical features do vary, and as early as 1745, Linnaeus proposed that humankind be classified into four main races: Europeans, Asiatics, Africans, and American Indians or Amerindians (Hughes and Kallen, 1974:6). In 1781, a German physiologist proposed a classification (based on head and skull shape): Caucasian (European), Negro, Mongol, Malayan, and American Indian. During the eighteenth and nineteenth centuries, classification of human populations became popular with physical anthropologists. Since the theory of evolution was becoming more acceptable also, many attempted to arrange races in a hierarchical order from primitive to highly civilized types. The genetic discoveries of Gregor Mendel revolutionized

and encouraged further interest in classification. Slowly the story of human development began to unfold.

American physical anthropologist Ernest Hooton expanded the list of physical criteria according to three primary divisions of humankind: Caucasoid, Mongoloid, and Negroid.

Hooton used seven criteria (see Table 18-1) to distinguish Caucasoid, Mongoloid, and Negroid racial types. Caucasoids have the lightest color of skin and eyes, whereas Negroids have the darkest, with Mongoloids falling in between. The nose and lip shapes of the Caucasoids are the narrowest, whereas the Negroids have the broadest and thickest. Mongoloids have straight, coarse hair, whereas Negroids have woolly or frizzy hair. Mongoloids have the most prominent cheekbones, and Caucasoids have the most hair on their bodies.

It quickly becomes apparent that there is a wide range of variation within each of the three types with respect to each of the criteria. Many schol-

TABLE 18-1. **Hooton's Criteria for Distinguishing Among the Three Races**

Criteria	Caucasoid	Mongoloid	Negroid
skin color	white, pink, or "ruddy" to light brown	yellow or yellow-brown	dark brown to black
eye color	all lighter shades, but never never black	medium-brown to dark brown	dark brown to black
hair type	straight to wavy, occasionally curled	straight (coarse in texture), and circular in cross-section	woolly to frizzy; oval in cross-section
nose shape	usually high-bridged and narrow	low root, short tip, medium width at nostrils	usually low; depressed, broad tip and nostrils
lip shape	medium to thin thickness; little or no eversion	medium thickness; variable eversion	usually thick, with obvious eversion
cheekbone	not prominent	projecting forward and laterally; may be covered by fat pad	variable, but usually more obvious than in Caucasoid
body hair (including beard)	medium to extremely variable	usually less than Caucasoid or Negroid	medium to scanty

SOURCE: Hughes and Kallen, 1974: page 9.

ars have questioned whether such a classification is still useful. However, because Caucasoids especially have made much of skin color and of some of the other criteria, we are forced to examine the differences and reasons for placing values on such physical characteristics.

Another major problem with this classification is that some of the world's populations do not fit into it, such as the East Indians of Asia, the original Indians of the two Americas, and most of the Pacific Polynesians and Melanesians. Indians from India represent roughly one-fifth of the world's population and they seem to fit the Caucasoid type in most respects, except that their skin color is considerably darker. They are classified as Caucasoid, but since skin color is often considered important by other Caucasians, they often treat East Indians as "coloreds." East Indians fit somewhere between the Caucasoid and Negroid types. Indians of North and South America seem to fit between the Caucasoid and Mongoloid types, but are usually classified as Mongoloid. The peoples of the Pacific Islands seem to fit best between the Mongoloid and Negroid categories, having somewhat darker skins than the Mongoloids.

For reasons such as these, many scholars have created more than three racial types.

Genetic and Skeletal Variations

Physical anthropologists analyze the skeletal characteristics and blood types of the three primary divisions discussed above. There is considerable evidence that Homo sapiens evolved over thousands of years, and minor skeletal differences evolved in different regions. Caucasoids, for example, have more pronounced brow ridges than the other two groups and a straighter (small jaws, prominent chin) facial profile, whereas Mongoloid cheekbones and jaws are prominent, and Negroid jaws protrude but have smaller chins and narrower palates (Hughes and Kallen, 1974:14). Blood types seem to have emerged from the three major geographical "breeding grounds" of Africa, Asia, and Europe. Of the ABO blood group sys-

tem, Caucasoids and Negroids have moderate evidence of A_2 genes; in Mongoloids, it is virtually absent. B type genes are low among Caucasoids, high among Mongoloids, and intermediate among Negroids. The RH (or Rhesus) factor is high among Caucasoids, but virtually absent among Mongoloids (Hughes and Kallen, 1974:15–16).

RACISM IN HISTORICAL PERSPECTIVE

With "race" difficult to define, and humanity difficult to classify into racial categories, why do we continue to try? It is because human beings need to simplify and order the universe to comprehend it. But more importantly, whites of European-Caucasian origin still judge others on the basis of skin color. Racial prejudice based on physical characteristics is a fact in North America, and we are forced to deal with the phenomenon of racism. Many North Americans believe that even behavior is determined by inherited characteristics that are derived from separate racial stocks — attributes that may be ranked as superior or inferior. This is racism. Indians, in both Canada and the United States, were placed on reserves (many were slaughtered), blacks in America were forced to become slaves, the Japanese during World War II were forcibly transferred to internment camps, and blacks and "coloreds" in South Africa still today live in ghettos and need passes to enter white territories. These are but a few examples of racism. Let us explore how such thinking developed over time.

Emergence of White European Dominance

Before the sixteenth century, Caucasian Europeans represented only one-sixth of the world population. However, when the Protestant Reformation began in the 1500s — at the same time that European explorers began to discover the rest of the world — ideas, inventions, and technology developed to enhance European power and dominance in the world. As industry flourished,

European populations exploded, so that they soon comprised one-third of the world population.

Europeans had traded with the Chinese, East Indians, and others for centuries, using Arabs and other agents. After Columbus, however, Europeans began trading with the East directly by sea, and so came into contact with people of different skin color, language, and culture. Spanish and Portuguese explorers found South and Central American Indians, and the British, French, and Dutch encountered Indian tribes in North America and the dark peoples on the coast of Africa. One dominant impression that these new experiences left was that other peoples of the world were not white. Skin color became an easy way of differentiating between Europeans and others.

Many Europeans were awed by some of the civilizations they found, but were also hard-pressed to justify their presence. Since European technology permitted extensive sea travel, it was only a matter of time before "white is superior" became a popular belief, first no doubt unconsciously and later consciously justified by various ideologies.

Colonialism

The patterns of contact varied. In some parts, mostly trading relationships developed; in others, exploitation was extensive, and in still other areas, pioneer settlers came to possess the land. Europeans created small, port enclaves on the coastlines of China, India, Indonesia, and elsewhere for the purpose of conducting trade. In North America, they built forts to trade European goods for furs with the Indians. In all of these trade relations, Europeans were a small minority, but they possessed sufficient technological superiority so that they could protect themselves and maintain their white superiority amidst colored peoples of many varieties.

Whereas the temptation to exploit was always present, the great Mayan, Aztec, and Inca civilizations of South America provided special opportunities for exploitation. In the 1530s, gold was found by the Spaniards, especially among the Inca

in what is today Peru. Small groups of powerful Spanish and Portuguese people subjugated, exploited, and sometimes enslaved native Indians to work in mines. Many European men, away from their families, exploited native women, and many married them and created families.

British, French, and Dutch colonies were established in what is today Canada and the United States. As Indians were increasingly pushed westward, white dominance and power increased, until after many battles, the last stand of the Métis and Indians took place; the white traders and agriculturists triumphed.

White European dominance over colored Negroid and Mongoloid, pre-industrial suppliers and servants was the pattern that emerged around the world. The colonial arrangements always benefited the whites, and in some places, especially in colonial America, black slaves were brought mainly from Africa to work the cotton fields of the Deep South. White dominance had taken the most blatantly inhumane course — the buying and selling of human beings as commodities. Some believed that God had created some peoples to be dominant and others subservient; and blacks were considered definitely inferior human beings.

These, then, are some of the historical reasons for the preoccupation of whites with skin color, and the classification of humans into races according to physical criteria.

IMMIGRATION AND SOCIAL STATUS

Immigration

We must remember that the Indians were the first migrants to the Americas. Anthropologists tell us that these earliest immigrants came at least 12 000 years ago. In Canada, most Indians were hunters and gatherers, although agriculture had begun among the Hurons and Iroquois in Southern Ontario, and large-scale fishing, chiefdoms, and a distinctive art had developed on the northwest coast. In Mexico, Central America, and Peru, the great civilizations of the Maya, Aztec, and Inca

The most inhumane manifestation of white dominance—the buying and selling of slaves.

were flourishing when European invaders invaded and exploited their land. It is a well-known fact that many American Indians had developed civilizations that rivaled white European development.

Since Europeans first settled what has come to be Canada, they now comprise 96 percent of the population. Barely 100 years ago, the two charter groups, the British and the French, laid the foundations of the Canadian confederation, so that Caucasian Europeans became the legal and dominant force in the shaping of the dominion. For the most part, immigration policy preferred North-European immigrants, so that very few non-Caucasians migrated. There were exceptions, however, when Chinese were brought in to build the railroad in British Columbia in the 1880s, or when laborers were needed in mines and factories in the North or in Southern Ontario. A gentleman's agreement was made with Japan, so that hardly any Japanese entered after the turn of the century. Often, special "head" taxes were imposed to discourage "the yellow hordes of Asia" from entering.

The new point-system introduced in the early 1970s was an important turning point in Canadian immigration policy. Immigration has become possible in three ways: (1) Close relatives in Canada willing to take responsibility for care and

The Norsemen were the first immigrants to arrive in North America, although colonialism—and with it, the dominance of the Caucasian race—did not take root until the sixteenth century.

maintenance can sponsor their parents, brothers, or sisters and have them enter Canada under the category "Sponsored Dependents." Since most Canadians are of North-European ancestry, this opportunity has further increased white immigration. (2) A category for "independent" applicants was introduced, permitting entrance to individuals if they can score fifty out of a possible 100 points. This category permits anyone in the world to compete, especially if they have sufficient educational, occupational, and language skills. (3) The "nominated" category is an intermediate version that requires applicants to score some points independently, but prior to settlement arrangements; having a relative in Canada can boost the chances of entrance.

The changes in the immigration pattern since the point system is evident in Table 18-2. In 1951, the ten countries that contributed the largest number of immigrants to Canada were all European and American. By 1981, six of the ten top contributors were from Asia and the Caribbean countries. A large proportion of these immigrants are highly visible (they are referred to as visible minorities). Since Canada is a large country with a relatively sparse population, and since the world pressure for living space is increasing, many people expect Canada to take in more refugees. Thus, if present trends continue, we can expect that the proportion of Mongoloids and Negroids (visible minorities) will increase. It is interesting to note that during economic downturns, there are usu-

TABLE 18-2. Leading Countries-of-Origin of Canadian immigrants, in descending order

1951	1960	1973	1981
Britain	Italy	Britain	Britain
Germany	Britain	United States	United States
Italy	United States	Hong Kong	India
Netherlands	Germany	Portugal	Vietnam
Poland	Netherlands	Jamaica	China
France	Portugal	India	Hong Kong
United States	Greece	Philippines	Philippines
Belgium	France	Greece	Poland
Yugoslavia	Poland	Italy	Haiti
Denmark	Austria	Trinidad	Portugal

SOURCE: *The Immigration Program*, Ottawa: Information Canada, 1974; Employment and Immigration Canada, 1981; *Immigration Statistics*, Ottawa; Supply and Services, 1983.

ally pressures from labor unions and others to restrict immigration. This conflict of interest can lead to changes in immigration laws, which have been part of the changing dynamics of Canada's history.

Demographic Characteristics

The number of Canadians of Mongoloid and Negroid origin increased from 3 percent in 1971 to between 4 and 5 percent in 1981. This increase in visible minorities — almost one million in 1981 — was due in part to a change in immigration policy. Whereas formerly the immigration policy favored North Europeans, the new point-system gave immigrants from the Third World a better chance to compete. Table 18-3 shows that roughly 90 percent of the Canadian population can be classified as Caucasian, 3.4 percent as Mongoloid, and 0.2 percent as Negroid. Roughly 6 percent were classified as being of multiple or mixed origins.

Native Indians represent about one-half of all visible minorities in Canada. In 1981, they formed a majority in the Northwest Territories, representing well over half of the 45 540 residents there. In addition to being a majority in the North, native peoples are concentrated in the five most westerly provinces, with the largest number in Ontario

TABLE 18-3. **Canadians by Racial and Ethnic Origins, 1981**

Racial/Ethnic Origin	Number		%
Total Population	24 083 500		
Caucasian	21 559 680		89.5
British	9 674 245	40.2	
French	6 439 100	26.7	
Other European	4 894 635	20.3	
Multiple (British/French)	430 255	1.8	
Indo-Pakistani Spanish	121 445	0.5	
Mongoloid	797 400		3.4
Native Indian	413 380	1.7	
Chinese	289 245	1.2	
Indochinese	43 725	0.2	
Japanese	40 995	0.2	
West Asian	10 055	0.0	
Negroid	45 215		0.2
African	45 215	0.2	
Multiple Origins	1 408 360		5.8
European/Other	1 330 275	5.5	
Native/Other	78 085	0.3	
Mixed Origins	272 845		1.1
Pacific Islands	155 290	0.6	
Latin American	117 555	0.5	

SOURCE: Statistics Canada, 1981. Update, 1983.

The Chinese represent the second largest visible minority group in Canada.

(84 000). About 6 percent of the population of Manitoba and Saskatchewan are Indians.

The Chinese comprised more than one-fourth of the visible minorities in 1981 and are concentrated in Ontario and British Columbia, mostly in Toronto and Vancouver, where the two, largest, Canadian Chinatowns are located. The Chinese have been a part of British Columbia's history, whereas their immigration to Ontario is more recent.

The Indo-Pakistani population of 121 000 is unique in that technically they are usually classified as Caucasian, since they fit Caucasian criteria, except for skin color. We discuss them here because they are a visible minority. Three-fourths of Indo-Pakistanis live in Ontario and British Columbia — again, mostly in Toronto and Vancouver (80 percent of the Vancouver population are Sikhs from the Punjab). The Indo-Pakistanis represent the third-largest visible minority.

Blacks represent the fourth-largest visible minority. The 1971 census listed 32 000 Negroes and 28 000 West Indians. About one-third of these reside in Nova Scotia, especially in Halifax. The new 1981 classification seems to have buried many blacks in other categories where they cannot be identified. However, based on the 1971 data and other more informal estimates, there must be about twice as many blacks as there are Africans. (We estimate that the 45 000 listed as Africans are mostly black.) The Negroid group, in any case, is considerably less than one percent of the Canadian population.

The Japanese are considered Mongoloids racially, and most are located in Ontario and British Columbia. During the 1940s, the Vancouver population was forcibly evacuated into the interior, and today they number only 40 000.

The 44 000 Indo-Chinese, who entered Canada largely during the 1970s, represent a multiethnic category of Vietnamese, Cambodians, Laotians, Philippinos, and Thais. Many came as refugees; one-third located in Québec and another third in Ontario, mostly in Montréal and Toronto. They add a small proportion to the Mongoloid racial group.

Thus, Canada's non-Caucasian minorities represent only 4 to 5 percent of the total population, and most of these are Mongoloid racially, represented by the native peoples and the Chinese.

In contrast to Canada's small, non-Caucasian population, the United States contains 17 percent of non-white peoples, especially Negroids. Of these, almost 12 percent are blacks, and these number more than the total population of Canada. Thus, it is not surprising that Americans are preoccupied with the question of race. Whereas in the past, the blacks lived predominantly in the Deep South, today they are found in large numbers in urban areas, especially in northern cities. The populations of many cities, such as Newark, Baltimore, Philadelphia, Cleveland, Detroit, and Chicago, are over half black or nearing a majority. Some of them have black mayors, and in many, there are ghettos that are almost exclusively black (Pinkney, 1975). There are no comparable areas or cities in Canada.

There are also 11.7 million Americans of other races, mostly Mongoloids, comprising about 5 percent of the total population. In addition, there are 14.6 million people of Spanish origin (Chicanos), who are considered Caucasians racially, but whose darker skin color makes them more visible. Chicanos often attract prejudice and discrimination.

In summary, compared with Canada, a much larger percentage of the American population are of the Negroid (11.7 percent) and Mongoloid (5.2 percent) races, which, along with the Spanish visible minority (6.4 percent), make up almost one-fourth of the total American population. Therefore, we would expect Americans to be more preoccupied with racial categories, problems, and issues than are Canadians. This tends to be true; however, the new immigration policy has brought more visible minorities to Canada, so that Canadians are becoming increasingly conscious of racial and physical differences, especially in larger cities such as Toronto and Vancouver.

Since the non-white percentage of Canada's population is very small, data on socioeconomic inequality tend to be limited.

Socioeconomic Inequality

Occupation, education, and income are the most commonly used indicators of socioeconomic status. We shall look at each in turn.

Table 18-4 shows which ethnic groups ranked above the Canadian mean income of $6004 in 1971 and which ranked below. The Japanese ranked well above the mean, placing second overall. If we use income as an indicator of equality, Japanese Canadians rank among the privileged. This ranking clearly shows that some non-whites are able to compete very well with whites in the marketplace.

In contrast, the other four non-white groups shown in Table 18-4 ranked the lowest. Li (1980: 369) compared the Japanese and Chinese income differences and found that although these two Asian groups were similar with respect to occupation, education, age, and sex distribution, the majority of Japanese had lived in Canada much longer (76 percent were Canadian-born) than the

TABLE 18-4. **Mean Income of Ethnic Groups, 1971***

Ethnic Groups	Number in Sample	Deviation from Mean Income ($)**
1. Jewish	1 318	+ 3 543.5
2. *Japanese*	185	+ 947.9
3. Austrian	187	+ 744.4
4. Russian	255	+ 348.0
5. British	36 809	+ 293.9
6. Czech	244	+ 104.5
7. Slovak	91	+ 83.5
8. Hungarian	597	+ 56.4
9. Polish	1 377	− 91.5
10. Italian	2 951	− 163.8
11. Scandinavian	1 554	− 195.0
12. German	5 609	− 223.2
13. Finnish	242	− 233.7
14. Other and unknown	3 415	− 324.9
15. Netherlands	1 759	− 383.6
16. French	20 008	− 423.5
17. Ukrainian	2 556	− 642.2
18. *Negro*	126	− 918.9
19. *Chinese*	501	− 1 025.7
20. *West Indian*	152	− 1 535.6
21. *Native Indian*	520	− 1 868.1
Canada	80 466	6 004.7

SOURCE: Peter S. Li, 1980, page 365.

* Fifteen years of age and over

** Measured in the number of dollars deviating above (+) or below (−) the national mean income of $6 004.70.

Chinese (20 percent Canadian-born) and had had time to accommodate to and compete in Canada. It should be noted that native Indians have lived here the longest, but they were forced onto reserves, which interrupted their ability to compete in the marketplace.

A recent study by Reitz (1980:152) compared twelve ethnic groups based on the 1961 and 1971 censuses and found that the Asians ranked with the Jews and British as having an above-average probability of obtaining the better jobs, and native peoples the lowest. (Most likely, the Japanese and professional Chinese, who have immigrated recently, have raised the Asian rank even more.)

These data show that being of the Mongoloid racial category and a visible minority does not deter members from competing well. In contrast, the average Indian and Inuit income was $2976, as compared with $5033 — the average Canadian income of selected ethnic groups.

With respect to education, the findings tend to follow the income and occupational trends. Native Indians were among those with less than nine years of education, although more and more are entering university today. Of nine ethnic groups in Toronto, the Chinese ranked third, and the West Indians seventh in number of years of education (Reitz et al., 1981:23).

In sum, Asians tend to rank toward the top; native peoples rank the lowest; and the West Indians and blacks near the bottom. Thus, we have some Mongoloid groups with a high socioeconomic rank and some with the lowest rank. Negroids rank fairly low. These data suggest that non-whites appear within the entire spectrum of the socioeconomic range.

Now we turn to the ideology of equality that we as Canadians support and theoretically subscribe to.

IDEOLOGY AND HUMAN RIGHTS

Our Heritage

Let us review briefly our heritage of religious, political, and economic ideologies to gain some perspective on the rights of all to equal opportunities.

The Western world has been profoundly influenced by the Judeo-Christian religious ideology. Although secularization has taken hold so that this ideology is no longer as dominant as it was in Europe during the Middle Ages, the majority of Canadians claim to be "Christian." According to the Judeo-Christian tradition, the worth of every human being was stressed, including the enemy.

Democratic political principles are in line with this ideology. Although British parliamentary freedom was at first intended for the elite, slowly freedom for all citizens was recognized and affirmed. The French call for "liberty, equality, and fraternity" was also intended to encompass the masses. Abraham Lincoln's "government for the people, by the people, and of the people" perhaps summarized the ideology best. It was enshrined in the American constitution, so that the freedom of speech and assembly, and the pursuit of life, liberty, and happiness were legal rights, upheld by the law.

In Canada, the British North America Act made no express mention of human rights or civil liberties, so that such rights were not legally entrenched until 1982, with the passing of the Canadian Bill of Rights, now part of the new Constitution. The rights apply to all Canadians, without discrimination by reason of race, national origin, color, religion, or sex.

Canada's religious and political ideologies converge, but our economic ideology often does not. Laissez-faire capitalism has as its basic tenets free enterprise, ownership of private property, rights to inheritance, and competition. Early capitalism tended to promote individual rights at the expense of the welfare of the masses.

Recently, Canada's government has adopted a modified socialist philosophy that advocates greater state control of some of the industries. According to this philosophy, education, welfare, health, transportation, and communication should be operated by the government for the benefit of all. Thus, we have a modified sociocapitalist economy, which tries to maintain individual freedom and the collective responsibility of all. Economic management and control, however, still lie mostly in the hands of those of North-European (especially British) origin. How, then, do Canadians of all origins and races have the chance to compete within the economic structure? Hughes and Kallen (1974:214) point out that "Despite a proliferation of human rights legislation, structural and institutional forms of racism persist in Canada today, and until we insist upon and work for the consistent enforcement of anti-racist legislation the truly 'just society' will remain a dream."

Some call for restructuring of our social institutions in order to promote equal human rights.

We have reviewed our heritage of ideologies, which to a large extent are a source of freedom for all. To what extent have these ideals been made into law? If the legal foundation of a *plural* society, in which all groups have equal rights, is laid, then racial equality should be much easier to achieve (Kallen, 1982).

Our Laws

The British North America Act of 1867 gave the members of the two founding nations of Canada, the British and French, what has been termed by Porter (1965) as "charter-group status": the act legalized their claims to ensure the perpetuation of their language and culture. Though legally of equal status, the French have always been junior partners in this alliance, since British political, economic, educational, and demographic influences have dominated. However, Québec has fought hard recently, through the Parti Québécois and the separatist movement, to correct the imbalance. Although the movement failed in its primary goal to secede from Canada, it has won in other respects. Canada's new constitution recognizes two official languages, which are now legally entrenched. At the same time as the British North America Act of 1867 gave charter-group status to the French and British, Canada's Indian peoples were forced off their lands. Specifically, about one-half of the Indian population was forced onto reserves to free the land for European settlers and to provide an administrative arrangement that would ensure control over them. Indians on the Prairies especially (most West-coast Indians to this day have not signed treaties), signed away their lands for a pittance. The reserves, often located in marginal regions, have always been on the periphery of modern industrial society. As a result, large numbers of young Indians have left reserves in search of jobs.

In the meantime, Indians today have become sufficiently organized to lobby for the right to self-

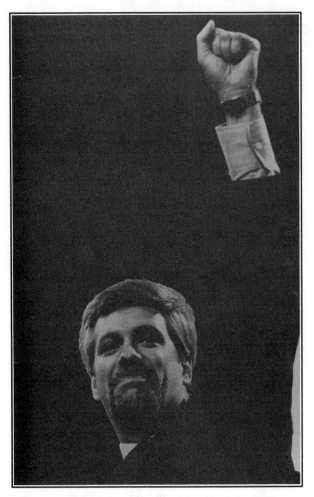

Pierre Marc Johnson, a vocal advocate for a strong French-Canadian identity, acceded to the leadership of the Parti Québécois in 1985.

What about the rights of more than one-fourth of our population, who are neither British, French, nor natives? This proportion of our population has been growing steadily. (See Chapter 21 on population.) Québec's struggle for equal rights inspired Canada's ethnic minorities to demand recognition for their contribution to the mosaic that makes Canada so unique. As a result, a multicultural policy was adopted and many programs are available for the perpetuation of individual ethnic cultures. Heritage-language programs in the public school system is just one example.

As noted previously, Canada's new immigration policy of a decade ago has resulted in a large increase in immigrants from the Third World, including Asians, South Americans, and blacks. A proportion of these new immigrants are also well-educated and increasingly demand equal rights and just treatment. The recent entrenchment of a charter of rights in the Canadian Constitution acknowledges the legal right of all Canadians to equal opportunity in Canadian society. Despite these legal statements on the part of government, racial tensions, prejudice, and discrimination exist in Canadian society. But the problem we face in carrying out this task is enormous.

COMPONENTS OF RACISM

In this section, we shall focus on ethnic stereotypes, prejudice, and discrimination, which seem to be growing in Canada.

Ethnic Stereotypes

Lippman (1922) was the first to use the concept of "stereotype" in the way that it is used today. Lippman assumed that his readers were familiar with the word, since it was used in the printing industry to refer to a plate made by molding a matrix of a printing surface, from which a cast was produced in type metal. According to Lippman's meaning of the concept, impressions can be accumulated and molded into oversimpli-

government. In the last decade or so, the government was forced to negotiate land settlements and recently to accept the aboriginal peoples' demands for special political rights. The new constitution of 1982 acknowledges for the first time that aboriginal peoples (the Indian, Inuit, and Métis) have rights. Since 1982, dialogue between them and the federal government has focused on trying to determine what these rights are. (See Asch, 1984.)

fied statements about anything — including groups of people — statements that are sometimes incorrect. Thus, images or stereotypes of minorities may be unfair or unjust.

Research on stereotypes in Canada has been fairly extensive. Studies show that Canadians often tend to judge minorities negatively on the basis of the stereotyped images that have been perpetuated (for example, images and imprints that may or may not arise out of a well-informed basis).

Prejudicial Attitudes

Prejudice has to do with negative attitudes about certain groups in society. Differential treatment of persons we come into contact with may be due to legitimate reasons, or they may be based on negative attitudes toward minorities, that is, on prejudice. It is often difficult to distinguish between legitimate and illegitimate reasons for differentiation.

Psychologists such as Allport (1954) say that all human beings have to categorize their experiences and must be selective in their perceptions and behavior because we are bombarded with many more sensory experiences than we can absorb and integrate. We naturally have to be selective in our categorization, and this process also permits favorable or unfavorable attitudes based on previous information, experiences, and sometimes stereotypes. No one can fully understand and assess his/her own predelections and values. Thus, it is quite easy to over- or under-compensate when we are faced with visible minorities, or faced with cultural behavior that we find strange.

Prejudice is a negative predisposition to behavior that may lead to discrimination (Hagan, 1977).

Forms of Discrimination

Discrimination is an expression of negative or illegitimate behavior, directed at minority groups. According to sociologist Francis (1972:272), "Restrictions on immigration and naturalization have been common, yet once immigrants have been admitted to potential membership, their differential treatment is relatively soon recognized as illegitimate."

Differential treatment is a clear form of discrimination. For Allport (1954:10), discrimination occurs "when the object of prejudice is placed at some disadvantage not merited by his own misconduct." The question becomes, what is disadvantage? Are ethnic jokes, for example, sufficiently effective in a high school setting so as to result in a disadvantage? In a study of nine high schools in Winnipeg (Driedger and Mezoff, 1981), ethnic jokes were reported by students regularly. Some students perceived these jokes as malicious, whereas others thought they were made "only in fun."

About one-third of the sample of students studied perceived discrimination. More specifically, two-thirds of the Jewish students reported discrimination, as did about one-half of the Polish, Italian, and French students, and one-third of the Ukrainian and German students also reported discrimination, while less than one-fifth of the Scandinavians and British reported discriminatory treatment. Discrimination seemed mostly to take the form of jokes, ridicule, and verbal abuse, although one-fifth of the Jewish students reported receiving hate literature, being physically attacked, and vandalized.

Two national surveys were done in 1976 and 1981 to determine to what extent there are prejudicial or discriminatory tendencies in the various regions of Canada (Bibby, 1982). In the 1981 study, 1265 respondents were asked whether they were at ease, or uneasy in the presence of various cultural and racial groups. It was found that only 9 percent stated that they were uneasy interacting with Orientals, but as many as 23 percent were uneasy associating with East Indians and Pakistanis. This trend was present in each of the five regions, although more Québecois and Maritimers were uneasy, especially with Asians and blacks, than the rest. Prairie Canadians and Québecois were least at ease with native Indians, and respondents of Ontario were least at ease with East Indians and Pakistanis.

When respondents were asked whether they approved of intermarriage between the various racial groups, the proportion of those who disapproved increased. Roughly 20 percent disapproved of white and native Indian intermarriage, and more than 37 percent disapproved of white/black intermarriage. Maritimers tended to disapprove the most, and Québecois were more open to intermarriage. There were also distinct regional trends. One-third to over one-half of Maritimers disapproved of marriage between whites and Asians, and between whites and blacks. Ontarians disapproved of white and East Indian/Pakistani intermarriage, and Prairie respondents disapproved of white and native Indian intermarriage.

When asked whether there was discrimination in their local community against racial or cultural groups, 55 percent of the respondents said there was. As many as 71 percent of the respondents in British Columbia reported discrimination, compared with the Maritimers, of whom only 37 percent said there was discrimination. The difference might be explained by the fact that British Columbians live in a more multicultural region, and have throughout their history interacted with Asians.

With visible minorities increasingly entering Canada, prejudice and discrimination are becoming greater problems, especially in such cities as Toronto. Now we turn to a comprehensive look at the structures of racism as reflected in the treatment of Indian peoples, the blacks, and the Japanese in Canada.

STRUCTURES OF RACISM

Indian Rights

Canada's Indians are legally categorized into two groups: (1) status Indians — those who are registered and therefore have a right to live on reserves, and (2) nonstatus Indians — those who cannot trace their lineage through the patrilineal line to ancestors provided for by the Indian Act of 1874, and therefore cannot live on reserves. Estimates claim that there are probably as many nonregistered Indians as there are registered. Frideres (1983:10) estimates that status, nonstatus, and Métis (of mixed blood) individuals together total about one million Canadians of Indian ancestry. Status Indians belong to one of 565 bands (a form of organization established by the government) that are dispersed among 2276 reserves (Price, 1979:52–53).

From the above, it is apparent that Indians have been dealt with differently throughout Canada, and so it is difficult to sort out which arrangements are legal and which Indians have which rights. Indians on the Atlantic coast and along the shores of the St. Lawrence made relatively few treaties with their white conquerors. After 1781, treaties were made in Southern Ontario and on the west coast. The majority (Treaties 1–11) were made beginning in 1871 on the Prairies and in the Northwest Territories (Frideres, 1983:11). It is important to note that no legal arrangements were made with Indians throughout half the Canadian lands.

Reserve Indians, under the Indian Act, came under the jurisdiction of the federal government. The reserve system gave the government tenure over Indian lands and the Indians were guaranteed welfare services, which made the reserve communities dependent wards of the government. The parcels of land allotted to the reserves were too small for Indians to continue being self-sufficient by hunting and trapping (Tanner, 1983:16–17). Furthermore, under pressure from whites, band councils often sold reserve lands for government projects, such as the extension of roads. Surrenders were also often made under severe pressures from non-native squatters (Frideres, 1983:93–95).

Thus, Canadians — both whites and Indians — are left with a legacy dating from colonial times. It is only in the last twenty or so years that the inadequacy and even illegality of the treaty terms

The reserve system failed because native peoples were treated as outcasts of Canadian society.

of settlement have come to light, largely because of the efforts of politicized Indian leaders such as Harold Cardinal, who exposed *The Unjust Society : The Tragedy of Canada's Indians*, in 1969. In addition to the reasons already stated, the reserve system failed because it shunted Indians to the periphery of Canadian society, where they do not learn the necessary skills to compete in a modern and white society. Many treaties have not been kept, in whole or in part, and the various interpretations of their terms often tend to diminish or deny Indian rights. It does not help the sit-

uation when the federal Indian Affairs department acts as trustees of their Indian wards. This last factor is one basis of the recent demand of the native peoples — the right to self-government. (See Asch, 1984, for detailed discussion.)

In sum, structures for dealing with our Indian minority were never adequate. The problem at hand is to unravel the meaning of "aboriginal rights." As late as 1982, with the new constitution, the government acknowledged "for the first time that there are 'aboriginal people' and 'aboriginal rights'." (Asch, 1984:1.)

Many Canadian blacks are descended from slaves brought to the New World in the seventeenth and eighteenth centuries. More recently, immigration from the West Indies has increased the black population in such urban centres as Toronto and Montréal.

Slavery of Blacks

The slave trade was an important part of the American economy and social structure. Today, prejudice and discrimination directed at the sizeable population of 26 million blacks is continuing evidence of inequality based on past injustices.

To a lesser extent, slavery also became a part of the social structure of early Canada. In 1628, a British ship brought the first black child to New France, the first, known black resident of Canada (Hill, 1981:3). Although the law of France forbade slavery, Louis XIV gave it limited approval, since there was a shortage of workers and servants in the colony. By 1709, full permission was given, and the practice of slavery in New France continued.

The British brought slaves to the New World as early as 1562, selling them to the Spanish American settlements, and the first shipload of twenty African slaves to reach British North America was landed at Jamestown, Virginia in 1619. A century later, when the French territory of Acadia was ceded to the British, New England settlers moved north, bringing with them their slaves to build Halifax in 1749. When the French were defeated by the British in 1760, the French slave-system was adopted by the British regime (Hill, 1981:5-6). Many officers, prominent citizens, and on occasion, clergymen, owned slaves. The slave trade was brisk.

When the British Empire Loyalists fled to Canada during the American rebellion around 1776, they also brought their slaves to Nova Scotia, to Upper and Lower Canada. Mohawk and Iroquois Indians, who had fought with the British, also moved north into Canada, and those who owned black slaves brought them along. Some black loyalists received land grants and later formed black settlements in Nova Scotia, the Niagara Peninsula, York (now Toronto), Kingston, and Prescott. Lieutenant-Governor Simcoe in Upper Canada worked hard to abolish slavery, and legislation to restrict slavery in 1790 preceded the 1803 decision that slavery was inconsistent with British law. By 1833, few slaves were left when the British Imperial Act abolished slavery throughout the Empire.

The underground railroad into Canada was a secret operation to hide, feed, and help blacks who were trying to escape slavery in the United States. These slaves came to southern Ontario, Québec, and New Brunswick, mostly areas where British Empire Loyalists had also settled. Canada became a haven for many blacks, especially Halifax, where until recently, one-third of Canada's blacks resided. The most segregated black community in Halifax has been cleared and dispersed (Clairmont and Magill, 1974), but other smaller communities still remain.

Recently, with the change in Canada's new immigration point-system, West Indians have greatly increased the black population, especially in urban areas such as Toronto. Hill (1960) and Ramcharan (1982) found considerable evidence of discrimination toward blacks and West Indians in Toronto. Race relations is especially interesting in Toronto, because in 1871, 96 percent of the population was of British origin, as compared to roughly one-half by 1981 (Kalbach, 1980). So many people of other origins have entered Toronto that it is today one of Canada's most multi-ethnic and multiracial cities. At least 28 000 blacks lived in Toronto in 1971 (Kalbach, 1980). Reitz (1981: 28) found that the West Indians had the lowest status jobs, the least job security, and the smallest income of nine groups compared in Toronto.

The recent influx of multiracial groups into Toronto has resulted in enough racial incidents that the government set up a task force to study the adequacy of the school system to cope with this problem. The task force found that "principals and teachers tended to be defensive about the possibility that there were incidents of conflict and confrontation that could be attributed to racist attitudes. Racism in children's lives in metro Toronto poses a serious challenge not only to the education system but to the future community." (Pitman, 1978:183–84.)

These findings suggest that blacks (and other racial minorities) are currently faced with racism and discrimination, which have not, for the present, grown to epidemic proportions.

Internment of Japanese Canadians

Our discussion of native Indian rights and the experience of blacks (beginning with slavery) have suggested that Canadian society is guilty of racial inequalities. The forced evacuation of Japanese from the west coast to the Canadian interior during the Second World War confirms this impression. In 1941, 21 175 Japanese lived on the west coast. A small minority of less than 8 percent was scattered throughout the rest of Canada. Ten years later, only 12 percent inhabited the west coast. The majority had been sent inland; 4527 to the provincial interior; 4757 to the Prairies and north; and 9737 to the eastern provinces (Nakamura, 1975:330). Three-fourths of these Japanese Canadians in 1941 were Canadian-born, and many had lived in Canada for several generations.

A small number of Japanese had begun to settle in Canada in 1884, and by 1894, about 1000 had entered Canada. These Japanese were good fishermen in Japan and found it natural to continue their trade on Canada's west coast. Indeed, they were able to compete so well that other Canadian fishermen soon saw them as a threat. Cries to stop Japanese immigration increased until, in 1908, Japan and Canada signed a "gentlemen's agreement" that effectively limited Japanese im-

The men's dormitory at Hastings Park in Vancouver, where Japanese Canadians were quartered prior to relocation in inland internment camps during World War II.

migration to less than 1000 per year. By 1908, 7985 Japanese had entered Canada (Nakamura, 1975:301).

Citizens in British Columbia had pressured previous governments to restrict the immigration of Asians in general, and the Chinese in particular. In 1907, political and labor leaders marched into Chinatown. A riot developed and thousands of dollars of damage was done. The Japanese, however, stopped the white troublemakers from entering their quarters on Powell Street. Thus, even before 1941, discrimination against Asians was commonplace.

To protect themselves, both Chinese- and Japanese-Canadians established segregated areas where they lived and built their social institutions. Prior to Pearl Harbor, the majority of Canada's Japanese lived in two large communities — 2151 in Steveston, a fishing community on the coast south of Vancouver, and 8427 in Vancouver itself (Nakamura, 1975:309). Steveston was a thriving community where Japanese was the language of communication and where the schools and religious and social organizations were Japanese. The same was true on Powell Street in the heart of Vancouver, where "Japantown" was a bustling enclave like many Chinatowns we know today.

The evacuation and relocation of these populations virtually destroyed the Japanese community on the west coast. Before the war, there were well over 200 Japanese organizations; few remained after the war. Japanese-language schools and newspapers were closed down, and along with them, culture, customs, and traditions (Nakamura, 1975:330). The evacuation took nine months. The Japanese were sent to road-camp projects, to old mining towns in British Columbia, and to sugar-beet projects in the Prairies. Some were deported to Japan. In the process, many families were broken up. The property, such as fishing boats, houses, businesses, and public buildings, was confiscated and often sold for a fraction of its value. Today, only a block of Japanese businesses remains on Vancouver's Powell Street (Petrie, 1982:11–46).

The destruction of these Japanese communities was made possible because of pressures exerted by west-coast politicians on Mackenzie King's government to enact anti-Japanese legislation. The American government succumbed to the same anti-Japanese pressures, which may have influenced Canadian politicians. The Japanese were a threat to west-coast labor unions, who pressured politicians to eliminate the Japanese fishermen from the industry. Evacuation solved the problem for them (Sunahara, 1980:94).

In general, the anti-Asian bias was sufficiently strong that very few objected to the injustices of the legislation of forced evacuation, confiscation of property, internment, and deportation. The war hysteria added fuel to the fire.

SUMMARY

1. The predominate classification of Homo sapiens into Caucasoid, Mongoloid, and Negroid groups is based on such characteristics as skin color, facial features, and head and body forms. These genetically inherited differences are attributed largely to evolutionary variations.

2. Racial inequalities exist because European Caucasians developed a sense of white superiority and dominance over Mongoloids and Negroids, which resulted in colonialism, invasion, exploitation, and slavery. The belief in racial superiority led to racism, which still exists in many parts of the world.

3. Canada is no exception where racism is concerned, although according to its heritage of ideologies, all Canadians should be treated equally; the Judeo-Christian religion holds that all human beings are of equal worth; democracy advocates freedom and participation for all; and the modified system of capitalism preaches freedom to compete, and to some extent social responsibility for those in need. In reality, however, not all have an equal place in Canadian society.

4. Immigration policies in the past preferred white Europeans. As a result, most Canadians are white, European Christians, with a small minority Mongoloid and Negroid in racial origin. The founding groups, the British and French, have special, legal privileges. Recently, the federal government has recognized that Canada is composed of many ethnic groups and has legislated a charter of rights for all, and a policy of multiculturalism.

5. Despite official recognition of equal rights for all, ethnic stereotypes and prejudicial attitudes are common. Increasingly, minorities such as the Jews, blacks, native Indians, and East Indians report discrimination, which occasionally erupts into violence.

6. Indeed, throughout Canada's history, examples of discrimination against minority groups, especially against non-whites, abound. Indians were slaughtered, their lands invaded, treaties made and broken. (It is only in the last two decades that native peoples are being compensated for historical wrongs and present-day exploitation of their lands.) Blacks were bought and sold in the past, and the Japanese Canadians were forcibly evacuated, their property confiscated, and their communities destroyed.

7. Canada's new immigration policy is making it easier for peoples from the Third-World countries to immigrate. The visible minorities are especially evident in urban areas such as Toronto. The

West and East Indians, together with the native Indians, occupy the lower-status jobs and therefore lower socioeconomic level. This situation does not portend well for the elimination of racial inequality in Canada.

GLOSSARY

Discrimination. Behavior aimed at depriving persons equal access to rights and opportunities available to others.

Ethnic stratification. The hierarchical ordering of ethnic or racial groups in a society.

Minority group. An ethnic or racial group that is subordinate to another group.

Plural society. One in which numerous ethnic/religious groups co-exist.

Prejudice. A feeling or attitude (usually negative) toward a person or group without sufficient cause.

Race. A category of people based on physical traits, the major one being skin color.

Racism. Any practice of discrimination, segregation, and so on, on the basis of superiority of one race over another.

Stereotype. Rigid opinions and judgements of others that create an exaggerated view, which is not easily changed, of a person or group.

Visible minorities. Those ethnic groups that differ from a white dominant society on the basis of physical characteristics such as color.

FURTHER READING

Broadfoot, Barry. *Years of Sorrow, Years of Shame: The Story of the Japanese Canadians in World War II.* Toronto: Doubleday Canada, 1977. The story of how Japanese Canadians were evacuated from the west coast into the Canadian interior; the sorrow, hardships, losses, and injustices that were experienced.

Frideres, James S. *Native People in Canada: Contemporary Conflicts.* Second edition. Scarborough, Ontario: Prentice-Hall, 1983. An account of native history, the Indian Act, treaties, Indian land claims, demographic and social characteristics, urbanization, native organizations, and government policy with regard to Canada's Indians, Métis, and Inuit.

Hughes, David R. and Evelyn Kallen. *The Anatomy of Racism: Canadian Dimensions.* Montréal: Harvest House, 1974. These anthropologists trace the evolution and origins of Homo sapiens, categorization of races, ethnic stratification of Canada's peoples, and the social processes of integration, as well as minority problems.

Kallen, Evelyn. *Ethnicity and Human Rights in Canada.* Toronto: Gage, 1982. Kallen examines the biological roots of race and racism and discusses the control of racial discrimination, ethnic identity, minorities and the structure of inequality, the persistence of ethnic stratification, the politicization of minority rights, and the recognition of individual and collective human rights.

Ramcharan, Subhas. *Racism: Nonwhites in Canada.* Toronto: Butterworth, 1982. This book includes a detailed examination of historical and contemporary experiences of members of racial groups in Canada, including the roles and status of Japanese, Chinese, East Indian, West Indian, Arab, and Filipino immigrants.

Ujimoto, K. Victor and Gordon Hirabyashi. *Visible Minorities and Multiculturalism: Asians in Canada.* Toronto: Butterworth, 1980. This is an edited volume of twenty-five readings contributed by as many authors, on the Chinese, Japanese, East Indians, Koreans, Vietnamese, and Southeast Asians.

CHAPTER NINETEEN

Ethnic and Minority Relations

ALAN B. ANDERSON

Few countries in the world today could legitimately claim to have a population consisting entirely of a single *ethnic group*. Most countries are pluralistic or multi-ethnic societies. This fact alone makes the study of ethnic relations a prominent field of enquiry within the social sciences, particularly sociology.

TOWARD A DEFINITION OF ETHNICITY

The concept of *ethnicity* — the country or people of origin of one's ancestors — is the basis of the formation of *ethnic groups*. A wide variety of terms have been used to refer to the ethnic subgroups of a society, including race, culture or subculture, nation, nationality, minority group, ethnic minority, ethnic group, and others. But these terms are not completely interchangeable.

"Race" can be either one (but not the only) component in identifying an ethnic group, or it can, in certain cases, be equated with an ethnic group. As you have already learned in Chapter 18, the concept of race has been used to set one particular group of human beings apart from another group on the basis of physical differences (real or imagined).

Other criteria of identification are cultural and are transmitted from generation to generation through the learning process. An ethnic group can be identified, or identifies itself, by a complex of traits, notably common origin, language, religion, and folkways.

In other words, an ethnic group is identified in terms of those characteristics that distinguish it from other groups and thus lead us to consider it a people apart (Akzin, 1964:36). Foremost among these characteristics, according to contemporary sociologists, are a common cultural tradition and a sense of being a distinct subgroup within a larger society.

Of course, we should not jump to the conclusion that all members of an ethnic group take an equal interest in their ethnic roots. Regarding this point, it is important to bear in mind that ethnic identification is not always objective; it may be subjective in the sense of awareness of, and interest in, one's ethnicity. This element is stressed by Canadian sociologist Vallee, when he defines an ethnic group as "made up of people who share ethnicity, who share some sense of peoplehood or consciousness of kind, who interact with one another in meaningful ways beyond the elementary family.... " (Vallee, 1975:167.)

Objective Components of Ethnicity: Language, Religion, and Folkways

In discussing language as a component of ethnicity, it is important to note that the degree of emphasis that an ethnic group places on speaking the language unique to that group varies from one group to another. Some ethnic groups place more emphasis on other factors, such as religion or folkways, as the key to their identity. In fact, some ethnic collectivities in certain societies never possessed a truly unique language. Previously colonized peoples considered as ethnic groups in Canada may have spoken only or primarily English (e.g., most West Indians) or French (e.g., Haitians) before immigrating to Canada. In fact, an ethnic group may lose its traditional language without necessarily ceasing to exist as an identifiable group; for example, few Canadian Jews still speak Yiddish, and few Canadians of Scottish descent can speak Gaelic. Even when retention of a unique language is stressed, ethnic groups differ in their propensity or ability to resist linguistic assimilation.

For many ethnic groups, religion has played an important role in stimulating or maintaining ethnic consciousness, and in providing the infrastructure for the organization of ethnic-oriented activities. As one observer has commented, "religion ... usually stands for more than faith — it is the pivot of the cultural tradition of a group." (Allport, 1954:415.) However, the salience of religion can decline, either through progressive secularization or through conversion to non-ethnic religions. Nevertheless, some sociologists have argued that religion may persist after other elements of ethnic consciousness have declined.

As should be obvious by now, the ethnic-religious link can be complex. An additional factor is that ethnoreligious groups tend to become subdivided into factions that represent various degrees of acceptance of change from conservatism to liberalism. For example, Doukhobors range from Sons of Freedom (or Zealots) through Orthodox to Independents; Jews can be Orthodox, Conservative, Reform, or Reconstructionist; Mennonites range from Old Order, through Bergthaler to Mennonite Brethren and General Conference Mennonites.

A wide variety of folkways, customs and traditions, contribute to the uniqueness of ethnic groups. They include the preparation and consumption of ethnic foods, wearing distinctive clothing, producing traditional crafts, performing folk music or dance, practising or using ethnic art, and following certain traditional behavior patterns.

Again, there is a great difference in the degree of participation between and within ethnic groups regarding folkways. Some ethnic groups in Canada retain strong folk cultures, such as the Ukrainian, whereas others do not.

Subjective Ethnicity: Perception, Stereotyping, Prejudice, and Discrimination

As with objective ethnicity, subjective awareness of, or interest in, ethnicity is highly variable. An

For many ethnic groups, preservation of the heritage tongue is only part of maintaining cultural identity.

individual claiming a certain ethnic origin (e.g., for the census) may not have much of an ethnic consciousness. An ethnic consciousness is not an automatic correlate of objective ethnicity. In other words, an individual who has been assigned to an ethnic group because of declared ethnic origin may not actually be a participant in the ethnic group or a practitioner of a traditional culture. People are assumed to be members of ethnic groups, not only in popular parlance, but also by sociologists and other academics, without careful consideration of the extent to which an ethnic category actually reflects group membership. This lack of conceptual clarity has proved problematic in aca-

demic studies of language use, religious trends, ethnic labor-force participation, intermarriage, integration and assimilation, the history of specific ethnic groups, multicultural education, and so on. Yet popular subjective perceptions of ethnicity are an important, omnipresent feature of ethnic relations. Sociologists are not only intent on correcting popular misconceptions, but they are also interested in studying attitudes as they affect ethnic identification and ethnic relations.

Although an ethnic group can be defined objectively, it may more accurately be regarded as a *perceived appearance group*; that is, an aggre-

A variety of cultural activities serve to reinforce ethnic identity, but not every ethnic group retains a strong folk culture.

gate, category, or group of people who are perceived as being distinguishable from a total population because of a unique characteristic or set of characteristics that has considerable social import in a particular social system (Anderson and Frideres, 1981:58).

Popular perceptions of ethnicity and ethnic behavior frequently assume the form of stereotypes. A *stereotype* is an exaggerated belief associated with a particular category of a national, ethnic, or racial group. To a considerable extent, ethnic- or racial-group stereotypes reflect the established relations of perceived appearance

groups in society (Anderson and Frideres, 1981: 58).

Sociologists have developed a typology of dimensions to measure stereotyping and have identified a number of processes that sustain stereotypes (Anderson and Frideres, 1981:74–76). These processes comprise (1) epithets: statements concerning perceived appearance groups that usually have a negative emotive meaning; (2) nicknames (usually derogatory), which provide a linguistic indicator of past and present relationships between the object group and the name-callers; (3) ethnic jokes, which are told because the teller accepts the underlying premises or assumptions about the ethnic group or individuals who are the brunt of the humor (presumably the listener must also share these assumptions, or the humor would be lost); (4) fictitious stories and publications purporting to be non-fiction, which have consistently denigrated selected ethnic groups; (5) mass media, which have served to label, compartmentalize, and overgeneralize about "ethnics."

Prejudice, closely linked to stereotyping, refers to categorical generalizations based on inadequate data. Prejudice and *discrimination* are also closely related. Whereas prejudice is a feeling or attitude, usually unfavorable or hostile, directed toward a person or group, discrimination is unfavorable treatment of groups on arbitrary grounds.

Also related to prejudice and discrimination are the concepts of *ethnocentrism* and *xenophobia*. Ethnocentrism is the view that one's own ethnic group — its norms, values, and culture — is superior to another group, or the tendency to judge other ethnic groups or cultures from the standpoint of one's own group or culture. Ethnocentrism often results from xenophobia — a fear, mistrust, or apprehension of "foreign" people or cultures.

Minority Group/Dominant Group

The origin of the concept of *minority group*, at least in an ethnic sense, is derived from the development of nation-states and nationalism in nineteenth-century Europe. It refers to any group of people "who, because of their physical or cultural characteristics, are singled out from others in the society in which they live for differential and unequal treatment and who, therefore, regard themselves as objects of collective discrimination." (Wirth, 1945:347.)

A more recent definition focuses on the balance of power rather than on perceived discrimination: a minority group is any group that is subordinate in power compared with the *dominant group*, "which has pre-eminent authority to function both as guardians and sustainers of the controlling value system, and as prime allocators of rewards in the society." (Shermerhorn, 1970: 12–13.)

Most sociological definitions of minority group and majority group (or dominant group) imply power relations, that is, relative disadvantage or advantage. However, the student of ethnic relations must be careful in applying these concepts to societies such as Canada. In fact, Canada reveals the limitations of these concepts, for several reasons. No single ethnic group in this country constitutes a statistical majority; every ethnic group is technically a minority. Even if the British-origin groups are combined (English, Scottish, Irish, Welsh), together they still comprise less than half the total Canadian population, although many writers have viewed them collectively as the dominant group, representing an Anglo-Canadian norm to which all others must conform. But defining this group or norm as a monolithic entity is no simple task. Historically, Anglo-conformity has been an effective vehicle for Anglo-Canadian dominance. But in contemporary analysis, the conflict situation implicit in sociological definitions is not applicable to every ethnic group in Canada (Anderson and Frideres, 1981:32).

ETHNIC PERSISTENCE AND CHANGE

In any pluralistic country such as Canada, a variety of factors contributing to the persistence of ethnic consciousness are offset by factors contributing to its decline. Both trends — persistence and change — co-exist, often within the same ethnic group. In the past, sociological attention has been devoted to loss rather than to retention. The present trend, the rediscovery or revival of ethnic consciousness among third-generation individuals in North America and Western Europe, has redirected sociological interest to retention. Loss of ethnic consciousness in the second generation and renewed interest in the third generation are common.

But the ethnic identity of the third generation (or later generations) is not necessarily identical to that of the first (immigrant) generation (Isajiw, 1975). For example, an immigrant (most likely completely of a single ethnic origin) may feel adamant about retaining the traditional language, religion, and folkways, and be an active participant in ethnic voluntary organizations, whereas the third-generation descendant (most likely of mixed parentage, or intermarried) may feel it is not essential to speak the language, or to attend an ethnic-religious parish, or to pursue certain folkways. Yet he/she may well retain a keen interest in ethnic customs and participate in ethnic associations whose membership consists largely of people born in Canada rather than immigrants (Isajiw, 1975).

Both the persistence of ethnicity, including the reinterpretation of ethnic identity, as well as its decline or loss, are affected by a range of factors external to the ethnic group per se: for example, by dominant-minority relationships, by multiculturalism and immigration policies and other political considerations, by education practices and policies, by economic trends, by structural conditions, and so forth.

Factors Making for Persistence

It is convenient to divide the factors making for ethnic persistence into attitudinal, ideological/demographic, and structural factors, although it should be understood that these are not discrete categories.

The first category concerns the attitudes of the group members about themselves. How do they view themselves? If they are "visible," in other words if they can be observed as different from others in the general population, this visibility may reinforce, or may even be the primary reason for their ethnic distinctiveness. Sociological generalizations about assimilation or integration may not be as applicable to "visible" minorities, since cultural attributes can be lost, changed, or de-emphasized far more easily than physical appear-

ance, unless visibility is restricted to clothing (as in the case of certain ethnoreligious groups, such as the Hutterites or Hassidic Jews.

In Canada, non-whites may be identified as "foreigners" longer than Canadians of European origin. Even third- or fourth-generation Canadians of Asian or Afro-Caribbean origin are not infrequently asked where they come from, although they are Canadian-born; yet even for European-origin groups in Canada, ethnic identity is likely to persist if salient criteria — ethnic consciousness, traditional language and religious affiliation, retention of folkways — continue to be emphasized by the group as a whole. Group pressure can be brought to bear on the individual member, so that failing to retain ethnicity may be regarded by the group as unethical.

Moreover, many writers have suggested that an official emphasis on Anglo-French biculturalism and bilingualism in Canada has contributed substantially to the preservation of ethnic cultures. In view of the longstanding emphasis on British and French Canadians as charter members of Confederation, the other Canadians have, by subtraction, felt obliged to claim their own ethnicity. Thus, every Canadian becomes a "hyphenated" Canadian: an English-Canadian, French-Canadian, Ukrainian-Canadian, Chinese-Canadian, and so on. In fact, ethnicity is likely to persist if conceptualization of national identity, in this case Canadian identity in general, is relatively weak or confusing compared to ethnic regional identities (Anderson and Frideres, 1981: 107).

A second set of factors relating to ethnic persistence are demographic/ecological. An initial question in this regard might be whether, or to what extent, the ethnic minority is socially and/or physically isolated from people of other ethnic origins. Canadian society includes many examples of a fairly advanced degree of ethnic self-segregation, such as among the Hutterites, Mennonites, and Amish, as well as the Sons of Freedom sect of Doukhobors and — most unusual in an urban set-

In many North American cities, the remains of the Jewish settlements of the turn of the century still retain their distinctive character. Immigrants, faced with such obstacles as quarantine and quota laws, have endured a long history of rejection in their struggle for acceptance. Their sense of alienation, and the need to seek security among one's own, did not end with the first generation.

ting—Hassidic Jews. Treaty Indian reserves provide an example of forced segregation. And there are innumerable examples of lesser degrees of ethnic segregation in the rural ethnic bloc settlements scattered throughout the Prairie provinces and in the urban ethnic neighborhoods found in most Canadian cities. The ability of an ethnic group to maintain such separation may depend on continuing immigration, so that a substantial proportion of people residing in an ethnic settlement or neighborhood are themselves immigrants. For example, a Chinatown may persist for decades, yet Chinese Canadians continuously move out of Chinatown and are replaced by new immigrants from Hong Kong or Vietnam. An ethnic minority consisting largely of immigrants is more likely to be concerned with adjusting to their new home-land, whereas one made up largely of Canadian-born would be concerned about maintaining their ethnic identity and culture from generation to generation.

The persistence of ethnic groups may be influenced by a variety of demographic considerations: (1) the size of the population of the group (locally, regionally, or nationally); (2) the group's proportion relative to total population of the community or neighborhood; (3) whether the ethnic population is growing, stable, or declining; and (4) whether the limits or boundaries of the settlement area are expanding, stable, or contracting. Moreover, sociological research on ethnic persistence takes basic demographic characteristics of the ethnic population into consideration, such as age, generation, sex, occupation, education, class, and residential and social mobility. Suffice it to say that very different conclusions about persistence can be drawn depending on precisely which segment of the ethnic population is studied.

Finally, the survival potential of ethnic communities will be enhanced if they are "institutionally complete." The concept of *institutional completeness* (Breton, 1964) is the extent to which the ethnic community controls its own institutions and social organizations. To what extent does the ethnic community control its own voluntary associations, mass media, schools, and churches? And to what extent do the group members tend to participate in ethnic associations, use ethnic media, send their children to ethnic schools or educational programs, or attend ethnic parishes?

Factors Making for Change

Ethnic identity change is usually measured in terms of intergenerational decline in the knowledge and/or use of the ethnic language, attendance at an ethnic church, practice of customs, marital endogamy, institutional completeness and participation in ethnic-oriented schools, voluntary associations, media, and so on.

Language loss may not necessarily be indica-tive of a decline of ethnic consciousness, although it is often closely linked to other processes affecting ethnic identification: widespread intermarriage between people of different ethnic origins; secularization, conversion, or de-emphasis of the link between ethnicity, language, and religion; discriminatory legislation against use of foreign languages in schools; the breakdown of the institutional completeness and enclosure of ethnic communities; and unfavorable demographic trends such as rural depopulation or a lack of replenishment of the ethnic group through continuing immigration.

We have noted that sociologists have used religion as a measure of ethnic identification. However, Canadian census data indicate that ethnic group members have been steadily abandoning their group's ethnic religious affiliation through intermarriage, as well as conversion and secularization. For example, by 1971 only a third (33.4 percent) of Canadians claiming Scandinavian origin were still Lutherans; more than half (52.7 percent) of Ukrainian Canadians were neither Orthodox nor Catholic; more than a quarter (29.1 percent) of Polish Canadians were no longer Roman Catholic; fully a third (33.1 percent) of Canadians of Czech descent were neither Catholic nor Lutheran; little more than half (55 percent) of the Dutch Canadians were Catholics, Reformed, or Mennonites; and so forth.

However, sociologists must be cautious about using only one factor in measuring ethnic identity change, since a change in one factor often affects another. This has been clearly illustrated in research on generational differences in ethnic identity retention in rural Saskatchewan (Anderson, 1982). The study, a survey conducted among a thousand respondents residing in rural ethnic bloc settlements, revealed a marked decline in almost all of the nine ethnoreligious groups represented: French Catholics; German Catholics; Mennonites; Hutterites; Ukrainian Orthodox; Ukrainian Catholics; Polish Catholics; Russian Doukhobors; and Scandinavian Lutherans. Every group (except the Hutterites) experienced a loss of ethnic consciousness from the first through the third generation. In particular, there was a decline in the use of the traditional mother tongue of the group and in attitudes opposing ethnic as well as religious intermarriage (although generally more opposition to religious than ethnic intermarriage was noted for each generation). There is no doubt that *intermarriage* between Canadians of different ethnic and/or religious backgrounds has weakened ethnic solidarity. The 1981 census revealed that a high percentage of Canadian-born family heads in some ethnic categories were married to spouses of different ethnic origins.

A vast sociological literature has been devoted to formulating theoretical models of ethnic identity change. To these we now turn.

SOCIOLOGICAL MODELS OF ETHNIC IDENTITY CHANGE

The most influential of early attempts to outline stages of ethnic contact relevant to ethnic minorities in North American cities was that of Robert Park. According to Park (1926, 1937, 1950), there are five cyclical stages of events that characterize race and ethnic relations.

1. *Invasion* refers to an alien ethnic group immigrating as a minority into the territory occupied by a majority ethnic group. The majority group believes it has superior status, but accepts the alien group because the latter is needed to perform specific functions unattractive to the majority or to supplement a labor shortage.

2. With social mobility, *competition* between majority and minority groups arises, especially for the same jobs sought by immigrants and poorer members of the majority group. Competition results in ethnic strife, prejudices, and stereotyping. The majority group feels it has the right to hold the best jobs and an advantaged position in society.

3. Therefore, *conflict* emerges. The majority group develops a conscious recognition that its aims and interests clash with those of the minority. Conflicts may lead to riots or annihilation, genocide or expulsion of the minority.

4. Failing annihilation or expulsion, *accommodation* may develop, wherein (a) the conflicting groups may achieve accommodation, (b) the minority group may withdraw into a ghetto situation, or (c) the minority may accept a degrading position.

5. The last of Park's stages is *assimilation*, which could involve (a) the merging of cultural differences, usually through the acceptance of the dominant culture by the minority at the expense of the minority's own culture, and/or (b) racial (physical) merging (amalgamation).

Later, Louis Wirth (1945:347–72), categorized ethnic minorities on the basis of their objectives: a minority could be (a) *pluralistic*, desiring peaceful co-existence with the majority and other minorities; (b) *assimilationist*, desiring absorption into the dominant group; (c) *secessionist*, if it sought both cultural and political independence; or (d) *militant*, if it went beyond the desire for equality toward a desire for domination: a total reversal of status.

Wirth directed more attention than Park toward differential minority response to attempted dominant control. Revisions of these and other models or typologies of ethnic relations enable the contemporary sociologist to provide a more sophisticated analysis of ethnic relations, particularly with regard to dominant social control and minority responses. To such an analysis we now turn.

ETHNIC MINORITY RESPONSE TO DOMINATION

Conflict and Dominant Social Control

Just as majority-group domination of minority groups ranges from eradication of the minority to accommodation, minority responses can vary from active resistance to passive acceptance of domination. We shall take some of the insights derived from sociological theories of social conflict and apply them to an analysis of social-control mechanisms employed by the dominant group.

There are two types of social conflict and conflict resolution: consensus or disconsensus (Aubert, 1963). Applied to ethnic relations, in a situation of *consensus conflict*, conflicting ethnic groups strive for the same goals, but these goals are not as attainable for some groups as for others. In Canada, for example, members of ethnic groups do not have equal access to all jobs in the labor market even though they may aspire to a certain occupation. The result is a disproportionate representation of certain ethnic groups in certain jobs (Porter, 1965). In a situation of *disconsensus conflict*, each ethnic group has different aims, as, for example, the demands of ethnic minorities for the teaching of heritage languages in the schools. In Québec, the anglophones lobby for English-language instruction, and francophones outside Québec for education in French.

From the perspective of the minority group, conflict can be viewed as having four functions (Himes, 1966):

1. Structural: Conflict can reduce the power differential between the minority group and dominant group, thereby restricting existing status differences.

2. Communication: Conflict can effectively serve to publicize a problem, bringing it to the attention of the public.

3. Solidarity: Conflict may increase group consciousness to such a degree that the group comes to resist dominant values.

4. Identity: Conflict can dispel the sense of alienation in the minority and replace it with a new sense of common purpose.

Canada's Indians are a good example of the way in which conflict can be functional, especially with regard to the native rights movement. Their plight was brought to public attention. As news of specific instances of conflict with authorities

Canada's native people population has demonstrated how conflict may generate unity and a sense of purpose. Here, publisher Juanita Rennie introduces her new magazine, *Sweetgrass*. The magazine, named for the herb used by shamans and symbolic of purification, aims to capture a national native people and non-native people readership.

spread from one Indian band to another, a sense of group consciousness developed, and a common purpose united the Indian peoples from coast to coast.

Anderson and Frideres (1981:233–58) have developed a theory concerning social control mechanisms and ethnic group mobilization in Canada. Briefly, they argue that ethnic minorities cannot fail to perceive various hindrances to their full integration within the Canadian socioeconomic system, just as these minorities view pressure to assimilate as a potential threat to their own interests and identity. As a result, some minority groups set forth their own explicit or implicit goals, then attempt to implement the resources available to them to achieve these goals (Breton, 1964). Their struggle to achieve a particular goal, for example, the use of their own ethnic language in school instruction, may be viewed as part of a broader movement for status recognition emerging from their specific position and role within the social system.

If the minority accepts its subordinate position in society, it can be considered to be low in discontent. The dominant group assesses the minority group's awareness level, that is, the minority's perception of its place in society and its relative discontent or passivity, as well as its leadership and ability to organize. If we apply this to the Canadian situation, the strength of the separatist movement in Québec resulted in the granting of major concessions to French Canadians. However, this move increased discontent among less numerous and powerful (but still fairly well organized) minorities, such as Ukrainian Canadians.

The dominant group can also control the desire of subordinate groups to want to change. This can be accomplished in five ways, according to Anderson and Frideres: through insulation, persuasion, selective participation, sanctions, and cooptation. Insulation is the process by which a minority group is kept from participating in the dominant social system; thus, the dominant group can control the minority group's access to, or mobilization of, resources.

An example is the forced segregation of Indians to reserves. Persuasion refers to strategies of the dominant group in persuading minority group members that they play a vital role in keeping society intact. Hence, the attempt during the Second World War to persuade Japanese Canadians that their forcible relocation, imprisonment, confiscation of property, and even exile was in "the best national interest."

Selective participation is a control mechanism combining influence and control. It serves to reduce minority power by allowing only limited participation in decision-making in economic, political, and social spheres.

Sanctions, both negative and positive, can be administered by the dominant group as a means of controlling undesirable or irresponsible action on the part of the minority. Negative sanctions are far more evident in white supremicist South Africa; however, government measures taken against "enemy aliens" during the First World War is a Canadian example. Finally, cooptation, limiting access to certain resources for minorities viewed as difficult or threatening, is a fifth means of controlling a minority group.

It should be pointed out that although all the above control mechanisms are theoretically available to the dominant group, in practice, one or another technique is applied at certain times under certain conditions. Because minority ethnic groups are constantly changing in what they perceive as vital aspects of their culture, as well as in their leadership and organization, the dominant group must continually alter the manner in which it deals with minority expectations. Let us turn now to the various ways in which ethnic minorities respond to varying degrees of dominant social control.

Genocide and Expulsion

Obviously, genocide is imposed on a minority and so is not strictly speaking a *reaction* to dominant control. *Cultural genocide* is the destruction of the culture of the group, in which sense the term has been applied to Canadian Indians by Harold Cardinal (1969), one of the first native activists. *Physical genocide* is the complete annihilation of a people; such an attempt is exemplified in the Nazi extermination of Jews and Gypsies during World War II, and in the less-publicized starvation of five to seven million Ukrainians by Stalin. In either form, annihilation is the result of conscious decision-making by the dominant group.

A second way to eradicate a minority is to expel it. Again, expulsion can assume two forms: it can be external, involving the relocation of the minority outside the country; such "repatriation" occurred when Japanese residents in Canada (some of them Canadian citizens) were sent "back" to Japan during the Second World War. Expulsion can assume the form of internal relocation, in which case the minority is forced to move from one region to another within the same country. Again, Japanese Canadians provide an example, when they were forcibly removed from the British Columbia coast and interred during the war. It is possible, of course, for a dominant group to combine genocide with expulsion, as in the case of the massacre and expulsion of an estimated 1.5 million Armenians in Turkey in 1915.

Assimilation, Anglo-Conformity, and Acculturation

In sociology, the concept of *assimilation* has a duplicity of meanings, reflecting the fact that it has been repeatedly redefined. Considerable confusion has resulted particularly from a failure to distinguish clearly between assimilation as a *state*, the final stage of ethnic identity change, and assimilation as a *process*. The process of being assimilated involves a gradual replacement of minority culture by elements of the dominant culture; in the end, a state of complete assimilation is achieved, in which the minority culture has been completely replaced, and the minority ceases to have an identity of its own. However, in pluralistic societies such as Canada, there are degrees of assimilation that vary between total and partial, as well as between individual group members and the group as a whole.

Sociologists have described a variety of conditions that hinder or retard assimilation. The rate and degree of assimilation depend on the relative isolation of the minority group from the dominant society, on the size and organization of the minority group, as well as on the degree and form of discrimination or social control practised by the majority group. Moreover, as mentioned previously, it is possible to reverse the process of assimilation: to return to one's roots after some degree of assimilation has taken place or to recapture an interest in one's ethnic identity after a generation or two. *Acculturation*, which is the process of acquiring cultural traits of another ethnic group, may take place without assimilation, which refers to both the acquisition of the perspective of the dominant group and the attempt to identify with it (Shibutani and Kwan, 1965:470, 497). In Canada, *Anglo-conformity* was clearly favored by the dominant group at least until after the Second World War, when official policy gradually gave way to an emphasis on cultural pluralism, although multiculturalism was not declared as an official policy until 1971 (and even today remains ill-defined). Anglo-conformity is a broad term that has as a central assumption the desirability of maintaining English institutions, the English language, and English-oriented cultural patterns. Throughout English-speaking Canada, Anglo-conformity was, and to a considerable extent still is, attempted through the school system, the writings of historians who praised British (not Canadian) ideals, and the institutionalization of British traditionalism. But it has ultimately failed because of the resistance of ethnic minorities, if not because of the ever-increasing heterogeneity of Canadian society (Jaenen, 1971:11).

Reference is seldom made by assimilation theorists to exploitation, whereas other theoretical approaches currently utilized in sociology stress exploitation as the driving force behind race and ethnic relations. Assimilation models typically emphasize cultural assimilation, the process through which cultural differences between diverse racial and ethnic groups diminish in contact situations. The inevitable conclusion drawn in countless sociological studies utilizing this approach is that assimilation is hastened or retarded in direct proportion to the similarity or dissimilarity of the groups in contact, with physical (racial) differences being more problematic than cultural. In short, race and ethnic relations are explained primarily in terms of innate physical and cultural differences between groups, since it is assumed that the degree of difference in turn accounts for prejudices, stereotyping, discrimination, and generally racism.

The Exploitation and Stratification of Ethnic Minorities

In contrast to the assimilation models, colonial models have emphasized exploitation and oppression of minority groups by the dominant group. In their analysis of race and ethnic relations, they stress European colonial domination, even though this domination could be indirectly exercised through upwardly mobile, middle-class members of the subjugated ethnic minority. Colonial models view the dominant group's pursuit of profit as the main motive for the exploitation of subjugated racial and ethnic minorities.

Class models have viewed the oppression of non-whites as an integral feature of capitalist exploitation experienced by all workers. There are obvious similarities between colonial models and class models, in that they both agree that capitalism is the basic source of exploitation of racial minorities. However, the main thrust of class models is on exploitation of workers; racism is a means of dividing the proletariat and a rationalization for exploiting non-whites (Geschwender, 1978:93, 102, 110). In their drive to make profits, capitalist employers attempt to reduce production costs by replacing higher-paid labor with cheap labor and exploiting existing racial differences.

Whereas colonial and class models have emphasized capitalist exploitation, sociologists in general have devoted attention to the close relationship between the subordination of ethnic minorities and social stratification. The term *ethnic stratification* is presently used in sociology to describe the following situations: (a) the internal stratification of a given ethnic group; (b) the subordinate status of the ethnic group in the total society; and (c) the mobility of ethnic group members and their entry into a non-ethnic social structure.

Three conditions must exist for a stratified system to emerge: ethnocentrism, competition, and differential power (Noel, 1968). Ethnocentrism is related to social stratification in that a particular ethnic group becomes the reference point for rating or scaling other ethnic groups. Competition exists between groups that strive for the same goal, such as land, better housing, jobs, and financial assets; the intensity of competition varies with the number, significance, and commonality of goals being sought. The third condition, differential power, refers to the ability of a particular group to impose its will on other groups.

There is ample evidence of ethnic stratification in Canada. Sociological research has indicated that some ethnic groups have higher levels of education, income, and status than others. The general absence of non-British in the Canadian business elite has been well documented by Porter (1965), Kelner (1970), and Clement (1975), among others. And research has repeatedly been conducted on ethnic (French, British, other) differences in income in Québec.

Where ethnic stratification exists, there is generally a degree of passive submission on the part of minorities regarding their disadvantaged subordinate status. The minority group finds it either necessary or advisable to accept, at least on a temporary basis, this situation. Passive submission characterized the Chinese response to discrimination during early periods of their settlement in Canada (Lee, 1976:47), and it was evident in the Japanese response to forced evacuation and resettlement in 1942 (Adachi, 1976:230). Passive submission, carried to an extreme, could lead to self-hatred if the dominant group's negative view of the minority group becomes internalized to such an extent that members become ashamed of their ethnic background and culture.

Ethnic Accommodation: Integration versus Segregation

Ethnic accommodation is characteristic of pluralistic societies and multinational states. The essential ingredient of *ethnic accommodation* is the acceptance, to greater or lesser extent, of the ethnic minority by the majority. The end result is either integration of the minority or segregation.

Integration should not be equated with assimilation. "The concept of integration rests upon a belief in the importance of cultural differentiation within a framework of social unity." Furthermore, "There may be economic absorption, but cultural pluralism, cultural absorption at some levels ... yet cultural differentiation and isolation at others ... and so on through many permutations which may arise because of variations in the social systems brought into contact through immigration." (Bernard, 1959:93-94.)

Yet accommodation and pluralism can also be characterized by segregation, which can be voluntary on the part of the minority or forced on the minority by the majority. Most sociological definitions of segregation refer to a state or process of a minority being spatially separated from other groups as the result of pressure placed on the subordinate group by the dominant group. Segregation can also occur without involving spatial or physical separation. An example of the former, of course, is the historic case of Canada's Indians being persuaded by the government to settle on reserves. Hutterite colonies are a good example of voluntary and spatial segregation. Examples of groups that segregate themselves voluntarily but not necessarily spatially include Hassidic Jews, Orthodox Doukhobors, Old Colony Mennonites, and Old Order Amish-Mennonites. Thus, patterns of segregation are quite complex.

North American Jews in general are an interesting case of partly involuntary, partly voluntary segregation. Most are the direct descendants of East European Jews who had been forced to live in ghettos.

Anderson and Frideres (1981:294) found that ethnic identity tends to persist in the Canadian West only as long as it remains positively valued and useful. Accommodation is sought when minority groups desire some degree of equality with the dominant group while remaining separate from the dominant group. The central question is, how much separation is possible or profitable without impeding effective integration?

North American Jews inherited a ghetto mentality that led them to congregate together upon immigrating to North American cities. Yet antisemitism cannot be discounted as having played an important role in perpetuating Jewish clustering, since certain residential areas were effectively closed to Jews. Whatever the explanation, Jews in Canada, and to a lesser extent in the United States, continue to reveal high residential concentration combined with high endogamy and institutional completeness.

It could be said that most, if not all, ethnic minorities (on the group level) are segregated to some extent, and that segregation is partly voluntary and partly involuntary. Vast rural areas of the Prairie provinces consist of ethnic bloc settlements, ranging in size from several hundred people around a single village to large settlements spread across thirty or more communities and populated by tens of thousands of people. According to Price (1959:270-71), there are three main processes by which these group settlements came into being. The first is an organized mass emigration of political or religious refugees from their homeland. Chain migration is the second; that is, the process whereby immigrants establish links with their friends and relatives in the homeland, a result of which is the consecutive emigration of these contacts to the settlement chosen by the original emigrants. The resulting settlements may reach the size of several thousands or more. The third process, gravitation, applies to settlements that are formed when migrants who have emigrated independently are drawn together into groups by mutual attraction, such as a common dialect or language, religion, cultural traditions, and so on.

Most Canadian cities contain clearly defined ethnic neighborhoods. Toronto has an Italian population estimated at more than a quarter of a million, as well as residential neighborhoods and/or commercial concentrations that are predominantly Chinese, East Indian, Portuguese, Jewish, Maltese, East European, West Indian, Korean, and Greek. Montréal contains Jewish, Greek, and Italian neighborhoods, as well as several areas in which the British-origin minority predominates. Vancouver has Chinese, Japanese, Jewish, Greek, French, German, and Mennonite concentrations, as well as several Indian reserves within its metropolitan boundaries. Winnipeg includes a French-Canadian town (St. Boniface), both poor and wealthy Jewish neighborhoods, an area settled almost entirely by Eastern Europeans, and a heavy concentration of native people.

It should be emphasized, however, that such urban ethnic concentrations can be misleading for several reasons. They do not necessarily contain most of the members of a particular ethnic group; for example, the Chinese do not always live in Chinatown. Second, their durability may depend on continuing immigration. Third, they vary greatly in size as well as in degree of institutionalization, and not all ethnic neighborhoods contain commercial strips. Fourth, they may reflect less of a propensity of an ethnic minority to congregate and more the apprehension (on the part of the majority) over the minority spreading into other residential areas. For example, large numbers of West Indians have been settled by the Metro Toronto Housing Authority in certain low-income apartment buildings in one outlying part of the city, turning some buildings into virtual black ghettos.

Voluntary segregation may be considered as one means available to ethnic minorities in accommodating to a new country.

Ethnic Revivalism and Separatism

The rediscovery or revitalization of an ethnic group's cultural heritage tends to be closely associated with ethnic separatism, the rejection of both assimilation and accommodation in order to achieve political and cultural independence, or at least autonomy, from the dominant society. Both ethnic revivalism and separatism imply the politicization of the ethnic minority; in fact, ethnic revivalism is invariably linked with ethnic nationalist movements.

The recent organization of Canada's Indians into a unified Assembly of First Nations is aimed at co-ordinating efforts to resist domination of the majority and to develop "self-determination." This demand for the right to autonomous self-government is indicative of both revivalism and secessionism. In Québec, no sooner than the separatist Parti Québécois came to power, it instituted new language legislation aimed at reinforcing French unilingualism. This legislation required all non-francophone children not born in Québec to attend French schools, and that all shop signs be exclusively in French. In 1980, the party held a referendum on sovereignty-association, which it defined as political (but not economic) independence from Canada. Although the referendum was unsuccessful, the secessionist movement was a response to years of domination by the Anglo majority.

Many examples of the close link between ethnic revivalism and separatism can be found in other countries. The United States, which has long prided itself on being a "melting pot" or "crucible," has had militant Black Power, Red Power, and Brown Power (Chicano or Mexican-American) movements. The foundation of the state of Israel in 1948 was accompanied by a revival of the dormant Hebrew language. Similarly, the Celtic Revival in the British Isles was associated

Militant Sikhs shout anti-government slogans in New Delhi, India, following the takeover of the Golden Temple in Amritsar by the Indian government.

with the Irish Home Rule and independence movements, and more recently with the "devolution" (decentralization) process as a response to Welsh and Scottish nationalism.

Ethnic revivalist and ethno-nationalist movements for regional/ethnic autonomy abound in most contemporary Western European countries. Some examples are found among Basques and Catalans in Spain, the Swedish-speakers in Finland, and the Lapps in Norway. Elsewhere in the world, ethnic separatist or nationalist movements continue to develop, most recently in India, where militant Sikhs are attempting to garner support for an independent state of Khalistan; in Sri Lanka, where the Tamil minority are pressing for their own state; in the Horn of Africa, where ethnic Somalis in Ethiopia, Kenya, and Djibouti continue to agitate for union with Somalia; and in the South Pacific, where Kanak rebels battle French colonial domination on the island of New Caledonia.

It is clear that, far from dying out through

assimilation or resting content with some form of accommodation, indigenous (non-immigrant) ethnic minorities in all of these countries are becoming increasingly politicized, anxious to revitalize their hereditary cultures and to gain more political autonomy, if not complete independence.

It seems appropriate to conclude this chapter with a brief discussion of how ethnic minority rights in Canada fit into a framework of multiculturalism.

MULTICULTURALISM AND MINORITY RIGHTS

Multiculturalism can be conveniently addressed by answering the following questions. First, how much attention has Canada, compared with other countries, paid to the rights of ethnic minorities? Second, how can ethnic minority rights be defined? Third, how do ethnic minority group members feel about their "rights"? Fourth, what are the implications of minority versus dominant group relations for minority rights? In other words, how dominant is the majority or dominant group, and in what ways? Fifth, what can we expect of Canada's multicultural policy?

Minority Rights in Canada

It is noteworthy that it took Canada's federal government almost a century since Confederation to develop specific human rights legislation regarding its ethnic minorities. No mention of such rights was found in the British North America Act, which served as the constitution of Canada until a formal constitution was legislated in 1982. This constitution does contain certain statements on the right of "official" (but not unofficial) language minorities to education in their own language. But it is far short of making anything except general pronouncements on the many other ethnic minorities comprising Canadian society. Even native rights were excluded from the original draft of the constitution; native leaders were not given an

effective voice to debate possible incorporation of native rights in the constitution until March, 1983.

The tardiness of national — and in many cases provincial — legislation on the rights of ethnic minorities may be accounted for in Canada's long history of discriminatory legislation against ethnic minorities: in 1885, a "head tax" levied on all oriental immigrants, which was increased tenfold in 1903; in 1923, an Oriental Exclusion Act prohibiting further oriental immigration, which was not repealed until 1947; decades of segregation of blacks in all-black schools in Western Ontario and Nova Scotia; the refusal of Canadian authorities to accept a reasonable quota of Jewish refugees from Europe after 1939; in 1942, the forced evacuation and deportation of Japanese from the British Columbia coast; and decades of discrimination and repression of European ethnic minorities through forced Anglo-conformity in the Canadian school system.

In view of this long — and apparently to some extent ongoing — history of institutional discrimination in Canada, one might wonder how effective the relatively recent human rights legislation will be in reducing the societal level of ethnic discrimination.

The Problem of Defining Minority Rights

Defining human rights or ethnic minority rights is problematic. Minority rights may even be in conflict with other, more general types of human rights. Thus, overtly racist groups such as the Ku Klux Klan often exploit a freedom-of-speech clause in order to spread hate propaganda; yet "incitement to hate" also constitutes an infringement of human rights. This confusion is often used as an excuse for failing to take immediate or effective legal action against human rights abuses.

Sociologists have constructed typologies of minority rights, drawing a distinction between collective, individual, and categorical rights (Kallen, 1982:75–77). Collective rights of an ethnic minority may consist of national group rights, in which

Originally begun in 1866 to conduct a campaign of terror against newly enfranchised blacks, the Ku-Klux Klan was officially disbanded in 1869. It was reorganized in 1915, when it extended its hostilities to Jews, Catholics, pacificists, the foreign-born, radicals, and labor unions. Officially disbanded once more in 1944, the Klan was again revived in recent years, and was involved in several violent confrontations with civil rights groups in the early 1980s.

ethnic collectivities have a territorial basis for their claims, or cultural group rights, referring to collective rights of a unique ethnocultural group. This conceptual distinction has its limitations, however. For example, French Canadians and native peoples might seem to be deceptively good examples of ethnic minorities with national group rights. The Québecois claim Québec as a virtual nation-state and French as the only official language in the province. But over a million French Canadians live outside Québec, and over a million non-French live in Québec. As for our native peoples, the leaders of organizations claiming to represent status Indians are currently pushing for self-government on reserves. Yet two-thirds of the native population consist of Indians who do not live on reserves, and Inuit and Métis who have interests of their own.

More significant is the problem that a distinction between "national" and "cultural" group rights seems to imply that cultural groups do not have a legitimate right to claim any territory. This may or may not make sense in Canada, where all the non-native ethnic groups could be defined as immigrant groups (that is, immigrants and their Canadian-born descendants). Yet it should be pointed out that in some countries, virtually every ethnic minority has a claim to its own territory, as well as education in its own language, along with a variety of other rights enshrined in the constitution of the country. For example, Yugoslavia is essentially an ethnic federation consisting of six republics, which are in effect nation-states of the six most populous ethnic or ethnoreligious groups: Serbs, Croats, Slovenes, Macedonians, Bosnians-Hercegovinians, and Montenegrins.

If a definition of cultural group rights suggests that these rights are pursued by the group as a whole, one must bear in mind that an ethnic population as a statistical category does not necessarily operate as a group with a common purpose. Such a definition assumes that members of ethnic collectivities positively value their distinctiveness and therefore are anxious to maintain it; however, this might be jumping to conclusions, given the complexity of subjective interest in ethnicity.

In-Group Support of Minority Rights

Ethnic collectivities, particularly ethnic minorities in North America, tend to become divided into traditionalists versus transitionalists. The former may be defined as "those actors closest to the ethnic core, for whom ethnic identity is most central and for whom ethnic alignment takes precedence over penetration of dominant institutions"; whereas transitionalists are "those actors (usually the numerical majority) for whom ethnic identity is less central and for whom the choice between ethnic alignment and penetration of dominant institutions is situationally determined." (Kallen, 1982:82.) The traditionalist identifies strongly with the collectivity, whereas the transitionalist only does so on occasion, if at all. Thus, the group solidarity of ethnic groups is variable.

The "Minority Syndrome"

The "minority syndrome" described by sociologists suggests that an ethnic minority is not simply a statistical category but disadvantaged and subordinate to a dominant group (which may not necessarily be a statistical majority). As Kallen (1982:110-11) has explained, a "majority defines the normative order of society," and "minority members tend to be regarded and treated by the dominant population as unworthy or undeserving of equal societal opportunities. It follows ... that the more abnormal or inferior the alleged minority attributes are considered, the more stigmatized the minority and the more insidious the forms of discriminatory treatment and denial of human rights." Moreover, this process can become accentuated for people having multiple minority status—that is, any combination of ethnic, racial, religious, class, sex, or physical disability.

It merits repeating that any analysis of dominant minority relations must take into consideration the extent to which the minority is voluntary or involuntary. In discussing relations between immigrant groups and the dominant group, Lieberson (1961) has pointed out (1) that unlike native peoples, immigrants cannot really "opt out" of the economy; (2) that immigrants tend to be under greater pressure to assimilate (if white); (3) that the dominant group ultimately controls the immigration process.

In outlining differential minority responses to dominant social control mechanisms earlier in this chapter, we have emphasized that varying degrees of domination are met with varying degrees of acceptance or resistance by the ethnic minority.

Canada's Multicultural Policy

The multicultural policy has been devoted, in the decade since its official inception in 1971, almost exclusively to selective financial support of ethnic performing arts and festivals and, to a lesser extent, ethnic writing and publishing, as well as academic "ethnic studies," conferences, and publications. Limited attention has, until recently, been paid to the most fundamental and pressing concerns of Canadian ethnic minorities, notably education and racism. Perhaps there is a shift in Canadian multicultural policy from a preoccupation with ethnic cultures to a new awareness of the concerns, problems, and rights of ethnic minorities.

In this regard, it is vital to note that the older, established immigrant groups tend to have rather different views of multiculturalism than newer immigrants. The former lay greater stress on the preservation of ethnic cultures, and hence are more likely to be content with the existing multicultural policy, although some of these established minorities have been pressing for more ethnic-oriented education in the public school system.

Education is almost exclusively within provincial jurisdiction, and few provinces, with the possible exception of Alberta, have met minority requests for the incorporation of ethnic history or languages into school curricula during the regular school hours. Piecemeal concessions have been

The main problem for new immigrants to Canada is that of racism, which limits opportunities with respect to employment, housing, and broad social contacts.

made to teach ESL (English as a Second Language) and certain "ethnic" languages after hours. One observer has commented that "the tendency in all public or state school systems is towards uniformity and centralization," toward processes that discourage educational recognition of cultural pluralism (Jaenen, 1972:199). Other critics confirm this observation: "Our schools, where much of this harm can be prevented, rather than tapping the rich cultural resources represented by our cultural minorities, are destroying them in the name

of conformity, efficiency and standardization." (Costa and Di Santo.)

Canadian multicultural policy has suffered from a lack of consistency, clarity, and continuity in both its interpretation and administration (Burnet, 1978). The main concern of newer immigrants, most of whom are non-white, is pervasive racism, which hinders their facility in finding suitable employment and housing, not to mention congenial social relations with other Canadians.

There are indications now that both the federal and provincial governments are realizing that multicultural policies and human rights legislation must be extended to deal more adequately with the vital concerns of ethnic minorities, particularly non-white immigrants being subjected to individual, institutional, and cultural racism.

GLOSSARY

Accommodation. The acceptance, to a lesser or greater extent, of an ethnic minority by the majority.

Acculturation. The acquisition of cultural traits of another ethnic group.

Assimilation. The gradual loss of a minority culture, which is replaced by a dominant culture.

Culture. That component of humanity that is created by humankind and is transmitted from generation to generation.

Discrimination. Unfavorable treatment of groups on arbitrary grounds.

Dominant group. The group that has the authority to function both as guardians and as sustainers of the controlling value system, and as prime allocators of rewards in the society.

Ethnic group. A minority group in a larger society that is identified or identifies itself by a complex of traits: notably, common origin, language, religion, and folkways.

Ethnicity. Descent from ancestors who shared a common culture or subculture manifested in distinctive ways of speaking and/or acting.

Ethnic stratification. The (a) internal stratification of an ethnic group; (b) the subordinate status of an ethnic group within the total society; or (c) the mobility of ethnic group members and their entry into non-ethnic social structure.

Ethnocentrism. The view that one's own ethnic group is superior to another group, or the tendency to judge other ethnic groups or cultures from the standpoint of one's own group or culture.

Folkways. Customs or practices that contribute to the uniqueness of ethnic groups, including ethnic foods, clothing, crafts, folk music, folk dancing, folk arts, and so on.

Minority group. Any group of people who, because of their physical or cultural characteristics, are singled out from others in the society. The concept implies a subordinate status vis-à-vis the dominant group.

In a statistical sense, any group of people constituting less than half a given population.

Multiculturalism. Accommodation of diverse ethnic groups within a single society or political state; may be equated with ethnic pluralism.

Perceived appearance group. A group of people who are perceived as being distinct from the total population because of unique characteristics that have high social import for a particular social system.

Pluralism. The co-existence of many cultural systems in one society.

Stereotype. An exaggerated belief associated with a particular subgroup, particularly of a national, ethnic, or racial group.

Traditionalist. A member of an ethnic group for whom ethnic identity takes precedence over identity with the dominant group.

Transitionalist. A member of an ethnic group whose ethnic identity becomes less important than identification of the dominant group.

Visible minority. People observable as different from others in the general population, usually on the basis of race or skin color.

Xenophobia. A fear, mistrust, or apprehension of "foreign" people or cultures.

FURTHER READING

Anderson, Alan B. and James S. Frideres (eds.) *Ethnicity in Canada: Theoretical Perspectives.* Toronto: Butterworth, 1981. A comprehensive discussion of theoretical perspectives and research on definitions of ethnicity — objective criteria, subjective perception and stereotyping; biculturalism, multiculturalism, and immigration; ethnic relations — conflict, racism, dominant social control, and minority subordination; minority responses and outcomes; and implications for Canadian multicultural policies.

Bienvenue, Rita M. and Jay E. Goldstein (eds.). *Ethnicity and Ethnic Relations in Canada.* 2nd edition. Toronto: Butterworth, 1985. A book of selected Canadian readings on ethnicity and ethnic relations, ethnic differentiation, ethnic inequalities, prejudice and discrimination, conflict and change.

Elliott, Jean Leonard (ed.). *Two Nations, Many Cultures: Ethnic Groups in Canada.* 2nd edition. Scarborough, Ontario: Prentice-Hall of Canada, 1983. A broad collection of case studies of native peoples, French Canadians within and outside Québec, ethnic minorities in Québec, and selected European and "third world" immigrant groups in the multicultural mosaic.

Friesen, John W. *When Cultures Clash: Case Studies in Multiculturalism.* Calgary: Detselig Enterprises, 1985.

Ishwaran, K. (ed.). *Canadian Families: Ethnic Variations.* Toronto: McGraw-Hill Ryerson, 1980. The theme of family, ethnicity, and religion in multicultural Canada is illustrated through case studies focusing on a variety of European-origin, native, and non-white ethnic groups.

Kallen, Evelyn. *Ethnicity and Human Rights in Canada.* Toronto: Gage Publishing, 1982. A thorough discussion of types of human rights and how they relate to ethnic inequality and multicultural policies in Canada.

Li, Peter and B. Singh Bolaria (eds.). *Racial Minorities in Multicultural Canada.* Toronto:

Garamond Press, 1983. Includes readings on Canadian immigration and multicultural policies, multicultural education, health care among ethnic minorities, ethnic family studies, institutional controls and ethnic organizations, and theoretical perspectives.

Mallea, John R. and Jonathan C. Young (eds.). *Cultural Diversity and Canadian Education: Issues and Innovations.* Ottawa: Carleton University Press, 1984.

Samuda, Ronald J., John W. Bury and Michel Laferriere (eds.). *Multiculturalism in Canada: Social and Educational Perspectives.* Toronto: Allyn & Bacon, 1984. All three of these comprehensive texts relate multicultural diversity to educational policies and practices in Canada.

CHAPTER TWENTY

Inequalities of Gender and Age

DENNIS FORCESE

A prominent political scientist recently observed that the equality issues that will dominate the 1980s in Canada are those of "aspirant groups" — women, the handicapped, native peoples, children, and the aged (Vickers, 1983:47–72). Other observers might add homosexuals and visible minorities to this list. Similarly, an inventory of the 1960s and 1970s in Canada would identify ethnic groups, youth, and regional populations as aspirant groups seeking some measure of equality with regard to income, power, respect, and general quality of life. Yet social science literature commonly refers to inequalities arising from the class structure of a society as the fundamental basis of inequality, a topic explored in Chapter 17.

But the operational inequalities — that is, the inequalities that people are conscious of and seek to amend, and that influence behavior — are those associated with distinctions that divide, as well as separate social classes. These are the very inequalities of aspirant groups, or "status groups," as Weber called them (1958). Status groups, as you already know, are persons distinguished by some common attribute or social location, and distinguishable in social esteem or honor and life style. Status groups are cross-cutting; that is, persons may belong to several. For example, one could be a male (sex), Jewish (ethnicity), lawyer (occupation), forty years old (age), living in Forest Hills, Toronto (region). Each status category describes his social situation in life.

The emphasis on class-based inequalities has subordinated, even trivialized, the relevance of status characteristics such as race, gender, and age. Marxist theorists have relegated such factors to secondary importance; however, empirical evidence suggesting the structural and behavioral relevance of status factors is all too evident. As Weberian theorists suggest, occupation, age, gender, race, and region all interact to form a nexus of inequality. Working-class women are more deprived and subordinate in power than working-class men; working-class native persons have less status and power than working-class Caucasians from charter-group backgrounds; elderly women are more deprived than women in their prime; and the privileges of an upper class are not equally available to men and women. In sum, structured or persisting inequality cannot simply be reduced to social class and therefore, in this chapter, we shall examine inequalities related to gender and age.

Gender and Age Inequality

Influenced by the feminist movement and an increased public awareness of the social situation of women, substantial literature has appeared on women and social inequality. There is no comparable literature, however, on the aged and inequality. Our society is preoccupied with the young and social problems concerning them, such as juvenile delinquency and youth unemployment. Indeed, it can be fairly stated that only a segment of the life span of Canadians has been seriously considered — that of adolescence and young adulthood. Unlike women's rights, there has been scant attention paid to "gray" rights.

However, the problems of the aged have begun to attract some attention. The attention is in part a spin-off from the concern with women's issues, for a disproportionate number of the aged are women. This awareness is also due to the increased aging of the population and to the financial and other burdens being placed on career-oriented and mobile individuals who are unable or unwilling

to care for their aged parents. The rather sudden reality of a situation wherein the state and its social agencies are ill-prepared to assume the burden of quality care for the aged may climax as the social crisis of the late twentieth century in Canada.

Nature versus Culture

Like race, the inequalities associated with gender and age derive remotely from biological inheritance, and more importantly, from social context and cultural interpretation. Even those individual or group characteristics that are biologically derived — for example, black or Caucasian, male or female, young or old — are socially defined and have value placed on them. Thus, differences in behavior associated with status groups are attributable not to biology but to social learning.

It is our fundamental premise that like other animals, and moreso, human beings learn and acquire the attitudes and behaviors (culture) featured in a given society at a given time. It follows, therefore, that these attitudes and behaviors can change and vary from one historical period to another, from one society to another.

Social differentiation by age and gender is a universal phenomenon. In simple societies, age, sex, and kinship are the only bases for forming distinguishable subgroups. Moreover, in all human societies, even the more complex, there is an expectation of "different behavior from males than from females." (Richards, 1977:172.) Noteworthy, too, is the fact that even in those societies dedicated to social change and achieved social roles, gender differentiation persists. For example, the People's Republic of China was conceived in a revolutionary commitment to equality, but has failed to achieve the same occupational or power opportunities for women as there are for men (Saunders, 1983). In fact, the official Communist party newspaper has declared that mothers should stay at home so that unemployed young people can have jobs (American Press, 3 June 1984). Gender is a convenient and effective basis

In spite of recent liberalization of gender roles, women still bear the primary burden of child care, regardless of their responsibilities outside the home.

for role allocation in society, but it is not a biological imperative.

GENDER DIFFERENTIATION

Men and women are different biologically, specifically with regard to functions in the reproductive process. The expressions of these reproductive capacities are interpreted socially and in turn have consequences for the social situation of men and women. Men, for example, are free of the biological responsibility in the event that conception takes place after intercourse. If conception occurs, women face a biological burden and consequences that extend throughout the nine-month gestation period. In addition, whether there are instinctual bases or not, social definitions have tended to attach postnatal responsibilities to women.

But the social definitions of responsibility vary enormously from society to society. In some, men have learned to experience labor pains and generally to simulate the female experience of childbirth. In others, the pain of childbirth for males is a version of culturally defined stress and anxiety. In some societies, women are free to relinquish child-care responsibilities as soon as a child is weaned. In others, women are held responsible in the belief that they have biologically-derived nurturing and child-care skills that continue until a child reaches adulthood — a stage itself subject to broad variation in definition. Even presumably straightforward and measurable biological differences — hormonal levels and associated emotional states or tension — vary by culture and therefore are shaped and expressed by learning (Saunders, 1982:219-20).

Men and women have traditionally been stereotyped in terms of a number of supposed, biologically based behaviors that vary from society to society and from class to class: women gather food and cook, or women must not do any physical work at all; men are hunters and warriors, or by "breeding," gentlemen of refinement and leisure. Female students do poorly in mathematics and science, but well in literature and the arts, and vice versa; only men are great composers, artists, or even great chefs; women are emotional and nonaggressive, whereas men are rational and aggressive. The list is endless.

All of these stereotypical characteristics of males and females are learned. Stereotypes are exaggerated social definitions that are stated as truisms, and they generally serve to prevent equal access to self-expression and activity by status groups.

The most taboo-ridden aspect of human behavior associated with gender definition is sexual expression. Often, it is presumed that the child-bearing and nurturing functions require restrained sexual conduct on the part of women, whereas men are allowed any number of partners and variety of sexual encounters. In our society, it is often stated that we have experienced a sexual revolution with regard to women. New birth control methods and greater female access to education and occupation have created a measure of freedom from biological responsibility for women comparable to that always enjoyed by men.

Sex-Role Differentiation, Past and Present

The key to the continuation of any human group is reproduction, child care, and nurturing. In some societies, procreation was replaced or supplemented by child theft from other groups, but generally reproduction is paramount. Thereafter, care and subsistence are fundamental. Men, because they did not bear children, were free to hunt and thereby to supplement the food supply. But in simple hunting-and-gathering societies, vegetable foodstuffs collected by women were usually the staples.

As you have already learned, horticulture and agriculture were probably developed by women. With controlled production of food, some of the uncertainty of subsistence was reduced and surplus was accumulated for the first time in human history. The female role in collecting foodstuffs became less crucial, and women came to be regarded as property, a form of conspicuous display. Women's work persisted in the fields and in the household, but it was far less intrinsic to the survival of the group, except for reproduction. Women were expected to perform tasks near the home.

While women tended the hearth, men were free to hunt or to make war. "There is no hunting and gathering society that makes hunting large game a regular part of the women's role ... nor one that confines men to activities around the home base." (Richards, 1977:26-27.) It follows from this fun-damental differentiation that basic sex roles become learned and expressed as social expectations (Richards, 1977:235-38).

Analyzing data from the Human Relations Area file, a repository of anthropological data from societies around the world, researchers have found, in addition to the interpretations of duties noted above, that socialization of girls tends to stress obedience and responsibility, and of boys, achievement and self-reliance (Barry et al., 1970:277).

Despite our society's increased stress on sexual equality, there still persist traces of similar training, with girls expected to be less aggressive but more obedient and responsible than boys. Hence, we still find that girls express lower educational and occupational aspirations, and are expected to assume responsibility for aged parents. The process of sex-role socialization is illustrated in the 1983 Canadian film of Alice Munro's short story, "Boys and Girls." Here, girls are relegated to traditional female activities despite inclination or talent, and boys assume responsibilities and privileges that are traditionally male.

Along with a more secure food supply and larger populations, there developed organized warfare, which served to emphasize the male of the species vis-à-vis power, prestige, and survival of the group. It is possible, as some anthropologists have argued, that the relegation of women to a subordinate status is associated with the transition from the communal social organization of simple societies to a family-oriented social organization in agrarian society. In simple societies, the sexual division of labor did not define women's work as inferior. But with the extended family as the unit of production in peasant agrarian societies, women's labor was exploited as "support labor." (Bourgeault, 1983.) Thus, for example, among Canadian native people, the status of women deteriorated with the European conquest and the imposition of European social organization. Finally, in the transition from agricultural to industrial society, women became part of the labor market. But unlike men, women were part of a labor reserve, periodically utilized as in the early industrial revolution, or in wartime, and otherwise relegated to jobs that derived from household labor (Connelly, 1978).

Socialization and Gender

Social roles are, as you have learned, related to the nature of economic organization and production, and to different levels of socioeconomic development. Human beings learn the behavior associated with social roles, along with their prestige and their rewards. This socialization process is both deliberate and unintended. As you learned in the chapter on socialization, we are taught to behave in one way or another. But we also learn by observation and imitation. The experiences and role models to which a person is exposed will influence that person's conception of role play, which together with the training received from infancy, will influence male and female adult behavior.

It may be argued that the most important institution in perpetuating traditional gender attitudes is the family, especially the two-parent family. But the learning of sex roles occurs in many institutions, from church to mass media. The directions that children receive in such settings are reinforced daily in peer-group interaction — in children's play, for example. Boys play with boys, and girls play with girls, and failure to segregate play is the object of concern and ridicule by other children and by adults. The nature of the play, the games, and the physical props, are also gender-specific.

Even modern formal education, with female-dominated preschool and primary teaching, has offered few occupational role models for girls other than those related to the household or traditional nurturing occupations such as teaching itself. Religious-oriented schools especially have stressed traditional conceptions of female role and female service and subordination. Public schools have also effectively streamed girls away from science subjects or vocationally oriented skills, except those again related to traditional domestic pursuits. Thus, home, school, play group, church, and the mass media all act to reinforce gender differentiation, one that is not premised on different but equal, but on different and unequal.

Culture and Patriarchy

In Canada and other settler societies, women from immigrant groups, such as the Italian and the Portuguese, are especially disadvantaged. They are subject to the cultural definition of traditional societies where the role of women does not favor education to the extent presently encouraged in our society. Usually, immigrant women survive in language ghettos that isolate them from their new society and relegate them to household or domestic labor. Confined to the household, they are not obliged, and have few opportunities, to acquire cultural attitudes more permissive of female equality.

Immigrant men are expected to be the providers. Therefore, even if their wives do work outside the home cleaning houses or offices, or in factories, it is supposed to be an interim activity, albeit an activity that frequently persists a lifetime and may be an important source of household income.

In the past, all women who worked had to do so to supplement the family income (an indication of low status) and they were generally from the working class. Today, this attitude — that women should not enter the labor force with a career in mind but rather to supplement the husband's income — persists in middle-class families, as well.

Many students of gender and roles have seized upon the notion of partiarchy to describe the web of cultural attitudes and practices that are associated with female subordination. Although they have been and are still being challenged, there is little doubt that traditional partiarchal notions of male supremacy persist. To the extent that changes in attitude have occurred, they are due to the increased female participation in higher education.

Between the 1950s and the 1980s, the percentage of women in post-secondary education has more than quadrupled.

Women and Education

Post-World War II Canada experienced an educational revolution. The number of people completing post-secondary education increased enormously, especially the number of females. Up until this time, higher education for women was discouraged. For the daughters of wealthy parents, education was at best a form of cultural finishing school, and for middle-class young women, a minority felt that higher education could be intellectually rewarding, but it was not usually a means to career. Education related to vocational or professional skills was discouraged generally, except for the traditionally female occupations of teaching and nursing. Education, consequently, was but a socially acceptable form of putting in time before marriage, rather than a career prerequisite.

These attitudes began to change in the 1950s, and especially in the 1960s. The major change was that of greater middle-class female participation in post-secondary education, one that still

TABLE 20-1. Percentage of female population aged eighteen to twenty-four in post-secondary education, 1951 to 1977

1951	4.6
1961	8.2
1966	10.8
1971	14.6
1976	18.0
1977	18.2

SOURCE: From Table 4.15, *Perspective Canada III*, 1980.

TABLE 20-2. Percentage of University Degrees Awarded to Women, Canada and the United States

		1962	1970	1976
First Degree	Canada	27.8	38.0	44.6
	USA	38.7	41.8	44.9
Second Degree	Canada	18.1	22.0	29.9
	USA	32.8	40.1	45.3
Ph.D.	Canada	8.1	9.3	15.5
	USA	10.7	14.3	22.9

SOURCE: From Table 15.17, *Canada III Perspectives*, 1980.

tends to follow the segregated pattern of young women in arts subjects and young men in applied fields. As indicated in Table 20-1 , female participation more than doubled in the period 1951 to 1966 and more than quadrupled since 1951 to 1977.

More recent data indicate a virtual equality of men and women in educational achievements measured by first degree and disregarding field. In contrast to 1961–62, when 16 500 men and only 6300 women received degrees, by 1981–82, the figures were 42 200 and 43 000, respectively (Statistics Canada, 1982). The equality deteriorates, however, when one examines graduate degrees, especially doctorates. In 1961–62, there were 290 Ph.D.'s awarded to men and thirty to women. By 1981–82, the disparity actually increased to 1400 male and 400 female Ph.D.'s (Statistics Canada, 1982). In the case of higher degrees, therefore, even in the humanities and the social sciences, female participation drops drastically. Consequently, employment at universities remains male-dominated.

A perspective of the Canadian situation may be gained in comparing Canada with the United States. Where, at the outset of the 1960s, women in the United States were, in far greater numbers, apt to complete a first degree; by 1976, the proportion was virtually identical in both countries. The number of Canadian women completing a graduate degree also increased from 1962 to 1976,

but their numbers are much less in the United States. (See Table 20-2.)

Occupational selection is related to the practice of "streaming" in the education of girls and boys, women and men. Already evident in high schools, more females than males choose subjects in the humanities as opposed to the sciences. This feature is true of nearly all developed societies, and not just Canada and the United States. Swedish researchers, for example, also identify curriculum-selection biases that stream women toward a limited occupational range. The so-called "advanced options" in Sweden, especially for lower-class girls, are not chosen, and middle-class girls are eventually selected out of the science and the industrial/vocational curricula (Sweden, 1979:23–28).

Work and Gender

It is also the case that although the number of Canadian and American women completing graduate degrees has increased, especially in the humanities and social sciences, the increase is not translated into comparable jobs for women. Thus, in Canada today we still find women relegated to traditional sectors of employment, even when the attitudes and qualifications of women are changing.

Part of the problem is that the occupational structure is not very permeable. Just as there is a youth unemployment problem because there are too few jobs, so there are relatively few opportunities for women to alter traditional occupational segregation. The lack of teaching opportunities at universities is an example, for even as the number of qualified women has increased, university expansion and employment have decreased. The exception has been employment opportunities in the public service, where jobs have increased more than in the private sector since World War II. It is therefore in the public sector that the number of women has increased markedly, because the number of jobs has increased. This increase also coincides with the political influence of feminism, and its stress upon labor-force participation by women.

Although more than 50 percent of women in modern Canada are employed and although social movements, intellectual opinion, and legislation have been oriented toward equal access for women, a widespread social attitude continues to emphasize household and child-raising duties as being the domain of women. Therefore, many women, who begin working upon graduating from school, later drop out of the labor force to have children (Saunders, 1982:235). The highest participation rate occurs between the ages of twenty and twenty-four.

Generally, men have access to a greater array of occupations and to jobs that have greater prestige, power, and economic return. At present, 75 percent of clerical workers are women and if sales and clerical jobs are merged, 60 percent of this category is filled by women (Armstrong and Armstrong, 1983:7–9). Thus, the least-paying jobs in our society are occupied by women.

Looking at banks, major offices, and the federal public service in the first thirty years of this century, Lowe (1980) argues that women have become an "administrative underclass," occupying a category of dead-end jobs undesirable to

TABLE 20-3. **Labor-Force Participation in Canada by Sex**

Year	Males	Females	Total	Participation Rates* Male	Participation Rates* Female	Participation Rates* Total
	(in 000's)			(percentage)		
1901	1 606	279	1 885	87.8	16.1	53.0
1911	2 381	418	2 799	90.6	18.6	57.4
1921	2 742	561	3 303	89.8	19.9	56.2
1931	3 291	751	4 042	87.2	21.8	55.9
1941	3 713	939	4 652	85.6	22.9	55.2
1951	4 087	1 147	5 223	83.9	23.5	53.7
1956	4 437	1,346	5 782	82.2	24.9	53.5
1961	4 782	1 739	6 521	79.8	28.7	54.1
1966	5 193	2 227	7 420	77.8	32.8	55.1
1971	5 800	2 831	8 631	76.1	36.5	56.1
1972	5 938	2 953	8 891	76.2	37.1	56.5
1973	6 127	3 152	9 279	76.8	38.7	57.5
1974	6 338	3 324	9 662	77.3	39.7	58.3
1975	6 499	3 515	10 015	77.2	40.9	58.8

* The participation rate is the number of persons in the labor force divided by the population aged 14 years and over.

NOTE: Newfoundland is not included from 1901 to 1941. Figures for 1901 to 1941 are adjusted to include residents of the Yukon and Northwest Territories, Indians on reserves and members of the armed forces, but exclude inmates of institutions.

SOURCE: From Table 6-1, *Perspectives Canada*, 1980.

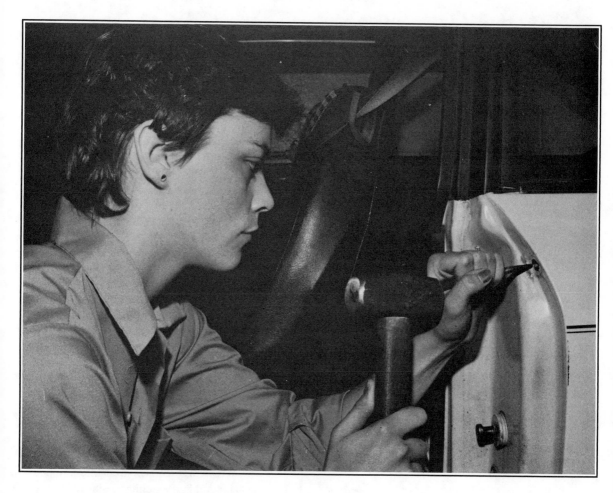

Although women still are largely socialized into "appropriate," gender-linked careers, some have chosen to compete for higher-paid, skilled blue-collar jobs traditionally held by men.

men. Lowe and others find a pattern of sexual stereotyping, segregation, and wage differences in the job market. More women have entered the labor force, but they still tend to enter female-dominated occupational sectors (Fox and Fox, 1983). At the point of entry, they secure salaries that reflect their educational level, moreso than males, but wage increments tend to top off as female careers fail to develop (Boyd, 1982:22).

Another feature of female labor force participation relates to hours of work. Female full-time workers tend to fill well-defined occupational roles that require relatively little overtime work. In contrast, men put in longer hours, with greater income and career consequences. However, when we consider part-time work, women work longer periods than men, but because they are in part-time positions, they gain scant income or career benefits. (Armstrong and Armstrong, 1983: page 52). In general, where women occupy identical occupational roles, they tend to receive less pay than do men.

Jeanne Sauvé, appointed Governor-General of Canada in 1983, is one of the few women in Canada to attain a powerful position in government.

Women's jobs also tend not to be unionized and to carry poor fringe benefits. In 1976, 42.5 percent of working men were unionized compared to only 26.8 percent of women (Saunders, 1982: 242). Canadian unions, historically, have consisted largely of male members and have been indifferent to the interests of women. Clerical and sales jobs have only been unionized in the last two decades.

Power and Gender

Not only are women deprived of equal opportunities vis-à-vis men in terms of range of jobs and income, they also seldom occupy positions of authority. Canadian researchers have found few women in high-ranking corporate and judicial positions (Clement, 1975:266 and Olsen, 1980:76–77). Only in 1984 was the first woman appointed to the Supreme Court of Canada, and only in 1984 do we have Canada's first female governor-general. There is some indication that women are now being recruited to fill prominent positions in major private or public organizations, but the incidence of career advancement to positions of authority is still slight.

American data indicate that in job sectors that allow for career advancement, male networking frequently blocks the promotion of women to these positions. This networking reinforces sex-role socialization, which fosters the belief that women are unsuitable for managerial roles. Thus, women become discouraged in competing with men. A striking example of this is the school system. The occupation of teaching has traditionally been female-dominated, especially at the primary levels. Yet the position of school principal has been, and still tends to be, occupied by males. Research suggests that women do achieve supervisory work roles, say in an office, but they tend not to achieve management positions that affect and determine hiring, promotion, or the pay of other employees (Institute for Social Research, 1983:5, 8).

A clue to reluctant female participation in politics may be found in the public musings of former Ontario premier, William Davis. He claimed that women tend to shun the unpleasantness and personal abuse that characterizes politics. Therefore, he suggested, even with the best good will, political parties find it difficult to recruit female candidates (*Toronto Star*, 24 June 1984). To the extent that such self-selection does influence participation, it may be so because of childhood socialization and male networking, discussed above.

It is a fact that there are very few women in elected political office, and that women will often contest seats when their party has scant prospects of winning. It seems that they drop out when electoral prospects in a riding improve (Kornberg et al., 1979:186–216 and Campbell, 1977:69–70). Remarking upon this phenomenon, the very successful female mayor of Ottawa recently declined to contest a federal seat in the city, precisely on the ground that she resented being courted, as other women have been, as a symbolic or sacrificial candidate.

Generally, then, women are in low-chance situations in politics. Vickers (1978) has found that most women in politics are found at the municipal levels, with participation dropping off at provincial and federal levels. In sum, although there

are prominent female role models in modern Canadian politics, their numbers are few.

Income and Gender

Until the second half of this century, it was acceptable for only those women who did not marry to work. To put it another way, working women were tolerated only until they would be supported by a spouse. Furthermore, the male spouse with a working wife suffered loss of prestige for not being able to support his family. A woman's social worth was

TABLE 20-4. Average Earnings of Women and Men in Selected Occupations

Occupation	Dollar Difference between 1965 and 1973	Women	Men
Managerial	1965	$ 3 351	$ 7 920
	1973	8 335	14 731
	Dollar difference 1965 to 1973	4 984	6,811
Professional and Technical	1965	4 226	7 602
	1973	7 770	13 500
	Dollar difference 1965 to 1973	3 544	5 898
Clerical	1965	3 263	4 713
	1973	5 584	8 483
	Dollar difference 1965 to 1973	2 321	3 770
Sales	1965	2 077	5 287
	1973	3 942	10 187
	Dollar difference 1965 to 1973	1 865	4 900
Services and Recreation	1965	2 099	4 120
	1973	3 368	7 796
	Dollar difference 1965 to 1973	1 269	3 676
Transportation and Communications	*1967	3 495	5 575
	1973	5 094	9 382
	Dollar difference 1967 to 1973	1 599	3 807

* 1965 figures were not available for women employed in Transportation and Communications.

SOURCE: Statistics Canada, Income Distribution by Size in Canada, 1973 (Catalogue No. 13-207) and (Catalogue No. 13 – 528).

derived from her mate's or parent's social worth. This calculation required women to be conspicuously idle whenever possible, or have their work confined to the household. Thus, both men and women were victims of social mores.

As already stated, the occupations available to women earned low wages or salaries, and the opportunities for career advancement were almost nil. These conditions were regarded as acceptable by both worker and employer because it was assumed that women were only short-term employees, eventually to be supported by a spouse, or because a woman's income was viewed as merely supplementing a husband's income. A related attitude was that wherever possible, the best jobs should be reserved for the "breadwinner" and not squandered on the temporary female worker, or on the female employee who was merely improving family income rather than providing necessities.

Even today, it is consistently true that women earn less than do men for identical work. In general, Canadian women earn 40 to 65 percent of men's wages (Saunders, 1982:242). (See Table 20-4.)

A recent survey commissioned by the Ontario Human Rights Commission compared the work experiences of 137 graduates of business schools. The sample consisted of seventy whites and sixty-seven persons from the visible ethnic minorities. There were several indications of preferential treatment of whites, but most striking difference related to gender. The greatest income differential was between white men and women (*Toronto Star*, 25 June 1983).

Similar disparities exist in the United States, where recent research indicates that working women earn two-thirds of the salary of working men for comparable work. This is greater than the publicized income gap between white men and black men. In addition, American researchers find that women are taught to aspire to lower-status and lower-income positions (Institute of Social Research, 1983:5).

With the increase in the number of women entering the labor force, there are some indications of improvement in their income. Since 1977, the income of Canadian women has been increasing more rapidly than have male incomes. In part, however, this is a function of recruitment of women into professional positions, and not of comparable salaries for comparable work. That is, there is some effort to recruit women, which may or may not result in continued income and career progress. According to Statistics Canada, women's earnings increased by 45 percent and men's by 25 percent in the period 1967–81, but in 1981, men earned an average of $18 200 and women an average of $9700 (Statistics Canada, 1984: 7).

It is also the case that women in the labor force increasingly make up a significant segment of family income. In the past, working women sustained working-class or lower middle-class households. Today, they are intrinsic to the quality of life of middle-class families. Since 1967, less than a twenty-year period, the number of married women in the labor force approximately doubled. Whether such labor-force participation will eventually lead to egalitarian families, including domestic roles for men, is yet to be seen.

Male Disadvantages

The social attitudes toward sex-role differentiation are an inhibiting factor for men as well as women. Men are discouraged from taking up careers in occupations such as nursing, or preschool or elementary-school teaching. Similarly, men are rarely afforded the option of part-time work, or of household and child rearing duties.

In many cultures, especially our own, women are expected to show emotion, men are not. Consequently, there is a tendency to distance men from their children, a tendency reinforced by the traditional sexual division of labor, relegating women to the household and men to the occupational labor force. The social definitions related to child care are especially evident in the instance of marital separation and child custody. The dominant

Our economy arbitrarily forces thousands of able-bodied, older workers into retirement.

practice is to have children placed in the care of women, even where men increasingly are interested in assuming child-care responsibilities.

The female domination of child care has marked economic consequences, as evidenced in the low-income of female-headed family units. In effect, the child-custody bias reinforces the weaker job and income opportunity of women, as evidenced by the incidence of below-the-poverty-line, single-head families: in 1976, 8.2 percent were male-headed, and 42.8 percent were female-headed (Statistics Canada, 1980: 37).

Unemployment and Gender

Unemployment systematically relates both to gender and to age. If we look at age groups in terms of two categories — the fifteen to twenty-four age group and twenty-five and over — we find that men and women experience similar unemployment rates in the first group. When we consider the second group, however, the pattern reverses and becomes more pronounced. Specifically, as the economy worsened from 1966 to 1977, more women experienced unemployment than men. It is in this age group that one would expect males to be developing careers, and women facing the prospect of dropping out of the labor force in order to meet child rearing responsibilities. Terminated or interrupted careers exacerbate female unemployment, as well as curtail career development. It is in this age group, also, that one finds female single parents coping with marriage breakdown and child custody. Consequently, there is a high incidence of below-poverty-line income.

At this point in our history, when we are striving to extend full employment opportunities to women, we are denying employment opportunities to the aged. And we are entering a period of a massive impoverished aged population, one that is predominantly female.

AGE AND SOCIAL STRUCTURE

Attitudes Toward Aging

All human beings pass through distinguishable biological phases, from birth through to maturation, aging, and death. The social behaviors and responsibilities, however, that are associated with biological phases, or even their demarcation points, are culturally specific. Meanings not only vary with society, but also with gender and with other subgroups within a society. In our society, aging as we are presently experiencing it is historically unique. Because of advancements in medicine and health care, not only are the elderly living longer, more of us are living longer. Despite this increased longevity, we are defined arbitrarily as nonproductive when we attain a certain age.

In pre-industrial societies, the aged are by and large venerated. Among the Inuit, the aged might be abandoned to death when physical disability renders them a burden to society. However, the aged are respected for their experience and knowledge. In contrast, our society relegates the aged to the social waste heap, imposing mandatory leisure and effective, albeit informal, isolation. Media images, consumer advertising, and job definitions are geared toward the young. At the same time, fear of aging proliferates to a degree that aging is psychologically resisted. Women seem especially vulnerable to the youth-culture emphasis, partly because so much of female socialization and media content stress physical appearance.

Television programs are guilty of stereotyping in negative ways. They tend to depict old men as "bad" and old people as unsuccessful and sickly (Hardert et al., 1984:106). Some recent aged "media" stars, such as the American actors George Burns, Art Carney, or, in his last film, Henry Fonda, have generated sympathetic presentations of elderly males — and because of Mr. Fonda's co-star, Katherine Hepburn, of elderly females — but the dominant impression conveyed still tends to be that of eccentricity, crankiness, and strangeness.

Our institutions also discriminate against the aged. Our economy restricts labor-force participation to the period of adult life that we define as vigorous and vital — which is given an arbitrary end at sixty-five (although this may change, pending the consequences of the Charter of Rights). Thereafter, without any test or measure, we are required to withdraw from the work activities that will have occupied most of our lives. This mandatory occupational withdrawal generally occurs with little societal preparation or assistance.

Age and Dependency

Throughout the world, irrespective of continued capacity to work, the aged are forced into dependency upon the state. State-administered programs in the developed nations are oriented toward moving the aged out of the labor-force and providing them with a minimal subsistence. The state therefore defines old age, and develops

the infrastructure to sustain those it has defined as aged (Myles, 1983:1-6).

Historically, the development of forced dependency may be related to the increased dependency on technology. For example, a machine-determined need for speed on the part of workers may have hastened the obsolescence of the older worker. The Depression accelerated the process with the need to phase out the older workers and to phase in the hitherto unemployed young (Myles, 1983:12-13). In the 1980s, we face a situation where increasing numbers of unemployed retired population, as well as unemployed young, are dependent on the taxation of the employed population and on state-administered transfer payments.

Governments may manipulate definitions of old age for fiscal reasons. For example, state expenditures may be reduced by raising the age of retirement. By this act, the definition and size of the elderly population is changed, the number of obsolescent and unemployed seniors reduced, and transfer payments to the aged are reduced. Or, conversely, in order to open up more positions for young workers, the retirement age may be lowered (Myles, 1984: 5-7). Thus, for example, the French government has lowered the age of mandatory retirement from sixty-five to sixty. In contrast, some members of the present Reagan administration in the United States are considering raising the definition of mandatory retirement beyond age sixty-five. Both governments are responding to fiscal needs and manipulating the labor force population by manipulating the definition of the "aged." The contrasting measures reflect government decisions regarding social priorities — specifically the dilemma posed by choosing between high taxation and income-maintenance payments whenever the unemployed aged population is large, versus high unemployment when more of the older population retain positions in the labor force (Myles, 1984).

Except for Canada and Ireland, payments to the elderly make up 50 percent or more of income-maintenance expenditures in the developed democratic societies (Myles:17). That is, in contrast to children's allowances, sickness benefits, unemployment aid or other forms of social assistance, the bulk of state payments go to support the elderly. The average expenditure for OECD (Organization for Economic Cooperation and Development) countries in 1972 was 62.4 percent — or all income-maintenance expenditures. The amount of Canada's payments was 39.4 percent, in contrast with 73.0 percent in the United States and 79.5 percent in Austria (Myles:18).

The retired population has been increasing for approximately two decades at a rate greater than the overall rate of population is increasing in Canada (Stone and Marceau, 1977:51). Moreover, the number will increase even more as the baby boom generation becomes aged. Between World War II and 1966, almost 7 million people — about one-third of Canada's population — were born (Kettle, 1980:19-20). In the next twenty years or so, these persons will form a vast group of aged obsolescents.

The prospect, as we approach the year 2000, is that of a large aged population to be supported by a pension or income-maintenance system that already is precarious. The alternative course, of which there are already indications, is that the policy of manadatory retirement will be altered, so that individuals will have the choice of working indefinitely or retiring. In Canada, the Charter of Rights has challenged the definitions of old age and retirement, but ultimately the definitions are at the discretion of the provincial government and the courts.

At 10 percent of the total population (National Council of Welfare, 1984: 4), Canada's aged population is one of the lowest in the industrialized world, lower than the United States, Great Britain, France, Sweden, and most other developed societies. The effects of an aging population are, therefore, more pronounced elsewhere than in Canada. The health-care services required, the income levels, as well as suitable housing and

TABLE 20-5. Age Distribution of Immigrants in Canada 1961–1977

Age	1961	1966	1971	1977
0-34	76.0	73.2	77.6	73.7
35-64	20.8	18.7	17.2	20.7
65 +	3.2	2.0	3.1	5.6

SOURCE: From Table 1.15, *Perspectives Canada III*, 1980.

recreational needs, are only beginning to have an effect in Canada.

The aged population of Canada is predominantly made up of the native-born. The immigrant populations have not yet reached the retirement age and consist of school-age children and working adults. (See Table 20-6.) Taken to an extreme, this situation portrays a foreign-born school population, and an aged population of native-born unemployed Canadians!

Since criminal offences in every society have been associated with youth, we could further project a declining crime rate, and a consequent potential for declining law-enforcement costs, with a projected increase in the aged population by 2000. Although there has been an increase in offences by the elderly, usually petty theft and shoplifting to supplement meagre incomes and food supply, the senior population is essentially law-abiding, despite significant deprivation.

Age and Work

Myles (1984:319) observes that "the power of the aged appears to have reached its zenith in the most highly developed agricultural economies due to their system of landholding and inheritance." In such a society, the aged have resources to be passed on to the young; there was a youthful dependency on the aged (Myles, 1980:318-21). In contrast, today's senior citizens suffer enormous losses. Not only are they denied legitimate access to most work, there is the consequent loss of income, power, and of prestige associated with career, as well as the personal satisfaction and sense of worth often associated with gainful employment.

At the turn of the twentieth century, North Americans were less likely to force people into retirement. In the United States, two out of three persons aged sixty-five and over were in the work force. By 1979, the proportion was one out of five (Hardert et al., 1984:111). In Canada, the proportion of seniors in the labor force was 59.6 percent in 1921; by 1951, it had declined to 39.5 percent and by 1977, to 15.5 percent (Myles and Boyd, 1982:275). Increasingly, therefore, we have eliminated senior Canadians from the world of work and relegated the majority to dependency. The shift is not a matter of declining skill, but rather a means of accommodating the entry of younger people into a declining labor market.

Age and Income

In our society, the elderly are supposed to have saved sufficient funds from previous employment to sustain themselves for the rest of their life. The value of these savings constantly depreciates, and therefore, the elderly have an ever-declining purchasing power. At the same time, the living costs of the aged may increase because of health problems, especially in societies such as the United States, where medical care is not free. Pension programs, a form of "deferred wage," benefit only the more privileged, and historically, have excluded women (Myles, 1980:334–35). Pensions such as Canada's Old Age Security, or the Canada and Québec Pension Plan, are meant to supplement the savings and private pension funds that the aged are supposed to have acquired while working. However, pension income rarely compensates for employment income. In 1976, only 38.8 percent of workers were covered by pension plans (Myles, 1980).

In 1984, Canada's "over-sixty-five" population, almost 2.5 million people, received Old Age Security payments of $263.78 a month. Additional income up to a combined total of $530 a month is available through the Guaranteed Income Supplement — a total well below Canada's poverty line (Zwarun, 1984:46). In recent public statements (July, 1984), the Minister of Finance declared that he had eliminated poverty among the aged; and yet by conventional standards, the aged are impoverished. In Ontario, as of February, 1984, elderly single persons received $8000 per year and couples $13 500 (*Toronto Star*, 1 July 1984).

Because women live longer than men, the lack of sufficient funds usually falls to women, the very persons who would not have had a private pension income because most would not have been employed full-time (Zwarun, 1984:48). Generally, women work on a part-time basis, and change jobs more frequently. Overall, fewer than 50 percent Canadians have private pension coverage.

Age and Poverty

It is estimated that 60 percent of single Canadians aged sixty-five and over live in poverty, and that the majority of these are women (National Council of Welfare, 1982). The concept of poverty is an arbitrary one, but it does indicate

TABLE 20-6. **Old Age Security, and Canada and Quebec Pension Plan Expenditures**

| | Millions of Current Dollars | | | | |
	1965–7	1961–2	1961–7	1971–2	1976–7
Old Age Security	419.9	686.6	1137.0	2205.4	4436.6
Canada and Quebec Pension Plan	—	—	0.1	189.6	1195.4
Total Social Security Expenditures	—	3539.0	5372.2	12 415.7	27 569.5

SOURCE: From Table 7.1, *Perspectives Canada III*, 1980.

relative conditions. In comparison (reflecting definition more than conditions), it has been estimated that in 1977, 14 percent of Americans sixty-five and over lived below the poverty line (Lowry, 1980:14).

The Canadian poverty line may be estimated for couples as $9220 or less annually, and for individuals as $5704 or less. In 1982, 60.4 percent of elderly women and 48.9 percent of elderly men were below the poverty line (National Council of Welfare, 1984:35–42). Perhaps the enormity of the problem can be better appreciated in terms of numbers: in 1981, there were 415 000 elderly women and 189 000 men below the poverty line (National Council of Welfare, 1984:24). These are the persons without private pensions or savings.

Generally, the circumstances of the elderly poor are mitigated only by mortgage-free home ownership. These homes incur operating costs, but those who own their own homes have shelter and considerable equity. The single aged are less well-off, with only 36 percent owning mortgage-free homes, compared with 66 percent of couples (National Council of Welfare, 1984: 57–63).

For the person approaching, or already into retirement, there is virtually no prospect of improving circumstances. The elderly usually have to make do with accumulated possessions, savings, and pensions. Except for the relatively wealthy upper middle-class and upper-class Canadians, the resources of the elderly are meagre, indeed.

Age and Gender

In 1981, approximately 57 percent of all aged were women (National Council of Welfare, 1984), and most were widowed. As mentioned, they lack the income that men have from private pension programs. In contrast, only 24.4 percent of the men are single. Women are left not only in economic deprivation, but also in emotional and social isolation. It is reported that single men tend to live with their family, and women more frequently in institutions (National Council of Welfare, 1984: 8, 14, 16).

It is not yet understood why women live longer than men. There may be some biological advantage; or there may be a causal relationship between work environment and life span. Perhaps job-related stress is also a factor; if so, the gender differences will decrease in future, with increased female labor-force participation.

Age and Isolation

Overall, not only are we experiencing growth in the number of elderly, but also we find a society that is not organized to assist the aged in the significant changes in their life circumstances. In our society, the practice of elderly parents living with their adult children is on the decrease. Social attitudes stressing the needs of young adults, as well as the social and geographical mobility required for employment, have virtually put a stop to traditional households consisting of several generations. Thus, for most aged persons, especially those handicapped by chronic disability, a state or privately operated "old-age" or nursing home becomes home. Such institutions increase the segregation, marginalization, and powerlessness that the elderly already experience by virtue of their age.

An image of old age prevails among middle-class Canadians that is captured in the euphemistic phrase "the golden age." It refers to that minority of retired Canadians with adequate savings and pension funds, who are able to enjoy this last phase of the life cycle by playing golf, by spending winters in sunny climes, and the like. However, many are not as fortunate, and as has been pointed out, the reality of old age is vastly different for many Canadians.

Another major source of anxiety is the deteriorating physical capacity experienced by the elderly, a condition that leads many to literally despair of their survival. A particular fear is related to crime. Media presentations that stress criminal violence probably affect all Canadians and their perceptions of personal safety, but they particularly affect old people. According to an Urban Victimization

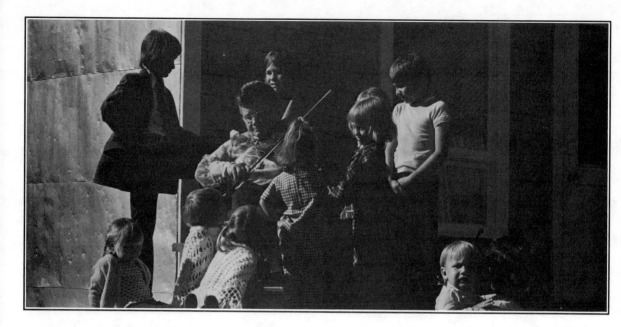

Woman fiddler surrounded by her grandchildren on the porch of her home in Île d'Orléans, Québec. In traditional societies, the elderly were respected, and extended families were the norm.

Survey conducted in 1982, 89 percent of all elderly men and women "felt unsafe walking alone in their own neighborhood after dark." (Statistics Canada, 1983: 6.)

MEN AND WOMEN: OLD BEFORE THEIR TIME

It is a disturbing irony that our society, like other industrial societies, has developed the means to increase longevity, but at the same time manages to denigrate those who live longer. In traditional pre-industrial societies, the elderly were respected for their wisdom, and extended families were the norm, with two or three generations living under one roof. Thus, the elderly were not isolated. Every generation had the opportunity to interact with members across the age groups. In contrast, our modern nuclear families have the eventual consequence of isolating individuals, in particular, elderly women who have lost their spouses because

of separation or death. The residential isolation of the generations is so common that many children do not know how to react to the aged. Contact with grandparents is increasingly not part of the socialization process and as a result, old people seem alien and strange.

The formidable problem for Canadian society over the next several decades will be to somehow accommodate the relatively new social objective of gender equality with the relatively old and disappearing value of the elderly. Canadian society seems effectively, albeit haltingly, to be achieving reduction of gender inequality. However, thus far, it has failed to come to grips with age inequality.

SUMMARY

1. Sexism and ageism are stereotypical attitudes and behavior that attribute characteristics, usually inferior, to women and to the elderly.

2. Both sexism and ageism are pervasive in our society, and they are related to the larger proportion of elderly women.

3. Age inequality is a much less recognized social problem than gender inequality.

4. Gender inequality has gradually been reduced over the previous several decades. More women achieve higher education and more women work.

5. Yet drastic disadvantages for women persist with regard to occupational range, salary, and power. Women earn less than men, are less often hired in managerial positions, and are seldom elected to political office.

6. The government has set an arbitrary age at which Canadians are forced into retirement.

7. Deprived of the right to gainful employment, many senior citizens suffer a profound loss of status, both psychological and economical.

8. Many aged are forced to live in institutions that effectively isolate them from normal social interaction.

GLOSSARY

Aged (Seniors). Adults who are arbitrarily defined as retired by law. In Canada, the age of retirement is sixty for women and sixty-five for men.

Ageism. Stereotypical attitudes and associated behavior that are based on attributing characteristics, usually inferior, to senior adults.

Gender inequality. Socially imposed disadvantages or privileges of opportunity and/or condition that are based on biological and social/cultural differences between males and females.

Patriarchy. The structure or social organization of power and privilege bestowed on males.

Poverty. A social condition of relative disadvantage caused by the lack of adequate income to meet the basic standard of living.

Sexism. Stereotypical attitudes and associated behavior that are based on attributing characteristics, usually inferior, to the opposite sex.

Socialization. The process of learning the attitudes and behavior of a society and the subgroup(s) to which one belongs.

Status (social). The position(s) that a person occupies (associated with roles) in society.

Stereotypes. Prevalent beliefs about social groups.

FURTHER READING

Armstrong, Pat and Hugh Armstrong. *A Working Majority.* Ottawa: Canadian Advisory Council on Status of Women, 1983. An ideal merger of commentary and basic data describing the condition of women in the Canadian labor force.

Government of Canada. *Perspectives Canada III.* Ottawa: Statistics Canada, 1980. The last statistical compendia published by Statistics Canada, providing a breadth of data on the social condition of Canadians, including data related to gender and age.

Government of Canada. *Sixty-five and Older.* Ottawa: National Council of Welfare, 1984. One of several excellent, brief reports presenting data on the condition of Canadians. Other National Council reports are included in the references.

Myles, John. *Old Age in the Welfare State: The Political Economy of Public Pensions.* Boston/Toronto: Little Brown and Co., 1984. A theoretically and empirically sophisticated overview of the social condition of the aged in Canada and other industrialized societies.

Saunders, Eileen. "Women in Canadian society." In D. Forcese and S. Richer (eds.), *Social Issues: Sociological View of Canada.* Scarborough, Ontario: Prentice Hall, 1982. A concise, clear exposition of theory and facts concerning the social condition of women.

Vickers, Jill and M. Janine Brodie. "Canada." In J. Lovenduski and J. Hills (eds.), *The Politics of the Second Electorate: Women and Public Participation.* London: Routledge and Kegan Paul, 1981. A comprehensive overview of the political role and participation of Canadian women by social scientists, whose several works in this area are definitive.

PART VI

Social Change in the Contemporary World

In previous chapters we focused on the beginning and the growth of the social system. We then discussed the basic elements of the social system. In this last section we shall examine the processes that are typical of modern societies.

Sociologists are not only interested in social changes, or important alterations in a social structure, but also in the persistence of traditions that fulfil certain functions necessary for the maintenance and survival of social life. Revolution, social movements, counter-revolutions, and resistance to social movements receive equal attention.

The chapter on population explores population characteristics and their dynamics. The effects of demographic change have far-reaching consequences in the ecosystem. Chapter 22, which deals with urbanization, underlines some of the effects of urban growth and the quality of life in our cities. Collective behavior and social movements, discussed in Chapter 23, invite our attention to people's organized efforts to bring about the changes they wish and to oppose those they deplore. The last chapter examines the nature of social change in relation to tradition and modernity, and provokes thought on whether or not modernity is beneficial to human life.

This last section of the book is designed to serve you with some reflective thoughts on the essential elements and social forms available in human society.

CHAPTER TWENTY-ONE

The Population Dimension of Society

WARREN KALBACH

In 1984, the world's population was estimated to have reached 4.76 billion people. National populations range in size from over a billion inhabitants in China, to the relatively small populations of under 100 000 living in the Seychelle Islands in the Indian Ocean and Vanuatu in the Pacific. *The rate of natural increase* (annual excess of births over deaths per 1000 population) is thought to be about 1.7 percent for the world as a whole, varying from a high of about 4 percent for Kenya, to zero or below for Hungary, Austria, and Germany. Variations in the standard of living throughout the world are reflected in recent estimates of infant mortality and the per capita gross national product (GNP). The former range from a low of 6.5, to over 200 infant deaths per 1000 live births in 1984, and the GNP ranged from an incredibly high U.S. $23 770 for the oil-rich United Arab Emirates, to less than U.S. $150 for some countries in Africa and South Asia (Population Reference Bureau, 1984).

In order to better understand the wide range of social and economic conditions existing in the world today, it is important to know something about the historical patterns of growth and the relative contributions made by the demographic processes of fertility, mortality, and migration. It is also important to understand how social factors can contribute to changes in these processes, as well as how population characteristics and processes can affect a country's social and economic structure, and in turn, the individual's behavior in that society. The purpose of this chapter is to provide both an introduction to the study of population and an appreciation of its importance.

Populations are aggregates of individuals bounded by national, regional, and cultural boundaries. "The scientific study of human populations, including their size, composition, distribution, density, growth and other demographic and socioeconomic characteristics, and the causes and consequences of changes in these factors" is known as *demography* (Population Reference Bureau, 1978:53). Within the broad discipline of demography, there are two major areas of interest: formal demography or demographic analysis, and social demography or population studies. The former deals almost exclusively with the "interrelationships between different components of a given population, and between components of a population and the pattern of population growth." (Matras, 1973:10.) Social demography, with its focus on the study of relationships between demographic phenomena and factors in the social milieu, clearly seeks to bridge the gap between the disciplines of sociology and demography.

Historically, most population research has been conducted at the *macro-level*; that is, populations (aggregates of individuals) are used as the unit of analysis rather than the individual. Thus, most analyses have been concerned with determining the relationships between population characteristics, rather than those between characteristics of individuals. This has been due, in part, to the fact that the results of national censuses have been released only in aggregate form for relatively large areas. However, with advances in computer technology, more detailed data have become available for smaller populations and for individuals. More recently, sampling techniques have been used to develop "public-use" census tapes, which permit correlation-type analyses of the characteristics of individuals without violating requirements of confidentiality. Census data on demographic,

social, and economic characteristics are playing an increasingly important part in social-science research.

Population research utilizes both macro- and micro-level perspectives. Both approaches can contribute to a fuller understanding of population behavior. At the macro-level, changes in the size, composition, and distribution of a population are the results of changes in fertility and mortality rates, and in the size and direction of migration streams. At the micro-level, the fertility, mortality, and migration behavior of individuals can be affected by the size and character of the population in which they live.

Of all the demographic characteristics, a population's *distribution by age and sex* is among the most important. At the macro-level, it indicates (1) the structure of a population with respect to the relative numbers of young and old; (2) the balance between the sexes; and (3) the size and character of the labor force. At the micro-level, age and sex identify the major stages of individual and family life cycles and their associated roles and statuses. Within specific cultural contexts, age and sex prescribe appropriate socialization patterns and determine eligibility for entering the labor force, getting married, and having children. The influence of age and sex on behavior is so strong and pervasive that valid comparisons between populations with respect to the basic demographic processes of fertility, mortality, and migration cannot be made unless the differences in age and sex compositions are taken into account.

The study of population transcends the boundaries of any single, intellectual discipline. Philosophers have speculated from time immemorial about the nature of human population and the causes and consequences of growth and change. The science of statistics, and the origins of modern demography and the social sciences, can be traced to Graunt's interest in death records in the mid-seventeenth century (Hutchinson, 1967:45). The biological and medical sciences have contrib-

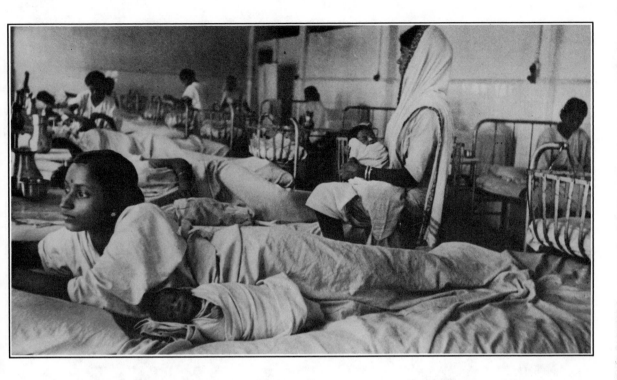

A maternity ward in India. Over-population has become a serious concern in many Third World nations. Government programs encouraging birth control or sterilization may meet with resistance owing to traditional values of the family.

uted significantly to our understanding of the nature of disease and the processes of life and death. However, after all is said and done, the main causes and consequences of population trends are social in nature. "Human society is the man-made environment within which the demographic processes take place" (Wrong, 1977:7), and so the study of population is an appropriate and legitimate concern of social scientists.

SOURCES AND IMPORTANCE OF POPULATION DATA

There are four major sources of population data: (1) complete or partial censuses of individuals living in a specifically defined area at a specified time; (2) registration systems that provide vital statistics for births, deaths, marriages, and divorce;

(3) continuing population registers that maintain complete records — including place of residence — of individuals throughout their lifetime; and (4) special surveys that collect data on items of current interest, such as unemployment rates in the provinces of Canada.

Modern systems of data collection, such as national censuses and vital registration systems, have a long, evolutionary history. They are the present-day counterparts of counting and record-keeping developed by early civilizations for creating inventories of food stores and population. As societies grew in size and developed more complex social and political institutions, the need for taxes to support governments and for conscription purposes made periodic population counts important. In modern times, censuses, registration systems, and surveys have come to be recog-

Recently China instituted a policy of "one family, one child," a restriction that runs counter to its tradition of large, extended families. While the allocation of scarce resources in the world's most populous nation poses a very real problem, it is difficult to imagine an entire generation of children growing up without siblings, aunts, uncles, or cousins.

nized as essential and legitimate government activities. They provide the data required for determining the legislative representation of a population, and for social and economic planning by business and government alike.

The first national census known to have been taken on a regular basis was in Sweden, a census that began in 1749 (Thomlinson, 1976:64). Most European countries were taking censuses of one kind or another at about the same time. In North America, the first census was taken in New France as early as 1666, but it was not until 1851 that Canada established the practice of regular decen-

nial censuses. Starting in 1886, an additional census was taken every fifth year in the Prairie provinces until 1956, when the mid-decade census was extended to all of Canada. Uniform collection of vital statistics was established in 1921 when legislation was enacted by most of the provinces, requiring compulsory registration of births, still-births, marriages, and deaths. Since then, detailed reports have been published annually by the Government of Canada.

Perhaps the best single source of comprehensive data on populations in the world today is the *Demographic Yearbook*, published annually by the United Nations since 1948. Another excellent source for basic, up-to-date population data for the major countries and regions of the world is the annual *World Population Data Sheet*, published by the Population Reference Bureau of Washington, D.C.

Collecting population data by means of national censuses is extremely difficult even under the best of conditions. The validity and reliability of census data depend largely on the level of educational attainment in the population, as well as on the degree of trust that people have in their government's intentions and ability to preserve the confidentiality of census information. The improvement in both the quality and quantity of Canada's census and vital statistics during the twentieth century represents an impressive degree of co-operation between the people of Canada and their government.

EXPLAINING POPULATION CHANGE: A HISTORICAL PERSPECIVE

There is considerable argument over the nature and seriousness of the world's over-population and the appropriate solutions. The debate persists, in part, because of the lack of accurate population data, the inadequacy of current population theories, and because of conflicting values and ideologies.

The current interest in population growth and the search for solutions to population problems is not new. The idea that excessive population growth tended to have negative consequences in terms of living standards, productivity, and social unrest had appeared long ago in the works of Confucius and other early Chinese scholars. The Greek philosophers, Plato and Aristotle, also discussed problems of attaining the good life in terms of an "optimum" population size that would provide for defence, minimize poverty and civil discord, and ensure effective government. Later, during the era of the Roman Empire, demographic concerns focused on stimulating population growth as a

means of preserving the empire against the effects of floods, famines, epidemics, wars, and revolutions (United Nations, 1953:21–22).

Interest in population-related problems appears to have declined during the medieval period as Christian writers became absorbed in more general moral issues. Poverty and want were perceived by some to be the natural byproducts of population growth; yet high levels of fertility were still favored as a means of countering the high mortality levels of the times (United Nations, 1953: 23). Thus, until the end of the eighteenth century, European writers appeared to favor population growth because a large population was thought necessary in the competition for political and economic dominance. However, worsening social and economic conditions that accompanied rapid industrialization and urbanization of the population began to attract attention to the plight of urban dwellers.

Malthus and Others

The publication of Malthus's *Essay on the Principle of Population* (1798), stimulated the controversy between the proponents of population growth and the prophets of "doom and gloom," who believed, like Reverend Malthus, that poverty and misery were the inevitable consequences of what Malthus saw as the natural tendency for population growth to outstrip subsistence levels. Malthus had little faith in the individual's ability to control growth through moral restraint or through social intervention to improve the plight of the poor. What he saw to be effective checks to growth included poverty, disease, and war. His moral values apparently kept him from fully appreciating the important role that contraceptives would play in controlling population growth. Not only did he fail to anticipate the extent to which Europeans would accept contraception, but he also underestimated their ability to increase their productivity and improve their standard of living. Nevertheless, his arguments generated considerable interest in the study of the determinants and consequences of population growth (Thomlinson, 1976:36–41).

Other, more optimistic writers of the time thought fertility was the only determinant of population growth. Sadler, for example, wrote in 1829 that the psychological capacity for reproduction varied inversely with population density, suggesting a natural law that would automatically keep population in check. This was followed a few years later by Doubleday's theory that human fecundity varied inversely with the amount and variety of available food, so that when starvation threatened, the individual's capacity for reproduction increased, thus ensuring survival (Thomlinson, 1976:47).

Marx and Others

Other arguments were generated by socialists and Marxists, who either denied the existence of a population problem or felt that it could be solved through the reorganization of society. Like Malthus, Marx had little faith in moral restraint as a population control, but he expected that fertility would decline as the standard of living improved and the exploitation of child labor diminished. Continuing population growth and problems of economic development in a number of socialist countries since World War II, particularly in China, have forced a reconsideration of the classical Marxist position regarding population growth as a unique capitalist problem.

Most population theories of the eighteenth and nineteenth centuries were single-factor theories shaped by the philosophical persuasions and biased observations of their advocates. There was, however, an awakening interest in the analysis of burial and christening records that was to have a profound effect on the development of population theory. John Graunt's analysis of births and deaths in London (1662) is thought by many to have been the precursor of modern demography. Sussmilch's work, based on parish records throughout Prussia, dealt with population size, composition, and components of growth and their interrelationships.

The publication of his work in 1741 was regarded as the first comprehensive treatise on population that attempted to develop a theory of probability (Petersen, 1975:147–48).

Pearl and Reed

The increasing use of official records stimulated interest in the study of population and in the development and testing of population theories. The growing accumulation of population statistics encouraged the search for relatively simple, mathematical growth models. A good example of this was the work of Pearl and Reed during the 1920s. Their population growth model, based on the logistic "S" curve, provided a good approximation of the actual pattern of population growth in the United States between 1920 and 1950 (Petersen, 1975:336–38). Subsequent attempts to project population growth were less successful, and in time the use of mathematical models was rejected by demographers as being overly simplistic and insensitive to many of the forces affecting population change. However, the work of Pearl and Reed stimulated interest in identifying distinctive stages of growth and in determining the relative importance of fertility and mortality for each stage. Later works (by Blacker and Cowgill, among others) led to the emergence of a new theory of the demographic transition.

Demographic Transition Theory: Thompson and Others

One version of the demographic transition model of population growth is the four-stage model depicted in Figure 21-1. Basically, it shows the transition from high to low levels of population growth that was thought to have occurred as the European population was transformed from a rural-agricultural society to an urban-industrial one over a period of 200 years. The determination of the actual number of stages in the transition is arbitrary, as they are only meant to illustrate the general sequence of events that accompanied urbanization and industrialization.

The evidence suggests that as living conditions improved and mortality declined, many more persons (particularly children) began to survive. Somehow during this process, individuals came to realize that large families were no longer an asset and began having fewer children. The process by which this change in attitude and practice came about is still not clearly understood, but that it happened, there is little doubt. It is this decline in fertility, which followed the improvement in mortality, that provides hope that the same thing will happen in those less-developed countries that have already achieved significant reductions in their mortality levels.

Subsequent research on population growth in many European countries has raised questions about demographic transition theory, especially concerning the inevitability of the sequence of the various stages (Hatt et al., 1955). Additional reservations about the theory's validity have been reinforced by the fact that the less-developed countries have not yet revealed a trend toward reduced

fertility following a rapid decline in mortality. Foreign-aid programs, imposed on them by the industrialized countries following World War II, improved basic living conditions in many areas, but did little to change the existing values that have supported and reinforced high-fertility levels for countless generations.

Multiphasic Response Theory: Kingsley Davis

The unanswered question concerning the dynamics of demographic transition theory is still, "What motivates the individual to have fewer children?" Kingsley Davis's multiphasic response theory suggests that individuals in populations are unlikely to reduce their fertility out of fear of poverty as much as out of fear of loss of status with respect to other members of their reference group during periods of economic growth (Davis, 1963). His studies of Europe and Japan indicate that families use every demographic means available to

FIGURE 21-1. The European Demographic Transition in Birth and Death Rates: 1750–1980.

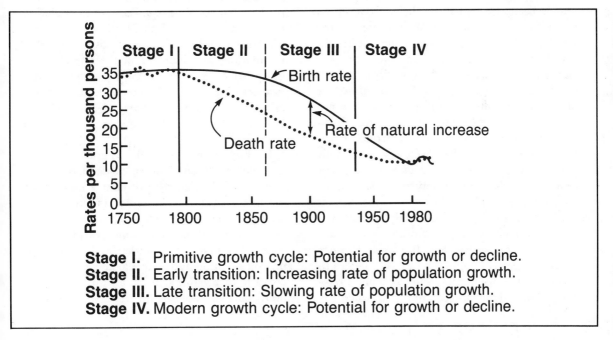

Stage I. Primitive growth cycle: Potential for growth or decline.
Stage II. Early transition: Increasing rate of population growth.
Stage III. Late transition: Slowing rate of population growth.
Stage IV. Modern growth cycle: Potential for growth or decline.

them in order to avoid any loss of status, including postponement of marriage, use of contraception, sterilization, abortions, and emigration.

Societies, as well as individuals, have responded to threats posed by sustained high levels of natural increase by increasing food production, stepping up the rate of industrialization, and improving transportation networks and other services that contribute to an improved standard of living, as well as encouraging emigration. From Davis's perspective, the key to triggering a multiphasic response in the less-developed nations experiencing rapid growth would appear to be economic development and an improved standard of living, rather than continuing and worsening poverty.

POPULATION DYNAMICS

Whether the world's population grows or declines is determined solely by the difference between its fertility and mortality rates, or its rate of natural increase. What little evidence there is suggests that population growth, for most of the time that human beings have inhabited the earth, has been intermittent and slow, flourishing in some areas while barely surviving or even dying out in others. During the course of human history, the pervasive pattern of fertility and mortality is thought to have been one of high fertility and almost as high, but variable, mortality. Common sense would have us believe that population growth is a direct response to an increase in fertility. However, when fertility is already close to maximum possible levels, growth is more likely to occur as a result of a decline in mortality rather than from an increase in fertility.

Improvements in the standard of living during the industrialization and urbanization of European populations were slow. But as death rates began to decline, population growth began to accelerate because fertility rates remained relatively high and unchanged. Moreover, when fer-

tility rates did begin to decline — for example, during the nineteenth century — population growth continued to increase because morality rates were declining at a faster rate.

The first phase of the world population explosion, triggered by this expansion of European population, extended from about 1650 to the 1920s. During the latter half of this transition, when declining fertility began to catch up with low mortality levels, population growth slowed significantly. With low fertility levels and mortality close to its lowest probable limits, an increase in the growth rate is more likely to occur as the result of an increase in fertility rather than from a further decrease in mortality. However, once individuals gain control over their fertility, the likelihood of a return to traditional patterns of high fertility seems remote.

Among the world's less-developed countries, the demographic picture has been different. Overall, these countries have been fairly quick to accept new technologies that would help them lower levels of mortality. They have not been as interested, or as successful, in reducing fertility levels. Given the fact that at the peak of European population expansion, about 1930, the less-developed countries still comprised about two-thirds of the world's population, any increase in their population growth-rate would have significant, global ramifications. Comparative data on population growth and fertility and mortality levels are given in Table 21-1. for major world regions and for selected countries.

It is important to remember that for the world as a whole and for most of the less-developed countries, population growth is a simple function of the difference between fertility and mortality. The only way population growth can be slowed is either to control fertility or to allow mortality to take its course. Without vast, unsettled lands, or any significant urban-industrial development, migration ceases to be a viable solution for the problem of overpopulation faced by the less-developed countries. The migration factor is of little significance. Yet there are a number of more-developed countries that are still open to international migration and where net migration can have a significant impact on national as well as regional population growth. In these cases, migration must obviously be taken into account when explaining total population change. The complete equation, which includes all the possible factors affecting population growth or decline, is as follows:

$$P2 = P1 + Births - Deaths + Immigration - Emigration$$

Where:

$P1 = population\ at\ the\ beginning$
$\quad\quad of\ the\ period$
$P2 = population\ at\ end$
$\quad\quad of\ the\ specified\ period$

TABLE 21-1. **Estimated Population and Rates of Increase, Total Fertility, and Life Expectancy for the World, Major Regions, and Selected Countries, 1984**

Region and selected countries	Population estimates mid-1983 (millions)	Natural increase (annual %)	Total fertility rate	Life expectancy at birth
World	4762	1.7	3.8	61
Europe	491	0.3	1.8	73
Sweden	8.3	0.0	1.6	76
West Germany	61.4	−0.2	1.4	73
Poland	36.9	1.0	2.3	71
Italy	57.0	0.2	1.6	73
USSR	274	1.0	2.5	69
North America	262	0.7	1.8	74
Latin America	397	2.4	4.2	64
Mexico	77.7	2.6	4.7	66
Haiti	5.5	2.2	5.5	52
Brazil	134.4	2.3	4.1	63
Argentina	29.1	1.5	2.8	70
Oceania	24	1.3	2.5	70
Africa	531	2.9	6.4	50
Egypt	47.0	2.7	5.3	56
Nigeria	88.1	3.2	6.9	49
Ethiopia	32.0	2.4	6.7	40
Zaire	32.2	2.9	6.1	47
South Africa	31.7	2.5	5.1	61
Asia	2782	1.8	4.0	58
Turkey	50.2	2.1	4.3	62
India	746.4	2.0	4.8	50
Indonesia	161.6	2.1	4.4	49
China	1034.5	1.3	2.6	65

SOURCE: Population Reference Bureau, *1984 World Population Data Sheet*, Washington, D.C., April, 1984.

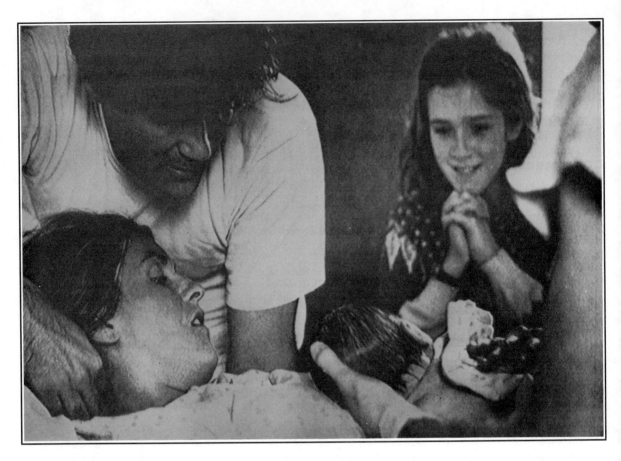

A doctor shows a newborn infant to his mother, father, and sister minutes after the birth. Families are now permitted to attend in the labor rooms of many North American hospitals.

The following section, which looks at Canada's demographic experience, examines each of these factors with respect to their contribution to the development of Canada's population.

CANADA'S DEMOGRAPHIC TRANSITION

Mortality

In New France, as in Europe before the demographic transition, mortality appeared to be high and relatively uncontrolled. Infectious diseases, frequent supply shortages, and crop failures were all contributing factors. For settlers born before 1700, the average number of years that one could expect to live was only thirty-five (Beaujot, 1978:8).

During the period of early settlement, more deaths tended to occur than births, and losses had to be made up through immigration. After 1763, and the assumption of control over New France by the British, the situation improved: estimates of mortality, based primarily on parish records, show significant declines. By the time of Confederation, the crude death rate of what had formerly been New France reached a level of about twenty-one deaths per 1000 population. It took another fifty years for the rate to fall to eighteen; and since the early 1920s, mortality for the total Canadian population has continued to show a consistent decline. By 1981, Canada's crude death rate reached a low of 7.0 (Statistics Canada, 1983b).

Decline in mortality does not apply to everyone. In Canada's early history, the elimination of infectious diseases produced the greatest reductions in mortality for the young of both sexes and for women in their child-bearing years. Today, significant reductions are still being achieved in infant mortality, and women are living longer than men. The number of years that older persons can expect to live has not increased very much, nor are their chances much better in an urban-industrial society such as Canada than in an underdeveloped country. The main consequences of the demographic transition with regard to decline in mortality have been (1) an increase in life expectancy, resulting from significant decreases in infant mortality (the number of infant deaths per 1000 live births); (2) an increase in life expectancy for women; and (3) an increase in degenerative diseases in urban-industrial populations that result in death.

Significant variations in infant mortality rates by region and within large, urban centres indicate that living conditions, life styles, and access to medical and health-care facilities are still associated with ethnic and socioeconomic status (Anderson, 1970). In 1981, infant mortality rates for the Yukon and Northwest Territories, with their predominantly Indian and Inuit populations, were respectively 7 and 144 percent higher than that reported for Ontario (Statistics Canada, 1983b). Infant mortality rates tend to be lower in the larger cities (Basavarajappa and Lindsey, 1976:307), and general mortality rates from all causes vary inversely with income levels in the largest cities (Wigle and Mao, 1980:6-7).

Two national health surveys, spanning a quarter of a century, show that differences in income levels and associated life styles and living conditions still contribute to the individual's chances for survival and risks of mortality from specific causes (Dominion Bureau of Statistics, 1960; Health and Welfare Canada, 1981). In 1950-51, access to medical help varied with income levels, as did the number of persons who received health care of any kind. Almost thirty years later, there is still evidence of significant differences in health between income groups. Low-income groups were found to have experienced relatively higher rates of mental disorders, heart disease, bronchitis, and emphysema than was the case for higher income groups (Abelson et al., 1983:12). The most recent health survey indicates that less than half the population reported no health problems, whereas a quarter reported problems serious enough to affect behavior. There is no doubt that there is room for improvement in the health of Canadians, further reductions in mortality, and increased life expectancy.

On reflection, it may appear that the historical improvement in mortality and longevity provides sufficient explanation for the aging of Canada's population. Certainly more people are living longer than ever before, but this does not provide a complete explanation for a population's aging. A population's age is an average determined by the total range of ages and the relative sizes of its constituent age groups. Because of this, a population can actually get younger if enough young persons are added to the population through immigration, or as a result of a large increase in birth rates. As paradoxical as it may seem, Canada's changing birth rate has had a much greater influence on the aging of its population than the significant improvement in mortality conditions and increase in longevity that has occurred during Canada's demographic transition. This has not been the case for the underdeveloped countries in the world, where significant reductions in mortality have primarily occurred among young children and infants. For countries that already have high fertility and relatively large, young-age groups, reductions in mortality have only served to maintain an already young population.

It is clear that one cannot completely assess the significance of mortality without some understanding of the nature of fertility and its contribution to population growth and change in Canada.

Fertility

The settlement of New France occurred prior to the fertility decline experienced in Europe during the latter part of the nineteenth century. It is likely that the early settlers would have brought to the New World the same attitudes that had sustained the high levels of fertility in Europe. From the 1660s until the mid-nineteenth century, fertility was thought to have varied between 45 and 65 births per 1000 population (Henripin, 1972:5), a level high enough to offset the effects of the high and variable rates of mortality that prevailed during that period. During the next fifty years of social, political, and economic development in Canada, estimates of fertility based on parish records for the Catholic population showed substantial declines. From forty-five births per 1000 population during the period 1851–61, the number fell to about thirty per 1000 during the last decade of the century (Dominion Bureau of Statistics, 1967: 241). As Canada continued to shift from an agricultural to an urban-industrial economy, the decline in fertility rates continued uninterrupted until the depression years of the 1930s.

The impact of returning veterans following World War II combined with the unprecedented postwar period of economic growth to produce the famous "baby boom" of the late 1940s and 1950s. Fertility peaked between 1953 and 1957 at slightly above twenty-eight births per 1000 population. However, economic conditions began to deteriorate in the late 1950s. With rising levels of unemployment, fertility began to decline again.

The worsening economy of the 1960s made early marriage and large families much less attractive than they had been during the early postwar

years. By 1971, a slight increase in the age at marriage suggested that men and women were beginning to postpone marriage, and fertility was about to fall below the level necessary to maintain population growth on the basis of natural increase alone. In the following decade, Canada's fertility reached a record low of 1.7 births per woman, which is well below the replacement level of 2.1 births per woman required to maintain a state of "zero" population growth (Statistics Canada, 1983b).

Not all women of the childbearing age participated to the same extent in the postwar baby boom. The fertility rates from five-year age groups of women between 1921 and 1981, shown in Figure 21-2., indicate that the fertility rates for older women (forty years of age and over) were unaffected and continued to decline throughout the entire thirty-year period. In contrast, all the younger women showed significant increases in fertility during the postwar period, with the greatest increases occurring in the under-thirty age category. The years of highest total fertility occurred in 1957 and 1961. The rates for either year would have produced an average of 3900 children per 1000 women, or just under four children per woman, had women actually experienced these particular rates while passing through their reproductive years.

Marriage rates have fluctuated since the peak year for marriages in 1946, partly in response to changing economic conditions but also as the result of the changing numbers of men and women entering the marriageable age group. Those that did marry were beginning to postpone having children, to increase the spacing between children, and/or to complete their families while still relatively young. These changes in the timing and number of children reflected the more effective control that women were achieving over their fertility. The "pill" appeared on the scene in 1960 and its use spread rapidly. There is little question that the development of this relatively inexpensive and convenient form of birth control played

FIGURE 21-2. Fertility Trends: Birth Rates by Age: Canada: 1921–1981.

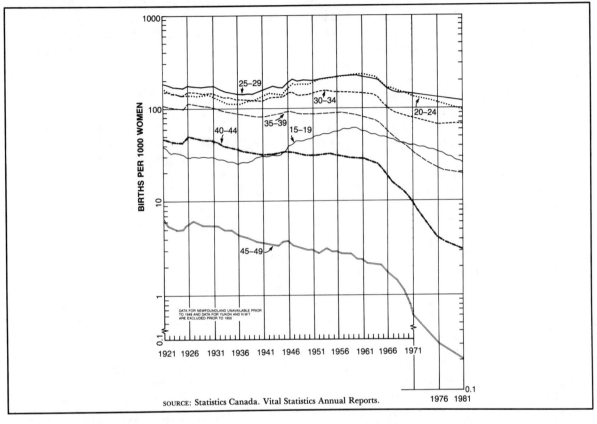

SOURCE: Statistics Canada. Vital Statistics Annual Reports.

a significant part in the fertility decline that followed the baby boom.

The long-term decline in fertility, like mortality, has not occurred uniformly throughout the Canadian population. It is generally believed that fertility began to decline first among the elite and upper socioeconomic classes of society in the urban centres. Even today, the lowest fertility is still to be found in the most urbanized areas among those with the most education, and highest incomes and occupational prestige (Kalbach and McVey, 1979: 101–12). There are also important regional differences. For example, the French-Canadian population of Québec at one time had one of the highest fertility levels in Canada. Yet today the fertility rate in this province has declined below

that of most other provinces because of a significant decline in the proportion of women who are marrying. Crude fertility rates in the Northwest Territories and in some of the Prairie provinces are today higher than Québec's, a consequence of their high-fertility, minority-group populations, such as the Inuit, Indians, and Hutterites. The increase among native peoples is accounted for by improving health conditions as well as increasing fertility. The Hutterites, in contrast to other groups, have managed to maintain the high fertility rates that they had when they first emigrated from Europe.

Today, most Canadians are living in a predominantly urban environment that is undergoing rapid social and economic change. At the same time, it is becoming increasingly difficult to achieve and maintain a standard of living and life style consistent with the increasingly educated urban dweller's expectations. As incomes fail to keep pace with either rising expectations or inflation, wives and other family members are pressured to seek employment to supplement the family income. Labor-force participation rates for women increased from 24 percent in 1951 to 52 percent in 1981 for all women, and from 11 to 51 percent for married women (Kalbach and McVey, 1979:274).

Changing social and economic conditions have encouraged women to continue working after marriage and/or to return to work as soon as possible after having children. The financial and emotional costs of having children, as well as the cost to one's freedom, are increasingly seen as disadvantages by urban, middle-class couples, and the financial costs are enough to discourage rural folk from having large families. The uncertainty about which way the Canadian economy will turn, and the feminist movement's aims of equal rights and self-realization for women encourages development of careers outside the home, while discouraging housekeeping and raising children.

There is a strong link between educational attainment and labor force participation for women in Canada. Because of this, labor force participation rates for women can be expected to increase to even higher levels. Both trends — increased educational attainment and greater labor-force participation — will tend to keep the fertility of Canadian women below the replacement level.

It should not be forgotten that the reduction of fertility to below replacement levels has been the result of the individuals achieving greater control over reproduction. When high fertility was ingrained in the cultural and institutional patterns of societies, prior to their demographic transition, its effects were more or less a constant, insofar as population change was concerned. After their transitions (Stage IV in Figure 21-1.) fertility has

become a more unpredictable factor of undiminished importance; yet with fertility presently at a record low level, its significance for growth tends to be overshadowed by the third and remaining component of the population equation, namely migration.

Migration

The early history of the exploration and settlement of North America could be characterized as one of relatively free movement, operating on a first-come, first-serve basis. Many came to improve their economic fortunes, while others wanted to sever their old-world ties and make a fresh start for themselves and their families. However, many came to escape religious and political persecution in the homeland, seeking a place to live in peace where they could preserve and perpetuate their particular culture. For a considerable period of time, immigration to the New World was unregulated and unchecked. As a consequence, the migration flow consisted of peoples of diverse cultural, religious, and political backgrounds.

More than forty-five million Europeans left Europe between the sixteenth and twentieth centuries, destined for North America (Bouvier et al., 1977: 6). With the introduction of the steamship in 1819 dawned a new era of cheap and fast transportation, which made possible the heavy flood of immigrants at the beginning of the twentieth century. It is estimated that some 1.5 million arrived in Canada between 1867 and 1895, but because of poor economic conditions, many moved on to the United States. In an effort to settle the Prairies, the government implemented special measures to encourage farmers to immigrate to Canada. As a result, by World War I, another three million persons entered Canada.

Between wars, economic fluctuations and uncertainty led to increasing restrictions on immigration and to a virtual shutdown during the Great Depression and for the duration of World War II. Following the war, economic expansion gen-

FIGURE 21-3. Origin of Immigrants to Canada by Last Country of Residence.

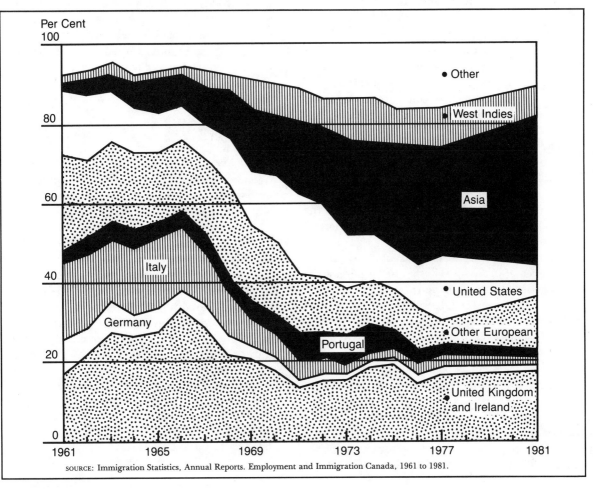

SOURCE: Immigration Statistics, Annual Reports. Employment and Immigration Canada, 1961 to 1981.

erated a new wave of immigration. Initially comprised of Europeans seeking to escape their war-ravaged homelands, the immigration stream changed in its ethnic composition as Canada liberalized its regulations during the 1960s and 1970s. Increasing numbers of immigrants came from the Caribbean, and Latin American and Asian countries, whereas the proportion coming from Europe dropped from three-quarters to less than half in a period of only twenty years. (See Figure 21-3.) Today, Canada operates under an annual quota

system, subject to periodic review, to fulfil its policy objectives of family reunification, refugee settlement, and labor-force needs.

As important as immigration has been for Canada's settlement, at no time since Confederation has the net migration for any decade accounted for more than half of the population growth. Its maximum contribution occurred between 1901 and 1911, when net migration accounted for 40 percent of the decade's growth. Although migration contributed only 26 percent to the overall growth during the decade of the postwar baby boom, the annual influx varied significantly but never exceeded 50 percent (Kalbach and McVey, 1979:47). In terms of numbers, the significance of net migration continues to be second to natural increase. The social, economic, and political significance of immigration will depend to an increasing degree on the patterns of distribution of the various ethnic and cultural populations in Canada's regions, including urban centres.

Prior to Confederation in 1867, Canada's economy was based on its natural resources and agriculture, and so population was predominantly rural. The three million or so immigrants who arrived between 1896 and 1914 were not all destined for the Prairies, and the character of the labor force showed the effects of increasing urbanization/industrialization that was pushing Canada through its demographic transition. Between 1901 and 1911, the urban population increased from 35 to 42 percent and surpassed 50 percent during the late 1920s and early 1930s (Stone, 1967:29). Postwar economic development and population growth boosted the urban population to 70 percent in 1961, and by 1981, 76 percent of the Canadian population resided in urban centres.

Variations in the timing, origin, and destination of the various immigrant streams to Canada over the years established a rather unique pattern of regional differences regarding ethnic and cultural composition, which has remained relatively unchanged over the years. At the same time, the populations of large urban centres differ visibly according to their ethnic and cultural, as well as their socioeconomic characteristics (Balakrishnan, 1976). The forces of urban growth have tended to blur the patterns of residential segregation. But they have not been eliminated, nor are they likely to be, as long as Canada continues to admit immigrants from diverse social, ethnic, and cultural origins.

The demographic equation identified in the previous section of this essay tells us that changes in the rate of a nation's population growth vary with changes in its rates of migration, fertility, and mortality. All three factors, at both the national and regional levels, have affected Canada's evolving character. The effects of the demographic transition, and Canada's migration experience on its age and sex structure and other population characteristics, are discussed in the following section.

POPULATION CHARACTERISTICS OF CANADA

Canada is typical of post-transition populations in that it is highly urbanized and enjoys a generally high standard of living. The relatively low and controlled levels of mortality and fertility have produced a mature and aging population with a high life expectancy at birth. Its uniqueness stems from its political and immigration history, which has produced a society dominated by two distinctive cultural groups — the British and the French. The positions of power of these two founding groups have been increasingly influenced by later waves of immigration from Europe and other countries (mentioned in the previous section). As a result, the bilingualism and biculturalism of the past has recently shifted toward a mix of bilingualism and multiculturalism.

Cultural Characteristics

At the time of Confederation, the British population was double the size of the French, and the two groups accounted for all but 8 percent of the country's population. Unlike the French, the British were heterogeneous, consisting of English, Irish, and Scottish origins and a mixture of Catholics and Protesant denominations. Today, the British and the French will account for two-thirds of the population, but the vast number of immigrants who settled here since the end of the nineteenth century to the present have added considerably to Canada's cultural diversity.

For almost two-thirds of the Canadian population, English was the first language learned.

French accounts for another quarter of the population, and the remaining 13 percent is made up of a wide variety of languages. Although the multilingual group is still relatively small, it has been growing more rapidly than the total population in recent years. Some individual language groups showed significant gains during the 1976–81 intercensal period. Indo-Pakistani groups, for example, increased by 100.3 percent; Armenian, 65.8 percent; Chinese, 69 percent; Spanish, 59.0 percent; and Semetic languages by 58.8 percent (Statistics Canada, 1982a).

The cultural mix of a population is also reflected in its religious composition. Both Catholic and Protestant religions have always been strongly represented in the Canadian population. However, with the more recent waves of immigration, Canada has become somewhat less Protestant as the immigration sources have shifted to predominantly Catholic countries, and more recently, to Eastern non-Christian populations. (See Figure 21.3.) At the beginning of the twentieth century, 42 percent of the population was Roman Catholic. By 1981, this figure rose to 47 percent. Eastern non-Christian and Jewish populations each contributed just over one percent of the total population, and those reporting no religious affiliation increased to 7.3 percent at the time of the 1981 census.

Changes in the ethnic and cultural origins and religious affiliations of the population have underscored the fact that the various groups that comprise the Canadian population have had significantly different demographic experiences. The French-Canadian population has sustained itself over the years through relatively high fertility. Recent declines in fertility and a slowing down of immigration from the British Isles, combined with a shift to other countries as sources of immigrants, will have a significant effect on the cultural composition of the Canadian population.

Age and Sex Structure

The sex ratio, or the number of males per 100 females, is a simple measure of the relative size of the male and female populations. There are only three factors that can affect the sex ratio of any population: (1) the sex ratio at birth; (2) the sex ratio of immigrants and emigrants; and (3) sex differences in mortality. The first has tended to be relatively constant over the years, varying only slightly between 105 and 106. Until recently, males tended to outnumber females among immigrants arriving in Canada, and if it were not for the fact that conditions for longevity have been improving more rapidly for women than for men, the sex ratio for the population of Canada would be considerably higher than it is today.

In 1981, the sex ratio for the total population was ninety-eight, compared to 105 at the beginning of the twentieth century. However, more males are still to be found in all but the oldest age groups in the rural areas of the country. In urban populations, the number of males generally exceed the number of females only in the younger age groups. Beyond the age of fifty, the sex ratio declines rapidly, and for the very elderly (ninety years and over), the sex ratio reached a low of forty-two in 1981 (Statistics Canada, 1982).

Unlike the sex ratio, a population's age distribution is affected more by variations in fertility. For example, the postwar baby boom has had a significant impact on the present age structure of the population. It is also a textbook example of the dynamics underlying population growth in post-transition populations. As mortality rates decreased and became more stabilized, fertility became the volatile and unpredictable factor in the population equation. The surge in childbearing was due to a favorable combination of economic expansion and to an end to wartime separations and the emergence of a more optimistic outlook that encouraged early marriage and an ideal family size of three to four children.

The increase in fertility during the late 1940s and throughout the following decade boosted the proportion of the population under fifteen years of age to a postwar high of 34 percent in 1961, temporarily slowing down the aging process for the population as a whole. With the passage of time, the babies blossomed into school-aged children, creating pressures for housing, food, clothing, and a wide range of goods and services for young people. As the baby boom generation ages, it will continue to play a significant role in shaping the nature of Canada's production and consumption patterns, and its social and political character as well. The progress of this generation through the age structure of the population can be traced in Figure 21-4., which shows that younger age groups following the boom have shrunk in relative size, whereas the older age groups have increased. According to the United Nations' Index of Aging, which is based on the proportion of the population sixty-five years of age and over, Canada shifted from the "early mature" population it reflected in 1881 (4.1 percent were sixty-five and over) to an "aged" population after 1971, when the proportion of sixty-five-and-over age category exceeded 8.0 percent (United Nations, 1956). By 1981, this proportion increased even more to 9.7 percent.

The impact that the baby boom generation has had, and will continue to have, on the population can readily be seen in the changes in size of the younger and older dependent-age groups relative to the economically active population, fifteen to sixty-five years of age. Just prior to 1981, these changes tended to be of a compensating nature. Between 1971 and 1981, the *total dependency ratio* — the ratio of the combined young and old age groups to the economically active population between fifteen and sixty-five years of age — increased only slightly from 60.4 to 61.8 percent. But, as the baby boom generation passes through the prime working ages and approaches retirement age, the dependency ratio will begin to change drastically, and the population of sixty-five and over will pose an increasingly heavy economic burden on those in the labor force. Compared to only 7.2 per cent in 1881, the old-age dependency ratio had increased to 14.3 percent

by 1981, and is expected to reach 16 percent by the end of the century and 24 percent by 2021 (Stone and Fletcher, 1980:16–19).

Marital Status and the Family

Since 1901, there has been a steady increase in the size of the married population, from 52 percent of the population (fifteen years of age and over) to 67 percent in 1961 (Kalbach and McVey, 1979: 311–12). The proportion has declined slightly to its present level of 63 percent (Statistics Canada, 1982). This recent decline, coupled with the significant increase in the divorced population, probably reflects the liberalization of divorce laws and a general acceptance of alternative life styles, as well as the constraining effects of the unfavorable economic conditions that have persisted during the last several decades. Between 1971 and 1981, the divorced population increased from 1.2 to 2.7 percent, and the proportion of husband-wife families declined slightly from 90.7 to 88.7 percent. By way of contrast, the proportion of the widowed population remained relatively steady at about 6 percent.

Variations in the rates of marriage, divorce, and mortality have a direct effect on the rates of family formation and dissolution, and average family size. The effects of mortality on family size, like those of fertility, are readily understood, but the significance of an increasing marriage rate on family size is less clear. However, if one remembers that most persons, at the time of marriage, have neither been previously married nor have had children, it is clear how an increase in the number of new marriages could reduce the average family size. In Canada, the decline in average family size since the early 1960s (from 3.9 to 3.3 persons per family) would appear to be more the result of the end of the baby boom years of high fertility, rather than a reflection of minor fluctuations that have occurred in the marriage rate. In any event, the effect of the rate of marriage on family size tends to be overshadowed by

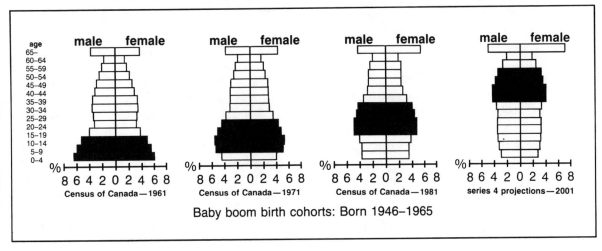

Baby boom birth cohorts: Born 1946–1965

SOURCE: Statistics Canada. Census of Canada, 1961, 1971, and 1981.

the impact of recent increases in divorce and the growing number of single-parent families.

In comparing the experiences of Canadian families over the last fifty to eighty years with those in the United States, it has been shown that Canadians have (1) consistently married two to three years later than their American counterparts; (2) spaced their children at closer intervals; (3) married off their last child earlier; and (4) tended to have longer marriages and longer periods of being together after their children have left home (Rodgers and Witney, 1981:727–38). However, this picture of the relatively stable Canadian family may give way, under the pressure of economic instability and other factors already discussed.

Social and Economic Characteristics

As we have already seen, the postwar economic boom speeded up the transformation of Canadian society. With regard to the economy, changes in the composition of the labor force reflected the increased need for managerial, professional, and technical workers, as well as for workers in clerical and service occupations. In contrast, the demand for workers in transportation and communication occupations has continued to decline, as well as for workers in farming and the other primary-type industries. Almost 40 percent of the male workers today are in occupations associated with crafts and production processes, and 21 percent are concentrated in the managerial, professional, and technical occupations. In contrast, 60 percent of the women in the labor force are employed in clerical and sales occupations, with another 23 percent in managerial, professional, and technical occupations (Statistics Canada, 1983h.).

Given the changes in Canada's economic structure, it is not surprising to find that the educational levels have continued to increase. The proportion of the population with secondary schooling increased from slightly more than one out of two persons in 1961, to four out of five in 1981 (Statistics Canada, 1984j.). The proportion of the population (fifteen years of age and over, not attending school full-time) that had some university education or a degree was about 6 percent in 1961. By 1981, the proportion increased to 15 percent. Part of this increase is due to the baby boom generation's moving through the educational system. Another part can be accounted for by a change in attitude toward the value of post-secondary education in a modern urban and highly industrialized society. Thus, the anticipated decline in the demand for post-secondary education after the baby boom population completed their schooling seems to have been offset by an increased demand for post-secondary education by subsequent generations. The increase in the proportion of those fifteen years of age and over with some post-secondary or university degrees since 1941 is clearly evident in Figure 21-5.

As mentioned previously, one of the most significant changes that has occurred during the postwar years has been the increased participation of women in the labor force, especially married women (Statistics Canada, 1984b). Between 1911 and 1981, their proportion of the labor force increased from 16.2 to 51.8 percent. In 1951, only 11 percent of married women worked outside the home; by 1981, this figure rose to 52 percent, compared to 62 percent for single women. Participa-

FIGURE 21-5. Education in Canada: 1941–1981. Percentage of Population Fifteen Years and Older.

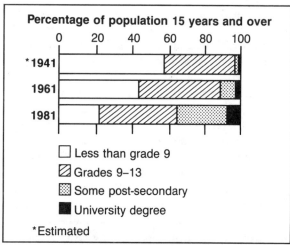

SOURCE: *Statistics Canada. Canada Update. Vol. 2, No. 2 (November, 1983).*

tion rates for single women, twenty years of age and over, rose almost as high as those for men in 1981 — 76 percent.

The increased participation of women in the labor force has come about for numerous reasons, but two are of particular importance: on the one hand, an increased interest in self-fulfillment in careers outside the home; on the other, the need to increase the family income (discussed previously).

The combination of these forces has created new stresses and strains within marriage and the family, and has increased the need for a redefinition and restructuring of family roles and expectations. The liberalization of the divorce laws and the changing nature of divorce settlements reflect an awareness of these problems and a need for innovative solutions.

COMING TO TERMS WITH DEMOGRAPHIC CHANGE

Canada

In contrast to the kinds of problems faced by the Third World countries today, Canada's present population problem stems from the slowing down of its rate of growth. Recent projections for Canada's population is twenty-eight to twenty-nine million by the year 2001, provided that fertility will average 1.7 births per woman by 1991 and remain constant thereafter, and given that annual net-migration will continue between fifty and seventy-five thousand persons (Statistics Canada, 1980: 37). Neither the present size of the population, nor that anticipated by the end of the century, poses an immediate problem. However, Canada will be faced with several major problems if fertility levels continue to fall below replacement levels. First, the aging process will continue unabated, increasing prospects for zero population growth, or an actual population decline. Secondly, if the fertility rate fails to increase, Canada will become more and more dependent on immigration to meet labor-force needs. The latter will have an important impact on the cultural character of this country if the recent shift to non-British and non-European countries as sources of immigrants is indicative of future trends.

Historically, Canada has been more concerned with population growth, the settlement of its vast agricultural lands in the West, and with exploitation of its natural resources, than it has been in limiting growth. Yet Canada does not have a general, overall population policy, as such. In the past, it used immigration policy to influence population growth and to shape the structure and cultural character of the country. From about 1910 until the end of the 1950s, immigration regulations were used to restrict entry of potential immigrants whose cultural and racial origins were in contrast to the two dominant cultural groups (Kalbach and McVey, 1979:44). Regulations have also been effectively employed to meet Canada's labor-force needs by bringing in workers whose skills were unavailable or in short supply among Canadians. Policies have also been implemented to encourage immigrants to settle in regions with labor-force shortages and in other areas that would benefit from economic development and population growth. Most recently, immigration of French-speaking people has been encouraged to reinforce Canada's French-language communities. Current policy is also geared to cutting back on the number of immigrants who would be seeking work in Canada during periods of relatively high unemployment.

A variety of government policies and social programs, although not thought of as being population policies, have been supportive of larger families. The family-allowance program, tax benefits for children, subsidized low-income housing, and national medicare plans based on need rather than ability to pay, are established features of Canadian society. It would be difficult, of course, to determine the extent to which these programs have contributed to Canada's relatively high fertility levels in the recent past. It is true that fertility levels in Canada have historically been higher than those in the United States, which has no national family allowance nor medicare program. However, it would appear that these social programs have not been sufficient to maintain high levels of fertility during the period of changing social and economic conditions following the post-baby boom era.

Canada has continued to use its immigration policy primarily as a means of meeting its immediate labor requirements, to permit family reunification and to fulfil its international obligations with respect to refugees. With continuing high levels of unemployment, it has cut off the flow of immigrants whose primary purpose in coming to Canada is to find employment.

Whereas immigration curtailment may be an acceptable short-term solution, its effects will be felt fifteen to twenty years from now, when the current small numbers of young people begin to enter the labor force at about the same time that the baby boom generation begins to approach retirement age. It will take increasingly bold and courageous action to come to terms with Canada's demographic future, particularly when it is realized that solutions to long-term problems may have immediate, but short-term negative consequences.

Prospects for Less-Developed Countries

The nature and magnitude of the population problem for the rest of the world is, perhaps, even more difficult to grasp because of its enormity, as well as its remoteness from the daily activities of Canadians. Of the estimated 4.8 billion people in the world in 1983, 76 percent or 3.6 billion live in the less-developed countries of the world. By the year 2000, the population in these countries is expected to increase to 5.0 billion and comprise almost 80 percent of a projected world population of 6.25 billion (Population Reference Bureau, 1984).

The sharp contrast in standard of living between the more- and less-developed countries can easily be seen in the following comparisons. The average per capita gross national product (GNP) in 1984 for the more developed countries was U.S. $9190, compared to only U.S. $750 for the less-developed ones. The significance of these differences in terms of the quality of life is reflected in the fifteen years difference between their estimated life expectancies at birth. It is also reflected in the difference between their infant mortality rates — nineteen versus ninety-four deaths per 1000 population, respectively, and in estimates of their total fertility. Women in the more-developed countries are now estimated to be averaging about two births during their childbearing years compared to 4.4 births in the less-developed areas of the world (Population Reference Bureau, 1984).

A further threat to the quality of life for these populations is posed by continuing migration from rural to urban areas. The numbers moving to the big cities pose a serious threat to the maintenance and expansion of municipal and other services required to support the normal everyday social and economic activities. In 1950, seven of the ten largest cities in the world were found in the industrialized countries. The two largest, New York and London, with 12.3 and 10.4 million people respectively, have been hard-pressed at times to maintain viable systems of transportation, food distribution, waste disposal, fire and police protection, health and welfare programs, and education facilities. Try to imagine the magnitude of the problems that will have to be faced and solved by a city of thirty-one million people, which is the projected population of Mexico City for the year 2000 (Murphy, 1981). A city of this size, in a country that is presently in serious financial difficulty, will make unprecedented demands on its resources. If this does not give one cause for concern, consider the fact that in the year 2000, the less-developed countries are expected to have about forty cities with populations of over five million, compared to only twelve cities in the industrialized nations (Van der Tak et al., 1979: 22).

Studies of differences in the production and consumption of goods in countries at various stages of development, and of the increasing costs of resource extraction and energy production, have raised serious questions about the probable success of efforts to raise the standard of living throughout the world to the same level as that currently enjoyed in North America and most European countries. However improbable this may be, it appears that any general improvement in living conditions for the overwhelming majority of the world's population will still depend upon (1) reducing fertility levels; (2) achieving some degree of economic development; and (3) increasing world food-production and achieving a more equitable distribution of food and natural resources. Realization of the latter seems to depend to an increasing extent on the willingness of the more-developed countries to reduce both their consumption of the world's resources and their degredation of the global environment.

Since World War II, two general strategies have been followed in attempts to slow down population growth. One is reflected in the postwar programs of economic and technical assistance to underdeveloped countries, to stimulate economic growth and improve standards of living. The expectations deriving from economic growth is that people will begin to control their fertility as they become aware of the fact that large families make it more difficult to share in the improved quality of life. The other strategy, complementing the first, is based on the belief that most people in the less-developed countries are already aware of the disadvantages of large families, but lack the knowledge and the means to limit the size of their families (Mauldin, 1965). Foreign-aid programs following World War II were successful in lowering mortality rates in the less-developed countries, but fertility remained fairly high and populations grew rapidly (Population Index, 1965: Table 21-2). A few areas that experienced postwar economic growth, such as Singapore, Taiwan, and Hong Kong, also ex-

In order to raise the worldwide standard of living, food production must increase while fertility levels decrease. As well, more-developed nations must assume greater responsibility for their use of global resources and degradation of the environment.

perienced a decline in their fertility. Since these populations were also targets of extensive family-planning education campaigns, it has not been possible to determine accurately just how much of the reduction can be attributed to either economic development or to the efforts of family-planning organizations.

Countries that have not experienced significant economic development have been less encouraging with regard to fertility reductions. Many Asian and African countries are still experiencing fertility rates between forty and fifty per 1000 population. India has been stubbornly resistant to officially sanctioned education programs, ranging from simple contraception to sterilization. China, with a population of over a billion people and a growth rate that will double its population

in fifty years, is perhaps faced with the severest test of any nation. Their officially sanctioned and strictly enforced programs of family limitation seem to be meeting with some success, even though their attempts to limit married couples to only one child have run counter to traditional Chinese values.

However, the strong resistance to India's recent attempts to introduce compulsory sterilization should serve as a reminder that the problem of achieving quick and effective population control is still an extremely complex and difficult one. Traditional attitudes and values involving family and marriage tend to be strongly ingrained and difficult to change. Whatever approach is taken, neither economic development nor family planning can be ignored. Experts still maintain that family-planning programs can ease population pressures more quickly than efforts to stimulate economic development to some critical threshold. Either way, the task of bringing a population and the expectations of its members into a more reasonable balance with its resources and capacity for the production and distribution of goods and services is an extremely difficult one. With continuing growth of the world's population, it will be increasingly difficult for countries, and individuals, to ignore the ultimate consequences.

SUMMARY

1. Given the social, political, and economic problems in the world today, it is important to study demographic processes, and how they affect and are affected by social, economic, and political institutions.

2. National censuses and continuous vital statistics registration systems have become the major means of collecting data on population, which are then used to analyze the dynamics of population change.

3. The pattern of mortality decline during Canada's settlement and economic development is one example of the dynamics of demographic transition.

4. Canada's postwar baby boom throughout the 1950s and subsequent decline in fertility to below replacement levels, is a good example of population dynamics.

5. Immigration played a significant role in Canada's early settlement and development. After Confederation, natural increase was the main source of population growth. Nevertheless, immigration from Third World countries today is expected to continue to add to Canada's ethnic and cultural diversity.

6. Canada, like other countries with low mortality and declining fertility rates, has a rapidly growing older population. If these trends continue, Canada will have to increase its immigration quota to meet labor-force requirements.

7. In addition to aging and a declining of population growth, changes in the economic structure, higher educational attainment levels, and increased labor-force participation of woman are the relevant factors underlying the current transformation of Canadian society.

8. As developing countries continue to urbanize without commensurate economic development, it will become incumbent for industrialized nations to provide them with technical assistance and other support.

GLOSSARY

Age-sex structure. The composition of a population in terms of the number or proportion of males and females, usually for five-year age groups. Generally displayed in the form of a special type of bar chart known as a "population pyramid."

Age-specific fertility rate. Number of births occurring in a specifc age group per 1000 women in that age group.

Baby boom. The unexpected and unprecedented increase in birth rates following World War II, between 1946 and the early 1960s, in Canada, the United States, Australia, and New Zealand.

Birth rate (also called the crude birth rate). The number of live births per 1000 population in a given year.

Death rate (also called crude death rate). The number of deaths per 1000 population in a given year.

Demographic transition. The historical shift from high to low levels of vital rates that occurred in a number of populations undergoing industrialization and urbanization. Declines in mortality preceeded declines in fertility causing high rates of population growth during the transition period.

Demography. "The scientific study of human populations, including their size, composition, distribution, density, growth and other demographic and socioeconomic characteristics, and the causes and consequences of changes in these factors." (Population Reference Bureau, 1978.)

Emigration. The process of leaving one country to become a permanent resident of another.

Immigration. Moving to one country from another to become a permanent resident.

Population. An aggregate of individuals bounded by national, regional, or cultural boundaries.

Rate of natural increase. The annual excess of births over deaths per 1000 population during a given period of time.

Sex ratio. The number of males per 100 females.

Total dependency ratio. The ratio of the economically dependent part of the population to the economically active part (i.e., the ratio of the population sixty-five years and over, plus those under fifteen years of age, to the working-age population between the ages of fifteen and sixty-five years).

Total fertility rate. The average number of children that would be born to a group of women during the course of their childbearing years if they experienced the age-specific fertility rates prevailing in a given year.

Vital statistics. Demographic data on births, deaths, marriages, and divorces in a population during a specified time period.

FURTHER READING

Beaujot, Roderic and Kevin McQuillan. *Growth and Dualism: The Demographic Development of Canadian Society.* Toronto: Gage, 1982. The most recent text on Canadian population. Its distinguishing feature is its comparative analysis of Canada's two founding nations.

Ehrlich, P.R. and A.H. Ehrlich. *Population, Resources, Environment.* San Francisco: W.H. Freeman, 1970. A comprehensive analysis of the worldwide population crisis and its impact on food supplies, resources and the environment. The authors' concern over the unprecedented challenge of rapid, global population growth is tempered by constructive proposals.

Hawkins, Freda. *Canada and Immigration: Public Policy and Public Concern.* Montréal: McGill-Queen's University Press, 1972. A comprehensive review and analysis of Canada's immigration policies during the postwar years, including federal-provincial relationships, overseas services, and the role of voluntary agencies.

Kalbach, W.E. and W.W. McVey, Jr. *The Demographic Bases of Canadian Society.* 2nd edition. Toronto: McGraw-Hill Ryerson, 1979. The first comprehensive text on Canadian population with chapters on the major components of population change and such population characteristics as ethnic origin, the foreign-born, religion, marital status and family, labor force, and housing.

Matras, Judah. *Introduction to Population: A Sociological Approach.* Englewood Cliffs, N.J.: Prentice-Hall, 1977. An excellent, general introductory demography text using U.S. data to illustrate population dynamics. There is also good coverage of world population trends and policy considerations. Techniques of quantitative description, measurement, and analysis of population change are presented in an appendix.

Richmond, A.H. and W.E. Kalbach. *Factors in the Adjustment of Immigrants and their Descendants.* Ottawa: Minister of Supply and Services, 1980. A comparative analysis of the social and economic characteristics of Canada's population by generation, ethnic origins, and country of birth; and an examination of changes in levels of economic achievement of immigrants during 1961–71.

Weeks, John R. *Population: An Introduction to Concepts and Issues.* 2nd edition. Belmont: Wadsworth, 1981. An introduction to concepts and issues in the study of population within the context of the current world situation.

Wrong, Dennis H. *Population and Society.* 4th edition. New York: Random House, 1977. The "classic" overview of population study, world population, components of population change, and an excellent introduction to the current population debate.

CHAPTER TWENTY-TWO

Urbanization

PETER McGAHAN

The modern age is an urban age. By 1970, the world's population stood at approximately 3.6 billion, of which 39 percent were urban residents. Indeed, almost one-fourth lived in cities of 100 000 or more, and the proportion of the world's population living in cities of 1 000 000 or more doubled between 1950 and 1970. Cities are defined as relatively large, densely populated settlements in which the majority of residents do not produce their own food.

This movement from a rural to an urban society in both Western and developing countries represents a social, demographic, and economic transformation of profound significance. In focusing on *urbanization* or urban growth in this chapter, we are concerned with only part of a much more complex process involving modernization, industrialization, and the development of complex forms of organization.

A sociological examination of the city entails study of the factors affecting urban growth, as well as the social and spatial organization of the urban community. The city is a *socio-spatial system*, the evolution and structure of which must ultimately be studied cross-culturally and historically. We shall first examine the process of urbanization, then review approaches to the study of urbanism and the nature of urban spatial structure, and conclude with a brief overview of contemporary issues in urban planning.

URBANIZATION

The Meaning of Urbanization

Urbanization as a demographic process involves (1) an increase in the number of urban areas or points of concentration in a society; (2) an increase in the size of individual cities; and (3) a general rise in the proportion of a society's total population living in urban areas. These increases tend to occur simultaneously.

When we examine urban growth from an ecological perspective, our focus is somewhat different. Human ecology is concerned primarily with the organization of functional requirements by which a local population maintains itself in a particular habitat. Urbanization represents an expansion or elaboration of that organization. It consists of a process of growth "from the simple, highly localized unit to the complex and territorially extended system." (Hawley, 1971:9.) The small trading centre that services only a modest hinterland and the large-scale metropolitan community with far-reaching links to other cities represent two disparate points along the urbanization continuum.

In defining what an urban area is, the Canadian census adopts a demographic criterion: those persons living in an area having a population concentration of 1000 or more and a population density of 400 or more per square kilometre.

In examining urban growth cross-culturally, we must be sensitive to the variations in the way countries define "urban". (In the United States, for example, the minimum population required for a place to be called urban is 2500; in Switzerland it is 10 000 + , and in Denmark 250 + .) "A numerical definition is the most basic criterion from which to develop data to either support or refute a claim that a place is a city. In some nations, India, for example, the definition of a city includes the factor that a certain percentage of the people living there not be involved in agriculture. Population density is a factor in other nations." (Exline, Peters, and Larkin, 1982:29.)

The Urban Transformation

Prior to the nineteenth century, urban development was sporadic. In the 40 000-year history of Homo sapiens, the first cities did not appear until approximately 3500 B.C., in that section of the Fertile Crescent lying between the Tigris and Euphrates rivers. These cities were made possible through advances made in stone-age technology. Improvements in methods of irrigation, cultivation, and transportation promoted the rise of cities — such as Ur, Kish, Ubaid — by making possible surplus food production that supported an urban population. A centralized social and economic organization evolved to exploit that surplus. This encouraged a more elaborate division of labor and craft specialization, and strong trade relations between centres. Almost all early cities were marked by "full-time specialists, large dense populations, great art, writing and numerical notation, exact and predictive sciences, levies that concentrate the surplus food production, the state, monumental public architecture, long-distance trade, and a class-structured society." (Gist and Fava, 1964:13.)

Early cities also emerged in the Indus River Valley (now West Pakistan) where, for example, the major centre of Harappa supported a population of 20 000 within an area of one square kilometre. However, the primitive state of medicine, the labor-intensive character of agriculture, and the rigid social stratification prohibited any sustained process of urban growth.

Ancient cities dotted the Western Hemisphere, as well, in Mexico and Guatemala. Mayan cities

Teotihuacan, the earliest large city of Middle America, was mysteriously abandoned and later destroyed by Cortez and his Spanish *conquistadores*.

emerged after 300 B.C., although less densely concentrated than those in Mesopotamia. The earliest large urban centre in Middle America was Teotihuacan ("place of the gods"), located fifty kilometers from present-day Mexico City. A religious and administrative centre, it covered nine to twelve square kilometres, with a population of approximately 75 000 at its peak between 150 and 750 A.D. Archeological evidence suggests that by 750 A.D., the city had been abandoned. The reason for this is not clear. One explanation might be "that the unending construction work [as revealed, for example, in its pyramids] was such a physical and economic burden on its inhabitants and tributary groups that the population might have nursed a growing rebellion which could have exploded in the overthrow of their traditional hierarchy." (Hardoy, 1973:71.)

Urban centres flourished in the Incan empire in the central Andes, one of the most developed pre-industrial civilizations.

With the fall of these civilizations, so too their cities inevitably declined. Such was the fate of Athens and Rome. After the demise of the Roman Empire, urban centres in Europe languished until the revival of trade in the tenth and eleventh centuries. But it was not until the Industrial Revolution in the eighteenth and nineteenth centuries that the urban transformation became a fixed feature of human history.

When we look back at the pre-industrial city, regardless of the culture within which it occurred, we are able to identify several common features (Sjoberg, 1960). Typically, it emerged within a feudal society. Dependent on animate sources of energy, such a society was able to produce sufficient food surplus to support a non-agricultural population. The pre-industrial city was small, containing rarely more than one-tenth of the society's total population. It was here that the society's elite were concentrated, at the apex of a highly stratified social order. The elite controlled political, religious, and educational institutions. Their rule was legitimated by tradition and sacred norms.

The most important economic activity in the pre-industrial city was the trading of local and imported goods and produce. What manufacturing existed was of a modest scale, executed by domestic craftsmen, organized into guilds.

The social order of the pre-industrial city was revealed in its spatial structure. The core of the city was the site of the most important religious and political activities, adjacent to which were the residences of the elite. (In contrast to the dominance of commercial activity in the core of the contemporary city, the pre-industrial city's market was not given spatial prominence.) The rest of the city was divided into wards or districts, within each of which were concentrated specific occupational or ethnic groups. The poorest residents lived on the outskirts, a significant contrast from what we see today in urban areas.

As modernization in the West proceeded, this pre-industrial urban profile receded. Beginning in the latter part of the fifteenth century, urban growth increased, particularly with the rise of modern nation-states. During the eighteenth century, urban development became pronounced in England because of several factors: (1) Construction of better roads and a variety of canals partly accounted for improved transportation. (2) Agricultural innovations were important: new methods of land drainage and cultivation of pasturage spread widely from the European continent; and increased mechanization helped meet the needs of an expanding population. Finally (3), the emergence of the factory system in the towns of England

TABLE 22-1. **Number and Population of Million-Cities, 1960 and 1975, in the Major Areas of the World**

Area	Number of Million-Cities*		Population of Million-Cities		Percentage of Population in Million-Cities	
	1960	1975	1960	1975	1960	1975
World Total	109	191	272	516	9.1	12.8
More developed regions	64	90	173	251	17.7	21.9
Less developed regions	45	101	99	265	4.9	9.2
Europe	31	37	73	93	17.3	19.3
U.S.S.R.	5	12	13	25	6.1	9.7
Northern America	18	30	52	80	26.2	32.9
Oceania	2	2	4	6	24.7	26.9
South Asia	16	34	32	88	3.7	6.8
East Asia	23	45	60	131	7.7	12.9
Africa	3	10	6	22	2.4	5.5
Latin America	11	21	31	71	14.5	21.9

*Cities which have a population of one million or more.

SOURCE: United Nations, *Concise Report on the World Population Situation in 1970–75 and Its Long-Range Implications* (New York: United Nations, 1974), 36.

TABLE 22-2. Distribution of Total and Urban Population by Urban Size Group, Rural Non-farm, and Rural Farm, Canada, 1981 (%)

Urban Size Group	Distribution of Total Population	Distribution of Urban Population
500 000 +	41.2	54.4
100 000 – 499 999	10.5	13.9
30 000 – 99 999	8.2	10.8
10 000 – 29 999	6.4	8.5
5000 – 9999	3.3	4.3
2500 – 4999	3.3	4.3
1000 – 2499	2.8	3.8
Rural Non-farm	20.0	—
Rural Farm	4.3	—
Total	100.0	100.0
(N)	(24 343 180)	(18 435 925)

SOURCE: 1981 Census of Canada. *Population*. Catalogue 92-902. Volume I. Table 2.

stimulated migration from the countryside. In the nineteenth century the introduction of the railway system permitted greater contacts between urban centres and their hinterland, and expanded markets. For all these reasons, urbanization (both demographically and ecologically) in England and elsewhere rapidly became the dominant feature of the modern age.

In 1800, less than 3 percent of the world's population lived in cities of 20 000 or more; by the 1950s, the proportion had risen to 20 percent — a rate of increase much faster than at any previous time in history. Only fifty cities of 100 000 population or more existed in 1800; by 1950, that number had grown to 900, and it has increased ever since (Davis, 1955). Table 22-1 shows the growth in the number of cities, each with a population of at least one million in almost every region of the world. Less developed regions especially reveal this trend. Between 1960 and 1975, a short fifteen-year period, the total population in the largest urban centres in underdeveloped countries almost

tripled. It is projected that by the end of this century, the number of cities of 100 000 population in the world will have doubled.

Despite this world-wide trend, there are still some striking differences among regions and nations. Levels of urbanization are highest in Australia, New Zealand, and North America, and lowest in many of the underdeveloped countries of Asia and Africa. These discrepancies, however, mask the much higher rates of urban increase that the latter continents have been experiencing in recent decades. The urban transformation has become a universal process.

Canada, about 100 years ago, was almost entirely rural. By 1981, 75.7 percent of the population resided in urban areas; only 4.3 percent lived on farms. Today, half (51.7%) of all Canadians live in cities of 100 000 population or more. In recent years, however, the rate of urban growth in Canada has declined.

Historical Types of Canadian Urban Communities

From the beginnings of permanent European settlement in Canada to the contemporary age, urban communities have exercised a central influence on the nation's social, political, and economic landscape. Within the broad range of such communities we can identify several types. Each of these represents a distinct form of ecological organization and stage of economic development, each a more complex territorial system of functional relationships than its predecessor.

The Early Colonial Town

This earliest type of community functioned simply as the agent of European metropolitan centres, as a garrison or administrative hub. These towns collected such staples as fur, lumber, and fish from the surrounding region and transmitted them back to Britain, France, and ultimately to other parts of western Europe. They were also the distribution points for economic and cultural

The great fire at Montréal, 1852. With their rapid expansion, Canada's early cities risked the spread of fire and disease due to crowding and lack of sanitary facilities.

imports from the mother country. Insofar as they preceded settlement of a region, colonial towns such as Kingston, York (Toronto), Québec, Montréal, and St. John's formed an urban frontier, a set of "nodes" connecting a relatively unsettled hinterland with an external metropolis. They had no developed local economy of their own, and their future depended on the potential growth of their own region at least partially (Stelter, 1975: 270-286).

The Commercial Centre

This type of urban community emerged in Eastern Canada after 1815 with the arrival of numerous British immigrants (Careless, 1978). Montréal experienced the greatest expansion during this stage of commercial development, gaining control over inland trade and commerce along the St. Lawrence River. Like the early colonial town, the commercial centre served as a centre for exporting staples — timber, lumber, potash, and wheat — to Britain. Its growth was directly linked to the ability of its merchants to exchange primary resources for British manufactured goods. Protected by a mercantilist system, the vitality of such commercial communities as Montréal, Hamilton, and Toronto reflected fluctuations in both the demand for these staples in the mother country and the capacity of the surrounding rural hinterland to meet this demand. In addition to its role in exporting staples, the commercial centre provided goods and services for an expanding hinterland.

The Commercial-Industrial and Metropolitan Community

A variety of factors promoted the growth of urban communities of greater scale in both Eastern and Western Canada. The growth of Toronto, Montréal, and Winnipeg (which was incorporated as a city in 1874, coinciding with its status as a commercial centre) was partly due to transportation improvements. In particular, the railroad provided an efficient means of long-distance transportation, which, in turn, widened the scope of the city's market and source of raw materials. Improvements in local transportation, such as the horse-drawn and electric street railways, encour-

TABLE 22-3. **Growth in Canada's Major Metropolitan Areas, 1976–1981**

Rank 1981	Rank 1976	Metropolitan Area	Population 1976*	1981	Percentage Change
1	1	Toronto	2 803 101	2 998 947	7.0
2	2	Montréal	2 802 547A	2 828 349	0.9
3	3	Vancouver	1 166 348	1 268 183	8.7
4	4	Ottawa-Hull	693 288	717 978	3.6
5	6	Edmonton	556 270A	657 057	18.1
6	9	Calgary	471 397A	592 743	25.7
7	5	Winnipeg	578 217	584 842	1.2
8	7	Québec	542 158	576 075	6.3
9	8	Hamilton	529 371	542 095	2.4
10	10	St. Catharines-Niagara	301 921	304 353	0.8
11	11	Kitchener	272 158	287 801	5.8
12	12	London	270 383	283 668	4.9
13	13	Halifax	267 991	277 727	3.6
14	14	Windsor	247 582	246 110	−0.6
15	15	Victoria	218 250	233 481	7.0
16	17	Regina	151 191	164 313	8.7
17	18	St. John's	145 400A	154 820	6.5
18	19	Oshawa	135 196	154 217	14.1
19	20	Saskatoon	133 793A	154 210	15.3
20	16	Sudbury	157 030	149 923	−4.3
21	21	Chicoutimi-Jonquière	128 643	135 172	5.1
22	22	Thunder Bay	119 253	121 379	1.8
23	23	Saint John	112 974	114 048	1.0
24	24	Trois-Rivières	106 031A	111 453	5.1

*Based on 1981 area.

A — Adjusted figures due to boundary changes.

SOURCE: *Canada's Cities*. Canada Update. Statistics Canada. Volume 2, No. 4 (March, 1984).

North American suburbs, designed to serve expanding metropolitan communities, are characterized by large numbers of recently constructed, single-family dwellings.

aged a wider dispersion of the city's population. In 1874, for example, Winnipeg consisted of an area little more than five square kilometres, of which only about one-fifth had been built up. By 1914, the city covered more than thirty-one square kilometres, with a population one hundred times larger. Such improvements coincided with industrial expansion. Between 1881 and 1891, for example, the number of industries located in Toronto increased by well over a thousand. Urban centres grew partly as places for the gathering and exporting of timber, lumber, and wheat from their sur-

rounding hinterlands. The income derived from this permitted cities such as Toronto and Winnipeg to diversify their economies, strengthen their industrial bases, and generate growth in the services they performed for their regions. A common pattern in nineteenth-century, urban growth was the competition between two or more centres for regional dominance — for example, Vancouver versus Victoria in British Columbia. In a developing region, not all communities could achieve an equally central position. Prosperity for one frequently meant decline for another.

The twentieth century has seen the increasing dominance of the *metropolitan community* (a territorial system in which a set of communities and surrounding area are linked together and to a central city). As transportation facilities became more advanced, *suburbanization*, or the outward movement of population, occurred on a larger scale. The metropolitan community expanded beyond the confines of cities because the cities were attracting more and more people, increasing the demand for housing. The availability of large tracts of vacant land on the periphery permitted construction of numerous single-family dwellings. As the metropolitan areas expanded, economic activities such as wholesaling and manufacturing dispersed as well, paralleling the decentralization of population.

Today, there are twenty-four metropolitan communities in Canada, containing about half the total population. Coinciding partly with variations in employment opportunities, migration and immigration flows, and rates of natural increase, these centres show contrasting rates of growth between 1976 and 1981. (See Table 22-3.) The population of Calgary, Edmonton, Saskatoon, and Oshawa has increased significantly, whereas such places as Sudbury and Windsor experienced an absolute decline. Dominating Canada's metropolitan system, of course, are Montréal and Toronto, which together contain one-fourth of the total population.

The Urban Region

As urbanization proceeds, cities and metropolitan communities themselves become linked through economic ties and population flows to form even more extensive territorial systems. These are *urban regions*. In Canada, the most important of these is the Windsor-Québec City urban axis. An area of almost 70 000 square miles, it contains more than 1800 municipalities, more than half of Canada's total population, and a large segment of its manufacturing employment (Yeates, 1975). Although the region encompasses numerous municipalities and is under the jurisdiction of two provinces, it functions as an identifiable unit with strong internal linkages. Toronto and Montréal economically dominate this region. Other examples of urban regions are the Edmonton-Calgary corridor and the Georgia Strait urban region, the latter a mosaic of communities with Vancouver's inner city as the focus. The formation of the urban region represents a complex state of urbanization.

The Single-Industry Community

Table 22-2 indicates that one-fifth of urban Canadians live in communities each with a population of less than 30 000. Many of these are single-industry communities. Although physically isolated from large metropolitan centres, their resource-extraction links them closely to the national economy. Examples are Sudbury, Fort McMurray, and Uranium City. They depend on an unstable economy, for as "the community of single industry seldom expands, it is vulnerable to changes in international markets, changes in technology, and in most instances it has a limited life expectancy, if for no other reason than that the sole reason for the town's existence may disappear." (Lucas, 1971:98.)

The National System of Cities

Ultimately, the metropolitan communities and urban regions are linked together loosely to form a national system of cities. Economic and demographic changes in one part of the country (such as oil development in Alberta and the increase in employment opportunities in Edmonton or Calgary) influence other sectors of this network (for example, outmigration from St. John's to Edmonton).

We have observed that the city is a socio-spatial system. When we examine how an urban community is socially organized, what shape its institutions take, and how social relationships and groups are structured within that system, we are studying *urbanism* (urban social life). To this topic we now turn.

URBANISM

The Classical Typological Perspectives

The theoretical models that exercised great influence in the study of cities were the *typological perspectives* (McGahan, 1982a), developed by Tönnies, Durkheim, and Simmel. They attempted to articulate the dramatic changes they witnessed in the late nineteenth- and early twentieth-centuries. The essence of typological perspectives is the explanation of the nature of urban social organization by contrasting it with non-urban social organization. As an example, let us look at the Gemeinschaft/Gesellschaft typology developed by Tönnies.

Ferdinand Tönnies (1855–1936), a German sociologist, believed that urbanization involves the emergence of a unique way of life, reflected in the types of associations and patterns of interaction, as well as in the nature of the central institutions of the city. To explain the impact of urbanization, he identified two types of social order. *Gemeinschaft* relations involve an underlying consensus or mutual understanding based on kinship, common locality of residence, or friendship, and the relationship exists for its own sake and cannot be arbitrarily terminated. In contrast, *Gesellschaft* relations are transitory and superficial, based on contract and exchange.

The purest form of Gesellschaft for Tönnies is the industrial-urban community, which has become dominant with the growth of capitalism. The institutions of the city clearly express this trend. Instead of traditional customs and mores characteristic of agricultural villages, there now exist formalized laws of contract. With the emergence of an industrially-based trade economy, impersonal forms of organization such as bureaucracies become prevalent. Kinship exercises a less central role in society.

This change from a rural-agricultural society, in which Gemeinschaft was prevalent, to an urban-industrial order, marked by the dominance of Gesellschaft, for Tönnies was both inevitable and regrettable.

During the 1920s and 1930s, a group of scholars led by Robert Park at the University of Chicago sought to systematize the insights of the European theorists and establish a more rigorous investigation of the contemporary urban community. Called the *Chicago School*, they saw the city as a social laboratory, as a context in which to understand the structure of different types of groups, such as the gang, and of inner-city neighborhoods. Reflecting the classical typological orientation, they were concerned especially with the disintegrating influences of city life and the problems in maintaining social control.

A central figure in the Chicago School, Louis Wirth (1897–1952) proposed a theory of urbanism. Taking size, density, and heterogeneity as the essential characteristics of the city, he suggested the types of social relationships and patterns of behavior that each of these determines. For example, he argued that the large population of the city promotes a wide range of individual differences. This, in turn, facilitates patterns of residential segregation in terms of language, ethnicity, and class. Such diversity necessitates reliance on formal mechanisms of social control, since the traditional sanctions of a small village are no longer adequate. The city's size and density also influence the development of impersonal, segmental, and superficial relationships between urban residents. Membership in groups is tenuous and specialized according to function. Primary-group ties become less prominent than secondary-group links. Large, dense, and heterogenous communities produce social instability.

Under these conditions, stress, individualism, and social disorganization are more likely to occur in the city than in a rural area. This theory of "urbanism as a way of life" is also called the *determinist theory*: the more a particular settlement increases in size, density, and heterogeneity, the more it will manifest these features of urbanism.

Modifications of the Classical Typological Perspective

The theories of Tönnies and Wirth were criticized subsequently as painting too broad and deterministic a picture of the differences between rural and urban social structures. Furthermore, their generalizations were found not to hold cross-culturally. Efforts to understand the nature of urbanism in more precise fashion have led to several modifications of the classical perspective (Fischer, 1976).

Compositional Theory

Such scholars as Herbert Gans and Oscar Lewis have argued that urban social life is a product of such factors as social class, ethnicity, and stage in the family life cycle, in other words, the composition of a city. If a particular urban area shows a different social pattern from that found in a specific rural settlement, it is because of variations in the composition of their respective populations. In addition, compositional theory denies that in cities primary-group relationships are inevitably weakened, or that size and density have significant social effects.

Subcultural Theory

This approach seeks to synthesize the determinist and compositional theories. In agreement with the former, subcultural theory argues that population concentration does indeed influence social life by causing the emergence of distinctive subcultures. The larger and denser the community, the greater its subcultural variety. Reinforcing this process is the influx of migrants from a variety of places. Large cities are also more likely to attract sufficient numbers to support the institutions needed for each subculture's vitality. Chinatowns, for example, are inevitably found in Canada's largest cities. Subcultural theory does not assume the disruption of primary-group ties. It depicts the city as a mosaic of social worlds, some of which may support unconventional or deviant behavior. Deviance is thus not a consequence of social disorganization, as Wirth had argued, but of subcultural strength: "With size comes 'community' — even if it is a community of thieves, counter-culture experimenters, avant-garde intellectuals, or other unconventional persons." (Fischer, 1975:1328–29.)

Chart 22-1. Competing Theories of Urbanism

Example: unconventional, deviant behavior* in the city

= Is a product of social disorganization and the breakdown in social norms in the city (*Determinist Theory*).

= Reflects the unique social composition of the city. In comparison to ruralites, city dwellers are more commonly young, without family responsibilities, highly educated, and members of minority groups. These are all features linked to unconventional life styles (*Compositional Theory*).

= In the city large numbers of people with similar interests congregate and form distinctive subcultures. These subcultures foster and sustain unconventional life styles and patterns of behavior (*Subcultural Theory*).

* Can range from deviant religious sects, to vice, to alternate life styles, and so forth.

Adapted from: Claude S. Fischer, *The Urban Experience*, 192–200.

Social Network Analysis

Complementing subcultural theory, social network analysis represents an alternative perspective in the study of the city's social life. It examines the structure and content of urbanites' networks and provides an understanding of the processes of communication and control, as well as of the flow of mutual aid and support. The urban community is seen as a complex of social networks in which individuals and collectivities are linked. Through

In 1985, a variety of construction projects were planned to revitalize Montréal's St. Catherine Street after years of neglect.

this approach we are able to recognize how urbanites' intimate ties, contrary to the classical assumption, have not eroded, but rather tend to be spatially dispersed. Such links are patterned so as to sustain distinctive subcultures, including viable ethnic communities.

Urbanism and Capitalism

Adopting a more general consensus model of social order, the Chicago School tended to ignore how urban institutions and the overall social organization of cities are shaped by the distribution of power and wealth characteristic of industrial capi-

talism. Urbanism and capitalism, the Marxist perspective argues, are closely linked: the form and functioning of urbanism reflect the dominant mode of production (Harvey, 1973). The institutions and ways of life in the city are affected by the conflicts inherent in the class relations of advanced capitalism; more to the point, they frequently support the continued concentration of power and wealth that is an essential part of the capitalist social order.

From this perspective, for example, we can gain an understanding of the growth of power of the property industry in Canada since the end of the Second World War. Because of its tremendous investments in urban property, this industry has changed the face of urban Canada. Every large city is marked by high-rise apartments, industrial parks, office towers, shopping centres, and suburban developments — each the creation of the property industry. Its activities have generated opposition from citizen groups, who have been more concerned with obtaining the lowest cost possible for accommodation and with maintaining the social and architectural character of their neighborhoods (Lorimer, 1972; 1978).

The development of specific institutions in the city can also be better understood from this perspective. Harring (1983) has recently documented how with industrialization the police in many American cities experienced a rapid expansion in the size of its force and substantial reorganization and centralization of its activities. This was a process, he argues, that benefited, and indeed was planned by, the ruling class. The bourgeoisie supported the police and aided their expansion as a weapon against an increasingly threatening and restive working class. The police gave protection to strikebreakers and adopted a variety of measures, some violent, to protect employers' property and undermine working-class opposition.

The value of the Marxist perspective in studying urban social organization is that it reasserts the impact that inequality and class relations have on the institutional life of cities.

URBAN ECOLOGY

Earlier we defined the city as a socio-spatial system. Urban ecology focuses on patterns of urban growth as well as on the spatial distribution of population and land-use types. We have viewed urbanization from an ecological perspective as the development of a complex territorial system of functional relationships. Here we consider the spatial correlates of this process; that is, how the internal spatial structure of the city reflects its growth.

With urban growth, sub-areas within the city become more specialized and differentiated in terms of population and land use. Several urban-growth models have been proposed, seeking to identify general patterns associated with this process.

Urban-Growth Models
Burgess's Concentric Zone Theory

This model represented a central theory of the Chicago School. Urban growth, Burgess proposed, necessitates expansion outward from the central business district. A series of areas evolves, depicted as a set of concentric zones in Figure 22-1 , in which Zone I is the central business district. The other sections of the metropolitan community are ordered around this inner core in the following way:

Encircling the downtown area there is normally an area in transition, which is being invaded by business and light manufacture. A third area is inhabited by the workers in industries who have escaped from the area of deterioration but who desire to live within easy access of their work. Beyond this zone is the 'residential area' of high-class apartment buildings or of exclusive 'restricted' districts of single family dwellings. Still farther, out beyond the city limits, is the commuters' zone—suburban areas, or satellite cities—within a thirty-to-sixty minute rise of the central business district.

(Burgess, 1967:50.)

FIGURE 22-1. **Models of the Internal Structure of Cities**

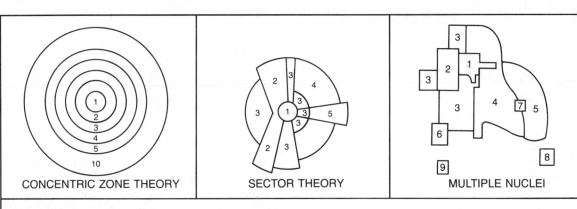

CONCENTRIC ZONE THEORY   SECTOR THEORY   MULTIPLE NUCLEI

THREE GENERALIZATIONS OF THE
INTERNAL STRUCTURE OF CITIES

DISTRICT
1. Central Business District
2. Wholesale Light Manufacturing
3. Low-class Residential
4. Medium-class Residential
5. High-class Residential
6. Heavy Manufacturing
7. Outlying Business District
8. Residential Suburb
9. Industrial Suburb
10. Commuters' Zone

Generalizations of internal structure of cities. The concentric zone theory is a generalization for all cities. The arrangement of the sectors in the sector theory varies from city to city. The diagram for multiple nuclei represents one possible pattern among innumerable variations.

From: Chauncy D. Harris and Edward L. Ullman, "The nature of cities," *The Annals*, 242 (November, 1945).

CN rail yards, Toronto. The growth of industries in a city tends to follow rail and transportation lines in elongated bands.

In the process of expansion outward, each zone tends to invade the next outer area. Immigration is an important stimulus to such expansion, and the distribution of the population among the different areas reflects this. The area in transition contains many of the city's slums. Not only are crime and vice disproportionately concentrated there, but also first-generation immigrant colonies. The zone of working-class homes, in contrast, contains second-generation settlements. Movement here frequently represents an attempt to escape from immigrant colonies, as families achieve greater economic security and become assimilated. The increasing suburbanization of Toronto's Italian population illustrates this movement. Farther out of the city live the affluent who can afford to live at such a distance from the core.

Burgess's scheme, therefore, captures the relationship between spatial and class structures. Nevertheless, it is not fully applicable to Canada's cities. For example, one analysis of changes in the spatial structure of Canada's largest metropolitan areas between 1961 and 1971 shows that in most Canadian cities the socioeconomic composition of residents in inner-city neighborhoods increased, while that of suburban areas decreased (Balakirshnan and Jarvis, 1979:227).

The Sector Theory

Hoyt found Burgess's rigid geometric pattern an unsatisfactory portrayal of the evolution of urban structure. He noted a number of anomalies this scheme ignored. For example, whereas a manufacturing zone did perhaps surround the central business district at one time, this is no longer the case; industries follow railroad and transportation lines in elongated bands rather than remaining near the central business district. Similarly, rental area maps do not show a series of concentric circles with a gradation of rents upward from the centre to the periphery in all sections of the city. Hoyt proposes, instead, that similar types of land use and population originate near the centre of the city and migrate outward in discernible sectors toward the periphery (Figure 22-1). For example, neighborhoods of high-rent or high socioeconomic status expand outward in the same wedge or sector along established lines of travel. Areas of lower status are correspondingly arranged in their own adjacent sectors. Edmonton illustrates this pattern. The sector theory thus presents urban growth as a set of discernible pie-shaped wedges, not concentric zones.

The Multiple Nuclei Theory

Both the concentric-zone and sector theories assume a single centre from which growth of a city extends outward. This assumption is less appropriate for the contemporary metropolitan community. Harris and Ullman (1945) observed that many twentieth-century North American cities are built around several discrete nuclei. The larger the city, the greater the number and diversity of these nuclei. These include, for example, (a) the wholesale and light manufacturing district, which locates near the focus of outside transportation facilities; (b) the heavy industrial district, which, because it requires large tracts of land, tends to be near the edge of the city; and (c) outlying suburban or satellite communities, which may arise with improvement in local transportation facilities. The multiple nuclei theory thus seeks to represent the full complexity of spatial patterns characteristic of the expanding metropolis.

Contemporary Urban Structure

One major process affecting the spatial distribution of urban population and types of land use is decentralization. In the late nineteenth century, the extension of streetcar service (for example, in Toronto) permitted a greater separation between place of residence and place of work. More importantly, it encouraged the development of residential suburbs. Such a trend intensified in the twentieth century as the automobile and other forms of local transport improved accessibility to all parts of the urban area. Today, both residents and business establishments have a greater choice of suitable places to locate within an urban area. Accompanying the outward diffusion of the population has been a redefinition of the functions of the central core. Wholesale and industrial establishments increasingly seek to locate in outlying areas where large tracts of vacant land exist, where property taxes are lower, and access to interurban transport lines are available. The creation of numerous shopping centres on the periphery since 1950 has led to an erosion of the core's prominence in retail business. But this trend has been partly compensated for by an expansion there in office buildings. The core of most of Canada's met-

The development of streetcar and bus routes enabled people to live at a distance from their place of work.

ropolitan areas has emerged as the preeminent office district for their respective regions.

When we examine the spatial distribution of populations in contemporary Canadian cities, we find, indeed, some convergence of the urban-growth models outlined above. That is, socioeconomic status follows a sectoral pattern, as Hoyt had proposed, whereas family status is distributed in concentric zonal fashion. An analysis of differences between neighborhoods within each Canadian metropolitan area reveals

... a widely known fact that, in most cities, age differences in the population are distributed in a

concentric zonal pattern. *Peripheral areas tend to be dominated by families in the early stages of child-bearing and child-rearing; inner suburbs tend to have a somewhat older age profile which approximates that of the city as a whole; and inner city areas are less family-oriented and have a disproportionate share of the city's elderly population, young singles who have left their parental home and childless couples.*

(Hill, 1976:31.)

The three largest metropolitan areas in Canada clearly reveal this pattern. In Montréal, Toronto, and Vancouver, the majority of households in the inner city do not contain children. Children are far more likely to be present in the outlying suburbs of each area.

Residential Mobility

This spatial distribution is a function partly of the sorting-out of people with similar economic, social, or ethnic characteristics. Other factors affecting residential mobility are the price of the dwelling unit, the type and location of residence, as well as individual life style preferences based on income and stage of life cycle. Certain spatial regularities emerge from all these conditions. For example, with respect to the concentric or zonal distribution of family status, as households move through the family-cycle stages (single or pre-family, young married couple, young family with children, mature family with older children, mature family without children, or widowed) their requirements for space change. This need can best be met by relocating at greater distances from the city centre. A concentric pattern is thus produced: households in the child-bearing and child-rearing stages reside on the periphery whereas pre-child or post-child households prefer the core or inner-zone areas. This pattern is evident in Toronto:

Young adults are generally located close to the City's core or Central Business District. Older fami-

lies tend to occupy the next ring out, then middle-aged families, then, in the newest suburban areas, young families. This very simplified model applies particularly well to a rapidly growing metropolis like Toronto. Over time, an 'invasion and succession' process takes place. The innermost ring expands as more young adults move into the core to take advantage of growing social and economic opportunities. They take over areas previously occupied by older families which have started to die. The next two rings remain basically stable, but their population gradually ages over time. They are replaced by a new generation of young adults moving into the core and continuing the process. Meanwhile, many of the young adults marry, form families, and move into new suburban housing built on the periphery, forming a new 'outer ring.'

(City of Toronto, 1980:21.)

Ethnic Residential Segregation

One central feature of Canada's urban spatial mosaic is residential segregation along ethnic lines. An ethnic community represents a form of social organization in which informal relationships and institutions develop to fulfil a range of the needs for members. Territorial segregation helps to strengthen such a community and provides the opportunities for necessary in-group contact.

An ethnic enclave is frequently the product of a variety of factors, including (1) the influence of social networks (friends and kin encourage their intimates to live nearby); (2) the desire to reside with neighbors of similar values and customs; (3) the ability to afford only low-income housing which is frequently concentrated in particular areas of the city; (4) the inability to speak the language of the host society; and (5) active discrimination on the part of the host society toward members of the ethnic group.

In general, ethnic residential segregation is more intense in larger cities. Some ethnic groups tend to cluster more than others. For example, there are more Italian, Indian, and Jewish ghettos in metropolitan Canada than any others. This pattern reflects the varying influences of the factors noted above.

Ecology of Crime

One persistent interest in urban ecology has been the environmental conditions under which crimes of different kinds occur and the spatial distribution of criminal activities. In their classic study of Chicago, for example, Shaw and McKay (1972) documented the extent to which differences in the economic and social characteristics of local areas correlated with variations in rates of delinquents. The areas of heaviest concentration of delinquents were located not far from the central business district. These neighborhoods were characterized by a rapid loss of population, low socioeconomic status, and a large foreign-born population. The rate of delinquency decreased steadily from the core to the periphery of the city, where neighborhoods with the opposite characteristics clustered and where a more stable institutional structure exercised informal social control.

A recent study (McGahan, 1982b; 1984) of the distribution of crime in St. John's, Newfoundland also found that the greater the proportion of multiple-family dwellings, of residents with low levels of education, and of lone-parent families (among other characteristics) in an area of the city, the more likely are the police to receive calls concerning crimes against the person and disturbances in the home.

It is important to remember, however, that such ecological analyses only portray the *conditions* under which crimes of different types seem to occur. They do *not* identify *all* the causes of crime.

The ecology of crime also seeks to examine how specific types of land use provide opportunities for crime. The broad span of unsupervised parking lots adjacent to new shopping malls, for example, offer opportunities for theft from unlocked cars. Similarly, the design of buildings may not be conducive to the kind of informal surveillance

The areas bordering on a city's central business district often experience the heaviest concentration of crime and delinquency.

by neighbors that discourages possible burglaries or break and entries.

URBAN PLANNING

The rapid growth of cities in Canada and in the rest of the world has led to a variety of problems and issues that have underlined the need for planning. In the preceding section we examined the nature of urbanization; here we wish to address how government seeks to control and direct that growth.

The history of the North American city in the twentieth century is one of increasing government intervention in urban processes. Although the emergence of urban planning as a bureaucratized activity and formal profession is a contemporary phenomenon, we must not ignore the historical roots of planning in Canada. Settlements as early as the 1700s reflected efforts to incorporate spatial plans. For example, the founding of Louisburg in 1726 was carefully planned as a military base and town to accommodate several thousand inhabitants.

Despite these roots, planning, both social and physical, was at an extremely rudimentary level throughout the nineteenth century. We find, for example, during the first half of the 1800s the continued failure of such communities as Saint John, Halifax, and St. John's to develop a systematic employment policy for the poor. Nor were the structural causes of unemployment directly attacked; instead, poverty was interpreted as a moral not an economic problem.

What urban reform measures were implemented between 1880 and 1920 reflected the values and interests of the dominant middle class (Rutherford, 1974). Creating an aesthetically pleasing environment by constructing civic monuments, for example, was one such measure and it was thought that this might remedy some of the major social problems existing in the largest cities. The less affluent were encouraged to internalize middle-class values and mores.

The urban middle class also encouraged municipal control of utility companies as a source of cheap, reliable power and transport facilities, which at the same time would enhance real-estate values and business profits, and make the city more attractive for industrial investment and expansion. The urban municipality was increasingly viewed as a business corporation that must be managed efficiently and economically. Administration was to be separated from politics, and civic government bureaucratized and run by experts. City-wide boards and commissions and the separation of legislative and executive functions were viewed as necessary instruments for a competent city government. They also served to insulate that government from political challenges to middle-class domination by the less affluent.

Modern city planning, as it began to emerge in Canada, thus reflected a middle-class ethos. It was also influenced by American reform ideology as well as by the efforts in Britain to regulate urban life through legislation. Urban growth in the early years of this century demanded regulation — but in a form that sustained the power and influence of the middle class. Municipal and housing reforms were encouraged, but in ways that would not undermine the desirable "bourgeois character of the city." (Rutherford, 1977.) This situation reminds us of the need to consider how the process of urban planning relates to the manner in which power is distributed in the city, an issue that the Marxist perspective emphasizes.

Urban planning policies and techniques frequently reflect and advance the interests of the dominant social class. North American urban renewal projects, for example, in many cases appear to have benefited the commercial and corporate interests encouraging these projects more than inner-city residents who are forced to relocate.

More generally, we should also recognize that planning policies often reflect how the urban community is conceptualized, according to what social model is used to portray its structure. Here urban planning intersects with competing sociological theories — the consensus versus conflict models, for example. Throughout its early stage of development Canadian urban planning assumed that urban structure is based on a fundamental consensus of interests and values, the middle-class ethos noted earlier. The biases inherent in the consensus perspective become evident when, as Lorimer (1978) and others have shown, we identify such conflicts of interest as that between the urban property industry and citizen groups. The conflict perspective advises us to see how planning efforts benefit or disadvantage competing groups. Planning is not a neutral activity, but relates directly to the structure of power and wealth in the urban community.

Issues in Urban Planning

Rapid urbanization is accompanied by a variety of serious problems that tax the ingenuity and imagination of urban planners. This is especially evident in Third World countries. For example, by 1990 the total population in Latin American cities over 20 000 will be 220 million, of which one-third to two-thirds will be squatters, people illegally occupying public or private land or buildings (Anthony, 1979). The squatter population has been growing much more rapidly than the total population. Most squatters are rural migrants seeking employment in the cities, which are incapable of supplying adequate low-cost housing for them. From salvage materials, they build their own shanties in the worst locations of the city.

The initial response to the emergence of these settlements was one that reflected the distribution of power and wealth in these societies. Squatters were viewed as "parasites"; their communities were demolished and the residents were relocated in public housing on the periphery. However, this only compounded the problem. The stock of low-cost housing was eroded even further. The resettled squatters faced increased expenditures, unacceptable distance from work, and alienation from the wider society.

More realistic experiments have been mounted in Columbia, El Salvador, Uruguay, and elsewhere to provide adequate housing and skills for squatters. These projects allow residents to acquire legal title to their land, an important prerequisite to community stability. Through various self-help and mutual-help schemes, the squatters are able to contribute to the upgrading of their settlements themselves. Although efforts are being made by the national governments in these countries to meet some of their needs, the task remains immense.

In many cities of developing nations, providing clean water to all inhabitants remains a problem. Fetching water from a local pump is often the responsibility of the children of a household.

In Canada, the continued growth of urban areas in the decades following World War II posed serious problems, ranging from the need for more efficient mass-transit systems and more adequate supplies of low-cost housing, to environmental decay. That such problems require a more comprehensive understanding of the interrelation among the demographic, ecological, economic, social, and political aspects of urbanization and urbanism for their solution is increasingly recognized. We can identify some of the central issues in contemporary urban planning.

Urban Renewal

In its simplest form, urban renewal can be defined as "the process by which the various parts of an urban area are repaired or replaced as they become physically deteriorated, obsolete, or suitable for alternate use." (Bunge, 1967.) During the last several decades in North American urban communities, an important attempt to change the inner-city physical environment has been initiated through the development of urban-renewal projects. These projects have varied greatly in scale and location, including such cases as the total destruction of Africville on the periphery of Halifax, the redevelopment of the Ross-Blanshard area of Victoria in the late 1960s, and the rehabilitation of the Strathcona area in Vancouver.

In the past, the Canadian urban-renewal program was characterized by several weaknesses. Its general objectives were not always clearly defined, and there was a vagueness in the exact meaning of "urban blight." More concretely, it was difficult to co-ordinate the responsibilities of the three levels of government — municipal, provincial, and federal — in carrying out renewal programs. This lengthened the time lag between the initiation of a renewal study and its actual implementation. Failure to consider the social consequences of renewal programs also became increasingly recognized as a serious shortcoming. When residents of inner-city areas slated for urban renewal identify strongly with many aspects of their neighborhood, relocation from it can have disruptive effects. As a result, more recent amendments to the National Housing Act have sought to give greater attention to the preservation and improvement of existing neighborhoods.

Urban Municipal Reorganization

One characteristic of urbanization (understood ecologically as the spread of a more comprehensive and intricate territorial division of labor) is the increasing irrelevance of urban municipal boundaries. That is, the "jurisdiction space" of a municipality does not parallel the functional inte-

gration of an area or region. The scope of such problems as the need to control environmental pollution, curb urban sprawl, and provide improved transportation systems extends beyond municipal boundaries. Furthermore, municipal fragmentation (that is, the co-existence of a number of distinct and independent municipalities within the same region) results in inefficient and costly duplication of services in the region, inequities in tax revenues and service expenditures among adjacent municipalities, and in inadequate planning. A variety of efforts have been made to reorganize urban municipalities in such a way that regional coordination and planning could be improved and political fragmentation reduced. These include (1) the creation of special-purpose agencies, such as a Transportation Authority, with responsibility for providing a particular service to adjacent municipalities; (2) the creation of a federated type of municipal government such as Metro Toronto; and (3) the extension of urban municipal boundaries, as occurred with the creation of Unicity Winnipeg in 1972.

This quest to adjust municipal boundaries to planning and administrative needs reflects an emphasis on economy and efficiency in the provision of services. Whether municipal reorganization adequately permits citizen participation in local decision-making remains a contentious issue.

New Community-Formation

In Britain, after World War II, a number of new towns were built in an attempt to regulate the spatial distribution of the urban population. The goal of this program, linked to regional development policies, was to create a series of viable communities that offered employment opportunities to their residents while encouraging decentralization of the population. Similarly, in Sweden the construction of new towns is viewed as an important strategy for creating a better-integrated social and physical environment.

Over the last several decades, many new communities have been constructed in Canada (Pressman, 1975). *Satellite towns*, such as Don Mills, outside Toronto, and Kanata, outside Ottawa, were developed to provide additional housing in a metropolitan area. Frequently financed and constructed by private companies, these are similar to suburbs in that they offer few employment opportunities for their residents, who must commute elsewhere to work. *Satellite cities* accommodate a larger population than towns and offer opportunities for employment within the cities themselves. Bramalea, Meadowvale, Erin Mills, and North Pickering are viewed as valuable channels for structuring regional growth and attaining a more balanced population distribution in an area.

An important issue is whether, in the long run, satellite towns and cities will be effective tools in redistributing the urban population.

National Urban Policy

The goal of such a national policy is to regulate the rate of growth and spatial distribution of urban development on a national level. The formulation of such a policy is more difficult to achieve in Canada than in countries such as Britain or Sweden, where the political system is more centralized, where there is greater public acceptance of government involvement in local affairs, and where a greater homogeneity of the population exists, such that a consensus on public goals is more feasible (Bourne, 1975).

The term "national urban policy" is a misleading one, since it suggests a uniform set of strategies in directing urban development, regardless of local circumstances. Such an approach is undesirable in a country like Canada that has significant regional differences. Urban and regional planning must be closely linked.

The Urban Future: Counter-Urbanization?

Urban planning seeks not only to react to problems but also to take account of emerging trends. In this light, we should observe that in Canada the last decade has represented the first time in a hundred years that the rate of population growth in rural areas has been greater than that in urban areas. With the exception of the Prairies and the Yukon, the proportion living in urban areas declined in all parts of the country. Rural fringe areas of large metropolitan areas are growing rapidly in population, as are medium-sized cities, that is, those with 30 000 to 99 000 residents. Increasingly, Canadians are locating outside the boundaries of large cities and metropolitan areas.

Called the "counter-urbanization" movement, this trend is not confined to Canada. A similar pattern is appearing in the United States, Europe, and even in some underdeveloped countries (Berry, 1978). This recent dispersal of population has been encouraged by, for example, the decentralization of rapidly expanding economic activities in the tertiary sector of the economy (such as the movement to small cities of research, and to development and consulting firms). Similarly, the wider distribution of transportation, education, and health facilities throughout the national urban network have made it more possible for Canadians today to settle in non-metropolitan areas without incurring significant liabilities.

If this trend continues into the next decade, Canada's settlement pattern will be marked by a slowdown in growth or even decline in the largest cities, a deconcentration of population, and significant diversity in the growth rates of individual communities. Insofar as planning in the past has assumed continued population concentration in metropolitan areas, government policies will need to be reoriented, with greater attention directed to the development of towns and small cities and to helping the largest communities adjust to this reversal.

We should also recognize that our urban future in Canada will be influenced by how other issues are resolved. These include (1) control over foreign ownership of urban-based corporations; (2) environmental pollution, especially in our urban centres; and (3) the range and quality of employ-

In Canada, rural fringe areas of large metropolitan areas are growing more rapidly than the cities themselves.

ment opportunities for women in both small cities and metropolitan communities. The quality of life for those living in Canada's national system of cities is equally dependent on the attention to these problems.

SUMMARY

1. In this chapter, we have focused on the city as a socio-spatial system. This entails analysis, first, of how this system has evolved, or of the process of urbanization. We examined some of the demographic and ecological dimensions of the urban transformation. This process in Canada has been manifested in the emergence of distinct types of urban communities — including the early colonial town, commercial centre, metropolitan community, and single-industry community. The urbanized nature of Canadian society is perhaps most fully revealed in the conception of it as a national system of cities.

2. The study of urbanism explains how urban communities are socially organized, what shape their institutions take, and how social relationships and groups are structured. Classical urban theory, as espoused by Tönnies and the Chicago School, was found to be inappropriate in understanding the complexity of urban social life. Alternate theories, such as the subcultural and the

Marxist, seek to articulate more fully how cities function socially and culturally.

3. The social order of cities is revealed in its spatial structure. Urban ecology pursues this link by examining how the spatial distribution of the population and types of land use are patterned and change with the growth of cities. The impact of improved systems of local transportation on this distribution is evident. With urban growth, subareas within the city become differentiated. A sifting and sorting of population takes place, in which those with similar economic, social, or ethnic characteristics concentrate in the same part of the city. The creation of ethnic spatial enclaves illustrates most vividly how the social and spatial aspects of an urban community are closely linked.

4. Urban planning represents an attempt to gain control of the development of cities. We have reviewed briefly some of the key issues here, and indeed some of the biases in city planning as it developed in Canada. It should be clear that, without adequate theories and models of urbanization and of urbanism, our efforts to direct the future growth of Canada's cities will inevitably falter. Our ability to implement urban policies is directly contingent on our understanding of how cities are demographically, ecologically, and socially changing.

GLOSSARY

Chicago School. Scholars at the University of Chicago in the 1920s and 1930s who established the study of urbanization as a distinctive empirical inquiry.

City. A relatively large, dense and permanent settlement in which the majority of residents do not produce their own food.

Colonial town. The earliest type of urban community in Canada, functioned as the agent of European metropolitan centres, as a garrison or administrative hub, as an entrepot.

Commercial centre. Type of urban community that emerged in early nineteenth century, characterized as a node for the gathering and exporting of staples, as a service centre for an expanding hinterland, and by the small scale of its economic enterprises.

Compositional theory. Argued that urban social life is a product of the social class, ethnic and family status characteristics of the urban population rather than the size, density of an urban community.

Concentric zone theory. Population and land use types vary in terms of distinctive concentric zones around the central business district.

Decentralization. A process of outward spread of the urban population from the core accompanied by diffusion of such economic activities as wholesaling and manufacturing.

Determinist theory. Argued that the size, density and heterogeneity of a city have important social consequences.

Ethnic residential segregation. A concentration of one or more ethnic groups in specific sections of the city.

Gemeinschaft. A primary group type relationship as exemplified in kinship and friendship.

Gesellschaft. A secondary group type relationship as exemplified in an economic exchange.

Metropolitan community. A localized territorial system in which a core community is economically and socially linked to surrounding areas. Defined in the 1981 Census as the main labour market area of an urbanized core (or continuously built-up area) having 100,000 or more population.

Modernization. A process of social change involving urbanization, industrialization, and bureaucratization.

Multiple nuclei theory. Sees the land-use pattern of many contemporary cities as being focused around several discrete nuclei.

National urban policy. An effort to regulate on a national level the rate of growth and spatial distribution of urban development.

Residential mobility. A movement of different categories of the population throughout the city. Accounts for the spatial distribution of those with particular economic, social or ethnic characteristics.

Satellite city. A new community developed to accommodate a relatively large population and to provide opportunities for employment; viewed as a valuable channel for structuring regional growth.

Satellite town. A new community developed to provide additional housing in a metropolitan area; offers few employment opportunities for its own residents.

Sector theory. Proposes that similar types of land use and population originate near the centre of the city and extend outward in discernible sectors toward the periphery. Focuses especially on the spatial distribution of socioeconomic status in the urban population.

Single-industry community. A community whose economic structure is based on one primary function such as resource extraction.

Social network analysis. Sees the urban community as a complex of social networks in which individuals and collectivities are linked.

Subcultural theory. Argues that population concentration leads to distinctive subcultures; interprets deviance in the city not as a consequence of social disorganization but of subcultural strength.

Typological perspective. A paradigm of classical urban theory that sought to explain the nature of urban social organization by contrasting it with the non-urban.

Urban ecology. Examines patterns of urban growth as well as the spatial distribution within cities of population and land-use types.

Urbanism. The nature of social life found within cities — their institutions, types of groups, and patterns of social relationships.

Urbanization: demographic meaning. The increase in the number of urban centres, in the size of individual cities, and in the proportion of the total population living in urban areas.

Urbanization: ecological meaning. An expansion of the organization or set of functional relationships through which a specific population is able to satisfy its daily needs. It consists of the process of growth from a highly localized unit to a complex, more comprehensive territorial system.

Urban municipal reorganization. An attempt to adjust the jurisdictional authority of a municipality to more fully coincide with the level of functional integration of an urban area.

Urban planning. A governmental attempt to direct and control the process of urbanization and the distribution of population and land use types with the city.

Urban population. Those persons living in an area having a population concentration of 1,000 or more and a population density of 400 or more per square kilometre.

Urban region. An extensive territorial system in which cities and metropolitan communities are linked through economic ties and population flows.

Urban renewal. The process by which various parts of the city are repaired or replaced as they become physically deteriorated, obsolete, or suitable for alternate use.

FURTHER READING

Artibise, Alan F.J. *Winnipeg: A Social History of Urban Growth, 1874–1914.* Montréal: McGill-Queen's University Press, 1975. This is a useful case study of urban development. Illustrates clearly the variety of factors associated with urban growth.

Bourne, L.S. *Urban Systems: Strategies For Regulation.* Oxford: Clarendon Press, 1975. Presents a general overview of the Canadian system of cities and its planning requirements, with comparisons to other countries.

Fischer, Claude S. *The Urban Experience.* New York: Harcourt Brace Jovanovich, 1976. Comparison of the determinist, compositional, and subcultural theories of urbanism.

Katz, Michael B. *The People of Hamilton, Canada West: Family and Class In A Mid-Nineteenth-Century City*. Cambridge: Harvard University Press, 1975. Presents the major demographic and social characteristics of the commercial city, ranging from household structure to patterns of inequality.

McGahan, Peter. *Urban Sociology in Canada*. Toronto: Butterworth, 1982. Elaborates on the themes presented in this chapter, introducing the major areas of study in urban sociology.

Michelson, William. *Man And His Urban Environment: A Sociological Approach*. Don Mills, Ontario: Addison-Wesley Publishers, 1970. Examines how the environment, as an ecological fact, influences human behavior.

Ray, D. Michael. *Canadian Urban Trends*. Toronto: Copp Clark, 1976. Presents a useful profile of the demographic characteristics of Canada's urban communities.

Schnore, Leo F. *The Urban Scene: Human Ecology and Demography*. New York: Free Press, 1965. Introduction to the nature of urban ecology, its theoretical roots, and some of its empirical interests.

Spelt, Jacob. *Urban Development In South-Central Ontario*. Toronto: McClelland and Stewart, 1972. Case study of urban development that illustrates the demographic and ecological meaning of urbanization.

Stelter, Gilbert and Alan F.J. Artibise. *The Canadian City: Essays In Urban History*. Toronto: McClelland and Stewart, 1977. Collection of articles relating to various aspects of the history of urban development in different sections of the country.

CHAPTER TWENTY-THREE

Collective Behavior and Social Movements

MARLENE MACKIE

Collective behavior, in one form or another, has occurred throughout history, in every society on earth. In our own contemporary society, it takes place in our downtown streets, athletic stadiums, stores, movie theatres, funeral parlors, and university classrooms. Our newspapers and newsmagazines are filled with accounts of collective behavior. This media interest is hardly surprising since this label includes some of the most colorful, dramatic, eccentric, and dangerous conduct of which human beings are capable.

These diverse types of behavior all involve *nonroutine social behavior*. Sociologists usually

Orson Welles delivers a radio broadcast from a New York studio in 1938, the same year his radio dramatization of H.G. Wells's fantasy, *The War of the Worlds*, caused widespread panic.

study normative behavior, which is patterned according to the common understandings in a culture. Collective behavior is one major exception.

Take the university classroom, for example. Most of what happens there is predictable. Even the first day of class, when everyone is a stranger, follows certain routines. A student who has registered for Introductory Sociology locates the appropriate lecture hall, finds an empty seat, faces the blackboard and ceases loud talking, laughing, and gum-chewing. The student opens a brand-new notebook and waits expectantly for someone to appear at the front of the classroom and begin talking authoritatively. The student plays the "student role." The professor plays the "professor role."

Though they have never met before, well-established norms guide the behavior of everyone concerned. Suppose the predictability of this classroom scene is shattered. The lights go out. An intruder points a rifle at the class. The situation is now undefined and the people in it are not sure what is happening or what they should do about it. Mutual influence and interaction will likely occur as the participants look to one another for cues.

The purpose of this chapter, then, is to discuss social behavior, which is to some extent outside established, predictable norms.

Collective Behavior Defined

A formal definition that elaborates on our shorthand definition of nonroutine social behavior is the following: Collective behavior is the specialty area within sociology which studies the social reactions to situations where the norms are nonexistent, ambiguous, or disputed (based on Turner and Killian, 1957:12). The key terms in this definition are worth emphasizing. *Norms*, you will recall, are rules or standards of conduct. They express cultural prescriptions for how people should feel, think, and act under a variety of circumstances. Collective behavior occurs when a situation is *not* covered by norms. The situation may be so novel that norms simply do not exist. In 1938, for example, millions of North Americans who were frightened by a radio dramatization of an invasion from Mars had absolutely no idea how to respond to this imminent problem (Cantril, 1940).

More unusual, though, are situations where participants are confused about the applicability of particular norms.

Collective behavior also occurs when norms are disputed. That is, the participants know perfectly well which norms apply but they choose to challenge the rules. On Easter Sunday, 1983, tens of thousands of English demonstrators formed a 22-kilometre human chain, linking three nuclear

Anti-nuclear protestors dance in a circle outside the Greenham Common Air Base, Easter, 1984, in protest of cruise missile storage there.

arms facilities. Their symbolic attempt to "break the nuclear chain" protested the norms of nuclear weapon testing and build-up. Collective behavior and deviance, then, sometimes overlap.

It is essential to remember that collective behavior is *social* behavior. The unit of analysis is the group, not the individual, as the sociologist studies interaction in collectivities, such as mobs, audiences, and social movements.

A final definitional point concerns the size of the collectivity. Most authorities (Lofland, 1981: 413) agree that for an episode to qualify as collective behavior, it must involve relatively large numbers of people. Although it is impossible to specify precisely how many people are required, it is intuitively clear that most phenomena of interest to the field, such as fads and riots, involve many participants.

THE SOCIOLOGY OF
COLLECTIVE BEHAVIOR

Before we proceed to discuss particular theories
and types of collective behavior, some general comments about this specialty area are in order.

The Importance of
Collective Behavior

There are three main reasons why sociologists
believe this specialty merits serious attention
(Milgram and Toch, 1969):

1. Understanding social change is one of sociology's fundamental tasks. Collective behavior, in
the form of crowds, riots, and social movements,
often catalyzes or accompanies historical change.
Therefore, its study helps sociologists make progress toward their general goal.
2. The study of collective behavior tells us something new about the ranges of social behavior of
which human beings are capable. Crowd behavior reveals extremes of heroism, on the one hand,
and savagery and destructiveness, on the other.
3. Sociological research of collective behavior can
be of help to professionals who concern themselves
with the prevention and control of some forms of
collective behavior, such as riots and disasters.

The State of Development of the Field
of Collective Behavior

Social analysts' fascination with mobs has a long
history. Gustave Le Bon, who is identified as the
founder of collective behavior, published *The
Crowd* in 1895. His book attempted to explain
the termoil of French political events, some of
which he himself experienced. The field became
a recognized sociological specialty when sociologists Park and Burgess (1921) coined the term "collective behavior."

It is therefore ironic that in comparison with
many other sociological specialties, collective
behavior remains an underdeveloped area. The
field is "long on ... speculative explanation and

short on demonstrable propositions" (Evans, 1969:
2), which lead to prediction. Strictly speaking,
many of the statements made in this chapter
should begin with precautionary words or statements, such as "perhaps" or "probably" or "we
think this is true." But that would make tedious
reading. Instead, we will warn readers at the very
beginning and let it go at that.

Two interrelated factors are responsible for collective behavior's relative lack of sophistication.
First, the area is theoretically weak. That is, it
currently lacks a satisfactory theoretical framework for explaining the wide range of phenomena embraced by the concept of "nonroutine social
behavior." Second, the subject matter of the sociology of collective behavior presents the researcher
with some unique methodological difficulties.
Some types, such as riots and disasters, are unpredictable and ephemeral. A researcher cannot
know about them in advance and be prepared to
study them. Moreover, sociology's usual methods,
such as the questionnaire and interview, are often
inappropriate. Imagine tapping a riot participant
on the shoulder and saying, "Pardon me, I'm a
sociologist. Do you mind answering a few questions?" However, a recent resurgence of interest
in the field is resulting in the development of
promising new theoretical and methodological
approaches. In time, the above deficiencies should
be rectified.

TYPES OF COLLECTIVITIES

In 1939, Herbert Blumer outlined a systematic
typology of collectivities (or groupings) where collective behavior occurs. This work provided the
basis for much recent research in collective behavior and mass communications. It still serves as
some of the modern field's basic vocabulary.

Before describing Blumer's types, it should be
pointed out that actual events are sometimes difficult to categorize, since they can embody elements of two or more types; also, over time, actual
episodes may transform from one type to another.

For example, a cheerful group of merrymakers, interfered with by the police, may turn into a nasty mob.

Blumer's first four types of collectivities are all characterized by a short time span and crowd participants in spatial contiguity. The last two types of collectivities usually have a somewhat longer life span. In addition, the participants do not share geographical space.

1. The *casual crowd* is a weak group form, with little interaction and scarcely any unity. Examples are "sidewalk superintendents" attracted by construction site activities; shoppers waiting for admission to a store; a ticket queue. Though the collective behavior in the casual crowd is "feeble" (to use Blumer's adjective), there is the potential for more dramatic developments. Suppose a shopper suddenly collapses with a heart attack. How will the witnesses handle this occurrence? When more intense forms of interaction occur, however, we are no longer dealing with a casual crowd.

2. The *conventional crowd* has two main characteristics: regularized, established ways of behaving (the football audience stands when the national anthem is played), and passive one-to-one relationship with an object of attention. Until behavior departs from the usual norms and interaction replaces the one-to-one fixation, collective behavior does not occur.

3. The *acting crowd* focuses on some external aspect of the environment. The acting crowd "is spontaneous and lives in the momentary present." It has "no conventions, established expectations, or rules." (Blumer, 1946:180.) Now we have fully-developed collective behavior that comes in three forms: the *acting, aggressive crowd* is a mob whose goal is to attack, lynch, kill, maim, loot, destroy; the *acting, escaping crowd* or panic-stricken crowd attempts to flee from danger; members of the *acting, acquisitive crowd* are in competition over some valuable reward that they believe to be in short supply. The sometimes violent behavior of 1983 Christmas shoppers, intent on acquiring scarce Cabbage Patch dolls, is an example.

Worshippers wave their hands during a hymn-singing session at the Charismatic Catholic Conference held in Kingston, Ontario. Highly expressive forms of worship have proliferated among many Christian denominations in recent years.

4. The *expressive crowd* has an internal goal: to change the mood, behavior, or self-image of the members themselves. Tension is released in a permissive setting through physical activity — laughing, shouting, dancing, praying, speaking in tongues.

5. The *mass* is composed of a large number of people who are physically separate, anonymous, and unorganized. Their individual activity takes the form of selecting a new fad or fashion, a party platform, a religious gospel, and so forth. When these lines of individual activity converge, the influ-

Early in this century, women rallied to shape public opinion regarding their rights in public and private life.

ence of the mass can be enormous. For example, in seventeenth-century Holland, a large part of the population was captivated by the get-rich-quick frenzy of the famous tulip craze. The price for one bulb of a variety called *Semper Augustus* rose to six thousand florins (the cost of a house). When the speculation fever subsided, fortunes were lost (Brown, 1965:719).

Contemporary interpretors emphasize that the individuals in a mass are not as psychologically isolated from one another as Blumer imagined. Decisions to choose a new fashion or political candidate or religion are influenced by primary group, as well as impersonal, mass media pressures.

6. The *public* refers to a collectivity that is confronted by an issue, divided in its ideas as to how to meet the issue, and that engages in debate over the issue. Should abortion be available on demand? Should nuclear weapons be tested? When the issue is resolved or supplanted by a more vital issue, the public fades away.

Public opinion is a critical determinant of the outcome of collective behavior episodes. For instance, the public regarded the British Suffragette Movement as "a strange, melodramatic, and unlovely phenomenon." (Smith, 1957:689.) Englishwomen were not granted the vote until after their contribution to World War I swayed public opinion (Mackie, 1983:291).

THEORIES OF COLLECTIVE BEHAVIOR

Emergent Norm Theory

Emergent norm theory, developed by Turner and Killian (1972), applies the perspective of symbolic interactionism to collective behavior. This approach takes as its starting point situations where the norms are nonexistent, ambiguous, or disputed. According to Turner and Killian, when a crowd confronts such a situation, the problem is resolved by the emergence of norms. The term "emergent" means both that norms are "hatched" on the spot and that they are, to some degree, specific to that situation.

Suppose a riot is underway in a large city. In the confusion, the content of liquor stores, jewellery stores, furniture stores is there for the taking. Will crowd members loot unprotected property? Sociologists report looting to be widespread during civil disturbances. Norms emerge among local residents that sanction looting. Large numbers of people openly help themselves to goods in a carnival atmosphere. What happens if a community is disorganized by a natural disaster, such as a flood? Under this circumstance, the emergent norms protect private property. The small amount of actual looting that does occur is done furtively by individuals from outside the stricken community. However, another type of emergent norm during disasters reinforces the stereotype of widespread looting. Private property rights are often suspended when food and blankets, for instance, become "community property" to be used for the common good (Quarantelli and Dynes, 1970).

The norms that emerge in unstructured situations respond to four general problems. First, unless the situation is self-evident, crowd participants attempt to define the situation. What is happening here? Second, there is a need to know what people in such situations are supposed to do. Third, crowd members are often concerned with the type of emotions appropriate here. Fourth, the unstructured situation requires leadership. Who will act first?

Let us take the example of a shopper who has suffered a heart attack and is slumped on the floor of a department store, surrounded by mystified bystanders. It is reasonable to suppose that certain norms emerge. This is an emergency. The woman on the floor is ill, not drunk or sleeping. She should be helped. The matter is serious, not funny. The emergent leader is the crowd member who steps forward to administer first-aid and who asks someone else to call an ambulance.

The challenge of emergent norm theory is to explain how the search for meaning occurs, how these new norms come into being. No simple answer exists. However, the crowd members' discomfort with ambiguity and consequent eagerness for "answers" are important factors. The emergent social reality is also facilitated by social pressures (exerted by crowd members) against nonconformity with the emerging definitions of the situation. The dominant crowd mood inhibits contrary behavior. The righteousness of crowds, the illusion of their unanimity, encourages behavior consistent with the emerging norms and discourages dissent. For instance, a reluctant member of a lynch mob, with no stomach for murder, will likely consider his/her own safety and withdraw, rather than attempt to dissuade the others.

Value-Added Theory and the Rioting Crowd

Smelser's (1962) work is the most systematic, general theory of collective behavior in existence. His very complex theory emerges from the functionalist perspective. It emphasizes social not psychological mechanisms.

An economist as well as a sociologist, Smelser borrowed the central concept of *"value-added"* from economics. At the simplest level, the notion of "value-added" acknowledges that collective behavior, like all social behavior, is caused by many factors. To be technically accurate, "value-added" means that any product (whether a commodity on the market or an episode of collective behavior) occurs through a series of stages. Each stage in the process adds its value to the final cost of the product. The stages must occur according to a certain pattern before the next stage can contribute its particular value to the finished product. Every stage in the value-added process is a necessary condition for the effective addition of value at the next stage. The sufficient condition for the final product is the combination of every necessary condition according to a definite pattern. As the value-added process progresses, it narrows the possibilities for what the final product might become (Smelser, 1962:14).

Clearly, an example is needed to help make sense of all this abstraction. Consider the steps by which beef on the hoof becomes tranformed into a T-bone steak on the barbeque. The beast is nurtured from calf to full-grown adult by the rancher, auctioned to the slaughter house buyer, and trucked to the slaughterhouse. Less than half the animal is eventually displayed in neat cuts under plastic wrap in the supermarket. A 1000 pound animal loses about a third of its weight at the packers. Few consumers are interested in braised hoofs or ears! The retailer lops off another 180 pounds or so of fat, bone, and waste. The choice pieces of the carcass amount to seventy-five pounds, and are dwarfed by the mound of stewing meat and pot roast. At every stage of the process, from rancher to trucker to packing plant to retail butcher, value is added and the cost goes up. The final cost of the T-bone steak reflects the pyramid effect of intervening costs. Moreover, the "causes" of the steak-producing process must occur in a certain *order*. The plastic wrap cannot go on before the slaughter occurs!

Smelser calls the "causes" of collective behavior "determinants." There are six determinants: (1) structural conduciveness; (2) structural strain; (3) growth and spread of a generalized belief; (4) precipitating event; (5) mobilization of participants for action; (6) operation of social control. These six determinants are the necessary conditions for the production of collective behavior. All six, taken together, are the "sufficient condition" for the production of collective behavior. Although each determinant has a general definition (which we will come to in a moment), each determinant comes in several varieties. The combination of varieties determines what kind of collective behavior will occur — a craze, panic, riot, or social movement.

Smelser's aim is to predict the occurrence of many types of collective behavior. However, it is impossible to think about all these forms simultaneously, so let's concentrate on the riot. The newsmagazine and newspaper descriptions that follow are illustrative material, not scientific data.

The Montréal Riot

The television scenes of sniper fire, shattered storefronts and armed soldiers patrolling the streets were all a familiar part of the newsreels of the sixties. The shock this time was that they came not via the U.S. networks, but live from Montreal. For the first time in any major Canadian urban center, the police and fire departments walked off their jobs in a wildcat strike, leaving a frightened city at the mercy of its own worst elements for 16 hours. The result was a night of lawlessness in the country's largest metropolis that caused one death, an estimated $2,350,000 in damages and, by the time it ended, the Quebec provincial police and the army had been called in.

(Time, 17 October 1969.)

The illegal strike precipitated an assortment of activities. At first, there was a carnival atmosphere as motorists ran red lights and ignored parking regulations. This lightheartedness did not last long. Sixty-one armed holdups occurred. Rioters attacked Mayor Drapeau's restaurant, smashing windows and chandeliers and setting draperies on fire. McGill University and the Queen Elizabeth Hotel, both English-Canadian symbols, became targets. Bank and store windows were smashed and looters ran rampant. Militant taxi drivers seized the opportunity to settle a long-standing grievance with the Murray Hill Limousine Service, which had exclusive airport rights. Limousines were overturned and set on fire. Molotov cocktails were thrown inside parked buses. Rifle fire was exchanged. Twelve persons were wounded and a provincial policeman fell dead (Hagan, 1977:192).

Structural Conduciveness

Smelser's most general determinant refers to social conditions that are permissive of a given sort of collective behavior. As far as riots are concerned, social cleavages are necessary. Because a large compact minority is required, and because such populations exist only in cities, race riots are urban phenomena. Further social conditions that permit riots to occur are an absence of adequately functioning grievance channels and a loosening of stable, social linkages. On hot summer nights and weekends, people are temporarily freed from familial and occupational roles and on the streets, available to riot (Smelser, 1968). Young people tend to be disproportionately involved in riots, partly because they are not yet securely linked into the responsibilities of adult roles. When effective grievance channels exist, people know they can complain about their troubles. When they do not, frustration builds.

Did structurally conducive conditions exist in Montréal prior to the October, 1969 riot? Remember that this determinant describes a situation that exists for weeks, months, even years before collective behavior actually takes place. Montréal was certainly a city with many cleavages, especially between French Canadians and English Canadians. In the two years before the riot, the terrorist fringe of the Québec separatist movement was involved in as many as 100 explosions — in suburban mailboxes, downtown office buildings and stores, the Stock Exchange (*Time*, 17 October 1969). The taxi dispute was also of long standing. Presumably, people felt complaining to authorities through formal grievance channels would do no good. Destructiveness took place at night when people were available for rioting.

Structural conduciveness is the most general determinant, necessary but far from sufficient. With the addition of further determinants comes a progressive narrowing of the range of possible outcomes.

Structural Strain

The second determinant describes a conflict between values and norms, a conflict between the way things ought to be and the way things actually are. Since the Quiet Revolution of the early 1960s, no part of Canada has been subject to more strain than Québec. Multi-ethnic frustrations characterized Montréal. A prolonged economic slump followed the boom of Expo year. Unemployment and taxes were higher than elsewhere in Canada. Shortages of public housing and welfare were acute. General societal values of equality and opportunity for all Canadians, respect for all ethnic groups, and so on, conflicted with actual Montréal conditions.

Growth and Spread of Generalized Beliefs

Such beliefs identify the source of strain, attribute certain characteristics to the source, and recommend that certain actions be taken to relieve the strain. Over time, the people dwelling in conditions of conduciveness and strain develop "theories" about their situation. Often scapegoating occurs as the "enemy" becomes symbolized. Different types of collective behavior situations involve different types of beliefs.

We can imagine various segments of the Montréal population discussing events. Though French-English enmity was not a prominent part of the riot, each ethnic group had complained about the other. Outrage likely grew among taxi drivers excluded from the lucrative airport franchise. Perhaps they spoke of violence as an appropriate reaction long before it happened. We know that many blamed Mayor Drapeau for their plight. Although "his 'politics of prestige' had conjured up Expo, Montreal's gleaming metro, baseball's Expos, and a vital downtown area," critics felt his "preoccupation with international prestige unfortunately (had) given a low priority to more basic concerns" of the urban poor (*Time*, 17 October 1969). Two weeks prior to the riot damage to the Mayor's restaurant, fifteen sticks of dynamite wrecked his home.

The range of possibilities narrows. A riot becomes increasingly probable. However, other responses can still occur. People under strain may turn to alcohol or drugs. They may form a social movement or take up religion. Or they may do nothing at all.

Precipitating Events

Smelser's fourth determinant is a dramatic event that gives the beliefs concrete substance. This "triggering" event is close in time to the collective behavior. Often the mass media mistake it for the sufficient cause.

A precipitating factor taken by itself cannot cause a collective episode. In order to do so, it must occur in the context of the other determinants of conduciveness, strain, and generalized belief.
(Milgram and Toch, 1969:558.)

Many of the U.S. race riots in the 1960s were precipitated by a confrontation between white policemen and black citizens, which was interpreted by black witnesses as discriminatory. What about Montréal?

The walkout of 3700 policemen undeniably precipitated the riot. Montréal's deteriorating finances made them believe a strike was their only recourse. However, in the Montréal case, the police do not seem to have been implicated in the riot-

ers' generalized beliefs. Instead, the strike provided the opportunity for looters, arsonists, burglars, taxi drivers, and separatists to act deviantly.

Mobilization of Participants for Action

Involved here are the leadership, communication, and organization required to mount a riot (or other form of collective behavior). Crowd mobilization depends on the appearance of leaders who stimulate action. Such leadership may involve demogogues seizing microphones to churn up the crowd. Or it may involve leadership by role models.

Role modelling among looters in Montréal illustrates mobilization for action. In the atmosphere of "mindless exultation," a man with two fur coats under his arm "gaily assured the crowd: 'one for the wife, one for the girl friend'." (*Time*, 17 October 1969). The *Toronto Star* (Hagan, 1977:194) reported as follows:

And a big guy—no kid this one—came out of the crowd and smashed Helmut [the owner of a radio and hi-fi store] on the side of the head, knocking him down among the wrecked display tables and broken glass.

The crowd caught the fever and in a second they were grabbing everything in sight. ... He watched helplessly as someone backed a small truck up to his window and the crowd loaded in color television and big hi-fi sets, and took more away in cars.

Operation of Social Control

Social control, unlike other controls, is a counter-determinant. It is its absence or ineffectiveness that makes collective behavior inevitable and determines how fast, how far, and in what directions the episode will develop.

The Québec and federal governments were slow to grasp the full import of the Montréal strike. More than five hours passed before the Québec National Assembly put Montréal under the jurisdiction of the Québec Provincial Police (QPP). Ten hours passed before the QPP Director returned from holiday and took command. The Québec Cabinet asked Ottawa for army help. The arrival of helmeted Van Doos (the Royal 22nd Regiment) and return of Montréal squad cars simultaneously brought sixteen hours of anarchy to an end (*Time*, 17 October 1969).

Social control also influenced the pattern of events when Halifax was hit by a police strike some thirteen years later. On Friday night, the first night of the strike, mobs set fires, threw rocks, broke windows, and looted. The Mayor charged that some of the striking patrolmen "egged on lawbreakers" that night. However, although the police strike continued, the trouble was not repeated the next weekend, partly because a local judge imposed hefty fines and jail sentences on the Friday night arrestees. Social control agents either encouraged or discouraged collective behavior. Rainy weather also helped dampen the hooliganism (*The Calgary Herald*, 9 June 1981).

Smelser's elegant scheme has drawn both positive and negative comments. The value-added logic has been an important contribution. His framework has proved to be an excellent heuristic device, useful for *post facto* interpretations of events such as the Montréal riot. With the wisdom of hindsight, nearly every detail fits. (The lack of connection between beliefs and precipitating event in the Montréal example was an exception.) Unfortunately, however, Smelser's theory does not predict very well, partly because his concepts are difficult to specify and to quantify. (What exactly constituted "strain" in Montréal and how much of it was required to produce a riot?)

Our discussion of the major theories of collective behavior is now concluded. We leave our general overview of the field and turn now to particular aspects and forms of collective behavior.

RUMOR: COMMUNICATION IN COLLECTIVITIES

Rumors are defined by sociologists as unverified accounts of events of public concern. The word "unverified" indicates that rumors are neither substantiated nor refuted. However, they are *not* necessarily false. Unlike "gossip," which is "small talk" about personal acquaintances, rumor is concerned with public issues (Rosnow and Fine, 1976:4).

The Genesis of Rumor

Two main types of rumors exist: *cognitive rumors* and *emotional rumors*. The content of the cognitive rumor reflects the search for information, described above. Emotional rumor expresses the deep feelings that are often aroused by social situations.

Rumor begins to circulate when people want to know about something, but there is a shortage of news from the regular, institutionalized channels of communication. For this reason, rumor has been described as "improvised news." (Shibutani, 1966.)

The rumor process is itself a form of collective behavior. As well, rumors are implicated in nearly every other type of collective behavior. Individuals search for information, in order to resolve ambiguity, the essence of collective behavior.

In the winter of 1967–68, the inner city of Detroit lay in ruins from the previous summer's race riot (Rosenthal, 1971). Racial tension was exacerbated by a four-month-old newspaper strike, which threatened to continue. Civic authorities established a Rumor Control Center, which citizens could call to check out the stories circulating in the absence of authoritative news. Ten thousand calls were recorded in one month! Some rumors were irrelevant. ("I heard the Mayor is going around with the WJR weather girl.") Some expressed racial fear. ("Blacks are going to kidnap and kill a young white boy from every suburb.") Some cognitive rumors sought to discover whether race riots would recur:

Mrs. H. heard from her neighbor who heard from her aunt who heard from a lady in Birmingham [Michigan] who heard from her neighbor who heard from her cleaning lady that the riot was to start July 1st. The lady in Birmingham had asked her cleaning lady to work on July 1st, and the [black] cleaning woman had responded by saying she could not work on July 1st as this was the day the riot was to start.

(Rosenthal, 1971:34–35.)

The Persistence of Rumor

Rumors, which arise out of ambiguity, persist because they continue to touch on people's uncertainties and anxieties. The last few years have seen many rumors concerning food products turned treacherous. A schoolyard rumor spread that Life Saver Bubble Gum contained spider eggs. McDonald's was rumored to be adding worms to its hamburger meat to boost protein content. Another rumor insisted that if a person drinks coke while eating Pop Rocks candy, his/her stomach will explode. Rosnow and Kimmel (1979) hypothesize that these stories reflect uncertainty and anxiety in our society about additives, cholesterol, and other health risks contained in food, which are communicated from parent to child. Fear about modern technology is reflected in the microwave story:

It seems there was an old lady who had been given a microwave oven by her children. After bathing her dog she put it in the microwave to dry it off. Naturally, when she opened the door the dog was cooked from the inside out.

(Brunvand, 1980:53.)

The actual amount of rumor in circulation is a function of three variables: the importance of the issue, the ambiguity surrounding the issue, and the anxiety or emotional arousal involved (Rosnow and Kimmel, 1979). Sometimes the issue is short-lived. People in a burning building grope through the smoke, seeking rumored exits. Either they find them quickly, or they do not. Sometimes the issue is part of the human condition and recurs throughout the centuries as folklore. For example, the castration rumor (the enemy castrates a young boy whose mother led him into danger) has erupted during many historical crises (Rosenthal, 1971).

The Termination of Rumor

In general, rumor ends when the situation out of which it arose is no longer problematic. Research data provide some particularities concerning the conditions for the termination of rumor (Shibutani, 1966:130 ff.):

1. Rumor construction terminates when verification or refutation from formal news channels occurs, providing that these channels are trusted. Where faith in the regular news sources is high, people rely on rumors only because of insufficient news from these sources.
2. Where institutional channels are not trusted, rumors may persist even after formal denials. This is especially likely when the rumors appear more plausible than official pronouncements (e.g., the Warren Commission report on President Kennedy's assassination).
3. When situations marked by intense collective excitement have run their course and tension is dissipated, rumors just disappear, even when no official announcement is made. When conventional perspectives are restored, many rumors appear ridiculous to the participants themselves.
4. When interest in the event is low and no action is needed, rumors may disappear as people become preoccupied with other matters. The public simply dissolves.

THE PANICKY CROWD

Laymen and social scientists alike are fascinated with the possibility that people caught in extreme stress situations — fires in hotels and high rise buildings, earthquakes, hurricanes — may "panic" and add to the injuries and loss of life caused by the physically destructive agent itself.

What Is Panic?

"*Panic*" is a dramatic but vague term, whose meaning has been stretched to apply to any kind of behavior that occurs when people feel afraid or worried. Many collective behavior theorists agree that the term has this meaning: panic is the disorganizing and maladaptive reaction in a collectivity to an occurrence perceived as dangerous. Fear-induced flight produced by limited access to escape routes results in the destruction of the group (based on Schultz, 1964:6–8).

Key elements of the above definition need clarification.

1. *Perceived Danger.* Panic occurs when crowd members *believe* themselves to be in peril. Whether their perception is accurate is beside the point. The Martians who frightened listeners in the 1938 "War of the Worlds" broadcast (Cantril, 1940) were figments of H.G. Wells's imagination. More recently, a stampede after a Bogota, Colombia soccer game killed twenty-four people and injured 250 others. The danger was quite disproportionate to the reaction. The stampede was provoked by drunken fans in the higher sections of the stadium, hurling lighted firecrackers and bottles, and urinating on people leaving the stadium at the end of the game (*The Calgary Herald*, 19 November 1982).

2. *Collectivity Disorganization.* Sociologists are interested in group panic, not individual panic. Although frightened individuals are necessary for collective panic to occur, fear does not invariably lead to the group falling apart. Springhill, Nova Scotia miners, trapped in 1958 in North America's deepest coal mine, were privately afraid. However, for reasons to be discussed later, their groups remained cohesive:

[The survivors] had been entombed in blackness for as long as nine days. Many of them ate bark, sucked coal, and drank their own urine; they exchanged wisecracks and they prayed, until they were brought up, like Lazarus, alive from the grave.

(Rasky, 1961:118.)

Group disorganization of an antisocial sort is graphically portrayed in an account of Chicago's 1903 Iroquois Theatre fire, which Eddie Foy, a vaudeville actor, witnessed:

… It was inside the house that the greatest loss of life occurred, especially on the stairways leading down from the second balcony. Here most of the dead were trampled or smothered, though many jumped or fell over the balustrade to the floor of the foyer. In places on the stairways, particularly where a turn caused a jam, bodies were piled seven or eight feet deep. Firemen and police confronted a sickening task in disentangling them. An occasional living person was found in the heaps, but most of these were terribly injured. The heel prints on the dead faces mutely testified to the cruel fact that human animals stricken by terror are as mad and ruthless as stampeding cattle. Many bodies had the clothes torn from them, and some had the flesh trodden from their bones.

(Foy and Harlow, 1928.)

The "disorganizing reaction of the collectivity" in our definition means the usual group norms are no longer operative. People hurt one another (antisocial behavior) or are simply oblivious to one another (nonsocial behavior). In short, where individualism prevails, the group as an organized entity ceases to function.

3. *Maladaptive Reaction.* The response to the perceived threat increases danger to self and others rather than reducing it. The Iroquois Theatre deaths were caused by the social reaction to the fire, not by the fire itself.

4. *Flight.* According to Quarantelli (1979:8), "the most notable outward manifestation of panic is flight." However, our definition of panic requires that the flight be maladaptive. Flight in and of itself is not sufficient to constitute panic. For instance, during the atomic bombing of Hiroshima, people fled the city. This was an adaptive response, since those who did not flee were killed by the rapid spread of fire (Schultz, 1964:7).

5. *Shortage of Escape Routes.* Panic is, in part, situationally determined in that the perceived scar-

city of exits creates anxiety and competition. Given escape routes that are actually limited (or inaccurately seen to be limited), the potentially adaptive character of flight becomes nonadaptive behavior as people quickly clog the few exits that do exist (Schultz, 1964:8). Radio reports of the Colombian soccer stampede said the crush occurred when fans piled up because exit doors had not been opened quickly enough at the end of the game (*The Calgary Herald*, 19 November 1982).

Under What Conditions Does Actual Panic Occur?

First of all, we must emphasize that the authenticated instances of mass panic are relatively few in number:

Although there has been war somewhere in the world almost continuously [over the last 80 years], it is a significant and somewhat astonishing fact that there have been few instances of mass panic directly connected with enemy attack on a civilian population. Moreover, studies of terrified people who have been stunned by an overwhelming disaster indicate that panic states are usually of short duration, and that excited and irrational behavior can usually be prevented or quickly brought to a stop if effective leadership and realistic information is provided.
(Janis et al., 1955, quoted in Schultz, 1964:119.)

Panic arises only under highly specialized circumstances. Five conditions give rise to the panic-producing situation (based on Janis et al., 1955, in Schultz, 1964:120).

1. **People perceive an immediate, severe danger.** The threat is so imminent that there is no time to do anything but try to escape. Often, there is foreknowledge of danger, as in tornados and airplane crashes.
2. **They believe that escape routes are limited.**
3. **They believe that escape routes are closing** (not closed), so that escape must be made quickly. Escape is possible, but only the first will do so. One reason the trapped Springhill miners did not panic was their conviction that escape was *not* possible.
4. **There is lack of authoritative communication to keep people informed.** Confusing escape instructions were allegedly at least partially responsible for the injury and death toll in the fire at Toronto's Inn on the Park Hotel (*The Calgary Herald*, 19 January 1981). One survivor said he went to the hotel desk to ask why the alarm had gone off and was told to return to his room. "It was crazy — I was out, safe, and they wanted me to go back up to the 11th floor and stay there."

Pushing and shoving, such as occurred in the Iroquois Theatre Fire, happens because the people at the back are not aware that the exits are already blocked. Some evidence shows that when people do know, they stop pushing and become resigned to their fate.
5. **There are signs that group bonds are disrupted.** People look for leadership and none is there. The usual norms of courtesy are being disregarded. The person feels alone in coping with the perceived danger (Turner and Killian, 1972: 85). As a corollary, social ties to others present in a crisis inhibit panic. Quarantelli (1979:11) describes the retrospective account of a man who was sitting with his son in a large theatre with only one exit when there was a shout of fire, and people started to flee: "With me was my young son. If he had not been there, I think I should have been one of those scrambling, screaming madmen but the thought held in my mind that I could not bear to have my son see me as those others were. . . . Also, I was responsible for him. . . ."

HYSTERICAL CONTAGION

For ten days back in 1944, a "phantom anesthetist" prowled the streets of Mattoon, Illinois (Johnson, 1945). A woman reported to the police that someone had sprayed her as she slept with a "sickish sweet-smelling" gas that paralyzed her. Twenty-eight other cases were eventually reported. Some Mattoon citizens armed themselves with shotguns and sat on their doorsteps waiting for the "mad gasser." After ten days of excitement, the episode was diagnosed as "hysterical contagion," the result of overactive imaginations.

A decade later, Seattle, Washington was hit by an epidemic of windshield pitting (Medalia and Larsen, 1958). Thousands of automobiles were reported to have suddenly developed bubbles in the windshield glass. Conjectured causes ranged from meteoric dust, to sandflea eggs hatching in the glass, but centered on radioactive fallout from H-bomb testing. The Mayor of Seattle made emergency appeals to the Governor and the President. Experts eventually determined that the windshield damage resulted from mass hysteria: people looking *at* their windshields, instead of *through* them.

Hysterical contagion is the dissemination within a collectivity of a symptom or set of symptoms for which no physical explanation can be found.
(Kerckhoff and Back, 1968:v.)

People collapse from "food poisoning," but no toxic element is found in the food. People become paralyzed from a mysterious "gas," but no gas is isolated. On the day of Elvis Presley's death, assembly-line workers fainted, but no physical reason for their collapse could be discovered.

As we have already seen, mass anxiety is not neatly proportionate to causes of fear. For example, Hollister, California is situated on the San Andreas fault, where earthquakes of three or more on the Richter scale occur once a month. The citizens of Hollister call their community the "Earthquake Capital of the World" and refuse to move (*Time*, 23 March 1982).

On the other hand, every once in a while, fear of a "mysterious force," such as an insane anesthetist or inexplicable, overnight damage to windshields, is disseminated through a collectivity. Although the particular content of the fear differs from case to case, all are inexplicable in terms of mechanical, chemical, or physiological causality (Kerckhoff and Back, 1968). Sociologists refer to these cases of "great scares from disproportionate causes" (Klapp, 1972:115) as "hysterical contagion."

Sociologists often approach the study of an episode of hysterical contagion by asking these four questions (Medalia and Larsen, 1958:181):

1. What is the origin of the mass delusion?
2. What is the pattern of its diffusion through the collectivity?
3. What persons are most susceptible and why?
4. What is the process of its disappearance?

In order to further general understanding of hysterical contagion, the case of *The June Bug* (Kerckhoff and Back, 1968; Kerckhoff, Back, and Miller, 1965) will be analyzed in terms of the above four questions.

The Case of the June Bug

"Montana Mills" is a textile processing and clothing manufacturing plant in the Southern United States. In the summer of 1962, the company was disrupted by an epidemic of insect bites that incapacitated sixty-two people. Symptoms ranged from minor skin irritations to fainting spells, severe pain, nausea, and feelings of disorientation. At first, some kind of insect in a shipment of cloth from England was suspected for the epidemic. The contagion spread so fast that on the two worst days, twenty-four and twenty persons came down with the symptoms. Then, just as suddenly, the complaints began to diminish.

Physicians and entomologists were unable to find any poisonous elements (insects, chemical irritants) capable of producing the symptoms. Eventually, they concluded that "the 'epidemic' of bites and pains had originated entirely in the minds of the victims, not in the physical conditions of the plant." (Kerckhoff, Back, and Miller, 1965.)

Sociologists Kerckhoff and Back were intrigued with the fact that sixty-two people supposedly were bit by this imaginary "June Bug" and got sick enough to require medical attention. The information they derived from interview-questionnaire research in the "Montana Mills" plant may be summarized according to the four questions just outlined.

Origin of the Delusion

Social strain in the textile plant was found to be the source of the hysterical contagion. The plant was not well organized. Channels of communication between management and workers were poor. The union was ineffective; employees feared loss of their jobs. June was the peak month in the production of clothing. Most of the plant had three shifts. However, the Dressmaking Department, were most of the victims worked, had only one shift. A great deal of overtime was required, often on short notice.

Kerckhoff and Back (1968) concluded that hysterical contagion occurs when people interact in a common setting in an atmosphere of unresolved tension. They develop a "theory" to explain their discomfort. The "theory" has to have some cultural legitimacy. In our society, evil spirits are "out." Instead, people decide something is wrong with the airconditioning or that someone has been putting saltpetre in the food. The insect "theory" was plausible in the American South. As the belief in this threat spreads, it adds yet another source of tension, namely, fear of the illness.

Pattern of Diffusion

Rumor and primary group influence were the mechanisms of diffusion of the June Bug hysteria. (The mass media played an important part in the Mattoon and Seattle episodes.) The first textile plant workers to display symptoms were social isolates, perhaps because friendless people need attention. During the second phase, the epidemic spread through friendship networks. Just before the hysteria was halted by the experts' insistence that the June Bug "theory" was unwarranted, it was becoming a general crowd response. In this latter phase, friendship had no bearing on the spread of hysteria.

Who Is Susceptible and Why?

As mentioned above, the June Bug victims who worked in the Dressmaking Department were under greater strain than the rest of the employees. As compared with workers in the Dressmaking Department who did not fall ill, the "affecteds" tended to be under even more personal strain. For instance, they were apt to have small children and to be especially worried about keeping their jobs.

In both the June Bug and Mattoon cases, most of the victims were women. (The Seattle windshield case was more complicated.) Why should this be so? Sociologists no longer accept Johnson's (1945) conclusion that women are just naturally more suggestible than men. Rather, so far as work-related hysteria is concerned, working women, saddled with traditional home responsibilities, often operate under a "double dose" of strain (Colligan and Stockton, 1978). As well, falling ill is a socially approved feminine reaction to strain. By contrast, men in a situation of work-centred strain, are more likely to get drunk or "punch someone out."

Process of Disappearance

How does the story end? Kerckhoff and Back (1968) support the conclusion reached earlier by Medalia and Larsen (1958:186) that "*interest* in a mass delusion may very well decline, while *belief* in the delusion persists." No more cases were reported after the experts' diagnosis of the June Bug phenomenon as a case of hysterical contagion. However, months later, the women involved in the epidemic still believed in the insect "theory." Moreover, most claimed to have actually seen the bug.

FADS, FASHIONS, CRAZES

When we think back over the decades, fads, fashions, and crazes provide much of the flavor of the times: flagpole sitting, dance marathons, bobbed hair (1920s); Monopoly, miniature golf, goldfish swallowing, bank nights (1930s); Frank ("The Voice") Sinatra, Dior's "New Look," "Kilroy was here" (1940s); hula hoops, saddle shoes, greasers, "Howdy Doody Time" (1950s); the Twist, the Beatles, Batman, James Dean (1960s); (Klapp, 1972:308; Skolnick, 1978); hippies and yippies, flower stickers on VWs, happy faces, streaking, Star Wars (1970s); Lady Diana hairstyles, gold bar hoarding, punk rock, video arcades, legwarmers, Trivial Pursuit (1980s).

In comparison with more ponderous historical events, this expressive form of collective behavior may seem inconsequential. However, sociologists take these matters very seriously indeed. For one thing, fads, fashions, and crazes are a fascinating form of social change. Some important changes (e.g., automobiles, movies) had faddish beginnings. For another, the pattern of social influence underlying these phenomena takes us to the very heart of sociological inquiry.

Some Terminological Distinctions

Fads, fashions, and crazes are all forms of collective behavior. Their novelty and unpredictability stimulate emergent norms. The "compelling power lies in the implicit judgement of an anonymous multitude." (Lang and Lang, 1961:466.) Finally, the adoption of fads, fashions, and crazes involves obsessiveness that surpasses everyday social behavior. Witness the Cabbage Patch Doll phenomenon.

Both fads and crazes involve exceptional preoccupation with the "object" for a limited duration, followed by a sudden decline in interest. Obsession reaches a peak, and is then followed by counterobsession (Turner and Killian, 1972: 129). The behavior appears ridiculous, stale, perhaps overly costly, or downright dangerous. Followers of fads and crazes are enthusiasts, not mere imitators. The 1974 streaking fad was quite imaginative. There were competitions for the best accessories (bowties, earmuffs) and best places (airports, football fields, the Eiffel Tower, and Academy Awards broadcasts). There were "snail walks" for oldsters, clothed streaks through nudist camps, and competitions for the longest streak, the largest streak, and the best "blue" (or coldest) streak (*Time*, 18 March 1974).

Crazes

These carry more serious consequences than the more trifling fads. Participants rearrange their lives for maximum indulgence in crazes. Groupies following rock bands may work only long enough to get travel money to be near their idols. Large sums of money may be made and lost in crazes such as gold booms or the Dutch tulip speculation. Crazes, such as the 1951 Russian Roulette craze, can be dangerous. Understandably enough, fewer people get involved in crazes than in fads.

Fashion

This involves diffusion in changes of taste. In comparison with fads and crazes, fashion is a more conventionalized, more widespread, and more manipulated form of collective behavior. Fashion is often big business, as designers and retailers place a variety of choices before the public. However, fashion failures, such as the much promoted midi style, show that the outcome is the result of collective processes, not industry manipulation. Fashions often involve continuity in style change. For example, over the years, women's skirt length slowly moves between the limits of thigh and floor. In contrast, fads and crazes involve discrete items and abrupt change. Over the last decade or so, T-shirts have been fashionable in recreational wear, sleeping attire, even formal dresses. However, designs on T-shirts reflect passing fads — timely slogans, happy faces, Garfield Cats, tie-dying.

Motives for Involvement in Fashions, Fads, and Crazes

The question most central for collective behavior specialists is why people get caught up in the

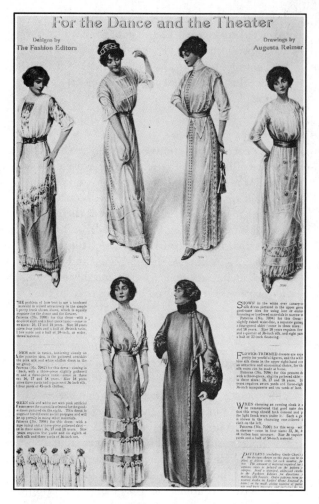

For the Dance and the Theater

Designs by
The Fashion Editors

Drawings by
Augusta Reimer

Fashion is usually a manipulated form of collective behavior in that designers and retailers profit through creating a variety of choices.

emerging fad, fashion, or craze. People sometimes participate because they seek to get rich quickly (e.g., gold crazes, pyramid sales schemes). Alternatively, they may conform to emergent fad and fashion norms in order to gain or keep reference group acceptance (e.g., teenagers' jargon and taste in clothes and music serve to demarcate insiders from outsiders). Also, we value the new and the up-to-date and scorn what is no longer "in." A long time ago, sociologist W.I. Thomas (1923) postulated the existence "Four Wishes," for (1) new experience, (2) security, (3) response, and (4) recogniton. Though this idiom borders on psychological reductionism, the "Four Wishes" all have some relevance for this mass behavior (Evans, 1969:591).

The "motives" discussion has concentrated on fashion behavior as a reflection of social status aspirations (Klapp, 1972:320). The idea here is that elites innovate and people further down the social ladder emulate these styles in order to differentiate themselves from those on even lower rungs of the ladder. In the classic statement of this "percolation thesis," Veblen (1899) observed that the moneyed classes consume, not to take care of their needs, but to symbolize their "honorific" social status. An example might be wealthy women's switch in taste in furs to chinchilla and sable when mink became easier for plebians to get (Klapp, 1972:320).

Some sociologists argue that the social status theory no longer fits North American society. In an article titled "The decline and fall of the status symbol" (1974), Blumberg proposed that in an abundant society, material possessions no longer confer the status they once did. So far as vacations, clothes, and meals out are concerned, credit cards mean that nearly everyone who feels like it can "pass" temporarily. (Does the "economic downturn" of the 1980s challenge Blumberg's argument?)

Finally, Klapp (1969) believes that fad and fashion behavior is symptomatic of the defects of mass society. Since modern societies deprive individuals of "psychological payoff," many seek to establish their identity through fashions and fads. Much of the search involves "ego-screaming," "Look at Me!" fashions. Women who shave their heads, or dye their hair green, men who have thirty-eight holes pierced in their ears or mimic Boy George are seeking attention. Klapp's (1969) view is that fad and fashion behavior today tell us more about psychological mobility, than about status mobility.

SOCIAL MOVEMENTS

Social movements are a major vehicle of social change. Their appearance is "a sign that the old social order is being challenged ... and an indication that new social worlds have been conceived." (Wilson, 1973:4.) Christianity, nazism, socialism, trade unionism, the civil rights movement, Black Power, Red Power, women's liberation, French-Canadian and Western-Canadian separatism — these and a host of other social movements have shaped the world we live in.

Characteristics of Social Movements

A social movement is a conscious, collective, organized attempt to bring about or resist large-scale change in the social order by noninstitutionalized means.

(Wilson, 1973:8.)

Social movement particpants are oriented to social change. They look at existing societal arrangements (or at somebody else's proposal for social change) and in effect say, "This is intolerable! We don't have to put up with this! Let's act together to remedy the situation!" "Acting together" implies organization, which may be more or less sophisticated. Organization involves norms for leadership choice, rights, and duties; criteria for membership; division of labor for getting tasks done; ideological pronouncements; norms for relations with outsiders; tactics. With regard to tactics, social movements often use non-institutionalized (rather innovative) means to bring about or prevent change. Tactics range from letters to the editor, petitions, boycotts, to civil disobedience, hijacking, kidnapping, bombing, and murder. The aim of tactics such as these is twofold: to attract members and to influence decision-makers either directly or indirectly through public opinion. Finally, social movements' deliberate attempts to change must be distinguished from accidental change that occurs through aggregate collective action, such as a collapse of the stock market.

Fashions and fads may serve to reinforce the ego in a society increasingly geared toward gratifying the mass rather than the individual.

Types of Change

All social movements are interested in change. However, the particular type of change varies. People can organize to *resist* some threatened change — a freeway through their neighborhood, easing of abortion laws, equal rights for some minority group. The Newfoundlanders' counter-movement defends the status quo in seal-hunt practices against the criticism of the Greenpeace and other protesters (Lamson, 1979).

On the other hand, movements that *promote* social change may be *radical* movements or *reform* movements. Radical movements attempt to make fundamental changes *of* the social system, whereas reform movements attempt to make more limited changes *within* the social system. The Canadian native rights movement encompasses subgroups with divergent philosophies (Boldt, 1980). The reform wing seeks integration of Indians into the existing system and social change through legitimate means. The radical wing advocates separatism and militant Red Power tactics. Smelser's (1962) *norm-oriented* and *value-oriented* movements make the same distinction. The former seeks to rectify societal strain through changing norms or rules, while the latter attempts to change societal values, or the basic principles that underlie the rules.

The broad field of collective behavior is conventionally divided into elementary collective behavior and social movements. Elementary collective behavior covers the forms discussed in previous sections of this chapter, which are "less structured, less organized, less oriented to change, and tend to have a shorter existence than social movements." (Wood and Jackson, 1982.) However, these distinctions are matters of degree and social movements have enough in common with elementary collective behavior forms to be included in the same specialty area. Neither type is institutionalized, or "widely accepted as binding in society." (Johnson, 1960:21, quoted in Wilson, 1973:9.)

Participation in Social Movements: the Psychological Approach

Few issues relating to the study of social movements have generated as much research and debate as the issue of recruitment. Who joins and why? (Zurcher and Snow, 1981:449 ff.) The underlying assumptions are: (1) that movement joiners differ in important ways from non-joiners, and (2) that the appeal of movements is centred in their ability to improve the life conditions or to ease the psychological tensions of a particular constituency of individuals. Put in terms of our earlier discussion of theories of collective behavior, structural strain (Smelser, 1962) creates tension for individuals and social movements, the result of emergent norms (Turner and Killian, 1972) that appeal to the needs of these individuals.

The following motivational orientations have been considered conducive to participation in social movements.

1. Pursuit of Meaning. Movement ideology often provides a simplified explanation of a complex, confusing environment (Cantril, 1941). Believe it or not, some people find comfort in the premise that humanity is being conquered by a powerful, pervasive conspiracy of Communists and Jews (Toch, 1965). Pamphlets put out by ultra-right wing movements use this "one cause" to explain the course of history, world-wide politics, fluoridation of water supplies, sex education, crime in the streets, and so on. Readers "experience the exhilarating feeling of living in a coherent — if dangerous — world." (Toch, 1965:53.)

2. Authoritarianism. Authoritarian personalities (Adorno et al., 1950), that is, individuals who are prejudiced, insecure, contemptuous of the weak, and admiring of strong leaders, are seen by some scholars (Lipset, 1963) as being especially susceptible to the appeals of movements on the radical left and right. Hoffer's (1951) "True Believer" compensates for feelings of self-inadequacy by submission to a powerful external cause or leader. Thus, the "omnipotence of Marxist doctrine" and the "infallible leader" of nazism are functionally equivalent in the sense that "the burning conviction that we have a holy duty toward others is often a way of attaching our drowning selves to a passing raft." (Hoffer, 1951: 8, 14.)

3. Search for Identity. A more recent but related explanation, is the notion that participation in social movements represents a search for identity, as does fad and fashion behavior (Klapp, 1969). Persons alienated from "self" search for a base for reconstituting the self. Accordingly, participants in such diverse movements as the Hare Krishna, the nuclear disarmament movement, and the women's liberation movement are seen to be seeking a sense of personal worth.

Crowd of enraged demonstrators overturns a streetcar, Winnipeg General Strike, June 21, 1919.

4. Quest for Community. Another theme is that social isolation leads to a "quest for community." (Aberle, 1966; Nisbet, 1954.) Individuals only weakly attached to kinship groups and local communities are seen to be susceptible to the appeals of ideologically diverse social movements, which become surrogate families. In the early 1970s, the Moonies used "love bombing," the "drenching" of prospective members in love and approval, as a recruitment technique. According to Lofland (1977:16), the objective was to produce a desire to "melt together" into the "loving, enveloping embrace" of Reverend Sun Myung Moon's "family."

5. Relative Deprivation. Probably the most popular explanation of movement participation is the idea that a sense of acute deprivation arises when what people think they should have exceeds what they actually have. The sense of deprivation is usually not absolute, but measured against that of reference groups. When the gap suddenly widens and becomes intolerable, people are thought to be especially prone to movement participation (Zurcher and Snow, 1981:452).

A farmer explains the appeal of "Bible Bill" Aberhart's Social Credit movement during the Great Depression of the 1930s (Horn, 1972:643):

Although we had sweat blood to build up productive farms we were broke. We could not buy clothes and we could not even pay our taxes although our granaries were full of grain, and the mortgage interest was piling up. And then Aberhart came.

His sonerous voice rolled out from the radio each Sunday and it contained a message of hope, and what was more to the point, some sensible economics.

(The Social Credit movement promised everyone $25 a month.)

There is explanatory merit in the argument that some people are more predisposed than others to movement participation. However, empirical studies have led to the conclusion that various psychological states are *conducive* to but not *sufficient* for movement participation. Frustration and discontent "fertilize the ground" for movement participation, but they do not lead to it themselves (Zurcher and Snow, 1981:454). The rest of the explanation of movement involvement, success or failure, lies in the sociological variables of movement organization and activities.

Social Movement Organization and Dynamics: the Sociological Approach

Sociological studies suggest that the key to understanding individuals' recruitment and commitment resides in a *transaction* between participants and movement. Attention is shifted from the individual's pre-affiliation psychology to the movement's organizational arrangements and strategies. The sociological perspective focuses on the linkage of personal motives to new behavior that supports the social movement interests (Zurcher and Snow, 1981:464).

Social Networks

One important question is this: which of the potential participants are most likely to be recruited into a given movement (or one movement rather than another)? One answer is that pre-existing social networks function as recruitment channels (Zurcher and Snow, 1981:454–55). Pinard's (1971) study of the rise of the Social Credit Party in Québec, Bibby and Brinkerhoff's (1974) study of the recruitment efforts of Western Canadian evangelical churches, and many other studies, conclude that recruitment occurs primarily through primary and secondary group ties. In other words, people are influenced to join their friends and acquaintances, rather than by impersonal appeals or abstract ideological argument.

Resource Mobilization Approach

The recent "resource mobilization" perspective (McCarthy and Zald, 1977; Zald and McCarthy, 1979) shifts the emphasis from structural strain and individual needs to the ongoing problems and strategic dilemmas of social movements. A primary assumption is that the aggregation of resources is critical for movement purposes. The approach is a utilitarian, cost-reward, supply-demand, conceptual framework. Therefore, it examines how a movement mobilizes a variety of resources — people, money, power, technical skills, mass media, and so on. It recognizes the importance of movement linkages to outside organizations in facilitating or frustrating access to resources (McCarthy and Zald, 1977). Often agencies of the larger society attempt to prevent a social movement from mobilizing resources.

The 1971 riot in Vancouver's Gastown area (*Time*, 18 October 1971) may be interpreted as an unanticipated result of police attempts to prevent a movement protesting Canada's marijuana laws from attaining the resource of social support. Two thousand hippies, tourists, and curious passersby gathered for what had been billed as "The Great Gastown Smoke-In and Street Jamboree." Vancouver police, who viewed the crowd as a challenge to authority, moved in with horses, motorcycles, and riot clubs. "Pandemonium broke loose" in what had been a "not unpleasant crowd."

So far, the resource mobilization approach is in an early stage of development. Only a few rigorous tests have been made (Wood and Jackson, 1982:143). Our discussion of psychological and sociological level approaches, taken together, serves to emphasize our conclusion that the study of social movements requires attention to both individual and organizational variables.

SUMMARY

1. The study of collective behavior is important because it helps us to understand social change,

reveals the ranges of human social behavior, and leads to solutions to practical problems.

2. For these reasons, collective behavior is an underdeveloped area within sociology: it lacks a satisfactory theoretical framework and it presents the researcher with unique methodological difficulties.

3. Turner and Killian's (1972) emergent norm theory and Smelser's (1962) value-added theory are the major theories of collective behavior.

4. Rumor occurs as individuals seek to resolve ambiguity in situations where more institutionalized communication channels are deficient. Rumors persist as long as they touch on people's uncertainties and anxieties. They terminate when situations are no longer problematic.

5. Panic (a relatively rare phenomenon) occurs when people perceive an immediate, severe danger and believe that the limited number of escape routes are closing, and that escape must be made quickly. There is lack of authoritative communication and signs that the group bonds are disrupted.

6. Hysterical contagion occurs when people, interacting in a stressful social situation, develop a plausible "theory" to explain their discomfort.

7. Sociologists have speculated that people get caught up in fads and fashions for these reasons: to get rich quickly; to win or keep reference group acceptance; to claim a higher social status and to differentiate themselves from their "inferiors"; to resolve identity problems produced by alienating aspects of mass society.

8. Social movements attempt to promote change or to resist change in the social order. In comparison with "elementary collective behavior," social movements tend to be more structured, more highly organized, more oriented to change, and less ephemeral.

9. Individual commitment to social movements and movement success or failure involve a transaction between participants and movements. The study of recruitment of individuals has included these motives: pursuit of meaning; the authori-

tarian personality; the search for identity; a quest for community; and relative deprivation. Organizational analysis has focused on social networks and "resource mobilization."

GLOSSARY

Acting crowd. A spontaneous collectivity whose goal is to manipulate some object in the external environment.

Casual crowd. A weak crowd form, with little interaction or awareness of group membership.

Collective behavior. The specialty area within sociology which studies the social reactions to situations where the norms are nonexistent, ambiguous, or disputed.

Conventionalized crowd. A collectivity characterized by established norms and a passive one-to-one relationship between audience members and object of attention.

Craze. A form of expressive collective behavior which resembles fads, except that the consequences are more serious.

Expressive crowd. A collectivity whose internal goal is to change the mood, behavior, or self-image of the members themselves.

Fad. A form of expressive collective behavior reflecting brief, but exceptional preoccupation with discrete items.

Fashion. Diffusion in changes of taste.

Hysterical contagion. The dissemination within a collectivity of a symptom or set of symptoms for which no physical explanation can be found.

Mass. A physically separate, heterogeneous collectivity, composed of a large number of anonymous individuals with little organization or direct interaction.

Panic. The disorganizing and maladaptive reaction in a collectivity to an occurrence perceived as dangerous. Fear-induced flight produced by limited access to escape routes results in the destruction of the group.

Public. A grouping of people who are confronted by an issue, divided in their ideas as to how to meet the issue, who engage in debate over the issue.

Rumors. Unverified accounts of events of public concern, which occur when there is a shortage of news from the regular, institutionalized means.

Social movement. A conscious, collective, organized attempt to bring about change or resist change in the social order by noninstitutionalized means.

Value-added. A term taken from economics which emphasizes the multi-causational nature of social behavior, as well as the pattern of causation.

FURTHER READING

Clark, Samuel D., J. Paul Grayson and Linda M. Grayson (eds.). *Prophecy and Protest: Social Movements in Twentieth-Century Canada.* Toronto: Gage, 1975. A collection of articles on Canadian social movements.

Shibutani, Tamotsu. *Improvised News: A Sociological Study of Rumor.* Indianapolis: Bobbs-Merrill, 1966. A sociological analysis of rumors in history.

Smelser, Neil J. *Theory of Collective Behavior.* New York: Free Press, 1962. A theoretically sophisticated treatment of collective behavior.

Turner, Ralph H. and Lewis M. Killian. *Collective Behavior.* 2nd edition. Englewood Cliffs, New Jersey: Prentice-Hall, 1972. A general text dealing with both elementary collective behavior and social movements, which is based upon emergent norm theory.

Zald, Mayer N. and John D. McCarthy (eds.). *The Dynamics of Social Movements.* Cambridge, Mass.: Winthrop, 1979. An edited collection of papers that utilizes the resource mobilization approach.

CHAPTER TWENTY-FOUR

Social Change, Modernity, and Tradition

JAYANT LELE

Ever since our species evolved on this earth, we have learned to live with change, and with changes in nature, in particular. The rhythms of nature have a certain inevitability about them, and out of that inevitability humankind fashioned a unique relationship to nature. The core of this relationship lay in the use of nature as a *partner* in social change as new modes of social co-operation became necessary in gaining nurture from nature. New modes of co-operation necessitated changes in social life, such as the family and the economy. Social change, then, is different from routine and recurrent changes that are experienced in daily life, or changes in the life cycle, such as maturation and aging. Social change occurs over a long period of time, primarily as a result of human action.

"Man survived the fiercest test of the Ice Ages because he had the flexibility of mind to recognize inventions and to turn them into communal property." (Bronowski, 1973:46.) These processes of adaptation and innovation have repeated themselves throughout history.

The discovery of inventions and turning them into communal property constitutes social learning. In a strict sense, only individuals, not societies, learn, but societies have ways of storing the fruits of individual learning as *social knowledge*. The social structure of a society acts as a channel for change in its capacity to store the results of innovative learning. The basis of this essay lies in

Failure to understand our relationship with nature may threaten our very survival.

answering the following questions: When do the results of accumulated individual learning come into focus and become the basis of new social structures? When does the cultural framework of a society (values, customs, and beliefs) undergo change?

There are no easy answers to these questions. Sociologists have searched deeply in human history for clues. As you have seen, Talcott Parsons (1977) made an attempt to combine the ideas of earlier scholars (Weber and Durkheim, in particular) with his own analysis of history to produce a theory of social change. Niklas Luhmann (1982) added new insights to Parsons's work by combining ideas of other thinkers such as Kant and Husserl. Jurgen Habermas (1979), another re-

nowned German sociologist, has brought to bear many of the salient features of Marx's theory of social change. In this and the next two sections, we shall draw on the ideas of these thinkers to sketch the process of social change, and to answer some of the questions raised.

When crisis situations are experienced by specific groups or classes in a society, they become disillusioned with the existing social order. They become critical not of the values and norms themselves, but of the interpretations that are put on them by those who are in control of society. They challenge these interpretations and suggest new ones, along with blueprints for a new social order. Parsons, Luhmann, and Habermas often differ on the causes and patterns of crisis, but agree on the source of social change; that is, the social knowledge stored in the social structure.

All three agree that a major source of crisis is humankind's relationship to nature. We interpret nature while working with it to gain survival. If our interpretations contravene or misunderstand the rhythms of nature, nature may administer surprises that prove fatal to a society's survival. The basic premise of this essay, then, is that in the game of ordered survival, there is no survival without order, but no order can survive if it flouts nature's laws. When confronted with such a crisis, those who challenge the social order can draw upon social knowledge that may have been ignored or dismissed at an earlier stage of the society's development.

Historically, however, this process does not take a uniform, linear path. Rather, societies differ in their response to an unexpected natural crisis: (1) a society may develop a new social order after overcoming the crisis; (2) it may establish an equilibrium with nature and thus postpone a crisis; or (3) it may not recognize a crisis and eventually become annihilated. In order to survive, societies must undergo social change. Some societies change faster and succeed in reducing their dependence on nature; others remain static over long periods or disappear. The alternative routes that a society can take are represented diagramatically below.

> Crisis → disequilibrium → innovation → new social order (e.g., Third World societies of Asia, Africa, and Latin America, which have advanced from tribal to complex societies).

> Equilibrium → postponement of crisis (e.g., recently discovered tribes in New Guinea and the Philippines that have, through isolation, maintained a low-level equilibrium with nature).

> Lack of recognition of crisis → no innovation → eventual annihilation. Many primitive societies that we know existed only from archaeological evidence.

Now we turn to the main source or agents of social change, both within societies and outside societies.

INTERNAL FACTORS OF SOCIAL CHANGE

Production and the Economy

The economy as an institution is devoted primarily to the production/distribution and the exchange of goods and services. In order to assess its contribution to social change, we need to ask the following questions about *each stage* of society's development: (1) What is the maximum level of control over nature? and (2) What is the form of organization that controls the economy? In hunting-and-gathering societies, kinship governed the procurement and distribution of goods and services. In industrial societies, bureaucracy controls the economy.

The level of control — how much a society can get out of nature and in what manner — directly depends on the available labor power. There are three important dimensions of labor power: its size, the associated technology, and the social organization of production. The size is determined by societal needs and by how they are to be met. Changing needs affect the size of labor power. Historically, the number of able-bodied workers was one of the determining factors in the survival of societies. For example, increases in population, and hence the number of workers, tended to accompany structural changes, and every successful structural change was accompanied by population increase. In turn, larger populations created greater need, allowed greater economic activity, and became a source of further social change.

As indicated, this pattern does not work independently of the other aspects of labor power, that is, technology and organization of production. For example, industrialization (production technology) led to substantial increases in production. At the same time, because of other technological innovations, leading to better sanitation and the preservation and distribution of food, mortality rates dropped and the population increased. Without the same technological developments and associated changes in the organization of food distribution, population increases mean famine and starvation for the masses. If there is an imbalance between these factors, havoc results.

One of the common solutions in history to an imbalance between population and productivity was mass migration. Since the Europeans were superior in naval and fighting power during the seventeenth and eighteenth centuries, they gained political control over much of the world. The colonies they established became one of the solutions for excessive population growth in the home country. Thus, immigrants from the Old World populated the New World. Malthus would have been surprised at the manner in which Western societies averted the potential crisis of overpopulation by making use of new technology!

In Europe and its settler colonies, because of the use of traditional and new methods of birth control, birth rates continued to drop despite rising population. With a rapidly changing technology, an increase in the size of labor power was not necessary in order to increase production. Conscious application of birth control methods had more to do with the changes in the social organization of production rather than changing technology. The advent of capitalism, according to Marx, was characterized by a practical asceticism, an attitude that regarded human procreation as a waste (Avineri, 1970:101).

Given the consequent worldwide imbalance between productivity — which accompanied the rapid growth of technology — and population growth, government policies encouraged or dis-

couraged migration in response to the perceived needs of the economy. Short-run interests of policymakers have often had long-term consequences for a country's economy. For example, in the first century after the British conquest of Canada, leaders manipulated migration successfully to reap the benefits of land speculation. Since then, Canada's economic development has been closely associated with, and often conditioned by, changing migration policies.

The second dimension of labor power, technology, is rooted in accumulated knowledge about nature, which is then applied by means of tools and techniques. Technology determines the productivity of labor. Hunting-and-gathering tribes, later agricultural societies, and the large colonial empires were all interested in improving the productivity of their labor force as much as we in the industrial world claim to be. It has always been the key to progress.

Gehlen (1980) attempts to reconstruct the entire history of our species as a history of technology. He sees the human subject as having, through successive stages, taken the various functions of his body and either enhanced them or transferred them to instruments fashioned out of nature. Beginning with the motor apparatus (hands, and legs), the process of transfer was followed with respect to energy production (the body as energy source) and the sensory apparatus (eyes, ears, and skin). With the invention of computers and Artificial Intelligence, this process seems to aim at augmenting if not replacing the functions of the brain, the control centre of all activities. Gehlen's reconstruction ignores the development of complex social structures and psychological processes (human self-understanding) that have accompanied or even produced these technological changes. He does, however, illustrate the importance of technology in enhancing the productivity of labor power. When carried to an extreme, the emphasis on the role of technology takes the form of *technological determinism*, which reverses the creative role of human societies in molding society. Gehlen argues that technology, as if by its own dynamics and without human intervention, affects the social order. Some sociologists have shown traces of such determinism (e.g., Veblen, 1922; Ogburn, 1950). Although the effects of technology on society are an important area for study, the central factor, social learning, should not be forgotten.

The third dimension, organization of production, has to do with co-ordinating labor by mobilizing it, training it, and then arranging it in the most efficient manner to ensure survival of the social order.

Furthermore, if the needs of a society change, the labor force must be reorganized to meet the change. But this must be done in keeping with changing environmental conditions for the human learning process to be viable. Innovation in technology must go hand in hand with innovations in the organization of labor.

Economy as the Institution of Control

Knowledge of nature's processes and the "know-how" to organize production changes over time. These changes are restricted by the way in which the labor force, technology, and production are controlled. As societies become more complex, they develop progressively more elaborate means to accomplish this task.

In hunting societies, control was minimal and no elaborate institutionalization of the economy occurred; that is, no stable and permanent division of resource and tasks existed. Land and the forests in which the hunt was conducted were equally shared by all, and division of labor lasted for the duration of the hunt. A more permanent division of labor existed along sex lines — women and children remained near the campsites during the hunt and collected vegetables and small animals nearby. Woman were probably the first cultivators of agriculture: the process of deliberate planting and nurturing of seeds. As you have already seen, the cultivation of food led to radi-

Caplin laid in an even pattern to dry in the sun, Nova Scotia.

cal structural changes in various human societies between 11 000 and 5000 B.C.

The major consequences of the food production (agriculture and animal husbandry) was the rise of surplus, and as a consequence, full-time crafts specialists emerged. It also gave rise to groups who began to control production and the distribution of surplus. This separation between producers and controllers, between the masses and leaders, grew more complex with an increasingly specialized division of labor. Today, large factories require a highly complex labor force, with many different departments, as well as supervisors and managers, who control the workers (at the bottom of the hierarchy) and who are responsible to owners (at the top). Each such unit is also integrated into the industry and institutions of

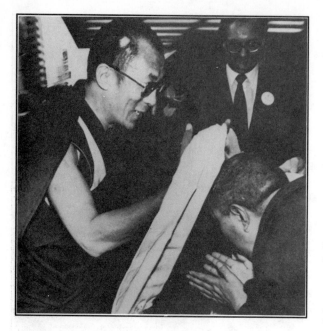

Prior to 1959, when the Chinese suppressed a revolt in Eastern Tibet, the Dalai Lama ruled over his countrymen as a priest-king. In many societies today, the distinction between church and state remains blurred.

change occurs through innovation and through confrontations between innovators and protectors of the status quo.

Religion and the Polity

Religion arose out of the need to explain the relationship between nature and humankind. Religious beliefs are as much a product of our imagination as are the innovations that improve our modes of survival and have been equally necessary to render coherence to the latter. They also change with changing economic relations. The polity, as the institution governing the distribution of a society's resources and surplus, grew out of the need to maintain social order. It also changes with the changes in the economy. The discrepancy between a society's capacity for increasing and redistributing surplus and the existing social order is usually experienced as a political crisis. The controllers of the social order then lose their legitimacy because they act as obstacles to change.

From a historical perspective, religion and government were once fused in the priest-king (in the Sumerian and Egyptian civilizations), who acted as custodian of the stored knowledge of a society. Even when the two spheres became differentiated, the political institution in some societies continued to draw upon religious explanations to justify decisions that affected the whole society. Kings claimed a divine right to rule. In this way, they also inherited an obligation to fulfil the expectations that a community of people associates with godliness. As a symbol of people's aspirations, kings are entitled to pomp and ceremony as a celebration of togetherness, but they are also presumably subject to containing and fulfilling all aspirations of their subjects to the best possible extent.

Leadership of this kind initially arises because it provides a society with innovative ways of fulfilling its needs. It is also conferred with certain advantages and privileges. It controls the minds and hearts of the people. Over a period of time, leaders develop a vested interest in that way of

finance and politics. Whether we speak of slow growth of the "know-how" of a hunting society or a highly organized flow, or of inventions and improvements to technology (through research and development, perspective planning, and so forth), discrepancies between increased potential for control over nature (technological possibilities) and the actual organization of that control (existing social institutions) are often a major source of crisis in the economy and social change. The specialized institutions within the economy of capitalism — property, money, profit, wages, markets, and legal contracts — and their combination are of recent origin.

Among other institutions that act as internal factors of social change, religion and polity evolved early in human history. Religious and political institutions also help us understand how social

In spite of India's entry into the space age, change comes slowly to the rural population. Farming techniques throughout the country have changed little in generations.

making sense — the means that conferred privileges on them. These leaders become involved in maintaining social order (the status quo) according to a successful blueprint. They either become incapable of recognizing the creative changes that occur in the economy, or it may not be in their interest to do so. They then seek to suppress change and try to persuade as many of their followers as possible to continue to believe in the status quo. Out of those whose life does not change because of the leaders resistance to change, new leaders arise. They have to battle with the established leadership in order to articulate and implement a new social order. The political institutions responsible for upholding social order thus turn into battlegrounds for social change.

EXTERNAL FACTORS OF SOCIAL CHANGE

Although potential for change is inherent in every society, some do not undergo radical structural change. Instead, changes take place over a long period of time, and attempts are made to absorb innovations within the existing cultural framework. But since a change in one area of given cultural produces change in other areas as well, the entire cultural framework undergoes change over time. This process may go unnoticed, sometimes for several centuries. For example, under the feudal social order, vast areas of forest and marsh were brought under cultivation, new towns were built, and inventions such as the plough and the harness were discovered. These changes spanned several centuries in a culture dominated by the clergy and the aristocracy. The impetus of all these innovations came, however, from the quiet and subservient mass of peasantry (Anderson, 1974).

The medieval period also illustrates the earlier point that some new ways of making sense get stored away as art, fiction, folklore, or counter-cultural activities (e.g., the alchemists of the sixteenth century). When these ideas reach a critical quantitative threshold, the existing cultural framework begins to crack from within, a revolutionary stage, of at times violent confrontations, emerges. The first signs of the end to feudalism came with peasant revolts, between the eleventh and the fourteenth centuries (Hilton, 1973).

The evolutionary process may be suddenly cut short and revolutionary change accelerated by the changes that occur in the organic-physical or social environment of a society. Since human beings are part of the organic-physical and social worlds, and affect them continually through their activity, the distinction between internal factors and external environment is more a matter of emphasis. The distinguishing feature of the environments of a society is that it can be controlled only minimally. A society must respond to changes in the environment by adapting its internal structure to these changes. External factors may require significant structural changes. For example, the Black Plague of the fourteenth century killed anywhere between 20 and 30 percent of the population of Europe and thus reduced the work force, thereby creating conditions for the eventual breakdown of feudalism (Braudel, 1967).

In simple, communal-type societies, the physical environment poses several limits on the capacity for change. There are aborigines in Australia who have never progressed beyond the hunting-and-gathering economy (Parsons, 1977). A possible explanation is that there were no suitable animals for domestication in their enivornment and hence a pastoral or agricultural society could not emerge.

Many societies probably disappeared in the face of unconquerable natural calamities.

The serious environmental challenges that are emerging today can hardly be described as external. Over the last few centuries, human innovation and adaptation have, because of the rapid development of the natural sciences, produced a unique relationship between nature and humankind. Scientific discoveries have led to an unprecedented growth of advanced technologies that use natural resources at rates that were unimaginable only a hundred years ago. In the process, massive amounts of waste matter are created. This is particularly true for North America, although the rest of the industrial world is not far behind. This process, in other words, begins with disequilibrium with nature, which leads to the destruction and depletion of nonrenewable resources and the creation of harmful waste material.

Another source of change is contact between two or more societies with substantially different internal structures and worldviews. When this happens, a diffusion of ideas and products may take place. Indeed, parts of the culture of any country can be shown to have been borrowed from another culture at some point in time (Murdock, 1934). An example of this is the Norman conquest of the British Isles in 1066, the result of which was the infusion of Norman culture into Anglo-Saxon culture.

Depending on its nature, contact can also be disastrous for some societies. For example, there is evidence to suggest that the impact of the European contact on the Indians in Canada was devastating for the latter. It may be summarized as the diffusion of disease, liquor, weapons, and wars. Dependency relations is another example of the detrimental effect that one society can have on another. With respect to Canada's current relationship to the United States, many Canadian observers (e.g., Williams, 1976) argue that this contact has placed Canada, the richest of all colonies, in the same disadvantageous position as many of the less-developed countries of Asia, Africa, and Latin America. Whether Canada should be viewed as a developed, imperialist power or as an underdeveloped hinterland specializing in primary production, is difficult to say, since it displays both types of characteristics (Clement, 1977; Naylor, 1980; Veltmeyer, 1980).

We now turn to the main theories that grew in the attempt to explain social change from eighteenth century to the present.

THEORIES OF SOCIAL CHANGE

Theories of the Enlightenment

The core concept in the theories that arose in the age of Enlightenment was reason. In the period preceding the rise of science (the Middle Ages), the religious theory of social change had interpreted reason as a divine faculty, an attribute of God. According to this theory, human beings behaved according to divine reason, if they acted conscientiously and correctly, that is, according to the moral norms of the society. In so doing, human beings gain true happiness in heaven, if not on earth.

The accomplishments of science changed the focus from the divinely interpreted norms of social action to norms that would ensure happiness on earth. The thinkers of the Enlightenment understood reason as the capacity of the human subject to apply general concepts to explain natural phenomena. They wanted to develop and apply similar concepts to the study of their society. They also believed in the idea of progress, which to them meant discovering the general principles of the social order in the same manner as they discovered the laws of natural science. In other words, progress meant implementation of reason by uprooting error, ignorance, and dogma.

Rousseau (1712–78) analyzed progress in terms of a paradox. He saw that as society develops and becomes more complex, it becomes harder for humankind to develop its potential. And herein

lies the paradox, for development of society creates the necessary conditions for that development. Like many other Enlightenment thinkers, he assumed that a scientific theory of society would necessarily be a critique of the existing institutions and a blueprint for a new society. To be a scientist of society was to be committed to change society if necessary. The rational criticism of oppressive institutions, religious as well as political, was considered to be an obligation.

Rousseau's ideas dominated the discussions of the philosophers of the French Revolution. The previous feudal society had been controlled by despots and priests who had lost touch with their people and who were also holding back the creative impulses of a new class of ambitious people (the bourgeoisie). Rousseau saw his task as exposing the untruth, not only of the objections directed against science, but also of the divine claims of the despots.

He argued that all social ills, moral depravity, dehumanization, and loss of human freedom were the outcomes of "the institution of inequality." To undo these wrongs, he advocated direct participation of all citizens in the decision-making process. However, Rousseau did not provide a plan of action, and left it to the theorists of the revolution to interpret his ideas in a revolutionary manner (Habermas, 1974:106).

The French Revolution struck a heavy blow to the old order. The new entrepreneurial class wanted to extend the potential for prosperity to a wider segment of society by making their emerging commercial-industrial economy the model of a new society. It was believed that a market economy would bring equal happiness to all. The masses who had enthusiastically participated in the revolution naturally felt it was their due to become equal participants in the making of the "General Will" of the new society as Rousseau had advocated. The slogans of equality, liberty, and fraternity had propelled them into courageous action, however misguided it might have seemed later. For the revolution marked the end of that dream. In the past, similar dreams had propelled the masses to action in the name of a divine community on earth.

The aftermath of the revolution made it clear to the newly emerged economic interests in Europe (some of which had been at the forefront of the revolution) that mass participation in the new political order would threaten their economic privilege. Thus, all over Europe, a strong negative response resounded to the theories of social change that characterized the Enlightenment. It was strongest in England, where the new capitalist class was also the strongest in Europe.

Evolutionary Theories

Theories of social change that arose in reaction to the Enlightenment and the revolution focused primarily on the maintenance of the status quo. They also spoke of reason and progress but with an entirely different interpretation. You have already been introduced to Compte as one of the fathers of sociology. Compte equated reason with science, which, in its methodology, rests on facts. This notion required that concepts explaining the social world be derived from the facts that constitute that world. Once the laws governing human society were discovered, Compte expected societies to be able to control their destiny, just as natural science can control nature. According to Compte, societies progress from theological and metaphysical stages to the final, positive stage, and hence his theory was evolutionary in perspective. Until both the positive stage and scientific reason have arrived in their full and final form, Western society would remain incapable of coping with the new challenges created by the "negative" philosophy of the Enlightenment.

Most theories of social change in the Comptean tradition were predicated on the assumption that Western industrial society, because of its enormous economic success, was approaching the most evolved form. Theorists who held this belief prescribed that the study of society should aim at understanding the laws of behavior, and not indulge in criticism, which cannot be based on scientific fact and hence would have only negative outcomes. The idea of the scientific method as objective, meaning merely descriptive and uncritical of the existing patterns, took root in mainstream sociology through positivism.

Even though Compte argued that social theories should be based on observation and analysis, his own theory of social change was not. Even though he insisted that theories should be verifiable, his was not. It was in fact a justification of scientific objectivism based on non-positive inferences (Habermas, 1971).

The early evolutionary theories were explicit in their beliefs that the movement from preindustrial to the industrial stage was progressive. Advocates spoke of the internal differentiation of social structures. The inner logic of growth and differentiation of structures seem to happen automatically according to these theories. In the theories of Herbert Spencer (1820–1903), a major theme was the submission of the individual to the laws of social evolution. Such theories fulfilled two functions. First, they provided justification for colonial expansion and the economic and political domination of other civilizations and societies. Merchants, missionaries, and civil servants saw colonialism as the noble way of civilizing the natives. Secondly, whereas Rousseau and other Enlightenment thinkers provided the impetus for a critical and scientific examination of social institutions, evolutionists placed the logic of development of social institutions beyond the pale of such criticism. In the extreme case, evolutionary theories such as "Social Darwinism" became a justification for the poverty, ignorance, and apathy of the underprivileged, and for the privileges of the rich.

Functional Theories

Functional theories of social change began to emerge when doubts about the superiority of the Western way of life arose because the economy did not produce a concomitant increase in the welfare of all people in all societies. More recent theories recognized that conflicting interests do arise within a given social order, and produce contradictory interpretations of such ideals as equality and honesty that superficially appear to be universally shared.

Talcott Parsons saw the evolution of societies from simple to complex as a process of problem-solving through cultural and social innovation. As societies become more complex and structurally differentiated, competing or conflicting interests result. These, in turn, trigger changes in the cultural pattern, which leads to the integration of the specialized roles and groups. Thus, according to Parsons, societies have to meet the internal challenges to their functioning produced by differentiation. They face external challenges to their integration, produced by the environment, including contact with other societies. These they must meet through further differentiation. Thus, social change was understood basically as the process of resolving problems of the society as a social system.

The major drawback of functional theories is that they do not take sufficient account of the role of the individual in the process of social change (Davis, 1959). Functionalists do speak of goal-oriented individuals engaged in meaningful social action, but their major concern is with institutions — their continuity and orderly development (Wrong, 1961; Gouldner, 1970). Their emphasis on culturally defined goals and properly socialized individuals makes the thoughts and actions of individuals seem to be socially implanted circuits of values, norms, and role expectations. Deviance from the norm is regarded as dysfunctional, and dominant values and norms are never questioned as ideologies. Conflict is considered to be functional only when a stable, integrated outcome is ensured.

Those who are generally discribed as conflict theorists (e.g., Simmel, Dahrendorf, Coser) are also mainly interested in the functions rather than the dysfunctions of conflict.

Dialectical Theory

Unlike conflict theory, Marx's dialectical theory of social change sees conflict as a symptom of something more basic. Marx speaks of *contradictions* rather than conflicts. Contradictions exist when the claims of a society diverge widely from the reality of people's experience. For example, if equality is a value in a society, those who experience inequality may demand that those who are in power fulfil the claim of equality. If such a change is possible, the leaders may agree to fulfil such a demand and thus the conflict may end in better integration. *Contradictions* remain when the fulfillment of the demands of one segment of society would necessarily require denying the legitimate claims of another. If both claims are of fundamental importance to the existence of the society, then the only resolution possible is for that society to move to a new social order that can go beyond the stalemate and make the claims non-contradictory. According to Marx, whether or not such a resolution succeeds depends on whether the *forces of production* have developed adequately. This dialectical view of social change takes into account both the explanation-justification (ideology) aspect of theory and the critical, blueprint (critique) aspect.

The basic contradiction of capitalism is that although production becomes more and more social (i.e., interdependence, based on equally necessary and valuable activities of all workers), the surplus is still harnessed by the few who own or control capital (including tools and machines). This contradiction expresses itself in conflicts between workers and capitalists. Marx argued that in order to resolve the contradiction, workers must struggle for a new blueprint of society. He called that blueprint *socialism*.

Marx's theory dealt primarily with capitalism in its early stages of development. However, later developments, such as the rise of multinational corporations and new international division of labor, called for major reinterpretations of Marx, which have greatly enriched our understanding of the dynamics of capitalism. Although tempered by a dialectical sense of the class structure in all societies, revisions of Marxist theories still seem to retain a Western orientation to the concepts of modernity and tradition, to which we now turn.

MODERNITY AND TRADITION

Even in the common-sense usage of the word, "tradition" refers to the past. It also implies continuity, in the sense that something from the past is transmitted to the present. Depending upon what that something is, there is usually a positive or a negative attitude that goes with it. (For example, television commercials advertise lemonades (food) as "good" and "old-fashioned," in contrast to laundry detergents (chemicals) that are always "new and improved.") Tradition implies communication between generations, and acknowledging tradition means that we recognize that we are part of history.

In sociology, "there is the pervasive absence of any analysis of the nature and mechanisms of tradition." (Shils, 1961:1426.) Today, sociologists most commonly use the term reference to "traditional society" in justaposition to "modern society."

The evolutionary and functional theories have drawn upon the Western experience of industrialization to find the contrasting attributes of tradition and modernity, which we shall examine later. The prevalent view of modernity often implies elimination of tradition. However, the impact of the past has certainly not disappeared from the Western societies.

In this essay, we shall treat tradition and modernity as dual concepts but not as substitutes for each other. Rather, I shall argue that one may become the other at different points of time. Such a view avoids the bias inherent in the idea that modernization is "good" and tradition is "bad." Although evolutionary and functional theories grant that societies may stagnate and others may undergo changes, they assume that societies that

advance take control of their natural resources and use them in their own best interests. In order to take control, it is necessary to have a sufficient knowledge of the natural world to be able to predict the outcome of the intent. These beliefs stem from a more basic belief in the scientific method of understanding and using empirical reality. However, societies are manipulated by individuals who control the societies, and so the results are often detrimental to the societies in question.

Belief in the scientific method as the only way of achieving control comes together in a widely believed interpretation of *modernity*: modernity is understood as the conscious application of a certain set of procedures in order to ensure a specific set of anticipated outcomes. The basic underlying model is that of scientific experimentation. In an experiment, one wants to know, on the basis of previous empirical knowledge, whether a particular outcome will follow a set of steps taken according to given rules. A prediction is made about the outcome, which takes the form of "if-then" statements. If the expected outcome does not occur, one has to question the assumptions on which the experiment was based.

The same logic can be applied to social events. We want to be able to predict the result of an action to achieve orderliness in our lives, which in turn orders our future. If we adhere to the norms and values of the society in which we live, we can expect predicted outcomes. Weber described this mode of thinking about life and nature as being unique to the West. This *"means-ends rationality"* contrasts with another mode of thinking called *value-rationality*. In the latter, a decision has to be made about how to act, and the criterion of choice cannot be empirical knowledge but value preferences. Scientific rationality comes into the picture insofar as all possible choices of action, with respect to the value preferences, are carefully looked at before a decision is made. This amounts to choosing the best strategy of action for attaining goals that are derived from the values.

A girl swings her axe into a cedar log during a totem pole carving lesson. The carved clan emblems are a feature of west coast native culture.

For Weber, "technical man" treats the world strictly in terms of "means-end rationality", whereas "cultured man" gives priority to value-rationality. Let us turn to an examination of the Western world in Weberian terms.

Modernity as Westernization

Transposed to the historical context of the late nineteenth- and early twentieth-century Europe, Weber's concept of Westernization meant (1) the prevalence of the capitalist mode of production; (2) the emergence of legal systems for the protection of private property and individual rights; and (3) the bureaucratic organization of authority (Giddens, 1971). The last of these developments was a cause of great concern for Weber, for he feared the consequences of "the total victory of 'technical man' (ruled by means-end rationality) over 'cultured man'." (Mommsen, 1970: page 186.) However, having attributed this trend

In choosing to wear the traditional *chador*, these Iranian women have voiced their doubts about the benefit of Western values to their society.

to a uniquely Western mode of thinking over and beyond the specific context of the development of capitalism, he felt that this "victory" was inevitable. The only counter-tendencies he could visualize were in terms of a vague, almost mystical belief in the human charisma.

The Enlightenment thinkers had attributed to rationality the critical function of organizing action against oppressive social institutions. Taking his cues from them, Marx developed a different, more universal conception of social change. For Marx, the roots of modernity were not in capitalism, but in the struggle for emancipation.

Modernity and Tradition: a Dynamic View

Proponents of modernization took Weber's idea of *traditional authority* (one that is legitimated

by custom) as resting in the past, and developed the argument that there is little impetus for change in societies based on traditional authority until they come into contact with Western thinking. Out of this conviction grew the belief that contact with, and imitation of, the West was by and large beneficial. However, in recent years, some rethinking about the dichotomous treatment of modernity and tradition has emerged, and more attention has been paid to those features of developing societies that are receptive to change and development and to those that are not (Ishwaran, 1981).

For Marx, as mentioned above, modernity occurs when outdated worldviews and beliefs are challenged. When leaders of the deprived classes see that change is necessary, they challenge the established rules for a new and more human social order. Studies of social movements show that history is full of examples of such battles, and their successes and failures. In Cuba in the recent past, peasants fought a successful battle against an oppressive regime and ideology, and implemented a new blueprint for their society. Similarly, oppressed peoples in South America, South Africa, and the Phillipines are currently fighting against outdated ideologies and social orders.

Thus, we can interpret modernity in two ways: according to the limited perspective of Western industrialization or according to challenges to the existing social order. In the latter view, modernity is both the means by which human beings can overcome nature and the oppression of human beings by society. With regard to the first way, Weber showed that the extension of rationalization to all domains of life becomes dehumanization: "We become preoccupied with getting the most from the least effort; we care less and less about the negative impact of such policies on people." (Ritzer, 1983:21.) If this is the case, can we trust the will and ability of the leaders in so-called modern societies to contain the growth of dangerous waste materials, to halt the rapid depletion of nonrenewable resources, and in the final analysis, to do away with the accumulating arsenals of total annihilation? In many Third World countries, the leaders are doing their best to imitate the Western experience at a highly accelerated pace. Many of them share the outlook of Western leaders, and measure progress by the same yardstick they use. Can we treat their aspirations and their desire for westernization as representative of the will of their people?

The masses in some Third World countries still live under the dictates of tradition. Even though the rulers, old and new, may interpret traditional values in their own interest, they still take their cues from the aspirations of their people. These dreams are about a future society, an ideal, *potential community*. As the forces of production in Third World countries develop, this ideal community will become more attainable. This will be made possible by means of modernity of tradition: life under the old ways will become more and more intolerable. If the rulers continue to justify old ways of ruling in terms of tradition, a critique of their false claims will become more and more persistent. That movements for the realization of unfulfilled dreams will increase is at the core of Marx's dialectical theory (Lefebvre, 1968: 5). Every society has the potential to change from within, creating new from the old. It is in this sense that modernity arises from tradition. As such, neither modernity nor revolution can be exported from one society to another to achieve effective social change.

Modernity versus Tradition: a Dichotomous View

The dichotomous view of modernity and tradition makes three assumptions:

1. Modernity and rationality are equated with science. This creates an impression that all relationships between nature and humankind and society before the rise of science were not based on fact, and those based on the scientific method are necessarily right.
2. Modernity necessarily gives rise to a plurality of religious beliefs, theories, views, and opinions, and hence there is no possibility and therefore no need to consider the restoration of a total worldview that considers a balanced relationship between nature and humankind and society as necessary for survival.
3. Modernity is dynamic and tradition is an obstacle or deadweight. The inner dynamics by which worldviews recurrently show their capacity to interpret and reinterpret reality are not understood and so tradition is denied relevance.

Let us look at each assumption in more detail.

It is true that science and industrialization have basically altered our ways of gaining nurture from nature. But a technical transformation of nature

Salvadoreans march through the streets of San Salvador to commemorate the anniversary of the death of Archbishop Monseigneur Oscar Arnulfo Romero, who in 1980 was assassinated by unknown gunmen while he said mass.

did occur before Galileo, and human beings did create and fulfil their needs before him. If meaningful existence and survival (with surplus) are the two basic criteria of potential for development, then our ancestors did not do too badly. In some ways, they probably did better. This is not to deny the liberating effects of science. It can liberate humanity from pain, hunger, cold, and toil. But it can also enhance the coercive power of the rulers and delay liberation from oppression. Marcuse (1964) has shown how science and technology, under conditions of increasing rationalization, lead to totalitarianism. The development of science also depends on the guiding interests of those who control it. Dehumanization and the advancement of science may reinforce each other.

In medieval Europe, the proponents of the scientific method were courageous, since science challenged the current potential and religious order. Under the forces of rationalization, science and technology become means of social control. The subtle suppression of inner freedom through development of mind- and personality-altering technologies, and of social freedom through electronic-surveillence techniques, have been well documented (Kahn and Wiener, 1969; Habermas, 1970). In a social, economic, and political climate charged with this obsession for control of nature and humankind, how can we make "science and technology subservient to the needs and goals of free men"? (Marcuse, 1969:56.)

Before advocating the transfer of science and technology to Third World countries where tradition still predominates, we must first ask how they will be affected. Whether science becomes beneficial or detrimental will depend on whether it serves all levels of society. For the masses to benefit, the internal structure of power must be such that the masses are able to demand change.

To understand how social change will affect society, we must learn to look at it objectively, without imposing our own culture's values on it. In this way, the disastrous effects that often arise from contact between two societies can be avoided, and a better understanding of different modes of thinking with respect to the relationship between nature and society can be achieved. A reappraisal of science, tradition, and modernity is essential if we are to meet some of the challenges that rationalization has produced for the West and for the rest of the world.

Tradition in the precapitalist Western society had the power to both integrate society and initiate its transformation. Although rulers invariably used religion to justify oppression, history also shows that religious leaders led massive and often successful rebellions against injustice. Even today, we witness Roman Catholic priests in El Salvador and Brazil working with the peasants in fighting oppression, with arms, if necessary. Similarly, in South Africa, clergy are in the forefront of the battle for liberation of black people from white oppression.

Despite the modernized and secular society in which we live, traditional values still survive in Canadian society. It has been suggested that traditional institutions such as the family and school still perpetuate traditional values along class lines; therefore it is said that achievement-orientation exists among the middle class and lack of motivation among the working class. Emphasis on self-discipline and renunciation of immediate gratification associated with the Protestant Ethic also persist in our society as values.

Sociologists such as Habermas (1970) and Giddens (1971), who offer a critique of modern society, have sometimes suggested revitalization of the Enlightenment ideas of freedom, equality, and community. However, social movements whose goal is mass participation in decision-making, and that attempt structural changes that would ensure the realization of this democratic ideal, cannot be expected to arise out of a "depoliticised public." (Habermas, 1970.) Thus, critical sociologists, while pointing out many of the problems of modern society, cannot seem to offer convincing solutions.

We may conclude that the two opposite views of tradition as dynamic worldview and as constraining ideology are but two sides of the same reality. Depending on the situation, one or the other manifests itself. In the Western experience, science arose at a time when tradition had become a dogmatic ideology. At about the same time, capitalism was propagated by a class that had been left out of the traditional sociopolitical order of princes and priests. Hence, attacks on the old order took the form of an attack on tradition, and modernity came to be associated with a break from tradition.

During the period of colonization, Western rulers (English, French, Dutch, and German) promoted the establishment of a class of local elites who became trained in the Western mode of thought and in so doing lost touch with much of their own past. At best, the elites became commuters between two cultures. As leaders of post-colonial societies such as Asia, Africa, and India, they are promoting a view of modernization that is consistent with Western prejudice; that is, they look upon tradition as an obstacle to change. At the same time, they have become adept at using traditional symbols to gain popular support for themselves. In the long run, they would like to see the people become "modern," like they are. They hope that when their people's sense of tradition does disappear, they will at the same time become willing to take "rational" orders from rational leaders.

Students of social change can better understand and explain their own social reality if they re-examine the prevalent notions about tradition, modernity, and change. They must also examine the direction taken by science and technology dur-

Despite a rapidly changing society, traditional values are still cherished in Canada.

ing the last two centuries and the impact of technology on everyday life. The perpetual threat of annihilation, of which we cannot help but be aware, and our apathy and/or inability to take concerted action toward overcoming it, or both legacies of a fractured sense of modernity. Tradition and modernity are not antithetical concepts.

Together, they constitute the basis of ordered survival and orderly change.

SUMMARY

1. Tradition, modernity, and social change are closely interrelated.

2. By studying the history of human civilization, we become familiar with how social change was brought about through adaptation and invention.

3. We also become sensitive to the revolutionary potential of tradition. A society's internal processes of differentiation and integration, operating through economic, political, and other institutions, may sometimes become accelerated by external factors such as the physical environment and contacts with other societies.

4. Most important is a society's level of control over its environment and over the adaptation required to exercise that control. Changes and challenges in the environment may, otherwise, threaten or accelerate the process of structural differentiation.

5. The most noteworthy example of social change is the industrialization of the Western world. It began with the overthrow of the feudal regime in Europe. When mass political participation threatened the new dominant classes, a strong reaction to the Enlightenment ideas emerged in Europe. It was reflected in the evolutionary and functional theories of social change, the first to attempt to discover the laws of social change.

6. Unilinear evolutionary theories were predicted on the assumption that Western industrial society was approaching the most evolved form. Functional theories address the problem of continuity and orderly development of institutions.

7. Weber understood modernity as the conscious application of scientific procedures in order to ensure predicted outcomes. He interpreted it as a uniquely Western mode of thinking, and capitalism as its major manifestation. For Marx, the roots of modernity were to be found not in capitalism but in man's struggle for emancipation.

8. Throughout human history, tradition—man's relationship to the past—is not merely passed down through generations. It has, in fact, shown two tendencies. One is that of providing justifications for a social order, no matter how oppressive it is. The other is to challenge such use by the rulers and to produce a critique of that order. Such

a critique may become a blueprint for a new society. This view of tradition avoids the enthnocentrism of the belief that modernization is good and suggests that tradition is still important for the future development of Western society.

GLOSSARY

Capitalism. The mode of production in which the means of production and the surplus (the wealth of the society) are privately controlled or owned.

Contradictions. Situations in which fulfilling legitimate demands of one segment of the society necessarily requires that legitimate claims of another segment be violated.

Dependency theory. A theory that shows that capitalist industrialization of the West has consequences for the Third World: namely, underdevelopment.

Diffusion. Transmission and incorporation of cultural traits, customs, techniques, and beliefs from one society to another as a consequence of contact.

Modernity. In conventional sociology, this refers to the frame of mind or social organization in which means-ends rationality is consciously at work.

Modernization theory. A theory that applies the lessons of the experience of the West to the development problems of the Third World.

Rationalization. Progressive penetration of means-ends rationality into all domains of social life.

Social change. Change in the basic and relatively stable patterns of social life, including institutions and social action.

Socialism. The mode of production in which the basic contradictions of capitalism will have been overcome, particularly class contradictions.

Social learning. The process by which innovations, inventions, and discoveries made by individuals are incorporated or stored away in social institutions. All inventions and innovations or discoveries normally occur within the existing institutional ways of making sense.

Tradition. A concept indicating attachment to the past.

FURTHER READING

Byrm, Robert J. and R. James Sacouman (eds.). *Underdevelopment and Social Movements in Atlantic Canada.* Toronto: New Hogtown Press, 1979. A collection of essays dealing with some responses by the working-class people of Atlantic Canada to the underdevelopment of their regions.

Eisenstadt, S.N. (ed.). *Readings in Social Evolution and Development.* Toronto: Pergamon Press, 1970. A valuable collection of essays on social change and development. Important ideas in evolutionary, functional, and dialectical theories of social change are discussed.

Frank, A.G. *Latin America: Underdevelopment or Revolution.* New York: Monthly Review Press, 1969. A classic in the literature on dependency, with a thought-provoking analysis of the ideological basis of the sociology of development. The second chapter deals critically with modernization theory.

Garner, Roberta Ash. *Social Change.* Chicago: Rand McNally, 1977. A long treatment of social change, amply illustrated with case studies. It deals with major historical epochs of social change and outlines basic concepts necessary for a full understanding of change.

Giddens, Anthony. *Sociology.* New York: Harcourt Brace Jovanovich, 1982. A brief but readable discussion of the discipline. Giddens presents some interesting comparisons between classical sociology and Marx's theory of society, particularly as they relate to the problems of social change.

Gouldner, Alvin. *The Coming Crisis of Western Sociology.* New York: Avon Books, 1970. A comprehensive critique of both functional and conflict theories. Gouldner's analysis of the ideological background of modern sociology is particularly good.

Lefebvre, Henri. *The Sociology of Marx.* New York: Random House, 1968. A comprehensive and lucid introduction to Marx's theory of society. It also deals with many contemporary problems from the Marxist perspective.

Marcuse, Herbert. *One-Dimensional Man.* Boston: Beacon Press, 1964. A classic in the critical theory tradition. Marcuse presents a penetrating analysis of the process of dehumanization in modern society.

Ogburn, William F. *Social Change.* New York: Viking Press, 1950. An early work on social change. Ogburn argues that cultural traits often fail to keep pace with technological innovations (culture-lag thesis) and thus gives primacy to technology over human creativity and social learning.

References

Abbey, Antonia
  1982 "Sex Differences in Attributions for Friendly
        Behaviour: Do Males Misperceive Females'
        Friendliness?" *Journal of Personality and Social
        Psychology*, Vol.42:830–38.

Aberle, D.
  1965 "A Note on Relative Deprivation as Applied
        to Millenarian and Other Cult Movements."
        In W.A. Lessa and E.Z. Vogt (eds.), *Reader
        in Comparative Religion: An Anthropologi-
        cal Approach.* 2nd ed. New York: Harper &
        Row, 537–41.

Ableson, J., P. Paddon and C. Strohmenger
  1983 *Perspectives on Health.* Ottawa: Statistics
        Canada, Supply and Services.

Acker, Joan
  1973 "Women and Social Stratification: A Case of
        Intelligent Sexism." *American Journal of Soci-
        ology*, Vol.78:936–45.

Adachi, Ken
  1976 *The Enemy That Never Was.* Toronto:
        McClelland & Stewart.

Adair, D. and J. Rosenstock
  1977 "Explaining Racial Attitudes Among Ado-
        lescents." *Multiculturalism*, Vol.1:1.

Agar, Michael
  1982 *The Professional Stranger.* Englewood Cliffs,
        N.J.: Prentice-Hall.

Agger, Robert et al.
  1972 *The Rulers and the Ruled.* Belmont, Calif.:
        Duxbury Press.

Akzin, Benjamin
  1964 *State and Nation.* Garden City, N.Y.:
        Doubleday/Anchor Books.

Albrecht, Stan L.
  1979 "Correlates of Marital Happiness Among the
        Remarried." *Journal of Marriage and the
        Family*, Vol.41,No.4:857–67.

Alexander, W.E. and J.F. Farrell
  1975 *Student Participation in Decision-making.*
        Toronto: Ontario Institute for Studies in Edu-
        cation.

Allport, Gordon W.
  1954 *The Nature of Prejudice.* Garden City, N.Y.:
        Doubleday/Anchor Books.

Anderson, Alan B.
  1982 "Generation Differences in Ethnic Identity
        Retention in Rural Saskatchewan." *Prairie
        Forum*, Vol.7:2.

Anderson, Alan B. and James S. Frideres
  1981 *Ethnicity in Canada: Theoretical Perspectives.*
        Toronto: Butterworth.

Anderson, Perry
  1974 *Passages from Antiquity to Feudalism.*
        London: Humanities Press.

Anderson, Perry
  1974 *Passages from Antiquity to Feudalism.*
        London: Verso Edition, NLB.

Anderson, U.M.
  1970 "Infant Survival Differentials in the City of
        Toronto: A Challenge to Health and Plan-
        ning and Research." *Canadian Family Physi-
        cian*, Vol.16(September):45–50.

Anisef, P., N. Okihiro and C. James
  1982 *Losers and Winners: The Pursuit of Equality
        and Social Justice in Higher Education.*
        Toronto: Butterworth.

Anthony, Harry Antoniades
  1979 *The Challenge of Squatter Settlements: With
        Special Reference to the Cities of Latin
        America.* Vancouver: University of British
        Columbia Press.

Armstrong, Hugh and Pat Armstrong
  1975 "The Segregated Participation of Women in
        the Canadian Labour Force, 1941-71." *Cana-
        dian Review of Sociology and Anthropology*,
        Vol.12:370–84.

Armstrong, Hugh and Pat Armstrong
1983 *A Working Majority, What Women Must Do for Pay.* Ottawa: Canadian Advisory Council on the Status of Women.

Armstrong, Pat and Hugh Armstrong
1984 *The Double Ghetto, Canadian Women and Their Segregated Work.* Revised edition. Toronto: McClelland & Stewart.

Arnopoulos, Sheila M.
1982 *Voices from French Ontario.* Montréal: McGill-Queen's University Press.

Aron, Raymond
1965 *Main Currents in Sociological Thought.* 1st translation by Richard Howard and Helen Weaver. New York: Basic Books.

Asch, Michael
1984 *Home and Native Land: Aboriginal Rights and the Constitution.* Toronto: Methuen.

Atkinson, A.B.
1975 *The Economics of Inequality.* Oxford: University of Oxford Press.

Atkinson, J.W. and D.C. McClelland
1948 "The Projective Expression of Needs." *Journal of Experimental Psychology*, Vol.38:405.

Aubert, V.
1963 "Competition and Dissensus: Two Types of Conflict and Conflict Resolution." *Journal of Conflict Resolution*, Vol.7(March):26–42.

Bachrach, P. and M.S. Baratz
1963 "Decisions and Non-decisions." *American Political Science Review*, Vol.57:632–42.

Bainbridge, W.S. and R. Stark
1982 "Church and Cult in Canada." *Canadian Journal of Sociology*, Vol.7,No.4:351–66.

Balakrishnan, T.R.
1976 "Ethnic Residential Segregation in Metropolitan Areas of Canada." *Canadian Journal of Sociology*, Vol.1,No.4:481–98.

Balakrishnan, T.R. and George K. Jarvis
1979 "Changing Patterns of Spatial Differentiation in Urban Canada, 1961-1971." *Canadian Review of Sociology and Anthropology*, Vol.16:218–27.

Balch, Robert W. and David Taylor
1977 "Seekers and Saucers: The Role of the Cultic Milieu in Joining a UFO Cult." *American Behaviorist Scientist*, Vol.20,No.6:839–60.

Bales, Robert (ed.)
1955 *Family Socialization and Interaction Process.* Glencoe, Illinois: Free Press.

Baltzell, E.D.
1958 *Philadelphia Gentlemen.* Glencoe, Illinois: Free Press.

Bandura, Albert
1969 *Principles of Behavior Modification.* New York: Holt, Rinehart and Winston.

Bandura, Albert
1973 *Aggression: A Social Learning Analysis.* Englewood Cliffs, N.J.: Prentice-Hall.

Bandura, Albert
1977 *Social Learning Theory.* Englewood Cliffs, N.J.: Prentice-Hall.

Banfield, Edward C.
1970 *The Unheavenly City Revisited.* Boston: Little, Brown.

Barry, I., Herbert and M. Bacon and I. Child
1974 "Cross-cultural Survey of Some Sex Differences in Socialization." In I. Alissa and W. Dennis (eds.), *Cross-cultural Studies of Behavior.* New York: Holt, Rinehart and Winston.

Basavarajappa, K.G. and J. Lindsay
1976 *Mortality Differences in Canada, 1960-62 and 1970-72.* Ottawa: Statistics Canada, Supply and Services.

Baum, Gregory
1975 *Religion and Alienation: A Theological Reading of Sociology.* Toronto: Paulist Press.

Beaujot, R.P.
1978 "Canada's Population: Growth and Dualism." *Population Bulletin*, Vol.33,No.2:3–47.

Bebbington, Andrew C.
1970 "The Effect of Non-response in the Sample Survey with an Example." *Human Relations*, Vol.23:169–80.

Becker, Gary S.
1964 *Human Capital.* New York: Columbia University Press.

Bendix, Reinhard
1962 *Max Weber: An Intellectual Portrait.* Garden City, N.Y.: Anchor Books.

Bendix, Reinhard
1963 *Work and Authority in Industry.* New York: Harper & Row, Harper Torchbooks edition.

Benedict, Ruth
1938 "Continuities and Discontinuities in Cultural Conditioning." *Psychiatry*, Vol.1:161–67.

Benedict, Ruth
1961 *Patterns of Culture.* (1934) Boston: Houghton Mifflin.

Beniger, James R.
1983 *Trafficking in Drug Users: Professional Exchange Networks in the Control of Deviance.* New York: Cambridge University Press.

Bennett, N.
1976 *Teaching Style and Pupil Progress.* Cambridge, Mass.: Harvard University Press.

Benson, Leslie
  1978   *Proletarians and Parties: Five Essays on Social Class*. Wellington, N.Z.: Methuen.
Berelson, B. (ed.)
  1974   *Population Policy in Developed Countries*. New York: McGraw-Hill.
Berg, I.
  1970   *Education and Jobs: The Great Training Robbery*. New York: Praeger.
Berger, J., T.L. Connor and M.H. Fisek (eds.)
  1974   *Expectation States Theory: A Theoretical Research Program*. Cambridge: Winthrop.
Berger, Peter
  1963   *Invitation to Sociology*. Garden City, N.Y.: Doubleday/Anchor Books.
Berger, Thomas R.
  1977   *Northern Frontier, Northern Homeland: The Report of the Mackenzie Valley Pipeline Inquiry*, Vol. 1. Ottawa: Supply and Services.
Bernard, Jessie
  1974   *The Future of Marriage*. New York: Macmillan.
Bernard, William S.
  1959   "The Integration of Immigrants in the United States." Paper presented at the UNESCO conference, April, 1956: cited in W.D. Borrie, *The Cultural Integration of Immigrants*. Paris: UNESCO.
Berreman, Gerald
  1960   "Caste in India and the United States." *American Journal of Sociology*, Vol.66 (September):120-27.
Berry, Brian J.L.
  1978   "The Counter-urbanization Process: How General?" In Niles M. Hansen (ed.), *Human Settlement Systems*. Cambridge, Mass.: Ballinger Publishing, 25-49.
Berscheid E. and E. Walster
  1979   *Interpersonal Attraction*. Reading, Mass.: Addison-Wesley.
Bettelheim, Bruno
  1959   "Feral Children and Autistic Children." *American Journal of Sociology*, Vol.64:455-67.
Bettelheim, Bruno and Morris Janowitz
  1964   *Social Change and Prejudice*. Glencoe, Illinois: Free Press.
Bibby, Reginald W.
  1977   "Religiosity in Canada: A National Survey." In C. Beattie and S. Crysdale (eds.), *Sociology Canada: Readings*. Toronto: Butterworth.
Bibby, Reginald W.
  1980   "Religion." In Robert Hagedorn (ed.), *Sociology*. Toronto: Holt, Rinehart and Winston.

Bibby, Reginald W.
  1982   "The Precarious Mosaic." *Intergroup Relations* (Project CAN80, Release No. 3.). Lethbridge: University of Lethbridge.
Bibby, Reginald W. and Merlin B. Brinkerhoff
  1974   "When Proselytizing Fails: An Organizational Analysis." *Sociological Analysis*, Vol.35: 189-200.
Bibby, Reginald and Merlin B. Brinkerhoff
  1976   "The Circulation of the Saints." In S. Crysdale and L. Wheatcroft (eds.), *Religion in Canadian Society*. Toronto: Macmillan.
Blake, Judith and David Kingsley
  1964   "Norms, Values, and Sanctions." In Robert E.L. Faris (ed.), *Handbook of Modern Sociology*. Chicago: Rand McNally.
Blau, Peter M.
  1964   *Exchange and Power in Social Life*. New York: John Wiley.
Blau, Peter M.and Otis Dudley Duncan
  1967   *The American Occupational Structure*. New York: John Wiley.
Blau, Zena Smith
  1981   *Aging in a Changing Society*. 2nd ed. New York: Franklin Watts.
Blauner, Robert
  1972   *Racial Oppression in America*. New York: Harper & Row.
Bloch, Marc
  1961a   *Feudal Society*. Translated by L.A. Manyon. London: Routledge and Kegan Paul.
Bloch, Marc
  1961b   *Feudal Society. Volume I: The Growth of Ties of Dependence. Volume II: Social Classes and Political Organization*. Chicago: University of Chicago Press.
Blood, Robert and D.M. Wolfe
  1960   *Husbands and Wives*. Glencoe, Illinois: Free Press.
Blum, J.
  1978   *The End of the Old Order in Rural Europe*. Princeton, N.J.: Princeton University Press.
Blumberg, Paul
  1974   "The Decline and Fall of the Status Symbol: Some Thoughts on Status in a Post-industrial Society." *Social Problems*, Vol.21:480-98.
Blumer, Herbert
  1946   "Collective Behavior." (1939) In Alfred McClung Lee (ed.), *Principles of Sociology*. 2nd ed. New York: Barnes and Noble, 167-222.

Blumer, Herbert
  1969 *Symbolic Interactionism: Perspective and Method.* Englewood Cliffs, N.J.: Prentice-Hall.
Boldt, Menno
  1980 "Canadian Native Leadership: Context and Composition." *Canadian Ethnic Studies*, Vol.12:15-33.
Boocock, Suzanne Spence
  1978 "The Social Organization of the Classroom." In R.H. Turner, J. Coleman and R.C. Fox (eds.), *Annual Review of Sociology.* 4th ed. Palo Alto, Calif.: Annual Reviews, Inc.
Boocock, Suzanne Spence
  1980 *Sociology of Education: An Introduction.* 2nd ed. Boston: Houghton Mifflin.
Boulet, Jacques-André and Laval Lavallée
  1983 *L'Évolution des Disparités Linguistiques des Revenus de Travail au Canada, 1970 à 1980.* Ottawa: Economic Council of Canada.
Bourgeault, Ron
  1983 "The Development of Capitalism and Subjugation of Native Women in Northern Canada." *Alternate Routes*, Vol.6:109-40.
Bourne, L.S.
  1975 *Urban Systems: Strategies for Regulation.* Oxford: Clarendon Press.
Bouvier, L.F., H.S. Shryock and H.W. Henderson
  1977 "International Migration: Yesterday, Today and Tomorrow." *Population Bulletin*, Vol.32, No.4:3-42.
Bowen, Kurt
  1983 *Protestants in a Catholic State: Ireland's Privileged Minority.* Montréal and Kingston: McGill-Queen's University Press.
Bowles, Samuel
  1971 "Unequal Education and the Reproduction of the Social Division of Labor." *Review of Radical Political Economics.* Illinois: 1-30.
Bowles, S. and H. Gintis
  1974 "IQ in the United States Class Structure." In Alan Gartner, Colin Greer and Frank Riessman (eds.), *The New Assault on Equality.* New York: Harper & Row.
Bowles, S. and H. Gintis
  1976 *Schooling in Capitalist America.* New York: Basic Books.
Boyd, Monica
  1982 "Sex Differences in the Canadian Occupational Attainment Process." *Canadian Review of Sociology and Anthropology*, Vol.19, No.1:1-28.

Boyd, Monica
  1983 "The Social Demographs of Divorce in Canada." In K. Ishawaran (ed.), *Marriage and Divorce in Canada.* Toronto: Methuen.
Boyd, M., D.L. Featherman and J. Matras
  1980 "Status Attainment of Immigrant and Immigrant Origin Categories in the United States, Canada, and Israel." In R.F. Tomasson (ed.), *Comparative Social Research*, Vol.3. Greenwich, Conn.: JAI Press.
Braithwaite, J. and V. Braithwaite
  1980 "The Effect of Income Inequality and Social Democracy on Homicide." *British Journal of Criminology*, Vol.20,No.1:45-53.
Braudel, Fernand
  1967 *Capitalism and Maternal Life, 1400-1800.* London: Weidenfeld and Nicolson.
Braverman, Harold
  1974 *Labor and Monopoly Capitalism: The Degradation of Work in the Twentieth Century.* New York: Monthly Review Press.
Bresner, Barry and T. Leigh-Bell
  1978 "Ontario's Agencies, Boards, Commissions, Advisory Boards and Other Public Institutions: An Inventory (1977)." *Government Regulation.* Toronto: Ontario Economic Council, 207-75.
Breton, Raymond
  1964 "Institutional Completeness of Ethnic Communities and the Personal Relations of Immigrants." *American Journal of Sociology*, Vol.70,No.2:193-205.
Breton, Raymond
  1978 "The Structure of Relationships Between Ethnic Collectivities." In Lee Driedger (ed.), *The Canadian Ethnic Mosaic.* Toronto: McClelland & Stewart.
Brinkerhoff, Merlin B. and Eugen Lupri
  1978 "Theoretical and Methodological Issues in the Use of Decision-making as an Indicator of Conjugal Power: Some Canadian Observations." *Canadian Journal of Sociology*, Vol.3, No.1:1-20.
Bronfenbrenner, Urie
  1970 *Two Worlds of Childhood: U.S. and U.S.S.R.* New York: Russel Sage Foundation.
Brookover, W.B. and E.L. Erickson
  1975 *Sociology of Education.* Homewood, Illinois: Dorsey Press.
Brown, John L. and R. Schneck
  1979 "A Structural Comparison Between Canadian and American Industrial Organizations." *Administrative Science Quarterly*, Vol.24: 24-47.

Brown, Roger
1965   *Social Psychology.* New York: Free Press.
Bruvand, Jan Harold
1980   "Urban Legends: Folklore for Today." *Psychology Today,* Vol.14(June):50-62.
Bryson, M.C.
1976   "The Literary Digest Poll: Making of a Statistical Myth." *The American Statistician,* Vol.30 (November):184-85.
Buchanan, James and Richard Wagner
1977   *Democracy in Deficit.* New York: Academic Press.
Bunge, John C.
1967   *Urban Renewal in Canada: An Assessment of Current Practice.* M.Sc. thesis. B.C.: Department of Community and Regional Planning, University of British Columbia.
Burgess, Ernest W.
1926   "The Family as a Unit of Interacting Personalities." *Family,* Vol.7,No.1:3-9.
Burgess, Ernest W.
1967   "The Growth of the City: An Introduction to a Research Project." In Robert Park and Ernest W. Burgess (eds.), *The City.* Chicago: University of Chicago Press, 47-62.
Burnet, Jean
1978   "The Policy of Multiculturalism within a Bilingual Framework: A Stocktaking." *Canadian Ethnic Studies,* Vol.10,No.2:107-13.
Campbell, Angus
1975   "The American Way of Mating: Marriage *si,* Children, only maybe." *Psychology Today,* May:39-42.
Campbell, Colin
1977   "Canadian Political Facts, 1945-1976." *Canadian Review of Sociology and Anthropology.* Toronto: Metheun.
Campbell, Colin and George J. Szablowksi
1979   *The Superbureaucrats.* Toronto: Macmillan.
Canada
1979   *The Task Force on Canadian Unity: A Future Together.* Ottawa: Queen's Printer.
Canadian Council on Social Development
1984   *Not Enough: The Meaning and Measurement of Poverty in Canada.* Ottawa: Canadian Council on Social Development.
Cantril, Hadley
1940   *The Invasion from Mars.* New York: Harper & Row.
Cardinal, Harold
1969   *The Unjust Society.* Edmonton: Hurtig Publishers.

Careless, J.M.S.
1978   *The Rise of Cities in Canada Before 1914.* Ottawa: Canadian Historical Association, Booklet No.32.
Carlton, R.A., L.A. Colley and N.J. Mackinnon
1977   *Education, Change, and Society: A Sociology of Canadian Education.* Toronto: Gage.
Carroll, William K.
1982   "The Canadian Corporate Elite: Financiers or Finance Capitalists." *Studies in Political Economy,* Vol.8:89-114.
Chappell, D., G. Gees, S. Schafer and L. Siegel
1971   "Forcible Rape: A Comparative Study of Offences Known to the Police in Boston and Los Angeles." In J. Henslen (ed.), *Studies in the Sociology of Sex.* New York: Appleton-Century-Crofts.
City of Toronto
1980   *Toronto in Transition: Demographic Trends in the Toronto Region.* Toronto: Planning and Development Department.
Clairmont, D. and F. Wien
1976   "Race Relations in Canada." *Sociological Forces,* Vol.9,No.2:185-97.
Clark, B.R.
1960   "The Cooling Out Function in Higher Education." *American Journal of Sociology,* Vol.65:569-76.
Clark, Mark and Barbara G. Anderson
1967   *Culture and Aging.* Springfield, Illinois: Charles C. Thomas.
Clark, S.D.
1971   *Church and Sect in Canada.* (1948) Toronto: University of Toronto Press.
Clarke, L. and D. Lewis
1977   *Rape: The Price of Coercive Sexuality.* Toronto: The Women's Press.
Clement, Wallace
1975   *The Canadian Corporate Elite.* Toronto: McClelland & Stewart.
Clement, Wallace
1977   *Continental Corporate Elite.* Toronto: McClelland & Stewart.
Clement, Wallace
1977   *Continental Corporate Power: Economic Lineages Between Canada and the United States.* Toronto: McClelland & Stewart.
Clement, Wallace
1981   *Hardrock Mining.* Toronto: McClelland & Stewart.
Clement, Wallace
1983   *Class, Power, and Property.* Toronto: Methuen.

Clinard, M. and W. Meier
1975 *Sociology of Deviant Behavior.* New York: Holt, Rinehart and Winston.

Cloward, R. and L. Ohlin
1960 *Delinquency and Opportunity: A Theory of Delinquent Gangs.* New York: Free Press.

Cohen, A.
1955 *Delinquent Boys.* New York: Free Press.

Cohen, E.G.
1972 "Sociology and the Classroom: Setting the Conditions for Teacher-Student Interaction." *Review of Educational Research,* Vol.42:448-49.

Coleman, James S.
1961 *Adolescent Society: The Social Life of the Teenager and Its Impact on Education.* New York: Free Press.

Colligan, Michael J. and William Stockton
1978 "The Mystery of Assembly-line Hysteria." *Psychology Today,* Vol.12(June):93-116.

Collins, Randall
1975 *Conflict Sociology: Toward an Explanatory Science.* New York: Academic Press.

Collins, Randall
1979 *The Credential Society.* New York: Academic Press.

Connelly, Patricia
1978 *Last Hired, First Fired: Women and the Canadian Work Force.* Toronto: Women's Press.

Cook, Alice
1975 *The Working Mother: A Survey of Problems and Programmers in Nine Countries.* Ithaca: New York State School of Industrial and Labor Relations, Cornell University.

Cook, R.A. and R.J. Coughlan
1974 "Work Attitudes." In H.J. Walberg (ed.), *Evaluating Educational Performance.* Berkeley, Calif.: McCutchan.

Cooley, C.H.
1909 *Social Organization.* New York: Scribner's.

Coombs, P.H.
1968 *The World Educational Crisis.* London: Oxford University Press.

Costa, E. and J. Di Santo
1972 "The Italian-Canadian Child, His Family, and the Canadian School System." In N. Byrne and J. Quarter (eds.), *Must Schools Fail?* Toronto: McClelland & Stewart.

Crysdale, Stewart
1977 *Sociology Canada.* Toronto: Butterworth.

Cuber, John F. and Peggy Harroff
1965 *The Significant Americans.* Baltimore: Penguin.

Cuneo, Carl J.
1978 "Class Exploitation in Canada." *Canadian Review of Sociology and Anthropology,* Vol.15:284-300.

Curtis, James E. and William G. Scott (eds.)
1979 *Social Stratification.* 2nd ed. Scarborough, Ontario: Prentice-Hall.

Dahrendorf, Ralf
1959 *Class and Class Conflict in Industrial Society.* Stanford: Stanford University Press.

Dahrendorf, Ralf
1965 *Gesellschaft und Democratie in Deutschland.* München: Piper Verlag.

Dalby, Liza C.
1983 *Geisha.* Berkeley: University of California Press.

Dalton, George
1968 "Introduction." In George Dalton (ed.), *Primitive, Archaic and Modern Economies: Essays of Karl Polanyi.* Garden City, N.Y.: Doubleday/Anchor Books, ix-lilv.

Davis, K.
1963 "The Theory of Change and Response in Modern Demographic History." *Population Index,* Vol.29,No.4:345-66.

Davis Kingsley
1940 "Extreme Social Isolation of a Child." *American Journal of Sociology,* Vol.45:554-64.

Davis, Kingsley
1947 "Final Note on a Case of Extreme Isolation." *American Journal of Sociology,* Vol.50: 432-37.

Davis, Kingsley
1955 "The Origin and Growth of Urbanization in the World." *American Journal of Sociology,* Vol.60:429-37.

Davis, Kingsley
1959 "The Myth of Functional Analysis as a Special Method in Sociology and Anthropology." *American Sociological Review,* Vol.24: 757-72.

Davis, Kingsley
1971 "Sexual Behavior." In Robert K. Morton and Robert Nisbet (eds.), *Contemporary Social Problems.* 3rd ed. New York: Harcourt Brace Jovanovich, 313-60.

Davis, Kingsley and Wilbert Moore
1945 "Some Principles of Stratification." *American Sociological Review,* Vol.10,No.2:242-49.

Demerath, N.H. III and Richard Peterson, (eds.)
1967 *System Change and Conflict.* London: Collier-Macmillan.

Denscomb, M.
1980 "Pupil Strategies and the Open Classroom." In P. Woods (ed.), *Pupil Strategies*. London: Croom Helm, 50–73.

Deutsch, Morton and Associates
1967 *The Disadvantaged Child*. New York: Basic Books.

Dewey, John
1922 *Human Nature and Conduct*. New York: Holt, Rinehart and Winston.

Dhingra, Harbans L.
1983 "Patterns of Ownership and Control in Canadian Industry: A Study of Large Non-financial Corporations." *Canadian Journal of Sociology*, Vol.8(Winter):21–44.

Dion, K., E. Berscheid and E. Walster
1972 "What is Beautiful is Good." *Journal of Personality and Social Psychology*, Vol.24:285–90.

Ditton, Jason
1977 *Part-time Crime: An Ethnography of Fiddling and Pilferage*. London: Macmillan.

Djilas, Milovan
1976 *The New Class*. New York: Praeger.

Dobb, Maurice
1946 *Studies in the Development of Capitalism*. London: Routledge and Kegan Paul.

Dollard, John, Leonard Dobb, Neal Miller, O.H. Mower and Robert Sears
1939 *Frustration and Aggression*. New Haven: Yale University Press.

Domhoff, William G.
1967 *Who Rules America?* Englewood Cliffs, N.J.: Prentice-Hall.

Domhoff, William G.
1983 *Who Rules America Now?* Englewood Cliffs, N.J.: Prentice-Hall.

Dominion Bureau of Statistics
1960 *Illness and Health Care in Canada: Canadian Sickness Survey, 1950–51*. Ottawa: Queen's Printer.

Dominion Bureau of Statistics
1967 *Canada Year Book, 1967*. Ottawa: Queen's Printer.

Doreber, A.L. and C. Kluckhohn
1952 *Culture, A Critical Review of Concepts and Definitions*. New York: Alfred A. Knopf and Random House.

Douglas, Mary
1966 *Purity and Danger*. London: Pelican Books.

Dreidger, Leo
1978 "Ethnic and Minority Relations." In Robert Hagedorn (ed.), *Sociology*. Toronto: Holt, Rinehart and Winston.

Driedger, Leo and Rodney Clifton
1984 "Ethnic Stereotypes: Images of Ethnocentrism, Reciprocity or Dissimilarity?" *Canadian Journal of Sociology*, Vol.6:1–17.

Driedger, Leo and Richard Mezoff
1981 "Ethnic Prejudice and Discrimination in Winnipeg High Schools." *Canadian Journal of Sociology*, Vol.6:1–17.

Drucker, Peter F.
1964 *The Concept of the Corporation*. New York: New American Library.

Duberman, Lucile
1976 *Social Inequality: Class and Caste in America*. Philadelphia: J.B. Lippincott.

Dulude, Louise
1981 *Pension Reform with Women in Mind*. Ottawa: Canadian Advisory Council on the Status of Women.

Duncan, Greg J., Richard D. Coe and Martha S. Hill
1984 *Years of Poverty, Years of Plenty*. Ann Arbor, Michigan: Institute for Social Research, University of Michigan.

Durand, John D.
1976 "The Population Statistics of China, A.D.2–1953." *Population, Studies XIII*, Vol.3:209.

Durkeim, Émile
1933 *The Division of Labour in Society*. Translated by Geo. Simpson. Glencoe, Illinois: Free Press.

Durkheim, Émile
1938 *The Rules of the Sociological Method*. Glencoe, Illinois: Free Press.

Durkheim, Émile
1964 *The Division of Labor in Society*. Glencoe, Illinois: Free Press.

Dworkin, A.
1980 *Our Blood: Prophecies and Discourses on Sexual Politics*. New York: Harper & Row.

Easterlin, Richard
1980 *Birth and Fortune: The Impact of Numbers on Personal Welfare*. New York: Basic Books.

Eddy, Mary Baker
1934 *Science and Health, with Key to the Scriptures*. (1875) Boston: published by the Trustees under the will of Mary Baker G. Eddy.

Edgerton, R.
1973 *Deviant Behavior and Cultural Theory*. Reading, Mass.: General Publishing.

Edwards, A.L.
1940 "Studies of Stereotypes: The Directionality and Uniformity of Responses to Stereotypes." *Journal of Social Psychology*, Vol.12:357–66.

Edwards, Richard
1979   *Contested Terrain.* New York: Basic Books.
Eggleston, John S.
1967   *The Social Context of the School.* London: Routledge and Kegan Paul.
Ehrlich, P.R. and A.H. Ehrlich
1970   *Population, Resources and Environment.* San Francisco: W.H. Freeman and Co.
Elkin, Frederick and Gerald Handel
1984   *The Child and Society.* 6th ed. New York: Random House.
Elliott, D. and D. Huizinga
1983   "Social Class and Delinquent Behavior in a National Youth Panel." *Criminology,* Vol.21, No.2:149-77.
Ellis, D.
n.d.   *The Wrong Stuff: A Sociological Introduction to the Study of Deviance.* Toronto: Collier-Macmillan.
Ellul, Jacques
1967   *The Technological Society.* New York: Random House.
Engels, Friedrich
1902   *The Origins of the Family, Private Property, and the State.* Chicago: Kerr.
England, R.W.
1954   "Some Aspects of Christian Science as Reflected in Letters of Testimony." *American Journal of Sociology,* Vol.59:448-53.
Erikson, E.H.
1963   *Childhood and Society.* 2nd ed. New York: W.W. Norton.
Escande, C.
1973   *Les Classes sociales au cégep.* Montréal: Parti Pris. Parti Press.
Espenshade, T.J.
1977   "The Value and Cost of Children." *Population Bulletin,* Vol.32,No.1.
Evans, Robert R. (ed.)
1969   *Readings In Collective Behavior.* Chicago: Rand McNally.
Exline, Christopher H., Gary L. Peters and Robert P. Larkin
1982   *The City: Pattern and Processes in the Urban Ecosystem.* Boulder, Colorado: Westview Press.
Eysenck, Hans
1975   *The Inequality of Man.* San Diego, Calif.: EDITS.
Fallding, Harold
1978   "Mainline Protestantism in Canada and the United States." *Canadian Journal of Sociology,* Vol.3,No.2:141-60.

Featherman, David L. and Robert M. Hausen
1978   *Opportunity and Change.* New York: Academic Press.
Feldmesser, Robert
1960   *Equality and Inequality Under Khruschev, Problems of Communism.* Washington, D.C.: U.S. Information Agency, 31-39.
Fels, Lynn
1981   *Living Together. Unmarried Couples in Canada.* Toronto: Personal Library.
Finley, M.I.
1973   *The Ancient Economy.* Berkeley: University of California Press.
Finley, M.I. (ed.)
1982   *Economy and Society in Ancient Greece.* Introduction by Brent D. Shaw and Richard P. Saller. New York: Viking.
Fischer, Claude S.
1976   "Toward a Subcultural Theory of Urbanism." *The American Journal of Sociology,* Vol.80: 1319-41.
Fischer, Claude S.
1976   *The Urban Experience.* New York: Harcourt Brace Jovanovich.
Fischer, Claude S.
1982   *To Dwell Among Friends.* Chicago: University of Chicago Press.
Forcese, Dennis
1975   *The Canadian Class Structure.* Toronto: McGraw-Hill Ryerson.
Forcese, Dennis and John Myles
1977   *Education and the Senior Adult.* Ottawa: Carleton University.
Ford, Clellan S. and Frank Beach
1951   *Patterns of Sexual Behavior.* New York: Harper & Row.
Foreign Investment Review Agency
1980   "Increased Domestic Control of Canadian Industry." *Foreign Investment Review,* Vol.3, No.2:2-3.
Form, William
1979   "Comparative Industrial Sociology and the Convergence Hypothesis." *Annual Review of Sociology,* Vol.5:1-25.
Fox, Bonnie and John Fox
1983   "Effects of Women's Employment on Wages." *Canadian Journal of Sociology,* Vol.8,No.3: 319-28.
Fox, Robin
1967   *Kinship and Marriage.* Harmondsworth: Penguin.
Foy, Eddie and Alvin F. Harlow
1928   *Clowning Through Life.* New York: Dutton.

Francis, E.K.
1976 *Interethnic Relations: An Essay in Sociological Theory.* New York: Elsevier.

Franke, R.H. and J.D. Kaul
1978 "The Hawthorne Experiments: First Statistical Interpretation." *American Sociological Review,* Vol.43:623-43.

Frankfurt Institute for Social Research
1972 *Aspects of Sociology.* Boston: Beacon Press.

Fraser, James G.
1969 *The Golden Bough.* London: MacMillan.

Freud, Sigmund
1933 *New Introductory Lectures on Psychoanalysis.* New York: W.W. Norton.

Freud, Sigmund
1962 *Civilization and Its Discontent.* New York: W.W. Norton.

Frideres, James S.
1983 *Native People in Canada: Contemporary Conflicts.* 2nd ed. Scarborough, Ontario: Prentice-Hall.

Friesen, D.
1968 "Academic-Athletic-Popularity Syndrome in the Canadian High School Society." *Adolescence,* Vol.3:39-52.

Fromm, Erich
1955 *The Sane Society.* New York: Holt, Rinehart and Winston.

Fuller, F.F. and O.H. Brown
1975 "Becoming a Teacher." In K. Ryan (ed.), *Teacher Education. Seventy-fourth Yearbook of the National Society for the Study of Education.* Part II. Chicago: University of Chicago Press.

Gagnon, John and W. Simon
1973 *Sexual Conduct.* Chicago: Aldine.

Gans, Herbert J.
1962 *The Urban Villagers.* New York: Free Press.

Gardner, R.C., D.M. Taylor and H.J. Feenstra
1970 "Ethnic Stereotypes: Attitudes and Beliefs?" *Canadian Journal of Psychology,* Vol.24: 321-24.

Gehlen, Arnold
1980 *Man in the Age of Technology.* New York: Columbia University Press.

Gerth, H. and C.W. Mills
1966 *From Max Weber.* New York: Oxford University Press, 180.

Geschwender, James A.
1978 *Racial Stratification in America.* Dubuque, Iowa: Wm. C. Brown.

Geuss, Raymond
1981 *The Idea of a Critical Theory: Habermas and the Frankfurt School.* Cambridge: Cambridge University Press.

Gherson, Joan
1978 "U.S. Investment in Canada." *Foreign Investment Review,* Vol.3,No.2:11-14.

Giddens, Anthony
1971 *Capitalism and Modern Social Theory.* London: Cambridge University Press.

Giddens, Anthony
1976 *Capitalism and Modern Social Theory.* Cambridge: Cambridge University Press.

Giddens, Anthony
1977 *Studies in Social and Political Theory.* London: Hutchinson.

Giddens, Anthony
1982a *Sociology.* New York: Harcourt Brace Jovanovich.

Giddens, Anthony
1982b *Sociology: A Brief but Critical Introduction.* New York: Harcourt Brace Jovanovich.

Gilbert, Dennis and Joseph Kahl
1982 *The American Class Structure: A New Synthesis.* Illinois: The Dorsey Press.

Gillespie, W. Irwin
1980 *The Redistribution of Income in Canada.* Toronto: Gage.

Gist, Noel P. and Sylvia Fleis Fava
1964 *Urban Society.* 5th ed. New York: Thomas Y. Crowell.

Giuliano, Vincent E.
1982 "The Mechanization of Office Work." *Scientific American,* Vol.247,No.3:48-64.

Glock, Charles Y., B.B. Ringer and E.R. Babbie
1967 *To Comfort and To Challenge.* Berkeley: University of California.

Glock, Charles Y. and R. Stark
1965 *Religion and Society in Tension.* Chicago: Rand McNally.

Goffman, Erving
1959 *The Presentation of Self in Everyday Life.* Garden City, N.Y.: Doubleday.

Goffman, Erving
1961a *Asylums: Essays on the Social Situation of Mental Patients and Other Inmates.* Garden City, N.Y.: Anchor Books.

Goffman, Erving
1961b *Encounters.* Indianapolis: Bobbs-Merrill.

Goffman, Erving
1974 *Frame Analysis.* New York: Harper & Row.

Goode, William J.
1982   *The Family.* 2nd ed. Englewood Cliffs, N.J.: Prentice-Hall.

Goodwin, D.
1977   *Delivering Educational Service.* New York: Teachers College Press, Columbia University.

Goodwin, Leonard
1972   *Do the Poor Want to Work? A Social-psychological Study of Work Orientations.* Washington, D.C.: Brookings Institution.

Gordon, Manuel
1977   *Researching Canadian Corporations.* Toronto: New Hogtown Press.

Gould, Julius and Wm. L. Kolb (eds.)
1964   *A Dictionary of the Social Sciences.* New York: Free Press of Glencoe, Inc.

Goyder, John
1985   *Canadian Journal of Sociology.* Vol.10 (in press).

Grabb, Edward G.
1984   *Social Inequality: Classical and Contemporary Theorists.* Toronto: Holt, Rinehart and Winston.

Graubard, A.
1972   "The Free School Movement." *Harvard Educational Review,* Vol.42:351-70.

Graunt, John
1662   "Natural and Political Observations Upon the Bills of Mortality." In Sir W. Petty (ed.), *The Economic Writings.* 1899. Cambridge: Cambridge University Press.

Greenberg, S. and Brenda Dervin
1970   *Use of the Mass Media by the Urban Poor.* New York: Praeger.

Grindstaff, Carl F.
1975   "The Baby Bust: Changes in Fertility Patterns in Canada." *Canadian Studies in Population,* Vol.2:15-22.

Gross, N., W.S. Mason and A.W. McEachern
1958   *Explorations in Analysis: Studies of the School Superintendency Role.* New York: John Wiley.

Guppy, Neil
1984   "Dissensus or Consensus: A Cross-national Comparison of Occupational Prestige Scales." *Canadian Journal of Sociology,* Vol.9:69-83.

Guppy, Neil and John G. Goyder
1984   "Consensus on Occupational Prestige: A Reassessment of the Evidence." *Social Forces,* Vol.62:709-25.

Habermas, Jürgen
1970   *Toward a Rational Society: Student Protest, Science and Politics.* Boston: Beacon Press.

Habermas, Jürgen
1976   *Legitimation Crisis.* London: Heinemann.

Habermas, Jürgen
1979   *Communication and the Evolution of Society.* Boston: Beacon Press.

Hagan, John
1977a *The Disreputable Pleasures.* Toronto: McGraw Hill-Ryerson.

Hagan, John
1977b "Finding Discrimination: A Question of Meaning." *Ethnicity,* Vol.4:167-76.

Hagedorn, Robert (ed.)
1983   *Sociology.* Toronto: Holt, Rinehart and Winston.

Hall, E.
1966   *The Hidden Dimension.* Garden City, N.Y.: Doubleday.

Hall, Richard H.
1975   *Occupations and the Social Structure.* Englewood Cliffs, N.J.: Prentice-Hall.

Hall, Richard H.
1978   "Professionalization and Bureaucratization." *American Sociological Review,* Vol.33: 92-104.

Hall, Richard H.
1982   *Organizations: Structure and Process.* Englewood Cliffs, N.J.: Prentice-Hall.

Hans, Valerie and Anthony N. Doob
1976   "Section 12 of the Canada Evidence Act and the Deliberations of Simulated Juries." *Criminal Law Quarterly,* 235-53.

Hardert, R.A., L. Grodon, M. Laner and M. Reader
1984   *Confronting Social Problems.* St. Paul, Minnesota: West Publishing Company.

Hardoy, Jorge E.
1973   *Pre-Columbian Cities.* New York: Walker and Company.

Hareven, Tamara K.
1974   "The Family as Process: The Historical Study of the Family Life Cycle." *Journal of Social History,* Vol.7:322-29.

Harring, Sidney L.
1983   *Policing a Class Society: The Experience of American Cities, 1865-1915.* New Brunswick, N.J.: Rutgers University Press.

Harris, Chauncy D. and Edward L. Ullman
1945   "The Nature of Cities." *The Annals,* Vol.242: 7-17.

Harvey, David
1973   *Social Justice and the City.* London: Edward Arnold.

Harvey, E. and R. Kalwa
1983   "Occupational Status Attainments of University Graduates." *Canadian Review of Sociology and Anthropology,* Vol.20:435-53.

Harvey, E. and J. Lennards
1973   *Key Issues in Higher Education.* Toronto: Ontario Institute for Studies in Education.

Hatt, P.K., N.L. Farr and E. Weinstein
1955   "Types of Population Balance." *American Sociological Review*, Vol.20,No.1:14–21.

Haupt, A. and T.T. Kane
1978   *Population Handbook.* Washington, D.C.: Population Reference Bureau.

Hauser, Robert M. and David M. Featherman
1973   "Trends in the Occupational Mobilty of U.S. Men, 1962–1970." *American Sociological Review*, Vol.38:302–10.

Havighurst, R.J. and D.U. Levine
1979   *Society and Education.* 5th ed. Boston: Allyn & Bacon.

Hawley, Amos
1971   *Urban Society: An Ecological Approach.* New York: The Ronald Press.

Health and Welfare Canada and Statistics Canada
1981   *The Health of Canadians: Report of the Canada Health Survey.* Ottawa: Supply and Services.

Hechter, Michael
1975   *Internal Colonialism: The Celtic Fringe in British National Development, 1536–1966.* Berkeley: University of California Press.

Hedley, R. Alan
1977   "Professional Bureaucracy: Community Mental Health Care Teams." *Organization and Administrative Sciences*, Vol.8:61–76.

Heider, Karl
1979   *Grand Valley Dani: Peaceful Warriors.* New York: Holt, Rinehart and Winston.

Heilbroner, Robert L.
1980   *The Making of Economic Society.* 6th ed. Englewood Cliffs, N.J.: Prentice-Hall.

Heise, David R.
1973   *Personality: Biosocial Bases.* Chicago: Rand McNally.

Henripin, Jacques
1972   *Trends and Factors of Fertility in Canada.* Ottawa: Statistics Canada, Supply and Services.

Herzog, J.
1962   "Deliberate Instruction and Household Structure." *Harvard Education Review*, Vol.32: 301–42.

Hess, Robert D. and Judith V. Torney
1967   *The Development of Political Attitudes in Children.* Chicago: Aldine.

Heyns, B.
1978   *Summer Learning and the Effects of Schooling.* New York: Academic Press.

Hill, Daniel G.
1981   *The Freedom-seekers: Blacks in Early Canada.* Agincourt, Ontario: Book Society of Canada.

Hill, Frederick
1976   *Canadian Urban Trends.* Vol.2, Metropolitan Perspective. Toronto: Copp-Clark.

Hill, Michael
1980   *A Sociology of Religion.* London: Heinemann.

Hill, Reuben and Paul Mattessich
1979   "Family Development Theory and Life-span Development." In E. Baltes and A. Birren (eds.), *Life-span Development and Behavior.* New York: Academic Press.

Hiller, Harry H.
1943   *French Canada in Transition.* Chicago: University of Chicago Press.

Hilton, Robert
1973   *Bond Men Made Free.* New York: Viking Press.

Hirschi, T.
1969   *Causes of Delinquency.* Berkeley: University of California Press.

Hite, Shere
1976   *The Hite Report: A Nationwide Study of Female Sexuality.* New York: Dell.

Hobart, Charles
1983   "Marriage or Cohabitation." In K. Ishawaran (ed.), *Marriage and Divorce.* Toronto: Methuen.

Hoffer, Eric
1951   *The True Believer.* New York: Time Inc.

Hoffman, Lois W.
1972   "Early Childhood Experiences and Women's Achievement Motives." *Journal of Social Issues*, Vol.28:164:205.

Hoggart, Richard
1958   *The Uses of Literacy.* London: Penguin.

Homans, George C.
1950   *The Human Group.* New York: Harcourt Brace.

Homans, George C.
1974   *Social Behaviour: Its Elementary Forms.* New York: Harcourt Brace Jovanovich.

Hopkins, Keith
1978   *Conquerors and Slaves: Sociological Studies in Roman History.* Cambridge: Cambridge University Press.

Horn, Michael
1972   *The Dirty Thirties: Canadians in the Great Depression.* Toronto: Copp-Clark.

Howitt, Dennis and Guy Cumberbatch
1975   *Mass Media Violence and Society.* New York: John Wiley.

Hughes, David R. and Evelyn Kallen
1974 *The Anatomy of Racism: Canadian Dimensions.* Montréal: Harvest House.

Hughes, E.C.
1943 *French Canada in Transition.* Chicago: University of Chicago Press.

Humphreys, Laud
1975 *Tearoom Trade.* 2nd ed. New York: Free Press.

Hunsberger, Bruce and L.B. Brown
1984 "Religious Socialization and Apostasy." *Journal for the Scientific Study of Religion*, Vol.23, No.3:239-51.

Hunter, Alfred A.
1981 *Class Tells: On Social Inequality in Canada.* Toronto: Butterworth.

Hunter, Floyd
19532 *Community Power Structure.* Chapel Hill: University of North Carolina Press.

Hutchinson, E.P.
1967 *The Population Debate.* Boston: Houghton Mifflin.

Iane, David
1982 *The End of Social Inequality? Class, Status and Power Under State Socialism.* London: George Allen and Unwin.

Inkeles, Alex
1968 "Society, Social Structure and Child Socialization." In John A. Clausen (ed.), *Socialization and Society.* Boston: Little, Brown, 117-21.

Institute for Social Research
1983 "Why Do Women Earn Less?" *ISR Newsletter* (Spring/Summer). University of Michigan.

Isajiw, Wsevolod W.
1975 "Immigration and Multiculturalism — Old and New Approaches." Paper presented at conference on Multiculturalism and Third World Immigrants in Canada, University of Alberta, Edmonton, September 3-5.

Ishwaran, K.
1976 *The Canadian Family.* Toronto: Holt, Rinehart and Winston.

Ishwaran, K.
1977 *Family, Kinship and Community.* Toronto: Holt, Rinehart and Winston.

Ishwaran, K. (ed.)
1981 "Bhaki Tradition and Modernization." In Jayant Lele (ed.), *Tradition and Modernity in Bhakti Movements.* Leiden: E.J. Brill.

Ishwaran K. (ed.)
1983 *The Canadian Family.* Toronto: Gage.

Ishwaran K. and Chan Kwok
1979 "The Socialization of Rural Adolescence." In K. Ishawaran (ed.), *Childhood and Adolescence in Canada.* Toronto: McGraw-Hill Ryerson, 97-119.

Jaenen, Cornelius
1971 "New Canadians and the Schools." Toronto: Department of the Provincial Secretary and Citizenship, Government of Ontario.

Jaenen, Cornelius
1972 "Cultural Diversity and Education." In N. Byrne and J. Quarter (eds.), *Must Schools Fail?* Toronto: McClelland & Stewart.

James, William
1950 *The Principles of Psychology.* New York: Dover Publications.

Jencks, Christopher, Marshall Smith, Henry Acland, Mary Jo Bane, David Cohen, Herbert Gintis, Barbara Heyns and Stephen Michelson
1972 *Inequality: A Reassessment of the Effect of Family and Schooling in America.* New York: Harper & Row.

Jencks, C.
1972 *Inequality.* New York: Basic Books.

Jensen, Arthur
1969 "How Much Can We Boost IQ and Scholastic Achievement?" *Harvard Educational Review*, Vol.39, No.1:1-123.

Jepson, H.
1976 "The Superintendent: The Man in the Middle." *ATA (Alberta Teachers' Association) Magazine*, Vol.56:34-36.

Johnson, Benton
1964 "Do Holiness Sects Socialize in Dominant Values?" In L. Schneider (ed.), *Religion, Culture and Society.* New York: John Wiley.

Johnson, Donald M.
1945 "The 'Phantom Anesthetist' of Mattoon: A Field Study of Mass Hysteria." *Journal of Abnormal and Social Psychology*, Vol.40: 175-86.

Johnson, E.H.
1983 *International Handbook of Contemporary Developments in Criminology: General Issues and the Americas.* Westport, Conn.: Greenwood Press.

Johnson, Leo A.
1977 "Illusions or Realities: Hamilton and Pinard's Approach to Poverty." *Canadian Review of Sociology and Anthropology*, Vol.14:341-46.

Johnson, Leo A.
1979 "Income Disparity and the Structure of Earnings in Canada, 1946-74." In James E. Curtis and William G. Scott (eds.), *Social Stratification: Canada.* 2nd ed. Scarborough, Ontario: Prentice-Hall.

Jones, J.
1972 *Prejudice and Racism.* Menlo Park, Calif.: Addison-Wesley.

Kahl, Joseph A.
1961 *The American Class Structure.* New York: Holt, Rinehart and Winston.

Kahn, Herman and A.J. Wiener
1969 "The Next Thirty-three Years: A Framework for Speculation." In Daniel Bell (ed.), *Towards the Year 2000.* Boston: Beacon Press.

Kalbach, Warren E.
1980 "Historial and Generational Perspectives of Ethnic Residential Segregation in Toronto, Canada: 1851-1971." Research Paper No. 118. Centre for Urban and Community Studies. Toronto: University of Toronto Press.

Kalbach, Warren E.
1983 "The Canadian Family: A Profile." In K. Ishwaran (ed.), *The Canadian Family.* Toronto: Gage.

Kalbach, Warren E. and Wayne W. McVey
1979 *Demographic Basis of Canadian Society.* 2nd ed. Toronto: McGraw-Hill Ryerson.

Kallen, Evelyn
1982 *Ethnicity and Human Rights in Canada.* Toronto: Gage.

Katz, Michael, Michael Doucet and Mark Stern
1982 *The Social Organization of Early Industrial Capitalism.* Cambridge, Mass.: Harvard University Press.

Kelley, H.
1967 "Attribution Theory in Social Psychology." *Nebraska Symposium on Motivation*, Vol. 15.

Kelner, Merrijoy
1970 "Ethnic Penetration into Toronto's Elite Structure." *Canadian Review of Sociology and Anthropology*, Vol.7,No.2:128-37.

Kerckhoff, Alan C. and Kurt W. Back
1968 *The June Bug: A Study of Hysterical Contagion.* New York: Appleton-Century-Crofts.

Kerckhoff, Alan C., Kurt W. Back and Norman Miller
1965 "Sociometric Patterns in Hysterical Contagion." *Sociometry*, Vol.28:2-15.

Kerr, N.D.
1964 "The School Board as an Agency of Legitimation." *Sociology of Education*, Vol.38: 34-59.

Kettle, John
1980 *The Big Generation.* Toronto: McClelland & Stewart.

Kimberly, John R.
1976 "Organizational Size and the Structuralist Perspective: A Review, Critique, and Proposal." *Adminstrative Science Quarterly*, Vol.21: 571-97.

King, Edmund J.
1966 *Education and Social Change.* Oxford: Pergamon Press.

Klapp, Orrin E.
1969 *Collective Search for Identity.* New York: Holt, Rinehart and Winston.

Klapp, Orrin E.
1972 *Currents of Unrest.* New York: Holt, Rinehart and Winston.

Koenig, Daniel J., Gary R. Martin and Lauren H. Seiler
1977 "Response Rates and Quality of Data." *Canadian Review of Sociology and Anthropology*, Vol.14:432-38.

Kohn, Melvin L.
1977 *Class and Conformity: A Study in Values, with a Reassessment.* Chicago: University of Chicago Press.

Kolenda, Pauline
1978 *Caste in Contemporary India: Beyond Organic Solidarity.* Menlo Park, Calif.: Benjamin Cummings.

Kornberg, Allan
1967 *Canadian Legislative Behaviour.* New York and Toronto: Holt, Rinehart and Winston, 23.

Kornberg, Allan, Joel Smith and Harold Clarke
1979 *Citizen Politicians-Canada.* Durham, N.C.: Carolina Academic Press.

Kovel, J.
1970 *"White Racism."* New York: Pantheon Books.

Kroeber, A.L. and C. Kluckhohn
1952 *Culture, A Critical Review of Concepts and Definitions.* New York: Alfred A. Knopf and Random House.

Kubat, Daniel and D. Thornton
1974 *A Statistical Profile of Canadian Society.* Toronto: McGraw-Hill Ryerson.

Lall, Sanjaya and P. Streeten
1977 *Foreign Investment, Transnationals and Developing Countries.* London: MacMillan.

Lambert, W., R.C. Hodgson, R.C. Gardner and S. Fillenbaum
1960 "Evaluational Reactions to Spoken Languages." *Journal of Abnormal and Social Psychology*, Vol.60,No.1:44-50.

Lamson, Cynthia
1979　*Bloody Decks and a Bumper Crop: The Rhetoric of Sealing Counter-protest*. St. John's, Newfoundland: Institute of Social and Economic Research, Memorial University of Newfoundland.

Landes, David S.
1969　*The Unbound Prometheus*. Cambridge: Cambridge University Press.

Landes, Ronald
1979　"Political Socialization Among Youth: A Comparative Study of English Canadian and American Children." In K. Ishawaran (ed.), *Childhood and Adolescence in Canada*. Toronto: McGraw-Hill Ryerson, 366–86.

Lane, David
1982　*The End of Social Inequality? Class, Status and Power Under State Socialism*. London: George Allen and Unwin.

Lang, Kurt and Gladys E. Lang
1961　*Collective Dynamics*. New York: Thomas Y. Crowell.

Lang, Ronald
1974　*The Politics of Drugs*. Lexington, Mass.: Lexington Books.

Larrain, Jorge
1979　*The Concept of Ideology*. Athens, Georgia: The University of Georgia Press.

Larson, Lyle E.
1976　"Toward a Conceptual Model of Heterosexual Love." In Lyle E. Larson (ed.), *The Canadian Family in Comparative Perspective*. Scarborough, Ontario: Prentice-Hall.

Latane, B. and J.M. Darley
1970　*The Unresponsible Bystander: Why Doesn't He Help?* New York: Appleton-Century-Crofts.

Laumann, Edward O.
1973　*Bonds of Pluralism: The Form and Substance of Urban Social Networks*. New York: John Wiley.

Lawrence, Paul R. and J.W. Lorsch
1967　*Organization and Environment: Managing Differentiation and Integration*. Boston: Harvard University Press.

Le Bon, Gustave
1960　*The Crowd*. New York: Doubleday.

Lee, C.E.
1976　"The Road to Enfranchisement: Chinese and Japanese in British Columbia." *B.C. Studies*, Vol.30(Summer):44–76.

Lefcourt, H.M.
1982　*Locus of Control: Current Trends in Theory and Research*. Hillsdale, N.J.: Earlbaum.

Lefebvre, Henri
1968　*The Sociology of Marx*. New York: Random House.

Lele, Jayant
1981　"The Bhakti Movement in India: A Critical Introduction." *Tradition and Modernity in Bhakti Movements*. Leiden: E.J. Brill.

Lemert, E.
1951　*Social Pathology*. New York: McGraw-Hill.

Lenski, Gerhard
1966　*Power and Privilege: A Theory of Social Stratification*. New York: McGraw-Hill.

Lenski, Gerhard and J. Lenski
1971　*Human Societies: An Introduction to Macro Sociology*. New York: McGraw-Hill.

Lenski, Gerhard and J. Lenski
1978　*Human Societies: An Introduction to Macro Sociology*. New York: McGraw-Hill.

Lerner, M.J.
1970　"The Desire for Justice and Reactions to Victims." In J. Macaulay and L. Berkowitz (eds.), *Altruism And Helping Behavior*. New York: Academic Press.

Leslie, Gerald
1979　*The Family in Social Context*. 4th ed. New York: Oxford University Press.

Lévi-Strauss, Claude
1963　*Structural Anthropology*. New York: Basic Books.

Lewis, Oscar
1959　*Five Families*. New York: Basic Books.

Lewis, Oscar
1966　*La Vida*. New York: Random House.

Li, Peter S.
1980　"Income Achievement and Adaptive Society: An Empirical Comparison of Chinese and Japanese in Canada." In K.V. Ujimoto and G. Hirobayashi (eds.), *Visible Minorities and Multiculturalism: Asians in Canada*. Toronto: Butterworth.

Lichtheim, George
1965　*Marxism: A Historical and Critical Study*. 2nd ed., revised. New York: Praeger.

Liebert, Robert M., John M. Neale and Emily S. Davidson
1973　*The Early Window: Effects of Television on Children and Youth*. New York: Pergamon Press.

Linz, Juan
1976　"Toward a Comparative Study of Fascism in Sociological and Historical Perspective." In W. Laqueur (ed.), *Facism*. Berkeley: University of California Press, 4–7.

Lippman, Walter
  1922 "Public Opinion." New York: Harcourt Brace.
Lipset, Seymour M.
  1963 *Political Man.* New York: Doubleday.
Lipset, Seymour M. and Reinhard Bendix
  1959 *Social Mobility in Industrial Society.* Berkeley: University of California Press.
Lockhart, Alexander
  1979 "Educational Opportunities and Economic Opportunities — The 'New' Liberal Equality Syndrome." In John A. Fry (ed.), *Economy, Class and Social Reality.* Toronto: Butterworth, 224–37.
Lofland, John
  1978 "Becoming a World-saver Revisited." In James T. Richardson (ed.), *Conversion Careers: In and Out of the New Religions.* Beverly Hills, Calif.: Sage, 10–23.
Lorenz, Konrad
  1966 *On Aggression.* New York: Harcourt Brace Jovanovich.
Lorenz, Konrad
  1981 *The Foundations of Ethology: The Principal Ideas and Discoveries in Animal Behavior.* New York: Springer Verlag.
Lorimer, James
  1972 *A Citizen's Guide to City Politics.* Toronto: James Lewis and Samuel.
Lorimer, James
  1978 *The Developers.* Toronto: James Lorimer.
Lortie, D.C.
  1975 *Schoolteacher.* Chicago: University of Chicago Press.
Lowe, Graham
  1980 "Women, Work and the Office in Feminization of Clerical Occupations in Canada, 1901–1931." *Canadian Journal of Sociology,* Vol.5, No.4:361–81.
Lucas, Rex A.
  1971 *Minetown, Milltown, Railtown.* Toronto: University of Toronto Press.
Luhmann, Niklas
  1982 *The Differentiation of Society.* New York: Columbia University Press.
Lupri, Eugen
  1985 *Spousal Violence.* Unpublished data.
Lupri, Eugen and James Frideres
  1981 "The Quality of Marriage and the Passage of Time." *Canadian Journal of Sociology,* Vol.6, No.3:283–305.

Lupri, Eugen and Donald L. Mills
  1983 "The Changing Roles of Canadian Women in Family and Work: An Overview." In Eugen Lupri (ed.), *The Changing Position of Women in Family and Society: A Cross-national Comparison.* Leiden: E.J. Brill.
Lupri, Eugen and Gladys L. Symons
  1982 "The Emerging Symmetrical Family: Fact or Fiction?" *International Journal of Comparative Sociology,* Vol.23:166–89.
Lyle, Jack and Heidi R. Hoffman
  1972 "Children's Use of Television and Other Media." In Eli Rubenstein et al. (eds.), *Television and Social Behavior, Reports and Papers.* Washington, D.C.: U.S. Government Printing Office.
Mackie, Marlene
  1983 *Exploring Gender Relations: A Canadian Perspective.* Toronto: Butterworth.
MacLean, Paul D.
  1973 *A Triune Concept of the Brain and Behavior.* Toronto: University of Toronto Press.
MacLeod, Henry
  1979 "The Cultural Transformation of the United Church of Canada, 1946–1977." Paper presented to the annual meeting of the Canadian Sociology and Anthropology Association.
Macpherson, C.B.
  1965 *The Real World of Democracy.* Toronto: Canadian Broadcasting Corporation, 1–2.
Malinowski, Bronislaw
  1929 *The Sexual Life of Savages in North-Western Melanesia.* London: Routledge and Kegan Paul.
Malarek, Victor
  1984 *Hey Malarek! The True Story of a Street Kid Who Made It.* Toronto: Macmillan.
Mann, W.E.
  1971 *Sect, Cult and Church in Alberta.* Toronto: University of Toronto Press.
Marcuse, Herbert
  1964a *One-dimensional Man: Studies in the Ideology of Advanced Industrial Society.* Boston: Beacon Press.
Marcuse, Herbert
  1969b *An Essay on Liberation.* Boston: Beacon Press.
Marshall, T.H.
  1950 *Citizenship and Social Class.* Cambridge: Cambridge University Press.
Martin, David A.
  1962 "The Denomination." *British Journal of Sociology,* Vol.13, No.1:1–14.

Martin, W.B.W.
1970 "Disparities in Urban Schools." *The Poor at School in Canada.* Ottawa: Canadian Teachers' Federation, 1-23.

Martin, W.B.W. and A.J. Macdonell
1982 *Canadian Education.* 2nd ed. Scarborough, Ontario: Prentice-Hall.

Marty, Martin E.
1980 "Foreward." In Ross P. Scherer (ed.), *American Denominational Organization, A Sociological View.* Pasadena, Calif.: William Carey Library.

Marx, Karl
1961 *Selected Writings in Sociology and Social Philosophy.* 2nd ed. T.B. Bottomore and M. Rubel (eds.). Harmondsworth: Penguin.

Marx, Karl
1964 *The Economic and Philosophic Manuscripts of 1844.* D.J. Struik (ed.). New York: International Publishers.

Marx, Karl
1967a *Capital.* 1st translation by Samuel Moore and Edward Aveling. Friedrich Engels (ed.). New York: International Publishers.

Marx, Karl
1967b *Capital: A Critique of Political Economy.* Vol. 1. New York: International Publishers.

Marx, Karl and Friedrich Engels
1970 *The German Ideology.* C.J. Arthur (ed.). New York: International Publishers.

Matras, Judah
1973 *Populations and Societies.* Englewood Cliffs, N.J.: Prentice-Hall.

Mauldin, W.F.
1965 "Fertility Studies: Knowledge, Attitude and Practice." *Studies in Family Planning*, Vol.7: 1-10.

Mayo, Elton
1960 *The Human Properties of an Industrial Civilization.* New York: Viking Press.

McCarthy, John D. and Mayer N. Zald
1977 "Resource Mobilization and Social Movements: A Partial Theory." *American Journal of Sociology*, Vol.82:1212-41.

McClelland, David
1961 *The Achieving Society.* Princeton, N.J.: Van Nostrand.

McGahan, Peter
1982a "Criminogenesis and the Urban Environment: A Case Study." *Canadian Police College Journal*, Vol.6:209-25.

McGahan, Peter
1982b *Urban Sociology in Canada.* Toronto: Butterworth.

McGahan, Peter
1984c *Police Images of a City.* New York: Peter Lang.

McKendry, T. and J.R. Wright
1965 "Home and School Association Activities in the Edmonton Area." *Alberta Journal of Educational Research*, Vol.11:90-95.

McNeill, William H.
1982 *The Pursuit of Power.* Chicago: University of Chicago Press.

McRoberts, Hugh A.
1982 "Social Mobility in Canada." In D. Forcese and S. Richer (eds.), *Social Issues: Sociological Views of Canada.* Scarborough, Ontario: Prentice-Hall.

Mead, George Herbert
1934 *Mind, Self and Society.* Chicago: University of Chicago Press.

Mead, George Herbert
1963 *Mind, Self and Society.* Chicago: University of Chicago Press.

Mead, George Herbert
1964 *On Social Psychology.* Chicago: University of Chicago Press.

Medalia, Nahum and Otto N. Larsen
1958 "Diffusion and Belief in a Collective Delusion: The Seattle Windshield Pitting Epidemic." *American Sociological Review*, Vol.23: 180-86.

Medea, A. and K. Thompson
1974 *Against Rape: A Survival Manual for Women.* New York: Farrar, Straus & Giroux.

Mehan, H.
1978 "Structuring School Structure." *Harvard Educational Review*, Vol.48:32-64.

Meighan, R.
1981 *A Sociology of Educating.* London: Holt, Rinehart and Winston.

Meissner, M., E.W. Humphreys, M.M. Scott and W.H. Scheu
1975 "No Exit for Wives: Sexual Division of Labour and the Cumulation of Household Demands." *Canadian Review of Sociology and Anthropology*, Vol.12:424-39.

Mendelssohn, Kurt
1974 *The Riddle of the Pyramids.* New York: Praeger.

Merton, Robert K.
1930 "Social Structure and Anomie." *American Sociological Review*, October:672-82.

Merton, Robert K.
1968 *Social Theory and Social Structure.* Revised edition. New York: Free Press.

Meyer, J.W., F. Ramirez, R. Rubinson and J. Boli-Bennett
1977 "The World Education Revolution, 1950-70." *Sociology of Education*, Vol.50:242-58.

Meyer, J.W., M. Hannan, R. Rubinson and G. Thomas
1979 "National Economic Development, 1950-70: Social and Political Factors." In J.W. Meyer and M. Hannan (eds.), *National Development and the World Systems*. Chicago: University of Chicago Press.

Michalos, Alex C.
1982 *North American Social Report: A Comparative Study of the Quality of Life in Canada and the USA from 1964 to 1974*. Vols.1-5. Boston: D. Reidel.

Mifflen, F.J. and S.C. Mifflen
1982 *The Sociology of Education: Canada and Beyond*. Calgary, Alberta: Detselig.

Milgram, Stanley and Hans Toch
1969 "Collective Behavior: Crowds and Social Movements." 2nd ed. In Gardner Lindzey and Elliot Aronson (eds.), *The Handbook of Social Psychology*, Vol.4:507-610. Reading, Mass.: Addison-Wesley.

Mills, C. Wright
1951a *The Power Elite*. New York: Oxford University Press.

Mills, C. Wright
1951b *White Collar: The American Middle Classes*. New York: Oxford University Press.

Mills, C. Wright
1956 *The Power Elite*. New York: Oxford University Press.

Mills, C. Wright
1959 *The Sociological Imagination*. (1972) New York: Oxford University Press and Penguin.

Mol, Hans
1976 "Correlates of Churchgoing in Canada." In S. Crysdale and L. Wheatcroft (eds.), *Religion in Canadian Society*. Toronto: Macmillan.

Mommsen, Wolfgang
1970 "Max Weber's Political Sociology and His Philosophy of World History." In Dennis Wrong (ed.), *Max Weber*. Englewood Cliffs, N.J.: Prentice-Hall.

Money-Kyrle, Roger
1951 *Psychoanalysis and Politics*. New York: W.W. Norton.

Montagna, Paul D.
1977 *Occupations and Society*. New York: John Wiley.

Montagu, Ashley
1964 *The Humanization of Man*. New York: Grove Press.

Moore, Wilbert E.
1963 "But Some Are More Equal Than Others." *American Sociological Review*, Vol.28:13-18.

Morris, William
1947 *On Art and Socialism*. London: John Lehmann Ltd.

Mowat, Claire
1984 *The Outport People*. Toronto: McClelland & Stewart (Seal Books).

Muncie, J. and M. Fitzgerald
1981 "Humanizing the Deviant: Affinity and Affiliation Theories." In M. Fitzgerald, G. McLennan and J. Pawson (eds.), *Crime and Society: Reading in History and Theory*. London: Routledge and Kegan Paul.

Murdoch, William W.
1980 *The Poverty of Nations*. Baltimore: Johns Hopkins University Press.

Murdock, Peter
1949 *Social Structure*. New York: Macmillan.

Murdock, Peter
1957 "World Ethnographic Sample." *American Anthropologist*, Vol.59,No.4:664-87.

Murphy, E.M.
1981 *World Population: Toward the Next Century*. Washington, D.C.: Population Reference Bureau.

Musgrove, Frank
1964 *Youth and Social Order*. Bloomington: Indiana University Press.

Mussen, Paul and Nancy Eisenberg-Berg
1977 *Roots of Caring, Sharing, Helping*. San Francisco: W.H. Freeman.

Myles, John
1980 "The Aged, the State and the Structure of Inequality." In J. Harp and J. Hofley (eds.), *Structural Inequality in Canada*. Scarborough, Ontario: Prentice-Hall.

Myles, John
1984 *Old Age in the Welfare State*. Boston: Little, Brown.

Myrdal, Gunnar
1957 *Economic Theory and Underdeveloped Regions*. London: Gerald Duckworth.

Nakamura, Mark
1975 "The Japanese." In Norman Sheffe (ed.), *Many Cultures, Many Heritages*. Toronto: McGraw-Hill.

National Council of Welfare
1979 *Women And Poverty*. Ottawa: National Council of Welfare.

National Council of Welfare
1984 *Sixty-five and Older*. Ottawa: National Council of Welfare.

Naylor, Tom
1980 "Dominion of Capital: Canada and International Investment." In P. Grayson (ed.), *Class, State, Ideology and Change.* Toronto: Holt, Rinehart and Winston.

Nelson, G.K.
1969 *Spiritualism and Society.* London: Routledge and Kegan Paul.

Nett, Emily M.
1981 "Canadian Families in Social-historical Perspective." *Canadian Journal of Sociology,* Vol.6,No.3:239-60.

Nettler, Gwynn
1976 *Social Concerns.* Toronto: McGraw-Hill Ryerson.

Newcomb, Theodore
1968 "Interpersonal Balance." In Robert P. Abelson et al. (eds.), *Theories of Cognitive Consistency: A Sourcebook.* Chicago: Rand McNally.

Newman, Peter C.
1975 *The Canadian Establishment.* Toronto: McClelland & Stewart.

Newman, Peter C.
1978 *The Bronfman Dynasty.* Toronto: McClelland & Stewart.

Newman, Peter C.
1981 *The Acquisitors.* Toronto: McClelland & Stewart.

Nietzsche, Friedrich
1966 *Werke in Drei Bänden.* (Herausgegeben von Karl Schlechta) München: Carl Hanser.

Nisbet, R.A.
1954 *The Quest for Community.* New York: Oxford University Press.

Nobel, Grant
1975 *Children in Front of the Screen.* Beverly Hills, Calif.: Constable.

Noel, D.
1968 "A Theory of the Origin of Ethnic Stratification." *Social Problems,* Vol.16,No.2:18-32.

Nottingham, Elizabeth
1971 *Religion: A Sociological View.* New York: Random House.

Novak, N.W.
1975 *Living and Learning in the Free School.* Toronto: McClelland & Stewart.

Ogmundson, Rick
1983 "Social Inequality." In Robert Hagedorn (ed.), *Sociology.* 2nd ed. Toronto: Holt, Rinehart and Winston.

Olsen, D.
1980 *The State Elite.* Toronto: McClelland & Stewart.

Omran, A.R.
1977 "Epidemiologic Transition in the U.S." *Population Bulletin,* Vol.32,No.2:3-42.

Ornstein, Michael D.
1983 "Class, Gender, and Job Income in Canada." In Robert V. Robinson (ed.), *Research in Social Stratification and Mobility.* Vol.2. Greenwich, Conn.: JAI Press.

Osberg, Lars
1981 *Economic Inequality in Canada.* Toronto: Butterworth.

Ostry, Sylvia
1967 *The Occupational Composition of the Canadian Labour Force.* Ottawa: Dominion Bureau of Statistics.

Ouston, S.
1984 "The School and Delinquency." *British Journal of Criminology,* Vol.32:38-47.

Padover, Saul K.
1978 *The Essential Marx: The Non-economic Writings.* New York: Mentor Books.

Parelius, A.P. and R.J. Parelius
1978 *The Sociology of Education.* Englewood Cliffs, N.J.: Prentice-Hall.

Pareto, V.
1935 *The Mind and Society.* New York: Harcourt Brace, 246.

Park, Robert Ezra
1926 "Our Racist Frontier in the Pacific." *Survey Graphic,* May.

Park, Robert Ezra
1937 "The Race Relations Cycle in Hawaii." In B.W. Doyle (ed.), *The Etiquette of Race Relations in the South.* Chicago: University of Chicago Press.

Park, Robert Ezra
1950 *Race and Culture.* Glencoe, Illinois: Free Press.

Park, Robert Ezra and Ernest W. Burgess
1921 *Introduction to the Science of Sociology.* Chicago: University of Chicago Press.

Parkin, Frank
1972 *Class Inequality and Political Order: Social Stratification in Capitalist and Socialist Societies.* London: Paladin.

Parkin, Frank
1979 *Marxism and Class Theory: A Bourgeois Critique.* London: Tavistock.

Parkin, Frank
1979 *Marxism and Class Theory: A Bourgeois Critique.* New York: Columbia.

Parsons, Talcott
1934 "Society." In *Encyclopedia of the Social Sciences,* Vol.14:225-31.

Parsons, Talcott
1937 *The Structure of Social Action.* New York: Free Press.

Parsons, Talcott
1942 "Age and Sex in the Social Structure of the United States." *American Sociological Review*, Vol.7:604–16.

Parsons, Talcott
1951 *The Social System.* New York: Free Press.

Parsons, Talcott
1964 "Christianity and Modern Industrial Society. In L. Schneider (ed.), *Religion, Culture and Society.* New York: John Wiley.

Parsons, Talcott
1966 *Societies: Evolutionary and Comparative Perspectives.* Englewood Cliffs, N.J.: Prentice-Hall.

Parsons, Talcott
1971 *The System of Modern Societies.* Englewood Cliffs, N.J.: Prentice-Hall.

Parsons, Talcott (ed.)
1972 *The Evolution of Societies.* Introduction by Jackson Toby. Englewood Cliffs, N.J.: Prentice-Hall.

Parsons, Talcott
1977 *The Evolution of Societies.* (Edited with an introduction by Jackson Toby.) Englewood Cliffs, N.J.: Prentice-Hall.

Parsons, Talcott and Robert Bales (eds).
1955 *Family: Socialization and Interaction Process.* Glencoe, Illinois: Free Press.

Patel, Dhiru
1980 *Dealing with Interracial Conflict: Policy Alternatives.* Montréal: Institute for Research on Public Policy.

Penrod, Steven
1983 *Social Psychology.* Englewood Cliffs, N.J.: Prentice-Hall.

Peter, Karl A.
1979 "Childhood and Adolescent Socialization Among Hutterites." In K. Ishawaran (ed.), *Childhood and Adolescence in Canada.* Toronto: McGraw-Hill Ryerson, 346–66.

Peterson, William
1975 *Population.* 3rd ed. New York: Macmillan.

Petrie, Anne
1982 *A Guidebook to Ethnic Vancouver.* Surrey, B.C.: Hancock House.

Phillips, David P.
1980 "The Deterrent Effect of Capital Punishment: New Evidence on an Old Controversy." *American Journal of Sociology*, Vol.86:139–48.

Piaget, Jean
1958 *The Growth of Logical Thinking from Childhood to Adolescence.* New York: Basic Books.

Pike, R.M.
1978 "Equality of Educational Opportunity." *Interchange*, Vol.9:30–39.

Pinard, M.
1971 *The Rise of a Third Party: A Study in Crisis Politics.* Englewood Cliffs, N.J.: Prentice-Hall.

Pincus, F.
1978 "Tracking in Community Colleges." In R.W. Nelson and D.A. Nock (eds.), *Reading, Writing, and Riches.* Scarborough, Ontario: Between the Lines, 171–94.

Pineo, Peter C.
1961 "Disenchantment in the Later Years of Marriage." *Marriage and Family Living*, Vol.23: 3–11.

Pineo, Peter C. and John Porter
1967 "Occupational Prestige in Canada." *Canadian Review of Sociology and Anthropology*, Vol.4, No.1:24–40.

Pirenne, Henri
1937 *Economic and Social History of Medieval Europe.* Translated by I.E. Clegg. New York: Harcourt Brace and World.

Piven, Frances F. and Richard A. Cloward
1971 *Regulating the Poor: The Functions of Public Welfare.* New York: Random House.

Polanyi, Karl
1957 *The Great Transformation.* Boston: Beacon.

Polanyi, Karl
1966 *Dahomey and the Slave Trade.* In collaboration with Abraham Rotstein. Seattle: University of Washington Press.

Polanyi, Karl
1971 "The Economy as Instituted Process." In Karl Polanyi, Conrad M. Arensberg and Harry W. Peason (eds.), *Trade and Market in the Early Empires.* Chicago: Henry Regnery, 243–70.

Polanyi, Karl
1977 *The Livelihood of Man.* Harry W. Pearson (ed.). New York: Academic Press.

Pollard, A.
1980 "Teacher Interest and Changing Situations of Survival Threat in Primary School Classrooms." In P. Woods (ed.), *Teacher Strategies.* London: Croom Helm, 34–60.

Population Reference Bureau
1978 *Population Handbook.* Washington, D.C.: U.S. Government Printing Office.

Population Reference Bureau
1984 *Population Data Sheet.* Washington, D.C.: U.S. Government Printing Office.

Porter, John
1965 *The Vertical Mosaic: An Analysis of Social Class and Power in Canada.* Toronto: University of Toronto Press.

Porter, J., M. Porter and B.R. Blishen
1982 *Stations and Callings.* Toronto: Methuen.

Posner, Judith
1980 "Old and Female: The Double Whammy." In V.W. Marshall (ed.), *Aging in Canada: Social Perspectives.* Don Mills, Ontario: Fitzhenry & Whiteside.

Pressman, Norman E.P.
1975 *Planning New Communities in Canada.* Ottawa: Ministry of State for Urban Affairs.

Presthus, Robert
1964 *Men at the Top: A Study in Community Power.* New York: Oxford University Press.

Presthus, Robert
1973 *Elite Accommodation in Canadian Politics.* London and New York: Cambridge University Press.

Presthus, Robert
1974 *Elites in the Policy Process.* New York and London: Cambridge University Press.

Presthus, Robert
1978 *The Organizational Society.* 2nd ed. New York: St. Martin's Press.

Presthus, Robert
1979 "The Politics of Accommodation." In R. Preston (ed.), *Perspectives on Revolution and Evolution.* Durham: Duke University Press.

Price, John
1979 *Indians of Canada: Cultural Dynamics.* Scarborough, Ontario: Prentice-Hall.

Pyke, S.W.
1975 "Children's Literature: Conception of Sex Roles." In Elia Zureik and Robert M. Pike (eds.), *Socialization and Values in Canadian Societies.* Vol.1. Toronto: McClelland & Stewart.

Quarantelli, E.L.
1979 "Panic Behavior in Fire Situations: Findings and a Model from the English Language Research Literature." Paper No.54. Disaster Research Center, Ohio State University.

Quarantelli, E.L. and Russel R. Dynes
1970 "Property Norms and Looting: Their Patterns in Community Crises." *Phylon,* Vol.31:168-82.

Radcliffe-Brown, A.R.
1952 *Structure and Function in Primitive Society.* Glencoe, Illinois: Free Press.

Ramcharan, Subhas
1982 *Racism: Nonwhites in Canada.* Toronto: Butterworth.

Ramirez, F.O. and J.W. Meyers
1980 "Comparative Education." In A. Inkeles, N.J. Smelser and R.H. Turner (eds.), *Annual Review of Sociology.* Palo Alto, Calif.: Annual Reviews, Inc., 369-99.

Rasky, Frank
1961 *Great Canadian Disasters.* Don Mills, Ontario: Longman.

Rehberg, R. and L. Hotchkiss
1972 "Education Decision-makers: The School Guidance Counselor and Social Mobility." *Sociology of Education,* Vol.45:339-61.

Reich, Michael
1981 *Racial Inequality: A Political Economic Analysis.* Princeton: Princeton University Press.

Reitz, Jeffrey G.
1980 *The Survival of Ethnic Groups.* Toronto: McGraw-Hill Ryerson.

Retiz, Jeffrey G., Liviana Calzavara and Donna Dasko
1981 "Ethnic Inequality and Segregation in Jobs." Research Paper No. 123. Centre for Urban and Community Studies. Toronto: University of Toronto.

Rhyne, Darla
1981 "Bases of Marital Satisfaction Among Men and Women." *Journal of Marriage and the Family,* Vol.43(November):941-55.

Ricardo, David
1953 *Principles of Political Economy and Taxation.* P. Straffa and M. Dobb (eds.). Cambridge: Cambridge University Press.

Richards, Cara
1976 *People in Perspective.* 2nd ed. New York: Random House.

Richer, S.
1974 "Middle-class Bias of Schools — Fact or Fancy?" *Sociology of Education,* Vol.47: 523-34.

Rinehart, James W.
1975 *The Tyranny of Work.* Don Mills, Ontario: Academic Press.

Ritzer, George
1983 *Sociological Theory.* New York: Alfred A. Knopf.

Robertson, Roland (ed.)
1969 *Sociology of Religion: Selected Readings.* Harmondsworth: Penguin.

Roethlisberger, F.J. and W.J. Dickson
1964 *Management and the Worker.* New York: John Wiley.

Rogers, R. and G. Witney
1981 "The Family Cycle in Twentieth-century Canada." *Journal of Marriage and the Family,* August:727-40.

Rosenthal, Marilynn
  1971 "Where Rumor Raged." *Transaction*, Vol.8:
    34–43.
Rosenthal, R. and L. Jacobson
  1968 *Pygmalion in the Classroom*. New York: Holt,
    Rinehart and Winston.
Rosnow, Ralph L. and Gary Alan Fine
  1976 *Rumor and Gossip: The Social Psychology of
    Hearsay*. New York: Elsevier.
Rosnow, Ralph L. and Alan J. Kimmel
  1979 "Lives of a Rumor." *Psychology Today*, Vol.13
    (June):88–92.
Rosow, Irving
  1967 *Social Integration of the Agent*. New York:
    Free Press.
Ross, James B. and Mary M. McLaughlin (eds.)
  1949 *The Portable Medical Reader*. New York:
    Viking Press.
Rothschild, Emma
  1982 "The Philosophy of Reaganism." *The New
    York Review of Books*, Vol.29,No.6(April):
    19–26.
Rotter, J.B.
  1966 "General Expectancies for Internal versus
    External Control of Reinforcement." *Psycho-
    logical Monographs*, Vol. 80.
Russell, Diana E.H.
  1982 *Rape in Marriage*. New York: Macmillan.
Ruston, J. Phillipe
  1980 *Altruism, Socialization, and Society*. Engle-
    wood Cliffs, N.J.: Prentice-Hall.
Rutherford, Paul
  1974 *Saving the Canadian City: The First Phase,
    1880–1920*. Toronto: University of Toronto
    Press.
Rutherford, Paul
  1977 "Tomorrow's Metropolis: The Urban Reform
    Movement in Canada, 1880–1920." In Gilbert
    A. Stelter and Alan F.J. Artibise (eds.), *The
    Canadian City: Essays in Urban History*.
    Toronto: McClelland & Stewart, 368–92.
Ryan, William
  1971 *Blaming the Victim*. New York: Random
    House.
Safilios-Rothschild, Constantina
  1977 *Love, Sex, and Sex Roles*. Englewood Cliffs,
    N.J.: Prentice-Hall.
Sahlins, Marshall
  1974 *Stone Age Economics*. London: Tavistock.
Sarason, S.B. and J. Doris
  1979 *Educational Handicap, Public Policy, and
    Social History*. New York: Free Press.

Saunders, Eileen
  1982 "Women in Canadian Society." In D. Forcese
    and S. Richer (eds.), *Social Issues: Sociologi-
    cal View of Canada*. Scarborough, Ontario:
    Prentice-Hall.
Saunders, Eileen
  1983 "Women, the Ecomony and the Sociological
    State: The Case of China." Carleton University,
    Ph.D. dissertation.
Schemerhorn, Ralph
  1970 *Comparative Ethnic Relations*. New York:
    Random House.
Schlesinger, Benjamin
  1978 *Remarriage in Canada*. Toronto: University
    of Toronto Press.
Schmookler, Andrew
  1984 *The Parable of the Tribes: The Problem of
    Power in Social Evolution*. Berkeley: University
    of California Press.
Schultz, Duane P.
  1964 *Panic Behavior*. New York: Random House.
Schur, E.
  1984 *Labelling Women Deviant: Gender Stigma
    and Social Control*. New York: Random
    House.
Science Council of Canada
  1976 *Study of Population and Technology. Impli-
    cations of the Changing Age Structure of the
    Canadian Population. Perceptions II*. Ottawa:
    Supply and Services.
Scott, W. Richard
  1975 "Organizational Structure." *Annual Review
    of Sociology*, Vol.1:1–20.
Scott, W. Richard
  1981 *Organizations, Rational, Natural, and Open
    Systems*. Englewood Cliffs, N.J.: Prentice-
    Hall.
Selznick, Philip
  1957 *Leadership in Administration: A Sociologi-
    cal Interpretation*. Levanston, Illinois:
    Peterson.
Service, Elman
  1979 *The Hunters*. Englewood Cliffs, N.J.:
    Prentice-Hall.
Sexton, Patricia Cayo
  1961 *Education and Income*. New York: Viking
    Press.
Shaw, Clifford R. and Henry D. McKay
  1972 *Juvenile Delinquency and Urban Areas*.
    Chicago: University of Chicago Press.
Shearing, Clifford D.
  DATE "How to Make Theories Untestable: A Guide
    to Theorists." *American Sociologist*, Vol.8
    (February):33–37.

Shibutani, Tamotsu
  1966 *Improvised News: A Sociological Study of Rumor.* Indianapolis: Bobbs-Merrill.
Shibutani, Tamotsu and Kian Kwan
  1965 *Ethnic Stratification: A Comparative Approach.* New York: MacMillan.
Shils, Edward A.
  1961 "The Calling of Sociology." In Talcott Parsons, E. Shils, K.D. Naegele and J.R. Pitts (eds.), *Theories of Society.* Glencoe, Illinois: Free Press.
Shils, Edward A.
  1963 "The Theory of Mass Society. In Philip Olson (ed.), *America as a Mass Society.* New York: Free Press, 30–47.
Simmel, Georg
  1908 "Der Streit." *Soziologie,* chapter 4. (English translation by Krut H. Wolff, *Conflict and the Web Group-Affiliations.* Glencoe, Illinois: Free Press, 1965.)
Simmel, Georg
  1950 *The Sociology of Georg Simmel.* Kurt Wolff (ed.). New York: Free Press.
Simmel, Georg
  1955 *Conflict and the Web of Group Affiliations.* Glencoe, Illinois: Free Press.
Simpson, George
  1971 *Émile Durkheim.* New York: Thomas Y. Crowell.
Sjöberg, Gideon
  1960 *The Preindustrial City: Past and Present.* New York: Free Press.
Skinner, B.F.
  1971 *Beyond Freedom and Dignity.* New York: Alfred A. Knopf.
Smelser, Neil J.
  1962 *Theory of Collective Behavior.* New York: Free Press.
Smelser, Neil J.
  1968 *Essays in Sociological Explanation.* Englewood Cliffs, N.J.: Prentice-Hall.
Smith, Goldwin
  1957 *A History of England.* 2nd ed. New York: Scribner's.
Smucker, Joseph
  1980 *Industrialization in Canada.* Scarborough, Ontario: Prentice-Hall.
Sowell, Thomas
  1981 *Markets and Minorities.* New York: Basic Books.
Spitz, René
  1945 "Hospitalism." *Psychoanalytic Study of the Child,* Vol.1:53–72.

Spitz, René
  1946 "Hospitalism: A Follow-up Report." *Psychoanalytic Study of the Child,* Vol.2:113–17.
Stack, Steven
  1980 "The Political Economy of Income Inequality: A Comparative Analysis." *Canadian Journal of Political Science,* Vol.13:273–86.
Stark R. and W.S. Bainbridge
  1980a "Networks of Faith: Interpersonal Bonds and Recruitment to Cults and Sects." *American Journal of Sociology,* Vol.85,No.6:1376–95.
Stark, R. and W.S. Bainbridge
  1981b "American-born Sects: Initial Findings." *Journal for the Scientific Study of Religion,* Vol.20,No.2:130–49.
Statistics Canada
  1972 *Salaries and Qualifications of Teachers in Public, Elementary and Secondary Schools.* (1973) Ottawa: Supply and Services, 44–45, Table 6.
Statistics Canada
  1974 "Historical-labour Force for Canada and Provinces." *1971 Census of Canada.* Ottawa: Supply and Services, Vol.3, Tables 2,3.
Statistics Canada
  1977 *Canada Year Book, 1976–77.* Ottawa: Supply and Services.
Statistics Canada
  1978 *Vital Statistics: Marriages and Divorces.* Ottawa: Supply and Services.
Statistics Canada
  1979a *Canada's Elderly.* Ottawa: Supply and Services.
Statistics Canada
  1979b *Canada's Families.* Ottawa: Supply and Services.
Statistics Canada
  1979c *Patterns of Fertility in Canada.* Ottawa: Supply and Services.
Statistics Canada
  1979d *Vital Statistics, 1977.* Ottawa: Supply and Services, Vol.1(Births),Table 6.
Statistics Canada
  1980a *Canada's Female Labour Force.* Ottawa: Supply and Services.
Statistics Canada
  1980b *Marriages and Divorces.* Ottawa: Supply and Services, Vol. 2.
Statistics Canada
  1980c *Perspectives Canada III.* Ottawa: Supply and Services.

Statistics Canada
1980d *Population Projections for Canada and Provinces, 1976–2001.* Ottawa: Supply and Services.

Statistics Canada
1980e *Salaries and Qualifications of Teachers.* (1981) Ottawa: Supply and Services.

Statistics Canada
1981a *Census of Canada.* Ottawa: Supply and Services.

Statistics Canada
1981b *Education in Canada.* Ottawa: Supply and Services.

Statistics Canada
1981c *The Labour Force.* Ottawa: Supply and Services, Vol.37:12.

Statistics Canada
1982a "Age, Sex and Marital Status." *1981 Census of Canada,* Ottawa: Supply and Services, Vol.1(Natural Sources), Table 3.

Statistics Canada
1982b "1981 Census-advance Information." *Statistics Canada Daily.* Ottawa: Supply and Services, Tuesday, 6 July 1982:15.

Statistics Canada
1982c *The Labour Force.* Ottawa: Supply and Services, Vol.38:12.

Statistics Canada
1982d *Salaries and Qualifications of Teachers in Public, Elementary and Secondary Schools.* (1983) Ottawa: Supply and Services.

Statistics Canada
1982e *Trends in Canadian Education, 1961–62 to 1983–84.* Ottawa: Supply and Services.

Statistics Canada
1983a *1981 Census of Canada: 20% Data Base.* Ottawa: Supply and Services.

Statistics Canada
1983b *Divorce: Law and the Family in Canada.* Ottawa: Supply and Services.

Statistics Canada
1983c *Labour Force — Occupation by Demographic and Education Characteristics. Canada, Provinces, Urban, Rival Non-farm and Farm.* Ottawa: Supply and Services.

Statistics Canada
1983d *Labour Force — Occupation Trends. Canada, Provinces.* Ottawa: Supply and Services.

Statistics Canada
1983e "Selected Social and Economic Characteristics." *1981 Census of Canada.* Ottawa: Supply and Services, Vol.3(Profile Series B), Table 1.

Statistics Canada
1983f *Vital Statistics 1981.* Ottawa: Supply and Services, Vol.1(Births and Deaths), Table 5.

Statistics Canada
1984a *Income Distribution by Size in Canada, 1983. Preliminary Estimates.* Ottawa: Supply and Services.

Statistics Canada
1984b *Women in the Work World.* Ottawa: Supply and Services.

Statistics Canada
1984c *Worked in 1980 — Employment Income by Occupation. Canada, Provinces.* Ottawa: Supply and Services.

Statistics Canada
1984d *Schooling in Canada.* Ottawa: Supply and Services.

Statistics Canada
1985 *Family Expenditure in Canada.* Ottawa: Supply and Services.

Stebbins, R.A.
1974 *The Disorderly Classroom: Its Physical and Temporal Conditions.* St. John's, Newfoundland: Faculty of Education, Memorial University of Newfoundland.

Stebbins, R.A.
1975 *Teachers and Meaning: Definitions of Classroom Situations.* Leiden: E.J. Brill.

Stebbins, R.A.
1981 "Classroom Ethnography and the Definition of the Situation." In L. Barton and S. Walker (eds.), *Schools, Teachers, and Teaching.* Sussex, England: Falmer Press, 243-64.

Stebbins, R.A.
1984 *The Magician: Career, Culture, and Social Psychology in a Variety Art.* Toronto: Clarke Irwin.

Stein, Aletha Huston and L. Friedrich (with Fred Vondracek)
1971 "Television Content and Young Children's Behavior." In Eli Rubinstein et al. (eds.), *Television and Social Behavior, Reports and Papers.* Washington, D.C.: U.S. Government Printing Office.

Steiner, Gary A.
1963 *The People Look at Television.* New York: Alfred A. Knopf.

Stelter, Gilbert A.
1975 "The Urban Frontier in Canadian History." In A.R. McCormack and Ian MacPherson (eds.), *Cities in the West.* Ottawa: National Museum of Man, 270-86.

Sternhell, Zeev
1976 "Fascist Ideology." In W. Laqueur (ed.), *Fascism*. Berkeley: University of California Press, 320-25.
Stinchcombe, Arthur L.
1968 *Constructing Social Theories*. New York: Harcourt Brace and World.
Stone, Leroy O.
1967 *Urban Development in Canada*. Ottawa: Queen's Printer.
Stone, Leroy O. and Susan Fletcher
1980 *A Profile of Canada's Older Population*. Montréal: Institute for Research on Public Policy.
Stone, Leroy O. and Claude Marceau
1977 *Canadian Population Trends and Public Policy Through the 1980's*. Montréal: McGill-Queen's University Press and Institute for Research on Public Policy.
Stryker, Sheldon
1972 "Symbolic Interaction Theory: A Review and Some Suggestions for Comparative Family Research." In E. Lupri and G. Lueschen (eds.), *Comparative Perspectives on Marriage and the Family*. Special issue of the *Journal of Comparative Family Studies*, Vol.3,No.1: 17-32.
Sudermann, M.
1979 "Sex Differences in High School Course Choice and Achievement." Research Report 79-09. Ottawa: Research Centre, Ottawa Board of Education.
Sunahara, M. Ann
1980 "Federal Policy and the Japanese Canadians: The Decision to Evacuate, 1942." In K.V. Ujimoto and G. Hirabayashi (eds.), *Visible Minorities and Multiculturalism: Asians in Canada*. Toronto: Butterworth.
Sweden
1979 *Step by Step*. Stockholm: National Committee on Equality Between Men and Women.
Sweden
1981 *Inequality In Sweden. Living Conditions*. Stockholm: National Central Bureau of Statistics.
Szymanski, Al
1976 "The Socialization of Women's Oppression: A Marxist Theory of the Changing Position of Women in Advanced Capitalist Society." *Insurgent Sociologist*, Vol.6,No.2:31-58.
Tannenbaum, F.
1938 *Crime and Community*. Boston: Ginn.

Taylor, Frederick W.
1911 *The Principles of Scientific Management*. New York: Harper.
Taylor, I., P. Walton and J. Young
1973 *The New Criminology: For a Social Theory of Deviance*. London: Routledge and Kegan Paul.
Taylor, Norman
1969 "The French-Canadian Entrepreneur and His Social Environment." In M. Roux and Y. Martin (eds.), *French-Canadian Society*. Toronto: McClelland & Stewart.
Tenner, Adrian (ed.)
1983 "Introduction." *The Politics Of Indianness*. St. John's, Newfoundland: Institute of Social and Economic Research, Memorial University of Newfoundland.
Tepperman, Lorne
1975 *Social Mobility in Canada*. Toronto: McGraw-Hill Ryerson.
The Economist
1980 *The World In Figures*. 3rd ed. New York: Facts on File, Inc.
Thomas, W.I.
1923 *The Unadjusted Girl*. Boston: Little, Brown.
Thomlinson, R.
1976 *Population Dynamics*. 2nd ed. New York: Random House.
Thompson, H.
1966 *Hell's Angels*. New York: Ballantine Books.
Thompson, James D.
1976 *Organizations and Beyond*. Lexington, Mass.: Lexington Books.
Thompson, Kenneth
1975 *Auguste Comte: The Foundation of Sociology*. New York: John Wiley.
Tiger, Lionel and Robin Fox
1968 *The Imperial Animal*. New York: Holt, Rinehart and Winston.
Tilly, Charles
1981 *As Sociology Meets History*. New York: Academic Press.
Toch, Hans
1965 *The Social Psychology of Social Movements*. Indianapolis: Bobbs-Merrill.
Tönnies, Ferdinand
1957 *Community and Society: Gemeinschaft und Gesellschaft*. (Translated and edited by C.P. Loomis.) East Lansing: Michigan State University Press.
Travers, E.P.
1978 "Eleven Pressures that Squeeze Superintendents — and Six Ways to Ease Them." *American School Board Journal*, 43-44.

Troeltsch, Ernst
  1931 *The Social Teaching of the Christian Churches.* (1911) Translated by Clive Wyon. London: George Allen and Unwin.

Tsui, A.O. and D.J. Boque
  1978 "Declining World Fertility: Trends, Causes and Implications." *Population Bulletin,* Vol.33,No.4:3–55.

Turk, A.
  1969 *Criminality and the Legal Order.* Chicago: Rand McNally.

Turner, Ralph H. and Lewis M. Killam
  1972 *Collective Behavior.* 2nd ed. Englewood Cliffs, N.J.: Prentice-Hall.

U.S. Bureau of the Census
  1980 *Statistical Abstract of the United States: 1980.* 101st ed. Washington, D.C.

U.S. Bureau of the Census
  1981 *Statistical Abstract of the United States: 1981.* 102nd ed. Washington, D.C.: 251, Table 251.

UNESCO
  1980 *Compendium of Social Statistics.* New York: United Nations.

Underhill, Frank
  1960 *In Search of Canadian Liberalism.* Toronto: MacMillan.

United Nations
  1953 *The Determinants and Consequences of Population Trends.* Population Studies, No. 17.

United Nations
  1956 *The Aging of Populations and the Economic and Social Implications.*

Valentine, Charles A.
  1968 *Culture and Poverty: Criticisms and Counterproposals.* Chicago: University of Chicago Press.

Vallee, Frank
  1975 "Multi-ethnic Societies: The Issues of Identity and Inequality." In D. Forcese and S. Richer (eds.), *Issues in Canadian Society.* Scarborough, Ontario: Prentice-Hall.

Van den Berghe
  1979 *Human Family Systems: An Evolutionary View.* New York: Elsevier North-Holland.

Van de Walle, E. and J. Knodel
  1980 "Europe's Fertility Transition." *Population Bulletin,* Vol.34,No.6:3–43.

Van der Tak, C. Haub and E. Murphy
  1979 "Our Population Predicament: A New Look." *Population Bulletin,* Vol.34,No.5:3–48.

Van Loon, Rick
  1970 "Political Participation in Canada." *Canadian Journal of Political Science,* Volume 3 September): 396–99

Vance, Rupert
  1932 *Human Geography of the South: A Study in Regional Resources and Human Adequacy.* Chapel Hill: University of North Carolina Press.

Vanfossen, Beth E.
  1979 *The Structure of Social Inequality.* Boston: Little, Brown.

Varga, Ivan
  1980 "Capitalism and the Return to Religion." *The Ecumenist,* Vol.18,No.4:54–59.

Veblen, Thorstein
  1899 *The Theory of the Leisure Class: An Economic Study of Institutions.* New York: Viking Press.

Veblen, Thorstein
  1922 *"The Instinct of Workmanship.* New York: Huebsch.

Veltmeyer, Henry
  1979 "The Capitalist Underdevelopment of Atlantic Canada." In R. Brym and J. Sacouman (eds.), *Underdevelopment and Social Movements in Atlantic Canada.* Toronto: New Hogtown Press.

Verba, Sidney and N.H. Nie
  1972 *Participation in America.* New York: Harper & Row, 12–15; 129–33; 335–48.

Vickers, Jill
  1978 "Where are the Women in Canada's Politics?" *Atlantis,* Vol.3,No.2:40–51.

Vickers, Jill and M. Janine Brodie
  1981 "Canada." In J. Lovenduski and J. Hills (eds.), *The Politics of the Second Electorate: Women and Public Participation.* London: Routledge and Kegan Paul.

Visher, E.B. and J. Visher
  1979 *Stepfamilies: A Guide to Working with Stepparents and Stepchildren.* New York: Brunner/Matel.

Vogel, Ezra
  1979 *Japan as Number One.* Cambridge: Harvard University Press.

Waller, W.
  1932 *The Sociology of Teaching.* New York: John Wiley, 196, 297.

Wallerstein, Immanuel
  1979 *The Capitalist World Economy.* Cambridge: Cambridge University Press.

Walster, E., G.W. Walster and E. Berscheid
  1978 *Equity: Theory and Research.* Boston: Allyn & Bacon.

Warner, W. Lloyd
  1949 *Democracy in Jonesville.* New York: Harper & Row.

Warner, W. Lloyd and Paul S. Lunt
1941 *The Social Life of a Modern Community.* New Haven: Yale University Press.
Watson, John
1924 *Behavior.* New York: W.W. Norton.
Weber, Max
1946 "Class, Status, Party." In Hans H. Gerth and C. Wright Mills (trans. and eds.), *From Max Weber: Essays in Sociology.* New York: Oxford University Press.
Weber, Max
1947 *From Wax Weber: Essays in Sociology.* Translated and edited by H. Gerth and C. Wright Mills. New York: Oxford University Press.
Weber, Max
1958a "Class, Status, Party." In Hans H. Gerth and C.Wright Mills (trans. and eds.), *From Max Weber: Essays in Sociology.* New York: Oxford University Press.
Weber, Max
1958b *The Protestant Ethic and the Spirit of Capitalism.* Translated by Talcott Parsons. New York: Scribner's.
Weber, Max
1964 *The Theory of Social and Economic Organization.* New York: Free Press.
Weber, Max
1968a *Economy and Society.* I.Guenter Roth and Claus Wittich (eds.). New York: Bedminster Press.
Weber, Max
1968b *Max Weber: On Charisma and Institution Building.* S.N. Eisenstadt (ed.). Chicago: University of Chicago Press.
Weber, Max
1978 "Socialism." In W.G. Runciman (ed.), *Max Weber: Selections in Translation.* Translated by E. Matthews. Cambridge: Cambridge University Press, 251–62.
Weiner B.
1982 "An Attributionally-based Theory of Motivation and Emotion." In N.T. Feather (ed.), *Expectations and Actions.* Hillsdale, N.J.: Earlbaum.
Wellman, Barry
1979 "The Community Question: The Intimate Networks of East Yorkers." *American Journal of Sociology,* Vol.84:1201–31.
Westley, William A. and Frederick Elkin
DATE "The Protective Environment and Adolescent Socialization." *Social Forms,* Vol.35:243–49.

White, O. Kendal, Jr.
1978 "Mormonism in America and Canada: Accommodation to the Nation-state." *Canadian Journal of Sociology,* Vol.3,No.2:161–81.
Whitehead, T. North
1938 *The Industrial Worker.* Cambridge, Mass.: Harvard University Press.
Whyte, William Foote
1943 *Street Corner Society.* Chicago: University of Chicago Press.
Whyte, William Foote
1955 *Street Corner Society: The Social Structure of an Italian Slum.* 2nd ed. Chicago: University of Chicago Press.
Wigle, D.T. and Y. Mao
1980 *Mortality Income Level in Urban Canada.* Ottawa: Health and Welfare.
Wilson, Bryan
1982 *Religion in Sociological Perspective.* New York: Oxford University Press.
Wilson, E.O.
1975 *Sociobiology: The New Synthesis.* Cambridge, Mass.: Harvard University Press.
Wilson, John
1973 *Introduction to Social Movements.* New York: Basic Books.
Wilson, N.K.
1983 "An International Perspective on Women and Criminology." In E. Johnson (ed.), *International Handbook of Contemporary Developments in Criminology: General Issues and the Americas.* Westport, Conn.: Greenwood Press.
Wood, James L. and Maurice Jackson
1982 *Social Movements: Development, Participation and Dynamics.* Belmont, Calif.: Wadsworth.
Wood, W.D. and P. Kumar (eds.)
1982 *The Current Industrial Relations Scene.* Kingston, Ontario: Industrial Relations Centre, Queen's University.
Woodward, Joan
1965 *Industrial Organization: Theory and Practice.* London: Oxford University Press.
Worsley, Peter
1982 *Marx and Marxism.* London: Ellis Horwood and Tavistock.
Worsley, Peter (ed.) et al.
1977 *Introducing Sociology.* Harmondsworth: Penguin.
Wright, Erik Olin
1979 *Class Structure and Income Determination.* New York: Academic Press.

Wrong, Dennis H.
1961 "The Oversocialized Conception of Man in Modern Society." *American Sociology Review*, Vol.26:183-93.

Wrong, Dennis H.
1964 "Social Inequality without Social Stratification." *Canadian Review of Sociology and Anthropology*, Vol.1:5-16.

Wrong, Dennis H.
1970 *Max Weber.* Englewood Cliffs, N.J.: Prentice-Hall.

Wrong, Dennis H.
1976 "Postscript 1975" In *Skeptical Sociology*. New York: Columbia University Press, 47-54.

Wrong, Dennis H.
1977 *Population and Society.* 4th ed. New York: Random House.

Wuthnow, Robert
1976 "The New Religions in Social Context." In Charles Glock and Robert Bellah (eds.), *The New Religious Consciousness*. Berkeley: University of California Press.

Yeates, Maurice
1975 *Main Street: Windsor to Quebec City.* Ottawa: Information Canada.

Young, Michael and Peter Willmott
1975 *The Symmetrical Family.* Harmondsworth, Middlesex: Penguin.

Zald, M.N. and McCarthy J.D.
1979 *The Dynamic of Social Movements: Resource Mobilization, Social Control, and Tactics.* Cambridge, Mass.: Winthrop.

Zurcker, Louis A. and David A. Snow
1981 "Collective Behavior: Social Movements." In Morris Rosenberg and Ralph H. Turner (eds.), *Social Psychology: Sociological Perspectives*. New York: Basic Books, 447-82.

Zwarun, Suzanne
1984 "Pension Dissention." *City Woman* (Summer):46-52.

Index